W9-DGL-404

Español Santillana is a collaborative effort by two teams specializing in the design of Spanish-language educational materials. One team is located in the United States and the other in Spain.

Published in the United States of America.

Español Santillana
Teacher's Edition Level 1B
ISBN-13: 978-1-61605-079-5
ISBN-10: 1-61605-079-9

Illustrators: **Bartolomé Seguí**, **Jorge Arranz**
Picture Coordinator: **Carlos Aguilera**

Cartographer: **Tania López**
Cartographic Coordinator: **Ana Isabel Calvo**

Production Manager: **Ángel García Encinar**

Production Coordinator: **Marisa Valbuena**, **Julio Hernández**

Design and Layout: **Alfonso García**, **Hilario Simón**, **Pedro Valencia**

Proofreaders: **Gerardo Z. García**, **María A. Pérez**, **Jennifer Farrington**, **José Ramón Díaz**, **Laurie Price**

Photo Researchers: **Mercedes Barcenilla**, **Amparo Rodríguez**

Santillana USA Publishing Company, Inc.
2023 NW 84th Avenue, Doral, FL 33122

Printed by Worzalla, Wisconsin.

3 4 5 6 7 8 9   18 17 16 15 14

Editorial Staff in the United States
Anne Smieszny
Ana Isabel Antón
Andrea Roberson

Editorial Staff in Spain
Susana Gómez
Cristina Núñez
Belén Saiz

Linguistic and Cultural Advisers in Latin America and in the United States

Antonio Moreno
Editorial Director, Santillana México

Mayra Méndez
Editorial Director, Santillana Puerto Rico

Luis Guillermo Bernal
Editorial Director, Santillana Guatemala

Cecilia Mejía
Editorial Director, Santillana Perú

Graciela Pérez de Lois
Editorial Director, Santillana Argentina

Manuel José Rojas
Editorial Director, Santillana Chile

Mario Núñez
Director of Professional Development, Santillana USA

Reviewers

Dr. Tamara Alsace
Buffalo, NY

Dr. Josefa Báez-Ramos
Seattle, WA

Mercedes Bernal
West New York, NJ

Miguel Castro
New Orleans, LA

Yvonne Davault
Mansfield, TX

Dr. Frances S. Hoch
Raleigh, NC

Petra Liz-Morell
Ridgefield Park, NJ

James Orihuela
Whittier, CA

Ana Sainz de la Peña
Allentown, PA

Eugenia Sarmiento
Centennial, CO

Thomasina White
Philadelphia, PA

Writers (Teacher's Edition)

María Inés García
Austin, TX

Lori Langer de Ramírez
Great Neck, NY

Andrea Roberson
Miami, FL

Miguel Santana
Tampa, FL

Writers (Student Book)

Dr. Miguel Santana
received his PhD in Hispanic literature at the University of Texas–Austin. Dr. Santana has taught Spanish at the elementary, high school, and college levels, and has worked as a Spanish editor and writer for numerous educational publishers in the United States. Miguel Santana is also an author of several novels.

Dr. Lori Langer de Ramírez
received her doctorate in curriculum and teaching from Teacher's College, Columbia University. She is chairperson of the ESL and World Language Department for Herricks Public Schools, New York. Dr. Langer de Ramírez is the recipient of many prestigious awards.

Eduardo Fernández Galán
received his *Licenciatura en Lingüística Hispánica* from the Universidad Complutense de Madrid. He has taught Spanish at Montgomery High School in Montgomery, New Jersey, and The College of New Jersey in Ewing.

Dr. Michele Guerrini
received her PhD in Romance languages from the University of Pennsylvania. She has worked as director of bilingual and EFL departments at Richmond Publishing in Spain and as an adjunct assistant professor of Spanish at The George Washington University in Washington, DC.

Cristina Núñez Pereira
received her *Licenciatura en Filología Hispánica* from the Universidad Nacional de Educación a Distancia and is a *Licenciada en Periodismo* from the Universidad Carlos III de Madrid.

Belén Saiz Noeda
received her *Licenciatura en Filología Hispánica* from Universidad de Alicante. She was a professor of Spanish language and culture and was in charge of Spanish teacher education at the Universidad de Alcalá and at other institutions.

María Inés García
received her masters in Spanish from Texas A & I University. She is a former director of the Languages Other Than English program for the Texas Education Agency, and was the Spanish specialist with the agency for 26 years.

María J. Fierro-Treviño
received her MA from the University of Texas–San Antonio. She was the director of Languages Other Than English program for the Texas Education Agency. She has taught Spanish at the secondary and college levels, and has worked as an instructional specialist, and as a presenter of professional-development seminars.

Contributors

Janet L. Glass
Dwight-Englewood School, Englewood, NJ

Dr. Frances S. Hoch
Raleigh, NC

Jan Kucerik
Pinellas County Schools Largo, FL

Dr. Dave McAlpine
University of Arkansas–Little Rock,
Little Rock, AR

Maria Elena Messina
Adrian C. Wilcox High School, Santa Clara, CA

Dr. Gerardo Piña-Rosales
North American Academy of the Spanish Language,
The City University of New York
(CUNY) Lehman and Graduate Center,
New York, NY

Advisers

Trina M. Gonzales-Alesi
John Glenn Middle School of International
Studies, Indio, CA

Paula Hirsch
Windward School, Los Angeles, CA

María Orta
Kennedy High School, Chicago, IL

Nina Wilson
Murchison Middle School, Austin, TX

Developmental Editor
Belén Saiz

Editorial Coordinator
Anne Smieszny

Editorial Director
Enrique Ferro

Índice

Español Santillana. Presentation

Scope & Sequence

Key Ideas for Today's Language Classroom

Student Book

Unidad puente. ¿Recuerdas?

Unidad 5. España

Unidad 6. Estados Unidos

Unidad 7. Argentina

Unidad 8. Chile

Appendices

Español Santillana

1. A motivating story

1. *Español Santillana* tells a story of travels and challenges.

Four pairs of enthusiasts of the Spanish language and Hispanic culture want to explore the Spanish-speaking world: its people, its cities, its regions, and its cultures.

Because of this, they have decided to create the *Fans del español* website and to travel to different countries in order to discover and show unique aspects of each place.

In each country, the four teams compete, taking on different *desafíos*, or challenges, that they must complete.

2. The challenges present exceptionally motivating situations and fascinating places.

Each unit presents four challenges related to the people, the regions, or the cultures of a country. For example, the teams participate in the ritual of the *voladores de Papantla* in Mexico, prepare a dish containing *paiche* fish in Iquitos, Peru, and compete in the Stairs Marathon in Valparaiso, Chile.

3. The students decide which team wins the challenge in each unit.

At the beginning of each unit, students discuss the challenges and make predictions about which pair will win. At the end of the unit, students take a vote to decide the winners of the challenge according to a previously established criterion: the most original, the most fun, the most relevant, and so on.

Active participation in the storyline promotes student involvement and motivation.

⚑→ TU DESAFÍO

The **Tu desafío** section that appears on certain pages is intended to motivate students and promote independent work.

Upon accessing the *Fans del español* website to do the proposed activity, students earn points, which they accumulate throughout the year.

In each unit there are four *desafíos.*

La lectura

El proyecto

Organization of the Unit: The Challenges

The first part of the unit tells the story of the challenges that the teams will face in each country.

1. *La llegada*

The initial pages contain three elements:

▶ A ***fotonovela*** that shows the arrival of the participants in the country. This section presents the vocabulary and the grammar of the unit in context. The story is followed by comprehension activities.

▶ A section with ***Expresiones útiles***.

▶ A page titled ***¿Quién ganará?*** where, students make predictions about which team will win this stage of the challenge.

2. The *Desafíos*

On these pages, the target linguistic concepts are developed in greater detail. Each ***Desafío*** comprises 8 or 10 pages in which vocabulary, grammar, and communication are developed.

3. *El encuentro*

After the challenges, a double-page titled ***Todo junto*** provides communicative activities that integrate the vocabulary and the structures taught throughout the unit.

As a closing to the story line, the four teams meet at a culturally significant place (***El encuentro***) and talk about the tasks they have completed, using the structures and the vocabulary presented in the unit. At the end, students vote for the team they consider the winner.

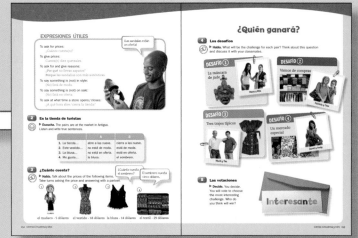
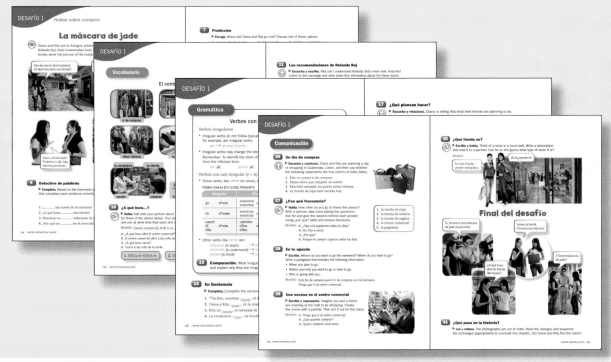
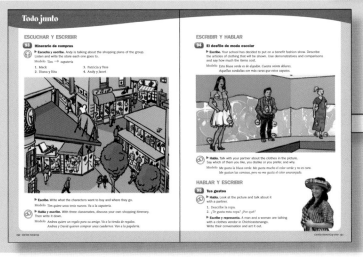
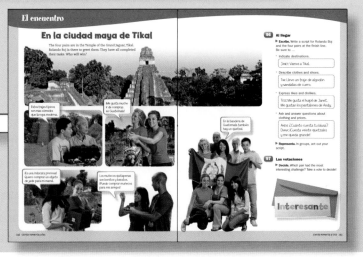

Organization of the Unit: The Structure of a *Desafío*

Each *Desafío* is organized into four sections.

The *Desafío* is the story of each team's challenge, and is therefore the basis of the story line. It also develops key vocabulary and grammar around a communicative function.

1. *El Desafío* (Presentation)

The **Desafío** begins with a **fotonovela**, in which the team's challenge is presented using the target vocabulary and grammar in a realistic context.

2. *El vocabulario*

On the **vocabulary** pages, the new words and phrases are presented with the support of images. Students use the vocabulary in follow-up activities.

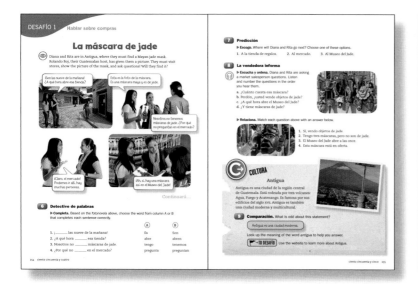

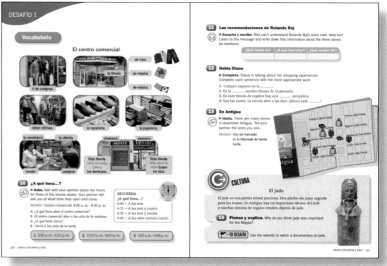

The "C-Boxes"

The linguistic material presented in each *Desafío* is complemented with boxes in which four of the five C's from the standards are developed: **Culture, Comparisons, Communities,** and **Connections**.

Communication is developed throughout the book in the vocabulary and grammar activities. A section at the end of each *Desafío* is also dedicated to Communication.

3. La gramática

On the **grammar** pages, students are given explanations of key structures, which are practiced along with the key vocabulary.

4. La comunicación

On the **communication** pages, there are progressively more open-ended activities allow students to apply the key vocabulary and grammar in communicative situations.

The *Desafío* ends with a ***fotonovela***, which is a continuation of and a conclusion to the initial *fotonovela*.

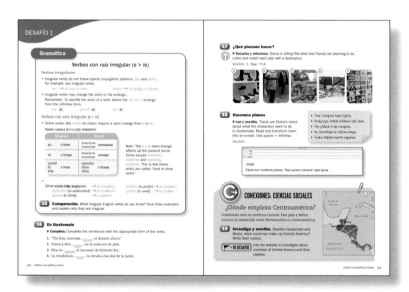

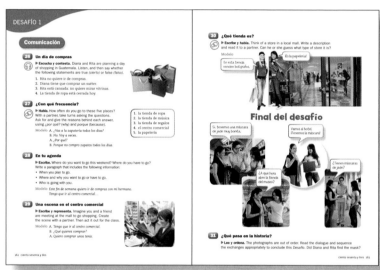

CULTURA

No más preocupaciones

Los muñecos qui...
Estos muñecos re...
preocupaciones (wo...
Por la mañana, tus...

59 Compara.

COMPARACIONES

El costo de la vida

El costo de la vi...
en una ciudad o...
¿Son iguales los...
ciudad? ¿Qué tie...
o las pequeñas?...
de los centros c...
(neighborhoods)?

87 Investig...

COMUNIDADES

MODA ... LTURA

Los trajes tradicion...
de un país. En Guate...
una especie de blusa...
común a muchas con...

39 Piensa y ex...

1. Is there a t...
   your count...
2. How do the...
   heritage of...

Alfredo Gálvez. *Tejedoras de Atitlán.*

CONEXIONES: ARTE

La perspectiva

Los artistas usan la perspectiva para representar en un cuadro la posición de los objetos. Los objetos más grandes parecen (*appear*) estar cerca y los objetos pequeños parecen estar lejos.

64 **Dibuja.** Draw three objects in perspective to illustrate the concept of demonstratives.

The Vocabulary

A careful selection.

Key vocabulary has been selected, considering the specifications of organizations dedicated to the instruction and evaluation of Spanish, including the *Instituto Cervantes* and the American Association of Teachers of Spanish and Portuguese (AATSP).
In general, the most commonly used and standard Spanish terms have been chosen, rather than regional variants. Whenever possible words close to their English counterparts (cognates) have been included. The basic criteria for the selection of vocabulary were frequency of use and relevance to students' everyday life, interests, and needs.

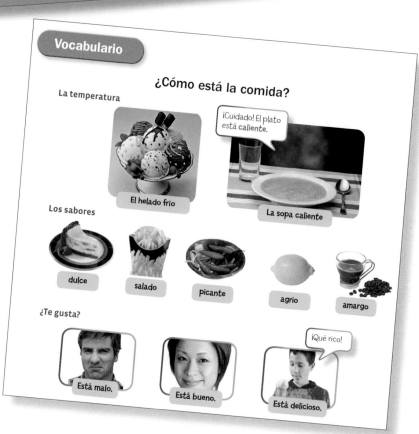

Organization by topic or situations.

The vocabulary is organized by topic or by situations related to the theme of the unit. For example, Unit 4, dedicated to the theme of food, includes words relating to foods and beverages, meals, and food stores.

Theme: Food

Desafío 1	**Foods and beverages**: pan, papa, maíz, sopa, verduras, frijoles, huevos, pollo, carne, pescado, helado, tarta, frutas, manzana, naranja, plátano, limón… **Meals**: desayuno, almuerzo, cena.
Desafío 2	**Food stores**: supermercado, mercado, panadería, pescadería, frutería, carnicería. **Actions in the kitchen**: cortar las verduras, mezclar la ensalada, cocinar, probar la comida.
Desafío 3	**At the table**: el mantel, la servilleta, el tenedor, el vaso, el plato, el cuchillo, la cuchara, la botella, la sal, la pimienta, el azúcar, la taza… **Actions and conditions related to food**: comer, beber, poner la mesa, limpiar la mesa, limpio, sucio.
Desafío 4	**Describing foods and beverages**: caliente, frío, dulce, salado, picante, agrio, malo, bueno, delicioso.

The instructional focus: work on many levels.

1. *Fotonovelas*

These include new vocabulary words and expressions that students can understand through their visual or verbal context. The activities help students focus on the lexical items and formulate hypotheses about their meaning.

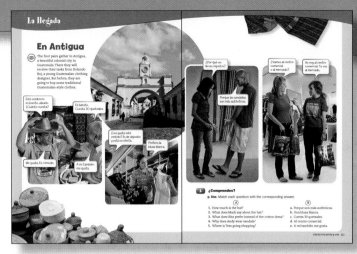

2. *Vocabulario*

The new words and expressions are presented on the vocabulary pages in each *Desafío* with the support of images. Students practice the vocabulary first in closed-ended activities (less difficult) and then in open-ended activities (more difficult), where they can apply the vocabulary in real-life situations.

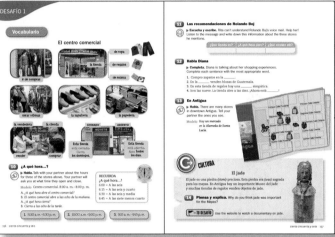

3. *Gramática, Comunicación,* and *Todo junto*

Key vocabulary is reinforced and used in different contexts, along with recycled vocabulary from previous units.

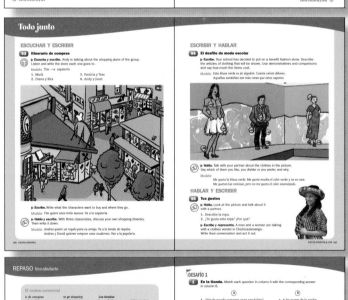

4. *Repaso*

At the end of the unit, vocabulary is reviewed and pre-assessment activities are included.

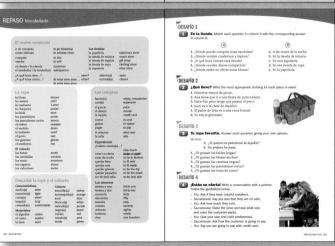

The Grammar

A decision guided by experience.

The selection and sequence of the grammatical elements was determined keeping three fundamental criteria in mind: the use of the structures, their productivity in communicative contexts, and their difficulty.

For example, the verbs *ser*, *estar*, and *tener* are presented before the verb *gustar* because they are more frequently used, they are more productive, and they present fewer difficulties for English speakers than the verb *gustar*.

Organization: Grammar linked to communicative functions.

In general, the presentation of grammar is linked to a communicative function. For example, in Unit 1, dedicated to the theme of personal life, the following functions and structures are learned:

Theme: Personal Life

Desafío 1 Identifying yourself and others	Subject pronouns The verb *ser*
Desafío 2 Describing people	Adjectives
Desafío 3 Describing family relationships	The verb *tener* Possessive adjectives and the preposition *de* (to show possession)
Desafío 4 Expressing states and feelings	The verb *estar*

Didactic Focus: the use of concise and organized information.

1. *Fotonovelas*

The *fotonovelas* include new structures that students can comprehend by their visual or linguistic context. The activities help students to focus on these structures and to formulate hypotheses about their meaning and usage.

2. *Gramática*

The grammar boxes present information in a concise and graphically organized manner. Each grammar box concludes with a comparison between Spanish and English.
The grammar activities are sequenced according to difficulty, from closed-ended activities to open-ended and personalized activities.

3. *Comunicación* and *Todo junto*

Key grammatical structures are reinforced by their application in open-ended, communicative activities.

4. *Repaso*

Key grammar is reviewed at the end of the unit by means of pre-assessment activities.

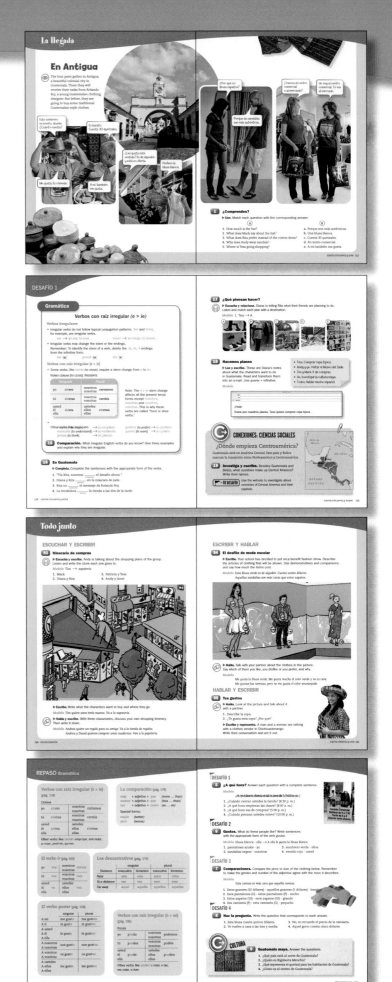

The *Mapas Culturales*

The *mapas culturales* propose a systematic study.

The *Mapa cultural* section offers an organized and systematic study of each country, analyzing its regions and some characteristic cultural aspects.

The first page contains **general information** about the country: its location, size, population, capital, etc.

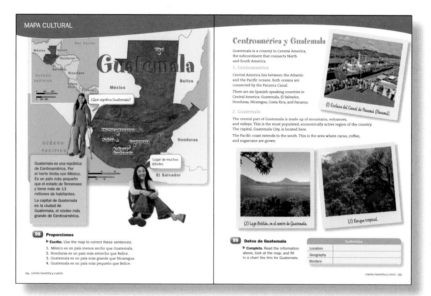

The notion of landscapes distinguishes large geographical regions, which allows students to create a **basic mental framework** about the zone or country. In Peru, for example, three major zones are defined: the coast, the Andes mountain range, and the jungle.

The *Mapa cultural* offers a selection of representative cultural aspects: places, people, traditions, customs, and folklore.

Culture in the *Mapas Culturales*

1A

México	Los desiertos y las ciudades del norte: los corridos La Ciudad de México: la antigua Tenochtitlán El centro: Guanajuato El sur: la población indígena
Puerto Rico	El Viejo San Juan El bosque tropical El Yunque La salsa, la esencia de Puerto Rico Los Estados Unidos y Puerto Rico
Guatemala	La gran ciudad maya de Tikal El quetzal: el ave de Guatemala Rigoberta Menchú: la lucha por la paz La marimba: sonido guatemalteco
Perú	Los incas, reyes de las montañas Las líneas de Nazca Los caballitos de totora Arequipa: una ciudad muy europea

1B

España	La España atlántica: la cuna del español La meseta: territorio de La Mancha Madrid: paraíso de pintores El sur: la herencia árabe
Estados Unidos	Judy Baca y el muralismo de Los Ángeles La comida tex-mex La pequeña Habana
Argentina	El tango Mafalda Buenos Aires Los ñoquis del 29 del mes
Chile	La Isla de Pascua Pablo Neruda El Festival Internacional de la Canción de Viña del Mar

Reading

Reading materials build competency for reading in Spanish.

The reading materials present an opportunity to practice the given vocabulary and grammatical structures, while improving students' ability to interpret new vocabulary and grammatical structures from specific contexts.

The use of numerous cognates makes the context more understandable and helps students to increase their vocabulary.

The readings work with different types of texts.

The readings present an outstanding aspect of the culture of a country and relate it to a type of text. The diverse selection of texts strengthens reading comprehension while suggesting models for language production.

Theme	Type of Text
• Teotihuacan	An informative text.
• The fortress of San Felipe del Morro	A travel blog.
• The market of Chichicastenango	A letter.
• The festival of Inti Raymi	A travel brochure.
• The Picasso painting *Guernica*	An art catalog.
• Hispanic Heritage Month	An invitation to a cultural festival.
• *La vuelta al mundo...* by Ricardo Mariño	A short story.
• *Oda a la manzana* by Pablo Neruda	A poem.

Each reading is linked to a comprehension strategy.

Each unit focuses on a specific reading strategy: identifying cognates, identifying key concepts, visualizing images from the text, formulating assumptions and questions, and so on. Applying these strategies, students develop their ability to read and understand Spanish texts.

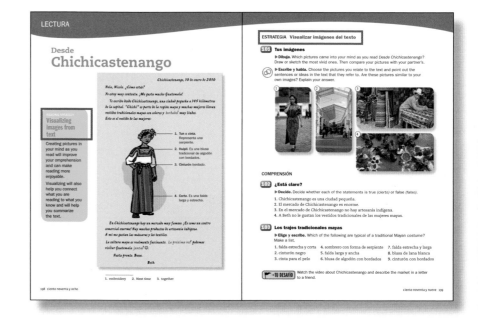

The Project

The project provides an opportunity for integrating and applying knowledge.

Each unit closes with a project that encourages students' creativity and communicative capacity, while activating vocabulary and grammatical structures that students have learned. Each project develops a communicative activity that integrates cultural and linguistic information.

Tareas propuestas en los proyectos

- Make a presentation about Diego Rivera.
- Organize a visit to the Casa Blanca Museum in San Juan, Puerto Rico.
- Arrange an exhibit of Guatemalan worry dolls.
- Create a restaurant menu and role-play serving the "customers."
- Make a poster about hygiene habits.
- Deliver a presentation about a distinguished Hispanic person in the United States.
- Create a travelogue.
- Participate in a campaign to protect endangered animals.

The activities are separated into steps.

Each project develops from a set of activities presented sequentially in separate steps. Each step is clearly defined and includes guidelines to help students complete the activities.

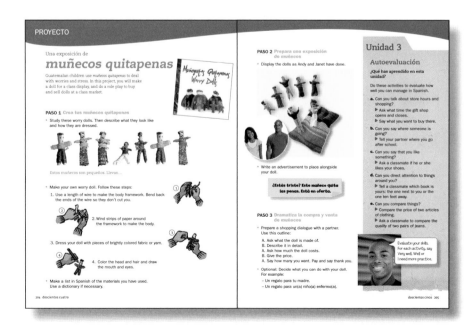

The *Teacher's Edition*

Keys for teaching and learning.

The pages at the beginning of each unit offer a broad overview as well as tools for the organization and planning of school activities.

Objectives, content, and evaluation criteria.

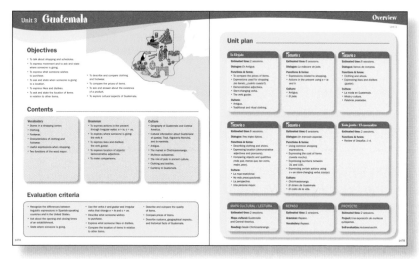

Outline of the unit and estimated time for completing each section.

Detailed description of the standars for learning Spanish in the unit.

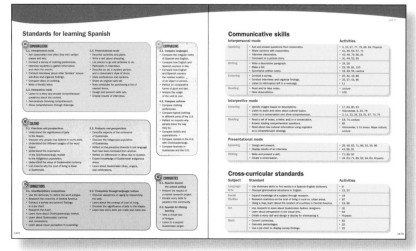

Communicative abilities practiced in the unit classified by skill (speaking, writing, listening, and reading) and by use (interpersonal, interpretative, and presentational).

Standards for other areas also discussed.

Detailed lesson plans for 50- and 90-minute classes.

Audio scripts.

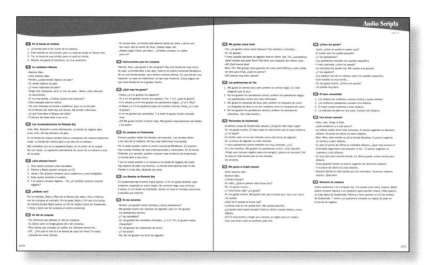

The instructional guides offer numerous resources for making the teacher's job easier.

General overview of the section.

Explanation of key educational and methodological solutions for interpreting the material.

Additional information about the cultural topics discussed.

Methodological proposals and suggestions: how to present the material, what to do with the class, how to prevent common errors, etc.

Differentiated instruction: developing learners, expanding learners, heritage language learners, special-needs learners, cooperative learning, multiple intelligences, critical thinking, etc.

Answer key.

Additional resources.

Technology

A wide variety of technological resources.

Español Santillana relies on broad technological support, including digital versions of print materials (books, workbooks, and teacher's guides), plus an extensive offering of specific resources: visual presentations, videos, audio materials, a webpage, and more.

Visual presentations in the *fotonovelas* and the challenges.

The *fotonovelas* that present the characters' arrival in the country and their challenges are supported by visual presentations that replicate the dialogues and the story. The visual presentations offer an excellent method for improving students' listening comprehension ability.

Videos for enjoying the Spanish-speaking world's cultures.

The unit begins with a video that gives students an overview of the country and the challenges that the characters will undertake.

Each *Mapa cultural* is also accompanied by a video that offers a detailed view of the country, its landscapes, and its most outstanding characteristics. In addition, each unit includes two other videos on significant cultural topics: the house of Frida Kahlo (Mexico), Old San Juan (Puerto Rico), the market of Chichicastenango (Guatemala), and so on.

The videos are highly evocative, serving to motivate students and reinforce their listening skills while promoting learning.

The audios, an invaluable tool.

The books are accompanied by an Audio CD containing recordings of all the listening activities. The Speaking and Listening Workbook (see page T29) is also accompanied by an Audio CD.

The webpages are a fundamental element of *Español Santillana.*

The webpage **Fans del español** (www.fansdelespañol.com) features the basic plot of the story. The characters decide to create the website *Fans del español* in order to share what they know about the Spanish-speaking world. Characters post information about themselves and about challenges that students can access on this webpage. In this manner, fiction takes on reality.

Additionally, the ***Español Santillana*** series is supported by the **Fans Online** website (campus.fansdelespañol.com), which offers countless activities, photogalleries, games, and other resources for the student, as well as an extensive bank of Assessment activities for the teacher to use (Online Assessments).

The digital versions of the Student Book and Teacher's Edition provide a complete multimedia experience.

Both the Student Book and Teacher's Edition are available in an interactive digital format:

▶ The ***Interactive Student Book*** contains numerous multimedia resources that enhance and complement learning Spanish: videos, visual presentations, audios, photogalleries, flashcards, etc. Students can listen to the pronunciation of the dialogues and vocabulary words, and can also use interactive tools such as highlighters and sticky notes.

▶ The ***All-in-One Digital Teacher's Edition*** brings together all of the elements that the teacher needs to plan and teach a class:

- The *Interactive Student Book* and its multimedia resources. This version of the *Student Book* is designed so that the teacher can project the pages onto a screen and can also activate the videos, the visual presentations, the audios, and other features.
- The *Teacher's Edition* pages.
- The *Teacher's Annotated Edition* of the *Practice Workbook* and the *Speaking and Listening Workbook*, with its corresponding audio tracks.
- The Assessment Program, with answer keys for the teacher.
- An editable version of the Lesson Plans, so that the teacher can personalize the lesson plans to his or her needs.

Three workbooks to practice with.

Español Santillana features three student workbooks:
the *Practice Workbook*, the *Speaking and Listening Workbook*,
and the workbook for heritage Spanish speakers
(the *Cuaderno para hispanohablantes*).

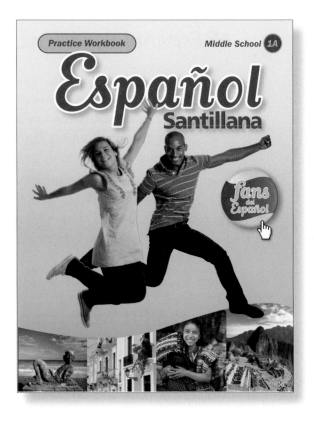

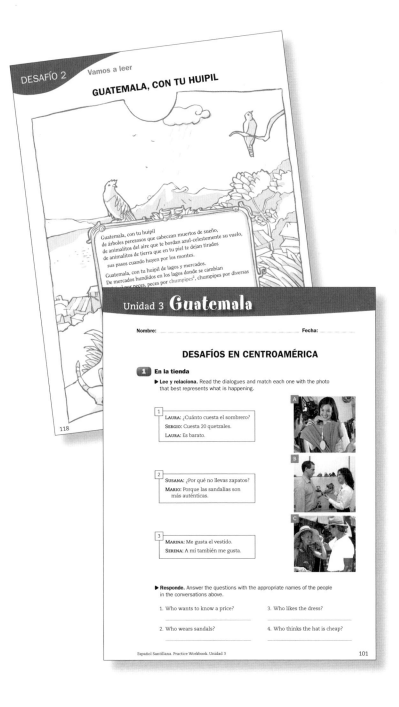

The *Practice Workbook* deepens the study of the language independently.

This is the perfect complement to the Student Book. Here students will find many opportunities to work with the linguistic and cultural contents of the series. It contains all the information (word glossaries and grammar summaries) that students need, and the activities have been designed so that students can work them out without having to consult other sources.

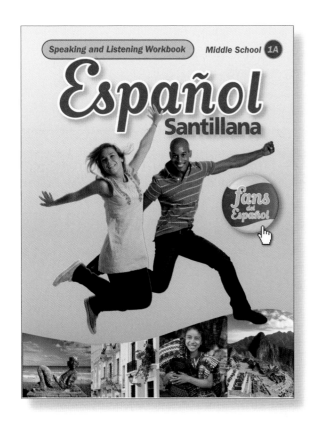

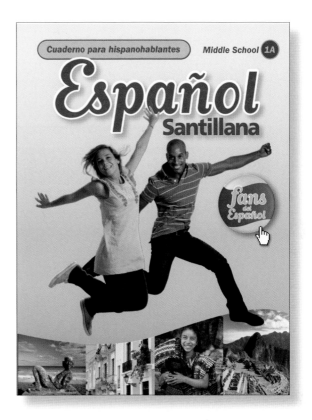

The *Speaking and Listening Workbook* consolidates two fundamental skills.

This workbook deals specifically with comprehension and verbal expression.

The listening activities can be used in the classroom or at home. The Audio CD that accompanies the workbook allows the students to work independently. In contrast, the speaking activities are designed to be used in the classroom.

The speaking and listening activities allow students to practice the key vocabulary and grammatical structures presented in the books.

The workbook for heritage Spanish speakers improves their reading comprehension and writing ability.

This workbook complements the *Español Santillana* textbook and is for heritage Spanish speakers capable of completing an activity in Spanish by themselves.
The workbook maintains the themes and structures of the Student Book, allowing heritage Spanish speaker to work with the textbook in class while completing tasks appropriate to their language level in the workbook.

The objectives of the workbook are the following:

- To develop reading comprehension (Reading).
- To expand students' vocabulary (Vocabulary).
- To improve students' handling of written expression for various purposes (Spelling, Writing).
- To encourage understanding of and appreciation for differences in cultural origins (Connections, Communities).

Scope and Sequence 1A

Unidad	Vocabulario	Gramática
Unit 1 **México** 30-87	• People • Physical characteristics • Personality traits • Family • States and conditions	• Subject pronouns • The verb *ser* • Adjectives
Unit 2 **Puerto Rico** 88-147	• The house • Furniture and objects in a house • Household chores • Leisure activities	• Nouns • Articles. Agreement with nouns • Expressing existence. The verb *haber* • Expressing location • Regular *-ar* verbs, present tense
Unit 3 **Guatemala** 148-205	• The shopping center • Clothing and footwear • Describing clothing and footwear • Shopping	• Stem-changing verbs (*e > ie*) • The verb *ir* • The verb *gustar*
Unit 4 **Perú** 206-263	• Foods and beverages • Food stores • At the table • Describing food	• Adverbs of quantity • Expressing want, preference, and rejection. The verbs *querer* and *preferir* • Irregular verbs in the *yo* form

Standards-based Teaching and Instructional Materials in the Spanish as a Foreign Language Classroom

Dr. David McAlpine University of Arkansas at Little Rock

The students in my *Methods of Teaching Second Languages* class don't believe me when I tell them that my best Spanish teaching experience in forty years was in a middle school classroom. It's true! Those of you just beginning your career in a middle school will soon learn, and those of you who are middle school "lifers" already know, that these youngsters in grades five through eight respond readily to content that is connected to their everyday lives and to instruction that actively involves them in the learning process. Your middle school Spanish students may show higher competencies in the three modes of communication than many of their high school counterparts because of their openness to learning new concepts, their curiosity about themselves and others, and their unabashed willingness to be a part of real-life situations.

How can the *Standards for Foreign Language Learning in the 21st Century* help create an engaging atmosphere for middle school students? Let's look at the five Cs and try to draw some classroom ideas from them.

Communication

This standard should be the easiest to meet, as middle school students enjoy listening, speaking, reading, and writing about themselves and others. Guiding the middle school student through tasks that involve problem solving will keep them engaged in the learning process as you move from meaningful listening to speaking activities, from age-appropriate readings to writing activities that range from interpersonal notes to other classmates to presentational products such as children's books and travel brochures.

Cultures

The paradigm of products, practices, and perspectives is just right for middle school students. They relish investigation of the strange and sometimes weird reasons why speakers of Spanish speak, act, and think as they do.

Connections

Middle school students are ready to see the connection of this new language with the other disciplines being explored in this novel educational structure. Should you be a part of a middle school "team" that allows you to collaborate on interdisciplinary lessons and projects, be sure to consider the unique contribution a second language makes to the development of communication skills, cross-cultural awareness, healthy attitudes, and 21st-century skills.

Comparisons

Students between the ages of 10 and 14 enjoy comparing and contrasting their first language and culture with that of the new language and culture. Having students work with authentic materials gives them the opportunity to see the similarities and differences between the Spanish language and that of their native language.

Communities

While it may be more difficult to take middle school students out of their classroom environment to use Spanish in culturally appropriate settings, many teachers have been successful with short-term, well-chaperoned study abroad trips. Others have developed service-learning projects where middle school students volunteer in Hispanic community centers and churches. Having your middle school students use their presentational language skills in the local elementary schools both provides a real-life language experience and enhances the middle school program. Of course, your middle school students are digital natives and are highly motivated by opportunities to use technology to communicate in Spanish, both within and outside our country.

Bibliography

Adair-Hauck, B. "Foreign Languages in the Middle Schools: A Curricular Challenge." *Pennsylvania Language Forum* 64 (1992): 12-18.

Curtain, Helena, and Carol A. Dahlberg. *Languages and Children—Making the Match: New Languages for Young Learners, Grades K–8*. 4th ed. Boston, MA: Pearson Allyn and Bacon, 2010.

Knop, C. K., and P. Sandrock. "The Case for a Sequential Second Language Learning Experience at the Middle Level." *Foreign Language Annals* 27 (1994): 77-83.

Met, M. "Current Foreign Language Practices in Middle Schools." *Foreign Language Annals* 27 (1994): 43-58.

National Standards in Foreign Language Education Project (NSFLEP). *Standards for Foreign Language Learning in the 21st Century*. Lawrence, KS: Allen Press, 2006.

Teaching and Learning: Language and Culture

Janet Glass Dwight Englewood School, Englewood,
New Jersey Rutgers University

Alfred Nobel's Peace Prize wished to reward "the person who shall have done the most or the best work for fraternity between nations." What could be more critical today? As teachers of world languages, our medium is language, but our message is one of cultural ambassador. Besides, what is more intriguing to a student than to learn how to make a new friend from another culture, to enter another world? This motivation is what stimulates our students' curiosity and helps them master the language. But once hooked, how can we make the most of their interest?

Five-Senses Culture

We can start by integrating culture into the whole language instruction process, making sure that culture underscores every language activity and is at the core of the unit. We can go beyond cultural "awareness" and try to experience the target culture in the classroom with smells, touches, simulations, tastes, rhythms, and video clips. Learning is enhanced when exchanges with people from the target culture happen early and often. As Byram et al. say in "Developing Intercultural Competence in Practice," "the task is rather to facilitate learners' interactions with some small part of another society and its cultures … and encouraging them to investigate for themselves the otherness around them." Let's lift it off the page!

Measuring Culture

When it comes to culture, students are always asking, "Does it *count*?" Although we have currently come a long way in measuring the language proficiency of our students, we are challenged to do as well with testing cultural appropriateness. Culture has to be taught systematically and then, assessed. How powerful it is to show students evidence of their own cultural competence, yet more exploration of how to best assess cultural competence is needed.

Seeing Our Own Culture with New Eyes

As language teachers, we also make the most of students' interest when we show how language shapes our thoughts, and leads to how we behave. Most of us don't become aware of our own cultural assumptions until confronted by another world view. When I was in Japan, for example, people frequently apologized as part of their daily conversation. They said, "Sorry I disturbed you" when calling someone on the phone. How does this habit of polite language reflect its culture? Accepting responsibility is a very high priority in Japan. As a result, we find it is a culture that discourages blame and is relatively free of lawsuits. Cultural instincts become internal, hidden, and subconscious. Through the target language, we strive to have our students uncover these influences, empathize with the people, and be able to interact in culturally appropriate ways.

Research Says

Meanwhile, research has confirmed what we have sensed. In a survey of young students studying language and culture, their responses to "People from other countries are scary" and "Hearing a language that's not English makes me nervous" was a resounding "No!" Students not in the program answered "Maybe" and "Yes."

So, as we make the foreign become familiar, the familiar will become a bit more foreign. By bringing cultural experiences into the classroom, measuring the outcomes, aiming for deep understanding and exchanges, we put linguistic and cultural abilities together and at the forefront of our shrinking world. *¡Sí, se puede!*

Bibliography

Byram, Michael, A. Nichols, and D. Stevens. "Developing Intercultural Competence in Practice." *Multilingual Matters Ltd*. 3 (2001).

Kennedy, Teresa, et al. "The FLES Attitudinal Inventory." *Foreign Language Annals*, ACTFL 33(3), May/June 2000: 278-289.

Wright, David A. "Culture as Information and Culture as Affective Process: A Comparative Study." *Foreign Language Annals*, ACTFL 33(3), May/June 2000: 330-341,

Motivation

Jan Kucerik Pinellas County Public Schools, Pinellas County, Florida

A seventh grade student known to his Spanish teacher as "Juanito" ambles reluctantly into his beginning Spanish classroom. He greets the teacher, not with an enthusiastic "Buenos días, señora," but instead with the question on the mind of many of his classmates, "What are we doing in here today?" Although we would like to believe that the question has been posed out of genuine interest in the classroom activities, we realize that Juanito's question is motivated by self-preservation. He worries that he might be unprepared for, or embarrassed by, the activities Señora has planned for the day.

What Motivates Our Students

Motivation is crucial to teaching and learning. Whenever we feel a desire or need for something, we are in a state of motivation. Juanito is motivated to survive the class period, and his teacher wants him to thrive and share her passion for the Spanish language and Hispanic culture. He has a need to feel safe, yet his teacher understands that he must take risks in order to acquire language. He wants to avoid struggle, and she knows that great effort is involved in negotiating meaning and learning from mistakes. Although human beings are motivated to learn from birth, students are often not motivated to learn what we want them to learn in the way that we want them to learn it. They do, however, select information and learning experiences that are important to them every day. Teachers continue to work tirelessly to motivate their students, but most focus on extrinsic motivators, which may not be enough to truly engage students in the long term. How do we make students feel connected to learning? How do we make them feel as if the learning could not happen without them? How do we create excitement for learning, resulting in students eagerly entering our classrooms each day?

Relationships Are Key

We rely on the standards and performance guidelines to articulate authentic tasks and clear goals. We persevere in our commitment to adjust the learning environment and the content to attract students. Most importantly, we recognize that our relationships with our students and their relationship with the learning process are crucial. Students must believe that they can be successful and experience incremental growth through learning experiences carefully designed around small chunks of meaningful language, leading to purposeful communication. Learning must be fun. Students are more likely to retain the language they acquire in a learning context that they enjoy.

They must feel that they are part of the learning environment, that they belong to the target culture, while they are acquiring their new language. They must understand the purpose of the lesson and have the freedom to select language that is important to them along the way.

Motivation and Learning

Students are motivated to take part in Spanish class when the context through which the language is presented and practiced is meaningful, serves a purpose, and relies on the students to bring it to life. Effective teachers understand the link between motivation and learning, and select language and cultural contexts that rely on the students to tell the story. "What are we doing in here today, Señora?" "We need you, Juanito, to help guide us on our learning journey."

Bibliography

Blaz, Deborah. *Foreign Language Teacher's Guide to Active Learning.* Larchmont, NY: Eye on Education, Inc., 1999.

———. *Bringing the Standards for Foreign Language Learning to Life.* NY: Eye on Education, Inc., 2002.

Curtain, Helena, and Carol A. Dahlberg. *Languages and Children—Making the Match.* Boston: Allyn and Bacon, 2004.

High, Julie. *Second Language Learning through Cooperative Learning.* San Clemente, CA: Kagan Publishing, 1993.

Marzano, Robert J., Debra J. Pickering, and Jane E. Pollock. *Classroom Instruction that Works.* Baltimore: ASCD, 2001.

Omaggio, Alice H. *Teaching Language in Context.* Florence, KY: Cengage and Heinle, 2000.

Patrick, Paula. *The Keys to the Classroom.* Alexandria, VA: The American Council on the Teaching of Foreign Languages, 2007.

Rogers, Spence. *21 Building Blocks Critical to Leaving No Child Left Behind.* Evergreen, CO: PEAK Learning Systems, Inc., 2003.

Rogers, Spence, Jim Ludington, and Becky Graf. *Teaching and Training Techniques: Lighting the Way to Performance Excellence.* Evergreen, CO: PEAK Learning Systems, Inc., 2003.

Rogers, Spence, Jim Ludington, and Shari Graham. *Motivation and Learning: A Teacher's Guide to Building Excitement for Learning and Igniting the Drive for Quality.* Evergreen, CO: PEAK Learning Systems, Inc., 1999.

Shrum, Judith L., and Eileen W. Glisan. *Teacher's Handbook: Contextualized Language Instruction.* Florence, KY: Cengage and Heinle, 2005.

Meeting the Needs of Middle Grades Students in the Foreign Language Classroom: A Call for Differentiated Instruction

Dr. Frances S. Hoch Raleigh, North Carolina

Middle school instruction is essential to the success of a K–12 Spanish language program, but it has often been the biggest stumbling block to full implementation. Middle school teacher faces many challenges such as insufficient contact time in language classes, designation as a "noncore" or exploratory subject, and, perhaps most significantly, a diverse student population.

The Different Skill Levels

Middle school Spanish students in the same classroom may be beginners, may have studied the language in elementary school, or may come from a home where Spanish is spoken. They may be gifted or struggling. They are at various stages of growth as they undergo many physical, emotional, intellectual, and social changes. They live in the moment and are most concerned about the opinions of their peers. It is the middle school Spanish teacher's responsibility to motivate these students, to teache them communication skills, and to help them understand and appreciate other cultures while meeting their personal and developmental needs as young adolescents.

How Do We Differentiate Instruction?

Differentiated instruction describes the variety of ways in which teachers respond to the needs and preferences of their students. Carol Ann Tomlinson suggests that teachers can differentiate in three areas: content, process, and product. Let's look at her model for the Spanish language classroom.

Content

Differentiating content can be accomplished by providing to students with choices. Students must meet basic content goals and objectives but they can accomplish them in different ways. Students may be able to select the topic and relevant vocabulary they wish to explore from a list of topics provided by the teacher. They may be given a choice of readings that address their interests and abilities. Teachers may also be able to provide direct instruction to those students who need it while allowing others to work independently.

Process

Process refers to the learning activities provided to students. Again, choice is important to address student needs and preferences. Middle school students often prefer to work in groups. Teachers should employ various flexible grouping strategies by sometimes mixing students of different abilities, and at other times grouping students according to interests or preferred learning styles. Students may be able to choose activities based on opportunities provided by the teacher or developed by the class.

Product

The product is the way in which students demonstrate what they have learned. Products may be oral and written tests, but they may also be graphic organizers, multimedia presentations, homework assignments, or journals, which students complete individually or in groups. All products should be judged according to a rubric that is clear to students before they begin. Student self-assessment is an evaluation tool. *Linguafolio*, a self-assessment system for foreign language students developed by NCSSFL (the National Council of State Supervisors for Languages), is one instrument that can assist students in monitoring their own language development.

Middle school is an important bridge in K–12 foreign language instruction which helps students progress toward communicative competence. Differentiated instruction can help these students experience success in the Spanish classroom and encourage them to continue studying the language in high school and beyond.

Bibliography

Blaz, Deborah. *Differentiated Instruction: A Guide for Foreign Language Instruction*. Larchmont, NY: Eye on Education, Inc., 2006.

Thiesen, Toni. "Differentiated Instruction in the Foreign Language Classroom: Meeting the Diverse Needs of All Learners." *Communique LOTECED* (2002).

Tomlinson, Carol A. *The Differentiated Classroom: Responding to the Needs of All Learners*. Alexandria, VA: ASCD, 1999.

Meeting the Needs of Heritage Speakers in a Spanish as a World Language Classroom

Maria Elena Messina Adrian C. Wilcox High School, Santa Clara, California

As middle school teachers take on the challenge of teaching Spanish to a small minority of heritage Spanish speakers (in a predominantly native English-speaking classroom), it is important to keep in mind the ultimate goals: to promote language acquisition and cultural awareness for both groups. This can be accomplished by differentiated instruction, by open-ended and cooperative activities that require linguistic and analytic ability, and by allowing both groups to contribute to completing tasks that promote equal-status behavior.

The Traditional Role of the Heritage Speaker

In the past, heritage speakers of Spanish were relegated to the role of "model" for the English speakers. While this gave them a higher status, it seldom met the need to increase their level of academic language. This resulted in discipline issues stemming from a lack of interest on the part of the student.

The Heritage and Native Speaker Backgrounds

Heritage speakers are American-born students whose home language is Spanish. Native speakers are recent immigrants from Spanish-speaking countries. Recent immigrants range from well-educated native speakers, at or above grade level in their primary language, to children whose formal schooling has been interrupted significantly. Heritage speakers can be at grade level in English and tend to have different levels of oral proficiency, but lack register development in Spanish since their formal education has been predominantly in English. Because of the differences in academic preparation in the target language, it is essential to determine each student's individual needs.

Spanish at the Middle School Level

The Center for Applied Linguistics has completed a comprehensive survey of K–12 foreign language programs nationwide, describing how schools are meeting the need for language instruction to prepare global citizens. The 2008 survey results indicate a serious "disconnect between the national call to educate world citizens with high-level language skills and the current state of foreign language instruction in schools across the country." According to the study, however, "Spanish has become increasingly popular over the last decade. In 2008, 88% of the elementary schools teaching a language reported teaching Spanish." Unfortunately, while the number of Spanish for Heritage Speakers programs is increasing at the high school level, they are practically none existent at middle schools. There are several reasons for this deficiency, including an insufficient number of heritage speakers to implement a program and a lack of appropriate materials. Because of this lack of dedicated programs, Spanish as a World Language programs must also embrace heritage speakers.

Meeting the Needs of English Speakers and Heritage Spanish Speakers: A Balancing Act

While the goals of Spanish instruction for heritage speakers are the same as those for their peers, the approach to reaching those goals is definitely different, and a true challenge for Spanish teachers in middle school.

The Curriculum

A successful second-language program will contain systematic differentiated instruction through which *all* students are guided to develop higher-order thinking skills which allow them to work independently, in pairs, and in groups. This program must teach language-learning strategies through authentic target language materials enhanced by the use of technology. Standards-based instruction, alternative assignments, and goals for heritage speakers that enable them to demonstrate mastery will foster engagement and motivation for both groups. Activities that raise the English speakers' level of confidence as well as the heritage speakers' level of academic language will promote a sense of community and enrich the relevance of learning.

Bibliography

Hall, Joan K., and A. Ramírez. "How a Group of High School Learners of Spanish Perceives the Cultural Identities of Spanish Speakers, English Speakers, and Themselves." *Hispania* 76(3) (1993): 613-620.

Jensen, Janis, Paul Sandrock, and John Franklin, *The Essentials of World Languages, Grades K–12: Effective Curriculum, Instruction, and Assessment.* Alexandria, VA: Association for Supervision and Curriculum Development, 2007.

Rhodes, Nancy C., and Ingrid Pufahl, *Foreign Language Teaching in U.S. Schools: Results of a National Survey.* Washington, DC: Center for Applied Linguistics, 2009.

Español
Santillana

fans
del
Español

Español Santillana is a collaborative effort by two teams specializing in the design of Spanish-language educational materials. One team is located in the United States and the other in Spain.

Published in the United States of America.

Español Santillana
Student Book Level 1B
ISBN-13: 978-1-61605-083-2
ISBN-10: 1-61605-083-7

Illustrators: **Bartolomé Seguí, Jorge Arranz**
Picture Coordinator: **Carlos Aguilera**

Cartographer: **Tania López**
Cartographic Coordinator: **Ana Isabel Calvo**

Production Manager: **Ángel García Encinar**

Production Coordinator: **Jesús A. Muela**

Design and Layout: **Marisa Valbuena, Javier Pulido, Alfonso García, Fernando Calonge**

Proofreaders: **Gerardo Z. García, Jennifer Farrington, Marta López, Lawrence Lipson**

Photo Researchers: **Mercedes Barcenilla, Amparo Rodríguez**

Santillana USA Publishing Company, Inc.
2023 NW 84th Avenue, Doral, FL 33122

1 2 3 4 5 6 7 8 9 10   15 14 13 12 11

Editorial Staff in United States
Anne Smieszny
Ana Isabel Antón
Andrea Roberson

Editorial Staff in Spain
Susana Gómez
Cristina Núñez
Belén Saiz

Linguistic and Cultural Advisers in Latin America and in the United States

Antonio Moreno
Editorial Director, Santillana México

Mayra Méndez
Editorial Director, Santillana Puerto Rico

Luis Guillermo Bernal
Editorial Director, Santillana Guatemala

Cecilia Mejía
Editorial Director, Santillana Perú

Graciela Pérez de Lois
Editorial Director, Santillana Argentina

Manuel José Rojas
Editorial Director, Santillana Chile

Mario Núñez
Director of Professional Development, Santillana USA

Reviewers

Dr. Tamara Alsace
Buffalo, NY

Dr. Josefa Báez-Ramos
Seattle, WA

Mercedes Bernal
West New York, NJ

Miguel Castro
New Orleans, LA

Yvonne Davault
Mansfield, TX

Dr. Frances S. Hoch
Raleigh, NC

Petra Liz-Morell
Ridgefield Park, NJ

James Orihuela
Whittier, CA

Ana Sainz de la Peña
Allentown, PA

Eugenia Sarmiento
Centennial, CO

Thomasina White
Philadelphia, PA

Writers

Dr. Miguel Santana
received his PhD in Hispanic literature at the University of Texas–Austin. Dr. Santana has taught Spanish at the elementary, high school, and college levels, and has worked as a Spanish editor and writer for numerous educational publishers in the United States. Miguel Santana is also an author of several novels.

Dr. Lori Langer de Ramírez
received her doctorate in curriculum and teaching from Teacher's College, Columbia University. She is chairperson of the ESL and World Language Department for Herricks Public Schools, New York. Dr. Langer de Ramírez is the recipient of many prestigious awards.

Eduardo Fernández Galán
received his *Licenciatura en Lingüística Hispánica* from the Universidad Complutense de Madrid. He has taught Spanish at Montgomery High School in Montgomery, New Jersey, and The College of New Jersey in Ewing.

Dr. Michele Guerrini
received her PhD in Romance languages from the University of Pennsylvania. She has worked as director of bilingual and EFL departments at Richmond Publishing in Spain and as an adjunct assistant professor of Spanish at The George Washington University in Washington, DC.

Cristina Núñez Pereira
received her *Licenciatura en Filología Hispánica* from the Universidad Nacional de Educación a Distancia and is a *Licenciada en Periodismo* from the Universidad Carlos III de Madrid.

Belén Saiz Noeda
received her *Licenciatura en Filología Hispánica* from Universidad de Alicante. She was a professor of Spanish language and culture and was in charge of Spanish teacher education at the Universidad de Alcalá and at other institutions.

María Inés García
received her masters in Spanish from Texas A & I University. She is a former director of the Languages Other Than English program for the Texas Education Agency, and was the Spanish specialist with the agency for 26 years.

María J. Fierro-Treviño
received her MA from the University of Texas–San Antonio. She was the director of Languages Other Than English program for the Texas Education Agency. She has taught Spanish at the secondary and college levels, and has worked as an instructional specialist, and as a presenter of professional-development seminars.

Contributors

Janet L. Glass
Dwight-Englewood School, Englewood, NJ

Dr. Frances S. Hoch
Raleigh, NC

Jan Kucerik
Pinellas County Schools Largo, FL

Dr. Dave McAlpine
University of Arkansas–Little Rock, Little Rock, AR

Maria Elena Messina
Adrian C. Wilcox High School, Santa Clara, CA

Dr. Gerardo Piña-Rosales
North American Academy of the Spanish Language, The City University of New York (CUNY) Lehman and Graduate Center, New York, NY

Advisers

Trina M. Gonzales-Alesi
John Glenn Middle School of International Studies, Indio, CA

Paula Hirsch
Windward School, Los Angeles, CA

María Orta
Kennedy High School, Chicago, IL

Nina Wilson
Murchison Middle School, Austin, TX

Developmental Editor
Susana Gómez

Editorial Coordinator
Anne Smieszny

Editorial Director
Enrique Ferro

Welcome to

The pairs

Andy Douglas y su hermana
Janet Douglas

Nosotros somos fans del español por la música. La música latina es muy divertida.

Tess Williams y su madre
Patricia Williams

Hay lugares fantásticos en el mundo hispano.

Español Santillana

Who we are

We are four pairs of fans of the Spanish language and of Hispanic cultures. Our objective is to get to know the Spanish-speaking world: its people, its landscapes, its cities, its customs, and its traditions. That's why we've created the website Fans del Español.

What we do

To reach our goal, we are going to travel to different Spanish-speaking countries with special missions: to find the most surprising place, the most fun customs and traditions, the most original recipe, and so on. In each country, we will take on Desafíos (challenges) that each pair will try to complete. Will we succeed?

You can follow our adventures through this book and on the website www.fansdelespañol.com.

Rita Delgado y su sobrina
Diana Robles

Hummm. Nosotras somos fans de la cocina hispana. Es deliciosa.

Tim Taylor y su abuelo
Mack Taylor

La gente hispana es maravillosa.

The countries of the challenges

What countries are the pairs going to visit? Let's find out. Do these activities.

1. Look at the photos and investigate. In which countries are these places located?

2. Look at the map and answer. What countries share borders with the countries represented by the photos?

3. Leaf through the book. What color corresponds to each country?

CANADÁ

OCÉANO ATLÁNTICO

ESTADOS UNIDOS

BAHAMAS

CUBA
REPÚBLICA DOMINICANA

MÉXICO
HAITÍ
JAMAICA
PUERTO RÍCO

BELICE
GUATEMALA HONDURAS
EL SALVADOR NICARAGUA

COSTA RICA PANAMÁ
VENEZUELA
GUYANA

COLOMBIA
SURI

ECUADOR

PERÚ

BOLIVIA

PARAGUAY

CHILE

URUGUAY
ARGENTINA

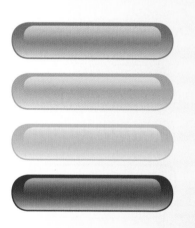

(1) Sevilla.

(2) Misión de Santa Bárbara.

OCÉANO
ATLÁNTICO

España

| 0 | 375 | 750 |
millas

| 0 | 375 | 750 |
kilómetros

yana Francesa

BRASIL

(3) Buenos Aires.

(4) Isla de Pascua.

Your participation counts!

1. Your vote decides the winner

In these challenges, you are going to play an important role. You will accompany us to each country. Pay close attention, because you are going to form part of the judging panel. In each country, you will evaluate which pair has done the best job or which task is the most interesting. Each time, you will help to decide the winning team.

2. Your challenge

You will also have your own challenge: TU DESAFÍO. During the course of the year, you will be able to accumulate points toward your challenge. To do this, watch for this symbol:

🚩 → **TU DESAFÍO**

When you see it, go to the *Fans del español* website. Just by participating, you will earn points. If at the end of the course you have accumulated enough points, you too will have won your challenge!

Contents

Unidad 5

España

Al otro lado del Atlántico

Video Program

Videos

- España. Al otro lado del Atlántico
- La Alhambra
- El monasterio de Silos
- Mapa cultural de España

Audiovisuales

En Madrid

Una vuelta ciclista

El azulejo perdido

El escudo de los reyes

Una receta antigua

www.fansdelespañol.com

Unidad 6

Estados Unidos

Desafíos en casa

DESAFÍO ③

DESAFÍO ④

Video Program

Videos

• Estados Unidos. Desafíos en casa
• La Calle Ocho (Miami)
• Los Grammy latinos
• Mapa cultural de los Estados Unidos

Audiovisuales

 En Washington DC

 Una partida de dominó

 Una noche en el museo

 Fotos de famosos

 ¡Vamos a jugar!

www.fansdelespañol.com

Unidad 7

Argentina

En tierra de gauchos

Video Program

Videos

- Argentina. En tierra de gauchos
- El tren a las nubes
- Las cataratas del Iguazú
- Mapa cultural de Argentina

Audiovisuales

 En Buenos Aires

 El tren a las nubes

 Un gaucho de la Pampa

 Las cataratas del Iguazú

 Sobres en la calle

www.fansdelespañol.com

Unidad 8

Chile

De vuelta a los Andes

Video Program

Videos

- Chile. De vuelta a los Andes
- Isla de Pascua
- Maratón de las Escaleras (Valparaíso)
- Mapa cultural de Chile

Audiovisuales

 En Santiago de Chile

 Las estrellas de Atacama

 Una estatua falsa

 El Maratón de las Escaleras

 La famosa Ruta W

www.fansdelespañol.com

Connecting Unit ¿Recuerdas?

Objectives

- To introduce people.
- To describe family members and friends.
- To describe people's physical features and personality traits.
- To identify how people feel.
- To claim and assign possession.
- To identify people and things.
- To express habitual actions.

- To talk about the parts of the house and household furniture.
- To express location, movement and existence.
- To conjugate and use regular and irregular verbs in the present tense.
- To express likes or dislikes and preferences.
- To talk about shopping.

- To talk about the color and cost of clothing.
- To describe place settings, foods, and drinks.
- To express quantity and comparison.
- To use direct and indirect object pronouns.

Contents

Vocabulary

- Family members.
- Personality traits and physical characteristics.
- Expressions describing states of being.
- Places and objects in the home.
- Chores and leisure activities.
- Stores and store hours.
- Clothing and colors.
- Place settings, foods and flavors.

Grammar

- The verbs *estar*, *ser*, and *tener*.
- Gender and number agreement in adjectives and nouns.
- Possessive adjectives.
- Definite and indefinite articles.
- Adverbs of location.
- The verb *haber* to express existence.
- *Ir a* + place.
- Verbs in the present tense.

- Adverbs of frequency.
- Stem-changing verbs *e > ie, o > ue,* and *e > i*.
- The verb *gustar*.
- Comparisons.
- Direct and indirect object pronouns.
- Irregular first-person verbs.
- Demonstratives.

Evaluation Criteria

- Ask for and give information about physical features, personality traits, and emotional states.
- Describe one's family members and friends in terms of personality and physical characteristics.
- Use the verbs *ser*, *estar*, and *tener* in descriptions, to express emotional states, and to express possession.
- Ask and give information about people and things.

- Recognize and use adjectives, nouns, articles, regular verbs, and adverbs of frequency.
- Describe the rooms and furnishings in a house.
- Talk about household chores and normal activities at home, and how frequently one does them.
- Use the verb *haber* to express existence.
- Ask about the opening and closing times of an establishment.
- State where someone is going.

- Use regular and irregular verbs in the present tense.
- Express what someone likes or dislikes and quantify how much one likes or dislikes something.
- Express the location of items in relation to other items.
- Compare people and things.
- Express for whom an action is performed and/or who benefits from it, and the corresponding pronouns.

Unit Plan

Preliminary pages

Estimated time: 1 session.

Functions & forms:
- Review the themes of book 1A.
- Preview the themes of book 1B.

1. IDENTIFICAR Y DESCRIBIR

Estimated time: 4 sessions.

Functions & forms:
- Introductions.
- Family members.
- Physical characteristics and personality traits.
- Temporary states and feelings.
- Describing people: The verbs *ser* and *estar*. Adjectives.
- Expressing possession: The verb *tener*. Possessive adjectives.
- Identifying people and things: Nouns. Articles.

2. EXPRESAR ACCIONES HABITUALES

Estimated time: 4 sessions.

Functions & forms:
- The house.
- Household chores and free-time activities.
- Expressing place, movement, and existence: Adverbs of place. The verbs *haber* and *ir*.
- Expressing habitual actions in the present: Regular verbs. Adverbs of frequency.
- Expressing habitual actions in the present. Stem-changing verbs.

3. EXPRESAR GUSTOS Y PREFERENCIAS

Estimated time: 4 sessions.

Functions & forms:
- Stores.
- Clothing.
- Foods.
- Expressing likes: The verb *gustar.* Adverbs of quantity. Comparisons.
- Object pronouns.
- Expressing habitual actions in the present: Irregular verbs in the *yo* form.
- Demonstratives.

REVIEW AND EVALUATION

Estimated time: 2 sessions.

Functions & forms:
- Review parts 1–3.

Evaluation: Test on the Connecting Unit.

Standards for Learning Spanish

COMMUNICATION

1.1. Interpersonal mode
- Read a conversation.
- Read a letter or an e-mail.
- Report a partner's answers in a table or diagram.
- Write a description for a guessing game.
- Have a conversation with a classmate.
- Interview a partner.

1.2. Interpretive mode
- Answer questions by filling in the blanks.
- Answer questions by matching.
- Answer questions in complete sentences.

- Use the prompts or pictures to write sentences.
- Identify the item that does not belong in a group.
- Listen to a passage and correct the information.
- Listen to a passage and summarize what you heard.
- Listen to descriptions and select the best answer.

1.3. Presentational mode
- Tell a partner about your family's chores.
- Read a description aloud to the class.
- Act out a situation with a partner.
- Describe the people seen in a photo.
- Write a description of a classmate.

CULTURE

2.1. Practices and perspectives
- Learn about how young adults feel before a big party.
- Learn about the distinct store hours for Hispanic-owned businesses.

2.2. Products and perspectives
- Understand the food choices in a Spanish-speaking country.

CONNECTIONS

3.1. Interdisciplinary connections
- Use verbs, adverbs, and/or adjectives to describe people.
- Use adverbs or demonstrative adjectives to say where people or objects are located.
- Fill in a graphic organizer.
- Fill in the blanks to create a clear and concise e-mail.

3.2. Viewpoints through language/culture
- Understand proper etiquette at a Spanish-speaking restaurant.

COMPARISONS

4.1. Compare languages
- Understand the many uses of the verb *tener* in Spanish and its significance in English.

4.2. Compare cultures
- Read an e-mail about a cultural event similar to a Sweet 16 party in the United States.

COMMUNITIES

5.1. Spanish beyond the school setting
- Complete a letter or e-mail to a friend in Spanish.
- Describe who and/or how often you perform certain chores and leisure activities at home.

5.2. Spanish for lifelong learning
- Observe and describe the clothing of the people around you.

Communicative Skills

Interpersonal Mode

		Activities
Speaking	• Have a conversation with a partner. • Interview a partner. • Describe people in a photo.	• 4, 6, 14, 24, 27, 28, 37, 44, 46, 50 • 20, 31 • 17
Writing	• Report a partner's answers in a table or diagram. • Write a paragraph based on a partner's description. • Write a conversation based on a real situation.	• 24, 29, 31 • 20 • 49
Listening	• Listen to and record a partner's answers. • Listen to a description for a guessing game.	• 29, 31 • 38
Reading	• Read a conversation. • Read a description for a guessing game.	• 40 • 38

Interpretive Mode

		Activities
Listening	• Listen to a passage and correct the information. • Listen to a passage and summarize what you heard. • Listen to descriptions and select the best answers.	• 2, 16, 35 • 5, 39 • 8, 15, 18, 22, 25, 32, 42
Reading	• Answer questions by filling in the blanks. • Answer questions by matching. • Answer questions in complete sentences. • Answer questions according to the clues provided.	• 1, 49 • 13, 21 • 33 • 40

Presentational Mode

		Activities
Speaking	• Talk about household chores. • Answer questions according to the pictures provided. • Act out a situation.	• 23, 29 • 33 • 40, 43
Writing	• Answer questions in complete sentences. • Write sentences based on prompts or pictures.	• 4, 31, 34 • 3, 7, 9, 10, 11, 17, 36, 41, 44, 45, 47

Cross-Curricular Standards

Subject	Standard	Activities
Language Arts	• Use verbs, adverbs, and/or adjectives to describe people. • Use adverbs or demonstratives to say where people or objects are located. • Fill in a graphic organizer. • Fill in the blanks to create clear and concise writing.	• 9, 42 • 25 • 10, 24, 31 • 12, 30, 49
Drama	• Act out a scene.	• 40, 43

Connecting Unit ¿Recuerdas?

Lesson Plans (50-Minute Classes)

Day	Objectives	Sessions	Activities	Time	Standards	Resources / Homework
1	To introduce book 1B, and the Connecting Unit	**Introduction** • Warm-Up: Book orientation • Forms and functions		5 m. 45 m.	1.2	
2	To introduce oneself and others, to identify people and to describe family relationships	**1. Identificar y describir – Vocabulario** (2–5) • Warm-Up: Independent Starter • Vocabulary: *Las presentaciones. La familia* • Vocabulary: *¿Cómo es? ¿Cómo está?*	 1–4 5–7	5 m. 25 m. 20 m.	1.1, 1.2, 1.3, 2.1	Audio Practice Workbook
3	To describe people	**1. Identificar y describir – Gramática** (6–7) • Warm-Up: Independent Starter • Grammar: *Describir personas: El verbo 'ser' y el verbo 'estar'. Los adjetivos*	 8–10	5 m. 45 m.	1.2, 1.3, 3.1, 4.1	Audio Practice Workbook
4	To express possession	**1. Identificar y describir – Gramática** (8–9) • Warm-Up: Independent Starter • Grammar: *Expresar posesión: El verbo 'tener'. Los adjetivos posesivos*	 11–14	5 m. 45 m.	1.1, 1.2, 1.3, 2.1, 3.1, 4.1, 4.2, 5.1	Practice Workbook
5	To identify people and things	**1. Identificar y describir – Gramática** (10–11) • Warm-Up: Independent Starter • Grammar: *Identificar personas y cosas: Los nombres. Los artículos*	 15–17	5 m. 45 m.	1.2, 1.3, 3.1, 4.1	Audio Practice Workbook
6	To talk about the parts of the house and furniture, and about household chores and leisure activities	**2. Expresar acciones habituales – Vocabulario** (12–15) • Warm-Up: Independent Starter • Vocabulary: *La casa* • Vocabulary: *Tareas domésticas y actividades de ocio*	 18–20 21–24	5 m. 20 m. 25 m.	1.1, 1.2, 1.3, 3.1	Audio Practice Workbook
7	To express place, movement, and existence	**2. Expresar acciones habituales – Gramática** (16–17) • Warm-Up: Independent Starter • Grammar: *Expresar lugar, movimiento y existencia: Adverbios y expresiones de lugar. El verbo 'ir'. El verbo 'haber'*	 25–28	5 m. 45 m.	1.1, 1.2, 1.3, 2.1, 3.1, 4.1, 5.1	Audio Practice Workbook
8	To express habitual actions in the present tense	**2. Expresar acciones habituales – Gramática** (18–19) • Warm-Up: Independent Starter • Grammar: *Expresar acciones habituales en el presente: Verbos regulares. Adverbios de frecuencia*	 29–31	5 m. 45 m.	1.1, 1.2, 1.3, 3.1, 4.1, 5.1	Audio Practice Workbook

Day	Objectives	Sessions	Activities	Time	Standards	Resources / Homework
9	To express habitual actions in the present tense	**2. Expresar acciones habituales – Gramática** (20–21) • Warm-Up: Independent Starter • Grammar: *Expresar acciones habituales en el presente: Verbos con raíz irregular (e > ie), (o > ue), (e > i)*	32–34	5 m. 45 m.	1.2, 1.3, 3.1, 4.1	Audio Practice Workbook
10	To talk about shopping clothing, and food	**3. Expresar gustos y preferencias – Vocabulario** (22–25) • Warm-Up: Independent Starter • Vocabulary: *Las tiendas. La ropa* • Vocabulary: *La comida*	35–38 39–41	5 m. 25 m. 20 m.	1.1, 1.2, 1.3, 2.1	Audio Practice Workbook
11	To quantify how much one likes something	**3. Expresar gustos y preferencias – Gramática** (26–27) • Warm-Up: Independent Starter • Grammar: *Expresar gustos en distinto grado: El verbo 'gustar'. La comparación*	42–44	5 m. 45 m.	1.1, 1.2, 1.3, 3.1, 4.1	Audio Practice Workbook
12	To express a point without repetition using direct and indirect objects	**3. Expresar gustos y preferencias – Gramática** (28–29) • Warm-Up: Independent Starter • Grammar: *Pronombres de objeto: Pronombres de objeto directo. Pronombres de objeto indirecto*	45–47	5 m. 45 m.	1.1, 1.2, 1.3, 3.1, 4.1	Practice Workbook
13	To express habitual actions in the present tense	**3. Expresar gustos y preferencias – Gramática** (30–31) • Warm-Up: Independent Starter • Grammar: *Expresar acciones habituales en el presente: Verbos irregulares en la primera persona. Los demostrativos*	48–50	5 m. 45 m.	1.1, 1.2, 1.3, 3.1, 4.1	Audio Practice Workbook
14	To integrate vocabulary and grammar	**Repaso** • Warm-Up: Independent Starter • Review		5 m. 45 m.	1.2, 1.3	Practice Workbook
15	To assess student proficiency	**Assessment** • Warm-Up: Last-minute questions and review • Assessment Test on Connecting Unit		5 m. 45 m.	1.2, 1.3	

Connecting Unit ¿Recuerdas?

Lesson Plans (90-Minute Classes)

Day	Objectives	Sessions	Activities	Time	Standards	Resources / Homework
1	To introduce book 1B and the Connecting Unit. To introduce oneself and others, to identify people and to describe family relationships	**Introduction / 1. Identificar y describir – Vocabulario** (1–5) • Warm-Up: Book orientation • Forms and functions • Vocabulary: *Las presentaciones. La familia* • Vocabulary: *¿Cómo es? ¿Cómo está?*	 1–4 5–7	5 m. 15 m. 35 m. 35 m.	1.1, 1.2, 1.3, 2.1	Audio Practice Workbook
2	To describe people. To express possession	**1. Identificar y describir – Gramática** (6–9) • Warm-Up: Independent Starter • Grammar: *Describir personas: El verbo 'ser' y el verbo 'estar'. Los adjetivos* • Grammar: *Expresar posesión: El verbo 'tener'. Los adjetivos posesivos*	 8–10 11–14	5 m. 40 m. 45 m.	1.1, 1.2, 1.3, 2.1, 3.1, 4.1, 4.2, 5.1	Audio Practice Workbook
3	To identify people and things. To talk about the parts of the house, furniture, and about household chores and leisure activities	**1. Identificar y describir – Gramática** **2. Expresar acciones habituales – Vocabulario** (10–15) • Warm-Up: Independent Starter • Grammar: *Identificar personas y cosas: Los nombres. Los artículos* • Vocabulary: *La casa* • Vocabulary: *Tareas domésticas y actividades de ocio*	 15–17 18–20 21–24	 5 m. 30 m. 25 m. 30 m.	1.1, 1.2, 1.3, 3.1, 4.1	Audio Practice Workbook
4	To express place, movement, and the existence of an object. To express habitual actions in the present tense	**2. Expresar acciones habituales – Gramática** (16–19) • Warm-Up: Independent Starter • Grammar: *Expresar lugar, movimiento y existencia: Adverbios y expresiones de lugar. El verbo 'ir'. El verbo 'haber'* • Grammar: *Expresar acciones habituales en el presente: Verbos regulares. Adverbios de frecuencia*	 25–28 29–31	 5 m. 40 m. 45 m.	1.1, 1.2, 1.3, 2.1, 3.1, 4.1, 5.1	Audio Practice Workbook
5	To express habitual actions in the present tense. To talk about shopping	**2. Expresar acciones habituales – Gramática** **3. Expresar gustos y preferencias – Vocabulario** (20–23) • Warm-Up: Independent Starter • Grammar: *Expresar acciones habituales en el presente: Verbos irregulares en la raíz e > ie, o > ue, and e > i* • Vocabulary: *Las tiendas. La ropa*	 32–34 35–38	 5 m. 45 m. 40 m.	1.2, 1.3, 3.1, 4.1	Audio Practice Workbook

Day	Objectives	Sessions	Activities	Time	Standards	Resources / Homework
6	To talk about food. To quantify how much one likes something	**3. *Expresar gustos y preferencias – Vocabulario / Gramática*** (24–27) • Warm-Up: Independent Starter • Vocabulary: *La comida* • Grammar: *Expresar gustos en distinto grado: El verbo 'gustar'. La comparación*	39–41 42–44	5 m. 40 m. 45 m.	1.1, 1.2, 1.3, 3.1, 4.1	Audio Practice Workbook
7	To express a point without repetition using direct and indirect objects. To express habitual actions in the present tense	**3. *Expresar gustos y preferencias – Gramática*** (28–29) • Warm-Up: Independent Starter • Grammar: *Pronombres de objeto: Pronombres de objeto directo. Pronombres de objeto indirecto* • Grammar: *Expresar acciones habituales en el presente: Verbos irregulares en la primera persona. Los demostrativos*	45–47 48–50	5 m. 40 m. 45 m.	1.1, 1.2, 1.3, 3.1, 4.1	Audio Practice Workbook
8	To integrate vocabulary and grammar, and to assess student proficiency	**Repaso / Assessment** • Review • Test on Connecting Unit		45 m. 45 m.	1.2, 1.3	Practice Workbook

Audio Scripts

Icons

The 🎧 symbol is used to refer to audio activities. The audio scripts for these activities are found in each unit at the end of the Overview section.

The 👁 symbol is used to refer to activities that are accompanied by a visual presentation. The scripts for these presentations are identical to the dialogues found in the fotonovelas in the Student Book.

The 💬 symbol is used to refer to speaking activities. These activities require spoken expression by the student and do not follow any particular script.

2 La familia de Alicia

Hola, me llamo Alicia y esta es mi familia. Mi padre se llama Carlos y mi madre se llama María. Tengo dos hermanos, Mario y Pedrito. También tengo dos primos, Carmen y Lucas. Son los hijos de mis tíos, Ana y Miguel. Mis abuelos se llaman Juan y Luisa.

5 ¿Cómo están?

1. –Hola, Janet. ¿Cómo estás?
   –Hola, Patricia. ¡Estoy emocionada!
   –¡Qué bien! ¿Y tu hermano Andy?
   –Está en su habitación. Está enfermo.
   –¿Qué le pasa?
   –Le duele la garganta y tiene fiebre.
2. –¿Estás contenta, Diana?
   –Sí, estoy muy contenta, tía. ¿Y tú, estás bien?
   –Pues no mucho. Estoy un poco triste.
   –¿Quieres salir a dar un paseo?
   –De acuerdo, vamos.
3. –¿Cómo estás, abuelo?
   –Estoy un poco cansado, Tim. Y tú, ¿cómo estás?
   –Yo estoy enojado.
   –¿Por qué?
   –Porque quiero ir al cine y nadie puede venir conmigo.

8 ¿Y tú cómo eres?

1. Mi profesora de Español se llama Guadalupe. Es muy joven.
2. Mis padres son muy altos.

3. Javier es un chico muy simpático.
4. Mi hermano Carlos es alto y atlético.

15 En buena compañía

1. chicas
2. profesores
3. hijos
4. hermana
5. niño

16 Rita y Alan

1. Mi hermana es rubia.
2. Mi abuela es delgada.
3. Mi tío es gordo.
4. Mi prima es simpática.
5. Mi madre es morena.

18 ¿Dónde está?

1. ¿Dónde está mi diccionario? Aquí hay un sofá, una estantería y un televisor, pero no veo mi diccionario.
2. ¡No encuentro mi celular! Aquí hay una estufa, un refrigerador y una mesa, pero ¿dónde está mi celular?
3. ¿Dónde está mi camiseta nueva? En este cuarto hay una cama, una mesita de noche y un armario, pero mi camiseta no está aquí.
4. No encuentro mi revista. Aquí hay una bañera, una ducha y un inodoro, pero no veo mi revista.
5. ¿Dónde está mi bicicleta? Aquí está el carro, pero no está mi bicicleta.

22 Primero las tareas domésticas

–Vamos a repartir las tareas, ¿de acuerdo? Tess, tú tienes que sacudir los muebles, ¿OK? Y Andy... ¿dónde estás, Andy?
–Aquí, en el jardín.
–Bien. Tú tienes que cortar el césped, ¿de acuerdo?
–Perfecto. Me gusta cuidar el jardín.
–Tim, hay mucha basura y tú eres fuerte.
–Vale. Yo saco la basura.
–Sí. Tim, la basura. Y Rita...
–¿Puedo pasear al perro?
–Sí, claro. ¿Y quién pasa la aspiradora?
–Pues yo. Yo puedo pasar la aspiradora.
–Gracias, Janet. Bueno, gracias a todos.

25 **¿De quién hablan?**

1. Está a la izquierda de Luis.
2. Está delante de Roy.
3. Está a la derecha de Marta.
4. Está detrás de Luis.
5. Está al lado de Roy.

29 **¿Quién cuida el jardín?**

1. Yo corto el césped.
2. Mis hermanas sacuden los muebles.
3. Pedro y yo paseamos al perro.
4. Tú tienes que barrer el suelo.
5. ¿Pueden ustedes limpiar el garaje?

32 **¿Quién hace cada cosa?**

1. Empezamos la clase a las nueve.
2. Mis hermanos nunca vuelven a casa tarde.
3. Nunca quieres lavar los platos.
4. Mi profesora siempre repite las preguntas.
5. Siempre pido ayuda a mi profesor.
6. Mi hermano mayor prefiere ir al cine.
7. Señores García, pueden pagar con tarjeta de crédito.

35 **De compras**

1. –Mira, Tess. Es un vestido de quinceañera.
   –Sí. Es muy elegante.

2. –Ese suéter es bonito.
   –Sí, es de lana. Es perfecto para el invierno.
3. –¿Cuánto cuesta la camisa?
   –Quince dólares.
4. –Tengo que comprarme unos zapatos nuevos.
   –¿Tienes dinero?
5. –Aquellos pantalones son un poco feos, ¿no?
   –No son feos, Diana. Es que... no están de moda.

39 **De compras en el supermercado**

–Diana, tenemos que preparar la comida. A ver... tenemos que comprar un kilo de arroz y unos huevos.
–Arroz y huevos. Bien. ¿Qué más?
–Tenemos que ir a la carnicería a comprar un pollo.
–Vale.
–Y en la frutería compramos manzanas y naranjas.
–Bien. Manzanas y naranjas.
–¿Necesitamos bebidas?
–¡Sí! Tenemos que comprar refrescos.

42 **¿A quién le gusta?**

1. A mí me gusta mucho la fruta.
2. A mi hermano le gustan mucho los frijoles.
3. A ustedes les gusta el pescado.
4. A nuestros amigos les gusta la verdura.
5. A ti te gusta mucho el arroz, ¿no?

¿Recuerdas?

The Unit

- This unit is a review of the main objectives of Middle School book 1A. Students will review the following topics:
  - Identifications and descriptions, expressing habitual actions, and expressing likes and preferences.
  - Vocabulary relating to the family, the home, daily activities, shopping, clothing, and food.
  - Expressing existence (*haber*), possession (*tener*), movement (*ir*), and likes (*gustar*).
  - Describing people and quantities.

Activities	Standards	Resources
¿Recuerdas?	1.2	

Teaching Suggestions

Warm-Up / Independent Starter

- Ask students to write the names of the participants shown on this page. Can they remember everyone's name? Do they know the family relationships between each of the pairs?

- Have students look at the objectives for this unit. Then divide the class into small groups and assign each group one of the objectives. Ask the groups to come up with an example for their assigned objective. Have students share their examples with the rest of the class.

Preparation

- In order to assess your students' proficiencies at this point in their studies, give them this performance pretest. If students are not able to perform certain tasks, this will be a good indication that you might need to spend some extra class time reviewing the corresponding structures or vocabulary.

1. **Identificar y describir**
- Have students
  - Introduce themselves.
  - Introduce a friend to another student.
  - Describe the physical characteristics of another student.
  - Talk about the emotions and conditions of another student.

Unidad

puente

¿Recuerdas?

You already know Spanish. You know how to introduce yourself, to greet people, to describe people, and to talk about your house and household chores. You can also buy items, ask for food in a restaurant, and express your likes and preferences.

This year, you are going to learn to do many other things in Spanish. You'll learn to express your feelings, to talk about your hobbies and free-time activities, and to give directions. But before we begin, let's review what you already know.

¿Estás preparado para el desafío?

¡Buena sue[rte]!

Review of the Previous Units

FLASH REVIEW OF MEXICO

In Mexico, students learned to identify and describe themselves and others, to describe family relationships, and to express physical states and feelings. They also learned about Mexican soccer, Frida Kahlo, a *quinceañera*, and the Papantla flyers.

FLASH REVIEW OF PUERTO RICO

In Puerto Rico, students learned to identify and describe places, to express existence and location, to express habitual actions, and to express obligation or necessity. They also learned about Old San Juan, the *coquí*, the bioluminescent bay, and the Camuy caves.

¿Recuerdas?

1. Identificar y describir

Vocabulario

Las presentaciones
La familia
¿Cómo es?
¿Cómo está?

Gramática

Describir personas:
– El verbo *ser* y el verbo *estar*
– Los adjetivos

Expresar posesión:
– El verbo *tener*
– Los adjetivos posesivos

Identificar personas y cosas:
– Los nombres
– Los artículos

2. Expresar acciones habituales

Vocabulario

La casa
Tareas domésticas y actividades de ocio

Gramática

Expresar lugar, movimiento y existencia:
– Adverbios y expresiones de lugar
– El verbo *ir*
– El verbo *haber*

Expresar acciones habituales en el presente:
– Verbos regulares
– Adverbios de frecuencia

Expresar acciones habituales en el presente. Verbos con raíz irregular

3. Expresar gustos y preferencias

Vocabulario

Las tiendas
La ropa
La comida

Gramática

Expresar gustos en distinto grado:
– El verbo *gustar*
– Adverbios de cantidad
– La comparación

Pronombres de objeto

Expresar acciones habituales en el presente:
– Verbos irregulares en la primera persona
– Los demostrativos

2. Expresar acciones habituales

- Have students
  - Name the parts of the house.
  - Describe where furniture and household objects are found in their house.
  - Name what chores they have and when they do them.
  - Describe what they feel like doing in their leisure time.

3. Expresar gustos y preferencias

- Have students
  - Say where they purchase their clothing.
  - Describe the clothing two of their classmates are wearing.
  - Describe their favorite foods and drinks.
  - Say where they buy their favorite foods and drinks.

Objectives

- In this unit, students will
  - Greet people and introduce friends.
  - Describe people, express possessions, and identify people and things.
  - Express place, movement, and existence.
  - Express habitual actions in the present tense.
  - Express likes and dislikes.
  - Talk about shopping, clothing, and food.
- By the end of the Connecting Unit students will have reviewed:
  - Vocabulary relating to the family, the home, daily activities, shopping, clothing, and food.
  - The verbs *ser, estar, haber, tener, ir,* and *gustar.*
  - Stem-changing irregular verbs, adverbs of frequency, possessive adjectives and demonstrative pronouns.

FLASH REVIEW OF GUATEMALA

In Guatemala, students learned to talk about shopping, to express likes, to describe and compare clothes and footwear, and to communicate while shopping. They also learned about Antigua, Guatemalan fashion, tradional Guatemalan clothing, and the Chichicastenango market.

FLASH REVIEW OF PERU

In Peru, students learned to express preferences and likes by degrees, to express necessity, to express actions, and to describe value. They also learned about typical Peruvian dishes like *paiche, seco de carne, ceviche,* and *suspiro limeño.*

Connecting Unit

1. IDENTIFICAR Y DESCRIBIR

Vocabulario – Las presentaciones. La familia

Presentation

- In this section, students will review:
  - Introductions.
  - Famiy and people.

Activities	Standards	Resources
Vocabulario	1.2, 2.1	
1.	1.2	
2.	1.2	Audio
3.	1.2	
4.	1.1, 1.2	

Teaching Suggestions

Warm-Up / Independent Starter

- Have students choose ten people from the vocabulary list and write the proper name of a person they know who represents each term. For example: *el chico* = Matt; *la profesora* = Mrs. Lee.

Preparation

- Ask students to work in groups of three to practice greeting and introducing each other. Have students rotate one student out of the group every minute, then repeat the introductions in a new group.

Activities

2. Ask students to create a family tree for a famous TV family with labels in Spanish such as the Huxtables from *The Cosby Show* or *The Simpsons*. Invite volunteers to show their family trees to the class and have the class describe the family relationships presented on the trees.

3. After completing the activity, have students use their answers to play a guessing game with a partner. One student will mix up their responses and read each one aloud to their partner. If his or her partner can guess the person being described, then they will go next. For example: *Es la tía de Diana.* → Rita.

4. When students finish, have each student introduce himself or herself to the class and then introduce a classmate. For example: *Hola, yo me llamo Kathy. Les presento a Tim.*

2

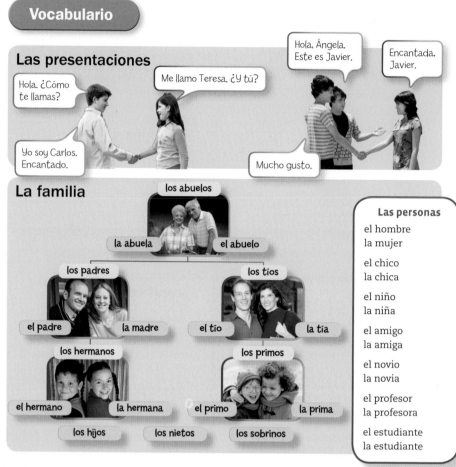

Vocabulario

Las presentaciones

- Hola. ¿Cómo te llamas?
- Me llamo Teresa. ¿Y tú?
- Yo soy Carlos. Encantado.
- Hola, Ángela. Este es Javier.
- Encantada, Javier.
- Mucho gusto.

La familia

- los abuelos
- la abuela
- el abuelo
- los padres
- los tíos
- el padre
- la madre
- el tío
- la tía
- los hermanos
- los primos
- el hermano
- la hermana
- el primo
- la prima
- los hijos
- los nietos
- los sobrinos

Las personas

el hombre
la mujer

el chico
la chica

el niño
la niña

el amigo
la amiga

el novio
la novia

el profesor
la profesora

el estudiante
la estudiante

1 **Mucho gusto**

▶ **Completa.** Choose the words that complete each conversation.

| Esta es | ¿Cómo te llamas? | Mucho gusto. | ¿y tú? | Te presento a |

1. A. ¿Cómo estás, Tess?
   B. Bien, ¿ _1_ ?

2. A. _2_ Ana López.
   B. Encantado, Ana.

3. A. _3_ mi novia Sara.
   B. _4_ .

4. A. ¿ _5_ ?
   B. Me llamo Alan.

2 dos

Differentiated Instruction

DEVELOPING LEARNERS

- Have students create a family tree with the names and the vocabulary words for each person. Then have students compare their family trees with their classmates to see if anyone has a family member by the same name. For example, if their grandfathers have the same name they will say:
  A. *Mi abuelo se llama Martin.*
  B. *Mi abuelo se llama Martin también.*

EXPANDING LEARNERS

- Ask students to copy the family tree of a classmate, and describe the relationships of five of the family members on the same paper, below the tree. When students have finished writing the relationships, have them trade papers with another partner and see if they can remember the names of the family members that they just wrote about. For example: *Es la madre de George.* → Marta.

1. IDENTIFICAR Y DESCRIBIR

Vocabulario – Las presentaciones. La familia

2 **La familia de Alicia**

 ▶**Escucha y corrige.** Listen to Alicia's description of her family and correct the information below.

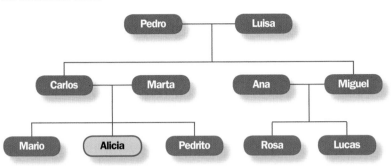

```
            Pedro ──────── Luisa
              │               │
     ┌────────┴────────┐  ┌───┴──────┐
  Carlos ── Marta      Ana ── Miguel
     │                   │
 ┌───┼─────┐        ┌────┴────┐
Mario Alicia Pedrito  Rosa   Lucas
```

3 **¿Quién es?**

▶**Escribe.** Write the relationship between the characters.

Modelo Rita ⟶ Diana

Rita es la tía de Diana.

1. Diana ⟶ Rita

2. Patricia ⟶ Tess

3. Tess ⟶ Patricia

4. Andy ⟶ Janet

5. Mack ⟶ Tim

6. Tim ⟶ Mack

4 **¿Qué tal?**

 ▶**Habla.** Get to know your classmates. Introduce yourself to a partner and find out how he or she is doing.

Modelo A. Hola. Me llamo Tom. ¿Y tú?
B. Yo me llamo Alan. ¿Cómo estás, Tom?
A. Bien, gracias. Te presento a Clara.
B. ...

tres 3

 AUDIO SCRIPT
See page XVII-I

Answer Key

1. 1. ¿y tú?
2. Esta es / Te presento a
3. Te presento a / Esta es
4. Mucho gusto.
5. ¿Cómo te llamas?

2. Marta changes to María.
Rosa changes to Carmen.
Pedro changes to Juan.

3. 1. Diana es la sobrina de Rita.
2. Patricia es la madre de Tess.
3. Tess es la hija de Patricia.
4. Andy es el hermano de Janet.
5. Mack es el abuelo de Tim.
6. Tim es el nieto de Mack.

4. Answers will vary.

Additional Resources

Fans Online activities
Practice Workbook

HERITAGE LANGUAGE LEARNERS

• There are many ways to greet someone in Spanish. Have students come up with a list of greetings, including gestures, and share them with their classmates. You may also have heritage students use non-heritage learners as their presenters.

CRITICAL THINKING

• Ask students to think about the different ways to formally introduce and greet someone in English. Then think about the different ways in Spanish. Are there the same number of ways to do each? Are some of the words cognates? Are these formal introductions commonly used or is it more common to use slang?

1. IDENTIFICAR Y DESCRIBIR

Vocabulario – ¿Cómo es? ¿Cómo está?

Presentation

- In this section, students will review:
  - Physical characteristics.
  - Personality traits.

Activities	Standards	Resources
Vocabulario	1.2	
5.	1.2	Audio
6.	1.1, 1.2	
7.	1.2	

Teaching Suggestions

Warm-Up / Independent Starter

- Ask students to look at the four people being described in the vocabulary and write the opposite of their descriptions. For example, the first boy is *alto, moreno, delgado y atlético*. Students will write the opposites: *bajo, rubio y gordo.*

Preparation

- Ask students to work in pairs to describe another person in the room. See if the partner can guess the person being described. For example: *Es inteligente.* → *Es la profesora.*
- Have students switch partners and repeat the process. Once students have finished, ask them to write a summary of all the people who were described in this exercise.

Activities

6. Have partners write two more descriptions about someone famous that they would both know and/or recognize. Student A should describe the person incorrectly. Student B should correct the mistaken impression. For example:
   A. *LeBron James es bajo.*
   B. *No, LeBron James no es bajo. Es alto.*

7. In small groups, ask students to act out each of the sentences out of order. The first student in the group to call out the correct *tener* phrase gets to go next. For example:
   Sentence 3: Student rubs her stomach.
   Student calls out: *Tienes hambre.*

4

Vocabulario

¿Cómo es?

Características físicas	Rasgos de personalidad

La señora es mayor, baja y rubia.

El chico es joven, alto y moreno. No es gordo. Es delgado y atlético.

Lara es graciosa y simpática. Es espontánea y atrevida.

Tom es serio y tímido. Es inteligente y estudioso.

¿Cómo está?

contenta   triste   emocionado   enojada   cansado   enfermo

Tengo hambre.   Tengo sed.   Tengo frío.   Tengo calor.   Tengo miedo.

5 ¿Cómo están?

▶ **Escucha y escribe.** Listen to the conversations and write how each person feels.

contenta   cansado   enojado   triste   emocionada   enfermo

1. Janet   2. Andy   3. Diana   4. Rita   5. Mack   6. Tim

Modelo 1. *Janet está emocionada.*

4 cuatro

Differentiated Instruction

DEVELOPING LEARNERS

- Ask students to describe how they usually feel on the following dates.
  1. *el primero de enero*
  2. *el catorce de febrero*
  3. *el cuatro de julio*
  4. *el treinta y uno de octubre*
  5. *el veintidós de noviembre*
  6. *el veinticinco de diciembre*

EXPANDING LEARNERS

- Have students write five sentences to express someone's feelings and his or her temporary physical conditions. For example, to describe *Tengo calor*, students could write the following sentences. *Es verano. Hace mucho sol. Estoy en el jardín.* Ask students to swap papers with a partner to see if he or she can guess what vocabulary word or phrase the scene is describing.

6 **No es cierto**

 **Habla.** Your partner isn't wearing his or her glasses today and is having trouble seeing. Help him or her describe the people in the photos.

Modelo Pedrito: guapo/feo
A. *Pedrito es **guapo**.*
B. *No, Pedrito no es guapo. Es **feo**.*

①

Carlos:
moreno/rubio

②

Don Luis:
joven/mayor

③

Toni:
alto/bajo

④

Paco:
delgado/gordo

7 **¿Qué siento cuando...?**

 Escribe. Describe how you would feel in each situation.

 miedo   frío   sed

 calor   hambre

Modelo Estoy en el Polo Norte. → *Tengo frío.*

1. Estoy en el desierto del Sahara. No tengo agua.
2. Nieva mucho. La temperatura es −5 °F.
3. Voy a pedir una pizza con jamón y queso.
4. ¡Tengo un examen de Matemáticas!
5. Hace sol. La temperatura es 100 °F.

cinco 5

 AUDIO SCRIPT
See page XVII-I

Answer Key

5. 1. Janet está emocionada.
   2. Andy está enfermo.
   3. Diana está contenta.
   4. Rita está triste.
   5. Mack está cansado.
   6. Tim está enojado.

6. 1. A. Carlos es moreno.
      B. No, Carlos no es moreno. Carlos es rubio.
   2. A. Don Luis es joven.
      B. No, don Luis no es joven. Don Luis es mayor.
   3. A. Toni es alto.
      B. No, Toni no es alto. Toni es bajo.
   4. A. Paco es delgado.
      B. No, Paco no es delgado. Paco es gordo.

7. 1. Tengo sed.
   2. Tengo frío.
   3. Tengo hambre.
   4. Tengo miedo.
   5. Tengo calor.

Additional Resources

Fans Online activities
Practice Workbook

HERITAGE LANGUAGE LEARNERS

• Have students describe the last time they felt the following emotions or physical states, in three or more sentences.
   1. emocionado(a)
   2. enojado(a)
   3. calor
   4. miedo

COOPERATIVE LEARNING

• In groups of three, ask students to write a short story in Spanish about a boy who feels every emotion in one day. Make sure students describe their character's physical traits at the beginning of their story. One student in the group will be the recorder, another student will be the team leader, and the third student will be the researcher. If there is a word that students don't know, then the researcher will look it up in the dictionary. Have a volunteer from each group read their story to the class.

Connecting Unit

1. IDENTIFICAR Y DESCRIBIR

Gramática – Describir personas

Presentation

- In this section, students will review:
  - Conjugations of the verbs *ser* and *estar* in the present tense.
  - Adjectives and adjective/noun agreement.

Activities	Standards	Resources
Gramática	1.2, 3.1, 4.1	
8.	1.2	Audio
9.	1.2	
10.	1.2	

Teaching Suggestions

Warm-Up / Independent Starter

- Ask students to think of a musical group that they like. Have them describe the physical characteristics and personality traits of the members of the group in 4–5 sentences.

Preparation

- Have students create a memory game. They will need 24 1.5 x 1.5 inch slips of paper. This can be achieved by folding two sheets of paper four times. Students will have eight pieces left over to use as teasers.
- Students will write two sets of all of the subject pronouns by category on separate slips of paper. Then they will write the conjugations for the verbs *ser* and *estar* on separate slips of paper.
- Have students turn over the slips of paper and mix them up. One student will turn over two slips of paper. If they match, that student goes again. If not, then the next person goes. The student with the most matches wins.

Activities

9. In pairs, ask students to take turns reading their answers while their partner points to the corresponding photo in the book.

10. Ask students to write one negative statement for each of the five photos. For example: *María no es rubia*.

6

Gramática

Describir personas

El verbo *ser* y el verbo *estar*

VERBO SER (TO BE). PRESENTE

Singular		Plural	
yo	soy	nosotros nosotras	somos
tú	eres	vosotros vosotras	sois
usted él ella	es	ustedes ellos ellas	son

VERBO ESTAR (TO BE). PRESENTE

Singular		Plural	
yo	estoy	nosotros nosotras	estamos
tú	estás	vosotros vosotras	estáis
usted él ella	está	ustedes ellos ellas	están

- The verb *ser* is used mainly to identify and to describe physical characteristics and personality traits.

  José **es** mi profesor de español. Él **es** alto, inteligente y simpático.

- The verb *estar* is used to express conditions and feelings.

  Ellos no **están** contentos.

Los adjetivos

- Spanish adjectives can be masculine or feminine, singular or plural.
- The **feminine** form is developed from the masculine form:

Masculine form	Feminine form	Examples
Ends in -o.	Changes -o to -a.	El niño es alto. → La niña es alta.
Ends in -e or in a consonant.	Does not change.	Mi padre es joven. → Mi madre es joven.

- The **plural** form is developed from the singular form:

Singular form	Plural form	Examples
Ends in a vowel.	Adds -s.	Ella es simpática. → Ellas son simpáticas.
Ends in a consonant.	Adds -es.	El profesor es joven. → Los profesores son jóvenes.

8 ¿Y tú cómo eres?

 ▶ **Escucha y elige.** Choose the adjective that corresponds to each description you hear.

1. joven/jóvenes
2. altos/alta
3. simpática/simpático
4. atlético/atléticas

6 seis

Differentiated Instruction

DEVELOPING LEARNERS

- Ask students to use the following clues to form sentences.
  1. *ellos / contento*
  2. *Martin / triste*
  3. *ellas / emocionado*
  4. *Julieta / enojado*
  5. *ellos / tímido*
  6. *Martin / inteligente*
  7. *ellas / atlético*
  8. *Julieta / joven*

EXPANDING LEARNERS

- Have students work in groups to play a game of "Pictionary." One student draws a person that shows a physical trait or emotion. His or her teammates guess which adjective is being pictured.

9 **Yo no estoy cansado**

▶ **Escribe.** Use the verb *estar* to say how the people in the photos feel.

Modelo *Marta está emocionada.*

Eva

Manuel y Martín

Javier

Liliana

Paula

Teresa

10 **Es simpática y está contenta**

▶ **Escribe.** Fill in a chart, like the one below, describing the people in the photos.

Modelo

¿Quién es?	¿Cómo es?	¿Cómo está?
María	Es morena y delgada. Es simpática.	Está contenta.

María

Carlos

Julia

Alberto

Luisa

 AUDIO SCRIPT
See page XVII-I

Answer Key

8. 1. joven
2. altos
3. simpático
4. atlético

9. 1. Eva está enferma.
2. Manuel y Martin están contentos.
3. Javier está triste.
4. Liliana está cansada.
5. Paula está nerviosa.
6. Teresa está enojada.

10. Answers will vary. Sample answers:
1. María es morena y delgada. Está contenta.
2. Carlos es rubio y alto. Está triste.
3. Julia es pelirroja y guapa. Está enferma.
4. Alberto es moreno y atlético. Está enojado.
5. Luisa es delgada y joven. Está cansada.

Additional Resources

Fans Online activities
Practice Workbook

HERITAGE LANGUAGE LEARNERS

• Many students, including heritage learners, have problems understanding the difference between the verbs *ser* and *estar*. Help these students by creating a poster with some general rules for the uses of each verb. Be creative with your rules, so students can remember them in the future.

TOTAL PHYSICAL RESPONSE (TPR)

• Read the following story to students. If they hear the verb *ser* or any of its conjugations they should stand up. If they hear the verb *estar* or any of its conjugations they should squat down.

Mi amigo Javier está en casa hoy. Es muy inteligente, y le gusta ir a la escuela, pero hoy no hay clases. Por eso, él quiere jugar al fútbol. Javier es alto, atlético y juega bien al fútbol. Mi amigo Javier está emocionado.

1. IDENTIFICAR Y DESCRIBIR

Gramática – Expresar posesión

Presentation

- In this section, students will review:
  - The verb *tener*.
  - Possessive adjectives.

Activities	Standards	Resources
Gramática	1.2, 3.1, 4.1	
11.	1.2	
12.	1.2, 2.1, 4.2	
13.	1.2	
14.	1.1	

Teaching Suggestions

Warm-Up / Independent Starter

- Ask students to write a list of five things that they have in their school bags or backpacks using the verb *tener*. For example: *Tengo mi cuaderno.*

Preparation

- Have students play this game of "20 questions" in small groups: each student draws the outline of a box on a piece of paper. Ask students to draw pictures of three of their favorite possessions in their box (for example, a book, a computer, a telephone, and so on). Students take turns asking each other if they have certain objects (for example: *¿Tienes una computadora?*). If the student has the item that they were asked about (for example: *Sí, tengo una computadora*), they draw an X over it. The last student with any objects remaining wins.

Activities

11. Ask students to pick five people they know and write a sentence about how old each person is. For example: *Mi hermana tiene catorce años.*

12. Have students write an e-mail back to the Mexican fan with their own information.

13. Invite students to write five sentences describing their extended families. For example: *Sarah es hija de mi tía; es mi prima.* Then ask them to draw a family tree showing these family relationships. Have them exchange papers with a partner for peer review.

Gramática

Expresar posesión

El verbo *tener*

VERBO TENER (TO HAVE). PRESENTE

Singular		Plural	
yo	tengo	nosotros nosotras	tenemos
tú	tienes	vosotros vosotras	tenéis
usted él ella	tiene	ustedes ellos ellas	tienen

Tengo dos hijos. Mis hijos **tienen** cinco y diez años.

- The verb tener usually means *to have*. And it also means *to be* when it expresses age or feelings.

  Yo **tengo** una computadora.   **Tengo** doce años.   **Tengo** miedo.

- To express obligation we can use tener que + infinitive.

  Tenemos que estudiar español.

Los adjetivos posesivos

- Possessive adjectives are used to show ownership. They agree with the noun they accompany, that is, they agree with the thing possessed, not with the owner.

  Nuestros amigos son simpáticos.

ADJETIVOS POSESIVOS

mi mis	*my*	nuestro, nuestra nuestros, nuestras	*our*
tu tus	*your (informal)*	vuestro, vuestra vuestros, vuestras	*your (informal)*
su sus	*his, her, your*	su sus	*their, your*

 11 **¿Qué tienes tú?**

▶ **Escribe.** Write sentences using the verb *tener*.

Modelo Jorge - 2 computadoras → *Jorge tiene dos computadoras.*

1. Tú - 16 años
2. Ustedes - 5 perros
3. Yo - 8 primos
4. Mis abuelos - 9 nietos
5. Mi hermana - 21 años
6. Usted - 3 gatos

Differentiated Instruction

DEVELOPING LEARNERS

- Pair students and tell them that to get to know each other better, they must ask each other at least ten questions using the verb *tener*. For example: *¿Tienes hermanos?* After a couple of minutes, have students switch partners and repeat the process.

EXPANDING LEARNERS

- Have students create a conversation between four people about the things they bring to class. Encourage students to act out their dialogue in front of the class. For example:
  A. *Hola, Juan. ¿Tienes mochila?*
  B. *Sí, tengo mochila. Es bonita.* (Student B holds up a backpack.)
  C. *Mi mochila es bonita también.* (Student C holds up a backpack.)
  D. *Sus mochilas son bonitas, pero mi mochila es fea.* (Student D holds up a backpack.)

12 Tengo una fiesta de quinceañera

▶ **Completa.** Janet received an e-mail from a Mexican fan. Fill in the blanks with the correct form of the verb *tener*.

Mensaje nuevo

Para:
Cc:
Asunto:

¡Hola, Janet!

Soy Rosa. ___1___ catorce años, pero mañana es mi cumpleaños. ¡Estoy muy emocionada y quiero invitarte a mi quinceañera! Es una fiesta muy divertida, con muchos invitados. Mis padres y yo ___2___ muchos amigos.

¿Ustedes ___3___ fiestas como la quinceañera en los Estados Unidos? En México es una tradición familiar. Mi prima también ___4___ quince años y celebramos juntas la fiesta de quinceañera. ¿Y tú, cuántos años ___5___, Janet?

¡Hasta pronto!

Rosa

13 ¿De quién es el primo?

▶ **Une y escribe.** Match the description in column A with the family member in column B to form a complete sentence.

A

1. El hijo de tu tío es
2. Los sobrinos de mi padre son
3. Las hijas de mi tía son
4. Luis es mi primo y el primo de mis hermanos; es
5. Pedro es el primo de mi amiga; es
6. Ana es la prima de Elena; es

B

a. mis primos.
b. su prima.
c. mis primas.
d. nuestro primo.
e. tu primo.
f. su primo.

14 Mi mejor amigo es simpático

▶ **Habla.** Can you describe your best friends? Talk to a partner about your best friends and those of your classmates.

Modelo A. Mi mejor amigo es simpático.
           ¿Cómo es tu mejor amigo?
        B. Mi mejor amigo es serio.
           ¿Cómo es la mejor amiga de Andrea?
        A. Su mejor amiga es muy simpática.

---

1. IDENTIFICAR Y DESCRIBIR
Gramática – Expresar posesión

14. You may also ask students to write a description of one of their classmates. Encourage students to share their descriptions with the classmate they just described and ask them if they think it is accurate or not.

Answer Key

11. 1. Tú tienes dieciséis años.
2. Ustedes tienen cinco perros.
3. Yo tengo ocho primos.
4. Mis abuelos tienen nueve nietos.
5. Mi hermana tiene veintiún años.
6. Usted tiene tres gatos.

12. 1. Tengo
2. tenemos
3. tienen
4. tiene
5. tienes

13. 1. e   4. d
2. a   5. f
3. c   6. b

14. Answers will vary.

Additional Resources

Fans Online activities
Practice Workbook

HERITAGE LANGUAGE LEARNERS

• Ask students to write a letter to a family member or a friend from their countries of origin that they have not seen in a while. Have them describe themselves and their families. Be sure they include their ages, descriptions of their personality and physical characteristics, names of possessions, and any other details they would like to include. If students would like to actually send their letters, encourage them to bring in stamps and an envelope.

MULTIPLE INTELLIGENCES:
Logical-Mathematical Intelligence

• Have students create a quiz with five word problems. Students will exchange papers and take each other's quiz. For example:
  A. *Si tengo tres hermanas y cuatro hermanos.*
     ¿Cuántos hermanos tengo?
  B. *Tienes siete hermanos.*

1. IDENTIFICAR Y DESCRIBIR

Gramática – Identificar personas y cosas

Presentation

■ In this section, students will review:
– Nouns.
– Masculine and feminine noun endings.
– Definite and indefinite articles.

Activities	Standards	Resources
Gramática	1.2, 3.1, 4.1	
15.	1.2	Audio
16.	1.2	Audio
17.	1.1, 1.2	

Teaching Suggestions

Warm-Up / Independent Starter

■ Ask students to write a paragraph of five sentences saying what each of their classmates / friends has with them in class today.

Preparation

■ Ask students to choose ten objects that they see in the classroom. Have them write a list of the ten objects in the singular, including their definite articles, and then ask them to write the same ten objects in the plural. Then switch to indefinite articles. For example:

el estudiante → los estudiantes
un estudiante → unos estudiantes
el libro → los libros
un libro → unos libros
la pared → las paredes
una pared → unas paredes

Activities

16. Have students work in small, mixed groups. Ask them to write six sentences about things they have in common and things that make them different. For example: *John y yo somos altos. Laura es baja.*

17. As an alternative to writing captions, have students write a brief story about each scene. Their scene should include a description of the people, where they are from, how they feel, and what they have.

10

Gramática

Identificar personas y cosas

Los nombres

• Spanish nouns can be **masculine** or **feminine**. Almost all nouns that end in -o are masculine, and those that end in -a are feminine.

• Nouns that refer to people usually have a masculine and a feminine form. The feminine form is developed from the masculine form:

Masculine form	Feminine form	Examples
Ends in -o.	Changes -o to -a.	el niño → la niña
Ends in a consonant.	Adds -a.	el profesor → la profesora

• Most Spanish nouns can be **singular** (one) or **plural** (more than one). The plural form is developed from the singular form:

Singular form	Plural form	Examples
Ends in a vowel.	Adds -s.	el primo → los primos
Ends in a consonant.	Adds -es.	el profesor → los profesores

Los artículos

• Spanish nouns are usually used with a definite or indefinite article. Articles agree with nouns in gender and number.

	SINGULAR		PLURAL	
	Masculino	Femenino	Masculino	Femenino
Definite articles	el	la	los	las
Indefinite articles	un	una	unos	unas

• Articles, like adjectives, agree in **gender** and **number** with the noun they accompany.

El niño es alto.   Es una niña muy simpática.
Los niños son altos.   Son unas niñas muy simpáticas.

15 **En buena compañía**

 ▶ **Escucha, elige y escribe.** Choose the article that agrees with the words you hear, then write the word with its corresponding article.

1. un/unas   2. los/las   3. la/los   4. una/unos   5. el/las

10 diez

Differentiated Instruction

DEVELOPING LEARNERS

• Have students practice the definite and indefinite articles by choosing four classroom objects to describe. Ask them to fill in a chart like the one below.

Object	Indefinite article	Definite article
cuaderno	Un cuaderno es necesario para la clase de español.	El cuaderno es pequeño.
pizarra	Hay una pizarra grande en nuestro salón de clase.	La pizarra está sucia.

EXPANDING LEARNERS

• Have five students sit in a circle. Each person is going to participate in "writing" ten sentences. The first person says an article and the second person says a person. From the third person on, each person has to say a word in Spanish that logically pushes the sentence forward to completion. Make sure students alternate going first. For example:
A. *El*
B. *El niño*
C. *El niño es*
D. *El niño es rubio*
E. *El niño es rubio y atlético.*

16 **Rita y Alan**

 ▶ **Escucha y escribe.** Rita and her friend Alan have discovered that their relatives are identical in all except gender. Listen and describe Alan's relatives based on Rita's descriptions of her family.

Modelo RITA: *Mi sobrina es alta.*
ALAN: *Mi sobrino es alto también.*

1. hermano   2. abuelo   3. tía   4. primo   5. padre

▶ **Escribe.** Now write the plural of Alan's descriptions.

Modelo *Mis sobrinos son altos.*

17 **En la foto**

▶ **Escribe.** Write the captions for these photos using the appropriate form of the indefinite article.

Modelo 1. *Una mujer y un niño.*

▶ **Habla.** Now, with a partner, describe the people in the photos using the appropriate form of the definite article.

Modelo 1. *La mujer es bonita y simpática. El niño es gracioso y está contento.*

HERITAGE LANGUAGE LEARNERS

• In English, the word *the* is used for all the definite articles, unlike Spanish. Ask students if there are any other times where one English word translates into many Spanish words; for example: *here, these, those.*

MULTIPLE INTELLIGENCES:
Intrapersonal Intelligence

• Ask students to write a journal entry about how they feel in Spanish class. Then write how they think their classmates around them feel about Spanish class. If they do not know the names of the students around them, then they should use articles when referring to them.

 AUDIO SCRIPT
See page XVII-I

Answer Key

15. 1. unas chicas
2. los profesores
3. los hijos
4. una hermana
5. el niño

16. 1. Mi hermano es rubio también.
2. Mi abuelo es delgado también.
3. Mi tía es gorda también.
4. Mi primo es simpático también.
5. Mi padre es moreno también.
▶ 1. Mis hermanos son rubios.
2. Mis abuelos son delgados.
3. Mis tías son gordas.
4. Mis primos son simpáticos.
5. Mis padres son morenos.

17. Answers will vary. Sample answers:
1. Una mujer y un niño.
2. Una chica y un chico.
3. Un hombre.
4. Un abuelo, una abuela y un niño.
5. Un niño y unas niñas.
6. Un hombre, una mujer y un niño.
▶ Answers will vary. Sample answers:
1. La mujer es pelirroja y delgada. El niño es gracioso y está contento.
2. La chica es alta y bonita. El chico es moreno.
3. El hombre es atlético.
4. Los abuelos son simpáticos. El niño está contento.
5. Los niños son inteligentes. Ellos están contentos.
6. Los padres son amables. El niño tiene hambre.

Additional Resources

Fans Online activities
Practice Workbook

2. EXPRESAR ACCIONES HABITUALES

Vocabulario – La casa

Presentation

- In this section, students will review:
  - Rooms in the house.
  - Objects and furniture in the house.

Activities	Standards	Resources
Vocabulario	1.2	
18.	1.2	Audio
19.	1.2	
20.	1.1, 1.2	

Teaching Suggestions

Warm-Up / Independent Starter

- Ask students to draw the floor plan for their house. Have them label each room and draw and label several objects in each room.

Preparation

- Have students walk around the room and compare their Independent Starters to those of other students in class. How many students have similar floor plans? Have them stand together and present their houses to the class naming all of the rooms and furniture in each room.

Activities

18. Before playing the audio for this activity, have students hypothesize what items each person has lost and in which rooms the participants will find them. After playing the audio, ask the class who had the most items and rooms of the house correct.

19. Ask students to write sentences telling which objects are located in each scene. For example: *En la cocina hay una estufa, un lavaplatos, un refrigerador y un microondas.*

20. Encourage students to organize their paragraphs before they begin by completing a Venn diagram. The headings should be: *Mi dormitorio*, *Su dormitorio*, and *Nuestro dormitorio*. To guide students' writings, let the class know that their paragraphs should be between five and ten complete sentences.

12

Vocabulario

La casa

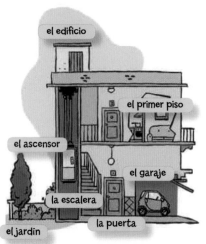

el edificio

el primer piso

el ascensor

el garaje

la escalera

la puerta

el jardín

El dormitorio

la cómoda

la cama

el armario

la mesita de noche

El baño

la ducha

el lavabo

el inodoro

la bañera

La sala

el sofá

el televisor

la estantería

la silla

la mesa

La cocina

el microondas

la estufa

el refrigerador

el lavaplatos

18 **¿Dónde está?**

▶ **Escucha y une.** Everyone has lost something. Listen and match each person with the part of the house where his or her lost item can be found.

(A)	(B)
1. Andy	a. el dormitorio
2. Tess	b. la cocina
3. Tim	c. el garaje
4. Rita	d. el baño
5. Janet	e. la sala

Differentiated Instruction

DEVELOPING LEARNERS

- Have students create labels for the rooms and furniture in their homes. Each vocabulary word will have its own Spanish label and should be decorated. Encourage students to post their labels around their homes for authentic practice and reinforcement of vocabulary.

EXPANDING LEARNERS

- In pairs, have students play a guessing game. One student will describe what room they are in and the other student will guess the room. For example:
  A. *En este cuarto hay una estufa, un lavaplatos y un refrigerador. ¿Dónde estoy?*
  B. *En la cocina.*

19 **Busca el intruso**

▶ **Identifica.** Identify the item that doesn't belong in each room.

Ⓐ
1. la estufa
2. el lavaplatos
3. el sofá
4. el refrigerador
5. el microondas

Ⓑ
1. el inodoro
2. la cómoda
3. el lavabo
4. la ducha
5. la bañera

Ⓒ
1. el armario
2. el sofá
3. la cómoda
4. la cama
5. la mesita de noche

Ⓓ
1. el sofá
2. la mesa
3. la silla
4. la estantería
5. la bañera

20 **¿Qué tienes en tu dormitorio?**

▶ **Habla.** What does your partner have in his or her bedroom? Ask five questions.

Modelo A. *¿Tienes una computadora?*
    B. *Sí, tengo una computadora en mi dormitorio.*

▶ **Escribe.** Write a paragraph comparing both bedrooms.

Modelo

El dormitorio de mi amiga Anne tiene una cama, un armario y una estantería grande.
Mi dormitorio tiene...

AUDIO SCRIPT
See page XVII-I

Answer Key

18. 1. e   2. b   3. a   4. d   5. c

19. A. 3   B. 2   C. 2   D. 5

20. Answers will vary. Sample answer:
A. *¿Tienes una cama?*
B. *Sí, tengo una cama grande.*
▶ Answers will vary.

Additional Resources

Fans Online activities
Practice Workbook

HERITAGE LANGUAGE LEARNERS

• Aside from the words on the vocabulary list, what other household objects or rooms in the house can heritage students think of? Have students create a new floor plan to share with the class that includes these objects.

SPECIAL-NEEDS LEARNERS

• For students with visual impairment, enlarge the vocabulary page so that they may easily identify the vocabulary words and the pictures that relate to each word. Take some time to go over each vocabulary word again to ensure student comprehension. You can also ask them to spell the words aloud for you, as a way of checking that they are able to see.

2. EXPRESAR ACCIONES HABITUALES

Vocabulario – Tareas domésticas y actividades de ocio

Presentation

- In this section, students will review:
  - Household chores.
  - Free-time activities.

Activities	Standards	Resources
Vocabulario	1.2	
21.	1.2	
22.	1.2	Audio
23.	1.1, 1.2	
24.	1.1, 1.2, 1.3, 3.1	

Teaching Suggestions

Warm-Up / Independent Starter

- Have students write a list of three chores that they have to do and three free-time activities that they enjoy doing.

Preparation

- Create a class chart of the favorite free-time activities of the students. Have them write their names on sticky notes. Create a bar graph on the board using the students' sticky notes to see which activities would be the most popular.

	Josefina		
Tomás	Patricia		Nicolás
Martina	Natalia	Pepe	Kathy
Ver la tele	Hablar por teléfono	Escuchar música	Leer revistas

Activities

21. Now have students say where they would do each activity in their homes. They may use all the rooms of the house, not just the three mentioned.

22. In pairs, ask students to talk about who in their home / family does the chores depicted in the photos. For example: *Tim tiene que sacar la basura. En mi casa, mi hermano saca la basura.*

23. Have students work in pairs to decide what each of them has to do to solve the following problems: *La casa tiene mucho polvo. El perro no está limpio.*

¡Hoy **tengo que** lavar los platos!

¡Yo **tengo ganas de** escuchar música!

Vocabulario

Tareas domésticas y actividades de ocio

limpiar el baño — pasar la aspiradora — barrer el suelo — sacudir los muebles

sacar la basura — cortar el césped — pasear al perro — cuidar a la mascota

ver la televisión — leer una revista — hablar por teléfono

21 **Cada actividad en su sitio**

▶ **Relaciona.** Match each activity with the part of the house where we do it.

1. lavar los platos
2. cortar el césped
3. cuidar a la mascota
4. leer una revista
5. ver la televisión

A — B — C

Differentiated Instruction

DEVELOPING LEARNERS

- Have students write out an hour-by-hour description of their typical Saturday around the house in the form of a schedule. Have them include what room they are in and what furniture or household objects are used. Students may compare their schedules with those of other students to see what they have in common.

EXPANDING LEARNERS

- Ask students to imagine their family has hired a housekeeper for the week. Have students write out a schedule and special instructions with chores for the housekeeper and also add in some free time.

22 **Primero las tareas domésticas**

 ▶ **Escucha y relaciona.** Listen and match the characters with their chores.

    1. Tess   **2.** Andy   **3.** Tim   **4.** Rita   **5.** Janet

23 **¡Más tareas!**

▶ **Habla.** Talk to a partner about what you have to do to solve each problem.

Modelo El baño no está limpio. (nosotros)
      → *Nosotros tenemos que limpiar el baño.*

> pasear al perro   leer una revista
>
> pasar la aspiradora   hablar por teléfono   lavar los platos

1. El suelo no está limpio. (yo)
2. Es el cumpleaños de tu amigo. (tú)
3. No funciona el lavaplatos. (nosotros)
4. Necesitan una receta para la fiesta. (ustedes)
5. El perro está muy nervioso. (ellos)

24 **¿Qué tienes que hacer los fines de semana?**

▶ **Habla.** Talk to a partner about what chores you have to do on the weekends.

Modelo A. Yo *tengo que ordenar mi dormitorio. Y tú, ¿qué tienes que hacer?*
       B. Yo *tengo que…*

▶ **Dibuja.** Draw a Venn diagram to compare your chores.

---

2. EXPRESAR ACCIONES HABITUALES

Vocabulario – Tareas domésticas y actividades de ocio

24. Now that they have discussed their weekend chores, ask students to write a list of other responsibilities that they have during the week. They can use a calendar chart.

 AUDIO SCRIPT
See page XVII-I

Answer Key

21. 1. A   4. C
      2. B   5. C
      3. B

22. 1. D   4. A
      2. B   5. C
      3. E

23. 1. Yo tengo que pasar la aspiradora.
      2. Tú tienes que hablar por teléfono.
      3. Nosotros tenemos que lavar los platos.
      4. Ustedes tienen que leer una revista.
      5. Ellos tienen que pasear el perro.

24. Answers will vary.
      ▶ Answers will vary.

Additional Resources

Fans Online activities
Practice Workbook

HERITAGE LANGUAGE LEARNERS

• Ask students to think about the free-time activities for teenagers in Spanish-speaking countries. Do students have the same amount of free time in Spanish-speaking countries as students in the United States? What are some of the activities common in their countries of origin and / or the countries they have visited?

TOTAL PHYSICAL RESPONSE (TPR)

• Have a volunteer read an hour-by-hour Saturday schedule aloud to the class. As he or she reads, have everyone else act out his or her chore or free-time activity. Repeat this process with another student until everyone in the class shows a clear understanding of the vocabulary.

2. EXPRESAR ACCIONES HABITUALES

Gramática – Expresar lugar, movimiento y existencia

Presentation

- In this section, students will review:
  - Adverbs of place.
  - The verbs *estar* and *ir*.

Activities	Standards	Resources
Gramática	1.2, 3.1, 4.1	
25.	1.2	Audio
26.	1.2, 2.1	
27.	1.1, 1.2	
28.	1.1	

Teaching Suggestions

Warm-Up / Independent Starter

- Have students choose five objects in the classroom—some close to their desks and some far away from them. Ask them to write five sentences describing these objects and telling where they are located by using adverbs of place.

Preparation

- Ask students to work in pairs to try and locate the objects that their classmates described in the previous activity.
- Have students write a list of five places where they go during the course of a week. For example: *El lunes voy a la biblioteca. El martes voy…*

Activities

25. Have students expand this activity by describing the physical attributes and/or feelings of each person in the illustration, and by specifying their location. For example: *Es alto y moreno. Está contento. Está detrás de Marta.* See if their partner can identify the person being described. (*Es Roy.*)

26. Complete this activity as a class. Read the letter and pause when you get to the blanks so students may call out the answers.

27. Have students continue the conversation by asking how many of those objects they have at home. For example:

   A. *¿Cuántos bolígrafos tienes en casa?*
   B. *Tengo cinco bolígrafos en casa.*

Gramática

Expresar lugar, movimiento y existencia

Expresar lugar. Adverbios y expresiones de lugar

- To say where things are located, use the verb estar with words that express place.

  El coquí está en el jardín.

- These words and phrases are also used to show location.

¿Dónde están los coquíes?

aquí · ahí · allí

al lado de **la flor**

cerca de **la flor**

lejos de **la flor**

detrás de **la flor** · encima de **la flor** · a la izquierda de **la flor**

delante de **la flor** · debajo de **la flor** · a la derecha de **la flor**

Expresar movimiento. El verbo ir

- To express where someone is going, use the verb ir *(to go)* and this formula:

  | ir a + place | Voy al cine.

  Remember: a + el = al

Expresar existencia. El verbo *haber*

- To say that someone or something exists, use the form hay *(there is, there are)*.

  Hay libros en la estantería.
  ¿Hay un lavaplatos en la cocina?

VERBO IR (TO GO). PRESENTE

	Singular		Plural
yo	voy	nosotros nosotras	vamos
tú	vas	vosotros vosotras	vais
usted él ella	va	ustedes ellos ellas	van

Differentiated Instruction

DEVELOPING LEARNERS

- Have students take out pencil and paper. Give students instructions for where to put the pencil in relation to the paper. For example: *El lápiz está a la derecha del papel.* Students will place their pencil to the right of the paper. As students begin to understand, speed up the instructions to see if students can keep up.

EXPANDING LEARNERS

- Have students create a board game. They will need to create the actual board with poster board, index cards with adverbs of place written on them, and dice. Since many schools prohibit students from bringing dice to school, please provide students with dice or some equivalent. To play, students will roll the dice and pick up one of the index cards. If he or she can locate an item in the classroom using the adverb of place on their index card, then they may move the number of spaces indicated on the dice.

25 **¿De quién hablan?**

 ▶ **Escucha e identifica.** Listen and identify the person being described.

Modelo Está a la izquierda de Ana.
→ Es Marta.

Rosa — Luis — Roy — Ana — Marta

26 **¿Vienes a la fiesta?**

▶ **Escribe.** Complete the letter with the correct form of the verb *ir*.

Hola, Nuria:

Mañana mis amigos y yo <u>vamos</u> a una fiesta. ¿ <u>1</u> tú también? <u>2</u> mucha gente nueva. Por ejemplo, <u>3</u> Sandra y Jenny, las primas de Javier.

Bueno, te escribo mañana. Ahora me <u>4</u> de compras con mi madre. Siempre <u>5</u> juntas a comprar.

Un beso.

Charo

27 **¿Cuántos hay?**

 ▶ **Habla.** With a partner, take turns asking about the number of objects below.

Modelo computadoras - 5
A. ¿Cuántas computadoras hay?
B. Hay cinco computadoras.

1 bolígrafos - 10   2 libros - 7   3 cuadernos - 20

4 mesas - 3   5 pizarras - 2

28 **¿Dónde están?**

▶ **Habla.** Talk to a partner about the items in your classroom. Say how many there are and where they are located in the classroom.

Modelo A. ¿Hay pizarras en la clase?
B. Sí, hay dos pizarras.
A. ¿Dónde están?
B. Están detrás de la mesa del profesor.

diecisiete 17

---

2. EXPRESAR ACCIONES HABITUALES

Gramática – Expresar lugar, movimiento y existencia

28. To extend this activity, have partners ask each other about different school areas. For example:

A. *¿Hay cafetería en la escuela?*
B. *Sí, hay una cafetería.*
A. *¿Dónde está?*
B. *Está al lado del gimnasio.*

 AUDIO SCRIPT
See page XVIIJ

Answer Key

25. 1. Es Roy.
2. Es Marta.
3. Es Ana.
4. Es Rosa.
5. Es Luis.

26. 1. Vas
2. Va
3. van
4. voy
5. vamos

27. 1. A. ¿Cuántos bolígrafos hay?
B. Hay diez bolígrafos.
2. A. ¿Cuántos libros hay?
B. Hay siete libros.
3. A. ¿Cuántos cuadernos hay?
B. Hay veinte cuadernos.
4. A. ¿Cuántas mesas hay?
B. Hay tres mesas.
5. A. ¿Cuántas pizarras hay?
B. Hay dos pizarras.

28. Answers will vary.

Additional Resources

Fans Online activities
Practice Workbook

HERITAGE LANGUAGE LEARNERS

• The verb *haber* is used to express existence. Ask students to research how people traveled during the pre-Industrial Revolution era in their countries of origin. Have students write a paragraph telling what kinds of transport means there were. Then have students compare the modes of transportation from those times with now.

MULTIPLE INTELLIGENCES:
Verbal-Linguistic Intelligence

• Ask students to get into groups of three, with one group member who identifies himself or herself as a verbal-linguistic learner. Two of the students will put themselves in different locations around the classroom and the verbal-linguist learner will describe where they are.

17

2. EXPRESAR ACCIONES HABITUALES

Gramática – Expresar acciones habituales en el presente

Presentation

- In this section, students will review:
  - Present tense regular verb conjugations.
  - Adverbs of frequency.

Activities	Standards	Resources
Gramática	1.2, 3.1, 4.1	
29.	1.1, 1.2, 1.3	Audio
30.	1.2, 3.1	
31.	1.1, 1.2, 3.1	

Teaching Suggestions

Warm-Up / Independent Starter

- Have students write a list of the free-time activities they do on a regular basis. They can use a chart like the one below to organize their responses.

nunca	rara vez	a veces
casi siempre	siempre	todos los días

Preparation

- Ask students to share their charts from the previous activity. They should read their responses to each other and see how their activities are similar or different. If they do the same activity with the same frequency, they can circle that activity on their charts.

- Review the subject pronouns and verb endings with the class. Use names instead of pronouns to assist students with this review. Remind students that any name followed by *y yo* will always use the *nosotros* conjugation and any name followed by *y tú* will always use the *ustedes* conjugation.

Activities

29. Have students read their sentences to a partner and then ask a question using the *tú* form based on each sentence. For example:

A. *Yo corto el césped. ¿Y tú? ¿Cortas el césped?*

B. *No, yo no corto el césped. Ellas sacuden los muebles. ¿Y tú? ¿Sacudes los muebles?*

A. *Sí ...*

18

Gramática

Expresar acciones habituales en el presente

Verbos regulares

VERBOS LAVAR (TO WASH), PRENDER (TO SWITCH ON) Y ABRIR (TO OPEN). PRESENTE

		Lavar	Prender	Abrir
Singular	yo	lavo	prendo	abro
	tú	lavas	prendes	abres
	usted, él, ella	lava	prende	abre
Plural	nosotros, nosotras	lavamos	prendemos	abrimos
	vosotros, vosotras	laváis	prendéis	abrís
	ustedes, ellos, ellas	lavan	prenden	abren

Adverbios de frecuencia

nunca   casi nunca   rara vez   a veces   muchas veces   casi siempre   siempre   todos los días

0 días al año

365 días al año

29 **¿Quién cuida el jardín?**

 ▶ **Escucha y une.** Listen and match each chore with the person or group.

Ⓐ   Ⓑ

1. cortar el césped   a. ustedes
2. sacudir los muebles   b. yo
3. pasear al perro   c. ellas
4. barrer el suelo   d. nosotros
5. limpiar el garaje   e. tú

Yo cuido el jardín.

▶ **Escribe.** Now write who does each chore in complete sentences and using the correct form of the verb.

 ▶ **Habla y escribe.** Tell your partner who does the chores at your house. Make a list of the chores people do at your partner's house.

Modelo

En mi casa	En casa de mi compañero(a)
Mi padre lava los platos.	Su hermana y él lavan los platos.

18 dieciocho

Differentiated Instruction

DEVELOPING LEARNERS

- Have students find three new verbs to conjugate in their textbooks, one with *-ar*, one with *-er*, and one with *-ir* endings. Then have students close their textbooks. Walk students through the process of conjugating verbs in order. First they will cross out the *-ar*, *-er*, or *-ir* and rewrite the verb without the ending six times. Next, in a different color, students will add the verb endings. Repeat this process until students have a clear understanding of how to conjugate verbs in the present tense.

EXPANDING LEARNERS

- Have student write a story using only the verbs *lavar*, *prender*, and *abrir*. They may also use adverbs of frequency. Have students read their stories to the class and vote for the most creative story.

30 Tareas domésticas para el fin de semana

▶ **Completa.** Tess is writing an e-mail to her friend Pancho about her chores. Complete the e-mail by using the correct form of the verbs in the boxes.

pasar	sacudir	pasear	limpiar

sacar	barrer	cortar	lavar

Mensaje nuevo

Para:
Cc:
Asunto:

¿Qué tal, Pancho?
Mi familia y yo tenemos muchas tareas domésticas los fines de semana.
Mi padre siempre _corta_ el césped los sábados. Mi hermano __1__
la basura y __2__ al perro. Mis hermanos y yo normalmente __3__
los platos y __4__ el baño.
Mi madre ordena la casa. ¿Tú __5__ el suelo de tu dormitorio?
Yo barro el suelo o __6__ la aspiradora y mi hermano __7__
los muebles.
¡Buen fin de semana!
Tess

---

31 ¿Con qué frecuencia?

▶ **Habla y escribe.** How often do you do each activity? Interview four classmates and record your answers in a chart like the one below.

lavar los platos	cortar el césped	ver la televisión	limpiar el baño
usar la computadora	hablar por teléfono	leer una revista	pasear al perro

Modelo A. *¿Con qué frecuencia lavas los platos?*
B. *Todos los días.*

	nunca	casi nunca	rara vez	a veces	muchas veces	casi siempre	todos los días
lavar los platos	✔			✔✔			✔
...							

---

2. EXPRESAR ACCIONES HABITUALES

Gramática – Expresar acciones habituales en el presente

31. You may want to create a chart on the board or on a transparency. Have students report their findings as you tally the results in the chart. What activities do students do more often? What activities are practiced less frequently? Is there an activity that no one does?

🎧 AUDIO SCRIPT
See page XVIIJ

Answer Key

29. 1. b   2. c   3. d   4. e   5. a
▶ Answers will vary.
▶ Answers will vary.

30. 1. saca
2. pasea
3. lavamos
4. limpiamos
5. barres
6. paso
7. sacude

31. Answers will vary.

Additional Resources
Fans Online activities
Practice Workbook

HERITAGE LANGUAGE LEARNERS

• Have students come up with a list of adverbs of frequency that have not been included in this list; for example, *a menudo*. Are these adverbs unique to certain countries around the Spanish-speaking world or are they common in all Spanish-speaking countries?

CRITICAL THINKING

• Ask students what they think determines how frequently they do something. For example: What determines how frequently they wash their hands or play video games? What determines how frequently they do their homework or play a sport? Is what determines their frequency internal or external factors, or both?

2. EXPRESAR ACCIONES HABITUALES

Gramática – Expresar acciones habituales en el presente

Presentation

- In this section, students will review stem-changing verbs: *e > ie, o > ue,* and *e > i.*

Activities	Standards	Resources
Gramática	1.2, 3.1, 4.1	
32.	1.2	Audio
33.	1.1, 1.2	
34.	1.2	

Teaching Suggestions

Warm-Up / Independent Starter

- Ask students to write a list of five things that they can and cannot do, using the verb *poder.* For example: *Yo puedo salir con mis amigos los fines de semana. ¡No puedo comprar unas sandalias en la papelería!*

Preparation

- Ask students to look at the three categories of stem-changing verbs. Using three different color markers, show students how the stem-changing verbs are conjugated. You can use black for the letters that do not change, red for stem changes, and blue for the verb endings.

Activities

32. Have students continue the activity by creating an oral quiz for their partners. They should write five sentences using five different verbs in different forms and ask their partners to guess the subject pronoun.

33. Ask students to write different answers to the five questions in this activity using the verb *preferir.* For example:

A. *¿Ustedes quieren ir al centro?*
B. *No, preferimos ir al parque.*

34. Have students write three additional personal questions using the stem-changing verbs on page 20. Then have each student interview his or her partner. For example: *¿Puedes comprar ropa cerca de tu casa? ¿Vuelas mucho en avión?*

Gramática

Expresar acciones habituales en el presente

Verbos con raíz irregular: *e > ie*

VERBO CERRAR (TO CLOSE). PRESENTE

Singular		Plural	
yo	cie**rro**	nosotros nosotras	cerramos
tú	cie**rras**	vosotros vosotras	cerráis
usted él ella	cie**rra**	ustedes ellos ellas	cie**rran**

- Other verbs *e > ie:*
  empezar *(to begin)* ⟶ yo empiezo
  entender *(to understand)* ⟶ yo entiendo
  pensar *(to think)* ⟶ yo pienso
  preferir *(to prefer)* ⟶ yo prefiero
  querer *(to want)* ⟶ yo quiero

Verbos con raíz irregular: *o > ue*

VERBO PODER (TO BE ABLE). PRESENTE

Singular		Plural	
yo	pue**do**	nosotros nosotras	podemos
tú	pue**des**	vosotros vosotras	podéis
usted él ella	pue**de**	ustedes ellos ellas	pue**den**

- Other verbs *o > ue:*
  costar *(to cost)* ⟶ cuesta(n)
  contar *(to count)* ⟶ yo cuento
  recordar *(to remember)* ⟶ yo recuerdo
  volar *(to fly)* ⟶ yo vuelo
  volver *(to return)* ⟶ yo vuelvo

Verbos con raíz irregular: *e > i*

VERBO PEDIR (TO ASK FOR). PRESENTE

Singular		Plural	
yo	pi**do**	nosotros nosotras	pedimos
tú	pi**des**	vosotros vosotras	pedís
usted él ella	pi**de**	ustedes ellos ellas	pi**den**

- Other verbs *e > i:*
  repetir *(to repeat)* ⟶ yo repito
  competir *(to compete)* ⟶ yo compito
  medir *(to measure)* ⟶ yo mido
  servir *(to serve)* ⟶ yo sirvo
  vestir *(to dress)* ⟶ yo visto

Differentiated Instruction

DEVELOPING LEARNERS

- Have students come up with a mnemonic device to remember the stem-changing verbs. For example, for the *o > ue* verbs, students can use **C**indy **C**an't **R**esist **V**ampire **V**ideos. (Make sure they realize that there are more stem-changing verbs and this mnemonic is only an example.) Once students have finished, you can make a class list to post in your classroom.

EXPANDING LEARNERS

- In pairs, have students relate the stem-changing verbs to the vocabulary from this section. They will write sentences such as: *Yo cierro la puerta de mi dormitorio antes de dormir* or *Yo me visto en el baño del gimnasio para la clase de Educación Física.*

32 ¿Quién hace cada cosa?

▶ **Escucha y relaciona.** Listen and match each statement with its pronoun.

Modelo 1. → e. nosotros

a. ellos   b. yo   c. tú   d. ella   e. nosotros   f. ustedes   g. él

33 ¿Quieres leer una revista?

▶ **Habla.** Tess would like to make plans with her partners, but everyone has something else to do. Use the photos to give Tess an excuse for each character.

Modelo Andy, ¿quieres ver la televisión?
→ *No puedo. Tengo que cortar el césped.*

1. Andy, Janet, ¿ustedes quieren ir al centro?
2. Mack, ¿Tim quiere visitar un museo?
3. Tim, ¿Diana y Janet quieren leer revistas?
4. Rita, ¿quieres ir al teatro?
5. Mamá, ¿quieres hablar por teléfono con los Estados Unidos?

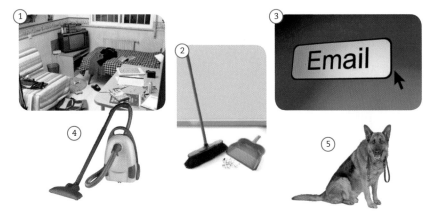

34 Unas preguntas

▶ **Escribe.** Answer the questions in complete sentences.

Modelo ¿Entienden ustedes el español?
→ *Sí, nosotros entendemos el español.*

1. ¿Prefieres barrer o pasar la aspiradora?
2. ¿Piensas hablar por teléfono con tus amigos hoy?
3. ¿Qué clase prefieres?
4. ¿Quieren ustedes ver la televisión?
5. ¿Los profesores repiten las preguntas en clase?

veintiuno 21

Gramática – Expresar acciones habituales en el presente

AUDIO SCRIPT
See page XVIIJ

Answer Key

32.
1. e	5. b
2. a	6. g
3. c	7. f
4. d	

33.
1. No podemos. Tenemos que ordenar el dormitorio.
2. No puede. Tiene que barrer el suelo.
3. No pueden. Tienen que escribir un correo electrónico.
4. No puedo. Tengo que pasar la aspiradora.
5. No puedo. Tengo que pasear al perro.

34. Answers will vary. Sample answers:
1. Prefiero barrer.
2. Sí, pienso hablar por teléfono con mis amigos hoy.
3. Prefiero la clase de Español.
4. No, no queremos ver la televisión.
5. Sí, los profesores repiten las preguntas en clase.

Additional Resources

Fans Online activities
Practice Workbook

HERITAGE LANGUAGE LEARNERS

• Ask heritage students to come up with a 10-question quiz using the stem-changing verbs. Tell students that they will administer this quiz to help their classmates practice the stem-changing verbs. Encourage students to be creative. They could, for example, design a "personality quiz" to discover their classmates' preferences (*preferir*), opinions (*pensar*), things they are and aren't able to do (*poder*), things they request (*pedir*), and so on. You may want to check the quiz for correct spelling and grammar use when students finish it.

COOPERATIVE LEARNING

• Pair heritage students with non-heritage learners. Heritage students will administer the 10-question quiz they created. Once students have finished the quiz, the heritage learners will check their answers. If students get all ten correct, then they are finished. If they get even one wrong, they will repeat the process with another heritage student. You may also want to check students' answers for correct spelling and grammar.

Connecting Unit

3. EXPRESAR GUSTOS Y PREFERENCIAS

Vocabulario – Las tiendas. La ropa

Presentation

- In this section, students will review:
  - Stores and shopping.
  - Clothing.
  - Colors.

Activities	Standards	Resources
Vocabulario	1.2	
35.	1.2	Audio
36.	1.2	
37.	1.1, 1.2	
38.	1.1, 1.2, 1.3	

Teaching Suggestions

Warm-Up / Independent Starter

- Have students draw a picture of a rainbow with the colors in ROYGBIV order (red, orange, yellow, green, blue, violet). Have them color in the rainbow and label the colors in Spanish.

Preparation

- Using a catalog or a magazine, ask students to work in pairs to talk about the clothing they see the models wearing. They should take turns pointing out different articles of clothing and saying if they like or don't like each one. For example: *Me gusta su camisa. No me gustan sus zapatos.*

Activities

35. Have students look at each image in this activity and say in which store they would be able to buy each one. For example: *Puedo comprar un suéter en la tienda de ropa.*

37. Have students pretend that they are out shopping with only $150. Based on the prices in the activity, ask them to tell a partner what they would buy with their money. For example: *Voy a una fiesta. Compro un vestido negro por 35 dólares y unos zapatos negros por 98 dólares.*

38. Allow the student who guesses correctly to read the next description. If no one guesses correctly, then the student being described will take the next turn.

22

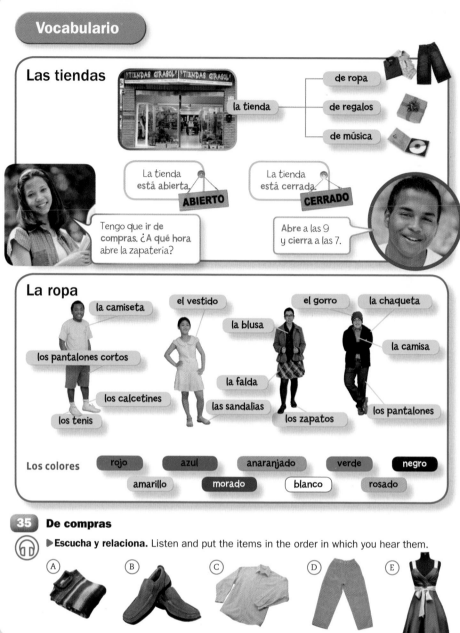

3. EXPRESAR GUSTOS Y PREFERENCIAS

Vocabulario

Las tiendas

la tienda — de ropa / de regalos / de música

La tienda está abierta. **ABIERTO**

La tienda está cerrada. **CERRADO**

Tengo que ir de compras. ¿A qué hora abre la zapatería?

Abre a las 9 y cierra a las 7.

La ropa

la camiseta, el vestido, el gorro, la chaqueta, la blusa, la camisa, los pantalones cortos, la falda, los calcetines, las sandalias, los zapatos, los pantalones, los tenis

Los colores: rojo, azul, anaranjado, verde, negro, amarillo, morado, blanco, rosado

35 De compras

▶ **Escucha y relaciona.** Listen and put the items in the order in which you hear them.

(A) (B) (C) (D) (E)

22 veintidós

Differentiated Instruction

DEVELOPING LEARNERS

- Ask students to choose one article of clothing (for example, *una camiseta roja*) and then list the names of students who are wearing that clothing item. Have them call out their list of names and see if the rest of the class can guess what article of clothing they all have in common.

EXPANDING LEARNERS

- Ask students to create a schedule in which they visit each of the four stores in activity 36. They should include the store, the item they need to buy, and the time they would visit each store. They can use a chart like the one below for their answers.

Necesito comprar...	Voy a...	A las...
unos tenis.	la zapatería.	tres de la tarde.

36 **¿Está abierta o cerrada?**

▶ **Lee y escribe.** Each store has different hours. Use the information below to say if they are open or closed at the times indicated.

Modelo   Tienda de ropa. 10:00 a. m. - 8:00 p. m. Ahora son las doce.
         → *Está abierta.*

Tienda	Horario	Ahora...
1. Tienda de regalos	9:00 a. m. - 6:00 p. m.	son las cuatro y media.
2. Tienda de música	8:30 a. m. - 5:00 p. m.	son las nueve de la mañana.
3. Tienda de ropa	9:00 a. m. - 8:00 p. m.	son las diez de la noche.
4. Zapatería	10:00 a. m. - 8:00 p. m.	son las tres de la tarde.

37 **¿Cuánto cuesta?**

 ▶ **Habla.** With a partner, talk about the prices of the following items.

Modelo   A. *¿Cuánto cuesta la falda amarilla?*
         B. *La falda amarilla cuesta veinticuatro dólares.*

Ⓐ Ⓒ Ⓓ Ⓔ Ⓑ

$ 35 $ 98 $ 18 $ 40 $ 69

38 **¿Quién es?**

▶ **Escribe.** Can you identify someone by his or her clothing? Choose a classmate and write a short description of their clothes.

Modelo

> Lleva una camiseta azul de algodón, unos pantalones cortos azules y unos tenis blancos.

 ▶ **Lee y habla.** Read your description aloud and see if your classmates can guess who is being described.

veintitrés 23

AUDIO SCRIPT
See page XVIIJ

Answer Key

35. 1. E   2. A   3. C   4. B   5. D

36. 1. Está abierta
2. Está abierta.
3. Está cerrada.
4. Está abierta.

37. A. A. ¿Cuánto cuesta el vestido negro?
B. El vestido negro cuesta treinta y cinco dólares.
B. A. ¿Cuánto cuestan los zapatos de cuero?
B. Los zapatos de cuero cuestan noventa y ocho dólares.
C. A. ¿Cuánto cuesta la camiseta roja?
B. La camiseta roja cuesta dieciocho dólares.
D. A. ¿Cuánto cuesta la blusa rosada?
B. La blusa rosada cuesta cuarenta dólares.
E. A. ¿Cuánto cuestan los pantalones vaqueros?
B. Los pantalones vaqueros cuestan sesenta y nueve dólares.

38. Answers will vary.
▶ Answers will vary.

Additional Resources

Fans Online activities
Practice Workbook

HERITAGE LANGUAGE LEARNERS

• Have students share their experiences of shopping in their countries of origin or a Spanish-speaking country they have traveled to. If students have not been outside the United States, have them compare their shopping experiences with the students who have traveled to a Spanish-speaking country. Students may also talk about their experiences shopping at a Latino-owned business in a Spanish-speaking neighborhood in the United States.

MULTIPLE INTELLIGENCES:
Bodily-Kinesthetic Intelligence

• Have students do a live rendition of "Rip the Runway." Students will get into groups of four. Each person will take turns doing his or her best catwalk. As they are walking, another group member will say what they are wearing and how much it costs. As the person is speaking, the "model" will point to that article of clothing to demonstrate their understanding of the vocabulary.

3. EXPRESAR GUSTOS Y PREFERENCIAS

Vocabulario – La comida

Presentation

- In this section, students will review:
  - Food and flavors.
  - Table settings and utensils.

Activities	Standards	Resources
Vocabulario	1.2	
39.	1.2	Audio
40.	1.1, 1.2, 1.3	
41.	1.2	

Teaching Suggestions

Warm-Up / Independent Starter

- Ask students to write a list of the foods they have eaten today. They can use a chart like the one below to organize their food.

bebidas	comidas	postres

Preparation

- Have students compare the foods they ate during the day. Then ask students to describe how the food they have eaten today usually tastes. For example: *Las frutas son dulces pero los huevos son salados.*

Activities

39. After listening to the dialogue, have students write the name of the utensil that they will need to eat each specific food. For example: *unos huevos → un tenedor.*

40. For every *falso* answer, have students rewrite the sentence to make it *cierto*. For every *cierto* answer, have students rewrite the sentence to make it *falso*. Then have students rewrite the conversation between the *mesero* and the *cliente* based on their new answers. Notice that only *cierto* answers will change in the conversation.

41. Ask students to write a sentence to describe each of the foods in the photos. For example: *El helado es dulce.*

24

Vocabulario

La comida

Señores, la carta.
el mesero

la servilleta
el cuchillo
el tenedor
el mantel
la cuchara
el plato
la botella
la sal
el vaso
la taza
la pimienta
el azúcar

Comidas

 la sopa

los frijoles

el pan

los huevos

 las verduras

el pollo con papas

la carne con arroz

el pescado con maíz

Postres

el helado

la torta

las frutas

Bebidas

el agua

el refresco

la leche

el jugo de naranja

Sabores

dulce

salado

picante

agrio

amargo

La sopa está caliente y el refresco está frío.

39 De compras en el supermercado

 ▶**Escucha y escribe.** Diana and Rita have to do some shopping. Listen and write what they buy.

24 veinticuatro

Differentiated Instruction

DEVELOPING LEARNERS

- Have students imagine they are creating a menu and serving it at a formal dinner. They must include an appetizer, main course, dessert, and drink. Once they have finished, ask students to work in pairs to design and set a table and take turns serving their meal. Students should describe what they have prepared and what they are serving.

EXPANDING LEARNERS

- Ask students to write a paragraph about a formal dining experience they have had or have seen on television. They should describe the scene, including table settings and the food served. Have volunteers read their descriptions to the class.

3. EXPRESAR GUSTOS Y PREFERENCIAS

Vocabulario – La comida

 40 **En el restaurante**

▶ **Lee y decide.** Read this conversation between a waiter and a client at a restaurant and decide if each statement is true *(cierto)* or false *(falso)*.

A la carta

MESERO: ¿Quiere ver la carta, señor?

CLIENTE: Sí, gracias. ¿Hay algún plato especial?

MESERO: Nuestra especialidad es la paella. Es arroz con carne o pescado.

CLIENTE: Pues quiero la paella.

MESERO: ¿Y para beber?

CLIENTE: Una botella de agua, por favor.

MESERO: ¿Quiere tomar postre?

CLIENTE: ¿Tienen helado?

MESERO: No, señor. Hay frutas y torta de chocolate.

CLIENTE: Entonces prefiero un café.

MESERO: ¿Cómo quiere el café?

CLIENTE: Con leche.

Aquí tiene la carta, señor.

1. El cliente no quiere ver la carta.
2. La paella lleva pescado.
3. El cliente pide un refresco.
4. De postre hay torta y helado.
5. El cliente pide un postre.
6. Al cliente no le gusta el café.

▶ **Representa.** Act out this situation with a partner.

 41 **¿Qué uso para cada comida?**

▶ **Escribe.** Write a sentence explaining what utensils you use to eat or drink each item.

Modelo *Para beber un jugo de naranja uso un vaso.*

①  ②   ③

④   ⑤  ⑥

🎧 **AUDIO SCRIPT**
See page XVIIJ

Answer Key

39. Arroz, huevos, pollo, manzanas, naranjas y refrescos.

40.
1. Falso	4. Falso
2. Cierto	5. Falso
3. Falso	6. Falso

41.
1. Para tomar un café uso una taza, un plato y una cuchara.
2. Para comer una ensalada uso un plato y un tenedor.
3. Para comer una sopa uso un plato y una cuchara.
4. Para tomar la leche uso un vaso.
5. Para comer la carne uso un plato, un tenedor y un cuchillo.
6. Para comer un helado uso una cuchara.

Additional Resources

Fans Online activities
Practice Workbook

HERITAGE LANGUAGE LEARNERS

• Ask students to give the class instructions on how to make a peanut butter and jelly sandwich. Do not give students any further instructions, other than to write a step-by-step guide to making the sandwich. Once students have finished, have volunteers read their instructions aloud. After the last volunteer reads, ask students if they open the cans / bottles, if they get the spoon or knife out of the drawer, if they put the sandwich on a plate, and so on.

CRITICAL THINKING

• What constitutes a formal dining experience? Ask students to think of the difference between casual dining and formal dining. Can they name some restaurants from each category? Is it worth paying the extra money for a formal dining experience? Why or why not?

3. EXPRESAR GUSTOS Y PREFERENCIAS

Gramática – Expresar gustos en distinto grado

Presentation

- In this section, students will review:
  - The verb *gustar*.
  - Adverbs of quantity.
  - Comparisons with *más … que, menos … que,* and *tan … como*.

Activities	Standards	Resources
Gramática	1.2, 3.1, 4.1	
42.	1.2	Audio
43.	1.1, 1.2, 3.1	
44.	1.1, 1.2	

Teaching Suggestions

Warm-Up / Independent Starter

- Ask students to write a list of five things they like and five things they don't like using the verb *gustar*. For example: *Me gustan los perros. No me gustan los gatos.*

Preparation

- Have students compare the items on their likes / dislikes list using phrases such as: *más … que, menos … que* and *tan … como*. For example: *Los gatos son más interesantes que los perros.*

- Then ask students to look at the glasses for the adverbs of quantity. Have students draw their own glasses like the ones in the grammar presentation and qualify how much they like the ten things they mentioned in their Independent Starter.

Activities

42. Have students respond to each sentence by giving their own feelings and adding adverbs of quantity like *nada, poco, bastante,* and *mucho*. For example: *A mi hermano le gustan los frijoles. A mí no me gustan nada los frijoles.*

43. Ask students to choose one of the dialogues and have them add a few more lines. Allow time for practice and then have students act out their dialogue in front of the class.

26

Gramática

Expresar gustos en distinto grado

El verbo *gustar*

- To express likes or dislikes, use the verb *gustar*.

VERBO *GUSTAR* (TO LIKE). PRESENTE

	Singular	Plural	
(A mí)	me gusta	me gustan	*I like*
(A ti)	te gusta	te gustan	*you like*
(A usted) (A él/a ella)	le gusta	le gustan	*you like he/she likes*
(A nosotros/as)	nos gusta	nos gustan	*we like*
(A vosotros/as)	os gusta	os gustan	*you like*
(A ustedes) (A ellos/a ellas)	les gusta	les gustan	*you like they like*

Note: To speak about one thing or an action, use the singular form *gusta*.

A María le gusta la sopa.

To speak about two or more things, use the plural form *gustan*.

A mí me gustan los postres.

Adverbios de cantidad

nada · poco · bastante · mucho

*No me gusta **nada** el pescado, pero me gusta **mucho** el chocolate.*

La comparación

- To express inequality regarding one characteristic, use these structures:

  más + adjective + *que* · *La torta es **más dulce que** la fruta.*

  menos + adjective + *que* · *Los refrescos son **menos sanos que** el agua.*

- To express equality, use this structure:

  tan + adjective + *como* · *Este sándwich está **tan bueno como** ese.*

42 **¿A quién le gusta?**

 ▶ **Escucha y escribe.** Listen and write the food each person likes.

1. yo	2. mi hermano	3. ustedes	4. nuestros amigos	5. tú

▶ **Escribe.** Now write complete sentences with your answers, using the correct form of the verb *gustar*.

Differentiated Instruction

DEVELOPING LEARNERS

- Ask students to write a short dialogue about a picky eater. One student can be the food server at a restaurant that offers many different dishes and food choices. The partner should refuse each offer, telling the server that he or she doesn't like whatever is being offered. For example:

MESERO: *¿Quiere carne con papas?*
CLIENTE: *No me gusta mucho la carne y no me gustan nada las papas.*

EXPANDING LEARNERS

- Have students imagine they are at a county fair and they are extremely hungry. With all the food vendors and their carts in front of them, how will they make a decision? Ask students to use the verbs *querer* and *preferir* to compare the flavors of the food they want and prefer. Then have them make their final decison.

3. EXPRESAR GUSTOS Y PREFERENCIAS

Gramática – Expresar gustos en distinto grado

43 **¿Qué prefieres?**

 ▶ **Habla.** What do you prefer to eat? Use the prompts below to act out three dialogues with a partner.

Modelo   [ensalada / arroz]

   A. ¿Quieres una ensalada?
   B. No, gracias. No me gusta nada
      la ensalada. Prefiero el arroz.
   A. A mí me gusta mucho la ensalada.

1. refresco / agua

2. pescado / carne

3. verduras / frijoles

RECUERDA

Los verbos **querer** y **preferir** tienen la irregularidad **e > ie** en el presente, como el verbo *cerrar*.

– querer (to want) ⟶ yo quiero,
               tú quieres,
               él quiere...

– preferir (to prefer) ⟶ yo prefiero,
                tú prefieres,
                él prefiere...

44 **¿Más o menos?**

▶ **Escribe.** Compare the foods and drinks below using an adjective from the box.

dulce	salado
picante	agrio
frío	caliente

Modelo

la carne   el pescado

La carne es más salada que el pescado.

①

la sopa   la ensalada

②

el maíz   las papas

③

la pimienta   el azúcar

④

el limón   la banana

 ▶ **Habla.** Give a partner your opinion about the foods and drinks above.

Modelo   A. ¿Qué te gusta más, el maíz o las papas?
          B. Me gustan más las papas porque no son tan dulces como el maíz.

---

44. Have students write three more food comparisons using the following descriptive words: *delicioso, saludable,* and *sabroso.* For example: *La sopa está tan deliciosa como la carne.*

🎧 **AUDIO SCRIPT**
See page XVIIJ

Answer Key

42. 1. A mí me gusta mucho la fruta.
     2. A mi hermano le gustan mucho los frijoles.
     3. A ustedes les gusta el pescado.
     4. A nuestros amigos les gusta la verdura.
     5. A ti te gusta mucho el arroz.

43. Answers will vary. Sample answer:
     1. A. ¿Quieres un refresco?
          B. No, gracias. No me gustan nada los refrescos. Prefiero agua.
          A. A mí me gustan mucho los refrescos.

44. Answers will vary. Sample answers:
     1. La sopa está más caliente que la ensalada.
     2. El maíz es más dulce que las papas.
     3. La pimienta es más picante que el azúcar.
     4. El limón es más agrio que la banana.
     ▶ Answers will vary.

Additional Resources

Fans Online activities
Practice Workbook

HERITAGE LANGUAGE LEARNERS

• There are many other ways to express and rate likes and dislikes in Spanish. Ask students to rewrite the grammar presentation using all new words. Then ask for volunteers to teach the class their new grammar lesson.

SPECIAL-NEEDS LEARNERS

• For students who have language difficulties, have a peer sit with them in a quiet location to review the vocabulary and grammar presentations learned so far in this section. Have the student who is helping point to a food from the vocabulary page and the student with special needs should point to the quantifying adverb. The student who is helping can assist his or her partner in forming a sentence with these two ideas.

3. EXPRESAR GUSTOS Y PREFERENCIAS

Gramática – Pronombres de objeto

Presentation

- In this section, students will review:
  - Direct object pronouns.
  - Indirect object pronouns.

Activities	Standards	Resources
Gramática	1.2, 3.1, 4.1	
45.	1.2	
46.	1.1, 1.2	
47.	1.2	

Teaching Suggestions

Warm-Up / Independent Starter

- Ask students to fill in a chart like the one below with examples of vocabulary that correspond with each direct object pronoun. For example:

lo	la	los	las
el gato	la silla	los libros	las camas

Preparation

- Have students write five sentences that express want using the verb *querer* and different direct objects. Ask them to replace the direct object with the appropriate direct object pronoun and rewrite the sentence. For example: *Yo quiero un helado.* → *Yo lo quiero.*

- Then have students work in pairs to write a related sentence using indirect object pronouns. For example: *Compro un helado para ti.* → *Te compro un helado.*

Activities

45. Have students write three more sentences indicating the chores they have to do in their homes and how often they do each chore. For example: *Tengo que sacar la basura. Yo la saco todos los días.*

46. Ask students to write two sentences about what they prefer to do instead of each chore. For example: *Yo no quiero poner la mesa. Prefiero escuchar música. Pero yo la escucho después de poner la mesa.*

28

Gramática

Pronombres de objeto

Pronombres de objeto directo

- To avoid repeating words that have already been mentioned, you can replace the direct object with a pronoun.

SINGULAR		PLURAL	
Masculino	Femenino	Masculino	Femenino
lo *him, it*	la *her, it*	los *them*	las *them*

- Direct object pronouns go normally before the conjugated verb and attached at the end of the infinitive.

  Quiero la camisa. → La quiero.
  Quiero comprar ese suéter. → Quiero comprarlo.

Pronombres de objeto indirecto

- Indirect object pronouns are the same as those used with the verb gustar.

Singular		Plural	
me	to me	nos	to us
te	to you (informal)	os	to you (informal)
le	to him, to her, to you (formal)	les	to them, to you

- Indirect object pronouns go before the conjugated verb and attached at the end of the infinitive.

  Traigo el desayuno a Juan. → Le traigo el desayuno.
  Tengo que pedir la carta al mesero. → Tengo que pedirle la carta.

45 **¿Quién lo barre?**

▶ **Escribe.** You are eager to help out today. Volunteer to do each chore.

Modelo Hay que barrer el suelo. → Yo lo barro.

| ① limpiar el baño | ② pasar la aspiradora | ③ cerrar las ventanas | ④ preparar el pescado | ⑤ comprar frutas y verduras |

Differentiated Instruction

DEVELOPING LEARNERS

- Some students have trouble understanding the difference between direct object pronouns and indirect object pronouns. Write the following sentences and have students underline the direct object and circle the indirect object in each sentence. Then students will rewrite the sentences twice, once using direct object pronouns and once using indirect object pronouns.
  1. *Yo quiero preparar una torta para mis amigas.*
  2. *Andy quiere comprar flores para su mamá.*

EXPANDING LEARNERS

- Have students write ten sentences that alternate randomly between direct object pronouns and indirect object pronouns. They may either tell a story or just write a list of sentences.

46 **¿Quién lo hace?**

▶ **Habla.** Discuss who does the following chores at your home with a partner.

Modelo

A. ¿Quién pone la mesa en tu casa?
B. *La* ponemos mis hermanos y yo.

① preparar la comida

② lavar los platos

③ comprar las frutas

④ hacer la ensalada

⑤ servir el café

47 **¿A quién?**

▶ **Escribe.** Rewrite the sentences using the indirect object pronouns from the box.

me	te	le	nos	os	les

Yo le sirvo la comida al cliente.

Modelo El mesero sirve la comida.   (a mí)
     → El mesero *me* sirve la comida.

1. Yo pido la tarjeta de crédito.   (a usted)
2. El mesero repite la pregunta.   (a nosotros)
3. Ellos piden agua.   (a la señora López)
4. ¿Tu madre sirve el desayuno?   (a ti)
5. Nosotros pedimos más helado.   (a ellas)

veintinueve 29

Gramática – Pronombres de objeto

47. For additional practice with indirect object pronouns, have students write three sentences describing some of the things a food server does. Students should use an indirect object pronoun and the verbs *servir, llevar,* and *pedir.* For example: *El mesero les sirve agua a los clientes. La mesera le lleva la carta a la señora. El mesero le pide la comida al cocinero.* Invite volunteers to read their sentences aloud.

Answer Key

45. 1. Hay que limpiar el baño.
     → Yo lo limpio.
   2. Hay que pasar la aspiradora.
     → Yo la paso.
   3. Hay que cerrar las ventanas.
     → Yo las cierro.
   4. Hay que preparar el pescado.
     → Yo lo preparo.
   5. Hay que comprar frutas y verduras.
     → Yo las compro.

46. Answers will vary. Sample answer:
   1. A. ¿Quién prepara la comida en tu casa?
     B. La prepara mi padre.

47. 1. Yo le pido la tarjeta de crédito.
   2. El mesero nos repite la pregunta.
   3. Ellos le piden agua.
   4. ¿Tú madre te sirve el desayuno?
   5. Nosotros les pedimos más helado.

Additional Resources

Fans Online activities
Practice Workbook

HERITAGE LANGUAGE LEARNERS

• Ask students to compare how direct object and indirect object pronouns are used in English and in Spanish. How are they similar and how are they different? Have students report their findings to the class, as this may help the students who are struggling to understand this concept.

MULTIPLE INTELLIGENCES:
Musical Intelligence

• Ask students to listen to or print the lyrics for the song "Te voy a llevar" by the rock band from Uruguay, No Te Va a Gustar. Have students scan the lyrics and find the direct and indirect object pronouns. Allow your musically-inclined students to sing the song for the class.

Connecting Unit

3. EXPRESAR GUSTOS Y PREFERENCIAS

Gramática – Expresar acciones habituales en el presente

Presentation

- In this section, students will review:
- – First-person irregular verbs.
- – Demonstratives.

Activities	Standards	Resources
Gramática	1.2, 3.1, 4.1	
48.	1.2	
49.	1.2, 1.3, 3.1	
50.	1.1, 1.2	

Teaching Suggestions

Warm-Up / Independent Starter

- Have students write a list of things they do each day using the verbs *hacer, poner, traer,* and *salir.* For example: *Por la mañana hago ejercicio. Me pongo la ropa y salgo de casa …*

Preparation

- Ask students to work in pairs to look for an action photo with two or more people in a magazine and describe the photo by using demonstratives. For example: *Esta señora lleva una chaqueta roja* (pointing to a woman in a red coat).

Activities

48. Have students rewrite the questions, replacing the articles with demonstratives. For example: *¿Quién pone esta mesa?* or *¿Quién pone aquella mesa?*

49. Guide students as they write similar conversations. Each participant in the conversation should have between four and six lines and students should choose original names for their restaurants and characters. Once students have finished, and for extra points, ask students to memorize their conversations to present to the class. Have the class vote on whose presentation had the best acting and a separate vote on whose presentation was the most creative.

50. Ask students to answer the questions according to who does each chore in their homes.

30

Gramática

Expresar acciones habituales en el presente

Verbos irregulares en la primera persona

- Some verbs are irregular in the present tense only in the first person. The rest of the forms follow the same pattern as the regular verbs.

VERBOS HACER (TO MAKE, TO DO), PONER (TO PUT), TRAER (TO BRING) Y SALIR (TO LEAVE). PRESENTE

		Hacer	Poner	Traer	Salir
Singular	yo	hago	pongo	traigo	salgo
	tú	haces	pones	traes	sales
	usted, él, ella	hace	pone	trae	sale
Plural	nosotros, nosotras	hacemos	ponemos	traemos	salimos
	vosotros, vosotras	hacéis	ponéis	traéis	salís
	ustedes, ellos, ellas	hacen	ponen	traen	salen

- Other verbs that are irregular only in the first person are:

  saber *(to know how)* ⟶ yo **sé**, tú sabes, él sabe…
  conocer *(to be acquainted)* ⟶ yo **conozco**, tú conoces, él conoce…
  ver *(to see)* ⟶ yo **veo**, tú ves, él ve…

Los demostrativos

- To indicate where something or someone is located in relation to the person speaking, use demonstratives.

DEMOSTRATIVOS

	SINGULAR		PLURAL	
Distance from speaker	Masculino	Femenino	Masculino	Femenino
Near	este	esta	estos	estas
At a distance	ese	esa	esos	esas
Far away	aquel	aquella	aquellos	aquellas

Me gusta **esta** camisa y **esa** falda.

48 ¿Quién pone la mesa?

▶ **Escribe.** Answer the following questions using a direct object pronoun.

Modelo   ¿Quién pone la mesa? (yo) ⟶ Yo la pongo.

1. ¿Quién pone los platos? (ellos)
2. ¿Quién trae el postre? (tú)
3. ¿Quién hace la cena? (papá)
4. ¿Quién corta la carne? (ella)
5. ¿Quién conoce al mesero? (nosotros)
6. ¿Quién sabe su nombre? (yo)

30 treinta

Differentiated Instruction

DEVELOPING LEARNERS

- Place textbooks, sheets of paper, and a ruler on desks around the room. Have students call out where the items are in relation to you. For example, you stand close to a book and students will say *Este libro*; you stand far away from a stack of papers and students will say *Aquellas hojas*. Repeat this process until you have practiced all the demonstratives.

EXPANDING LEARNERS

- In groups of three, have students create a dialogue similar to one of those in activity 49. Ask students to repeat the dialogue several times so that different students get to play different roles. For fun, they can change the style of each dramatization (for instance, making one rendition funny, one sad, one mysterious, etc.) by changing their tone of voice and gestures to match each mood.

49 **Salimos a cenar**

▶ **Completa.** Two friends are having dinner at a restaurant in downtown Lima. Complete their conversations using a demonstrative from the box.

aquella	aquellos	aquel	esa	este

LUISA: Aquí está el restaurante El limeño. ¿Entramos?
EVA: A mí no me gusta ___1___ restaurante. Prefiero ___2___ de allí.
LUISA: ¿El restaurante El Inca?
EVA: Sí. Es muy famoso por la comida indígena.

MESERO: ¿Quieren sentarse en ___3___ mesa, señoras?
LUISA: Yo prefiero ___4___, más cerca de la ventana.

EVA: ¡Tengo hambre! ¿Dónde está nuestro mesero?
LUISA: Un momento. Está con ___5___ clientes.
EVA: ¡Aquí viene el mesero!

▶ **Escribe y representa.** With a partner, write a conversation similar to one of the ones above using at least three demonstrative adjectives.

50 **No, yo no la pongo**

▶ **Habla.** Talk to a partner about who does the following activities.

Modelo poner la mesa (mi madre)
    A. *¿Tú pones la mesa en tu casa?*
    B. *No, yo no pongo la mesa en mi casa. La pone mi madre.*

1. saber hacer paella (mis padres)
2. conocer buenas recetas (mi hermana)
3. traer la cena (Pedro)
4. hacer la comida (mi padre)
5. servir la sopa (mi madre)
6. hacer la compra (todos)

---

3. EXPRESAR GUSTOS Y PREFERENCIAS

Gramática – Expresar acciones habituales en el presente

Answer Key

48. 1. Ellos los ponen.
2. Tú lo traes.
3. Papá la hace.
4. Ella la corta.
5. Nosotros lo conocemos.
6. Yo lo sé.

49. 1. este
2. aquel
3. esa
4. aquella
5. aquellos
▶ Answers will vary.

50. 1. A. ¿Tú sabes hacer paella?
   B. No, yo no sé hacer paella. La hacen mis padres.
2. A. ¿Tú conoces buenas recetas?
   B. No, yo no conozco buenas recetas. Las conoce mi hermana.
3. A. ¿Tú traes la cena?
   B. No, yo no traigo la cena. La trae Pedro.
4. A. ¿Tú haces la comida en tu casa?
   B. No, yo no hago la comida. La hace mi padre.
5. A. ¿Tú sirves la sopa en tu casa?
   B. No, yo no sirvo la sopa. La sirve mi madre.
6. A. ¿Tú haces la compra en tu casa?
   B. No, yo no hago la compra. La hacemos todos.

Additional Resources

Fans Online activities
Practice Workbook

HERITAGE LANGUAGE LEARNERS

• Ask students to imagine they are having a party at their house. The party can be to celebrate a special holiday, a special occasion, or just a regular Saturday get-together. Have students write a narrative about what people typically bring and do, what time people arrive and leave, what type of music is played, etc.

MUTIPLES INTELLIGENCES: Visual-Spatial Intelligence

• Ask students to create and illustrate a comic strip where Pongo the Dog, Traigo the Bird, and Hago the Cat have to pick up trash as part of a recycling project. Students must use demonstratives to accent their story.

Unit 5 Española

Objectives

- To identify the body parts and their basic functions.
- To make descriptions using the five senses.
- To organize daily hygiene routines.
- To use reflexive pronouns.
- To talk about physical and emotional conditions.
- To discuss basic illnesses, basic remedies, and healthy lifestyle choices.

- To give commands and advice.
- To express habits.
- To explore cultural aspects of Spain.

Contents

Vocabulary
- Body parts.
- The five senses.
- Personal hygiene products.
- Daily hygiene routines.
- Medical staff and their workplace.
- Basic remedies.
- Healthy lifestyle habits.

Grammar
- To express the actions of the five senses.
- To use reflexive pronouns.
- To say something hurts.
- To express physical and emotional states.
- To give commands.

Culture
- The geography and history of Spain.
- *La Vuelta Ciclista a España*.
- The steep mountain pass called *El Angliru*.
- Cubism.
- *La Alhambra*.
- *El Hostal de los Reyes Católicos*.
- *El Camino de Santiago*.
- *El Obradoiro* in Santiago de Compostela.
- *El monasterio de Silos*.
- *El Guernica* by Pablo Picasso.

Evaluation Criteria

- Identify body parts.
- Describe surroundings using the five senses.
- Identify daily hygiene products.
- Describe and compare good daily hygiene habits.

- Identify medical professions and their workplaces.
- Express what hurts.
- Identify and describe the symptoms of an illness.
- Express emotions.

- Give and follow commands.
- Identify basic remedies for common illnesses.
- Choose healthy lifestyle habits and illness prevention.

Unit Plan

La llegada

Estimated time: 2 sessions.

Dialogue: *En Madrid.*

Forms & functions:
- Body parts.
- Medical professions and buildings.
- To express how someone feels.
- To wish someone to feel better.
- To say where something hurts.

Culture:
- Madrid.

DESAFÍO 1

Estimated time: 5 sessions.

Dialogue: *Una vuelta ciclista.*

Forms & functions:
- Body parts and five senses.
- Expressing actions of the five senses: The verbs *ver, oír, oler,* and *decir.*

Culture:
- *La Vuelta Ciclista a España.*
- *El Angliru.*
- *¿Lo ves o no lo ves?*

DESAFÍO 2

Estimated time: 5 sessions.

Dialogue: *El azulejo perdido.*

Forms & functions:
- Personal hygiene products and routines.
- Expressing habitual actions: Reflexive pronouns.

Culture:
- *La Alhambra.*
- *Los productos de higiene personal.*

DESAFÍO 3

Estimated time: 6 sessions.

Dialogue: *El escudo de los reyes.*

Forms & functions:
- Medical staff and buildings.
- Common symptoms and illnesses.
- Expressing physical conditions: The verbs *doler* and *sentirse.*

Culture:
- *El Hostal de los Reyes Católicos.*
- *El Camino de Santiago.*
- *El Obradoiro.*

DESAFÍO 4

Estimated time: 5 sessions.

Dialogue: *Una receta antigua.*

Forms & functions:
- Basic remedies and healthy lifestyle habits.
- To give commands and advice: Affirmative *tú* commands.

Culture:
- *El monasterio de Silos.*
- *La belleza física.*

Todo junto / El encuentro

Estimated time: 2 sessions.

Dialogue: *En la Plaza Mayor.*

Forms & functions:
- Review of *Desafíos 1–4.*

Culture:
- *Los horarios de los españoles.*
- *La Plaza Mayor.*

MAPA CULTURAL / LECTURA

Estimated time: 2 sessions.

Mapa cultural: *España.*

Reading: *El Guernica.*

REPASO

Estimated time: 2 sessions.

Vocabulary: *Repaso.*

Grammar: *Repaso.*

PROYECTO / EVALUACIÓN

Estimated time: 5 sessions.

Project: *Un póster sobre hábitos de higiene.*

Self-evaluation: *Autoevaluación.*

Standards for Learning Spanish

COMMUNICATION

1.1. Interpersonal mode
- Participate in a discussion on a given topic.
- Describe people in a photo or drawing.
- Interview a classmate.
- Compare pictures and/or charts with a partner.
- Compare morning routines and hygiene with a partner.
- Ask and answer questions about illness and a healthy lifestyle.
- Discuss agreement or disagreement based on an audio recording.
- Prepare a presentation with a partner.
- Discuss and compare responses to a questionnaire with a partner.

1.2. Interpretive mode
- Answer questions based on a picture story, reading, or audio recording.
- Read or listen to a conversation.
- Put pictures in order based on a conversation or captions.
- Take notes based on an audio recording or reading passage.
- Draw a picture based on a description or an audio recording.

1.3. Presentational mode
- Act out at a skit or dialogue.
- Report findings to the class.
- Present an individual or group project.
- Share opinions with a group or the class.

COMPARISONS

4.1. Compare languages
- Compare reflexive and non-reflexive verbs.
- Explore reasons for using articles versus possessive adjectives.
- Understand how accent marks can change the meaning of a word.
- Recognize the difference between *tú* commands and verbs conjugated in the *usted* form.

4.2. Compare cultures
- Compare personal hygiene products in the United States with those in Spanish-speaking countries.
- Compare concepts of health and medicine in the United States with those in Spanish-speaking countries.
- Use artwork to understand the happenings of a specific time period.

CULTURE

2.1. Practices and perspectives
- Learn about the leader in a bicycle race.
- Describe the use of hygiene products in Spanish-speaking countries.
- Compare community schedules in Spanish-speaking countries with those in the United States.
- Identify and understand the Arabic influence in Spain.

2.2. Products and perspectives
- Describe hygiene products used in Spanish-speaking countries.
- Identify cubism as an art style.
- Understand the uses and history of the *Hostal de los Reyes Católicos*.
- Use artwork to understand the happenings of a specific time period.
- Reflect on the idea of beauty in other time periods and in different cultures.

COMMUNITIES

5.1. Spanish beyond the school setting
- Convince the judges why a particular team should win.
- Visit a website to watch a video on a cultural event or famous figure.

5.2. Spanish for lifelong learning
- Identify and label the hygiene products students use on a daily basis.
- Use the Internet to find information about famous Spanish landmarks.
- Research and identify ways to live a healthier lifestyle.

CONNECTIONS

3.1. Interdisciplinary connections
- Draw an original work of art.
- Interpret a painting or drawing.
- Use spelling as a vocabulary resource.
- Implement and practice reading strategies.
- Locate political and geographical divisions.
- Look at and/or read a map.
- Describe illness prevention.
- Express healthy eating habits and exercise routines.

3.2. Viewpoints through language / culture
- Interpret the meaning of artworks by Hispanic artists.
- Understand the feelings and motivations behind a pilgrimage.
- Identify the changes in health and medicine over time and between cultures.

Communicative Skills

Interpersonal Mode

		Activities
Speaking	• Describe people in visual display to a partner. • Compare morning routines and hygiene with a partner. • Discuss and compare responses to a questionnaire with a partner. • Talk about aches and pains with a classmate.	• 6, 8, 11, 20, 23, 27 • 35, 36, 38, 40, 86, *Proyecto* • 65, 66, 70, 72 • 45, 51, 54, 56, 84, R3*
Writing	• Write health tips or slogans with a partner. • Create a chart to compare a partner's answers.	• 62, 79, 87 • 22, 31, 86, *Proyecto*
Listening	• Interpret a classmate's answers. • Understand a partner's clues in order to exchange information.	• 19, 36, 56, 72, *Proyecto* • 23, 51
Reading	• Understand a personal reflection or survey.	• 21, 30, 50

*R = *Repaso*

Interpretive Mode

		Activities
Listening	• Demonstrate an understanding of an audio recording.	• 2, 12, 17, 21, 26, 29, 30, 34, 39, 49, 61, 64, 70, 78, 81, 85
Reading	• Use the context in order to complete a text. • Understand a descriptive, informative, or explanatory passage along with its images. • Interpret a reading or a picture story. • Understand the main idea of a text and synthesize it into a title.	• 18, 67, 69, 79, R4 • 20, 23, *Proyecto* • 6, 7, 20, 25, 32, 38, 43, 44, 48, 50, 57, 63, 68, 72, 88, 93, 95 • 94

Presentational Mode

		Activities
Speaking	• Act out a skit or dialogue. • Report findings to the class. • Present an individual or group project. • Share opinions with a group or the class.	• 6, 67, 83, 85, 89 • 19, 36, 62, 74 • 23, 89, *Proyecto* • 4, 5, 61, 81, 87, 90
Writing	• Write a descriptive paragraph or e-mail. • Create an informative and / or decorative poster.	• 13, 21, 22, 23, 39, 42, 82 • 23, 63, *Proyecto*

Cross-Curricular Standards

Subject	Standard	Activities
Language Arts	• Write a descriptive paragraph or e-mail. • Implement and practice reading strategies.	• 13, 21, 22, 23, 39, 42, 82 • *Lectura*
Social Studies	• Locate political and geographical divisions. • Look at and / or read a map.	• *Mapa cultural* • *Tu desafío*, 91
Art	• Draw an original work of art. • Interpret a painting or drawing.	• 20, 23, 55 • 80, 84, *Lectura*
Health and Phys. Ed.	• Describe illness prevention. • Express healthy eating habits and exercise routines.	• 62, 63 • 68, 70, 74, 75, 78, 79, *Proyecto*

Lesson Plans (50-Minute Classes)

Day	Objectives	Sessions	Activities	Time	Standards	Resources/ Homework
1	To introduce Spain	**España** (32–33) • Warm-Up: Country orientation • Spain • Images and functions		5 m. 15 m. 30 m.	1.2, 2.2, 4.1	Video Practice Workbook
2	To introduce Spain and to discuss the pairs' challenges	**La llegada** (34–37) • Warm-Up: Independent Starter • Presentation: *En Madrid* • *Expresiones útiles* and *¿Quién ganará?*	 1 2–5	5 m. 15 m. 30 m.	1.1, 1.2, 1.3, 4.1	Visual Presentation Audio Practice Workbook
3	To talk about the body and feelings	**Desafío 1 – Una vuelta ciclista** (38–39) • Warm-Up: Independent Starter • *Fotonovela: Una vuelta ciclista* • *Cultura: La Vuelta Ciclista a España*	 6–8 9	5 m. 35 m. 10 m.	1.1, 12, 1.3, 3.1, 3.2, 5.1, 5.2	Visual Presentation *Tu desafío*
4	To learn the parts of the body and the five senses	**Desafío 1 – Vocabulario** (40–41) • Warm-Up: Independent Starter • Vocabulary: *Partes del cuerpo* • *Cultura: El Angliru*	 10–13 14	5 m. 35 m. 10 m.	1.1, 1.2, 3.1, 3.2, 5.2	Audio Practice Workbook *Tu desafío*
5	To express actions of the five senses	**Desafío 1 – Gramática** (42–43) • Warm-Up: Independent Starter • Grammar: *Los verbos 'ver', 'oír', 'oler' y 'decir'* • *Cultura: ¿Lo ves o no lo ves?*	 15–19 20	5 m. 35 m. 10 m.	1.1, 1.2, 2.2, 3.1, 3.2, 4.1, 5.1, 5.2	Audio Practice Workbook *Tu desafío*
6	To integrate vocabulary and grammar	**Desafío 1 – Comunicación** (44–45) • Warm-Up: Independent Starter • *Comunicación:* Review main vocabulary and grammar	 21–23	5 m. 45 m.	1.1, 1.2, 1.3, 3.1	Audio Practice Workbook
7	To assess student proficiency	**Desafío 1 – Evaluación** (45) • Warm-Up: *Final del desafío* • Quiz on *Desafío 1*	 24	30 m. 20 m.	1.2	*Tu desafío*
8	To express habitual actions	**Desafío 2 – El azulejo perdido** (46–47) • Warm-Up: Independent Starter • *Fotonovela: El azulejo perdido* • *Cultura: La Alhambra*	 25–27 28	5 m. 30 m. 15 m.	1.1, 1.2, 1.3, 3.2, 4.2, 5.2	Visual Presentation Audio Video *Tu desafío*
9	To learn about personal hygiene	**Desafío 2 – Vocabulario** (48–49) • Warm-Up: Independent Starter • Vocabulary: *La higiene personal* • *Comparaciones: Los productos de higiene personal*	 29–31 32	5 m. 35 m. 10 m.	1.2, 2.1, 4.2	Audio Practice Workbook *Tu desafío*
10	To learn about reflexive verbs	**Desafío 2 – Gramática** (50–51) • Warm-Up: Independent Starter • Grammar: *Los verbos reflexivos* • *Conexiones: La adolescencia*	 33–36 37	5 m. 35 m. 10 m.	1.1, 1.2, 1.3, 3.1, 4.1	Audio Practice Workbook

Day	Objectives	Sessions	Activities	Time	Standards	Resources/Homework
11	To integrate vocabulary and grammar	**Desafío 2 – Comunicación** (52–53) • Warm-Up: Independent Starter • *Comunicación*: Review main vocabulary and grammar	38–41	5 m. 45 m.	1.1, 1.2, 3.1, 5.2	Audio Practice Workbook
12	To assess student proficiency	**Desafío 2 – Evaluación** (53) • Warm-Up: *Final del desafío* • Quiz on *Desafío 2*	42	30 m. 20 m.	1.2	
13	To express physical states	**Desafío 3 – El escudo de los reyes** (54–55) • Warm-Up: Independent Starter • *Fotonovela: El escudo de los reyes* • *Cultura: El Hostal de los Reyes Católicos*	43–46 47	5 m. 35 m. 10 m.	1.1, 1.2, 1.3, 2.2, 3.2, 5.2	Visual Presentation *Tu desafío*
14	To learn about symptoms and illnesses	**Desafío 3 – Vocabulario** (56–57) • Warm-Up: Independent Starter • *Vocabulary: Síntomas y enfermedades* • *Cultura: El Camino de Santiago*	48–51 52	5 m. 35 m. 10 m.	1.1, 1.2, 3.1, 4.2	Audio Practice Workbook
15	To tell what hurts	**Desafío 3 – Gramática** (58–59) • Warm-Up: Independent Starter • *Grammar: El verbo 'doler'* • *Conexiones: El Obradoiro*	53–56 57	5 m. 35 m. 10 m.	1.1, 1.2, 2.2, 3.1, 4.1, 5.2	Audio Practice Workbook
16	To express emotional and physical states	**Desafío 3 – Gramática** (60–61) • Warm-Up: Independent Starter • *Grammar: El verbo 'sentirse'* • *Conexiones: Los gérmenes y la salud*	58–62 63	5 m. 35 m. 10 m.	1.1, 1.2, 1.3, 2.2, 3.1, 4.1, 5.2	Audio Practice Workbook
17	To integrate vocabulary and grammar	**Desafío 3 – Comunicación** (62–63) • Warm-Up: Independent Starter • *Comunicación*: Review main vocabulary and grammar	64–66	5 m. 45 m.	1.1, 1.2, 1.3	Audio Practice Workbook
18	To assess student proficiency	**Desafío 3 – Evaluación** (63) • Warm-Up: *Final del desafío* • Quiz on *Desafío 3*	67	30 m. 20 m.	1.2	*Tu desafío*
19	To give commands and advice	**Desafío 4 – Una receta antigua** (64–65) • Warm-Up: Independent Starter • *Fotonovela: Una receta antigua* • *Cultura: El monasterio de Silos*	68–70 71	5 m. 30 m. 15 m.	1.1, 1.2, 3.1, 3.2, 4.2, 5.2	Visual Presentation Audio Video *Tu desafío*
20	To learn basic remedies	**Desafío 4 – Vocabulario** (66–67) • Warm-Up: Independent Starter • *Vocabulary: Remedios básicos* • *Conexiones: Mi pirámide*	72–74 75	5 m. 35 m. 10 m.	1.1, 1.2, 1.3, 3.1	Audio Practice Workbook *Tu desafío*
21	To give commands	**Desafío 4 – Gramática** (68–69) • Warm-Up: Independent Starter • *Grammar: El imperativo afirmativo de 'tú'* • *Conexiones: La belleza física*	76–79 80	5 m. 35 m. 10 m.	1.1, 1.2, 2.1, 3.1, 3.2, 4.1, 4.2	Audio Practice Workbook

Day	Objectives	Sessions	Activities	Time	Standards	Resources/Homework
22	To integrate vocabulary and grammar	**Desafío 4 – Comunicación** (70–71) • Warm-Up: Independent Starter • *Comunicación*: Review main vocabulary and grammar	81–82	5 m. 45 m.	1.1, 1.2, 1.3	Audio Practice Workbook
23	To assess student proficiency	**Desafío 4 – Evaluación** (71) • Warm-Up: *Final del desafío* • Quiz on *Desafío 4*	83	30 m. 20 m.	1.1, 1.2, 1.3	
24	To integrate language in context	**Todo junto** (72–73) • Warm-Up: Independent Starter • *Todo junto* • *Cultura: Los horarios de los españoles*	84–87 88	5 m. 35 m. 10 m.	1.1, 1.2, 1.3, 2.1, 4.2	Audio Practice Workbook
25	To integrate language in context	**El encuentro** (74–75) • Warm-Up: Independent Starter • *El encuentro: En la Plaza Mayor*	89–90	5 m. 45 m.	1.2, 1.3	
26	To learn about Spanish customs and traditions	**Mapa cultural – España** (76–79) • Warm-Up: Independent Starter • *Mapa cultural: España*	91–93	5 m. 45 m.	1.1, 1.2, 1.3, 2.2, 3.1, 3.2, 5.2	Video Practice Workbook
27	To learn about *El Guernica*	**Lectura – El Guernica** (80–81) • Warm-Up: Independent Starter • *Lectura: El Guernica*	94–96	5 m. 45 m.	1.1, 1.2, 2.1, 2.2, 3.1, 3.2, 4.2, 5.2	*Tu desafío*
28	To review vocabulary	**Repaso – Vocabulario** (82–83) • Warm-Up: Independent Starter • *Repaso: Vocabulario*	1–4	5 m. 45 m.	1.1, 1.2	Practice Workbook
29	To review grammar and culture	**Repaso – Gramática** (84–85) • Warm-Up: Independent Starter • *Repaso: Gramática*	5–9	5 m. 45 m.	1.2, 2.1, 2.2, 5.2	Practice Workbook
30	To create a healthy lifestyles poster	**Proyecto – Hábitos de higiene** (86–87) • Warm-Up: Read the project outline • Work on project		5 m. 45 m.	1.1, 1.2, 1.3, 3.1	
31	To create a healthy lifestyles poster	**Proyecto – Hábitos de higiene** (86–87) • Warm-Up: Read the project outline • Work on project		5 m. 45 m.	1.1, 1.2, 1.3, 3.1	
32	To present projects	**Proyecto – Hábitos de higiene** (86–87) • Warm-Up: Prepare presentations • Project presentations		5 m. 45 m.	1.1, 1.2, 1.3, 3.1	
33	To present projects	**Proyecto – Hábitos de higiene** (86–87) • Warm-Up: Prepare presentations • Project presentations		5 m. 45 m.	1.1, 1.2, 1.3, 3.1	
34	To assess student proficiency	**Assessment** • *Autoevaluación* (87) • Test on Unit 5		10 m. 40 m.	1.2, 1.3	

Lesson Plans (90-Minute Classes)

Day	Objectives	Sessions	Activities	Time	Standards	Resources/ Homework
1	To introduce Spain and to discuss the pairs' challenges	**España / La llegada** (32–37) • Warm-Up: Country orientation • Spain • Images and functions • Presentation: *En Madrid* • *Expresiones útiles* and *¿Quién ganará?*	 1 2–5	 5 m. 10 m. 20 m. 20 m. 35 m.	1.1, 1.2, 1.3, 2.2, 4.1	Visual Presentation Audio Video Practice Workbook
2	To learn about the body, feelings, and the five senses	**Desafío 1 – Una vuelta ciclista / Vocabulario** (38–41) • Warm-Up: Independent Starter • *Fotonovela: Una vuelta ciclista* • *Cultura: La Vuelta Ciclista a España* • Vocabulary: *Partes del cuerpo* • *Cultura: El Angliru*	 6–8 9 10–13 14	 5 m. 35 m. 10 m. 30 m. 10 m.	1.1, 1.2, 1.3, 3.1, 3.2, 5.1, 5.2	Visual Presentation Audio Practice Workbook *Tu desafío*
3	To express actions of the five senses and to integrate vocabulary and grammar	**Desafío 1 – Gramática / Comunicación** (42–45) • Warm-Up: Independent Starter • Grammar: *Los verbos 'ver', 'oír', 'oler' y 'decir'* • *Cultura: ¿Lo ves o no lo ves?* • Comunicación: Review main vocabulary and grammar	 15–19 20 21–23	 5 m. 30 m. 10 m. 45 m.	1.1, 1.2, 1.3, 2.2, 3.1, 3.2, 4.1, 5.1, 5.2	Audio Practice Workbook
4	To assess student proficiency and to express habitual actions	**Desafío 1 – Evaluación / Desafío 2 – El azulejo perdido** (45–47) • Warm-Up: *Final del desafío* • Quiz on *Desafío 1* • *Fotonovela: El azulejo perdido* • *Cultura: La Alhambra*	 24 25–27 28	 25 m. 20 m. 30 m. 15 m.	1.1, 1.2, 1.3, 3.2, 4.2, 5.2	Visual Presentation Audio Video Practice Workbook *Tu desafío*
5	To learn about personal hygiene and reflexive verbs	**Desafío 2 – Vocabulario / Gramática** (48–51) • Warm-Up: Independent Starter • Vocabulary: *La higiene personal* • Comparaciones: *Los productos de higiene personal* • Grammar: *Los verbos reflexivos* • Conexiones: *La adolescencia*	 29–31 32 33–36 37	 5 m. 30 m. 10 m. 30 m. 15 m.	1.1, 1.2, 1.3, 2.1, 3.1, 4.1, 4.2	Audio Practice Workbook *Tu desafío*
6	To integrate vocabulary and grammar and to assess student proficiency	**Desafío 2 – Comunicación / Evaluación** (52–53) • Warm-Up: Independent Starter • Comunicación: Review main vocabulary and grammar • *Final del desafío* • Quiz on *Desafío 2*	 38–41 42	 5 m. 45 m. 20 m. 20 m.	1.1, 1.2, 3.1, 5.2	Audio Practice Workbook
7	To express physical states, symptoms, and illnesses	**Desafío 3 – El escudo de los reyes / Vocabulario** (54–57) • Warm-Up: Independent Starter • *Fotonovela: El escudo de los reyes* • *Cultura: El Hostal de los Reyes Católicos* • Vocabulary: *Síntomas y enfermedades* • *Cultura: El Camino de Santiago*	 43–46 47 48–51 52	 5 m. 35 m. 10 m. 30 m. 10 m.	1.1, 1.2, 1.3, 2.2, 3.1, 3.2, 4.2, 5.2	Visual Presentation Audio Practice Workbook *Tu desafío*

Day	Objectives	Sessions	Activities	Time	Standards	Resources/ Homework
8	To tell what hurts and to express emotional and physical states	**Desafío 3 – Gramática** (58–61) • Warm-Up: Independent Starter • Grammar: *El verbo 'doler'* • *Conexiones: El Obradoiro* • Grammar: *El verbo 'sentirse'* • *Conexiones: Los gérmenes y la salud*	 53–56 57 58–62 63	 5 m. 30 m. 10 m. 35 m. 10 m.	1.1, 1.2, 1.3, 2.2, 3.1, 4.1, 5.2	Audio Practice Workbook
9	To integrate vocabulary and grammar and to assess student proficiency	**Desafío 3 – Comunicación / Evaluación** (62–63) • Warm-Up: Independent Starter • *Comunicación*: Review main vocabulary and grammar • *Final del desafío* • Quiz on *Desafío 3*	 64–66 67	 5 m. 45 m. 20 m. 20 m.	1.1, 1.2, 1.3	Audio Practice Workbook *Tu desafío*
10	To give commands and advice and to learn basic remedies	**Desafío 4 – Una receta antigua / Vocabulario** (64–67) • Warm-Up: Independent Starter • *Fotonovela: Una receta antigua* • *Cultura: El monasterio de Silos* • Vocabulary: *Remedios básicos* • *Conexiones: Mi pirámide*	 68–70 71 72–74 75	 5 m. 30 m. 15 m. 30 m. 10 m.	1.1, 1.2, 1.3, 3.1, 3.2, 4.2, 5.2	Visual Presentation Audio Video Practice Workbook *Tu desafío*
11	To give commands and to integrate vocabulary and grammar	**Desafío 4 – Gramática / Comunicación** (68–71) • Warm-Up: Independent Starter • Grammar: *El imperativo afirmativo de 'tú'* • *Conexiones: La belleza física* • *Comunicación*: Review main vocabulary and grammar	 76–79 80 81–82	 5 m. 30 m. 10 m. 45 m.	1.1, 1.2, 1.3, 2.1, 3.1, 3.2, 4.1, 4.2	Audio Practice Workbook
12	To assess student proficiency and to integrate language in context	**Desafío 4 – Evaluación / Todo junto** (71–73) • Warm-Up: *Final del desafío* • Quiz on *Desafío 4* • *Todo junto*	 83 84–87	 30 m. 20 m. 40 m.	1.1, 1.2, 1.3	Audio Practice Workbook
13	To integrate language in context	**Todo junto / El encuentro** (73–75) • Warm-Up: Independent Starter • *Cultura: Los horarios de los españoles* • *El encuentro: En la Plaza Mayor*	 88 89–90	 5 m. 20 m. 65 m.	1.2, 1.3, 2.1, 4.2	Audio
14	To learn about Spanish customs and traditions	**Mapa cultural / Lectura** (76–81) • Warm-Up: Independent Starter • *Mapa cultural: España* • *Lectura: El Guernica*	 91–93 94–96	 5 m. 45 m. 40 m.	1.1, 1.2, 1.3, 2.1, 2.2, 3.1, 3.2, 4.2, 5.2	Video Practice Workbook *Tu desafío*
15	To review vocabulary, grammar, and culture	**Repaso – Vocabulario / Gramática** (82–85) • Warm-Up: Independent Starter • *Repaso: Vocabulario* • *Repaso: Gramática*	 1–4 5–9	 5 m. 40 m. 45 m.	1.1, 1.2, 2.1, 2.2, 5.2	Practice Workbook

Day	Objectives	Sessions	Activities	Time	Standards	Resources/ Homework
16	To create a healthy lifestyles poster	***Proyecto*** (86–87) • Warm-Up: Read the project outline • Work on project		5 m. 85 m.	1.1, 1.2, 1.3, 3.1	
17	To present projects	***Proyecto*** (86–87) • Warm-Up: prepare presentations • Project presentations		5 m. 85 m.	1.1, 1.2, 1.3, 3.1	
18	To present projects and to assess student proficiency	***Proyecto / Assessment*** (86–87) • Warm-Up: Prepare presentations • Project presentations • *Autoevaluación* • Test on Unit 5		5 m. 30 m. 10 m. 45 m.	1.1, 1.2, 1.3, 3.1	

2 ¿Cómo se sienten?

–Hola, María. ¿Cómo te sientes hoy?

–Me duele un poco la cabeza.

–Y tú, Javier, ¿cómo estás?

–No me siento bien.

–¿Qué te pasa?

–Me duelen los pies.

–Pedro, ¿tú cómo te sientes?

–Bien, doctora.

–Estupendo. Y tú, Rosalía, ¿cómo estás?

–Mal... Estoy enferma.

12 ¿Fátima, Armando o la doctora Galdón?

Mi amiga Fátima tiene el pelo negro y los ojos azules.
La doctora Galdón es muy atractiva. Tiene el cuello largo, las piernas largas y la cara muy bonita.
¿Y Armando? Armando tiene el pelo rubio, una nariz grande y es delgado. Es muy gracioso y muy buena persona.

17 ¿Qué hacen los participantes?

–Mamá, hay algo que me produce alergia.

–Sí, hija, tienes los ojos rojos.

–No puedo oler nada. Esta alergia es horrible. Y tampoco oigo muy bien.

–¿Puedo apagar la radio? No me gusta esta música tan moderna de los jóvenes.

–Claro. Mamá, ¿adónde vas?

–Voy al restaurante del hotel. Hay un espectáculo de flamenco.

–¿Flamenco?

–Sí. Tim y Mack quieren ver el espectáculo y voy con ellos.

–Buena idea. Nos vemos después de la cena.

–Descansa, Tess.

–Sí, mamá. Hasta luego.

–Adiós, hija.

21 El ciclista Antonio López

La Vuelta Ciclista a España ofrece muchos servicios a los ciclistas. Por ejemplo, tenemos doctores y enfermeros en todas las etapas. Para las piernas y los pies cansados, hay salas de terapia muscular y sesiones de relajación. Y en los hoteles los ciclistas tienen salas de juegos para hablar con los compañeros y divertirse.

26 Hotel Baños Reales

El Hotel Baños Reales está cerca de la Alhambra. Es un hotel barato con todos los servicios de un hotel caro. Para la higiene personal hay productos en las habitaciones a disposición de los clientes. En los baños hay jabón gratis. La crema de afeitar tiene productos naturales ¡y huele muy bien! Para relajarse y descansar, el hotel tiene un *spa* con servicios de primera clase.

29 La rutina de Janet

Para llegar a tiempo a la excursión, Janet tiene que levantarse antes de las ocho. Después tiene que ducharse y cepillarse los dientes. Luego tiene que ponerse desodorante, vestirse, peinarse y, finalmente, maquillarse. Es una rutina simple, pero con Janet nunca sabes si es posible. Ella es una chica muy especial.

34 Un día para descansar

–¿Qué haces, Janet?

–Me visto con ropa cómoda para ir al *spa*.

–¿Y qué haces en el *spa*?

–Me lavo la cara con agua mineral y me ducho con un gel hidratante.

–Pues yo me lavo las manos con un jabón de frutas y me afeito con una crema de maracuyá.

–¿Y no te duchas en el *spa*?

–No, yo me baño en el *jacuzzi*.

–¡Me gusta mucho el *spa* del hotel!

39 Para descansar en Granada

Para descansar en Granada tienen que visitar el Hotel Spa Lanjarón. El hotel ofrece baños de aguas termales. El agua especial de Lanjarón es relajante y buena para la salud. También tenemos un gimnasio, abierto durante todo el día. Los productos de higiene personal son naturales y de muy buena calidad. Las habitaciones son grandes y cómodas. Y la comida del restaurante de nuestro hotel es muy sana y deliciosa. ¡Les esperamos pronto en el Hotel Spa Lanjarón!

49 Los dolores de mi amiga

–Hola, Carolina. ¿Qué te pasa?

–¡Ay, doctora, me duele todo!

–A ver, ¿qué te duele?

–La cabeza.

–¿Tienes tos?

–No, no tengo tos, pero tengo fiebre.

–¿Te duele el estómago?

–No.

–¿Y la espalda?

–Sí, me duele la espalda y todo el cuerpo.

–Tienes que descansar este fin de semana, Carolina. No debes salir de casa. Y vuelve a verme el lunes.

–De acuerdo. Gracias, doctora.

55 Una visita al hospital

Me siento muy mal. Me duele mucho la cabeza. Y después de caminar todo el día, me duelen mucho los pies y las piernas. Me siento cansada y débil. ¿Qué puedo hacer?

61 **En la consulta de la doctora**

–Doctora Galdón, mi tía Rita y yo nos sentimos mal.

–¡Vaya, Diana! ¿Qué te pasa?

–Me duele mucho la cabeza.

–¿Y a ti, Rita?

–Yo tengo fiebre.

–¿Y te duele algo?

–Sí, el estómago.

–Doctora, ¿estamos muy enfermas? ¿Qué tenemos?

–Tienen un resfriado y están un poco débiles. Tienen que descansar, beber agua y jugos naturales, y comer bien para estar fuertes.

64 **¿Cómo te encuentras?**

1. Me duele mucho el estómago.
2. Me duele la cabeza y tengo fiebre.
3. Me siento muy bien.
4. Me siento mal. Estoy muy cansada.
5. Me duele la garganta.

70 **Una vida sana**

Escucha, Tim. Es muy importante estar sano. Debes comer bien y seguir una dieta sana. También debes acostarte temprano porque es importante descansar: es necesario dormir ocho horas al día. Y tienes que hacer deporte y gimnasia. ¡Mírame a mí! ¡Yo soy mayor, pero estoy en muy buena forma!

73 **Un gimnasio nuevo**

¿Quieres hacer deporte y mantenerte en forma? ¡Este es tu gimnasio! Tenemos muchas actividades. ¿Te gusta comer bien y beber jugos naturales? ¡Visita nuestra cafetería! Nuestros alimentos son muy sanos y naturales. ¿Te gusta caminar o correr? Ven a visitarnos: tenemos espacios especialmente diseñados para hacer ejercicio. No esperes a mañana y visítanos hoy mismo. ¡Te esperamos! Pero recuerda: no está permitido traer mascotas al gimnasio.

78 **Buenos consejos**

–¿Qué hago para mantenerme en forma, Tim?

–Puedes correr, es muy sano.

–Pero es muy aburrido…

–Entonces camina.

–No me gusta caminar…

–Pues… pasea a tu perro todos los días. Hay un parque muy bonito cerca de tu casa.

–No, no me gusta ese parque. Y tengo alergia a las flores. ¿Qué más puedo hacer?

–Debes comer bien y tomar alimentos saludables: frutas, verduras…

–No me gustan las verduras.

–¡Uf, qué difícil eres, Diana!

81 **Los remedios de la abuela**

–Tim, querido, ¿hay algún problema?

–Nada serio, abuela. Es que tengo un resfriado.

–Toma frutas y jugos naturales.

–También me duele un poco el estómago y me siento un poco débil.

–Toma una sopa de pollo. Es muy buena para el estómago.

–¿Y qué puedo tomar para la garganta?

–Toma té con miel y limón. El té con miel y limón es muy bueno para el dolor de garganta.

–Ah, y al abuelo le duelen los pies.

–Eso no es nada. Debe darse un masaje con crema o con un poco de aceite.

–¡Gracias, abuela! ¡Eres un sol!

85 **Esmeralda está enferma**

–¡Ay, Rodrigo! ¡Ayúdame! Me siento débil.

–¡Mi amor, mi vida, mi corazón! Descansa.

–Me duele la cabeza.

–Toma este medicamento. ¡Te vas a sentir mucho mejor!

–Me duele todo: la espalda, los brazos, las piernas… ¡Ay, Rodrigo!

–Voy a llamar al doctor Martínez.

–Las manos y los pies… ¡no los siento! ¿Qué hago, Rodrigo?

–Vamos al hospital, cariño. Necesitas ayuda.

–No, Rodrigo. Quédate a mi lado. Te necesito.

España

The Unit

- The theme for Unit 5 is the human body. The participants of the challenge will learn about body parts, hygiene, healthcare, and basic remedies.

- In Madrid, the four pairs will try to complete different tasks assigned to them by their host, Dr. Galdón.

  – *Desafío 1*. Tess and Patricia are at the Granada-Sierra Nevada stage of the *Vuelta Ciclista a España*. Their task is to get an autographed T-shirt from the race leader.

  – *Desafío 2*. Andy and Janet are in the Alhambra in Granada. Their challenge will be to locate a specific tile among the hundreds that decorate this palace.

  – *Desafío 3*. Diana and Rita are at the *Hostal de los Reyes Católicos* in Santiago de Compostela, in search of the royal family's coat of arms.

  – *Desafío 4*. Tim and Mack are in Silos, at the famous *monasterio de Silos*, in search of a remedy for a stomachache.

Activities	Standards	Resources
España	1.2, 2.2, 4.1	Video

Teaching Suggestions

Warm-Up / Independent Starter

- Ask students to look at the four locations in Spain. There is a lot of history behind these places. Are there similar places in the United States? Ask students to name four similar places in the United States, tell their location, and a historical fact about each. For example, the Alamo in San Antonio, Texas, was the location of important battles during the Texas Revolution.

Spain

- Spain is a country in the European Union located on the west coast of Europe. The capital of Spain is Madrid. Different populations have contributed to Spain's diversity. Iberians, Celts, Phoenicians, Romans, Visigoths, and Arabs have been some of the peoples who have settled Spain throught its history.

Unidad 5

España

Al otro lado del Atlántico

DESAFÍO 1

DESAFÍO 2

▶ **To talk about the body and the senses**

Vocabulario
Partes del cuerpo

Gramática
Los verbos *ver, oír, oler y decir*

La Vuelta Ciclista a España

La Alhambra

▶ **To express daily routine**

Vocabulario
La higiene personal

Gramática
Los verbos reflexivos

The Challenge

DESAFÍO 1

La Vuelta Ciclista a España

As an annual competition, the Tour of Spain began in 1955. Each year in September, about 150 cyclists spend three weeks trekking over 2000 miles across Spain. The course is divided into 21 stages and the leader of each stage wears a gold jersey to identify him as the leader, although in 2010 the leader's jersey was red.

DESAFÍO 2

La Alhambra

The Alhambra was originally a Muslim fortress and palace complex. It sits on a plateau overlooking the city of Granada, in southern Spain. The palace was built between 1238 and 1358 on the site of a 9th century citadel. The Arabic word *alhambra* means "the red," which probably refers to the color of the bricks with which the walls of the Alhambra were built. Today, the Alhambra is one of Spain's most-visited tourist attractions.

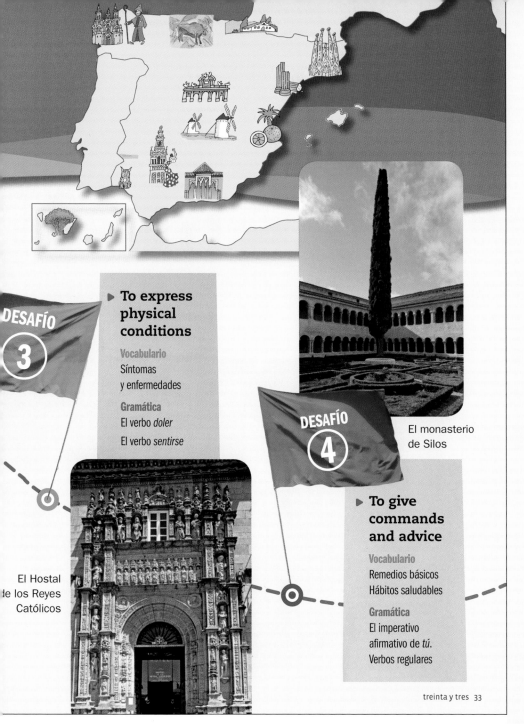

■ Have students read each objective under the photos, then discuss how each place relates to the objective.

■ Focus students' attention on the map of Spain. Ask students how Spain's location played a role in its exploration of the Americas.

Picture Discussion

■ Use the photos to have students share any information they have on the four topics.

La Vuelta Ciclista a España

■ Ask students to name all of the cycling competitions they have heard of. For example, the *Tour de France*, *Giro d'Italia*, or any local tours in your area. Also ask how long they think these tours last. Then, ask students if they think they would ever participate in a tour.

La Alhambra

■ Let students know that there were no cement or brick factories in those times to mass-produce the materials we use today for building our homes. Ask students how long do they think it took to build this extremely detailed fortress.

El Hostal de los Reyes Católicos

■ Ask students if they know what the differences are between hostel, hotel, and motel. Ask them to discuss the benefits and disadvantages of each. Break students into groups and ask each group to make a case for the best place to stay during their travels.

El monasterio de Silos

■ Ask students if they know where they can find monks and nuns here, in the United States. Do they dress and perform the same rituals as those in the Silos Monastery? Is it common for monks to record a CD?

Objectives

■ By the end of Unit 5, students will be able to
  – Talk about body parts and their basic functions.
  – Describe their daily hygiene routines in the present tense.
  – Express personal habits using reflexive verbs.
  – Talk about physical and emotional states.
  – Talk and give advice about basic remedies and healthy habits.

▷ DESAFÍO 3

El Hostal de los Reyes Católicos

This beautiful building was founded at the end of the 15th century by the Catholic Monarchs, Fernando and Isabel. It originally began as a pilgrim hospital, it was then converted into a hostel and it is now regarded as one of the oldest and most luxurious hotels in the world. The *Hostal de los Reyes Católicos* is located in Obradoiro Square, a central point for the pilgrims of the *Camino de Santiago* (Saint James' Way). Its location is ideal for walking around Santiago de Compostela as it is a short distance from the main tourist attractions.

▷ DESAFÍO 4

El monasterio de Silos

The Silos Monastery is famous for its meticulous landscaping, wall carvings, and very old religious sculptures that line the walls of the complex. Above all, the monastery is internationally famous for the Gregorian chanting of its Benedictine monks. These monks live, work, and worship here daily, and around sundown, they chant.

La llegada

Presentation

- In this section, the participants have arrived in Madrid, the capital of Spain. They will receive clues about how to find their hostess, Dr. Galdón, at a hospital. The context of health and hygiene will help students learn about Spain's traditions.

- Students will be introduced to:
  - Present tense of irregular verbs.
  - Reflexive verbs.
  - The verb *doler*.
  - Regular affirmative *tú* commands.

Activities	Standards	Resources
Fotonovela	1.2	Vis. Pres.
1.	1.2, 1.3	

Teaching Suggestions

Warm-Up / Independent Starter

- Ask students to study the dialogue in silence for a moment and then answer the following questions:
  - What does Dr. Galdón do to entertain her patients?
  - What word describes Dr. Galdón's personality?
  - Who do you think finds Dr. Galdón first?

Preparation

- Read the speech bubbles to the students using a different voice for each character. Ask students to raise their hands as they hear and see words they recognize, such as cognates and vocabulary from previous lessons. After reading all the captions, review the words students recognized.

La fotonovela

Before Viewing

- Ask students to describe what they see in the photo of the hospital. Are they familiar with hospitals and the people who work there? Have they been to a hospital? Invite them to share their experiences.

After Viewing

- Have volunteers re-enact the dialogue. Have them stand in front of the class and act it out.

En Madrid

The four pairs meet in Madrid. They visit a hospital to find Dr. Galdón, their Spanish host. Dr. Galdón will assign a task to each pair. But they are in for a surprise!

> Tienen que pensar con la cabeza...

> La doctora se maquilla para entretener a sus pacientes.

> Los pacientes de la doctora son niños.

> La doctora es muy graciosa.

Differentiated Instruction

DEVELOPING LEARNERS

- In pairs, have students reread the dialogue and answer the following comprehension questions using complete sentences to thoroughly analyze the *fotonovela*.
  - *¿Cuántas personas hay en la fotonovela?*
  - *¿Qué llevan?* Be sure to mention the material, color, and fit.
  - *¿Qué hay detrás de las personas?*

EXPANDING LEARNERS

- Have students use the *fotonovela* to create a brainstorm web with the word *hospital* as its center. Have students look at the photos and supply all the words that relate to a hospital. Have them use a bilingual dictionary to look up the words. Select five cognates from their answers and write them on the board. Give students the opportunity to realize how easy it is to increase thematic vocabulary by using cognates.

Perdón, señora. ¿Es usted la doctora Galdón?

No. Yo trabajo en el hospital, pero no soy la doctora Galdón. Soy enfermera. ¿Te sientes mal?

Yo soy médica, pero no soy la doctora Galdón. ¡Lo siento!

Sí. Yo soy la doctora Galdón. Espera un minuto... ¿Te duele la cabeza, mi amor?

Activities

1. Have students review their sentences with a partner. Then have each one write one more question that has two possible answers and exchange it with their partner.

Answer Key

1. 1. b   2. a   3. b   4. b   5. b
  1. Las parejas están en un hospital.
  2. La doctora Galdón trabaja en un hospital.
  3. La doctora Galdón es muy graciosa.
  4. La doctora se maquilla.
  5. A la niña le duele la cabeza.

Additional Resources

Fans Online activities

Practice Workbook

---

1 **¿Comprendes?**

▶ **Escoge y escribe.** Choose the correct answer for the questions, then write a complete sentence for each.

1. ¿Dónde están las parejas?   a. En un parque.   b. En un hospital.
2. ¿Dónde trabaja la doctora Galdón?   a. En un hospital.   b. En una escuela.
3. ¿Cómo es la doctora Galdón?   a. Es muy tímida.   b. Es muy graciosa.
4. ¿Qué hace la doctora?   a. Se afeita.   b. Se maquilla.
5. ¿A quién le duele la cabeza?   a. A Diana.   b. A la niña.

Modelo 1. *Las parejas están en un hospital.*

HERITAGE LANGUAGE LEARNERS

• Have students research and write down synonyms for *hospital* or names of other medical facilities; for example, *dispensario médico, clínica, consultorio, sanatorio.* Have them explain the similarities and differences between these facilities and a hospital.

COOPERATIVE LEARNING

• Have students break into groups of four. One person in each group will look at one of the four scenes in the *fotonovela.* Their job will be to explain the scene to the group. Make sure that each group has an equal division of skill levels. As the student explains the scene, if what he or she says is correct, the rest of the group will nod in agreement. If it is incorrect, then the rest of the group will shake their heads. If the student does not get it right on the third try, someone else in the group should explain what is going on in the scene.

Unit 5
La llegada

Presentation

- In this section, students will learn useful expressions for asking about how someone feels and for saying how they feel.

Activities	Standards	Resources
Expresiones útiles	1.2, 4.1	
2.	1.2, 1.3	Audio
3.	1.2, 1.3	
4.	1.1, 1.2	
5.	1.1, 1.2, 1.3	

Teaching Suggestions

Warm-Up / Independent Starter

- Ask students to count back five calendar days and write down how they felt each day. Have them use a five-column chart.

Preparation

- Review the *Expresiones útiles* in the box. You may want to invite volunteers to the front of the class and have them perform short dialogues. Have them point to *cabeza* and *estómago* and to role-play various gestures for *Me siento bien* and *Me siento mal* as they talk.

- Make students aware that they should ask questions and use the expression *Cuídate* with people they address in the *tú* form. You may want to share the formal and plural equivalents: *¿Qué le pasa?, ¿Qué les pasa?, ¿Cómo se siente?, ¿Cómo se sienten?, Cuídese, Cuídense.*

Activities

2. Before playing the audio, ask students to work in pairs to review the *Expresiones útiles*. If time allows, have partners role-play a conversation between a doctor and a patient in which they use some of the expressions on the list. Then ask them to switch roles.

3. After students have completed this activity, ask volunteers to act out each scenario. The rest of the class should say the right expression for each representation out loud.

36

EXPRESIONES ÚTILES

To ask how someone feels:
> ¿Cómo estás?
> ¿Qué te pasa?
> ¿Cómo te sientes?
> ¿Te sientes bien/mal?

To say how you feel:
> Me siento bien/mal.
> Estoy enfermo(a).

To wish someone to feel better:
> Que te mejores.
> Cuídate.

To say where something hurts:
> **Me duele** la cabeza.
> **Me duelen** los pies.

¡Me duele la cabeza!

2 ¿Cómo se sienten?

▶ **Escucha y une.** Listen to the dialogue between Dr. Galdón and her patients. Match the people (column A) with how they feel (column B).

(A)	(B)
1. A María	a. se siente bien.
2. A Javier	b. le duele la cabeza.
3. Pedro	c. está enferma.
4. Rosalía	d. le duelen los pies.

3 ¿Qué dicen?

▶ **Elige.** Choose the right expression for each picture.

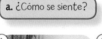

| a. ¿Cómo se siente? | b. Cuídate. | c. Me duelen los pies. | d. Me duele la cabeza. |

①  ②   ③   ④

36 treinta y seis

Differentiated Instruction

DEVELOPING LEARNERS

- Ask students to find and collect pictures that represent each of the *Expresiones útiles* in magazines. After they have collected all the pictures, have students organize them into mini-books to keep with them and use whenever relevant.

EXPANDING LEARNERS

- Have students look at activity 3 as a model for drawing three new pictures that represent three different *Expresiones útiles*. Once done, students will exchange their papers and write captions for the new pictures.

¿Quién ganará?

4 **Los desafíos**

▶ **Habla.** What will be the challenge for each pair? Think about this question and discuss it with your classmates.

DESAFÍO ①

Una vuelta
ciclista

Tess y Patricia

DESAFÍO ②

El azulejo perdido

Andy y Janet

DESAFÍO ③

El escudo
de los reyes

Rita y Diana

DESAFÍO ④

Una receta
antigua

Mack y Tim

5 **Las votaciones**

▶ **Decide.** You decide.
You will vote to choose
the most exciting challenge.
Who do you think will win?

Emocionante

HERITAGE LANGUAGE LEARNERS

- There are many other expressions for describing how someone feels or to express that something hurts. Have students brainstorm a list of appropriate terms and organize them on a two-column chart: one column with the *Expresiones útiles* from the book and the second column with the list created by the group. Have them share their expressions with the class and ask them to look at which list is longer and tell how many different countries these words come from.

MULTIPLE INTELLIGENCES:
Verbal-Linguistic Intelligence

- Write the expressions *Me siento bien* and *Me siento mal* on the board. Erase the words *bien* and *mal*. Have students complete the phrases with other Spanish words they know.

¿Quién ganará?

4. Encourage students to share their ideas and elicit answers if they are not sure about the different *Desafíos*.

   Remind students about the four challenges:

   1. Tess and Patricia need to get an autographed T-shirt from the leader of the *Vuelta Ciclista a España*.
   2. Andy and Janet are at the Alhambra, in Granada. There they need to find a specific tile among the hundreds that decorate this palace.
   3. Diana and Rita are in Santiago de Compostela and their task is to find the coat of arms of the royal family.
   4. Tim and Mack are in Silos and they have to find the pharmacy of the old Silos Monastery and get a remedy for a stomachache.

5. In this unit, students will vote to choose the most exciting challenge. Let the students discuss their different opinions and then help them to reach an agreement. You may also divide students into groups of four. Each person will represent one of the participants. The "participant" who has the most compelling argument in each group will go to the front of the class. Then the "participants" who have the most representation in front of the class are the ones who will win the pre-vote.

AUDIO SCRIPT
See page 31K

Answer Key

2. 1. b   2. d   3. a   4. c
3. a. 3   b. 1   c. 4   d. 2
4. Answers will vary.
5. Answers will vary.

Additional Resources

Fans Online activities
Practice Workbook

DESAFÍO 1

Hablar del cuerpo y de los sentidos

Presentation

- In *Desafío 1,* Tess and Patricia need to get an autographed T-shirt from the leader of the *Vuelta Ciclista a España.* Their search will take them to the Granada-Sierra Nevada stage of the race.

- Students will learn vocabulary for the body and senses, and irregular verbs in the present tense.

Activities	Standards	Resources
Fotonovela	1.2	Vis. Pres.
6.	1.1, 1.2, 1.3	
7.	1.2, 1.3	
8.	1.1	
9. Cultura	1.1, 1.2, 2.1, 3.1	
Tu desafío	1.2, 3.2, 5.1, 5.2	

Teaching Suggestions

Warm-Up / Independent Starter

- Write the following sentences on the board. Students will review the present tense conjugation of *o > ue* verbs using the verb *poder.*
  1. *Yo ... aprender mucho de España en esta unidad.*
  2. *Tú ... comparar tus respuestas con las mías.*
  3. *El profesor ... poner una prueba sorpresa.*

Preparation

- Have students read the task and then model the pronunciation of *Una vuelta ciclista.* Activate prior knowledge by asking them to describe what they know about similar competitions. How is this event similar or different from ones they have seen on TV or in their hometowns?

 La fotonovela

Before Viewing

- Read through the speech bubbles and introduce the vocabulary, pointing out cognates such as *comentarista, líder,* and *accidente.*

After Viewing

- Have students draft one yes / no question based on each photo of the *fotonovela.* Guide students with an example like *¿Puede Patricia ver la ...?*

Una vuelta ciclista

 Tess and Patricia are at the Asturias stage of the *Vuelta Ciclista a España* (Bicycle Tour of Spain). Their task is to get an autographed T-shirt from the leader of the race. First, they have to figure out who he is!

> ¿Quién gana la etapa, Tess? No puedo ver nada.

> Yo tampoco veo nada y no oigo al comentarista.

> Mira, el líder tiene problemas. Le duele la pierna izquierda.

> ¡Cuidado! ¡Un accidente!

> Un golpe fuerte en la cabeza. ¿Puede ver? ¿Me oye?

> Me duele la cabeza. ¡Qué dolor!

Continuará...

---

6 **Detective de palabras**

▶ **Completa.** Use words from the *fotonovela* to complete these sentences.

1. ¿Quién _____ la etapa, Tess?
2. Yo tampoco _____ nada.
3. Le _____ la pierna izquierda.
4. ¿Puede ver? ¿Me _____?
5. Me _____ la cabeza.

 ▶ **Habla y representa.** With a partner, decide who said each line and act out the dialogue.

Differentiated Instruction

DEVELOPING LEARNERS

- Have students work in pairs to read the speech bubbles from the *fotonovela* aloud. Encourage them to use gestures and vocal intonation, emphasizing the questions and exclamations. Then ask them to create a simple timeline with the main action from the *fotonovela.*

EXPANDING LEARNERS

- Ask students to imagine they have to write a cover story about a cycling race for their school newspaper. Have one student conduct an interview of five questions with a "cyclist," asking about his or her training, preparation, equipment, etc. Make sure students record their answers in order to write their article.

¿Comprendes?

▶ **Escribe.** Answer the questions in complete sentences.

1. ¿Qué problema tiene Patricia?
2. ¿Qué problema tiene Tess?
3. ¿Qué problema tiene el líder?
4. ¿Qué le duele al ciclista del accidente?

 ¿Qué ves?

▶ **Habla.** Patricia took these photos in Spain. Take turns describing the people, their physical characteristics, and their clothes.

Modelo A. *¿Qué ves?*
B. *Veo a un ciclista. Lleva una camiseta amarilla
y unos zapatos amarilllos.*

 **CULTURA**

La Vuelta Ciclista a España

La Vuelta Ciclista a España es una carrera por etapas (*stages*). Durante tres semanas, ciclistas internacionales participan en una carrera por las ciudades, los campos y las montañas de España. El líder lleva un jersey amarillo.

La Vuelta Ciclista a España es una competición tan importante como el *Tour de France* y el *Giro d'Italia.*

9 **Piensa.** Why do you think the leader wears a yellow jersey?

🚩→ **TU DESAFÍO** Visit the website to learn more about the *Vuelta Ciclista a España.*

treinta y nueve 39

Hablar del cuerpo y de los sentidos

Activities

7. Ask students to read the comprehension questions Before Viewing the visual presentation. After students answer the questions, ask volunteers to use them as a script to perform in front of the class.

8. To expand this activity, have students cut out action pictures from a magazine and repeat the process. Ask students to include a description of the person as well as his or her clothes.

 CULTURA

La Vuelta Ciclista a España

This international cycling race started in 1935. Though there were years in which it had to be canceled due to political unrest in the country, the *Vuelta* has been an annual competition since 1955. The route changes annually. The color of the leader's jersey has also changed throughout the years, but it has been golden since 1999. However, the novelty in the 2010 *Vuelta* was that the leader wore a red jersey to mark the 75th anniversary of the event.

Answer Key

6. 1. gana 4. oye
2. veo 5. duele
3. duele
▶ Answers will vary.

7. 1. Patricia no puede ver.
2. No puede ver y no puede oír al comentarista.
3. Le duele la pierna izquierda.
4. Le duele la cabeza.

8. Answers will vary.

9. Answers will vary.

Additional Resources

Fans Online activities

HERITAGE LANGUAGE LEARNERS

• Ask students to imagine they are at this race with Tess and Patricia. Have students write speech bubbles that go along with Tess and Patricia's dialogue. Then, in groups of three, have students act out their new / expanded dialogues.

CRITICAL THINKING

• In this lesson, students learn about the *Vuelta Ciclista a España.* Allow students to discuss why this event is not as popular in the United States as the *Tour de France.* Divide the class into groups and have them list their reasons in order of relevance. Then, have them suggest how they could help popularize this event.

DESAFÍO 1

Vocabulario – Partes del cuerpo

Presentation

- The vocabulary box presents words related to parts of the body and the senses.

Activities	Standards	Resources
Vocabulario	1.2	
10.	1.2, 1.3	
11.	1.1	
12.	1.2, 1.3	Audio
13.	1.3, 5.1	
14. Cultura	1.1, 1.2, 3.1, 3.2	
Tu desafío	1.2, 3.1, 5.2	

Teaching Suggestions

Warm-Up / Independent Starter

- Write this activity on the board. Students will review clothes vocabulary.

  Match each clothing item with the body part it corresponds to.

  1. *guantes*   a. *cabeza*
  2. *pantalones*   b. *ojos*
  3. *sombrero*   c. *manos*
  4. *zapatos*   d. *piernas*
  5. *gafas*   e. *pies*

Preparation

- Model the pronunciation of the words in the vocabulary presentation and have students repeat the words out loud. You may want to bring a variety of clothes or objects that relate to each specific vocabulary item to the class. Hold up each item as you ask volunteers to relate it to the new vocabulary.

Activities

11. This is a good opportunity to review singular and plural. Write down *los dedos* on the board and ask students which would be the singular form. You may repeat the activity with each response.

12. You may want to expand this activity by asking students to come up with five sentences related to different body parts and their functions. For example: *Para caminar usamos las piernas.*

40

DESAFÍO 1

Vocabulario

Partes del cuerpo

Acciones

ver   oír   oler   saborear   tocar

10 **Acciones habituales**

▶ **Completa.** What do these people enjoy doing? Complete the captions with the appropiate infinitive.

oír

oler

saborear

ver

tocar

1 _____ una comida.   2 _____ un perfume.

3 _____ un cuadro.   4 _____ música.   5 _____ un instrumento.

Differentiated Instruction

DEVELOPING LEARNERS

- To reinforce the parts of the body vocabulary, ask students to create sticky notes. Have them read a word and paste it onto the appropriate body part. Continue the process with each vocabulary word. Then, have them remove the sticky notes as you randomly call out the vocabulary words.

EXPANDING LEARNERS

- Review the adjectives that describe physical characteristics. Ask students to come up with a body part that can be described by any of those adjectives. Challenge them, individually, to volunteer to use the adjectives in a sentence to describe a classmate's body part: *Los dedos de John son delgados y largos, El pelo de Ashley es rubio y corto.*

11 Características físicas

 ▶ **Habla.** With a partner, describe this character. Use the words in the boxes.

Modelo *Tiene las orejas grandes.*

piernas	pies
brazos	nariz
cabeza	ojos
manos	orejas

largo	corto
grande	pequeño
alto	bajo
gordo	delgado

12 ¿Fátima, Armando o la doctora Galdón?

 ▶ **Escucha y escribe.** Patricia meets three special people in Spain. Listen and write the name of the person who has each of these physical traits.

Fátima   Armando

La doctora Galdón

1. ojos azules
2. nariz grande
3. pelo negro
4. piernas largas

5. cara bonita
6. cuerpo delgado
7. pelo rubio
8. cuello largo

13 Autorretrato

▶ **Escribe.** Write a paragraph describing at least three of your physical characteristics and the things you like to see, hear, smell, and touch.

Modelo *Soy alta, morena y tengo los ojos negros. Me gusta oír música pop.*

CULTURA

El Angliru

El Angliru es un puerto de montaña muy alto. Está en el norte de España, en Asturias. La Vuelta Ciclista a España pasa a veces por El Angliru. El Angliru es una de las etapas más difíciles de la carrera, pero también es una zona natural muy bonita.

14 Piensa. What body parts would need to be very strong in order to bicycle up a mountain like *El Angliru*?

▶ **TU DESAFÍO** Visit the website to learn more about the Asturias region.

---

13. You may expand this activity to include the concept of comparisons by asking volunteers to compare themselves with a classmate. This could be a group activity. Have students put their paragraphs in a container and pick them out one by one. One member picks out one and reads it to the group. Have them guess the writer.

 AUDIO SCRIPT
See page 31K

CULTURA

Alto de El Angliru

This mountain is also known as *La Gamonal*. Its highest point reaches 1,573 m (5,160 ft.) above sea level. The *Vuelta Ciclista a España* targets three levels of increasing difficulty while traversing the *Angliru*. The steepest part of the ascent has an inclination of 23.6%, maintained for 3 km (1.9 miles). This mountain has elevated the prestige of the entire race and, although a bit controversial for the amount of accidents, cyclists know what to expect.

Answer Key

10.
1. saborear
2. oler
3. ver
4. oír
5. tocar

11. Answers will vary.

12. Fátima: 1, 3
Armando: 2, 6, 7
La doctora Galdón: 4, 5, 8

13. Answers will vary. Sample answer: Tengo los ojos azules, el pelo negro y me gusta ver la televisión.

14. Answers will vary.

Additional Resources

Fans Online activities
Practice Workbook

41

HERITAGE LANGUAGE LEARNERS

- Ask volunteers to model and expand vocabulary in front of the class and talk about the joints and other components that link parts of the body. For example: *la muñeca* (wrist) *une el brazo con la mano, el tobillo* (ankle) *une la pierna con el pie, el cuello une la cabeza con el torso, el hombro* (shoulder) *une el torso con el brazo.* Then ask other students questions based on the information shared: *¿Qué une la pierna con el pie?* Model the answer and have students repeat it.

MULTIPLE INTELLIGENCES:
Musical-Rhythmic Intelligence

- Have groups of students create a call and response chant using the new vocabulary. Have them perform it for the class. Students call out a word they know and their partners say the new vocabulary word that starts with the same syllable, for example, *Perú* would trigger *pelo*.

DESAFÍO 1

Gramática – Los verbos *ver*, *oír*, *oler* y *decir*

Presentation

- This grammar presentation uses verbs related to the senses to introduce present tense irregular conjugations.

Activities	Standards	Resources
Gramática	1.2, 3.1, 4.1	
15.	1.2, 4.1	
16.	1.1, 1.2, 3.1	
17.	1.2, 1.3	Audio
18.	1.2, 1.3	
19.	1.1, 1.3	
20. Cultura	1.1, 1.2, 2.2, 3.1, 3.2	
Tu desafío	1.2, 3.1, 5.1, 5.2	

Teaching Suggestions

Warm-Up / Independent Starter

- Use the new verb *saborear* to remind students of regular conjugation patterns. Have them write the correct forms for each of the following subjects: *yo, tú, María, Sergio, los niños, nosotras, ustedes*.

Preparation

- Go over the grammar presentation with the class. Have students create four tables like the ones in their book. Then have them fill up as many cells as possible. Go over their answers and ask them why the usual memorization patterns do not apply with these verbs.

Activities

15. Elicit from students that *tocar* is a regular verb. Use *tocar* to reinforce regular conjugation patterns. Use *beber* and *vivir*, which also relate thematically.

16. Use this activity to reintroduce direct object pronouns. Ask students what does the word *la* in the answer refer to. What is the benefit of using direct object pronouns when we speak?

18. Make sure students read the whole paragraph before completing it. To boost their confidence, remind them to identify cognates.

Gramática

Los verbos *ver*, *oír*, *oler* y *decir*

- The verbs ver *(to see)*, oír *(to hear)*, oler *(to smell)*, and decir *(to say, to tell)* express actions that our senses perform. All four verbs are irregular.

VERBO VER (TO SEE). PRESENTE

Singular		Plural	
yo	veo	nosotros nosotras	vemos
tú	ves	vosotros vosotras	veis
usted él ella	ve	ustedes ellos ellas	ven

VERBO OÍR (TO HEAR). PRESENTE

Singular		Plural	
yo	oigo	nosotros nosotras	oímos
tú	oyes	vosotros vosotras	oís
usted él ella	oye	ustedes ellos ellas	oyen

VERBO OLER (TO SMELL). PRESENTE

Singular		Plural	
yo	huelo	nosotros nosotras	olemos
tú	hueles	vosotros vosotras	oléis
usted él ella	huele	ustedes ellos ellas	huelen

VERBO DECIR (TO SAY, TO TELL). PRESENTE

Singular		Plural	
yo	digo	nosotros nosotras	decimos
tú	dices	vosotros vosotras	decís
usted él ella	dice	ustedes ellos ellas	dicen

Note:
1. In Spanish, the letter h is always silent. Do not pronounce it in the irregular forms of oler.
2. Spanish words that start with the sound ue are spelled hue.

15 **Piensa.** Although the verbs tocar *(to touch)* and saborear *(to taste)* refer to the senses, they are not included here. Why do you think that is?

16 **¿Qué haces?**

 ▶ **Habla.** What do you do with these things? Ask your partner using direct object pronouns in your responses.

Modelo
A. *¿Qué haces con una flor?*
B. *La veo, la huelo, la toco.*

1. una televisión
2. una radio
3. una guitarra
4. un perfume
5. un trabalenguas *(tongue twister)*
6. un perro

Differentiated Instruction

DEVELOPING LEARNERS

- Write the verb *oler* on the board and ask volunteers to read its conjugations aloud. Stress that the letter *h* is silent in Spanish. Encourage students to list other initial *h* Spanish words. Or write *hombre, hola, hay, horario, historia, hotel, hablar,* and *hermano* on the board and have students read them aloud to practice pronunciation.

EXPANDING LEARNERS

- Students can write a paragraph describing a hard day. Ask them to use the verbs *ver, oír, oler, tocar,* and *decir* in more than one conjugation. Advise them to refer to the grammar presentation for accuracy.

17 ¿Qué hacen los participantes?

 ► **Escucha y contesta.** Tess and Patricia are talking about their experiences in Spain. Listen and answer the questions in complete sentences.

1. ¿Quién no puede oler ni oír bien? ¿Por qué?
2. ¿Por qué apaga la radio Patricia?
3. ¿Adónde va Patricia?
4. ¿Quién quiere ver un espectáculo de flamenco?

18 Un día difícil

► **Completa.** Tess is not having a great day. Fill in the blanks with the appropriate form of the verbs *oler, oír, ver,* and *decir.*

Un mal día

Estamos en un restaurante típico, pero no me siento bien. No ___1___ la carta porque tengo los ojos irritados, y no ___2___ al mesero porque la música está muy alta. Además, no ___3___ la comida porque tengo la nariz roja. Mamá me ___4___: «No estás enferma». Pero yo me siento mal.

19 Una encuesta

► **Escribe.** Write five questions using the sense verbs.

Modelo *¿Qué programas de televisión ves?*

 ► **Habla.** Use your questions to interview five classmates. Report your findings to the class.

Pablo Ruiz Picasso.
Retrato de Dora Maar.

CULTURA

¿Lo ves o no lo ves?

El cubismo es un estilo artístico de principios del siglo xx. Los artistas cubistas representan los objetos desde distintas perspectivas. El español Pablo Picasso es un famoso pintor cubista. Fíjate en el cuadro de la fotografía. ¿Qué ves en él?

 20 Dibuja y habla. Draw a picture of a partner using Picasso's cubist style. Compare your picture with your partner's. Talk about what you see in each drawing.

 → TU DESAFÍO Use the website to learn more about Pablo Picasso.

HERITAGE LANGUAGE LEARNERS

• Students can interview other heritage speakers. Have them exchange their questions with a partner and answer them in writing. Each pair should compare and contrast their answers in a Venn diagram using three categories: "What partner A likes," "What partner B likes," and "What we both like" as the intersection.

MULTIPLE INTELLIGENCES: Verbal-Linguistic Intelligence

• Have students act as directors of a partner's cubist drawing. They must tell their partner where to place body parts in their portrait by giving them clues. For example: *Veo con los brazos.* Encourage them to use all the new vocabulary.

Gramática – Los verbos *ver, oír, oler* y *decir*

19. You may modify this activity for small groups. After students have interviewed four classmates, they compare and tabulate their answers.

 AUDIO SCRIPT
See page 31K

 CULTURA

Pablo Picasso

This Spanish artist was one of the co-founders of cubism. The main characteristic of this avant-garde art movement of the early part of the 20th century is the abstract representation of reality seen from multiple viewpoints. Picasso's *Guernica*, a depiction of the bombing of a town by the same name, is probably one of the most famous paintings in the world. The *Guernica* is on permanent display at the *Museo Reina Sofía* in Madrid.

Answer Key

15. Students should be able to infer that *tocar* is a regular *-ar* verb; therefore, it does not directly relate to the grammar point.

16. Answers will vary.

17. 1. Tess. Porque tiene alergia.
2. Porque no le gusta la música moderna de los jóvenes.
3. Va al restaurante del hotel.
4. Mack y Tim quieren ver un espectáculo de flamenco.

18. 1. veo 2. oigo 3. huelo 4. dice

19. Answers will vary. Sample answer:
1. ¿Qué ves en un parque normalmente?
► Answers will vary.

20. Answers will vary.

Additional Resources

Fans Online activities
Practice Workbook

DESAFÍO 1

Comunicación

Presentation

- This section integrates all of the contents of the entire *Desafío* and provides additional practice using the four skills.

Activities	Standards	Resources
21.	1.2, 1.3	Audio
22.	1.1, 1.3, 3.1	
23.	1.1, 1.2, 1.3, 3.1	
24. Final del desafío	1.3	
Tu desafío	1.2, 5.1	

Teaching Suggestions

Warm-Up / Independent Starter

- Have students answer the following questions in writing.
  - *¿Te duele algo ahora?*
  - *¿Cuál es tu sentido favorito? ¿Por qué?*
  - *¿Qué características tiene un buen ciclista?*
  - *¿Qué partes del cuerpo asocias con cada sentido?*

Preparation

- Have students review the spread and read the *fotonovela*. Ask them: *¿Quién es Antonio López? ¿Por qué es importante? ¿Dónde está? ¿Por qué lo buscan Tess y Patricia?* Have students use the vocabulary and grammar from this *Desafío* to create one more scene to the *fotonovela*.

Activities

21. Modify the activity by having students act it out as a real situation.

22. Have students complete a mind map to brainstorm before writing their e-mails. Students should list at least three activities for each of the five senses. Once students have finished brainstorming, remind them that every e-mail should have a greeting, a body, and a closing.

23. Wrap this up by having students vote on which monster is the most original one. Which has the most extraordinary features? You may display the highest-ranked monsters on the bulletin board.

Comunicación

 21 **El ciclista Antonio López**

▶ **Lee y escribe.** In his blog, Antonio López wrote about his experiences during the *Vuelta Ciclista a España*. Read the text and list his problems.

> **La etapa de El Angliru**
>
> 22 de septiembre. Asturias
>
> Hoy es un día difícil. Desde mi cuarto veo El Angliru y, lo confieso, estoy nervioso. Tengo los ojos rojos, me duele el cuello, tengo las piernas y los pies cansados... Pero hoy es un día importante. ¡Quiero ganar esta etapa! Gracias a todos los fans por sus mensajes electrónicos. ¡Nos vemos en la carrera!

▶ **Escucha y escribe.** An organizer of the *Vuelta* is describing services available for cyclists. Listen and take notes about the services that Antonio López could use.

▶ **Escribe.** Using the blog entry and the listening activity above, write an e-mail to Antonio López. Suggest services that could help him.

22 **Personaliza tus sentidos**

▶ **Escribe.** Write an e-mail describing things you like to do with your five senses. Write a sentence for each one and explain your reasons.

Modelo

OÍR. Me gusta oír música en español porque aprendo vocabulario nuevo.

 ▶ **Habla.** Read your e-mail to several classmates. Fill in a chart like the one below to compare your likes.

Modelo

A tus compañeros	A ti
A César le gusta oír música en español.	A mí también me gusta. / A mí no me gusta.

Differentiated Instruction

DEVELOPING LEARNERS

- Have students look at the photo of Antonio López and brainstorm a list of body parts that may be hurting him. Write *Me duele(n)* on the board. Students should read the sentence and substitute the words on their lists, accordingly.

EXPANDING LEARNERS

- Ask students to talk about their health. Do they often feel sick? What part of the body hurts them most often? What do they usually do to resolve the issue? Have students write their answers and share them with the class.

23 Adivinanzas con sentido

▶ **Crea y escribe.** Create a monster by drawing or making a collage. Then write a paragraph to describe your monster's body and how it sees, hears, smells, tastes, touches, and walks. Notice that Spanish does not use possessive adjectives with body parts.

> **Mi monstruo**
>
> El monstruo tiene tres ojos. Tiene tres dedos en las manos...

▶ **Habla.** In a group, display your artwork along with that of your classmates. Then take turns describing your monsters. Who can be the first to guess which monster is being described?

Final del desafío

①  ②  ③

24 ¿Qué pasa en la historia?

▶ **Escribe.** Write a caption for each photograph using the five senses. Include details about what the participants hear from the crowd, see, smell, taste, and touch, and what the people are wearing.

Modelo   1. *Patricia y Tess buscan al ciclista con el jersey amarillo.*

 → TU DESAFÍO   Earn points for your own challenge! Listen to the questions for your *Minientrevista Desafío 1* on the website and write your answers.

cuarenta y cinco 45

 AUDIO SCRIPT
See page 31K

Answer Key

21. 1. Está nervioso.
2. Tiene los ojos rojos.
3. Le duele el cuello.
4. Tiene las piernas y los pies cansados.
   ▶ 1. Sesiones de relajación.
      2 y 3. Doctores y enfermeros.
      4. Salas de terapia muscular.
   ▶ Answers will vary.

22. Answers will vary. Sample answers:
OÍR. Me gusta oír libros en CD.
VER. Me gusta ver deportes en la tele.
TOCAR. Me gusta tocar el agua.
DECIR. Me gusta decir secretos a mis amigos.
OLER. Me gusta oler perfumes florales.
   ▶ Answers will vary.

23. Answers will vary. Sample answer:
Este monstruo no tiene ojos, pero ve con los dedos. Tiene tres narices y cuatro manos. No camina porque no tiene piernas.
   ▶ Answers will vary.

24. Answers will vary. Sample answers:
1. ¿Dónde está el campeón? ¿Lo ves?
2. A. ¿Puede firmar esta camiseta amarilla, por favor?
   B. Sí, claro.
3. ¡Y ahora, una foto!

Additional Resources

Fans Online activities
Practice Workbook

HERITAGE LANGUAGE LEARNERS

• Have students create a song or riddle using the vocabulary for body parts and five senses. They will share their work with other native speakers in the class and choose the best three creations to teach to the rest of the class.

MULTIPLE INTELLIGENCES:
Bodily-Kinesthetic Intelligence

• Ask students to come up with a cheer routine that involves the parts of the body and the verbs associated with the senses. They must perform their routine in front of the class while the other students write down the sequences of letters to form words. Guide them with the following example: *Dame una B. Dame una R. Dame una A. Dame una Z. Dame una O. ¿Qué dice? ¡Brazo!*

45

DESAFÍO 2

Expresar acciones habituales

Presentation

- In *Desafío 2*, Andy and Janet are at the Alhambra, in Granada, Spain. There they need to find a tile similar to the one in the photo they have.

- In this lesson, students will
  - Read and listen to information about personal hygiene using reflexive verbs.
  - Learn how to place direct object pronouns.

Activities	Standards	Resources
Fotonovela	1.2, 2.2, 3.1	Vis. Pres.
25.	1.2	
26.	1.2, 1.3	Audio
27.	1.3	
28. Cultura	1.1, 1.2, 3.2, 4.2	Video
Tu desafío	1.2, 3.2, 5.2	

Teaching Suggestions

Warm-Up / Independent Starter

- Have students read the dialogue below and ask them to notice the pronouns attached to the infinitive verbs. Then have them circle each subject pronoun and underline each attached pronoun.
  A. *Yo necesito afeitarme.*
  B. *¿Tú necesitas afeitarte? Yo necesito lavarme las manos.*

Preparation

- Have students read the speech bubbles with a partner and write lists of the cognates and the words they can't identify. Review their lists as a class.

 ### La fotonovela

Before Viewing

- Ask students why they think that finding a tile in the Alhambra would be a difficult task. Also, raise awareness about the Arab influence in Spain by asking them to look at the photos carefully, paying special attention to the architectural details.

After Viewing

- Ask students to compare modern hygiene habits with the hygiene available at the time of the Arab's presence in Spain.

46

El azulejo perdido

 Andy and Janet are at the Alhambra in Granada, Spain. Their task is to find an *azulejo* (tile) among the hundreds of tiles that decorate this fortress. Where will they find it?

Continuará…

25 **¿Comprendes?**

▶ **Completa.** Look at the *fotonovela* to choose the best option to complete the sentences.

1. Andy dice que necesita _____	a. afeitarse	b. bañarse
2. Andy quiere _____	a. lavarse las manos	b. lavarse los pies
3. Janet tiene en su mochila _____	a. jabón	b. champú
4. Janet tiene que encontrar _____	a. un baño	b. un azulejo

Differentiated Instruction

DEVELOPING LEARNERS

- Recycle nouns and adjectives using new vocabulary. Have students classify the words in the dialogue that would fit under a column labeled *Nombres*. With their lists as a springboard, have students use adjectives to create simple sentences like *El jabón es natural*.

EXPANDING LEARNERS

- Have students talk about the type of stores where one would typically buy such products. Then have them work in pairs to role-play a salesperson/customer situation.

35 Rutinas de la mañana

▶ **Habla.** What do the four pairs do each morning? Talk with a partner to compare their morning routines with yours.

Modelo 1. A. *Diana y yo nos levantamos a las siete de la mañana. ¿Y tú?*
B. *Yo me levanto a las siete y media.*

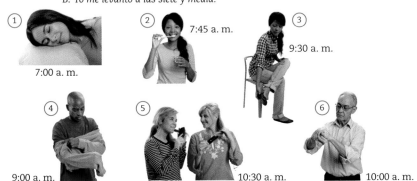

① 7:00 a. m.

② 7:45 a. m.

③ 9:30 a. m.

④ 9:00 a. m.

⑤ 10:30 a. m.

⑥ 10:00 a. m.

36 Horarios

▶ **Escribe y habla.** Find out about your partner's routine. Write at least four questions and interview him or her.

Modelo *¿A qué hora te lavas la cara?*

▶ **Presenta.** Now present your findings to the class in a timeline.

Modelo 6:00 a. m.   12:00 p. m.   6:00 p. m.   12:00 a. m.
                    se lava

Josefina se lava la cara a las ocho y cuarto.

CONEXIONES: SALUD

La adolescencia

La adolescencia es un período de cambios mentales y físicos. Durante la adolescencia es muy importante mantener una rutina sana. Acostarte y levantarte temprano, comer una dieta equilibrada *(balanced)* y mantener buenos hábitos de higiene puede ayudarte a sentirte bien.

37 Piensa. How do you feel when you skip breakfast or when you don't sleep enough? Can you concentrate at school?

cincuenta y uno 51

Gramática – Los verbos reflexivos

36. Have students work in groups to compare and contrast their sentences. How are they alike? How are they different? Have them illustrate their results using a Venn diagram. If time allows, play a game of "How well do you know me?" For example: *¿A qué hora me levanto?* Each correct response gets a point.

37. Before students read the *Conexiones* section, have them talk about how they feel this morning. Select different students to explain why they feel that way. Ask two or three students to read the paragraph aloud. Monitor their pronunciation. After the reading, have students express the main idea and supporting details.

AUDIO SCRIPT
See page 31K

Answer Key

33. *Lavarse* is a reflexive verb. This means that the subject of the sentence is the recipient of the action of the verb.

34. 1. Janet se viste con ropa cómoda.
2. Andy se baña en el *jacuzzi*.
3. Janet se lava la cara con agua mineral.
4. Janet se ducha con un gel hidratante.
5. Andy se afeita con una crema de maracuyá.
6. Andy se lava las manos con un jabón de frutas.
▶ Answers will vary.

35. Answers will vary. Sample answer:
Janet se cepilla los dientes a las ocho menos cuarto de la mañana. Yo me cepillo los dientes a las ocho.

36. Answers will vary.
▶ Answers will vary.

37. Answers will vary.

Additional Resources

Fans Online activities
Practice Workbook

HERITAGE LANGUAGE LEARNERS

• If you have students who have recently arrived in the United States, have them share the similarities and differences that they have noticed associated with their personal routine. For example: Did they wake up and get up at the same time in their country of origin? Did they shower in the morning or in the evening?

MULTIPLE INTELLIGENCES:
Bodily-Kinesthetic Intelligence

• Provide index cards with reflexive verbs for volunteer students to act out in front of the class. For example: *Se ducha a las siete de la mañana*, or *Nos vestimos antes de venir a la escuela.* You may divide the class into two teams and turn the activity into a game. Remind volunteers not to speak during their performance.

Unit 5

DESAFÍO 2

Comunicación

Presentation

- In this section, students will
  - Communicate simple ideas about personal hygiene.
  - Read and talk about morning schedules.

Activities	Standards	Resources
38.	1.1, 1.2	
39.	1.2, 1.3, 3.1	Audio
40.	1.1, 1.3, 5.1	
41.	1.3	
42. Final del desafío	1.2	

Teaching Suggestions

Warm-Up / Independent Starter

- Have students use reflexive verbs to express three things they do every morning.

Preparation

- Before you begin the activities, you may want to ask students to explain in their own words how the vocabulary and the grammar in *Desafío 2* relate to the context of personal hygiene. Elicit questions about reflexive verbs and pronoun placement.

Activities

38. Review how to tell time before doing this activity. Use the times provided on the chart to ask students ¿*Qué hora es?* Write each response on the board. Use a clock to quiz students about as many times as possible.

39. Students can use their e-mail as a script for a phone conversation. They should work in pairs and role-play a phone call between a possible guest and an employee at a resort.

40. Students can survey the class to find out which classmates have the most similar schedules among them. As they ask around, monitor them to assure that they are using Spanish to form their questions. Give them about a minute for each interaction and prompt them to speak to each other. Ask for volunteers to report their findings.

52

Comunicación

 38 **Una persona organizada**

 ▶ **Habla.** Read the schedule Janet has prepared for tomorrow morning. Tell your partner how this schedule compares with your own daily schedule.

Modelo *Janet se levanta a las siete menos cuarto, pero yo me levanto a las siete.*

6:45 a. m.	7:15 a. m.	7:30 a. m.	7:45 a. m.	7:50 a. m.	8:00 a. m.
Levantarme	Ducharme	Vestirme	Cepillarme los dientes	Peinarme	Maquillarme

39 **Para descansar en Granada**

▶ **Escucha y escribe.** Lanjarón is a spa resort in the Sierra Nevada. Listen to the spa's radio advertisement and list three special features you would like.

▶ **Escribe.** According to what you heard, write an e-mail to a nearby resort. Ask if they offer the same features.

Modelo

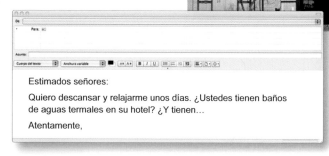

De:
Para:
Asunto:
Cuerpo del texto   Anchura variable

Estimados señores:

Quiero descansar y relajarme unos días. ¿Ustedes tienen baños de aguas termales en su hotel? ¿Y tienen…

Atentamente,

 40 **Así lo hago yo**

 ▶ **Escribe y habla.** Write your schedule, then compare it with a partner's. Report your findings to the class.

Modelo *Yo me levanto a las siete. Sandra se levanta a las siete y media. Las dos nos duchamos a las ocho.*

52 cincuenta y dos

Differentiated Instruction

DEVELOPING LEARNERS

- Ask students to compare their morning routines on a school day, on a weekend day, and on vacation. What do they have in common and how are they different? Include times and routine in the discussion.

EXPANDING LEARNERS

- Ask students to brainstorm other verbs in English that may be reflexive in Spanish. Have them think of their personal hygiene routine as a springboard for remembering. Some examples might include: to floss, to get a haircut, and to trim your nails (*utilizar el hilo dental, cortarse el pelo, cortarse las uñas*). Next, have the students use a bilingual dictionary to find translations for these verbs. Have them tell you which of the verbs are reflexive and which are not. Ask them how they know.

41 **Tu higiene diaria**

▶ **Escribe.** Write sentences describing when you use each item.

Modelo 1. *Uso el desodorante todos los días.*

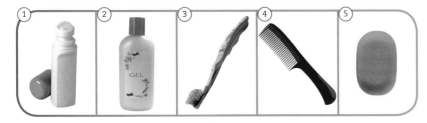

Final del desafío

Nuestro desafío en Granada

Lunes

Tenemos un plan: acostarnos a las nueve
de la noche para levantarnos a las seis de la mañana.
¡Es un buen plan! No nos duchamos por la mañana
porque nos duchamos por la noche. Por la mañana
nos lavamos las manos y la cara, nos ponemos
desodorante y nos cepillamos los dientes.
Después vamos a la Alhambra.

Martes

¿Y nuestro plan? Janet no está en el dormitorio.
Tampoco está en el autobús turístico. ¿Dónde está?
¡Está en el *spa* del hotel! ¿Y el azulejo? No lo
tenemos. ¡Adiós al desafío en España! Es la primera
prueba fallada. ¡Qué mal!

42 **¿Qué pasa en la historia?**

▶ **Lee y escribe.** Andy is not very happy with Janet at the end of this challenge.
Read his blog for the beginning and end of the *Desafío*, and find out why. Then write
Janet's blog entry for the same days.

HERITAGE LANGUAGE LEARNERS

• Have students talk about their favorite
hygiene products from their country of
origin. Students should explain why they like
these products. Ask them if they have found
substitute products here or which products
have they found here that they like.

MULTIPLE INTELLIGENCES:

Verbal-Linguistic Intelligence

• After students write Janet's blog entry, ask
several of them to recite it for the class while
pretending to be Janet. Guide the students
with their performance, telling them to think
about Janet's personality and how she might
feel, having not completed the task.

Unit 5
DESAFÍO 2
Comunicación

41. You may jumpstart this activity by showing
images of real product advertisements from a
Spanish newspaper or the Internet. As you show
each advertisement, have students explain what
the product is for.

42. Make sure students understand the reading
clearly before writing Janet's blog entry. If
necessary, have them discuss Janet's morning
from the opposite perspective. Students should
write a detailed sequence of events using
vocabulary from the *Desafío*, and reflexive verbs
and verb phrases. The blog must support Andy's
acknowledgement of a failed task.

 AUDIO SCRIPT
See page 31K

Answer Key

38. Answers will vary. Sample answers:
   1. Janet se levanta a las siete menos
      cuarto, pero yo me levanto a las seis.
   2. Ella se ducha a las siete y cuarto, pero
      yo me ducho a las seis y cuarto.
   3. Ella se viste a las siete y media; yo me
      visto a las seis y media.

39. Answers will vary.
   ▶ Answers will vary.

40. Answers will vary. Sample answer:
   Michael se ducha con agua fría, yo me
   ducho con agua caliente. Los dos nos
   duchamos por la mañana.

41. Answers will vary.

42. Answers will vary.

Additional Resources

Fans Online activities
Practice Workbook

53

Unit 5
DESAFÍO 3
Expresar estados físicos

Presentation

- Diana and Rita are in Santiago de Compostela. Their task is to find the coat of arms (*escudo*) of the royal family.

- In this section, students will preview grammar and vocabulary to express emotional and physical states.

Activities	Standards	Resources
Fotonovela	1.2, 3.2	Vis. Pres.
43.	1.2, 1.3	
44.	1.2, 1.3	
45.	1.1	
46.	1.1	
47. Cultura	1.2, 2.2, 3.2	
Tu desafío	1.3, 3.2, 5.2	

Teaching Suggestions

Warm-Up / Independent Starter

- Write *¿Cómo te sientes?* on the board. Have students write the answer and illustrate it in the manner of the *fotonovela*.

Preparation

- As a group, discuss the importance of being able to get yourself medical help while in another country. What are the universal symbols that may help you if you are in trouble? Have students independently list and draw any they may know.

La fotonovela

Before Viewing

- Have students go over each frame of the *fotonovela*. Have them think about the implications of feeling sick while on vacation. Ask them to chose one photograph and describe the character in it.

After Viewing

- Have students close their books and dictate the dialogue to them. Read the phrases twice. Students should be able to form complete sentences.

54

El escudo de los reyes

Diana and Rita are in Santiago de Compostela at the famous *Hostal de los Reyes Católicos*. Their task is to find the *escudo* (coat of arms) of the royal family on the side of this old hospital. Can they find it?

Continuará...

43 Detective de palabras

▶ **Completa.** Complete the questions.

1. ¿Cómo te _____?
2. ¿_____ enferma?
3. ¿Necesitas _____ al médico?
4. ¿Quieres _____?

▶ **Escribe.** Write the answers to each question according to the dialogue.

Modelo   ¿Estás enferma? → No, no estoy enferma.

54 cincuenta y cuatro

Differentiated Instruction

DEVELOPING LEARNERS

- Some students might need guided help while performing activity 46. Have students rewrite the questions and their answers as a script. Challenge them to perform the dialogue twice, the first time with their script in hand, the second time, from memory.

EXPANDING LEARNERS

- Have students continue the story of the *Desafío*. After Diana and Rita finish sightseeing, they go to the doctor. Students should write a sample dialogue of the doctor speaking with Diana. Have them use the information given about Diana's condition. The doctor should give Diana one or two recommendations. For example:

  DOCTOR: *Hola, Diana. ¿Cómo estás?*
  DIANA: *Hola, doctor. No me siento bien.*
  DOCTOR: *¿Qué te duele?*
  DIANA: *Me siento débil y cansada.*
  DOCTOR: *Tienes que descansar y comer bien.*

44 **¿Comprendes?**

▶ **Escribe.** Decide whether each statement is true *(cierto)* or false *(falso)*. If it is false, make it true.

1. Diana se siente bien.
2. A Diana le duele la cabeza.

3. Diana no quiere ir al médico.
4. Diana no quiere descansar.

 45 **¡Me duele!**

 ▶ **Habla.** Does it hurt? Look at the pictures and ask a partner. Take turns asking and answering.

Modelo A. *¿Te duele la espalda?*
B. *Sí, me duele la espalda.*

 **46** **Una visita al médico**

 ▶ **Habla.** Imagine you don't feel well and you go to the doctor. With a partner, take turns playing the role of doctor and patient.

Modelo DOCTOR(A): *Buenos días, ¿cómo está?*
PACIENTE: *Buenos días, doctor(a). No me siento bien. Me duele la cabeza.*

CULTURA

El Hostal de los Reyes Católicos

El Hostal de los Reyes Católicos está en Santiago de Compostela, en Galicia, en el noroeste de España. Tiene más de 500 años. Originalmente era *(it was)* un hospital y un parador *(state-run hotel)* para los peregrinos *(pilgrims)* del famoso Camino de Santiago. Hoy muchos peregrinos y turistas descansan allí.

47 **Piensa.** How do you feel after a long trip? Where do you rest? What do you do to rest?

▶→ **TU DESAFÍO** Visit the website to learn more about the *Hostal.*

Activities

45. To modify this activity, have students act out what is hurting them instead of using the pictures.

46. As an extension of this activity, have students playing the role of doctor ask the "patient" questions like: *¿Te duele el estómago?, ¿Te duele la cabeza?* The student playing the patient should answer using complete sentences. Have partners switch roles and repeat the activity. If time allows, invite volunteer pairs to role-play the activity in front of the class.

47. Have students work in small groups to compare their answers. How are their experiences after a long trip similar? How are they different?

Answer Key

43. 1. sientes   3. ir
2. Estás   4. descansar
▶ Answers will vary.

44. 1. Falso. Diana no se siente bien.
2. Falso. A Diana no le duele la cabeza.
3. Cierto.
4. Cierto.

45. 1. A. ¿Te duele la rodilla?
  B. Sí, me duele la rodilla.
2. A. ¿Te duele el estómago?
  B. Sí, me duele el estómago.
3. A. ¿Te duele el pie?
  B. Sí, me duele el pie.
4. A. ¿Te duele la cabeza?
  B. Sí, me duele la cabeza.

46. Answers will vary.

47. Answers will vary.

Additional Resources

Fans Online activities

HERITAGE LANGUAGE LEARNERS

• Ask students that come from Spanish-speaking countries about the similarities and differences concerning medicine and healthcare. Are there more pharmacies and hospitals in their country than in the United States? Do doctors visit patients at home? Do students need to have a medical checkup before the start of the school year? Are there community health centers or do people go to large hospitals to receive routine medical care? Is healthcare expensive in relation to the United States?

MULTIPLE INTELLIGENCES:
Musical-Rhythmic Intelligence

• Teach students this line from a popular Spanish song: *Me duele la cabeza, / me duele el corazón. / El médico me ha dado / jarabe de limón.* Go over its meaning and have students come up with two more lines and a melody for it.

DESAFÍO 3

Vocabulario – Síntomas y enfermedades

Presentation

- In this section, students will learn:
  - To express how they feel using the verbs *tener*, *sentirse*, and *doler*.
  - Vocabulary for symptoms and illnesses.
  - To ask and say where to go for medical help.

Activities	Standards	Resources
Vocabulario	1.2	
48.	1.2, 1.3, 5.1	
49.	1.2, 1.3	Audio
50.	1.2, 1.3, 5.1	
51.	1.1, 1.3	
52. Cultura	1.2, 3.1, 4.2	

Teaching Suggestions

Warm-Up / Independent Starter

- Have students draw a picture of themselves and label as many body parts as they can.

Preparation

- Before students open their books, write the question *¿Cómo te sientes?* on the board. Next to it list the adjectives *enfermo, sano, fuerte, débil, cansado*. Model pronunciation of the question and answer it by acting out each adjective with a pantomime. For a second round, have students open their books and point to the image that corresponds to your pantomime.

Activities

48. To extend this activity, pair students to discuss what questions they might be asked at each location. For example: *¿Cómo te sientes? ¿Tienes fiebre?*

50. After students finish their writing activity, have them use the information in the health survey as a script for a dialogue. Have one student be the receptionist and the other the patient.

52. You may also ask students to think about why people go on pilgrimages.

56

Vocabulario

Síntomas y enfermedades

¿Cómo te sientes?

Estoy enfermo, doctora. Me siento débil y cansado.

la enfermera

el enfermo

la médica

la farmacia

¿Qué te pasa?

Tengo dolor de cabeza y fiebre, y también tengo tos.

Tienes un resfriado.

el hospital

Me duele...

la garganta | el estómago | la espalda

Me duelen...

los oídos | las muelas

---

48 **¿A la farmacia, al médico o al hospital?**

▶ **Escribe.** Decide whether you would go to the pharmacy, to the doctor, or to the hospital for each problem.

¿Adónde vas?

Modelo *Voy a la farmacia.*

1. tienes dolor de cabeza
2. tienes tos
3. tienes fiebre
4. te sientes débil

5. tienes un resfriado
6. te duelen los oídos
7. te sientes mal
8. te duele el brazo

56 cincuenta y seis

Differentiated Instruction

DEVELOPING LEARNERS

- Have students rank symptoms from the least serious to the most serious. Have them compare lists with other classmates. Tell students that some symptoms may fit into two categories.

EXPANDING LEARNERS

- Have students write sentences about what they like to do when they stay home sick. Have them include activities that make them feel better. For example: *Cuando tengo un resfriado, me gusta ver la televisión; Cuando me siento mal, me gusta beber té caliente.*

49 **Los dolores de mi amiga**

 ▶ **Escucha y decide.** Listen to the conversation between Dr. Galdón and her patient. Tell which of these problems the patient has.

1. dolor de cabeza   2. fiebre   3. tos   4. dolor de estómago   5. dolor de espalda

50 **Una encuesta de salud**

▶ **Escribe.** You are at a doctor's office. Fill out this health survey with information about how you feel today.

Doctor Emilio Guzmán
Medicina General
Madrid

Bienvenido(a) a la oficina del doctor Guzmán. Por favor, responde a nuestra encuesta de salud. ¡Gracias!

1. ¿Cómo te sientes hoy?
2. ¿Estás cansado(a)?
3. ¿Tienes dolor…
   a. de cabeza?   b. de espalda?   c. de estómago?   d. de brazos?   e. de piernas?
4. ¿Tienes tos o fiebre?
5. ¿Con qué frecuencia vas al médico?
6. ¿Qué haces para mantenerte sano(a)?

51 **¿Qué te pasa?**

 ▶ **Habla.** In pairs, take turns being a doctor and a patient and role-play different health problems. The patient mimes the problem and the doctor guesses.

Modelo   A. *[softly coughs]*
         B. *Tienes tos.*

 CULTURA

El Camino de Santiago

Desde el siglo X, miles de peregrinos de todo el mundo recorren cada año el Camino de Santiago. El Camino lleva *(leads)* a la catedral de Santiago de Compostela, en el noroeste de España. Santiago de Compostela, Roma y Jerusalén son los principales lugares de peregrinación para los cristianos.

52 **Compara.** The *Camino de Santiago* is a Christian pilgrimage. Do you know of any pilgrimage sites from other religions?

 AUDIO SCRIPT
See page 31K

 CULTURA

El Camino de Santiago

The *Camino de Santiago* has existed for over a thousand years. More than 100,000 pilgrims travel to the city each year from all over Europe and other parts of the world. The pilgrims carry minimal possessions with them and often walk for weeks at a time with nothing but a walking stick. If you travel to this region you will see individuals or groups walking along country roads, and even major highways, towards Santiago.

Answer Key

48. Answers will vary.

49. 1, 2 y 5.

50. Answers will vary. Sample answers:
   1. Me siento bien.
   2. No, no estoy cansada.
   3. Sí, tengo dolor de cabeza.
   4. No, no tengo tos.
   5. Voy al médico dos veces al año.
   6. Como alimentos saludables y hago ejercicio.

51. Answers will vary.

52. Answers will vary. Sample answer:
   The pilgrimage to Mecca is important for Muslims. It is an annual holy journey, or Hajj, across Saudi Arabia.

Additional Resources

Fans Online activities
Practice Workbook

HERITAGE LANGUAGE LEARNERS

• Have students play a guessing game to practice vocabulary words. Students will create clues for their teammates to guess. They should also use their personal knowledge of the language to come up with similar terminology. For example: some students may say *Estoy resfriado* instead of *Tengo gripe*. Other students may say *gripa* instead of *gripe*, since that is the term used in some Spanish-speaking countries.

MULTIPLE INTELLIGENCES:
Musical / Kinesthetic Intelligence

• Use the Spanish lyrics for the tune of the well-known song "If you're happy and you know it, clap your hands" *(Si estás contento y lo sabes, da una palmada)*, substituting the word *contento* with new vocabulary. You may increase the difficulty and fun by asking students to create verses such as: *Si estás cansado y lo sabes, ¡tienes fiebre!*

57

DESAFÍO 3

Gramática – El verbo *doler*

Presentation

- In this section, students will learn to express feelings of pain using the irregular verb *doler*.

Activities	Standards	Resources
Gramática	1.2, 3.1, 4.1	
53.	1.1, 3.1, 4.1	
54.	1.1, 1.2, 1.3	
55.	1.2, 1.3, 3.1	Audio
56.	1.1, 1.3	
57. Conexiones	1.2, 2.2, 3.1, 5.2	

Teaching Suggestions

Warm-Up / Independent Starter

- Have students review definite articles by writing the appropriate one for each of the following words:
  1. *cabeza*
  2. *ojos*
  3. *mano*
  4. *piernas*
  5. *brazo*
  6. *pies*

Preparation

- Before students open their books, conjugate the verb *gustar* out loud. Then have a volunteer from the class do the same. Now introduce the verb *doler* and explain the similarities and differences in conjugation. Choose another volunteer to conjugate *doler* out loud.

Activities

54. Extend this activity by having students ask questions before talking about the other characters. For example: *A Rita le duelen los pies.* → *¿Le duelen los pies a Andy también?* → *Sí, a Andy también le duelen los pies.*

55. Extend this activity by having students suggest things Rita could do to feel better.

56. To reinforce this activity, keep students in pairs. Have student one act out a scenario of someone in pain. Then have student two guess what the person is feeling.

57. Extend this activity by asking students to find out which different architectural styles converge in the cathedral.

58

> ## Gramática

El verbo *doler*

- To say that something hurts, use the verb *doler* *(to hurt, to ache)*.

  Me duele la cabeza.

- The verb *doler* is an irregular verb with an o > ue stem change (like *poder*).

- *Doler* follows the same rules as the verb *gustar*:
  1. It is always paired with an indirect object pronoun: me, te, le, nos, os, les.
  2. Usually only two of its forms are used: the singular *duele* and the plural *duelen*.

     Me **duele** la cabeza.   Me **duelen** los pies.

- Sometimes to clarify the meaning of the pronouns, you can include a prepositional phrase.

  A María le duele la mano.

VERBO DOLER (TO HURT, TO ACHE). PRESENTE

	Singular	Plural
(A mí)	me **duele**	me **duelen**
(A ti)	te **duele**	te **duelen**
(A usted) (A él/a ella)	le **duele**	le **duelen**
(A nosotros/as)	nos **duele**	nos **duelen**
(A vosotros/as)	os **duele**	os **duelen**
(A ustedes) (A ellos/a ellas)	les **duele**	les **duelen**

53 **Piensa.** Why do you think Spanish uses a definite article when referring to a body part, and not a possessive adjective like *my* or *his*? Why is it necessary to use the possessive adjective in English?

54 **¡Ay, qué dolor!**

 ▶ **Habla.** With a partner, take turns saying what aches and pains each person has.

Modelo Rita - los pies → *A Rita le duelen los pies.*
  1. Tim - los brazos
  2. Janet y Diana - las piernas
  3. Nosotros - el estómago
  4. Tú - los ojos
  5. Yo - los oídos
  6. Ellos - la cabeza
  7. Ustedes - la mano
  8. Mack - la espalda

> ### Differentiated Instruction

DEVELOPING LEARNERS

- Recycle the structure from the previous lesson *¿Cómo te sientes?* Use this structure in combination with the verb *doler*. Have students work in pairs and create a dialogue with questions and answers. For example:

  A. *¿Cómo te sientes hoy, Mark?*
  B. *Me siento mal, Kathy.*
  A. *¿Por qué?*
  B. *Me duele la cabeza.*
  A. *Tienes que ir a la farmacia.*

- Be sure students give a recommendation on what the student should do according to their problem. For example: *ir al médico, a la farmacia, al hospital.*

EXPANDING LEARNERS

- Have students work in small groups to create a travel brochure of Santiago de Compostela. They should include facts and images in their brochure. For example: *Santiago de Compostela está en la región noroeste de España. La catedral de Santiago es famosa. Hay muchos restaurantes buenos.*

Left page

 55 **Una visita al hospital**

 ▶ **Escucha, dibuja y escribe.** Rita tells the nurse at the hospital what is bothering her. Draw a picture of Rita and label the part that hurts.

56 **¿A ti qué te duele?**

▶ **Escribe.** Write a sentence to say what part of the body hurts each person.

Modelo Carlos  → *A Carlos le duelen los pies.*

① Pepe   ② Luis   ③ Jaime   ④ Sofía   ⑤ Elena

 ▶ **Habla.** Now interview a classmate to see if these body parts ache.

Modelo

¿A ti te duelen los pies?

Si, me duelen los pies.

¿Y la cabeza?

No, no me duele la cabeza.

CONEXIONES: ARTE

El Obradoiro

La fachada (*front*) del Obradoiro es la parte más característica de la catedral de Santiago de Compostela. Está en la Plaza del Obradoiro. Allí llegan (*arrive*) los peregrinos que hacen el Camino de Santiago.

57 **Investiga.** Use the Internet to find out when the *catedral de Santiago de Compostela* and the *fachada del Obradoiro* were built.

cincuenta y nueve 59

HERITAGE LANGUAGE LEARNERS

- Have heritage students talk about similarities and differences among the terms *hotel, motel,* and *hostal.* Have them report their discussion in a compare and contrast table.

SPECIAL-NEEDS LEARNERS

- Students who have trouble remembering the conjugation of the verb *doler* can create a memory game with pictures. Have students use the pictures from activity 56, *¿A ti qué te duele?*, as a guide. As they flip through the pictures, they must say a correct sentence to describe each one and make sure that the pronoun they use matches. Students can role-play in pairs or do this activity in small groups.

Right page

DESAFÍO 3

Gramática – El verbo *doler*

 AUDIO SCRIPT
See page 31K

 CONEXIONES: ARTE

Santiago de Compostela

Santiago de Compostela is an old city turned New Age. The city's rich history becomes apparent when visiting the old town, or *zona vieja*, and seeing the cathedral, the Rajoy palace, and the *Hostal de los Reyes Católicos*. These places showcase Santiago's architectural legacy. A younger crowd fills the streets of the new town, or *zona nueva*, where the University of Santiago de Compostela is located.

Answer Key

53. When referring to a body part in Spanish, an indirect object pronoun is used in conjunction with the verb showing possession. Therefore, a possessive adjective is not needed.

54. 1. A Tim le duelen los brazos.
2. A ellas les duelen las piernas.
3. A nosotros nos duele el estómago.
4. A ti te duelen los ojos.
5. A mí me duelen los oídos.
6. A ellos les duele la cabeza.
7. A ustedes les duele la mano.
8. A Mack le duele la espalda.

55. Answers will vary.

56. 1. A Pepe le duele la cabeza.
2. A Luis le duele la espalda.
3. A Jaime le duele el estómago.
4. A Sofía le duele la pierna.
5. A Elena le duele el brazo.
▶ Answers will vary.

57. Construction of the present cathedral began in the 11th century. The Obradoiro facade was built in the 18th century.

Additional Resources

Fans Online activities
Practice Workbook

DESAFÍO 3

Gramática – El verbo *sentirse*

Presentation

■ In this section, students will learn:

– To express emotional and physical states using the verbs *sentirse* and *encontrarse*.

– To use *si* to express condition.

Activities	Standards	Resources
Gramática	1.2, 3.1, 4.1	
58.	1.1, 2.2, 3.1, 4.1	
59.	1.2, 1.3	
60.	1.2, 1.3	
61.	1.1, 1.2, 1.3	Audio
62.	1.1, 1.2, 1.3	
63. Conexiones	1.2, 1.3, 3.1, 5.2	

Teaching Suggestions

Warm-Up / Independent Starter

■ Have students make a list of all the verbs that can be used to promote a healthy lifestyle. For example: *hacer ejercicio, estudiar, cocinar*. If students have enough time, they should conjugate these verbs for additional practice.

Preparation

■ Have students complete these five sentences that express conditions:

– *Si como mucho…*

– *Si me duele el estómago…*

– *Si como verduras…*

– *Si hago mucho ejercicio…*

Ask them to use the vocabulary learned so far in this unit.

Activities

60. To extend this activity for additional speaking practice, have students state the possible outcomes for themselves. For example: *Si hago deporte, me siento bien*.

62. To elaborate on this topic, point out any differences in the students' remedies for the same health problems. Inquire if this is related to cultural / regional differences. Do any of these remedies come from their family traditions?

Gramática

El verbo *sentirse*

● In order to express physical and emotional states, use the verb sentirse *(to feel)*.

Me siento bien.   Juanita se siente contenta.

● Sentirse is an e > ie stem-changing verb (like cerrar) used with a reflexive pronoun.

VERBO SENTIRSE (TO FEEL). PRESENTE

Singular		Plural	
yo	me siento	nosotros nosotras	nos sentimos
tú	te sientes	vosotros vosotras	os sentís
usted él ella	se siente	ustedes ellos ellas	se sienten

● The verb encontrarse can be used to express the same meaning as sentirse. Encontrarse is an o > ue stem-changing verb (like poder).

Hoy me encuentro muy bien.   Patricia se encuentra enferma hoy.

Sentences with si

● To express what you do if something happens, use this construction:

Si + condition …   Si me siento enfermo, voy al médico.

58 **Piensa.** What do the words sí and si mean in Spanish? Can you think of any other word pairs that are differentiated by only an accent mark?

59 **¿Cómo se sienten?**

▶ **Escribe.** Write sentences about how these people feel. Use the verb *sentirse* and the words in the boxes.

Modelo Yo *me siento bien.*

enfermo(a)   emocionado(a)

cansado(a)   bien

① ella

② nosotros

③ ellos

④ tú

Differentiated Instruction

DEVELOPING LEARNERS

● To reinforce stem-changing verbs have students write ten sentences using the verbs *doler, poder, empezar*, and *cerrar*. They may create a story with their sentences if they would like. Then, have students exchange their papers to read and proofread each other's sentences.

EXPANDING LEARNERS

● In groups, have students find a before and after picture from a magazine or the Internet. The before picture should be of someone who does not feel well, and the after picture should be of someone who has recovered. When students have found their pictures, have each of them narrate a story about how their character feels, what he or she did to get better, and how they feel now.

60 ¿Cómo se sienten?

▶ **Escribe.** How do the people below feel if they do the activities indicated?

Modelo Voy al parque.
→ *Si voy al parque, me siento bien.*

1. Mi madre hace deporte.
2. Nosotros visitamos a un amigo.
3. Tú haces un regalo.
4. Tus amigos duermen poco.
5. Ustedes comen mucho.

61 **En la consulta de la doctora**

 ▶ **Escucha y elige.** Diana and Rita explain their symptoms to Dr. Galdón. Choose the answer that summarizes the situation at the doctor's office.

1. a. A Diana le duele la cabeza.
   b. Diana tiene un resfriado.
   c. Diana tiene sueño.
2. a. A Rita le duele un brazo.
   b. Rita tiene hambre.
   c. Rita tiene fiebre.
3. a. A Rita le duele el estómago.
   b. A Diana le duele el estómago.
   c. Diana come mucho.
4. a. Tienen un resfriado.
   b. Tienen tos.
   c. Están fuertes.
5. a. Tienen que ir al hospital.
   b. Tienen que beber refrescos.
   c. Tienen que descansar.

 ▶ **Habla.** In small groups, discuss what the doctor said and say whether you agree or disagree with her.

62 **¿Qué hacer si te encuentras mal?**

▶ **Escribe y habla.** With your partner, prepare a presentation about five common health problems and their remedies. Then report your findings to the class.

Modelo *Si tienes fiebre, toma una ducha fría.*

CONEXIONES: CIENCIAS

Los gérmenes y la salud

Vivimos en un mundo lleno de gérmenes (*germs*). La mejor forma de evitar la gripe (*influenza*) y otras enfermedades es lavarse las manos con frecuencia. Si quieres mantenerte fuerte (*strong*) y sano (*healthy*), tienes que beber mucha agua, comer alimentos saludables y descansar bien.

PROTÉJASE Y PROTEJA A LOS DEMÁS
Medidas de prevención frente a la Nueva Gripe

Al toser, cúbrase la boca

Lávese las manos frecuentemente

Mas información: Tfno 012
www.madrid.org

63 **Escribe.** What are some ways that you try to keep yourself healthy? Make a poster to illustrate the benefits of living a healthy life. For example: *Cuando como bien, tengo mucha energía.*

 AUDIO SCRIPT
See page 31L

 CONEXIONES: CIENCIAS

Los gérmenes y la salud

The World Health Organization (WHO) recommends regular hand-washing to reduce the number of germs that cause the common cold and other illnesses. This means before eating, after using the bathroom, and after being in public places where germs can be passed. The WHO also recommends building up the body's immune system to fight off these germs. Some examples of immune system boosting foods and drinks are orange juice, fish high in Omega-3 fatty acids, garlic, and yogurt.

Answer Key

58. *Sí* is used to express assent (yes); *si* is used to express condition (if). *Mí* and *mi, él* and *el,* and *tú* and *tu.*

59. 1. Ella se siente bien.
2. Nosotros nos sentimos cansados.
3. Ellos se sienten emocionados.
4. Tú te sientes enfermo.

60. 1. Si mi madre hace deporte, se siente bien.
2. Si nosotros visitamos a un amigo, nos sentimos bien.
3. Si tú haces un regalo, te sientes bien.
4. Si tus amigos duermen poco, se sienten mal.
5. Si ustedes comen mucho, se sienten mal.

61. 1. a   2. c   3. a   4. a   5. c.
▶ Answers will vary.

62. Answers will vary.

63. Answers will vary.

Additional Resources

Fans Online activities
Practice Workbook

HERITAGE LANGUAGE LEARNERS

- Have students create a campaign for the nurse's office at school in Spanish. They should create posters, a radio ad, and a video if the resources are available. Have them use vocabulary and grammar structures from previous *Desafíos*.

CRITICAL THINKING

- Ask students to think about alternative ways to prevent the spreading of germs. Most students already know to cover their mouths when they sneeze and to wash their hands frequently, but what else can they do to avoid getting sick? For example, can they build their immune systems by taking vitamins, drinking orange juice? Will staying home from school when they feel sick help to prevent germs from spreading?

DESAFÍO 3

Comunicación

Presentation

- In this section, students will review and practice:
  - Grammar and vocabulary to express feelings of pain.
  - Grammar and vocabulary to express emotional and physical states.

Activities	Standards	Resources
64.	1.2, 1.3, 5.1	Audio
65.	1.1, 1.3	
66.	1.1, 1.2	
67. Final del desafío	1.1, 1.2, 1.3	
Tu desafío	1.2, 5.2	

Teaching Suggestions

Warm-Up / Independent Starter

- Have students complete the sentences with the correct word from the following group: *fiebre, tos, ducho, voy, cansado.*
  - *Si paseo en bicicleta cuatro horas, me siento …*
  - *Si tengo … , no voy a la escuela.*
  - *Tengo … y no puedo hablar.*
  - *Me … todas las mañanas.*
  - *Me duele el cuerpo entero, … al hospital.*

Preparation

- Have student pairs ask each other about what they do when they feel ill. For example: *Si te sientes enfermo, ¿ves televisión?* Or *Si estás enfermo, ¿vas al médico?* Have students interview five classmates and present their findings to the class.

Activities

64. Have students compare their answers in a group. Students should try to convince each other of the best remedy for each of the students in the listening activity. Circulate among the students to monitor participation and Spanish usage.

65. Take a class poll for each question and see how many students answered *casi siempre*, *a veces*, and *nunca* to each question. Overall, do you have a healthy class? Use this question to evoke a class discussion.

DESAFÍO 3

Comunicación

64 **¿Cómo te encuentras?**

▶ **Escucha y relaciona.** Some people went to the nurse's office today. Listen and match the statements you hear with the pictures.

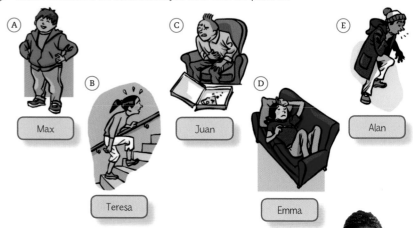

(A) Max   (B) Teresa   (C) Juan   (D) Emma   (E) Alan

▶ **Escribe.** Write a description, a diagnosis, and a remedy for each picture above.

Modelo   *A Teresa le duele la cabeza y tiene fiebre. Tiene gripe. Tiene que descansar.*

65 **Problemas de salud**

▶ **Decide.** The school nurse is collecting information. Answer the questions about yourself to help her.

1. ¿Te duele la cabeza?
2. ¿Comes alimentos sanos?
3. ¿Vas al médico?
4. ¿Haces deporte?
5. ¿Te acuestas temprano?
6. ¿Bebes más de un litro de agua al día?

	a. casi siempre	b. a veces	c. nunca
1.	a. casi siempre	b. a veces	c. nunca
2.	a. casi siempre	b. a veces	c. nunca
3.	a. casi siempre	b. a veces	c. nunca
4.	a. casi siempre	b. a veces	c. nunca
5.	a. casi siempre	b. a veces	c. nunca
6.	a. casi siempre	b. a veces	c. nunca

▶ **Habla.** Compare your responses to the questions with a partner. Do you both have the same answers?

Differentiated Instruction

DEVELOPING LEARNERS

- Students should practice the *si* structure in combination with the verbs *doler* and *sentirse.* You may require them to use family vocabulary. For example: *Si mi madre trabaja mucho, le duele la cabeza.*

EXPANDING LEARNERS

- Have students prepare pairs of index cards with a description of a person who is not feeling well on one card and a cut-out photo that fits the description on the other. Make enough pairs of cards so that all of the students can participate. Students should be able to find the card that completes the pair by circulating around the classroom asking questions. For example: *¿Tienes gripe? No, estoy débil.*

66 El Camino de Santiago

▶ **Habla.** You and a friend are going to walk the *Camino de Santiago*. With a partner, talk about the possible problems below and suggest solutions.

Modelo A. ¿*Qué hacemos si tenemos sed?*
B. *Si tenemos sed, bebemos agua.*

1. tener un resfriado
2. tener frío
3. sentirse mal
4. tener tos
5. doler los pies
6. estar débiles

Final del desafío

¡Ay, tía, ___1___ mucho los pies! Hoy no me encuentro ___2___.

Por allí hay un ___3___. ¿Vamos al ___4___?

¡Tía, mira! ¡El ___5___ está en la otra pared!

67 ¿Qué pasa en la historia?

▶ **Escribe y representa.** Complete the dialogue above. Then in groups act out the ending of the *Desafío*.

→ TU DESAFÍO Earn points for your own challenge! Listen to the questions for your *Minientrevista Desafío 3* on the website and write your answers.

AUDIO SCRIPT
See page 31L

Answer Key

64. 1. C   2. D   3. A   4. B   5. E
▶ Answers will vary.

65. Answers will vary.
▶ Answers will vary.

66. Answers will vary. Sample answers:
1. Si tenemos un resfriado, vamos a la farmacia.
2. Si tenemos frío, nos vestimos con la ropa apropiada.
3. Si nos sentimos mal, buscamos un doctor.
4. Si tenemos tos, no hablamos.
5. Si nos duelen los pies, descansamos.
6. Si estamos débiles, comemos.

67. 1. me duelen
2. bien
3. hospital
4. médico
5. escudo

Additional Resources

Fans Online activities
Practice Workbook

HERITAGE LANGUAGE LEARNERS

• Have students write a descriptive paragraph about themselves, their daily routine, what they do when they feel sick, etc. Require them to use vocabulary and grammar from the *Desafío*. For example: *Si estoy cansado después de la escuela, duermo una hora. Me gusta dormir porque es bueno para mí.* Monitor students' progress and provide guidance accordingly.

MULTIPLE INTELLIGENCES:
Naturalist Learners

• Have students visualize what types of landscapes they would see if they were to walk the *Camino de Santiago*. Would the landscape be flat or hilly? Would they see lots of trees or only a few? How green are the regions they would walk through? You may ask students who are good artists to create pieces that illustrate their visualizations.

63

Unit 5
DESAFÍO 4
Dar órdenes y consejos

Presentation

- Tim and Mack are in Silos. They have to find the pharmacy of the old Silos Monastery and get a remedy for a stomachache.

- In this section, students will learn:
  - Basic remedies vocabulary.
  - Regular affirmative *tú* commands.

Activities	Standards	Resources
Fotonovela	1.2, 3.1	Vis. Pres.
68.	1.1, 1.2, 1.3	
69.	1.2	
70.	1.1, 1.2, 1.3, 5.2	Audio
71. Cultura	1.2, 3.2, 4.2	Video
Tu desafío	1.2, 3.1, 3.2, 5.2	

Teaching Suggestions

Warm-Up / Independent Starter

- Write the following sentences on the board. Have students fill in the blanks with the proper form of each verb.
  - *Tú ... (beber) poca agua. ¡Bebe más!*
  - *Tú no ... (compartir) tu comida. ¡Comparte!*
  - *Tú no ... (vivir) saludablemente. ¡Vive mejor!*
  - *Tú no ... (leer) nada. ¡Lee!*
  - *Tú no ... (dormir) ocho horas. ¡Duerme más!*

Preparation

- Use the Warm-Up above to preview the differences between *tú* conjugations and informal singular commands.

 La fotonovela

Before Viewing

- As a group, discuss what living a healthy lifestyle means. Is this definition universal? What benefits are there from having a healthy lifestyle? Ask students about their opinions regarding home remedies and drugstore medications.

After Viewing

- Have students brainstorm possible remedies that Tim and Mack might find at the pharmacy. Allow students to share how stomachaches and other minor ailments are treated at their homes.

64

Una receta antigua

Tim and Mack are in Silos, in the province of Burgos. They have to find the old pharmacy of the Silos Monastery and ask for a remedy to cure a stomachache. Will they do it?

Mira, abuelo. Aquí está el monasterio de Silos...

Bien. Está lejos, pero estamos en forma, ¿verdad?

Y tú también. Eres joven, comes bien y te cuidas.

Claro. Tú eres una persona muy sana, abuelo. Haces deporte y comes alimentos saludables.

¡Mira, el monasterio! Camina rápido, abuelo. Dentro está la farmacia.

Continuará...

68 **Detective de palabras**

▶ **Completa.** Using the *fotonovela*, fill in the missing verb to complete each statement.

1. _____, abuelo.   a. Mirar   b. Mira
2. _____ en forma.   a. Estamos   b. Tenemos
3. Tú _____ deporte.   a. hago   b. haces
4. _____ alimentos saludables. a. Come   b. Comes
5. _____ rápido, abuelo.   a. Camina   b. Caminas

 ▶ **Habla.** With a partner, take turns asking and answering questions about the healthy lifestyle habits mentioned in the dialogue.

Modelo A. *¿Estás en forma?*
        B. *Sí, estoy en forma.*

Differentiated Instruction

DEVELOPING LEARNERS

- Remind students how to turn sentences into questions. Use the sentence from the *fotonovela Haces deporte,* and model question formation: *¿Haces deporte?*

EXPANDING LEARNERS

- Have students prepare an interview with a celebrity who they consider to be healthy. Students must create at least five questions to ask. For example: *¿Con qué frecuencia haces deporte?*

69 Camino del monasterio

▶ **Completa.** These are signs that Tim and Mack see on the way to the monastery. Complete them with the verbs in the box.

cuida
toma
bebe

1.  _____ alimentos saludables: come frutas y verduras.

2.  agua mineral: sana y natural.

3.  tu cuerpo: visita al médico regularmente.

70 Una vida sana

 ▶ **Escucha y elige.** Mack is telling Tim what he must do to stay healthy. Select the recommendations that Mack makes to Tim.

1. Tienes que comer bien.
2. Tienes que acostarte temprano.
3. Tienes que dormir doce horas al día.
4. Tienes que hacer deporte.
5. Tienes que ver poca televisión.

 ▶ **Habla.** Check off the things that you do to stay healthy and compare your answers with a partner's. Who lead a healthier lifestyle? Explain.

Modelo *Yo estoy sano. Como bien, me acuesto temprano...*

 **CULTURA**

El monasterio de Silos

El monasterio de Silos está en Burgos, en el norte de España. Es del siglo XI y es famoso por su arquitectura. Uno de los lugares más interesantes del monasterio es la antigua farmacia.

El coro (*choir*) de los monjes (*monks*) del monasterio es muy famoso.

71 **Piensa.** How do you think that the concept of health and medicine has changed since the pharmacy of the monastery was built?

 TU DESAFÍO Use the website to learn more about the Benedictine monks of Silos.

Dar órdenes y consejos

Activities

68. Use this activity to recycle the structure *sentirse + si*. Divide students into pairs. Then have each student ask their partner whether or not they participate in a specific activity, and how that activity makes them feel.

69. Extend this activity by having students create two new signs that have to do with a healthy lifestyle.

71. Elicit from students that medicine has improved with time.

 AUDIO SCRIPT
See page 31L

 CULTURA

El monasterio de Silos

In the Middle Ages, the monks of the Silos Monastery ran a hospital. They also had a pharmacy where they made their own remedies. This pharmacy has been preserved and modern-day visitors can see how medicine was practiced centuries ago. The pharmacy boasts a collection of close to 400 jars where the monks stored their remedies and potions.

Answer Key

68. 1. b   2. a   3. b   4. b   5. a
▶ Answers will vary.

69. 1. Toma
2. Bebe
3. Cuida

70. 1, 2, 4.
▶ Answers will vary.

71. Answers will vary.

Additional Resources

Fans Online activities

HERITAGE LANGUAGE LEARNERS

• In many Spanish-speaking countries, and where there is a large concentration of indigenous cultures, one can find ancient or common remedies that do not require a trip to the pharmacy. Ask students if they know of or use any remedies from their country of origin to cure a stomachache. If they do not know of a remedy, then have students research one.

SPECIAL-NEEDS LEARNERS

• For students with hearing disabilities, provide scripts before listening to activity 70. Tell students they should read the script as many times as necessary to understand the basic theme. As you play the recording, have them follow the words with their fingers the first time. Then challenge students to listen to the passage without the script. Ask them to describe the basic theme using their own words.

DESAFÍO 4

Vocabulario – Remedios básicos

Presentation

- In this section, students will learn vocabulary about illness prevention and basic remedies.

Activities	Standards	Resources
Vocabulario	1.2	
72.	1.1, 1.2, 1.3	
73.	1.2, 1.3	Audio
74.	1.1, 1.3	
75. Conexiones	1.2, 3.1	
Tu desafío	1.2, 5.2	

Teaching Suggestions

Warm-Up / Independent Starter

- Have students fill in the blanks with the appropriate reflexive pronouns.
  - Andy … mantiene en forma; hace mucho deporte.
  - Yo … mantengo en forma; no como alimentos no saludables.
  - Nosotros … mantenemos en forma; paseamos en bicicleta todos los días.
  - Tú … mantienes en forma; vas al gimnasio todos los días.
  - Ustedes … mantienen en forma; hacen ejercicio casi todos los días.

Preparation

- On the board, draw a scale from one to ten for rating healthy choices. Explain to students that one represents the least healthy choice and ten the healthiest. Then invite volunteers to share what they did this morning. Write their answers and keep tabs.

Activities

72. Extend this activity by writing the following items on the board: *tomar vitaminas, dormir bien, tomar una ducha fría, llevar bufanda.*

74. To complete this activity as a class, ask five students to write one of their questions on the board. When they finish, read each question aloud. Students will raise their hands to reply stating their frequency. Are their lifestyles healthy?

Vocabulario

Remedios básicos

los medicamentos

tomar medicamentos

Hábitos saludables

beber mucha agua

comer bien

descansar

¡Estás en forma!

Sí, hago ejercicio y me cuido mucho.

correr

caminar

hacer deporte

72 **Hábitos sanos**

 ▶ **Escribe y habla.** How well do you take care of yourself? Write questions for each answer. Then interview your partner.

Modelo No, no tomo medicamentos. → ¿Tomas medicamentos?

1. Sí, como bien.
2. No, no hago deporte.
3. No, no camino.
4. Sí, me cuido mucho.
5. Sí, corro todos los días.
6. No, descanso poco.

66 sesenta y seis

Differentiated Instruction

DEVELOPING LEARNERS

- Break students into pairs so that they can compare their answers for activity 74. Encourage students to use their new vocabulary during the comparison. For example:
A. ¿Por qué corres todos los días?
B. Porque quiero estar en forma.

EXPANDING LEARNERS

- Students should think about what would be their ideal healthy lifestyle. What type of exercise would they do and how often? What would their diet consist of? Would they take vitamin supplements? What are the most important vitamins they need? How does school fit into this picture? Then they should write a paragraph outlining a typical day describing their ideal lifestyles.

73 **Un gimnasio nuevo**

 ▶ **Escucha y escribe.** A new gym is advertising on the radio. Listen and decide whether you can or cannot do these activities there.

Modelo hacer deportes → *Sí puedo hacer deportes.*

1. llevar a mi perro
2. comer bien
3. beber jugos naturales
4. correr
5. comprar medicamentos
6. caminar

74 **Una encuesta**

 ▶ **Escribe y habla.** Write five questions using words from page 66. Then interview four classmates. Record their answers in a table like the one below. Do they live healthy?

Modelo

	Todos los días	A veces	Casi nunca	Nunca
¿Con qué frecuencia haces deporte?	John	Ellen Brad	Emily	

CONEXIONES: CIENCIA Y SALUD

Mi pirámide

La pirámide de nutrición es un esquema para seguir una dieta equilibrada. Según la pirámide, hay seis tipos de comidas: cereales *(grains)*, verduras, frutas, leche, carnes y legumbres, y aceites. La pirámide también recomienda hacer ejercicio y beber agua.

El gobierno de los Estados Unidos tiene una página en Internet donde *(where)* puedes diseñar tu plan. ¡Visítala!

75 **Investiga.** Create your own personalized food pyramid online. Does anything surprise you about the recommended daily portions of each food?

 TU DESAFÍO Visit the website to learn more about food and health.

sesenta y siete 67

Vocabulario – Remedios básicos

75. Elaborate on this activity by having students share information from their food pyramids. If time permits, have them present their pictures to the class.

 AUDIO SCRIPT
See page 31L

 CONEXIONES: CIENCIA Y SALUD

Vida saludable

In order to maintain a healthy lifestyle the World Health Organization (WHO) recommends that everyone eat a healthy diet that includes fruits and vegetables and excludes excessive amounts of fats, simple sugars, and salt. Exercise is also an important part of healthy living. Developing a healthy balance of both diet and daily exercise will significantly decrease one's chances of lifestyle-induced diseases.

Answer Key

72. 1. ¿Comes bien?
2. ¿Haces deporte?
3. ¿Caminas?
4. ¿Te cuidas mucho?
5. ¿Corres todos los días?
6. ¿Descansas mucho?

73. 1. No puedo llevar a mi perro.
2. Sí puedo comer bien.
3. Sí puedo beber jugos naturales.
4. Sí puedo correr.
5. No puedo comprar medicamentos.
6. Sí puedo caminar.

74. Answers will vary.

75. Answers will vary.

Additional Resources

Fans Online activities
Practice Workbook

HERITAGE LANGUAGE LEARNERS

• Have students prepare a three-minute presentation highlighting the healthy aspects of Latin culture. Students should compare healthy foods, habits, and exercise regimes or sports activities.

MULTIPLE INTELLIGENCES:

Bodily-Kinesthetic Intelligence

• If students have recording capabilities, break them into groups. Students should then write a short script for an exercise video. They must determine the director, the photographer, and the actors. If possible, have them share the video with the class.

Unit 5
DESAFÍO 4

Gramática – El imperativo afirmativo de *tú*. Verbos regulares

Presentation

■ In this section, students will learn to use regular informal affirmative commands.

Activities	Standards	Resources
Gramática	1.2, 3.1, 4.1	
76.	1.2, 3.1, 4.1	
77.	1.3	
78.	1.2, 1.3	Audio
79.	1.1, 1.2, 1.3	
80. Conexiones	1.2, 2.1, 3.1, 3.2, 4.2	

Teaching Suggestions

Warm-Up / Independent Starter

■ Tell students they are talking to a friend who has some minor problems. Use the correct form of the verbs in parenthesis.
  – ¿ ... hambre? ¡Come! (tener)
  – ¿ ... cansado? ¡Duerme ocho horas! (estar)

Preparation

■ Before students open their books, have a brief discussion about when it is appropriate to use an affirmative *tú* command. Discuss the tone, what it implies and if it should be used with everyone.

Activities

76. Encourage students to come up to the board and prove that their rule holds true. Have them conjugate a regular verb as an example while they explain their rule.

77. To expand this activity have students write a sentence or two creating a story for the people to whom they are giving the commands. For example: *Linda tiene muchos amigos. Cuando camina, ella habla mucho por teléfono. ¡Camina más rápido, Linda!*

78. Have students create a conversation, based on the advice given and the excuses presented regarding this activity, to perform for the class. They may use gestures and props if appropriate.

Gramática

El imperativo afirmativo de *tú*. Verbos regulares

- To tell someone what to do, use a command.
  Camina más rápido, por favor.

- These are the command forms that we use when talking to one person:

IMPERATIVO AFIRMATIVO. VERBOS REGULARES

Caminar	Comer	Escribir
camina	come	escribe

- Notice that for regular verbs, the *tú* command is the same as the *tú* form in the present tense without the final -s.

  tú caminas → camina
  tú comes → come
  tú escribes → escribe

Imperativos y pronombres objeto

- Object and reflexive pronouns are placed attached to the end of the *tú* command.

  Dame ese libro.   Lávate las manos.

76 **Piensa.** Devise a simple rule to form the *tú* command from the usted form of the present tense.

77 **¿Qué hago?**

▶ **Escribe.** The people below need some directions. Tell them what to do, using the verbs in the boxes.

Modelo 1. *¡Camina más rápido!*

 1 caminar

 2 comprar

 3 beber

 4 comer

 5 tomar

68 sesenta y ocho

Differentiated Instruction

DEVELOPING LEARNERS

- Have students go through their book and select the verbs taught in previous lessons. Ask students to create a table for the conjugation of *tú* affirmative commands. In addition, have them use each of the verbs in an original sentence.

EXPANDING LEARNERS

- Have students pretend they are personal trainers. Have them create flyers advertising their services and philosophy as trainers. Encourage students to use the *tú* commands when possible. For example: *¡Trabaja duro conmigo y vive bien!* Display their flyers around the room.

78 Buenos consejos

▶ **Une y escucha.** Tim and Diana are talking about what they do to lead a healthy life. Match Tim's advice with Diana's excuses. Then listen and check.

CONSEJOS	EXCUSAS
1. Corre.	a. Tengo alergia a las flores.
2. Camina.	b. No me gusta caminar.
3. Pasea al perro por el parque.	c. No me gustan las verduras.
4. Come bien.	d. Es muy aburrido.

79 Para vivir mejor...

▶ **Lee y completa.** Read this poster with tips to living a healthy lifestyle and complete it using the *tú* commands.

cepillarse

beber

practicar

comer

lavarse

cuidarse

HÁBITOS SALUDABLES

1. Las frutas y verduras son muy saludables. <u>Cómelas</u> todos los días.
2. Los jugos naturales tienen muchas vitaminas. <u> 1 </u> para desayunar o para almorzar.
3. <u> 2 </u> las manos siempre antes de comer.
4. <u> 3 </u> los dientes después de comer.
5. El deporte es muy bueno para ti. <u> 4 </u> habitualmente.
¡<u> 5 </u> más y vive mejor!

▶ **Escribe.** With a partner, write three more health tips.

CONEXIONES: ARTE

La belleza física

Las ideas sobre la belleza humana no son iguales para todos. Mira estos dos cuadros.
La pintura de la izquierda es la original, del español Diego Velázquez (1599–1660); la pintura de la derecha es del pintor colombiano Fernando Botero (1932). ¿Te parecen bonitas?

Diego Velázquez.
La infanta Margarita de Austria.

Fernando Botero.
La princesa Margarita.

80 Piensa. What is considered beautiful in your culture? What do people do to meet that ideal?

sesenta y nueve 69

DESAFÍO 4

Gramática – El imperativo afirmativo de *tú*. Verbos regulares

80. You may ask students to provide their own definitions of "physical beauty." Tell them that depending on the place and time, this idea can change. Certain general observations concerning beauty, however, can be made. Elicit from students the popular saying "Beauty is in the eye of the beholder."

 AUDIO SCRIPT
See page 31L

 CONEXIONES: ARTE

La belleza física

Some may wonder how these two artists could paint two completely different portraits of the same person. Diego Velázquez sat with Margaret of Austria and painted the original work of art. Fernando Botero's painting is an interpretation of Velázquez's painting. Botero was inspired to recreate this painting after studying Diego Velázquez's artwork in Spain. Botero is known for exaggerated body shapes in his artwork.

Answer Key

76. For regular verbs, the *tú* command is the same as the *usted* form of the verb in the present tense.

77. Answers will vary. Sample answers:
2. Compra los medicamentos en la farmacia.
3. Bebe jugos naturales.
4. Come frutas y verduras.
5. Toma tus medicamentos.

78. 1. d   2. b   3. a   4. c

79. 1. Bébelos   4. Practícalo
2. Lávate   5. Cuídate
3. Cepíllate

80. Answers will vary.

Additional Resources

Fans Online activities
Practice Workbook

HERITAGE LANGUAGE LEARNERS

• Have students talk about the differences and similarities regarding the concept of beauty in the United States and their countries of origin. If they conclude that they are very similar, ask them to think about the American influence around the world. Are there any relationships between these concepts? Ask them to share their points of view.

MULTIPLE INTELLIGENCES:
Musical Intelligence

• Students with musical abilities will create a song using *tú* affirmative commands. They should use the melody of the popular song "Livin' la vida loca" by Ricky Martin and write lyrics to fit the title *Vive la vida sana*. This could also be a group project for extra credit. Have them create the video for the song and share it with the class.

Unit 5
DESAFÍO 4
Comunicación

Presentation

■ In this section, students will review and practice:
- Vocabulary about illness prevention and basic remedies.
- Using affirmative *tú* commands to give advice.

Activities	Standards	Resources
81.	1.1, 1.2, 1.3	Audio
82.	1.3	
83. Final del desafío	1.1, 1.2, 1.3	

Teaching Suggestions

Warm-Up / Independent Starter

■ Students should write a short paragraph about anything that ails them on a regular basis. For example: *Tengo sueño, Estoy cansado, Tengo hambre*, and so on. Students may also draw pictures and write captions for their descriptions.

Preparation

■ Break the students into pairs. Using the paragraphs they created in the Warm-Up exercise, have each student offer a remedy for his or her partner's problem. For example:
A. *Tengo dolor de estómago.*
B. *Toma té caliente.*

Activities

81. Extend this activity by keeping the students in groups and having them discuss what advice their own grandmothers would give. Students should use the images on the left side of activity 81 as a guide.

82. Guide this activity by having students break into pairs. Each pair decides who will play Tim and who will play Agustín. Tim will interview Agustín about his lifestyle changes. Agustín will use the pictures in activity 82 to create his story.

83. As an extension or homework assignment to this activity, have students research the properties of mint tea and how to prepare it. Challenge them to write a simple recipe using affirmative *tú* commands.

Comunicación

81 Los remedios de la abuela

▶ **Escucha y elige.** Tim isn't feeling well, and Mack's feet hurt. Tim decides to call his grandmother. Listen and choose the advice she gives for each problem.

El problema es...

El remedio es...

▶ **Habla.** In small groups, discuss the advice that Tim's grandmother gave him. Use the images above to assist you.

Modelo *Si te duele la cabeza, descansa.*

70 setenta

Differentiated Instruction

DEVELOPING LEARNERS

• Begin a two-column chart on the board with the headings *Problema* and *Remedio*. Next, begin to fill the chart by writing in some problems. For example: *dolor de cabeza* or *fiebre*. Then fill in the *Remedio* column: *Toma un medicamento, Visita al médico*, etc. Be sure to highlight the affirmative command form of the verb so that students can make the connection. Students should fill in the rest of the table with at least three more examples.

EXPANDING LEARNERS

• Have students create a recipe for one of their favorite remedies; for example, *sopa de pollo*. The recipe should include instructions using the vocabulary from this unit. If time permits, students can also create an illustration for their recipe. You may create a class cookbook to display in the classroom.

82 **Una transformación personal**

▶ **Escribe.** While in Burgos, Mack made a new friend: Agustín Ramos.
Write a story about Agustín's lifestyle change.

Final del desafío

a. Perdón, señor, buscamos un remedio para el dolor de estómago.

b. Termina la manzana. abuelo. ¡Ya estamos en el monasterio!

c. ¡Vaya! Té de menta. ¿Es todo?

d. El mejor remedio es el té de menta.

e. Tengo que estar en forma. Comer frutas es bueno para la salud.

Para el dolor de estómago bebe té de menta.

83 **¿Qué pasa en la historia?**

▶ **Escribe y representa.** Rewrite the speech bubbles in the correct order according to the scenes above. Then act out the ending of the *Desafío* with a partner.

🎧 **AUDIO SCRIPT**
See page 31L

Answer Key

81. 1. A 2. B 3. A 4. B
▶ Answers will vary.

82. Answers will vary. Sample answer:
Me llamo Augustín Ramos. Tengo cuarenta y un años. Normalmente tomo alimentos no saludables y no hago ejercicio. Pero esta semana tengo una rutina diferente. Hago ejercicio todos los días y como muchas frutas y verduras. Me siento sano y en forma.

83. 1. e, b
2. a, d
3. c

Additional Resources

Fans Online activities
Practice Workbook

HERITAGE LANGUAGE LEARNERS

• Have students write about plants or other natural remedies that are used in Spanish-speaking countries. For example: *aloe vera,* or *sábila* in Mexico, is used to treat cuts and skin wounds. Students should research this topic and give a brief presentation to the class. Visual aides should be included in the presentation.

MULTIPLE INTELLIGENCES:

Bodily-Kinesthetic / Musical Intelligence

• To practice vocabulary and review grammar from this *Desafío*, break students into small groups and arrange them in a circle. Students will be playing a musical memory game. They should slap their lap with both hands twice, clap their hands together twice and then snap each finger one at a time to create an ongoing rhythm while going around the circle.

• First, one student chooses a vocabulary word or a sentence that uses grammar from this *Desafío*. The next student says what the first student said as well as something new.

71

Todo junto

Presentation

- Students will talk about their bodies and senses, express habitual actions, and talk about symptoms, illnesses, and basic remedies.

- In this section, students will use:
  - Expressions used for showing how you feel.
  - Present tense of irregular verbs like *doler.*
  - Reflexive verbs like *sentirse.*
  - Informal *tú* commands.

Activities	Standards	Resources
84.	1.1, 1.2	
85.	1.1, 1.2, 1.3	Audio
86.	1.1, 1.2	
87.	1.1, 1.2, 1.3	
88. Cultura	1.2, 2.1, 4.2	

Teaching Suggestions

Warm-Up / Independent Starter

- Have students rewrite these sentences to form a logical conversation:
  - *Estoy un poco enfermo.*
  - *¿Cómo te sientes?*
  - *No, voy a mi casa.*
  - *¿Qué te duele?*
  - *¿Vas al médico?*
  - *Me duele el estómago y tengo fiebre.*

Preparation

- To help students prepare for integrating and using everything they learned in Unit 5, have them create a concept map. Have them identify the linguistic goal of each *Desafío* as the main topic, and its vocabulary and grammar as support. Have them use their concept maps as tools for developing a five-question quiz for a classmate.

Activities

84. You may bring an actual *Operation*™ game and allow student pairs to use it. Only those who complete the activity successfully can take their turn at the "operating table."

HABLAR

84 **Un juego de mesa**

 ▶ **Habla.** You and your partner are playing Operation. Point to different parts of the patient's body and say what hurts or what problem he has. Your partner will "operate" by telling you how to fix or prevent the problem.

Modelo A. *Doctor, me duele el estómago.*
        B. *Bebe jugo de frutas.*
        A. *También me duele la cabeza.*
        B. *Tienes que descansar.*

ESCUCHAR Y ESCRIBIR

85 **Esmeralda está enferma**

 ▶ **Escucha y escribe.** Esmeralda, the main character from a radio soap opera, is feeling sick today, and her boyfriend, Rodrigo, is trying to find out what's wrong with her. Listen and write Rodrigo's suggestions for each problem.

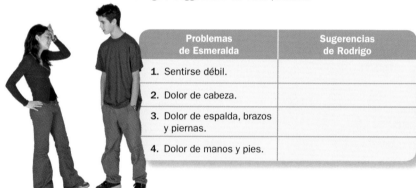

Problemas de Esmeralda	Sugerencias de Rodrigo
1. Sentirse débil.	
2. Dolor de cabeza.	
3. Dolor de espalda, brazos y piernas.	
4. Dolor de manos y pies.	

▶ **Escribe y representa.** According to what you heard, write your own ending to the scene. Perform your original ending for the class.

Differentiated Instruction

DEVELOPING LEARNERS

- Some students may need more time for these activities. Divide the class into three groups and assign the activities accordingly. As each group presents its activity, have the others identify the key points of each. If you have time, assign teams a second activity.

EXPANDING LEARNERS

- Challenge students to create an *integración* activity. Explain that this section incorporates the communicative goals of the unit. Ask students for a relevant context in which to implement these goals. Divide them into groups to brainstorm and then have them write individually. You can allow them to exchange their activity with others to resolve it.

ESCRIBIR Y HABLAR

 86 **Mi rutina**

▶ **Escribe.** Indicate your daily routine by filling in a chart like this one.

MI HORARIO	
7:00 a. m.	Me levanto.
8:00 a. m.	
_____ a. m.	

 ▶ **Habla.** Compare your daily routine with your partner's. Then explain the differences.

Modelo

> Carlos se levanta a las siete y yo me levanto a las siete y cuarto.

ESCRIBIR Y HABLAR

87 **Anuncios**

▶ **Escribe.** With your partner, write slogans for these products using the *tú* command.

Modelo   *Lávate las manos con el jabón POMPAS.*

lavarse   cepillarse   bañarse   afeitarse

 ▶ **Habla.** With your classmates, vote to decide the most original slogans.

 CULTURA

Los horarios de los españoles

Los horarios de los españoles con frecuencia sorprenden a los visitantes.

En general, los españoles se levantan entre las 7 y las 8 de la mañana, y se acuestan entre las 11 y las 12 de la noche.

Muchas tiendas cierran a mediodía. ¡Pero en España «mediodía» significa las 2 p. m., no las 12 p. m.! Después del descanso para la comida, las tiendas abren a las 5 y cierran sobre *(about)* las 8 de la tarde. Los españoles comen y cenan tarde.

ABIERTO

Horario Comercial
Mañana de 9 a 1´30
Tarde de 5 a 9
Sábado tarde abierto

La siesta es una costumbre española muy popular. Pero los españoles no duermen la siesta a diario. ¡Tienen que trabajar y estudiar!

88 **Compara.** What are the similarities and differences between your community's schedules and Spanish habits?

---

85. Discuss the *Escribe y representa* part of the activity with students. Have them skim through the vocabulary and grammar goals of each *Desafío*, and make them aware of the need to implement all of them in their scripts. After they write, have them review their scripts for specific examples of the communicative goals of each *Desafío*.

86. Students may create comparison and contrast charts to respond to this activity.

 AUDIO SCRIPT
See page 31L

Answer Key

84. Answers will vary.

85. 1. Descansar.
  2. Tomar un medicamento.
  3. Llamar al doctor.
  4. Ir al hospital.
  ▶ Answers will vary.

86. Answers will vary. Sample answers:
  8 a. m. Me ducho.
  11 a. m. Almuerzo en la cafetería.
  1 p. m. Me ducho, después de la clase de gimnasia.
  ▶ Answers will vary.

87. Answers will vary.
  ▶ Answers will vary.

88. Answers will vary.

Additional Resources

Fans Online activities
Practice Workbook

HERITAGE LANGUAGE LEARNERS

• Ask students if they know of similar schedules in other countries. Write the normal schedule for your community on the board, then ask for volunteers to put the other countries' schedules next to it to compare them.

CRITICAL THINKING

• Have students look at and describe Grant Wood's *American Gothic*. There have been many interpretations of this painting, including some that are comical. Ask students to think about their ideas of beauty and answer the following questions:

– Are the people in this painting attractive?
– Do their standards of living and access to mass media influence their appearance?
– Do you think they would ever change their appearance based on social standards?

73

Unit 5
El encuentro

Presentation

- The participants have undergone their individual challenges and are now meeting in the *Plaza Mayor* in Madrid to demonstrate successful completion of their tasks.

Activities	Standards	Resources
Fotonovela	1.2	
89.	1.3	
90.	1.1	

Teaching Suggestions

Warm-Up / Independent Starter

- Have students look at each of the participants' faces without reading the speech bubbles and guess whether each of them completed their task. Have students write two sentences for each picture saying if they think the tasks were completed, and why or why not.

Preparation

- Read the speech bubbles to the class using different voices to represent the different participants speaking. Then ask the class if their guesses were correct.
- Draw students' attention to Janet's speech bubble that says *Perdona, Andy. ¡Me siento muy mal!* Ask students if they think Janet is sick. She is not sick, but she feels bad. She feels apologetic. Let students know that the phrase *Me siento mal* is used for both emotional and physical states.

La fotonovela

- Ask students to study the pictures and read the text in the speech bubbles to themselves, then share their impressions with the rest of the class.
- Have students write the names of the different characters and talk about how they might feel or what they have achieved.
- Ask students to share their opinions about what the characters have accomplished. Have them point to the characters and say how they might feel.

74

En la Plaza Mayor

The four pairs meet in Madrid after attempting their individual tasks. Did the characters complete their tasks successfully?

¡Tenemos el jersey del líder de la Vuelta Ciclista!

Perdona, Andy. ¡Me siento muy mal!

¡El té de menta es el mejor remedio para el dolor de estómago!

Este es el escudo. Está en el Hostal de los Reyes Católicos.

Differentiated Instruction

DEVELOPING LEARNERS

- Ask students to create a chart like the one below to organize their thoughts before beginning their script. You will check their charts to make sure they are on the right track before they begin writing.

Desafío 1 — Unidad 5 — Desafío 3

Desafío 2 — Desafío 4

EXPANDING LEARNERS

- Have students write one more speech bubble per picture to continue the conversation. Have them perform the new dialogue in front of the class.

Al llegar

▶ **Escribe.** At the meeting point in Madrid, the four pairs talk to Dr. Galdón. Choose one of the characters and write a script for their conversation. Be sure to include the following points:

- How he or she feels.

> DOCTORA GALDÓN: ¿Cómo te encuentras, Diana?
> DIANA: No me siento bien, doctora.

- What body parts hurts him or her.

> DOCTORA GALDÓN: ¿Te duele la cabeza?
> DIANA: Sí, un poco. Y también me duele la garganta.

- What he or she has to do to feel better.

> DOCTORA GALDÓN: Tienes un resfriado, Diana. Tienes que ir a la farmacia y comprar estos medicamentos.
> DIANA: Gracias, doctora.

▶ **Representa.** In pairs, act out your script for the class, or videotape it to show to the class.

Las votaciones

▶ **Decide.** Which pair has done the most exciting challenge? Take a vote to decide.

¿Vamos al Museo del Prado?

¡Sí! ¡Buena idea!

Emocionante

Activities

89. Divide the class into pairs and ask each group to read the captions together. You may want to review question words with the class. They may use the dictionary to prepare the interviews. Divide the class into four groups, to represent each pair in the *Desafío*. Then, within each group, have students evenly divide the questions among the group members. They will come together for their presentation. After all the groups have presented, you can decide who wins this stage of the challenge.

90. On the board, write the names of the members of each pair in the challenge and tally the results of the class vote for the winning pair. If time allows, let students present to the class and explain briefly why they have chosen their winning team.

Answer Key

89. Answers will vary.

90. Answers will vary.

HERITAGE LANGUAGE LEARNERS

- The participants are in the *Plaza Mayor*, in Madrid, the capital of Spain. Have students research the main town squares of three capital cities in Spanish-speaking countries, including their families' country of origin. Have them present a similarities and differences chart for comparing the town squares.

SPECIAL-NEEDS LEARNING

- For students who have visual impairments or reading difficulties, record your voice reading the dialogue for them. Be sure to use different voices for the characters saying their names before you read their parts. Play the recording at least twice for them.

75

MAPA CULTURAL

España

Presentation

▪ This section presents Spain through its geographic location and topographic diversity. The map of the country serves as a reference point for additional cultural readings and activities that expand on the skills students learned in this unit.

▪ Students will
– Become familiar with facts about distinct regions of Spain.
– Recognize Spain's geographical features.

Activities	Standards	Resources
Mapa Cultural	1.2, 3.1, 5.2	Video
91.	1.2, 1.3, 3.1, 5.1	
92.	1.2, 1.3, 3.1, 5.1	

Teaching Suggestions

Warm-Up / Independent Starter

▪ Students should scan the Unit 5 *Mapa cultural* for cognates and unknown words. Have them list them and complete a chart with the following headers: *Cognados | Significado ‖ Palabras nuevas | Significado*. You may allow them to use a bilingual dictionary or the glossary of this book.

Preparation

▪ Invite students to share what they know about Spain. You may have them scan Unit 5 for images. Then have students look at the Map and read the information on page 76. Share the following facts with them.
– Country: Spain.
– Capital: Madrid.
– Official languages: Castilian Spanish (official); Catalan (17%), Galician (7%) and Basque (2%), are official regionally.
– Government: Parliamentary monarchy.
– Area: 194,898 square miles (smaller than the state of Texas).
– Population: 46,951,532 (January 1, 2010 est.).
– Currency: Euro.

▪ Have students write complete sentences using these facts. Reinforce this vocabulary asking them questions in Spanish. For example: *¿Cuál es el idioma oficial de España? ¿Cuál es su población?*

MAPA CULTURAL

España es una monarquía parlamentaria situada en el sur de Europa. Su territorio comprende la mayor parte de la Península Ibérica, los archipiélagos de Baleares y Canarias, y las ciudades de Ceuta y Melilla, en el norte de África. La capital de España es Madrid.

91 **Disfruta España**

▶ **Escribe.** Look at the map, read the statements, and write where these people should go. Use affirmative *tú* commands.

Modelo Paula quiere ir a una ciudad de la costa atlántica.
   → *¡Visita Cádiz!*

1. Juan quiere ver una ciudad en la costa del mar Cantábrico.
2. Luis quiere ir a una ciudad de la costa mediterránea.
3. Cristina quiere conocer la capital de España.
4. Susana quiere conocer el centro de España.

España es un país grande, pero es más pequeño que el estado de Texas.

76 setenta y seis

Differentiated Instruction

DEVELOPING LEARNERS

• With their books open, have students draw a map of Spain and label:
  – A northern and western border shared with two countries
  – The capital city
  – The bodies of water on the west and east coasts
  – The Pyrenees and Sierra Nevada mountain chains
  – Andalusia
  – Barcelona

EXPANDING LEARNERS

• Working in pairs, have students create an itinerary for a backpacking trip through Spain. Students should answer the following questions:
  – Where will they leave from and when?
  – What city will they fly into?
  – How will they travel in Spain?
  – What cities/places do they want to visit? Why?
  – How long will they stay?

Los paisajes de España

España es un país con una geografía y una cultura muy variadas.

1. La España atlántica

El norte del país es la **España atlántica**. Es una zona de paisajes verdes, entre el mar y la montaña, y pueblos marineros que viven de la pesca y el turismo.

(1) Lago Enol (Asturias).

(2) Paseo de la Castellana (Madrid).

(3) Playa en Cádiz (Andalucía).

2. La meseta y Madrid

El interior de España es una extensa **meseta** con campos de cereales y viñedos. La abundancia de castillos da nombre a dos de sus regiones: **Castilla y León** y **Castilla-La Mancha**.

3. El sur

Andalucía es la región de España situada en el sur de la Península Ibérica. Sus playas están bañadas por el **océano Atlántico** y el **mar Mediterráneo**. Sus paisajes, sus pueblos blancos y su clima convierten a esta región en un gran destino turístico.

92 **Esto es España**

▶ **Relaciona.** Match this photo with one of the three Spanish regions you have just read about.

▶ **Responde.** If you were to live in Spain, which region would you choose? Why? Make a chart with your reasons.

Geography

• Spain occupies most of on the Iberian Peninsula, between the Atlantic Ocean and the Mediterranean Sea. It is bordered by Portugal and France, both of which are part of Europe. Like the United States, Spain has territories outside the mainland, including the Balearic Islands and the Canary Islands.

Landscape

• Spain's landscape is mostly dominated by mountain ranges. The most well-known are the Pyrenees in the north, Sierra Nevada in the south, and the Cantabrian Mountains in the northwest. The other small but appealing part of the Spanish landscape is its coastal plains and river valleys. These tourist magnets run along the Atlantic Ocean and the Mediterranean Sea.

Culture

• Spain is a culturally diverse country with strong Roman and Muslim influences. Spain has an important artistic heritage (El Greco, Velázquez, Goya, Picasso, Dalí). Many of Spain's traditions, like the running of the bulls in Pamplona, or *la Tomatina* in Buñol, Valencia, are well known throughout the world. Spanish iconic folklore expressions such as flamenco have contributed to Spain's character.

Activities

92. You may extend this activity by having students find photos to illustrate three regions of their homeland that parallel Spain's distinct regional geography. Then have them explain to a classmate why they chose to highlight those particular regions.

Answer Key

91. 1. ¡Visita Bilbao!
2. Sample answer: ¡Visita Barcelona!
3. ¡Visita Madrid!
4. ¡Visita Toledo!

92. El sur.
▶ Answers will vary.

HERITAGE LANGUAGE LEARNERS

• Students should choose one cultural element from the three regions presented on page 77 and thoroughly research the topic. For extra credit, have them do a brief presentation in class.

COOPERATIVE LEARNING

• Break students into groups of four. Have students compare two cities in the United States with two cities in Spain. Two students will work on Spain and two will work on the United States. Have them use a Venn diagram and come up with their own list of features to classify. Each pair will then exchange information with the others. All the cities' similarities will go in the center of the Venn diagram.

Unit 5
MAPA CULTURAL
España

Presentation

- In this section, students will continue to explore the northern area of Spain, the region of *La Mancha* (famous for the setting of *Don Quijote* by Cervantes), the capital city of Madrid (with the *Museo del Prado*), and the south (heavily influenced by the Arabs).

Activities	Standards	Resources
Mapa Cultural	1.2, 2.1, 2.2, 3.1, 5.2	
93.	1.2, 1.3, 3.1, 3.2	

Teaching Suggestions

Warm-Up / Independent Starter

- Have students list the following:
  - Two bodies of water that border Spain.
  - Two languages spoken in Spain other than Spanish.
  - The name of the peninsula where Spain is located.
  - The name of one mountain range.
  - The name of an American state larger than the total area of Spain.

Preparation

- Ask students to research the following topics before the reading:
  - Spanish is a Romance language.
  - The Spanish Empire between the 15th and 19th centuries.
  - The Moorish conquest in the 8th century.
  - The Prado Museum.

- Have students read pages 78 and 79 of the *Mapa cultural*. Next, read each segment aloud to the class. Model pronunciation and then ask the class to read together. Ask for volunteers to explain where the following are located and if possible, students should elaborate on these topics using the information they gathered from the reading:
  - *El Monasterio de San Millán.*
  - *La Mancha.*
  - *El Museo del Prado.*
  - *Arquitectura tradicional árabe.*

78

1. La España atlántica: la cuna del español

La lengua española nació en el norte de España. Desde allí se extendió hacia el sur y luego pasó a América.

(1) *Monasterio de San Millán de la Cogolla (La Rioja), cuna del español.*

(2) *Molinos de viento en Consuegra (Toledo).*

2. La meseta: territorio de La Mancha

En la meseta está **La Mancha,** una región que es el escenario de las aventuras de **don Quijote.** Él es el protagonista de la novela más famosa de la lengua española, *El ingenioso hidalgo don Quijote de La Mancha,* escrita por **Miguel de Cervantes.** Los molinos de viento son característicos del paisaje de **La Mancha.**

3. Madrid: paraíso de pintores

Madrid, la capital de España, es una ciudad moderna con una intensa vida cultural. En esta ciudad está el **Museo del Prado,** uno de los museos de pintura más importantes del mundo. Aquí hay obras de los más famosos pintores españoles, como **Francisco de Goya** y **Diego Velázquez.**

(3) *Fachada del Museo del Prado (Madrid).*

The Hispanic World

La España atlántica: la cuna del español

Spanish was essentially born a Romance language and its origin can be traced to northern Spain. It developed from Vulgar Latin but also has Celtiberian, Basque, and Arabic influences. King Alfonso X favored the development of the language in the 13th century, and Spanish rapidly spread worldwide over the following centuries. It is believed that there are now more than four hundred million native Spanish speakers, which makes Spanish the most widely spoken of all the Romance languages.

La meseta: territorio de La Mancha

La Mancha is undoubtedly connected to Cervantes's *Don Quijote*, written at the beginning of the 17th century. We immediately imagine an arid plateau full of imposing white windmills. Miguel de Cervantes's masterful literary creation captured the essence of Spain in the late 16th century, but it also gave us a portrait of Spain's dry and desolate central plateaus.

4. El sur: la herencia árabe

En España la influencia árabe es muy importante, especialmente en **Andalucía**. Las construcciones árabes más famosas son los jardines y palacios de la **Alhambra**, en **Granada**, y la **Mezquita de Córdoba**.

(4) La Alhambra (Granada).

(4) Mezquita de Córdoba.

93 **Investigación: Barcelona**

The eastern part of the Iberian Peninsula is the Mediterranean, where there are large cities such as Barcelona and Valencia.

▶ **Lee y completa.** Read the text and complete the graphic organizer by assigning the characteristics that correspond to Madrid, to Barcelona, or to both.

Madrid   Barcelona

gran ciudad

- ☐ edificios modernistas
- ☐ templo de la Sagrada Familia
- ☐ museo del Prado
- ☐ puerto mediterráneo
- ☐ grandes avenidas
- ☐ capital de España

Barcelona es una gran ciudad situada en la costa mediterránea. Tiene grandes avenidas, bellos edificios modernistas y un templo muy famoso: la Sagrada Familia.

La Casa Batlló (Barcelona).

Activities

93. To modify this activity, have students work in pairs. They should read the text silently and then together. Have them discuss each one of the items on the list. After the diagram is completed, students should modify the paragraph about Barcelona and write a new one titled *Madrid y Barcelona, dos ciudades españolas.*

Answer Key

93. – Madrid: Museo del Prado, capital de España.
   – Barcelona: edificios modernistas, puerto mediterráneo, templo de la Sagrada Familia.
   – Both: gran ciudad, grandes avenidas.

Additional Resources
Fans Online activities
Practice Workbook

Madrid: paraíso de pintores

The *Museo del Prado* in Madrid has one of the largest and most important collections of European art in the world. The Prado's collection comprises approximately 7,600 paintings and 6,300 drawings in addition to thousands of sculptures, historical documents, and prints. *Las Meninas* by Velázquez and the two *Majas* by Goya are some of the masterpieces that can be seen at the Prado. It opened its gates in 1819 and is regarded as one of the world's finest art museums. Additional information can be found at the museum's official website: http://www.museodelprado.es.

El sur: la herencia árabe

The history of Al-Andalus began when North African invaders launched raids on the Iberian Peninsula in the early 8th century. It ended in 1492, when Boabdil, the last king of Granada, handed over the keys of Spain's last Moorish bastion to the Catholic monarchs, Fernando and Isabel. Today there is still a strong imprint of Arabic culture in southern Spain. The Alhambra in Granada, for example, is the most magnificent Islamic monument in Europe. It is estimated that several thousand words in current Spanish usage can be traced to the Arabic language.

LECTURA

El *Guernica*

Presentation

- In this section, students will focus on asking questions as a reading strategy. Students will learn about the Spanish Civil War and Picasso's rendering of the bombing of Guernica. In addition, they will increase their understanding of Spanish culture and history by analyzing elements of this painting.

Activities	Standards	Resources
Lectura	1.2, 2.1, 3.1, 3.2, 4.2	
94.	1.2, 1.3	
95.	1.3, 2.2, 3.1	
96.	1.1, 1.3	
Tu desafío	1.2, 3.1, 5.2	

Teaching Suggestions

Warm-Up / Independent Starter

- Students should brainstorm about what the important components of reading comprehension are. Ask students to make a list of all the question words they can think of. Give them a hint and write the word *who* on the board.

Preparation

- Before reading the passage, ask the class if anyone has ever seen this painting before. If so, let the students share what they know. You may use the following information to fill students in on background about Picasso and the bombing of Guernica.

  – Pablo Picasso, born in Malaga, Spain, on October 25, 1881, is one of the most renowned artists of the 20th century. He was a very influential painter and sculptor, and was one of the creators of cubism.

  – The bombing of Guernica on April 26, 1937 was an aerial attack on this Basque town during the Spanish Civil War. This attack was coordinated by the German and Italian armed forces and caused many civilian deaths and the destruction of the town.

  – Ask students if they recall the definition of *cubism*. Guide them in their recollection by drawing several cubes on the board. Then have students study the painting on page 80.

80

Pablo Ruiz Picasso. *Guernica.*
Óleo sobre lienzo. 349,3 × 776,6 cm.

Pablo Ruiz Picas

READING STRATEGY
Ask questions

Asking questions about a text's content, structure, and language helps you understand the text more clearly. It also makes reading fun.

Ask questions before, during, and after reading. Keep in mind the key questions about any matter or story: *who*, *what*, *where*, *when*, and *why*.

El *Guernica*,
de Pablo Picasso

El *Guernica*, de Pablo Ruiz Picasso (1881–1973), es un famoso cuadro del Museo Reina Sofía de Madrid.

Picasso pinta esta obra en 1937, durante la Guerra Civil española (1936–1939), cuando los aviones destruyen el pueblo de Guernica. Picasso quiere representar en el cuadro el dolor, la muerte[1] y el horror de la guerra.

El *Guernica* es un cuadro lleno de simbolismo. A la izquierda hay un toro, símbolo de la brutalidad. Debajo del toro, una mujer llora con su hijo muerto en brazos. Más abajo hay un hombre muerto con una espada rota[2] y una flor en la mano como un símbolo de esperanza[3]. En el centro hay un caballo enloquecido[4]. A la derecha hay una mujer desesperada en medio del fuego.

---

1. death   2. broken sword   3. hope   4. crazy

80 ochenta

Differentiated Instruction

DEVELOPING LEARNERS

- Have students form questions using the question words and nouns. For example: *¿Qué es un lápiz? ¿Quién tiene un lápiz?* Continue in this manner until students have practiced all of the question words. Have students reread the passage. Then return to the activity and have students answer the questions about the passage.

EXPANDING LEARNERS

- Have students analyze the painting closely and ask them to find two more images to describe. Can they think of what these images might symbolize? Have students share their interpretations in a class discussion.

ESTRATEGIA Hacer preguntas

94 **¡Cuántas preguntas!**

▶ **Responde.**

1. ¿Qué es el *Guernica*?
2. ¿Quién es Pablo Ruiz Picasso?
3. ¿Cuándo pinta Picasso el *Guernica*?
4. ¿Dónde está el *Guernica*?
5. ¿Qué representa el *Guernica*?

Museo Nacional Centro de Arte Reina Sofía

AMPLIACIÓN:
Pza. Emperador Carlos V s/n
28012 Madrid

Santa Isabel,52
28012 Madrid
www.museoreinasofia.es

COMPRENSIÓN

95 **¿Qué significa?**

▶ **Escribe.** What do these *Guernica* fragments represent? Write a sentence that explains the meaning of each one according to the information in the reading.

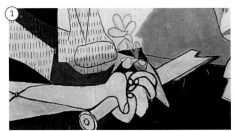

96 **¡Qué gran historia!**

▶ **Escribe.** Write another title for the reading. Then compare it with a partner's. Which title is clearer? Which is more original?

→ TU DESAFÍO Earn points for your own challenge! Visit the website and get information about Picasso's work.

ochenta y uno 81

HERITAGE LANGUAGE LEARNERS

• Have students choose another Spanish artist to research; for example, Diego Velázquez or Salvador Dalí. Students should follow the format of the *Guernica* passage and try to provide similar information. Make sure each student chooses a major work from the artist and discusses the style and context of the work in relation to the historical period. Have students write three short paragraphs.

MULTIPLE INTELLIGENCES:
Visual-Spatial Intelligence

• Ask students what the word *símbolo* means. Discuss if *simbolismo* should be apparent to everyone without explanation. Inquire if Picasso used symbolism in his painting. Then have students create or think of several images that can be used as symbols; for example, a white dove symbolizes peace. Volunteers can present their pictures to the class.

■ Have a volunteer read the *Reading strategy* section aloud and compare it to his or her list from the Warm-Up exercise. Elicit from students how these questions help them identify key concepts and supporting details from every reading.

Activities

94. Have students answer these questions in writing. To reinforce practice of question words, have them rewrite the questions using a work of art with which they are familiar. For example: *¿Qué es el David de Miguel Ángel? Es una escultura.*

95. Extend this activity by having students express their opinion about each detail of the painting. They can use the structures *me gusta, no me gusta,* or *pienso que.*

96. Before completing this activity briefly discuss the characteristics of a good title. What is the purpose of a title? Should it be short or long? Discuss examples of what students consider a good title.

Answer Key

94. Answers will vary. Sample answers:
1. El *Guernica* es una pintura.
2. Pablo Picasso es un pintor español.
3. Picasso pinta esta obra en 1937.
4. El *Guernica* está en el Museo Reina Sofía de Madrid.
5. El *Guernica* representa el dolor, la muerte y el horror de la guerra.

95. Answers will vary. Sample answers:
1. Un hombre muerto con una espada rota y una flor en la mano como un símbolo de esperanza.
2. Una mujer llora con su hijo muerto en brazos. Representa la muerte.
3. Un toro, símbolo de la brutalidad.
4. Es la imagen de un caballo enloquecido.

96. Answers will vary.

Additional Resources

Fans Online activities

81

REPASO

Vocabulario

Presentation

- In this section, students will review vocabulary for:
  - The body and the senses.
  - Expressing habits.
  - Symptoms and sickness.
  - Basic remedies.
  - Expressing how you feel.
- Students will complete practice activities for the four *Desafíos*.

Activities	Standards	Resources
1.	1.2, 1.3	
2.	1.3	
3.	1.1, 1.3	
4.	1.2, 1.3	

Teaching Suggestions

Warm-Up / Independent Starter

- Have students identify and list all the new vocabulary words in the following paragraph:

  ¿Cómo me siento? Me siento mal. Estoy un poco enfermo. Me duele la cabeza. También me duelen las piernas y la espalda. Por aquí hay un hospital, pero no me gusta ir al médico. Hoy voy a acostarme temprano para dormir ocho horas. Si me acuesto pronto y duermo bien, por la mañana me levanto con energía.

Preparation

- Divide the vocabulary words among your students. Ask them to draw an image on an index card for each word. After students finish their drawings collect the cards and shuffle them.
- Divide the class into teams and have them take turns guessing one card at a time. If one team doesn't know a vocabulary word, the next team gets a chance to win the point.

Activities

1. To extend this activity, have students make up sentences using each pair of words. Ask for volunteers to share some of their sentences with the class.

REPASO Vocabulario

Partes del cuerpo

		La cabeza	
el brazo	arm		
el cuerpo	body	la boca	mouth
la cabeza	head	la cara	face
el cuello	neck	la nariz	nose
el dedo	finger, toe	los ojos	eyes
los dientes	teeth	las orejas	ears
la espalda	back	el pelo	hair
el estómago	stomach	**Acciones**	
la garganta	throat	oír	to hear
la mano	hand	oler	to smell
las muelas	teeth	saborear	to taste
los oídos	ears	tocar	to touch
el pie	foot	ver	to see
la pierna	leg		

La higiene personal

el cepillo	hairbrush
el cepillo de dientes	toothbrush
el champú	shampoo
la crema de afeitar	shaving cream
el desodorante	deodorant
el gel	gel
el jabón	soap
la pasta de dientes	toothpaste
el peine	comb
la toalla	towel

Acciones

acostarse	to go to bed
afeitarse	to shave
bañarse	to take a bath
cepillarse	to brush (one's hair, teeth)
ducharse	to take a shower
lavarse	to get washed, wash (up)
levantarse	to get up
maquillarse	to make (oneself) up
peinarse	to comb (one's hair)
vestirse	to get dressed

Síntomas y enfermedades

el dolor	pain, ache
la fiebre	fever
la gripe	flu
el resfriado	cold
la tos	cough
el hospital	the hospital
la farmacia	the pharmacy
el/la médico(a)	doctor
el/la enfermero(a)	nurse
el/la enfermo(a)	patient

¿Cómo te sientes?

Estoy enfermo(a).	I am sick.
Me siento débil.	I feel weak.
Me siento bien.	I feel fine.
Me siento mal.	I don't feel well.

¿Qué te pasa?

Me duele(n)...	I have a … ache.
Tengo dolor de...	I have a … ache.

Remedios básicos y hábitos saludables

los medicamentos	medications, medicines
tomar medicamentos	to take medicine(s)
beber mucha agua	to drink a lot of water
caminar	to walk
comer bien	to eat well (a healthy diet)
comer mal	to eat badly (an unhealthy diet)
correr	to run
cuidarse	to take care of oneself
descansar	to rest
estar en forma	to be in shape
hacer deporte	to play sports
hacer ejercicio	to exercise

Differentiated Instruction

DEVELOPING LEARNERS

- Bring objects to the class (such as an orange, an apple, or a comb) and have students brainstorm all the new vocabulary words that relate to it. For example, if you brought an orange, a student may say *oler*, *nariz*, *boca*. You may increase the difficulty of the exercise by having them use the word in a complete sentence: *Huelo la naranja con la nariz.*

EXPANDING LEARNERS

- You may have students draw a "Vocabulary Bingo" card with nine terms from the review lists. As you call out words at random, students should place marks over the corresponding drawings. When a student marks an item on the card, he or she gets the chance to use the word in a complete sentence to win the game.

DESAFÍO 1

1 **El cuerpo.** Match each action with the corresponding part of the body.

1. ver
2. tocar
3. oír
4. saborear
5. oler

a. las manos
b. la boca
c. la nariz
d. los oídos
e. los ojos

DESAFÍO 2

2 **La higiene.** What objects do you need to do the actions below? Write sentences.

Modelo *Para ducharte necesitas gel y una toalla.*

1. peinarte   2. lavarte el pelo   3. cepillarte los dientes   4. lavarte las manos

DESAFÍO 3

3 **¿Qué les pasa?** With a partner, take turns asking and answering about each person's problem.

Modelo 1. A. *¿Qué le pasa a Diana?*
              B. *Le duele la boca.*

(1)
Diana

(2)
Mack

(3)
Tess

(4)
Tim

(5)
Janet

DESAFÍO 4

4 **Tim está enfermo.** Rita is worried about Tim.
Complete their conversation using the words from the box.

RITA: ¿Qué te pasa, Tim? ¿Te ___1___ bien?

TIM: No. Me ___2___ mal. Me ___3___ mucho las piernas y ___4___

RITA: Puede ser la gripe.

TIM: Además estoy ___5___ y no como bien.

RITA: Tienes que ir al ___6___

TIM: Sí, tienes razón. Tengo que ___7___

| encuentras |
| cansado |
| cuidarme |
| la cabeza |
| duelen |
| médico |
| siento |

ochenta y tres 83

HERITAGE LANGUAGE LEARNERS

- Bring Spanish magazines or newspapers to the class. Challenge heritage speakers by having them scan the pages and identify the vocabulary from this unit within the pages of these materials. Turn this activity into a game by allocating a specific number of words and/or a time limit.

MULTIPLE INTELLIGENCES:
Visual-Spatial Intelligence

- For words that are not cognates, have students draw a visual mnemonic device that will help them remember the word. For example, a man sitting on top of a giant hand may help students remember *mano*.

Unit 5
REPASO
Vocabulario

2. Turn this into a communication activity by separating students into pairs. Each pair should create a short story about each of the actions. For example, when do they perform these actions?, how frequently do they perform them?, etc.

3. Encourage students to elaborate on this activity by asking and answering *¿Por qué?* questions.

4. Before students complete this activity, have them categorize the words in the list on the right as nouns, adjectives, or verbs.

Answer Key

1. 1. e   2. a   3. d   4. b   5. c

2. 1. Para peinarte necesitas un peine o un cepillo.
2. Para lavarte el pelo necesitas champú.
3. Para cepillarte los dientes necesitas un cepillo y pasta de dientes.
4. Para lavarte las manos necesitas jabón.

3. 1. A. ¿Qué le pasa a Diana?
B. Le duelen las muelas.
2. A. ¿Qué le pasa a Mack?
B. Le duele el estómago.
3. A. ¿Qué le pasa a Tess?
B. Le duele la cabeza.
4. A. ¿Qué le pasa a Tim?
B. Le duelen las piernas.
5. A. ¿Qué le pasa a Janet?
B. Le duele la mano.

4. 1. encuentras
2. siento
3. duelen
4. la cabeza
5. cansado
6. médico
7. cuidarme

Additional Resources

Fans Online activities
Practice Workbook

83

REPASO

Gramática

Presentation

- Students will review the following grammatical structures presented in the unit:
  - Irregular verbs for the senses.
  - Reflexive verbs.
  - Expressing feelings of pain using the irregular verb *doler*.
  - Expressing emotional or physical states using the verb *sentirse*.
  - The regular affirmative *tú* command.

Activities	Standards	Resources
5.	1.2, 1.3	
6.	1.2, 1.3	
7.	1.2, 1.3, 5.1	
8.	1.2, 1.3	
9. Cultura	1.3, 2.1, 2.2, 5.2	

Teaching Suggestions

Warm-Up / Independent Starter

- Ask students to write four sentences describing what they do after they wake up each morning. Tell students to keep to the theme of their weekly morning routines. For example: *Me lavo los dientes con cepillo y pasta de dientes.*

Preparation

- Review the grammar page with the class. Remind students of the following:
  - Reflexive verbs refer to the subject of the sentence.
  - The verb *doler* is always paired with an indirect object pronoun.
  - The verb *encontrarse* can be used to express the same meaning as *sentirse*.

Activities

5. To extend this activity, have students complete it individually and then break them into pairs. Have students ask each other questions pertaining to things they sense around the room. For example: *¿Oyes la voz de la profesora?*

6. Provide extra practice of reflexive verbs by having students come up with sentences about their family's daily routine.

REPASO Gramática

Los verbos *ver, oír, oler* y *decir* (pág. 42)

	VER	OÍR	OLER	DECIR
yo	veo	oigo	huelo	digo
tú	ves	oyes	hueles	dices
usted, él, ella	ve	oye	huele	dice
nosotros(as)	vemos	oímos	olemos	decimos
vosotros(as)	veis	oís	oléis	decís
ustedes, ellos(as)	ven	oyen	huelen	dicen

Los verbos reflexivos (pág. 50)

LAVARSE

yo	me lavo	nosotros nosotras	nos lavamos
tú	te lavas	vosotros vosotras	os laváis
usted él ella	se lava	ustedes ellos ellas	se lavan

El verbo *doler* (pág. 58)

	singular	plural
A mí	me duele	me duelen
A ti	te duele	te duelen
A usted A él A ella	le duele	le duelen
A nosotros A nosotras	nos duele	nos duelen
A vosotros A vosotras	os duele	os duelen
A ustedes A ellos A ellas	les duele	les duelen

El verbo *sentirse* (e > ie) (pág. 60)

SENTIRSE

yo	me siento	nosotros nosotras	nos sentimos
tú	te sientes	vosotros vosotras	os sentís
usted él ella	se siente	ustedes ellos ellas	se sienten

Oraciones con *si* (pág. 60)

To say what happens if a condition arises, use a clause with *si*.

Si tengo fiebre, no voy a clase.

El imperativo afirmativo de *tú*. Verbos regulares (pág. 68)

CAMINAR	COMER	ESCRIBIR
camina	come	escribe

Differentiated Instruction

DEVELOPING LEARNERS

- If students are having a hard time remembering direct object pronoun substitution from activity 5, have them identify the direct objects in the questions. For example, *los partidos de fútbol* in *¿Ven ustedes los partidos de fútbol?* Point out that this is a plural masculine direct object, therefore, the appropriate pronoun is *los*. Review the rest of the pronouns in this manner and review their placement.

EXPANDING LEARNERS

- To expand on the verb *sentirse,* have students write an e-mail to a friend telling how they feel in five distinct situations.
  Or you may provide the following situations:
  - *Cuando llueve.*
  - *Cuando no tengo amigos en una fiesta.*
  - *Cuando estoy feliz.*

DESAFÍO 1

 5 **¿La hueles?** Answer the questions using the words in parentheses.

Modelo ¿Hueles la carne? (no - la pizza) → *No, no la huelo. Huelo la pizza.*

1. ¿Ven ustedes los partidos de fútbol? (no - los documentales)
2. ¿Oyes la radio por la noche? (no - mis CD)
3. ¿Hueles la fruta? (no - el café)
4. ¿Dices tu apellido en clase? (no - el nombre)

DESAFÍO 2

 6 **Rutinas.** Write sentences using the appropriate form of the verbs.

Modelo tú - cepillarse los dientes con frecuencia
  → *Tú te cepillas los dientes con frecuencia.*

1. Mis padres - levantarse muy temprano siempre
2. Mis hermanos y yo - ducharse por la noche
3. Mi hermana mayor - maquillarse todos los días
4. Mi abuelo - afeitarse cuatro veces por semana

DESAFÍO 3

 7 **¿Qué haces si…?** What do you do in these situations? Write sentences.

Modelo sentirse débil → *Si me siento débil, descanso y como bien.*

1. doler la cabeza   2. sentirse enfermo(a)   3. encontrarse mal   4. doler los oídos

DESAFÍO 4

 8 **Órdenes.** What would you say to the characters in these situations? Use a verb from the box to write a command. Include a reflexive or direct object pronoun.

ducharse
comprar
leer
acostarse

Modelo Andy tiene un examen a las 9 de la mañana → *¡Levántate!*

1. Mack tiene un correo electrónico de la madre de Tim.
2. Tess tiene mucho sueño.
3. Tim está muy sucio: pelo, cara, manos…
4. Janet necesita unos medicamentos.

 ## CULTURA

9 **Conoce España.** Answer the questions.

1. Where can you see the influence of Arabic culture in Spain today?
2. What do you know about the *Camino de Santiago*?
3. What historic event did Picasso want to reflect in his painting *Guernica*?

ochenta y cinco 85

---

7. Complete this activity as a class. Ask students to help you create a list of five potential remedies for each situation on the board. Students will select two items from each category to form their sentences.

8. Challenge students to turn this exercise into a scene from the story. Have volunteers perform it.

9. Elicit as much information about Spain as they can recall from the unit. Write their answers on the board.

Answer Key

5. 1. No, no los vemos. Vemos los documentales.
   2. No, no la oigo. Oigo mis CD.
   3. No, no la huelo. Huelo el café.
   4. No, no lo digo. Digo el nombre.

6. 1. Mis padres se levantan muy temprano siempre.
   2. Mis hermanos y yo nos duchamos por la noche.
   3. Mi hermana mayor se maquilla todos los días.
   4. Mi abuelo se afeita cuatro veces por semana.

7. Answers will vary.

8. 1. Léelo.
   2. Acuéstate.
   3. Dúchate.
   4. Cómpralos.

9. 1. Mostly in Andalusia.
   2. It is a religious pilgrimage.
   3. The Spanish Civil War.

Additional Resources

Fans Online activities
Practice Workbook

HERITAGE LANGUAGE LEARNERS

• Encourage heritage students to share information about when to use *tú* commands. Have students create a poster to illustrate their points.

MULTIPLE INTELLIGENCES:

Verbal-Linguistic Intelligence

• Have students use the questions in activity 5 to create a summary of the information presented in Spanish. They should pay careful attention to vocabulary, grammar, and flow. After students have finished their writing, have them exchange paragraphs with a partner for peer editing.

PROYECTO

Hábitos de higiene

Presentation

- In this section, students will apply the vocabulary, grammar and cultural information they have learned in Unit 5 to complete a project on healthy hygiene habits. The project offers an opportunity for students to receive further practice with reflexive verbs, body and hygiene vocabulary, frequency expressions and regular affirmative *tú* commands. Students will follow step-by-step instructions to create a group poster.

Activities	Standards	Resources
Paso 1	1.3, 5.2	
Paso 2	1.1, 1.3, 3.1, 5.1	
Paso 3	1.1, 1.3, 3.1, 5.2	
Paso 4	1.3, 3.1, 5.2	

Teaching Suggestions

Warm-Up / Independent Starter

- Use the cues to make sentences.
  - si / ir / baño / lavarse / manos
  - cuando / estar / cansado / Raúl / acostarse / temprano
  - si / comer / cebolla / cepillarse / los dientes
  - si / hacer / calor / vestirse / ropa / ligera
  - cuando / sentise / mal / Alexa / ir / médico

Preparation

- Review the formation of reflexive verbs with students. Remind them that most of the verbs associated with hygiene are reflexive.
- Then have students make a list of the body parts associated with hygiene. When they have finished, have students use the reflexive verbs and names of body parts to complete *Paso 1*.

Step-by-Step Instructions

Paso 1

- Break students into small groups. Then have them interview each other and make a list of the reported hygiene habits. Members of the group should take turns posing the question *¿Qué haces para mantenerte sano?* Point out to students that each of them must provide a list of at least five daily habits.

PROYECTO

Un póster sobre

hábitos de higiene

In this project you will make a healthy habits poster.

PASO 1 **Escribe una lista de los principales hábitos de higiene**

Make a chart of your hygiene habits, and indicate how often you practice each one.

PASO 2 **Haz una encuesta para conocer los hábitos de higiene de tu grupo**

- In a group, interview your classmates about their good hygiene habits *(hábitos de higiene)*. Then make a list of what they do.

  Modelo
  A. ¿Qué hábitos de higiene tienes?
  B. Ducharme, lavarme la cara…

- Interview your classmates again to discover how often they do each activity and complete a chart like the one below. Use frequency expressions from the box.

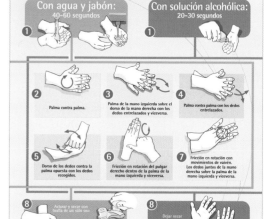

Técnica para una correcta higiene de manos

¿Con qué frecuencia te lavas el pelo?

Yo me lavo el pelo tres veces a la semana.

Expresiones de frecuencia
nunca
a veces
todos los días
una vez a la semana
(dos) veces a la semana

Hábito de higiene	Frecuencia
Lavarse el pelo	Tres veces a la semana

Rubric for Evaluation

	Content	Organization	Presentation
1 point	Limited relevance. Information is incomplete or not based on research. Little Spanish is used.	Inefficient use of class time. Information is disorganized or unclear.	Communication is unclear. Many errors in vocabulary and grammar.
3 points	Basic information is correct. Relevant information but lacks significance. Spanish is used most of the time.	Class time is used well. Information and content are mostly organized but lack some clarity.	Good communication. Mostly correct vocabulary and grammar.

PASO 3 Analiza los hábitos de tu grupo

- Find out the recommended frequency for each activity. Consult your school nurse or do research.

  A. *¿Con qué frecuencia hay que cepillarse los dientes?*

  B. *Dos o tres veces al día.*

- How healthy are your habits? Compare the information in your chart with your research to draw conclusions.

  Nosotros nos cepillamos los dientes una vez al día. Eso no está bien. Hay que cepillarse los dientes dos o tres veces al día.

PASO 4 Crea tu póster: *Diez hábitos de higiene*

- Select the ten most important habits on your chart and illustrate them.
- Express each habit as a command. Include frequency expressions.

DIEZ HÁBITOS DE HIGIENE

1. Lavarse las manos

   Lávate las manos antes de comer.

2. Cepillarse los dientes

Unidad 5

Autoevaluación

¿Qué has aprendido en esta unidad?

Complete these activities to evaluate how well you can communicate in Spanish.

Evaluate your skills. For each item, say Very well, Well, or I need more practice.

a. Can you talk about your body?
  ▶ Ask your partner what part of the body he or she uses to smell a flower, hear a CD, or touch a pet.
  ▶ Ask your partner to say what body parts are used to eat a sandwich and to get dressed.

b. Can you talk about healthy habits?
  ▶ Ask your partner how often he or she takes a shower and goes to bed at midnight.
  ▶ Tell your partner three things he or she should do to stay healthy.

c. Can you report a pain or an ailment?
  ▶ Role-play with a partner. Pretend to be sick or have a pain in a part of your body.
  Look at your partner and ask how he or she feels. Ask what pain(s) or what ailment he or she has.

d. Can you suggest a remedy for common pains or ailments?
  ▶ Discuss with your partner what you usually do when you have a health problem.

ochenta y siete 87

	Content	Organization	Presentation
5 points	Relevant, interesting information. Many details and significance are highlighted. Spanish is used exclusively.	Class time is used wisely. Information and content are clearly organized visually and logically.	Clear communication. Correct and complete vocabulary and grammar.

PROYECTO

Hábitos de higiene

Paso 2

- While the students compile their information in a two-column chart, list the *Expresiones de frecuencia* on the board and review their meanings. For slower-paced learners, use gestures to reinforce comprehension. Before students calculate the average frequency for each group habit, review the mathematical process.

Paso 3

- Allow students to research recommended hygiene habits on the web. You may assign this as homework the day before the activity is scheduled. After making their comparisons, students should create a sentence stating how healthy the group's habits are.

Paso 4

- Refer students to *Desafío* 4 for additional help on regular affirmative *tú* commands.
- Have students share their posters with the class in an oral presentation.

Evaluation

- Explain how the project will be evaluated by distributing copies of the rubric chart and discussing it.
- Encourage students to refer to the rubric chart as they prepare their projects. It may be helpful to correlate points with traditional grade scales and indicate how the project will count toward the final grade.

Content

- Explain the importance of using reflexive verbs and affirmative *tú* commands to communicate ideas about healthy habits.

Organization

- Every part of the outline in the instructions should be included in the final presentation.

Presentation

- Students should use as much Spanish as possible. They should check grammar and vocabulary. Encourage creativity and a presentation style that will hold their classmates' attention.

Estados Unidos

Objectives

- To identify professions and workplaces.
- To express future career paths.
- To give commands.
- To express free-time activities.
- To talk about intentions.
- To demonstrate interest in certain hobbies.
- To express the continuation of an action.
- To show interest or disinterest in sports.
- To associate sports with sports equipment.
- To express understanding the differences between the Spanish words for "to play."

Contents

Vocabulary

- Professions.
- Workplaces.
- Free-time activities.
- Hobbies.
- Equipment used for certain hobbies.
- Sports and sporting equipment.

Grammar

- Irregular affirmative *tú* commands.
- 'Ir a' + infinitive.
- Present progressive.
- Present participle.
- Stem-changing verbs (*u* > *ue*).

Culture

- *La Calle Ocho*.
- Little Havana and Maximo Gomez Park.
- Bilingual professions.
- Journalist Cristina Saralegui.
- The Hispanic Society of America Museum.
- Central Park.
- Latin Grammy Awards.
- *La Fiesta Noche del Río*.
- Tejana music.
- The Latino influence on the United States.
- Baseball.
- *Jai alai*.
- To explore the cultural aspects of the United States.

Evaluation Criteria

- List and associate professions and workplaces.
- Give commands.
- Talk about free-time activities and hobbies.
- Express an action currently in progress.
- Associate sports with sports equipment.
- Correctly conjugate stem-changing verbs (*u* > *ue*).
- Tell what is going to happen in the future.

Unit Plan

La llegada

Estimated time: 2 sessions.

Dialogue: *En Washington DC.*

Forms & functions:
- Professions and workplaces.
- Hobbies and free-time activities.
- Sports.
- To ask and answer what someone does for a living.
- To express a desire.
- To express aproval.

Culture:
- Washington DC.

DESAFÍO 1

Estimated time: 5 sessions.

Dialogue: *Una partida de dominó.*

Forms & functions:
- Professions and workplaces.
- To give commands and advice: Irregular *tú* commands.

Culture:
- *La Calle Ocho.*
- *Profesiones bilingües.*
- *Cristina Saralegui.*

DESAFÍO 2

Estimated time: 5 sessions.

Dialogue: *Una noche en el museo.*

Forms & functions:
- Hobbies.
- Expressing the intention to do something: Future actions with *ir a* + infinitive.

Culture:
- *La Sociedad Hispánica de América.*
- *Central Park.*

DESAFÍO 3

Estimated time: 6 sessions.

Dialogue: *Fotos de famosos.*

Forms & functions:
- Free-time activities.
- Expressing the continuation of an action: Present continuous and gerund.

Culture:
- *Los Grammy Latinos.*
- *La Fiesta Noche del Río.*
- *La música tejana.*
- *La influencia latina en los Estados Unidos.*

DESAFÍO 4

Estimated time: 5 sessions.

Dialogue: *¡Vamos a jugar!*

Forms & functions:
- Sports and sports equipment.
- Sports related vocabulary.
- To talk about sports: the verb *jugar* (stem-changing verbs *u > ue*).

Culture:
- *El béisbol.*
- *La popularidad de los deportes.*
- *El jai alai.*

Todo junto / El encuentro

Estimated time: 2 sessions.

Dialogue: *En Grant Park.*

Forms & functions:
- Review of *Desafíos 1–4.*

Culture:
- *Grant Park.*

MAPA CULTURAL / LECTURA

Estimated time: 2 sessions.

Mapa cultural: *Estados Unidos.*

Reading: *Celebramos la Herencia Hispana.*

REPASO

Estimated time: 2 sessions.

Vocabulary: *Repaso.*

Grammar: *Repaso.*

PROYECTO / EVALUACIÓN

Estimated time: 5 sessions.

Project: *Un cartel sobre un hispano famoso.*

Self-evaluation: *Autoevaluación.*

Standards for Learning Spanish

COMMUNICATION

1.1. Interpersonal mode
- Discuss the challenges of the participants.
- Comment about a reading.
- Ask and answer questions from a partner.
- Talk to a partner about their opinions and preferences.
- Gather information from a partner.
- Interview a classmate.
- Have a conversation.
- Make comments based on a picture.
- Play a guessing game.

1.2. Interpretive mode
- Answer questions by matching.
- Listen to a conversation and answer questions.
- Read a story, blog or e-mail, and fill in the blanks.
- Read cultural information and answer the questions.
- Answer questions according to the clues provided.
- Match activities, pictures, or places using an audio recording.

1.3. Presentational mode
- Create a conversation to share with classmates.
- Create a presentation.
- Create a poster or drawing to share with classmates.
- Write an e-mail.
- Write the answer to questions according to a reading or picture story.
- Summarize findings based on an audio recording.
- Write sentences or questions with the clues given.
- Listen to a classmate and/or follow his or her instructions.

CULTURE

2.1. Practices and perspectives
- Read a picture story depicting cultural aspects of the United States.
- Understand cultural gatherings/rituals of different Spanish speakers.
- Investigate popular sports in Spanish-speaking countries and reasons for their popularity.

2.2. Products and perspectives
- Learn about geographical, historical, and cultural aspects of the United States.
- Recognize symbols of Hispanic culture in the United States.

CONNECTIONS

3.1. Interdisciplinary connections
- Understand history of states and cities in the United States that were once ruled by Spanish speakers.
- Recognize those sports that have come from Spanish-speaking cultures.
- Organize community physical activities.
- Identify the geographic locations of large populations of Spanish-speakers in the United States.
- Graphically organize thoughts in order to write a comparative analysis.
- Research famous Hispanics in the United States.

3.2. Viewpoints through language/culture
- Understand the influence of Spanish-language journalism.
- Determine the type of artifact that best represents American culture.
- Learn about the culture of a place whose words have been borrowed.
- Recognize the places that are a national symbol for a particular country.
- Learn about the history of a site that has Hispanic influence.
- Recognize the influence of Spanish-speaking sports figures in the United States.
- Understand the origins and influence of *jai alai*.

COMPARISONS

4.1. Compare languages
- Understand that the denotation of a verb can change depending on the noun used.
- Compare the present progressive in English and in Spanish.
- Understand the meaning of spelling changes in Spanish.
- Understand the differences between the Spanish words for "to play" and their English equivalents.

4.2. Compare cultures
- Question the purpose of community cultural entertainment.
- Compare sports in the Spanish-speaking world and in the United States.

COMMUNITIES

5.1. Spanish beyond the school setting
- Talk about potential professions.
- Organize a Career Fair.
- Talk about plans for after school in the community.
- Plan a family sports outing.

5.2. Spanish for lifelong learning
- Think about the influence of journalism on Hispanic Americans.
- Create a set of dominoes using Spanish professions instead of dots.
- Plan an Olympic Sports Day at school or in the community.
- Investigate and make a poster celebrating Hispanic Heritage.

Communicative Skills

Interpersonal Mode

		Activities
Speaking	• Talk to a partner about their opinions and preferences. • Engage in simple conversation with a partner. • Role-play with a partner. • Exchange information with classmates.	• 27, 28, 34, 47, 65, 69, 72, 77, 79 • 10, 12, 19, 41, 52, 60, 72, 84, *Proyecto* • 20, 21, 40 • 37, 39, 57, 81, 83
Writing	• Create a poster or drawing to share with classmates. • Write a journal entry or e-mail response with personal information.	• 20, 74, 79, 80, 92, *Proyecto* • 21, 39
Listening	• Understand a partner's clues in order to exchange information. • Determine preferences based on an audio recording.	• 34, 88 • 65, 69
Reading	• Share an e-mail or an instant message to a friend.	• 21, 56, 59

Interpretive Mode

		Activities
Listening	• Obtain information from a conversation. • Identify the main ideas of an oral text.	• 7, 11, 16, 19, 25, 27, 50 • 25, 33, 36, 46, 61, 65, 69, 73, 76, 83
Reading	• Obtain literal information from a narrative or informational text. • Understand a picture story. • Use the context in order to complete a text. • Use clues to decipher the meaning of a text. • Relate the information in a text to personal experiences.	• 1, 24, 45, R1, R3, • 6, 23, 42 • 2, 8, 15, 21, 56, 59, 63, 84 • 17, 37, 43, 60, 82, R5, R7 • 35, 66, 87

Presentational Mode

		Activities
Speaking	• Present a skit to classmates. • Create a presentation.	• 28, 29, 37, 41, 62, 69, 72, 77, 78, 84 • 3, 40, 62, 79
Writing	• Write sentences or texts with the clues given. • Write and present descriptions about oneself and others. • Write an e-mail.	• 3, 12, 17, 20, 23, 28, 29, 32, 33, 34, 38, 43, 47, 60, 64, 67, 68, 73, 75, 82, 90 • 6, 24, 42, 52, 81 • 21, 39, 85

Cross-Curricular Standards

Subject	Standard	Activities
Language Arts	• Understand the origin of words. • Graphically organize to write a paragraph.	• 30, 58 • 89, 90
Art	• Study how Spanish history in the Americas influenced modern times. • Study landmarks. • Understand the history of sports in different countries.	• 58, 88, 92 • 26, 28, 35 • 70, 75
Social Studies	• Draw an original artwork. • Study art museums.	• 80 • 26
Music	• Recognize and celebrate music and fine arts. • Investigate the *tejano* genre of music.	• 44, 48 • 53

Lesson Plans (50-Minute Classes)

Day	Objectives	Sessions	Activities	Time	Standards	Resources/ Homework
1	To introduce the United States	**Estados Unidos** (88–89) • Warm-Up: Country orientation • The United States • Images and functions		5 m. 15 m. 30 m.	1.2, 2.2, 4.1	Video Practice Workbook
2	To introduce the United States and to discuss the pairs' challenges	**La llegada** (90–93) • Warm-Up: Independent Starter • Presentation: *En Washington DC* • *Expresiones útiles* and *¿Quién ganará?*	 1 2–5	5 m. 15 m. 30 m.	1.1, 1.2, 1.3, 2.2, 4.1	Visual Presentation Practice Workbook
3	To talk about professions and to give commands	**Desafío 1 – Una partida de dominó** (94–95) • Warm-Up: Independent Starter • *Fotonovela: Una partida de dominó* • *Cultura: La Calle Ocho*	 6–8 9	5 m. 30 m. 15 m.	1.1, 1.2, 1.3, 2.1, 4.2	Visual Presentation Audio Video
4	To learn professions and workplaces	**Desafío 1 – Vocabulario** (96–97) • Warm-Up: Independent Starter • Vocabulary: *El trabajo* • *Comunidades: Profesiones bilingües*	 10–12 13	5 m. 35 m. 10 m.	1.1, 1.2, 1.3, 5.1	Audio Practice Workbook
5	To give commands	**Desafío 1 – Gramática** (98–99) • Warm-Up: Independent Starter • Grammar: *Imperativo afirmativo. Verbos irregulares* • *Cultura: Cristina Saralegui*	 14–17 18	5 m. 35 m. 10 m.	1.1, 1.2, 1.3, 3.1, 3.2, 4.1, 5.2	Audio Practice Workbook *Tu desafío*
6	To integrate vocabulary and grammar	**Desafío 1 – Comunicación** (100–101) • Warm-Up: Independent Starter • *Comunicación*: Review main vocabulary and grammar	 19–21	5 m. 45 m.	1.1, 1.2, 1.3, 5.1	Audio Practice Workbook
7	To assess student proficiency	**Desafío 1 – Evaluación** (101) • Warm-Up: *Final del desafío* • Quiz on *Desafío 1*	 22	30 m. 20 m.	1.2, 1.3, 2.1, 5.2	*Tu desafío*
8	To express intention	**Desafío 2 – Una noche en el museo** (102–103) • Warm-Up: Independent Starter • *Fotonovela: Una noche en el museo* • *Cultura: La Sociedad Hispánica de América*	 23–25 26	5 m. 35 m. 10 m.	1.1, 1.2, 1.3, 3.2, 4.2, 5.1	Visual Presentation Audio
9	To learn about free-time activities	**Desafío 2 – Vocabulario** (104–105) • Warm-Up: Independent Starter • Vocabulary: *Los pasatiempos* • *Conexiones: Las palabras prestadas*	 27–29 30	5 m. 35 m. 10 m.	1.1, 1.2, 1.3, 3.1, 3.2	Audio Practice Workbook
10	To express intention	**Desafío 2 – Gramática** (106–107) • Warm-Up: Independent Starter • Grammar: *'Ir a' + infinitivo* • *Conexiones: Central Park*	 31–34 35	5 m. 35 m. 10 m.	1.1, 1.2, 1.3, 3.1, 3.2, 4.1, 4.2, 5.1	Audio Practice Workbook
11	To integrate vocabulary and grammar	**Desafío 2 – Comunicación** (108–109) • Warm-Up: Independent Starter • *Comunicación*: Review main vocabulary and grammar	 36–39	5 m. 45 m.	1.1, 1.2, 1.3	Audio Practice Workbook

Day	Objectives	Sessions	Activities	Time	Standards	Resources/ Homework
12	To assess student proficiency	***Desafío 2 – Evaluación*** (109) • Warm-Up: *Final del desafío* • Quiz on *Desafío 2*	40	30 m. 20 m.	1.1, 1.3	
13	To talk about actions that are happening at a particular moment	***Desafío 3 – Fotos de famosos*** (110–111) • Warm-Up: Independent Starter • *Fotonovela: Fotos de famosos* • *Cultura: Los 'Grammy' Latinos*	41–43 44	5 m. 30 m. 15 m.	1.1, 1.2, 1.3, 2.1, 3.2, 5.1, 5.2	Visual Presentation Video *Tu desafío*
14	To learn about free-time activities	***Desafío 3 – Vocabulario*** (112–113) • Warm-Up: Independent Starter • Vocabulary: *Tiempo libre* • *Conexiones: La Fiesta Noche del Río*	45–47 48	5 m. 35 m. 10 m.	1.1, 1.3, 1.2, 3.2	Audio Practice Workbook
15	To talk about actions that are happening at a particular moment	***Desafío 3 – Gramática*** (114–115) • Warm-Up: Independent Starter • Grammar: *El presente continuo* • *Conexiones: La música tejana*	49–52 53	5 m. 35 m. 10 m.	1.1, 1.2, 1.3, 3.1, 3.2, 4.1	Audio Practice Workbook
16	To speak using the present participle	***Desafío 3 – Gramática*** (116–117) • Warm-Up: Independent Starter • Grammar: *El gerundio* • *Conexiones: La influencia latina en los Estados Unidos*	54–57 58	5 m. 35 m. 10 m.	1.1, 1.2, 1.3, 3.1, 3.2, 4.1	Audio Practice Workbook
17	To integrate vocabulary and grammar	***Desafío 3 – Comunicación*** (118–119) • Warm-Up: Independent Starter • *Comunicación*: Review main vocabulary and grammar	59–61	5 m. 45 m.	1.1, 1.2, 1.3	Audio Practice Workbook
18	To assess student proficiency	***Desafío 3 – Evaluación*** (119) • Warm-Up: *Final del desafío* • Quiz on *Desafío 3*	62	30 m. 20 m.	1.2, 1.3	
19	To talk about sports	***Desafío 4 – ¡Vamos a jugar!*** (120–121) • Warm-Up: Independent Starter • *Fotonovela: ¡Vamos a jugar!* • *Cultura: El béisbol*	63–65 66	5 m. 35 m. 10 m.	1.1, 1.2, 1.3, 2.1, 3.2,	Visual Presentation Audio
20	To learn sports and sports equipment vocabulary	***Desafío 4 – Vocabulario*** (122–123) • Warm-Up: Independent Starter • Vocabulary: *Los deportes* • *Conexiones: La popularidad de los deportes*	67–69 70	5 m. 35 m. 10 m.	1.1, 1.2, 1.3, 3.2, 4.2	Audio Practice Workbook
21	To learn stem-changing verbs	***Desafío 4 – Gramática*** (124–125) • Warm-Up: Independent Starter • Grammar: *Verbos con raíz irregular (u > ue)* • *Cultura: El jai alai*	71–74 75	5 m. 35 m. 10 m.	1.1, 1.2, 1.3, 2.1, 3.1, 3.2, 4.1, 5.1	Audio Practice Workbook *Tu desafío*
22	To integrate vocabulary and grammar	***Desafío 4 – Comunicación*** (126–127) • Warm-Up: Independent Starter • *Comunicación*: Review main vocabulary and grammar	76–79	5 m. 45 m.	1.1, 1.2, 1.3, 3.1, 5.1, 5.2	Audio Practice Workbook

Day	Objectives	Sessions	Activities	Time	Standards	Resources/ Homework
23	To assess student proficiency	**Desafío 4 – Evaluación** (127) • Warm-Up: *Final del desafío* • Quiz on *Desafío 4*	80	30 m. 20 m.	1.2, 1.3, 3.1	*Tu desafío*
24	To integrate language in context	**Todo junto** (128–129) • Warm-Up: Independent Starter • *Todo junto*	81–84	5 m. 45 m.	1.1, 1.2, 1.3, 3.1	Audio Practice Workbook
25	To integrate language in context	**El encuentro** (130–131) • Warm-Up: Independent Starter • *El encuentro: En Grant Park*	85–86	5 m. 45 m.	1.1, 1.2, 1.3	
26	To learn about customs and traditions in the United States	**Mapa cultural – Estados Unidos** (132–135) • Warm-Up: Independent Starter • *Mapa cultural: Estados Unidos*	87–89	5 m. 45 m.	1.1, 1.2, 1.3, 2.2, 3.1, 3.2	Video Practice Workbook
27	To learn about Hispanic Heritage celebrations	**Lectura – Celebramos la Herencia Hispana** (136–137) • Warm-Up: Independent Starter • *Lectura: Celebramos la Herencia Hispana*	90–92	5 m. 45 m.	1.1, 1.2, 1.3, 3.1, 3.2, 5.1, 5.2	*Tu desafío*
28	To review vocabulary	**Repaso – Vocabulario** (138–139) • Warm-Up: Independent Starter • *Repaso: Vocabulario*	1–4	5 m. 45 m.	1.2, 1.3, 4.1	Practice Workbook
29	To review grammar and culture	**Repaso – Gramática** (140–141) • Warm-Up: Independent Starter • *Repaso: Gramática*	5–9	5 m. 45 m.	1.3, 2.1, 2.2, 4.1, 5.2	Practice Workbook
30	To create a presentation to celebrate Hispanic Heritage in the United States	**Proyecto – Un hispano famoso** (142–143) • Warm-Up: Read the project outline • Work on project		5 m. 45 m.	1.1, 1.2, 1.3, 3.1, 5.2	
31	To create a presentation to celebrate Hispanic Heritage in the United States	**Proyecto – Un hispano famoso** (142–143) • Warm-Up: Read the project outline • Work on project		5 m. 45 m.	1.1, 1.2, 1.3, 3.1, 5.2	
32	To present projects	**Proyecto – Un hispano famoso** (142–143) • Warm-Up: Prepare presentations • Project presentations		5 m. 45 m.	1.1, 1.2, 1.3, 3.1, 5.2	
33	To present projects	**Proyecto – Un hispano famoso** (142–143) • Warm-Up: Prepare presentations • Project presentations		5 m. 45 m.	1.1, 1.2, 1.3, 3.1, 5.2	
34	To assess student proficiency	**Assessment** • *Autoevaluación* (143) • Test on Unit 6		10 m. 40 m.	1.2, 1.3	

Lesson Plans (90-Minute Classes)

Day	Objectives	Sessions	Activities	Time	Standards	Resources/ Homework
1	To introduce the United States and to discuss the pairs' challenges	**Estados Unidos / La llegada** (88–93) • Warm-Up: Country orientation • The United States • Images and functions • Presentation: *En Washington DC* • *Expresiones útiles* and *¿Quién ganará?*	 1 2–5	 5 m. 10 m. 20 m. 20 m. 35 m.	1.1, 1.2, 1.3, 2.2, 4.1	Visual Presentation Video Practice Workbook
2	To talk about professions and work places, and to give commands	**Desafío 1 – Una partida de dominó / Vocabulario** (94–97) • Warm-Up: Independent Starter • *Fotonovela: Una partida de dominó* • *Cultura: La Calle Ocho* • Vocabulary: *El trabajo.* • *Comunidades: Profesiones bilingües*	 6–8 9 10–12 13	 5 m. 30 m. 15 m. 30 m. 10 m.	1.1, 1.2, 1.3, 2.1, 4.2, 5.1	Visual Presentation Audio Video Practice Workbook
3	To give commands and to integrate vocabulary and grammar	**Desafío 1 – Gramática / Comunicación** (98–101) • Warm-Up: Independent Starter • Grammar: *Imperativo afirmativo. Verbos irregulares* • *Cultura: Cristina Saralegui* • Comunicación: Review main vocabulary and grammar	 14–17 18 19–21	 5 m. 30 m. 10 m. 45 m.	1.1, 1.2, 1.3, 3.1, 3.2, 4.1, 5.1, 5.2	Audio Practice Workbook *Tu desafío*
4	To assess students' proficiency and to express intention	**Desafío 1 – Evaluación / Desafío 2 – Una noche en el museo** (101–103) • Warm-Up: *Final del desafío* • Quiz on *Desafío 1* • *Fotonovela: Una noche en el museo* • *Cultura: La Sociedad Hispánica de América*	 22 23–25 26	 25 m. 20 m. 30 m. 15 m.	1.1, 1.2, 1.3, 2.1, 3.2, 4.2, 5.1, 5.2	Visual Presentation Audio *Tu desafío*
5	To learn about free-time activities and to express intention	**Desafío 2 – Vocabulario / Gramática** (104–107) • Warm-Up: Independent Starter • Vocabulary: *Los pasatiempos* • *Conexiones: Las palabras prestadas* • Grammar: *'Ir a' + infinitivo* • *Conexiones: Central Park*	 27–29 30 31–34 35	 5 m. 30 m. 10 m. 30 m. 15 m.	1.1, 1.2, 1.3, 3.1, 3.2, 4.1, 4.2, 5.1	Audio Practice Workbook
6	To integrate vocabulary and grammar and to assess student proficiency	**Desafío 2 – Comunicación / Evaluación** (108–109) • Warm-Up: Independent Starter • *Comunicación*: Review main vocabulary and grammar • *Final del desafío* • Quiz on *Desafío 2*	 36–39 40	 5 m. 45 m. 20 m. 20 m.	1.1, 1.2, 1.3	Audio Practice Workbook

Day	Objectives	Sessions	Activities	Time	Standards	Resources/ Homework
7	To talk about free-time activities and actions that are happening at a particular moment	**Desafío 3 – Tomando fotos de los famosos / Vocabulario** (110–113) • Warm-Up: Independent Starter • *Fotonovela: Fotos de famosos* • *Cultura: Los 'Grammy' Latinos* • Vocabulary: *Tiempo libre* • *Conexiones: La Fiesta Noche del Río*	 41–43 44 45–47 48	 5 m. 30 m. 15 m. 30 m. 10 m.	1.1, 1.2, 1.3, 2.1, 3.2, 5.1, 5.2	Visual Presentation Audio Video Practice Workbook *Tu desafío*
8	To talk about actions that are happening at a particular moment and to speak using the present participle	**Desafío 3 – Gramática** (114–117) • Warm-Up: Independent Starter • Grammar: *El presente continuo* • *Conexiones: La música tejana* • Grammar: *El gerundio* • *Conexiones: La influencia latina en los Estados Unidos*	 49–52 53 54–57 58	 5 m. 30 m. 10 m. 35 m. 10 m.	1.1, 1.2, 1.3, 3.1, 3.2, 4.1	Audio Practice Workbook
9	To integrate vocabulary and grammar and to assess student proficiency	**Desafío 3 – Comunicación / Evaluación** (118–119) • Warm-Up: Independent Starter • *Comunicación*: Review main vocabulary and grammar • *Final del desafío* • Quiz on *Desafío 3*	 59–61 62	 5 m. 45 m. 20 m. 20 m.	1.1, 1.2, 1.3	Audio Practice Workbook
10	To learn sports and sporting equipment vocabulary	**Desafío 4 – ¡Vamos a jugar! / Vocabulario** (120–123) • Warm-Up: Independent Starter • *Fotonovela: ¡Vamos a jugar!* • *Cultura: El béisbol* • Vocabulary: *Los deportes* • *Conexiones: La popularidad de los deportes*	 63–65 66 67–69 70	 5 m. 30 m. 15 m. 30 m. 10 m.	1.1, 1.2, 1.3, 2.1, 3.2, 4.2	Visual Presentation Audio Practice Workbook
11	To learn stem–changing verbs and to integrate vocabulary and grammar	**Desafío 4 – Gramática / Comunicación** (124–127) • Warm-Up: Independent Starter • Grammar: *Verbos con raíz irregular (u > ue)* • *Cultura: El jai alai* • *Comunicación*: Review main vocabulary and grammar	 71–74 75 76–79	 5 m. 30 m. 10 m. 45 m.	1.1, 1.2, 1.3, 2.1, 3.1, 3.2, 4.1, 5.1, 5.2	Audio Practice Workbook *Tu desafío*
12	To assess student proficiency	**Desafío 4 – Evaluación** (127) • Warm-Up: *Final del desafío* • Last minute questions • Quiz on *Desafío 4*	80	40 m. 30 m. 20 m.	1.2, 1.3, 3.1	*Tu desafío*
13	To integrate language in context	**Todo junto / El encuentro** (128–131) • Warm-Up: Independent Starter • *Todo junto* • *El encuentro: En Grant Park*	 81–84 85–86	 5 m. 40 m. 45 m.	1.1, 1.2, 1.3, 3.1	Audio Practice Workbook

Day	Objectives	Sessions	Activities	Time	Standards	Resources/ Homework
14	To learn about customs and traditions in the United States	***Mapa cultural / Lectura*** (132–137) • Warm-Up: Independent Starter • *Mapa cultural: Estados Unidos* • *Lectura: Celebramos la Herencia Hispana*	 87–89 90–92	 5 m. 45 m. 40 m.	1.1, 1.2, 1.3, 2.2, 3.1, 3.2, 5.1, 5.2	Video Practice Workbook *Tu desafío*
15	To review vocabulary, grammar, and culture	***Repaso – Vocabulario / Gramática*** (138–141) • Warm-Up: Independent Starter • *Repaso: Vocabulario* • *Repaso: Gramática*	 1–4 5–9	 5 m. 40 m. 45 m.	1.2, 1.3, 2.1, 2.2, 4.1, 5.2	Practice Workbook
16	To create a presentation celebrating Hispanic Heritage in the United States	***Proyecto*** (142–143) • Warm-Up: Read the project outline • Work on project		 5 m. 85 m.	1.1, 1.2, 1.3, 3.1, 5.2	
17	To create a presentation celebrating Hispanic Heritage in the United States	***Proyecto*** (142–143) • Warm-Up: Prepare presentations • Project presentations		 5 m. 85 m.	1.1, 1.2, 1.3, 3.1, 5.2	
18	To present projects and to assess student proficiency	***Proyecto / Assessment*** (142–143) • Warm-Up: Prepare presentations • Project presentations • *Autoevaluación* • Test on Unit 6		 5 m. 30 m. 10 m. 45 m.	1.1, 1.2, 1.3, 3.1, 5.2	

7 Las mujeres también juegan

1. Mi nombre es Alina Álvarez. Soy doctora de Medicina Familiar. Me gusta mucho jugar al dominó.
2. Yo soy Mercedes Alarcón. Me dedico a dar clases de Matemáticas. Trabajo en una escuela de Secundaria.
3. Me llamo Aurora Paredes. Soy empresaria. Tengo una tienda de ropa.
4. Yo me llamo Sandra García. Trabajo de mesera en un restaurante cubano.

11 Futuros profesionales

1. Hola, soy Janet. Me gusta mucho la música. Estudio en la universidad porque quiero ser maestra de Música.
2. ¿Qué tal? Soy Tim. Yo quiero ser jugador profesional de tenis.
3. Les habla Diana. Sí, a mí me gusta mucho la fotografía. Quiero ser una fotógrafa famosa.
4. Hola, soy Andy. Quiero ser entrenador de fútbol americano... Pero también quiero ser médico. Médico o entrenador, no sé. Tengo tiempo para decidir, ¿verdad?
5. Yo soy Tess. Me gusta la tecnología. Quiero dedicarme a diseñar y a construir edificios. Sí, quiero ser ingeniera como mi mamá.

16 La jueza Estrella Rodríguez

Me gusta mucho ser jueza. Es una profesión honorable. Si quieres ser juez, sé una persona honesta y di siempre la verdad. La honestidad es muy importante en este trabajo. También debes prestar atención a tu comunidad y ayudar a la gente. Y, sobre todo, sé responsable y estudia mucho. En esta profesión tienes que conocer bien las leyes. ¡Buena suerte, Tim!

19 Héroes de la comunidad

1. Soy Elena Rosas, empleada de la fábrica de ropa. No puedo asistir al evento porque mi jefe está enfermo. Hoy no tengo el día libre. Lo siento.
2. Buenos días, soy el ingeniero Fabián Candelas. Le hablo para confirmar mi presentación en el evento. Muchas gracias por invitarme.
3. Sí, buenas tardes, habla la señora Esperanza Esparza. Soy abogada. Gracias por invitarme. Voy a estar allí a las siete. Hasta pronto.
4. Hola, habla Juan Hernández. Soy secretario en una oficina de abogados. No puedo asistir al evento. Lo siento mucho.
5. Hola, soy Cristóbal Barrios, el entrenador del equipo de fútbol de la universidad. Estoy muy contento de poder colaborar en este evento. Me gusta hablar con los jóvenes.
6. Hola, soy Marisa Jiménez. Soy médica. Le llamo para confirmar mi asistencia al evento. Muchas gracias.

25 Vamos a pasear por Nueva York

–Diana, ¿vamos a pasear por Central Park?
–Sí, buena idea. Después voy a tomar fotos de la ciudad. ¿Quieres venir conmigo?

–No, yo voy a visitar el Metropolitan Museum. Nos vemos luego.
–De acuerdo. ¿Sabes? Mis padres van a visitar Nueva York en verano.
–¡Ah, qué bien! Podemos recomendarles algunos lugares interesantes.
–Oye, Rita, ¿vas a ver a Patricia?
–Sí, Patricia y yo vamos a ir de compras a Times Square. ¿Sabes qué va a hacer Tim?
–Va a visitar la Estatua de la Libertad.

27 Una chica muy interesante

¡Hola! Soy Diana y tengo muchos hobbies. Me gusta bailar, cantar y tocar el piano. En la escuela tenemos que actuar en obras de teatro, pero no me gusta. ¿Qué más...? Me gusta mucho caminar y montar en bicicleta. Son mis actividades favoritas. Pero no me gusta nadar. También me gusta escuchar música y leer libros. Y no me gusta nada ver la televisión. ¿Y a ti, qué te gusta?

33 Los planes de Rita

Estos son mis planes. Ahora Andy, Tim y yo vamos a jugar al baloncesto en el gimnasio. No juego bien al baloncesto, pero quiero hacer ejercicio. Esta tarde Diana, Tess y yo vamos a pintar en Central Park. Me gusta pintar flores. Esta noche voy a leer en mi habitación. ¡Tengo un libro muy interesante! Mañana por la mañana voy a montar en bicicleta con mi sobrina Diana. Y por la tarde voy a tocar el piano en el *lobby* del hotel. Y la próxima semana voy a cantar en el restaurante del hotel. Es la noche del karaoke y me gusta mucho cantar.

36 Actividades en el parque

Hola, tía Rita. Hoy es la celebración del Día de la Hispanidad en Central Park. Tengo muchas ganas de bailar y de escuchar música latina. También quiero ver obras de arte de artistas hispanos. ¡Estoy muy orgullosa de ser hispana! Después podemos almorzar algo típico de Nueva York, pero con sabor latino. Llámame. ¡Hasta pronto!

46 ¡Qué suerte!

1. Soy Mack. Yo quiero el reproductor de música para escuchar mi música favorita.
2. Soy Tess y quiero el celular para mandar mensajes a mis amigos.
3. Soy Diana. Yo quiero la cámara de fotos. Voy a usarla para tomar fotos en la quinceañera de mi prima.
4. Soy Andy. Quiero el televisor para ver mis programas favoritos.
5. Soy Tim y quiero la cámara de video. La voy a usar para grabar la graduación de mi amigo.

50 Una escuela de arte

–Alicia, ¡me encanta tu presentación! Bailas muy bien.
–Gracias, Tess. Mira, te quiero presentar a algunos amigos. Este es Nelson.
–Hola, Tess.
–Encantada, Nelson. ¿Qué haces?
–Soy músico. Estoy grabando una canción nueva.

–Hola, Tess. Yo soy Beatriz. Estoy filmando una película muy interesante. Pero no soy actriz; soy la directora de la película.

–¿Cómo estás, Tess? Yo soy Teresa y esta es Kate. Estamos tomando fotografías.

–Yo me llamo Elena. Estoy editando unos programas nuevos de la Fiesta Noche del Río para la televisión.

–Nosotros somos Héctor y Sergio. Hoy estamos grabando una radionovela para la próxima semana. ¿Te gusta escuchar la radio?

–Sí, claro. Encantada de conocerlos a todos. ¡Hay muchas especialidades interesantes en esta escuela!

55 ¡Está durmiendo!

1. ¡Psst! ¡Psst! ¡Despierta! ¡Tienes que empezar la sesión de fotos!
2. ¡Mira, es Shakira! ¡Shakira!, ¡Shakira!, ¿puedo hacerme una foto contigo?
3. ¡Qué canción más bonita! Me gusta mucho.
4. ¿Dónde están los chicos de Maná? ¡No están aquí! ¿Tienen su ropa para el evento? ¿Necesitan más ropa?

61 Adivina qué

1. Estoy en el cine. Todos están mirando la pantalla. ¿Qué estoy haciendo?
2. Estoy en una biblioteca. Todos están en silencio. ¿Qué estoy haciendo?
3. Estoy en casa con mi familia. Los platos están sobre la mesa. ¿Qué estoy haciendo?
4. Estoy en la calle. Quiero hacer planes para el fin de semana con mis amigas. ¿Qué estoy haciendo?
5. Estoy en el parque con unos amigos y tengo una cámara en la mano. ¿Qué estoy haciendo?

65 Para estar en forma

Este es mi plan para estar en forma. Voy a hacer ejercicio todos los días. También voy a comer bien y voy a tomar muchas frutas y verduras. No debo tomar muchos refrescos y sí beber más agua durante el día. El agua es buena para la salud. Además quiero montar en bicicleta. Y ahora voy a correr porque hoy tengo un partido de béisbol y tengo que hacer un jonrón.

69 ¿Ver o jugar?

1. A mí me gusta ver el baloncesto en la televisión. Pero me gusta más jugar al fútbol.
2. Yo prefiero jugar al tenis. Y no me gusta jugar al voleibol, pero sí me gusta ver los partidos en la televisión.

3. Me gusta mucho jugar al baloncesto. También me gusta ver la natación en la televisión.
4. A mí me gusta ver los partidos de béisbol en el estadio. Y también me gusta jugar al béisbol.
5. Me gusta mucho ver los partidos de fútbol americano en la televisión. Y para jugar, prefiero el golf.
6. Me gusta jugar al béisbol. Y a veces veo el boliche en la televisión.

73 Adivina...

1. Buenas tardes, soy Andy. Janet y yo vamos al parque. Necesitamos un bate, un guante y una pelota.
2. ¡Hola! Habla Tim. Mi abuelo y yo vamos al estadio. Necesitamos un balón y un casco.
3. Hola, habla Diana. Mi tía y yo vamos al centro recreativo. Necesitamos dos raquetas y una pelota.
4. Hola, soy Tess. Yo voy al parque con Patricia. Solo necesitamos un balón.

76 Primero las tareas

–Andy, ¡tienes muchas tareas! Primero tienes que pasar la aspiradora, así que no puedes jugar al fútbol. Y esta tarde tampoco puedes jugar al baloncesto porque tienes que hacer una torta de chocolate para el cumpleaños de mamá.

–Yo quiero jugar al béisbol.

–No, no puedes jugar al béisbol porque tienes que llamar a nuestros abuelos.

–¿Y al tenis? ¿Puedo jugar al tenis?

–No, tienes que lavar los platos.

–Janet, si yo hago todas las tareas domésticas, ¿qué vas a hacer tú?

–Yo… voy a nadar. ¡Hasta luego, Andy!

83 ¿Qué ves?

1. Diana y Rita están en el parque. Diana está pintando y Rita está hablando por teléfono.
2. Andy, Tim y Janet están en un concierto. Andy está bailando y escribiendo mensajes con el celular, Janet está bailando y Tim está grabando a Andy y a Janet con su cámara.
3. Tess y Patricia están en una cafetería. Patricia está tomando una torta y té. Y tiene una cámara de fotos en la mano. Tess está hablando por teléfono. Ella está tomando una torta y un jugo de naranja.

Estados Unidos

The Unit

- The theme for Unit 6 is work and free-time activities in the context of different regions of the United States. The participants will perform a variety of tasks relating to sports and other free-time activities.

- The participants face the following challenges:
  - *Desafío 1*. Tim and Mack are in Miami. Their task is to win a game of dominoes in a Little Havana competition.
  - *Desafío 2*. Diana and Rita are at the Hispanic Society of America Museum in New York City. Their task is to spend the whole night in the museum.
  - *Desafío 3*. Tess and Patricia are at the Latin Grammy Awards in San Antonio, Texas. They have been asked to take photos of the musicians at the event before the show begins.
  - *Desafío 4*. Andy and Janet are in Dodger Stadium in Los Angeles. One participant will play with the team and try to hit a home run before time runs out.

Activities	Standards	Resources
Estados Unidos	1.2, 2.2, 4.1	Video

Teaching Suggestions

Warm-Up / Independent Starter

- Have students use the communicative goals of the unit as guides for their own learning expectations. They should write three things they would like to learn under each category.

The United States of America

- The United States is located in North America; two of its 50 states are not contiguous (Alaska and Hawaii). The capital of the United States is Washington DC, a federal district. Second only to Mexico, the United States is the country with the most Spanish speakers. The cities highlighted in this unit showcase four major areas of concentration for Hispanics.

Unidad 6

Estados Unidos

Desafíos en casa

DESAFÍO 2

DESAFÍO 1

▶ **To give commands and advice**

Vocabulario
El trabajo

Gramática
Imperativo afirmativo.
Verbos irregulares

Museo de la Sociedad Hispánica de Nueva York

▶ **To express intention**

Vocabulario
Los pasatiempos

Gramática
Ir a + infinitivo.
Expresiones temporales de futuro

Parque del Dominó de Miami

The Challenge

⚑ DESAFÍO 1

Parque del Dominó de Miami
Playing dominoes is a popular pastime in Miami—especially in Maximo Gomez Domino Park in the neighborhood called Little Havana, or *La Pequeña Habana*, where the famous *Calle Ocho* is located.

⚑ DESAFÍO 2

Museo de la Sociedad Hispánica de Nueva York
The Hispanic Society of America Museum, located in Manhattan (New York City), includes a free museum and reference library for studying of the arts and cultures of Spain, Portugal, and Latin America.

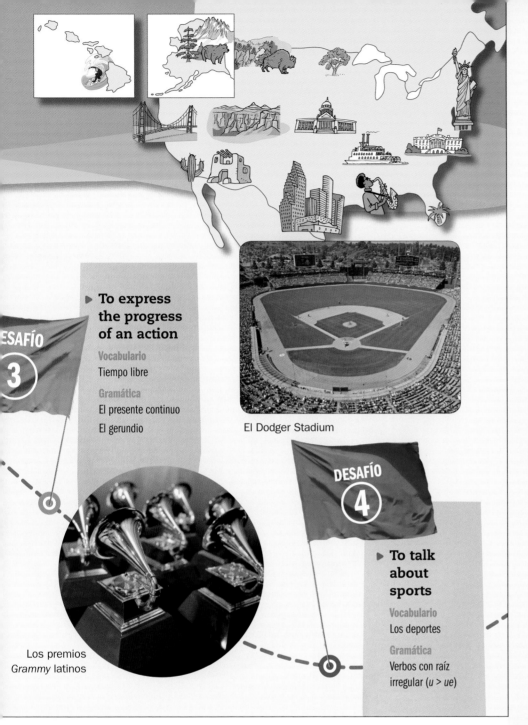

■ Have students look at a map of the United States. Ask them to locate each of the four places to which the participants will travel. Have students work in small groups to brainstorm everything they know about each of the places. Have any students ever visited Miami, New York, San Antonio, or Los Angeles?

Picture Discussion

■ Have students look at the photos, and ask them to work in pairs to share information. Suggested questions: What do they think will be asked of the participants? How long will each task take? Which task would they like to take part in?

Parque del Dominó de Miami

■ Ask students if they know of a park, or other public area in their town, where people gather to play games such as chess, dominoes, and checkers.

Museo de la Sociedad Hispánica de Nueva York

■ This picture can lead to a discussion about the architectural style of many major museums. Why do most large museums have imposing facades and pillared entrances? Could the period when the building was planned and completed influence its architecture? Are there any similar buildings in their town?

Los premios *Grammy* latinos

■ Let students know that the name *Grammy* is derived from the original name for this award: the Gramophone Award. Ask students to look at the photo and tell what the trophy represents. Have them talk about the evolution of music-playing devices from the gramophone to the players they now use.

El Dodger Stadium

■ Ask students to share what they know about baseball (game rules, sports equipment necessary to play, characteristics of the field, major teams, most important leagues, etc.).

Objectives

■ In this unit students will learn about professions and professional advice. By the end of the unit students will be able to
 – Speak about professions.
 – Use commands.
 – Give advice.
 – Express intent.
 – Describe actions.
 – Talk about habits and sports.

To express the progress of an action

Vocabulario
Tiempo libre

Gramática
El presente continuo
El gerundio

DESAFÍO 3

El Dodger Stadium

Los premios *Grammy* latinos

DESAFÍO 4

To talk about sports

Vocabulario
Los deportes

Gramática
Verbos con raíz irregular (*u > ue*)

DESAFÍO 3

Los premios *Grammy* latinos

The Latin Grammy Awards show represents a relatively new addition to the world of award shows, but it is steadily gaining in popularity. It is an annual event that takes place in the fall and acknowledges the impact and influence that Latino music has had around the world.

DESAFÍO 4

El Dodger Stadium

Dodger Stadium is the home to the Los Angeles Dodgers in California. Over the years, many famous baseball players have called Dodger Stadium their home. About 56,000 fans can pile into the stadium at one time to watch the home team take on any of the 29 other Major League Baseball teams.

La llegada

Presentation

- In this section the four pairs arrive in Washington DC. There they meet Mr. and Mrs. Goldberg, who will share with them their individual tasks in each of the four cities/states that they will visit.

- The dialogue previews:
  - Professions.
  - Free-time activities.
  - Present progressive.
  - *Querer* + infinitive.

Activities	Standards	Resources
Fotonovela	1.2	Vis. Pres.
1.	1.2, 2.2, 4.1	

Teaching Suggestions

Warm-Up / Independent Starter

- Have students write a list of all the words they already know relating to professions and free-time activities. When they have finished, these words can be compiled into a class list and displayed on the board or in a poster to be hung in the classroom as the students work through Unit 6. As new words appear in the unit, have students add them to the class list.

 La fotonovela

Before Viewing

- Ask students to look at the photos on page 91. Have them try to predict the profession or favorite activity of each person. As a class, discuss the following question: Is it possible to tell what a person does for a living just by looking at him or her? Why or why not?

While Viewing

- As students listen to the dialogue, ask them to make a note of any words that are new to them. Alternatively, they can write a list of five words that they have heard before.

After Viewing

- In small groups, have students summarize the dialogue and report back to the class by re-enacting the *fotonovela*.

En Washington DC

The four pairs meet in Washington DC, where they will receive tasks from Mr. and Mrs. Goldberg, their American hosts.

¡Bienvenidos! Yo soy John Goldberg. Soy abogado. Trabajo en una oficina.

¡Hola! Yo soy Jane Goldberg. Me dedico a las computadoras. Soy ingeniera.

90 noventa

Differentiated Instruction

DEVELOPING LEARNERS

- Have students select one of the professions mentioned in the spread. Have them enunciate each of the letters in the noun. Model pronunciation of the word and then have them repeat it. Carry on the activity until all the new words are covered.

EXPANDING LEARNERS

- Have students describe the people in the photo. What are they doing? How do they look? Then have them select one person and find the word in the spread that refers to his or her profession. Ask them if they know any people in real life that have the same job. Have them talk about this person and his or her profession. What kind of job does this person have? What are his or her responsibilities?

Hola. Yo también quiero ser ingeniera.

Yo quiero ser entrenador de fútbol americano y médico.

Diana quiere ser fotógrafa. Nos está tomando fotos.

Yo quiero jugar al tenis toda mi vida. Voy a ser un jugador profesional.

Una sonrisa, por favor. ¡Perfecto, Tess! ¡Muy bien, Patricia!

Activities

1. After doing the activity, have students create a picture dictionary by defining the words on the right (*la oficina, las computadoras, el abogado, la fotógrafa, el médico,* and *el entrenador*) and cutting photos or drawings from magazines to accompany the definitions. They should organize the dictionary pages alphabetically.

You may want to expand this activity by asking students to make a list of the feminine and masculine forms of each profession word mentioned in the *fotonovela*. For example: *el abogado → la abogada; el médico → la médica.* Let students know that some profession words do not change. In those cases, the article changes to let us know whether we are talking about a man or a woman. For example: *el periodista → la periodista; el pianista → la pianista; el piloto → la piloto.*

Answer Key

1. 1. c   2. a   3. b   4. e   5. d

Additional Resources

Fans Online activities
Practice Workbook

---

1 ¿Comprendes?

▶ **Une.** Match each question with the corresponding answer.

(A)

1. ¿Qué es el señor Goldberg?
2. ¿Dónde trabaja el señor Goldberg?
3. ¿A qué se dedica la señora Goldberg?
4. ¿Qué quiere ser Andy?
5. ¿Qué quiere ser Diana?

(B)

a. En una oficina.
b. A las computadoras.
c. Es abogado.
d. Fotógrafa.
e. Médico y entrenador.

HERITAGE LANGUAGE LEARNERS

• Encourage students to share terms they know that refer to jobs and professions. List them on the board and have other students try to guess their meanings. Erase the words from the board. Ask heritage learners to make a list with all the words they can remember. Focus on spelling.

SPECIAL-NEEDS LEARNERS

• Many students with listening disabilities may benefit from fragmentation reading and repetition. Do an initial reading of the dialogues aloud, pausing after each word. Have students repeat each word after you. Elongate the sentences, phrase by phrase, until students can link the words' meanings together.

La llegada

Presentation

- In this section, students will
  - Ask and answer questions about what someone does for a living.
  - Express a desire.
  - Express approval.

Activities	Standards	Resources
Expresiones útiles	1.2, 1.3, 4.1	
2.	1.2	
3.	1.1, 1.2, 1.3	
4.	1.1, 1.2	
5.	1.1, 1.2, 1.3	

Teaching Suggestions

Warm-Up / Independent Starter

- Ask students what their parents' current jobs or professions are and write them on the board in Spanish.
- Have students identify which of these jobs or professions are easily recognizable and which ones are not. Do the same regarding their parents' free-time activities.
- Finally, ask students to look at the expressions of approval listed in *Expresiones útiles* and translate them into English.

Preparation

- Review the *Expresiones útiles* by using them in personalized contexts. For instance, you can write the following sentences on the board: *Me dedico a la medicina. Soy doctora. Este niño es mi paciente. Él quiere ser médico también. ¡Perfecto!* Have students locate the three communicative goals in the paragraph. Then have them work in groups to practice creating other contexts.

Activities

2. Have students write a brief autobiographical statement about what activities they do now and what they want to do in the future. Ask them to read their statements aloud while you tally their responses regarding their future plans. Have them talk briefly about the requirements for some of their chosen future professions.

92

EXPRESIONES ÚTILES

Quiero jugar al tenis.

To ask and answer what someone does for a living:
  –¿A qué te dedicas?
  –Me dedico a las computadoras.

  –¿En qué trabajas?
  –Soy jugador profesional de fútbol.

To express a desire:
  –Yo **quiero ser** médica.
  –Y yo **quiero estudiar** fotografía.

To express approval:
  ¡Perfecto!
  ¡Muy bien!
  ¡Excelente!

2 **¿Qué expresión usas?**

▶ **Completa.** Complete the dialogues with the missing words.

1. –¿A qué te ___1___?
   –Soy ingeniera.

2. –¿En qué ___2___?
   –___3___ entrenador de tenis.

3. –Yo quiero ser ingeniero.
   –Yo también. ___4___ estudiar Ingeniería.

4. –Hablo español, inglés y francés.
   –¡___5___!

3 **Mucho gusto, señor Goldberg**

▶ **Escribe.** Tim sits down for an interview with Mr. Goldberg. Use the expressions above and the dialogue to create a comic strip with Tim and Mr. Goldberg.

▶ **Representa.** With a partner, perform your comic strip for the class.

¿Qué quieres ser, Tim?

Quiero ser jugador de tenis.

Differentiated Instruction

DEVELOPING LEARNERS

- Have students organize the expressions into three columns: questions, answers, and interjections. Ask students to share how they know where to list each expression.

EXPANDING LEARNERS

- In pairs, have students write lines of dialogue that connect to each expression. Encourage them to think about statements that might provoke interjection responses (for example: *¡Excelente!* or *¡Perfecto!*), and to include appropriate answers to the question expressions.

¿Quién ganará?

4 Los desafíos

 ▶ **Habla.** What challenge will each pair face? Think about this question and discuss it with your classmates.

DESAFÍO ①

Una partida de dominó

Tim y Mack

DESAFÍO ②

Una noche en el museo

Diana y Rita

DESAFÍO ③

Fotos de famosos

Tess y Patricia

DESAFÍO ④

¡Vamos a jugar!

Andy y Janet

5 Las votaciones

▶ **Decide.** You decide. You will vote to choose the most multicultural challenge. Who do you think will win?

Multicultural

noventa y tres **93**

3. Ask students to work in small groups to create 3–4 more frames for the comic strip. They can create their own frames, or use an online resource such as Make Beliefs Comix (www.makebeliefscomix.com).

¿Quién ganará?

4. Have students look at the pictures and ask them which pair they think has to face the most multicultural challenge. Elicit different answers. Remind students of the different challenges:

   1. Tim and Mack participate in a dominoes competition in Little Havana, Miami.
   2. Diana and Rita have to spend the whole night at the Hispanic Society of America Museum in New York City.
   3. Tess and Patricia have to take photos of the musicians at the Latin Grammy Awards ceremony in San Antonio, Texas.
   4. Andy and Janet are in Dodger Stadium. One of them will play with the team and try to hit a home run.

Answer Key

2. 1. dedicas
   2. trabajas; Soy
   3. Quiero
   4. Answers will vary.

3. Answers will vary. Sample answer:
   A. ¿A qué te dedicas?
   B. Me dedico a las computadoras.
   ▶ Answers will vary.

4. Answers will vary.

5. Answers will vary.

Additional Resources

Fans Online activities
Practice Workbook

HERITAGE LANGUAGE LEARNERS

- Ask heritage students to think about other ways to express interjections in *Expresiones útiles*. How do people express approval in their native country or culture? For example: *¡Chévere!* in Colombia, *¡Qué padre!* or *¡Padrísimo!* in Mexico, etc. Have the students share their expressions with the class.

SPECIAL-NEEDS LEARNERS

- Students with learning disabilities often benefit from color-coding words and phrases to classify different parts of speech.
- Have students copy the following questions and expressions. Tell them that the colors represent the following parts of speech: red = verb, blue = question word, green = preposition, purple = noun, yellow = personal pronoun.
  – ¿A qué te dedicas?
  – ¿En qué trabajas?
  – Yo quiero ser médica.
  – Yo quiero estudiar fotografía.

93

DESAFÍO 1

Dar órdenes y consejos

Presentation

- In *Desafío 1*, Tim and Mack are in Miami. Their task is to win a dominoes game in a Little Havana competition, despite the fact that most of the participants are world-class players.

- In this section students will learn:
  - Professions vocabulary.
  - Irregular informal commands.

Activities	Standards	Resources
Fotonovela	1.2, 2.1	Vis. Pres.
6.	1.2, 1.3	
7.	1.2	Audio
8.	1.2, 1.3	
9. Cultura	1.1, 1.2, 2.1, 4.2	Video

Teaching Suggestions

Warm-Up / Independent Starter

- To recycle the conjugation of the verb *ser*, have students answer the following questions:
  - *¿Cuál es tu ciudad favorita?*
  - *¿Cuáles son tus deportes favoritos?*
  - *¿Quiénes son tus mejores amigos?*

Preparation

- Ask students to imagine walking on *Calle Ocho*, the most famous street in Little Havana, where most of the street signs are in Spanish, and the language being spoken is also Spanish. What might a student do to communicate with the local residents? How might they decipher the signs? What kinds of foods might be served in the restaurants? What kinds of stores might they find on *Calle Ocho*?

La fotonovela

Before Viewing

- Ask a student volunteer to read the introduction to the task. Ask students to look at the pictures and tell what they find surprising or interesting. What scenes and people do they see in the background? Are there any women playing dominoes?

Una partida de dominó

Tim and Mack are in Miami. Their task is to win a dominoes game in a Little Havana competition. But they don't know most of the players are world-class contenders! What a difficult task!

En Internet hay información sobre la Calle Ocho.

Ven a jugar al dominó con nosotros

Abuelo, pon buena cara. No todos los jugadores son expertos.

Yo soy profesor de Matemáticas. Uso el dominó en mis clases.

¿Yo?... Yo no trabajo. Soy estudiante de Secundaria.

Yo trabajo en un hospital. Soy médico. ¿En qué trabajas tú, joven?

Continuará...

6 Detective de palabras

▶ **Completa.** Using the *fotonovela*, choose the word that completes each sentence.

1. No todos los _____ son expertos.   a. jugadores   b. profesionales
2. Yo soy _____ de Matemáticas.   a. profesor   b. estudiante
3. Trabajo en un _____.   a. hospital   b. médico
4. Soy _____ de Secundaria.   a. jugador   b. estudiante

▶ **Responde.** Answer the questions according to the dialogue.

1. ¿Quién usa el dominó en sus clases?
2. ¿Dónde trabaja el médico de la foto?
3. ¿Quién no trabaja? ¿Por qué?

Differentiated Instruction

DEVELOPING LEARNERS

- Help students identify the professions on this spread by asking them yes / no questions. For example: *¿Una vendedora vende cosas? ¿Una bibliotecaria lee libros?* After students respond, you may reformulate the questions using the verb *hacer*. *¿Qué hace una vendedora?*

EXPANDING LEARNERS

- Dominoes is a very popular game in Latin communities. Ask students to research the game and prepare a presentation on its history, strategies, and rules of dominoes. Then arrange for a set of dominoes to be brought in and allow students to play in class. If several students know the game, a tournament may be organized.

7 **Las mujeres también juegan**

 ▶ **Escucha y escribe.** In Miami, Tim and Mack meet an interesting group of players. Listen to the conversations and write the name of the person and her profession.

Mercedes Aurora

Alina Sandra

a. mesera de un restaurante cubano

b. profesora de Matemáticas

c. empresaria de una tienda de ropa

d. doctora de Medicina Familiar

8 **Ven a la Calle Ocho**

▶ **Completa.** Before the tournament, Tim writes a blog for domino lovers. Complete his text with the appropriate forms of the verb *ser*.

> El Parque del Dominó
>
> 5 de mayo. Miami
>
> Mi abuelo y yo ___1___ de California. Sabemos jugar al dominó, pero no ___2___ expertos. El Parque del Dominó ___3___ el escenario de nuestra prueba en Miami. Ustedes ___4___ muy buenos jugadores y yo no ___5___ un jugador profesional, ¡pero vamos a ganar!

CULTURA

La Calle Ocho

La Calle Ocho es la calle principal de la Pequeña Habana, un importante barrio hispano de Miami. En esta calle hay restaurantes, teatros, galerías y negocios de personas de origen cubano. Muchos cubano-americanos se reúnen (*meet*) para conversar (*talk*) y jugar al dominó en el parque Máximo Gómez, conocido como «Parque del Dominó».

9 **Piensa.** Why do communities provide public forums for cultural entertainment such as Miami's Maximo Gomez Park?

noventa y cinco **95**

After Viewing

■ Ask students who they think won the game of dominoes. Why? Did any of the players seem better suited to play dominoes well based on their profession? Why or why not?

Activities

7. After students complete the activity, have them act out the different professions in a charades-like game to see if their classmates can guess the profession.

 AUDIO SCRIPT
See page 87K

CULTURA

El Parque del Dominó

Maximo Gomez Park—the site of a lot of domino playing in the area—was named after Máximo Gómez y Báez (1836–1905), a military commander in Cuba's War of Independence (1895–1898). The area where the park is located is unofficially named Little Havana.

Answer Key

6. 1. a 2. a 3. a 4. b
  ▶ 1. El profesor de Matemáticas.
    2. En un hospital.
    3. Tim, porque es estudiante.

7. 1. Alina, doctora.
    2. Mercedes, profesora.
    3. Aurora, empresaria.
    4. Sandra, mesera.

8. 1. somos   4. son
    2. somos   5. soy
    3. es

9. Answers will vary.

Additional Resources

Fans Online activities

HERITAGE LANGUAGE LEARNERS

• Encourage heritage students to reseach and compile specific words or phrases used during and for the game. Create a list of the sayings and vocabulary on the board.

MULTIPLE INTELLIGENCES:

Logical-Mathematical Intelligence

• Review numbers using domino tiles. Bring a set to the class and pick tiles at random. Each student who is shown a tile has to name the number of dots on each side. The next student adds up the total and calls it out. Then the next one counts the sum back to zero.

Unit 6
DESAFÍO 1

Vocabulario – El trabajo

Presentation

- In this section, students will learn words related to professions, different types of work, and places of work.

Activities	Standards	Resources
Vocabulario	1.2	
10.	1.1, 1.2	
11.	1.2, 1.3	Audio
12.	1.1, 1.2, 1.3, 5.1	
13. Comunidades	1.1, 1.2, 5.1	

Teaching Suggestions

Warm-Up / Independent Starter

- Have students brainstorm a list of the jobs or professions that they already know in Spanish. Ask them to choose one job or profession and develop a concept map around it. Challenge them to include at least ten related words.

Preparation

- Ask students to look at the pictures for the professions vocabulary. Have students separate the vocabulary into a chart like this one:

Persona	Lugar
la abogada	la oficina
el maestro	la escuela

Activities

10. Alternatively, have students write down the answers for this activity.

12. Are there other people who do the jobs listed? For example: who else might teach students? Have students brainstorm different types of jobs that might relate to the descriptions.

13. In order to help students, ask them to look at jobs posted on several job-placement sites. Have them make a list of ads that mention the need for more than one language for the job (for example: "bilingual a plus" or "knowledge of Spanish required"). Have them report to the class about how many jobs they found that require / recommend knowledge of more than one language and what those jobs were.

96

Vocabulario

El trabajo

Las profesiones

 Soy directora de un hospital. Soy médica.

¿En qué trabajas?

Lugares de trabajo

 Trabajo en una oficina.

 Somos empleadas de una fábrica.

 Trabajo en una escuela.

 Trabajo en una obra.

 la abogada
 el secretario
 la entrenadora
 el maestro
la ingeniera

10 **¿De quién es?**

▶ **Habla.** With a partner, take turns asking and answering about the profession with which these items are associated.

Modelo 1. A. ¿De quién es el portafolios?
B. Es de la abogada.

 (1) el portafolios
(2) la raqueta
(3) las tizas
(4) el casco
(5) los auriculares

▶ **Habla.** Now ask and answer questions with your partner about the places where the professions above are performed.

Modelo A. ¿Dónde trabaja la abogada?
B. La abogada trabaja en una oficina.

Differentiated Instruction

DEVELOPING LEARNERS

- Have students create a list with the names of five friends. Have them pair the names with the professions they would most likely be successful in as adults.

EXPANDING LEARNERS

- After breaking students into pairs, have them practice a dialogue using the provided vocabulary to say what they are interested in, what job or profession they would like to have, and where they would work.

11 Futuros profesionales

 ▶ **Escucha y escribe.** The characters are talking about their future careers. Listen to their statements and report the information.

Modelo 1. *Janet quiere ser maestra de Música.*

| ① Janet | ② Tim | ③ Diana | ④ Andy | ⑤ Tess |

12 Tareas y profesiones

▶ **Escribe.** Write what professional would do each of the following tasks.

1. dirigir la construcción del aeropuerto
2. enseñar a los estudiantes
3. organizar la agenda del día
4. preparar a los atletas
5. defender a sus clientes
6. curar a los enfermos

▶ **Escribe.** Write sentences about each professional's job.

Modelo 1. el ingeniero
→ *Los ingenieros dirigen la construcción del aeropuerto.*

 ▶ **Habla.** Now talk with a classmate about the professions above. Which would you prefer to have and why? Which would you not like to have?

COMUNIDADES

PROFESIONES BILINGÜES

En muchas profesiones es necesario hablar dos o más lenguas. Abogados, enfermeros, médicos y policías son ejemplos de personas que pueden usar el español en su trabajo diario. Si hablas varias lenguas, puedes tener más y mejores trabajos.

13 Piensa. What jobs in your community require speaking a second language? How might you use Spanish in your future profession?

noventa y siete 97

 AUDIO SCRIPT
See page 87K

COMUNIDADES

Profesiones bilingües

In the current global economy, there is a tremendous need for workers who are proficient in more than one language. Since there are more than 40 million Spanish speakers in the United States, companies that offer services to Spanish speakers tend to make more profit than those that do not. Therefore, companies are often willing to pay Spanish-speaking employees more.

Answer Key

10. Answers will vary. Sample answer:
   A. ¿De quién es la raqueta?
   B. Es de la entrenadora.
   ▶ Answers will vary. Sample answer:
   A. ¿Dónde trabaja la entrenadora?
   B. La entrenadora trabaja en la escuela.

11. 2. Tim quiere ser jugador profesional de tenis.
   3. Diana quiere ser fotógrafa.
   4. Andy quiere ser o médico o entrenador.
   5. Tess quiere ser ingeniera.

12. 1. el/la ingeniero(a)   4. el/la entrenador(a)
   2. el/la maestro(a)   5. el/la abogado(a)
   3. el/la secretario(a)   6. el/la médico(a)
   ▶ 2. Los maestros enseñan a los estudiantes.
   3. Los secretarios organizan la agenda del día.
   4. Los entrenadores preparan a los atletas.
   5. Los abogados defienden a sus clientes.
   6. Los médicos curan a los enfermos.

13. Answers will vary.

Additional Resources

Fans Online activities
Practice Workbook

97

Unit 6
DESAFÍO 1

Gramática – Imperativo afirmativo. Verbos irregulares

Presentation

▪ In this section, students will learn:
- Irregular informal commands.
- How to form commands with pronouns.

Activities	Standards	Resources
Gramática	1.2, 3.1, 4.1	
14.	1.1, 1.2, 3.2, 4.1	
15.	1.2, 1.3	
16.	1.2, 3.1	Audio
17.	1.2, 1.3	
18. Cultura	1.1, 1.2, 3.2, 5.2	
Tu desafío	1.2, 5.2	

Teaching Suggestions

Warm-Up / Independent Starter

▪ Have students look at the informal commands in the grammar boxes. Have them brainstorm about times in their personal lives during which they may have used such commands in their home language. For instance, yelling at a younger sibling: *Leave my room!*; talking to a friend: *Come here!*

Preparation

▪ Now ask students to think of how these commands might sound in Spanish. Yelling at a younger sibling: *¡Sal de mi cuarto!* Talking to a friend: *¡Ven aquí!*

▪ Have students provide random examples for you to translate and ask them to focus on tone rather than meaning. Ask them if the commands sound the same in both languages. You may want to recycle the Spanish phrase *por favor*.

Activities

14. A homophone is a word that is pronounced the same as another word, but differs in meaning; for example: *sal* = salt and leave! Ask students to think about any other homophones in Spanish that they may know. Here are some examples:

tú (you)   *tu* (your)
sí (yes)   *si* (if)

Gramática

Imperativo afirmativo. Verbos irregulares

• Some common tú commands have irregular conjugations.

VERBOS IRREGULARES. IMPERATIVO

tener (to have)	hacer (to do)	poner (to put)	venir (to come)	salir (to leave)		ser (to be)	decir (to say)	ir (to go)
ten	haz	pon	ven	sal		sé	di	ve

Ten un buen día.
Haz una ensalada.
Pon el libro en la estantería.
Ana, ven a la cocina, por favor.

Sal de tu cuarto, por favor.
Sé sincera.
Di la verdad.
Ve a casa de tus abuelos.

• To form the tú command of tener, hacer, poner, venir, and salir, detach the infinitive ending:

ten-er → ten   hac-er → haz   pon-er → pon
ven-ir → ven   sal-ir → sal

• If the tú form of a verb is irregular in the present tense, it is also irregular in the tú command.

tú empiezas → empieza   tú duermes → duerme

• Remember that object and reflexive pronouns follow and are attached to the command.

Hay que poner la mesa. Ponla, por favor.   Hazle una hamburguesa.

14 **Piensa.** How would you know if someone was using sal to mean *salt* or *leave*?

15 **Consejos de los profesionales**

▶ **Completa.** Using the verbs above, complete these professional recommendations with the appropriate command form.

Para ser un buen maestro, __1__ paciencia con los estudiantes.

Para saber qué hace un ingeniero, __3__ a mi fábrica.

Para trabajar bien, __5__ cada cosa en su lugar.

Para ser una buena entrenadora, __2__ ejercicio con tus atletas.

Para ser una buena secretaria, __4__ ordenada.

Differentiated Instruction

DEVELOPING LEARNERS

• Write the *tú* commands of the charted verbs on the board. Have students read each aloud as their classmates act out the commands. This can be played like a "Simon says" game in which one student (or a small group of students) calls out a command as their classmates act each one out.

EXPANDING LEARNERS

• List the irregular *tú* commands on the board. Have students use them in complete sentences. For example: *Juan, ten paciencia con la mascota.* Ask each student to elaborate and give a reason for each command. For example: *Juan no tiene paciencia con la mascota.*

16 La jueza Estrella Rodríguez

▶ **Escucha y decide.** Listen to Judge Rodríguez talking to Tim at a school Career Fair, and point out which pieces of advice Tim receives.

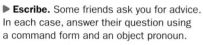

1. Sé honesto.
2. Ve a los eventos culturales de la Calle Ocho.
3. Sé una persona responsable.
4. Pon atención a las personas de tu comunidad.
5. Haz tus tareas todos los días.
6. Di siempre la verdad.

> Estudia mucho, Tim.

17 Consejos para la vida diaria

▶ **Escribe.** Some friends ask you for advice. In each case, answer their question using a command form and an object pronoun.

> ¿Dónde pongo los libros?

1. ¿Dónde pongo los libros? - en la estantería
2. ¿Cuándo hago mis tareas? - después de clase
3. ¿Cuándo saco la basura? - antes de cenar
4. ¿Dónde hago deporte? - en el gimnasio de la escuela
5. ¿Dónde compro la ropa? - en el centro comercial
6. ¿Cuándo ordeno mi dormitorio? - durante el fin de semana

> **Ponlos** en la estantería.

CULTURA

Cristina Saralegui

La periodista *(journalist)* Cristina Saralegui es famosa en todo el mundo hispano gracias a su programa de televisión *El show de Cristina*. Cristina es de origen cubano y vive en Miami. Para ella la clave del éxito es «hablar claro, hablar con mi acento, con mi corazón…».

18 **Piensa.** How does being a talk-show host and a magazine editor contribute to Cristina's influence on Hispanic Americans? Would you like to be in her position?

▶ **TU DESAFÍO** Use the website to learn more about Cristina Saralegui.

Gramática – Imperativo afirmativo. Verbos irregulares

16. Have students act out a scene from *Judge Judy*. In small groups, students can brainstorm a simple case / problem. Then have them bring their case to the "judge" and ask her to give her ruling using commands.

17. Have students design a poster for the classroom using commands and suggestions for how to succeed in Spanish class.

AUDIO SCRIPT
See page 87K

CULTURA

Cristina Saralegui

Cristina Saralegui was born in Cuba in 1948. She and her family immigrated to the United States in 1960. Although she started her career as a journalist, she is better known as the host of her world-famous *El show de Cristina*. According to *People Magazine,* Cristina is one of the most influential and successful Hispanic figures in the United States.

Answer Key

14. By using context clues.

15. 1. ten 3. ven 5. pon
2. haz 4. sé

16. 1. sí 3. sí 5. no
2. no 4. sí 6. sí

17. 1. Ponlos en la estantería.
2. Hazlas después de clase.
3. Sácala antes de cenar.
4. Hazlo en el gimnasio de la escuela.
5. Cómprala en el centro comercial.
6. Ordénalo durante el fin de semana.

18. Answers will vary.

Additional Resources

Fans Online activities
Practice Workbook

HERITAGE LANGUAGE LEARNERS

- Using what they already know about Cristina Saralegui, ask students to write a paragraph about her in the first person. They should talk about her strengths as a journalist and editor. What personal qualities make her successful? Students should use *tú* commands in their writings to give personal advice as if coming from Cristina.

SPECIAL-NEEDS LEARNERS

- To assist students with listening disabilities, provide a script that students can read the night before. Have students read the script aloud and record themselves. Students will be able to recognize the listening passage when they listen to it in class.

DESAFÍO 1

Comunicación

Presentation

- In this section, students will practice:
  - Professions vocabulary.
  - Irregular informal commands.
  - The verb *ser*.

Activities	Standards	Resources
19.	1.1, 1.2, 1.3	Audio
20.	1.1, 1.2, 1.3, 5.1	
21.	1.1, 1.2, 1.3, 5.1	
22. Final del desafío	1.2, 1.3, 2.1, 5.2	
Tu desafío	1.2, 1.3, 5.2	

Teaching Suggestions

Warm-Up / Independent Starter

- Have students identify the affirmative commands in these sentences. Have students transform the ones that are not into affirmative commands.
  - *No voy a la tienda.*
  - *Ven a la clase de Español mañana.*
  - *Compra tus propios lápices.*
  - *No tomas tus vitaminas.*

Preparation

- Ask students to think about what profession or job they might like to have in the future. If they don't know the name for it in Spanish, have them look it up in a Spanish-English dictionary. Gather all the students' dream professions and create an *Adivina quién* (Guess Who?) chart with the information as shown in the example below.

abogado	*maestra*	*ingeniera*
dentista	*veterinaria*	*cantante*
secretaria	*entrenador*	*jugador de béisbol*
contador	*maestro*	*médico*

- Give students a copy of the chart and have them walk around the room asking their classmates questions to find out who chose which profession. The student who fills in each square with the name of a classmate wins!

Comunicación

19 **Héroes de la comunidad**

▶ **Lee y habla.** A middle school in Miami is hosting a Career Day. Read the announcement, then talk with a partner about why you would attend this event. Which professionals would you like to talk to? What questions would you ask?

Modelo A. ¿Quieres asistir al evento?
B. *Sí, quiero asistir porque quiero hablar con un ingeniero…*

Héroes de la comunidad visitan la escuela

Hoy, martes 23, trabajadores de la comunidad visitan nuestra escuela. El evento «Todos podemos ser héroes» es a las doce del mediodía en el gimnasio. Ven y habla con médicos, enfermeras, ingenieros, secretarios, empresarios y empleados de fábricas. ¡Aprovecha esta oportunidad para empezar a decidir tu futuro!

 ▶ **Escucha y escribe.** Some of the guests for this event have left messages for the principal. Listen and note who is attending and who is not.

1. Elena Rosas
2. Fabián Candelas
3. Esperanza Esparza
4. Juan Hernández
5. Cristóbal Barrios
6. Marisa Jiménez

20 **Un estudiante organizado**

▶ **Escribe.** You are organizing a Career Fair in your school. Draw up a schedule for seven community workers.

Modelo

Agenda para el evento

1. Maestro de español. Cafetería, a las 10 de la mañana.
2. Ingeniero. Biblioteca, a las 11:15 de la mañana.

Sí, quiero trabajar con niños y me gusta el español.

¿Quieres hablar con el maestro de Español?

Ve a la cafetería. El maestro habla a las diez de la mañana.

 ▶ **Habla.** With a partner, role-play host and student. Use your schedule and make sure to include informal commands in your conversation.

Differentiated Instruction

DEVELOPING LEARNERS

- Have students make a flow chart summarizing the rules of irregular *tú* commands formation. Have them number each step and use the different verbs to illustrate it.

EXPANDING LEARNERS

- Ask students to write three questions for three different occupations they are interested in. Next, break students into pairs and have them role-play student and professional using the lists of questions they created. Encourage students to use commands when playing the role of the professional.

21 El consejero informal

▶ **Lee y escribe.** You write the advice column in your class's newspaper. Read the e-mail that a classmate has sent you and take notes on the student's problems.

Querido consejero:

Tengo problemas. No tengo muchos amigos y no voy bien en la escuela. No tengo paciencia y por eso no hago mis tareas todos los días. No pongo atención en la clase de Historia porque no me gusta. No digo siempre la verdad a mis padres y no voy al parque con mis amigos. ¿Puedes ayudarme?

Gato Triste

▶ **Escribe y representa.** Write a response to Gato Triste. Then role-play the situation with a partner using irregular commands.

Modelo A. *No voy bien en la escuela.*
         B. *Pon más atención y estudia más.*

Final del desafío

¿Qué hago, Tim?
¿Con qué ficha salgo?

Sal con la ficha nueve y ocho.

22 Juego de dominó

▶ **Crea y escribe.** You have to help Tim and Mack win the dominoes game! Create your own dominoes set, using professions and related words instead of numbers. Write the rules to your new game in Spanish, using the irregular *tú* commands (*pon, ten, haz*, etc.).

▶ **Juega.** Now play your dominoes game with a partner.

 → TU DESAFÍO Earn points for your own challenge! Listen to the questions for your *Minientrevista Desafío 1* on the website and write your answers.

HERITAGE LANGUAGE LEARNERS

• Hispanic work cultures and environments differ from those of the United States in several aspects. For example: the Spanish tradition of a *siesta* (nap after lunch, usually at home) has been adopted by many Spanish-speaking countries. Ask students if there is a tradition of the *siesta* in their home countries. Encourage them to ask their parents or a family member if they are not sure. Have students set up a debate in which one side argues for a *siesta* break for your school and the other argues against it.

MULTIPLE INTELLIGENCES:

Interpersonal Intelligence

• Have students think about the kinds of jobs that they would be best suited for in the future. Then ask students to create a "career test" by writing a list of ten questions to ask their partners. The questions should be aimed at determining the kinds of jobs their partners might be well suited for. For example: Do you enjoy working on your own, or working as part of a team? Then in pairs, have students interview each other. Finally, using their partner's answers, ask students to write a report that gives recommendations for their future careers.

Activities

19. Ask students to think about the profession that they would most like to see represented at a Career Day in their school. Next have them write their names on sticky notes. Create a bar graph on the board using the students' sticky notes to see which career would be the most popular.

20. Ask students to imagine what would happen if one of their guests for Career Day didn't show up! Have them write a list of three commands they would use to tell a friend or assistant what to do. For example: *Haz una llamada a la directora. Di el problema a la directora. Ve a mi oficina para…*

21. Ask students to write a similar letter, but this time from Gato Triste's mother or father. What might Gato's parents say about his behavior?

22. Have students try their hand at playing dominoes. You may wish to bring a set of dominoes to class, or ask students if they have one at home that they can bring.

> 🎧 **AUDIO SCRIPT**
> See page 87K

Answer Key

19. Answers will vary. Sample answer: Quiero asistir porque quiero hablar con un entrenador.

▶ 1. no   4. no
  2. sí   5. sí
  3. sí   6. sí

20. Answers will vary.
▶ Answers will vary.

21. Answers will vary.
▶ Answers will vary.

22. Answers will vary.

Additional Resources

Fans Online activities
Practice Workbook

DESAFÍO 2

Expresar intención

Presentation

- In *Desafío 2*, Diana and Rita are at the Hispanic Society of America Museum in New York City. Their task is to spend the whole night in the museum.

- In this section students will learn:
  - Words of intention.
  - Words for basic free-time activities.
  - Simple future.

Activities	Standards	Resources
Fotonovela	1.2	Vis. Pres.
23.	1.2, 1.3, 5.1	
24.	1.2, 1.3	
25.	1.2, 1.3	Audio
26. Cultura	1.1, 1.2, 3.2, 4.2	

Teaching Suggestions

Warm-Up / Independent Starter

- Have students brainstorm three activities that they would do if they were somehow locked into their school overnight (for example: *cantar, estudiar, jugar baloncesto*).

Preparation

- Ask for a student volunteer to read the introduction to Diana and Rita's challenge. How many students would do the same as Rita? How many would want to do the same as Diana? Learning what they could not do, how many students think they would become bored?

La fotonovela

Before Viewing

- Ask students to look at the pictures and tell what they find surprising or interesting. What type of art do they think they might find in this museum? In what ways might this museum be different from or similar to a museum that they have already visited?

After Viewing

- Ask students to guess what Diana and Rita do all night in the museum. What would they do if they were asked to spend a night in a museum?

102

Una noche en el museo

Diana and Rita are at The Hispanic Society of America Museum in New York City. Their task is to spend the whole night in the museum. What will they do to pass the time?

¡Toda la noche en el museo! ¡Me gusta la prueba! ¿Qué vamos a hacer?

¡Yo voy a ver muchas obras de arte! Mira este cuadro de Joaquín Sorolla.

Yo voy a escribir mensajes a mis amigos y voy a hablar por teléfono con ellos.

¡Pero Diana, no podemos usar el teléfono ni la computadora!

¡¿Qué?! ¿No vamos a poder hablar por teléfono ni usar la computadora durante toda la noche?

Continuará...

23 **Detective de palabras**

▶ **Completa.** Diana and Rita want to do different things in the museum. What are their plans? Complete their statements.

RITA: Yo voy a ___1___.
DIANA: Yo voy a ___2___ y voy a ___3___.

▶ **Escribe.** What are your plans for today? Write three sentences to express them.

Modelo *Hoy voy a jugar al fútbol con mis amigos.*

102 ciento dos

Differentiated Instruction

DEVELOPING LEARNERS

- Have two volunteers read the dialogue between Diana and Rita. Briefly discuss what the dialogue is about. Assist students by asking specific yes / no questions. For example: Does Diana want to talk on the phone? Does Rita want to look at art?

EXPANDING LEARNERS

- Have students choose an American city they want to visit and do research on it. What and where are the museums dedicated to Americans with Hispanic heritage in that city? Have students write a paragraph that answers the following questions: *¿Qué ciudad vas a visitar? ¿Cómo se llama el museo? ¿Qué puedes ver en el museo?*

24 ¿Qué quieren hacer?

▶ **Escribe.** Using the *fotonovela*, write what Diana and Rita want to do, and tell whether they can do each activity or not.

Modelo   *Rita quiere ver obras de arte. Puede ver muchas obras de arte en el museo.*

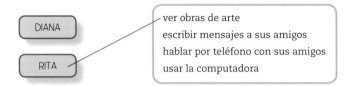

DIANA

RITA

- ver obras de arte
- escribir mensajes a sus amigos
- hablar por teléfono con sus amigos
- usar la computadora

25 Vamos a pasear por Nueva York

▶ **Escucha y une.** Diana and Rita are talking about their plans in New York. Listen and match the people in column A with the actions in column B.

(A)	(B)
1. Diana y Rita	a. va a tomar muchas fotos.
2. Diana	b. van a ir a Central Park.
3. Rita	c. va a ir a la Estatua de la Libertad.
4. Los padres de Diana	d. va a visitar el Metropolitan Museum.
5. Rita y Patricia	e. van a ir a Nueva York en verano.
6. Tim	f. van a ir de compras a Times Square.

CULTURA

La Sociedad Hispánica de América

La Sociedad Hispánica de América es una organización fundada en 1904 para promover las culturas hispanas. Tiene una importante colección de arte y objetos culturales de España, Portugal, Latinoamérica y las islas Filipinas. Entre los artistas más famosos con obras en el museo están Diego Velázquez, Bartolomé Murillo y Francisco de Goya. También hay libros y manuscritos raros y especiales.

26 **Piensa.** What items would you choose to put in a museum that promotes American culture, arts, and literature?

ciento tres 103

HERITAGE LANGUAGE LEARNERS

• Draw students' attention to the New York City landmarks on this spread. Have them share what they know about New York City's Hispanic presence. Ask them which other cities in the United States are similar in this regard. Have them think about the reasons these cities have developed such large concentrations of Hispanics.

TOTAL PHYSICAL RESPONSE (TPR)

• Have students suggest at least five things Diana and Rita could do at the museum. Write the list on the board. As you read each sentence, have students perform the action. For example: *ver obras de arte.*

Activities

25. Have students visit the following website to learn more about New York City's top attractions: http://gonyc.about.com/od/bestofnewyorkcity/tp/topattractions.htm. Then ask students to make a postcard of their favorite site using a photo from the website on one side, and a message to a friend (in Spanish, of course!) on the other side.

26. Have students work in pairs to research what to put in this museum. Have them explore this website: http://www.hispanicsociety.org/hispanic/collections.htm.

AUDIO SCRIPT
See page 87K

CULTURA

La Sociedad Hispánica de América

Archer Milton Huntington (1870–1955) founded The Hispanic Society of America on May 18, 1904. The Hispanic Society hosts a free museum and reference library. The library houses thousands of manuscripts and over 250,000 books. In addition to its permanent collection, the Society holds special exhibitions.

Answer Key

23. 1. ver muchas obras de arte
2. escribir mensajes.
3. hablar por teléfono.
▶ Answers will vary.

24. Answers will vary.

25. 1. b   2. a   3. d   4. e   5. f   6. c

26. Answers will vary.

Additional Resources

Fans Online activities

Unit 6

DESAFÍO 2

Vocabulario – Los pasatiempos

Presentation

- In this section, students will learn:
  - Words related to basic free-time activities.
  - Artistic activities.
  - Sports activities.

Activities	Standards	Resources
Vocabulario	1.2	
27.	1.1, 1.2, 1.3	Audio
28.	1.1, 1.2, 1.3	
29.	1.1, 1.3	
30. Conexiones	1.1, 1.2, 3.1, 3.2	

Teaching Suggestions

Warm-Up / Independent Starter

- Ask students to list all the vocabulary in alphabetical order.

Preparation

- Ask students to look at the pictures for the pastimes and to write a list of their five favorite activities in alphabetical order. Then students can walk around the room to find out which classmates share the same favorite activities (this can be continued for the rest of the activities on the list). Sample dialogue:

  A. ¿Cuál es tu actividad favorita?
  B. Mi actividad favorita es nadar.
  A. Mi actividad favorita es leer un libro.

Activities

27. Have students debate the best and worst activities.

28. Sometimes we do activities in untraditional places. Ask students to think of unusual places for doing different things. For example:

En la piscina, me gusta leer.
En el jardín, me gusta tocar el piano.

29. Have students brainstorm five items that their classmates might need to buy in order to practice their favorite activities. For example:

Para tocar el piano necesitas comprar un piano.
Para bailar necesitas comprar zapatos nuevos.

104

Vocabulario

Los pasatiempos

 bailar

 cantar

 tocar el piano

 actuar

 pintar

 caminar

 hacer deporte / practicar deportes

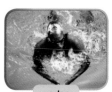 montar en bicicleta

 nadar

 viajar

 escuchar música

 leer un libro

escribir mensajes

27 **Una chica muy interesante**

 ▶ **Escucha y clasifica.** Listen as Diana talks about her likes and dislikes and classify her activities and pastimes in a table like the one below.

Me gusta mucho	Me gusta	No me gusta	No me gusta nada
	bailar		

 ▶ **Escribe y habla.** Use a similar table to classify your own likes and dislikes. Then talk with a partner about them.

Modelo No me gusta nada pintar. ¿A ti te gusta?

104 ciento cuatro

Differentiated Instruction

DEVELOPING LEARNERS

- Have students make flashcards with the new vocabulary from page 104. They should write the Spanish word on one side and the English one on the other. Ask students to work in pairs to help each other practice.

EXPANDING LEARNERS

- Ask students to choose five of their favorite activities from the ones listed on page 104. Have them say when and where they can do each activity, and why they like each one. Have them fill in a chart with their answers like the one below.

	¿Cuándo?	¿Dónde?	¿Por qué?
cantar	Por la tarde	En la escuela	Es divertido

- Have the student write a sentence with all the information from the chart. For example:
  Me gusta *cantar* *por la tarde* *en la escuela* porque *es divertido*.

104

28 **¿Adónde voy?**

 ▶ **Habla.** Ask your partner about the places below, using the verb *poder*, and say whether you like or don't like the activity mentioned. Take turns.

Modelo A. *¿Qué podemos hacer en el jardín?*
　　　　 B. *Podemos leer.*
　　　　 A. *¡Qué bueno! Me gusta mucho leer.*

1. En Times Square…
2. En Central Park…
3. En la Estatua de la Libertad…
4. En la Manhattan Artistic Academy…
5. En el jardín del hotel…

▶ **Escribe.** When, where, and with whom do you do the activities above in your city? Write sentences.

Modelo *En verano, leo buenos libros en la biblioteca con mis hermanos.*

29 **Tu favorito**

▶ **Escribe.** Choose and rank some activities from the *Vocabulario* according to your preference. Write five sentences.

Modelo *Me gusta más bailar que hacer deporte.*

 ▶ **Habla.** In a group, talk with your classmates and compare your choices.

Modelo A. *A mí me gusta más bailar que hacer deporte. ¿Y a ustedes?*
　　　　 B. *A mí me gusta mucho hacer deporte. Me gusta jugar al tenis…*

 CONEXIONES: INGLÉS

Las palabras prestadas

El español y el inglés intercambian palabras y expresiones. Por ejemplo, los nombres de algunos deportes, como el *golf*, el *voleibol* y el *fútbol*, vienen del inglés. En cambio, las palabras en inglés *rodeo*, *lasso* y *salsa* tienen su origen en el español.

30 **Piensa.** Do you know any other words in English that come from Spanish? What can we learn about the culture of a place whose words we have borrowed?

HERITAGE LANGUAGE LEARNERS

• To learn more about each other, have students bring in pictures of themselves doing something that is typical in their or their family's country of origin. Ask students to talk about the activity in detail. Who else is in the picture? Where did it take place? For how long have they been interested in the activity? Does anyone else in the class share the same interest?

MULTIPLE INTELLIGENCES:

Bodily-Kinesthetic Intelligence

• Have students bring sports equipment or accessories they use for their hobbies to the class. On an index card, each student should write what it is and what it is used for in Spanish. Students place the item and the card on their desk. Have everyone walk around and examine what was brought in. At the end of the activity, vote on who gets the Strangest Item Award.

Vocabulario – Los pasatiempos

 AUDIO SCRIPT
See page 87K

 CONEXIONES: INGLÉS

Las palabras prestadas

Along with many words borrowed from Spanish in the English language, many place names in this country also come from the Spanish language—especially in the southern part of the country which was once Mexican territory. Ask students to write a list of place names that come from Spanish. They can arrange them in a chart like the one below.

States	Cities	Others
Colorado	El Paso	Sierra Nevada

Answer Key

27. Me gusta mucho: caminar y montar en bicicleta.
　　 Me gusta: tocar el piano, bailar, cantar, escuchar música y leer libros.
　　 No me gusta: actuar en obras de teatro y nadar.
　　 No me gusta nada: ver la televisión.
　　 ▶ Answers will vary.

28. Answers will vary. Sample answer:
　　 A. ¿Qué podemos hacer en Central Park?
　　 B. En Central Park podemos montar en bicicleta.
　　 A. ¡Qué bueno! Me gusta montar en bicicleta.
　　 ▶ Answers will vary. Sample answer:
　　 En primavera, monto en bicicleta con mis amigos.

29. Answers will vary. Sample answer:
　　 Me gusta más cantar que bailar.
　　 ▶ Answers will vary.

30. Answers will vary.

Additional Resources

Fans Online activities
Practice Workbook

105

DESAFÍO 2

Gramática – *Ir a* + infinitivo

Presentation

- In this section, students will learn:
  - How to express intention.
  - *Ir a* + infinitive.
  - Future time expressions.

Activities	Standards	Resources
Gramática	1.2, 3.1, 4.1	
31.	1.2, 3.2, 4.1	
32.	1.2, 1.3	
33.	1.2, 1.3	Audio
34.	1.2, 1.3, 5.1	
35. Comunidades	1.1, 1.2, 3.2, 4.2	

Teaching Suggestions

Warm-Up / Independent Starter

- Have students write about one thing that they are going to do after school and one thing that they plan to do tomorrow.

Preparation

- Have students create a timeline with the time expressions, placing the earliest time expression on the left and the latest one on the right. For example:

```
+------------+------------+------------
hoy        mañana      mañana
           por la mañana  por la tarde
```

- Encourage students to use the timeline to talk about things they do at those specific times.

Activities

31. Ask students to provide more examples using forms of the verb *ir* in two similar sentences. For example: *Yo voy a tener un examen en la escuela mañana* and *Yo voy a la escuela.*

34. Ask for volunteers to share their plans with the rest of the class and tell who else is doing the same.

35. Ask students to think about places in the Spanish-speaking world that they have seen or heard about where people engage in outdoor and sports activities. What types of activities do the people do in those places?

Gramática

Ir a + infinitivo

- To express the intention to do something, use this structure:

  | ir a + infinitivo | Ellos **van a trabajar** en Nueva York.   Yo **voy a viajar** a México.

  The structure *ir a* + infinitive is one way to express the future.

- Notice that only ir is conjugated; the second verb remains in the infinitive.

  Nosotras **vamos a escuchar** música.

Expresiones temporales de futuro

- When you express intention or future plans, you can use some adverbs:

ahora   luego   hoy   mañana
        después

Luego vamos a ir al parque.   Mañana voy a descansar.

- To be more specific about the time, you can use these expressions:

esta mañana	mañana por la mañana	la próxima semana	el próximo año
esta tarde	mañana por la tarde	la semana que viene	el año que viene
esta noche	mañana por la noche		

Esta noche vamos al cine.   Yo **voy a ir** a México el próximo año.

31 **Compara.** What is the difference between Yo voy a comprar verduras mañana and Yo voy al mercado? Do you use the same verb *(to go)* to express both ideas in English?

32 **Nuestro calendario**

▶ **Escribe.** Read Diana's notes and write what people are going to do.

Modelo   Próxima semana. Tess al parque.
→ *La próxima semana Tess va a ir al parque.*

1. Hoy, 2:00 p. m. Todos al restaurante.
2. Hoy, 7:00 p. m. Yo al gimnasio.
3. Mañana, 8:00 p. m. Tim a la biblioteca.
4. Esta tarde, 6:00 p. m. Rita y yo al cine.

Differentiated Instruction

DEVELOPING LEARNERS

- Write the sentences below on the board. Tell student to fill in the blanks with the proper forms of *ir*. Next, ask them to circle the infinitive in every sentence. When the activity is complete, discuss how the Spanish structure compares to the English *going to*.

1. … a lavarme el pelo hoy. (Voy)
2. Él … a comer a las seis de la tarde. (va)
3. Mis amigos y yo … a ir al cine esta noche. (vamos)
4. María … a dormir toda la mañana. (va)
5. Ustedes … a llamar a Rita a las cuatro de la tarde. (van)

EXPANDING LEARNERS

- Have students write a tentative schedule for tomorrow. Then have them work with a partner to coordinate the following day's activities. Students should use the plans they have already made and try to work around them. For example:

A. ¿Qué vas a hacer mañana, Pedro?
B. Voy a ir al médico a las ocho.
A. ¿Quieres ir al cine a las cinco de la tarde?
B. No puedo, voy a ir al gimnasio a las cinco.

33 **Los planes de Rita**

 ▶ **Escucha e identifica.** What activities will Rita be doing in New York? Listen and write the letter of each activity in the order you hear.

 (A)

(B)

(C)

(D)

(E)

(F)

 ▶ **Escucha y escribe.** Listen again and write a sentence saying what Rita does at each time.

Modelo *Ahora Rita va a jugar al baloncesto con Andy y Tim.*

1. ahora   **2.** esta tarde   **3.** esta noche

4. mañana por la mañana   **5.** mañana por la tarde   **6.** la próxima semana

34 **Mañana voy a...**

▶ **Escribe.** What are your plans for tomorrow morning, afternoon, and evening? Write sentences telling two things you will do at each time.

 ▶ **Habla.** Now talk with two classmates about your plans. Who else is going to do the same things as you?

COMUNIDADES

CENTRAL PARK

Central Park es un famoso parque de Nueva York. Ofrece muchas actividades para jóvenes y mayores. Visitantes de todo el mundo pasan tiempo allí, porque pueden caminar, ver animales, asistir al teatro o a conciertos. Central Park es un oasis en medio de la ciudad.

35 **Compara.** Do you have something like Central Park where you live? Where do people go in your community for outdoor activities? Do visitors from other countries ever go there?

HERITAGE LANGUAGE LEARNERS

• In some Latin countries, people have a tendency to be more relaxed about punctuality. Discuss the phenomenon of «Latin time» with students. Ask them how this could affect making plans and organizing events.

COOPERATIVE LEARNING

• For further practice, have small groups plan a party celebrating an upcoming holiday. Students should plan where, when and what the theme is, how many people are going to come and which activities are going to take place. Designate responsibilities for planning. Once all the information is gathered, have students design the invitation.

 **AUDIO SCRIPT**
See page 87K

COMUNIDADES

Central Park

Located in Manhattan, Central Park is one of the most recognized landmarks of New York City. It opened in 1859 and was declared a National Historic Landmark in 1963. Concerts, exhibitions, and other forms of entertainment bring more than 25 million visitors each year.

Answer Key

31. The first sentence expresses the intention to do something in the future, while *Yo voy al mercado* refers to the action of going and that action's destination. In English we use the same verb (to go) to express both ideas.

32. 1. Hoy a las dos todos van a ir al restaurante.
2. Hoy a las siete de la tarde voy a ir al gimnasio.
3. Mañana a las ocho de la tarde Tim va a ir a la biblioteca.
4. Esta tarde a las seis Rita y yo vamos a ir al cine.

33. 1. E   2. C   3. F   4. B   5. A   6. D
▶ 2. Esta tarde Rita va a pintar en Central Park con Diana y Tess.
3. Esta noche Rita va a leer en su habitación.
4. Mañana por la mañana va a montar en bicicleta.
5. Mañana por la tarde va a tocar el piano.
6. La próxima semana va a cantar en el restaurante del hotel.

34. Answers will vary.
▶ Answers will vary.

35. Answers will vary.

Additional Resources

Fans Online activities
Practice Workbook

DESAFÍO 2

Comunicación

Presentation

- In this section, students will practice:
  - How to express intention.
  - *Ir a* + infinitive.
  - Future time expressions.
  - Words related to basic free-time activities.
  - Artistic and sports activities.

Activities	Standards	Resources
36.	1.2, 1.3	Audio
37.	1.1, 1.2, 1.3	
38.	1.1, 1.3	
39.	1.1, 1.3	
40. Final del desafío	1.1, 1.3	

Teaching Suggestions

Warm-Up / Independent Starter

- Have students create a weekly / monthly agenda page with several of their most important activities for the week.

Preparation

- After students have completed their Independent Starter, have them talk about each activity they will do, when they will do it, and with whom, in pairs. Then ask students to switch pairs and report what their former partner will do this week to their new partner.

- Students can then work together to create a comparison checklist of the activities they have in common.

Activities

36. Have students rate each activity according to their own tastes by saying if they like it a lot (for example: *Me gusta mucho la comida latinoamericana*), if they like it (for example: *Me gustan los conciertos*), if they don't like it (for example: *No me gusta bailar*), or if they don't like it at all (for example: *No me gusta nada asistir a las exposiciones de arte*).

You may want to create a bar graph to record the results of the class on the board. Which activity do students like the most? Which the least?

Comunicación

36 Actividades en el parque

 ▶ **Lee y escribe.** Read the advertisement. Then write an itinerary for Diana at the celebration. Make sure to tell her what she is going to do at each place.

Modelo *Esta noche vas a…*

 ▶ **Escucha y escribe.** Listen to the message Diana left for Rita. Decide which Hispanic Day activities they are going to do.

Modelo *Diana y Rita van a ir al concierto de música tropical para bailar y escuchar música latina.*

LOS HISPANOS ♥ NY

¡La Gran Manzana está de fiesta!

¡Celebra el Día de la Hispanidad en Central Park! Esta noche vamos a celebrar un concierto de música tropical. ¡Vas a mover tu cuerpo con los ritmos del merengue y la salsa! Mañana por la mañana vamos a asistir a una exposición de esculturas de formas y colores extraordinarios.

También vamos a celebrar un torneo de juegos de mesa. Después vamos a tener un almuerzo con comida latinoamericana.

¿Quieres venir? Puedes comprar tus boletos en el Museo de la Sociedad Hispánica de América.

37 Un guía neoyorquino

 ▶ **Habla.** You are volunteering as a guide in New York. Your partner will tell you what a group of tourists are going to do this afternoon. Use the information to suggest where they can go.

Modelo señora López - leer un libro

1. patricia - pintar
2. los empresarios - bailar
3. yo - nadar
4. la profesora de música - caminar y ver animales
5. nosotros - ver cuadros de pintores hispanos
6. todos - escuchar música latina

La señora López va a leer un libro esta tarde.

Ella puede leerlo en Central Park.

38 Tengo curiosidad

▶ **Escribe.** What are your classmates' future plans? Write five interview questions about the things they intend to do in the near and distant future. Use a different time expression in each.

Modelo *¿Vas a escribir correos electrónicos hoy?*

▶ **Habla.** Use your questions to interview three classmates. Report your findings to the class.

Differentiated Instruction

DEVELOPING LEARNERS

- Before beginning the activities in this spread, have pairs of students practice *ir a* + infinitive. Student A should call out a verb and student B should say when he or she is going to do the activity. For example:
  A. *comer*
  B. *Voy a comer a la una de la tarde.*
- Have students take turns as they work through the personal pronouns.

EXPANDING LEARNERS

- Tell students they've been given the opportunity to lead a tour through one of their favorite places. Have them create a three-day itinerary for a group of tourists. The itinerary should be diverse in its activities. Encourage students to state why they have planned certain activities.

39 Las vacaciones ideales

▶ **Habla.** In a small group, talk about where you are going to travel during your next vacation and what you are going to do there. Tell when you will do each thing.

¿Qué van a hacer el próximo verano?

Vamos a ir a California.

Yo voy a nadar en el océano.

Mi hermano y yo vamos a hacer deportes acuáticos.

▶ **Escribe.** Write an e-mail summarizing the plans for your friends.

Modelo

Mensaje nuevo

Para:
Cc:
Asunto:

¡Hola a todos!
El próximo verano yo voy a…

Final del desafío

Esta noche voy a…

Y yo…

También vamos a…

40 ¡Qué museo más interesante!

▶ **Escribe.** Complete the speech bubbles according to the photos. Then add yourself into the scenes of the challenge. What will you do in the museum all night?

▶ **Representa.** Act out this ending for your classmates.

HERITAGE LANGUAGE LEARNERS

• Elicit recommendations from students about special places in their countries of origin that a visitor should try. Ask students details about the location. What are the hours of operation? What does the place look like? What are typical items found on restaurant menus? Have them create a schedule for one full day.

MULTIPLE INTELLIGENCES:

Logical-Mathematical Intelligence

• Have students calculate the distance between their town and New York City. Ask them to determine flight times between these two locations. All results (statistics) should be written in Spanish. Write the following information on the board: *De Tampa, Florida, a Nueva York hay 1164 millas. Vamos a viajar en carro.* Have students present their findings to the class including pertinent information by following the examples given.

---

38. Have students write out the answers to their own interview questions. Ask them to compare their answers with their classmates' answers. Do they all have similar answers? Very different? In what ways?

39. To expand this activity, have students compare their summer vacation plans. Ask them if they will see each other during their vacations. Invite volunteers to report to the class. For example: *El próximo verano, Sara va a visitar a sus abuelos en Austin. Yo voy a ir a Florida. No nos vamos a ver.*

 AUDIO SCRIPT
See page 87K

Answer Key

36. Answers will vary. Sample answer:
Esta noche vas a ir a un concierto de música tropical y vas a bailar ritmos latinos. Mañana por la mañana vas a asistir a una exposición de esculturas. Después vas a poder participar en un torneo de juegos de mesa. Luego vas a almorzar comida latinoamericana.
▶ Answers will vary.

37. Answers will vary. Sample answers:
1. Patricia va a pintar esta tarde.
2. Los empresarios van a bailar mañana por la tarde.

38. Answers will vary. Sample answer:
¿Vas a nadar después de la escuela?
▶ Answers will vary.

39. Answers will vary.
▶ Answers will vary.

40. Answers will vary.
▶ Answers will vary.

Additional Resources

Fans Online activities
Practice Workbook

Unit 6

DESAFÍO 3

Expresar el desarrollo de una acción

Presentation

- In *Desafío 3*, Tess and Patricia are at the Latin Grammy Awards in San Antonio, Texas. They have been asked to take photos of the musicians at the event before the show begins.

- In this section students will learn:
  - Ways to express development of an action.
  - Vocabulary relating to technology and entertainment.

Activities	Standards	Resources
Fotonovela	1.2, 2.1	Vis. Pres.
41.	1.2, 1.3	
42.	1.2, 1.3	
43.	1.2, 1.3	
44. Cultura	1.1, 1.2, 2.1, 3.2, 5.1	Video
Tu desafío	1.2, 5.2	

Teaching Suggestions

Warm-Up / Independent Starter

- Have students look at the pictures and write simple captions for each one without looking at the *fotonovela*. Then ask students to look at the speech bubbles on the page to see how close they are to what they wrote.

Preparation

- Have students brainstorm a list of Latin singers and groups that they know of. Ask them to try to name one or two songs for each, and then rate them with a "thumbs up" or a "thumbs down."

 La fotonovela

Before Viewing

- Ask a student volunteer to read the introduction to the task. Ask students to look at the pictures and tell what they find surprising or interesting. Which singers and musical groups do they think will attend this year's Latin Grammys?

After Viewing

- Have students act out the *fotonovela* in small groups. Ask them to predict the end of the scene. Do the women take the photos in time?

110

Fotos de famosos

 Tess and Patricia are at the Latin Grammy Awards in San Antonio, Texas. Their task is to take photos of the musicians at the event. Will they find all the musicians in time to take their pictures before the show begins?

¡No lo puedo creer! ¡Estamos en los Grammy latinos! ¡Hoy vamos a un gran concierto!

¡Es increíble! Yo veo los Grammy latinos en la televisión todos los años.

¡Mira, allí está Juanes. ¿Tienes la cámara?

Sí, la tengo en la bolsa... creo... La estoy buscando...

¡Rápido, Tess! ¡Juanes está saliendo! ¡Estás perdiendo la oportunidad!

Continuará…

41 **Detective de palabras**

▶ **Relaciona.** Match each phrase with a picture.

1. ver la televisión
2. ir a un concierto
3. tomar una foto

(A)   (B)   (C)

▶ **Habla.** How much do you like to do these activities? How often do you do them? Compare your answer with a partner's.

Modelo A. ¿Te gusta ver la televisión?
B. Sí, me gusta mucho ver la televisión.

A. ¿Cuándo ves la televisión?
B. La veo todas las tardes.

Differentiated Instruction

DEVELOPING LEARNERS

- Have students re-create the *fotonovela* using simple stick figures. Encourage them to use chunks of language from the actual *fotonovela* and/or to rewrite the scenes/dialogue in their own words. They can use an online comic strip generator like Make Beliefs Comix to create their scenes: www.makebeliefscomix.com.

EXPANDING LEARNERS

- Have students extend the action from the *fotonovela* by adding 2–3 more musicians to the scene and imagining Tess and Patricia's reactions to each one.

42 ¿Comprendes?

▶ **Escribe.** Answer the questions.

1. ¿Dónde están Tess y Patricia?
2. ¿A qué espectáculo asisten hoy?
3. ¿De quién toman fotos?
4. ¿Qué está buscando Tess en su bolsa?

43 ¿Qué estás haciendo?

▶ **Escribe.** Tess thinks that the people below are doing a certain thing, but Patricia disagrees. Write a sentence based on each picture.

Modelo TESS: *Marcos está comiendo una empanada.*
PATRICIA: *¡No! Marcos está comiendo una hamburguesa.*

La familia está paseando en **coche**.

② Sara está tocando **la guitarra**.

③ Rafa está jugando en **el parque**.

④ Susi está bebiendo **agua**.

⑤ Tom está apagando **la computadora**.

CULTURA

Los *Grammy* latinos

Desde el año 2000, el *Grammy* latino es un premio muy prestigioso para los cantantes, músicos o grupos musicales latinos. La gala de los *Grammy* latinos se celebra todos los años en otoño. El músico más premiado es el cantante colombiano Juanes, con 17 *grammys*.

44 Piensa. Have you ever seen the Latin Grammy Awards? Which Latin singer is your favorite?

→ TU DESAFÍO Visit the website to learn more about the Latin Grammy Awards.

HERITAGE LANGUAGE LEARNERS

• Ask students what they know about the Latin Grammy Awards. Does anyone have a favorite singer or band? Have them discuss what types of Latin music are popular in different regions of the United States and with which populations.

CRITICAL THINKING

• Have students think about different music genres. Ask them to analyze the following questions: Why do music genres exist? Why is it necessary to differentiate between distinct types of music? Why do we need award ceremonies to recognize Latin music specifically? Have students partner up to discuss their answers.

Expresar el desarrollo de una acción

Activities

41. Have students extend the phrase by saying where they would do each activity. For example: *Veo la televisión en mi casa.*

44. Ask the students who has seen both the Latin Grammys and the Grammys. As a class, brainstorm the similarities and differences between the two award shows. You can use a Venn diagram to organize the answers by filling in the traits that the two shows have in common in the middle of the two circles.

AUDIO SCRIPT
See page 87K

CULTURA

Los *Grammy* latinos

Since its inception in 2000, the Latin Grammy Awards have been held in different cities: Los Angeles, New York, Las Vegas, Miami, and Houston. As of 2010, San Antonio has not yet hosted this event. However, for the purposes of this book, the Latin Grammy Awards are taking place in San Antonio because of the large Hispanic influence in this city.

Answer Key

41. 1. B   2. C   3. A
▶ Answers will vary.

42. 1. Tess y Patricia están en San Antonio, Texas.
2. Hoy asisten a los *Grammy* latinos.
3. Toman fotos de Juanes.
4. Tess está buscando la cámara.

43. 1. ¡No! La familia está paseando en bicicleta.
2. ¡No! Sara está tocando el piano.
3. ¡No! Rafa está jugando en el gimnasio.
4. ¡No! Susi está bebiendo leche.
5. ¡No! Tom está apagando la luz.

44. Answers will vary.

Additional Resources

Fans Online activities

Unit 6
DESAFÍO 3
Vocabulario – Tiempo libre

Presentation

- In this section, students will learn:
  – Words related to modes of communication.
  – Words related to artistic activities.

Activities	Standards	Resources
Vocabulario	1.2	
45.	1.2	
46.	1.2, 1.3	Audio
47.	1.1, 1.2, 1.3	
48. Conexiones	1.1, 1.2, 3.2	

Teaching Suggestions

Warm-Up / Independent Starter

- Ask students to list the top five communication media in their own lives. The teacher can also share the top five communication media that were popular when he or she was a middle school student. Which ones are still popular? (For example: the phone.) Which ones are no longer as popular? (For example: the fax.)

Preparation

- Have students look at the pictures on the page. Ask them to classify the vocabulary words into groups such as "things to do" (*Actividades*) and "things to use" (*Objetos*).

Activities

46. Ask students to verbally describe one of the electronic gadgets to a partner. Play "Guess What?" (*Adivina qué*) to see if their partners can guess which gadget format is being described. For example:
A. *Es negro. Lo usamos para hacer llamadas...*
B. *Es un teléfono.*
Then have students ask their partners if they use this gadget, how often they use it, and what actions they do with it.

47. Ask students to rate the activities by level of importance in their lives. Have them write their names on sticky notes. Create a bar graph on the board using the students' sticky notes to see which activity is the most popular.

Vocabulario

Tiempo libre

> A mí me gusta **escuchar la radio**. Y a ustedes, ¿qué les gusta hacer en su tiempo libre?

> A mí me gusta mucho **tomar fotos** y **grabar** con mi cámara.

> Yo prefiero **jugar a los videojuegos** y **escribir correos** a mis amigos.

> A mí me gusta mucho **ir al cine**. Me gusta **ver películas** de terror.

tomar fotos — la cámara de fotos

grabar — la cámara de video

ver una película — la película

jugar a los videojuegos — el videojuego

45 En mi tiempo libre

▶ **Relaciona.** Match each activity with the related object.

1. grabar
2. escuchar
3. tomar
4. ver
5. jugar

(A)  (B)  (C)  (D)  (E)

Differentiated Instruction

DEVELOPING LEARNERS

- Reinforce vocabulary by bringing images of communication media and artistic free-time activities to class. Point to one of the pictures and say *Esto es una cámara*. Next, point to the same picture and ask a student *¿Qué es esto?* Repeat this procedure with all of the images. Then point to one and ask a student a question using an incorrect noun. For example: *¿Es esto una cámara?* (pointing to a TV). Have students provide the correct vocabulary word in a complete sentence.

EXPANDING LEARNERS

- Have students write about *El día perfecto*. Ask them to describe the perfect morning, afternoon, and evening using the vocabulary from the *Desafío*. Students may want to *ver la televisión, escuchar la radio, tomar fotos, ir al cine*, etc. Recycle the '*ir a*' + *infinitivo* structure and plan the perfect day for the following week.

46 **¡Qué suerte!**

▶ **Escucha y escribe.** The local electronics store is giving away free gadgets to the first fifty customers. Listen and write what the characters say they will do with their item.

Modelo las noticias → *Patricia quiere la radio para oír las noticias.*

① ② ③ ④ ⑤

a. la graduación de su amigo **b.** la quinceañera de su prima

c. sus programas favoritos **d.** mensajes a sus amigos **e.** su música favorita

47 **¿Qué prefieres?**

▶ **Une, escribe y habla.** Write questions choosing a phrase from each column to talk to your partner about your preferences.

Modelo *¿Prefieres grabar un video o ir al cine?*

Ⓐ Ⓑ Ⓒ Ⓓ

	B	C	D
¿Prefieres	1. grabar un video 2. tomar fotos 3. escuchar la radio 4. jugar a los videojuegos 5. escribir correos electrónicos	o	a. mirar fotografías? b. grabar canciones? c. ver una película? d. ir al cine? e. hablar?

CONEXIONES: ARTE

La Fiesta Noche del Río

San Antonio es una ciudad del sur de Texas con mucha influencia hispana. La ciudad es famosa por su *River Walk*, o Paseo del Río. El *River Walk* es una zona para pasear y divertirse *(enjoy oneself)* a lo largo del río San Antonio. Hay hoteles, restaurantes, tiendas y teatros. Allí se celebra la Fiesta Noche del Río. Los actores bailan, cantan y actúan según las tradiciones de México, Argentina, España y los Estados Unidos.

48 **Relaciona.** What type of event would you like to attend at the River Walk?

---

48. Have students visit the official website of the San Antonio River Walk at http://www.thesanantonioriverwalk.com/. Ask them to pick out one of the upcoming events and write a brief description in Spanish.

AUDIO SCRIPT
See page 87K

CONEXIONES: ARTE

La Fiesta Noche del Río

The *Fiesta Noche del Río* is an event that has taken place at the Arneson River Theater on the San Antonio River Walk since 1958. It is sponsored by the Alamo Kiwanis Club and is aimed at raising funds for children's charities in the San Antonio community. The *Fiesta Noche del Río* features the songs and dances of Mexico, Spain, Argentina, and Texas.

Answer Key

45. 1. E 2. A 3. C 4. B 5. D

46. 1. Diana quiere la cámara para tomar fotos en la quinceañera de su prima.

2. Andy quiere el televisor para ver sus programas favoritos.

3. Tim quiere la cámara de video para grabar la graduación de su amigo.

4. Tess quiere el teléfono celular para escribir mensajes a sus amigos.

5. Mack quiere el reproductor de música para escuchar su música favorita.

47. Answers will vary. Sample answer: ¿Prefieres tomar fotos o mirar fotografías?

48. Answers will vary.

Additional Resources

Fans Online activities
Practice Workbook

HERITAGE LANGUAGE LEARNERS

• By looking at the artisitic expression and mass media of a culture, one can tell a lot about life in that society. Ask students to share what they know about Hispanic media and entertainment. What are some differences between Latin and Anglo cultures in this respect? You may ask if "reality shows" are a phenomenon in Spanish television.

MULTIPLE INTELLIGENCES:

Intrapersonal Intelligence

• Ask students to reflect on their preferences regarding media and artistic free-time activities. If the vocabulary listed on the spread does not support their preferences, allow them to use a dictionary. Have them describe what they like and why. Encourage them to present their preferences to the class.

DESAFÍO 3

Gramática – El presente continuo

Presentation

- In this section, students will learn:
  - How to express developing actions.
  - The present progressive (*estar* + present participle).

Activities	Standards	Resources
Gramática	1.2, 3.1, 4.1	
49.	3.1, 4.1	
50.	1.2, 1.3	Audio
51.	1.3	
52.	1.1, 1.3	
53. Conexiones	1.1, 1.2, 3.1, 3.2	

Teaching Suggestions

Warm-Up / Independent Starter

- Show students a photograph from a magazine or clip art that includes many different people doing different activities. Have students write a list of three things that they see happening in the picture.

Preparation

- Create a class list by writing all the students' words on the board. You can turn this into a competition by breaking students into small groups and asking them to write as many descriptive sentences as they can about the image. The group with the most sentences wins.

- In pairs, have students practice forming the gerund with verbs of their choice. For example:
  A. *hablar*   B. *hablando*

Activities

49. Ask students if they use the present progressive in English a lot during the day. When do they most use it? What are some examples of sentences that they use frequently?

51. Ask students to take turns eavesdropping on their neighboring group as they play charades. One student watches and then turns around to act out what he or she saw. The partner should say what the other person is doing, in the 3rd person singular. For example: *Ella está escuchando música.*

114

Gramática

El presente continuo

- In Spanish we use the present progressive (presente continuo) to talk about actions that are happening at the moment of speaking.

  –¿Qué **estás haciendo**, Luis?
  –Estoy **escuchando** música.

Formación del presente continuo

- The present progressive is formed as follows:

  | estar + gerundio | Pablo **está haciendo** la comida y María **está escribiendo**.

- The gerundio (present participle) is formed by adding these endings to the verb stem:
  1. -ando for -ar verbs: escuchar → escuchando
  2. -iendo for -er and -ir verbs: hacer → haciendo   escribir → escribiendo

- Notice that in the present progressive, only estar is conjugated.

  VERBO TRABAJAR (TO WORK). PRESENTE CONTINUO

	Singular		Plural
yo	estoy trabajando	nosotros nosotras	estamos trabajando
tú	estás trabajando	vosotros vosotras	estáis trabajando
usted él ella	está trabajando	ustedes ellos ellas	están trabajando

49 **Piensa.** What are some uses of the present progressive in English? How are those similar to or different from the present progressive in Spanish?

50 **Una escuela de arte**

 ▶ **Escucha y escribe.** Listen and write what the people below are studying in performing arts school.

Modelo *Alicia está estudiando baile.*
1. Nelson
2. Beatriz
3. Teresa y Kate
4. Elena
5. Sergio y Héctor

a. fotografía
b. radio
c. televisión
d. música
e. cine

Differentiated Instruction

DEVELOPING LEARNERS

- Have students create memory aids to remember the endings for the present progressive. For example, they could write a two-column chart of -ar verbs with their -ando endings on a flashcard. They can do the same for -er and -ir verbs.

EXPANDING LEARNERS

- Have students list five to ten times of the day and write what they are doing at that moment. For instance, if a student writes 7:00 a. m., then he or she may say *Estoy levantándome.* Challenge them to be creative and give eloquent descriptions for each selected time.

51 **Sin palabras**

▶ **Representa.** Act out an action from page 112 and see if your classmates can guess what you are doing.

Modelo ¡Estás escuchando música!

52 **Tess, la fotógrafa**

▶ **Escribe y habla.** At the Latin Grammys, Tess took this photo for her school newspaper. Write sentences to caption what each person is doing. Then talk with a classmate about each person's actions.

Modelo A. ¿Qué está haciendo María?
　　　　B. María está hablando por teléfono.

CONEXIONES: MÚSICA

La música tejana

Un tipo de música muy popular en Texas y en otros lugares de los Estados Unidos es la música tejana. Los instrumentos principales en la música tejana son el acordeón, el piano eléctrico y la guitarra eléctrica. Un cantante muy famoso de música tejana es Jay Pérez.

53 **Piensa y compara.** Have you ever heard *Tejano* music? What are the primary instruments in the music that you like to listen to?

ciento quince 115

Gramática – El presente continuo

52. After looking again at the photo, have students say one thing that each person is not doing. For example: *María no está nadando.*

 AUDIO SCRIPT
See page 87K

 CONEXIONES: MÚSICA

La música tejana

Tejano music is the name given to forms of folk and popular music originating from the Hispanic populations in central and southern Texas. Sometimes called Tex-Mex, this music combines the folk, country, rock and blues of Texas. Artists like the late "Queen of Tejano" Selena Quintanilla, La Mafia, Jay Pérez, and Mazz have opened international borders for Tejano music. While the lyrics of most Tejano music are appropriate for school-aged students, some songs might cause issues in school.

Answer Key

49. The present progressive is used a great deal more in English than in Spanish, and not always for the same purposes. In Spanish, the simple present tense is more often used for expressing current developing actions rather than the present progressive. For example: *I am coming – Voy.*

50. 1. d　2. e　3. a　4. c　5. b

51. Answers will vary.

52. Answers will vary. Sample answer:
　　A. ¿Qué está haciendo Jorge?
　　B. Está bebiendo agua.

53. Answers will vary.

Additional Resources

Fans Online activities
Practice Workbook

HERITAGE LANGUAGE LEARNERS

• Encourage those students with a personal connection to Tex-Mex culture to enrich the information presented in this *Desafío*. What are their memories of this culture? How would they compare entertainment and free-time activities with those of the United States? What are some of their favorite pastimes?

MULTIPLE INTELLIGENCES:

Intrapersonal Intelligence

• Provide students with the situations below. Ask students to reflect on how they feel in each of them and finish the sentences accordingly. You may want to have them write a journal entry.

1. *Cuando estoy jugando al béisbol…*
2. *Cuando estoy viendo la televisión…*
3. *Cuando estoy bailando…*
4. *Cuando estoy escuchando música…*

115

DESAFÍO 3

Gramática – El gerundio

Presentation

- In this section, students will learn:
  - How to express a progressive action.
  - Irregular present participles.
  - The present progressive with object pronouns.

Activities	Standards	Resources
Gramática	1.2, 3.1, 4.1	
54.	4.1	
55.	1.2, 1.3	Audio
56.	1.2, 1.3	
57.	1.1	
58. Conexiones	1.1, 1.2, 3.1, 3.2	

Teaching Suggestions

Warm-Up / Independent Starter

- Make flashcards by asking students to illustrate three of the verbs in the present progressive form. They should put their illustrations on the front and the sentences on the back. Have classmates guess the sentence.

Preparation

- Use photographs or illustrations from random books and magazines to present the concept of the present progressive. After you show each image to the students, state what the person is doing. Have students repeat after you. Then ask for volunteers to go to the board and write what they just heard.

Activities

54. Ask students to try to pronounce *creer* and *traer* with the *-iendo* ending to help them understand why we use *-yendo*.

55. Before listening to the audio, have students try to describe scenes using the prompts. For example: *Está durmiendo.* → *La persona está en la cama. Está cansada.*

57. In groups of three, have students choose one photo and say one thing that each person is going to do (*ir a* + infinitive) after the activity in the scene. For example:

1. *Después, Patricia va a comer algo.*

Gramática

El gerundio

- Remember that the present participle (gerundio) is formed by adding the endings -ando or -iendo to the stem of the verb.

  trabaj-ar → trabaj**ando**   hac-er → hac**iendo**   escrib-ir → escrib**iendo**

Verbos irregulares en gerundio

- Most present participles are regular. The only irregular ones occur in verbs that have e > i or o > u stem changes.

VERBOS IRREGULARES EN GERUNDIO

E > I		O > U
decir → diciendo	servir → sirviendo	dormir → durmiendo
medir → midiendo	vestir → vistiendo	morir → muriendo
pedir → pidiendo		poder → pudiendo

- When the stem of an -er or -ir verb ends in a vowel, the ending -iendo is written -yendo.

  leer → leyendo   Estoy **leyendo** un libro.
  oír → oyendo   Estamos **oyendo** música.

El gerundio con pronombres objeto y reflexivos

- Object pronouns and reflexive pronouns can either be placed before estar or attached to the present participle.

  Luis **se** está vistiendo.   Luis está vistiéndo**se**.
  Ellas **lo** están diciendo.   Ellas están diciéndo**lo**.

54 **Piensa.** Why might -yendo be a better ending than -iendo for verbs like creer and traer?

55 **¡Está durmiendo!**

 ▶ **Escucha y completa.** Tess can hear but she can't see what is going on in the crowd. Listen and complete the following sentences to describe the situation. Use the present progressive form of the verbs in the box.

1. Un fotógrafo _____.
2. Un fan _____ una foto a Shakira.
3. Una chica _____ una canción muy bonita.
4. Los chicos del grupo Maná _____.

> dormir
> oír
> vestirse
> pedir

Differentiated Instruction

DEVELOPING LEARNERS

- The change from *-iendo* to *-yendo* in some verbs may cause pronunciation difficulties. Model pronunciation slowly using *leyendo* and *oyendo* as examples. Divide each of these verbs into syllables and have students repeat them after you.

- Reinforce the pronunciation differences between the consonant *y* and the vowel *i*. Ask students when is this consonant pronounced as a vowel.

EXPANDING LEARNERS

- Have students browse through magazines or pictures in their textbooks. As they browse have them create a table of infinitives and present participles for each picture. Make sure the list includes at least ten verbs. When students finish, have them write an original story using all of the verbs.

56 **¿Qué estás haciendo?**

▶ **Completa.** Tess and Diana are on the phone talking about their plans for the evening. Fill in the missing present participles in the dialogue.

> TESS: ¡Hola, Diana! ¿Cómo estás? ¿Qué estás ___1___ ?
> hacer
>
> DIANA: Me estoy ___2___ . ¿Y tú?
> vestirse
>
> TESS: Estoy ___3___ un libro muy interesante... ¿Cómo está Rita?
> leer
>
> DIANA: Está mejor, gracias. Es solo un resfriado. Ahora está ___4___ .
> dormir
> ¿Quieres salir a comer conmigo?
>
> TESS: Hoy no puedo. Mi madre está ___5___ una pizza... ¿Quieres venir?
> pedir
> Estamos ___6___ el último disco de Juanes. ¡Es fantástico!
> escuchar

57 **Haciendo todo a la vez**

▶ **Habla.** With a partner, say the things that each person is doing in the photos below.

1. Patricia...   2. Andy...   3. Mack y Tim...

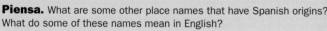

CONEXIONES: HISTORIA Y GEOGRAFÍA

La influencia latina en los Estados Unidos

En los Estados Unidos hay muchos lugares con nombres españoles: ciudades como Los Ángeles, Santa Fe y San Diego; y estados como Florida, Colorado y California. Estos lugares pertenecieron (belonged) a España o a México. Hoy conservan los nombres y muchas costumbres latinas.

58 **Piensa.** What are some other place names that have Spanish origins? What do some of these names mean in English?

ciento diecisiete 117

AUDIO SCRIPT
See page 87L

CONEXIONES: HISTORIA Y GEOGRAFÍA

La influencia latina en los Estados Unidos

The Latin influence is not only felt in the typical geographical areas where Hispanics have concentrated in this country. Lately, it seems latinos are everywhere and are being portrayed well beyond the old typical clichés. TV shows like *Ugly Betty*, movie stars like Salma Hayek and Penélope Cruz, and political figures such as Supreme Court Justice Sonia Sotomayor are reminders of the advancement of Latinos in the United States.

Answer Key

54. You can also explain to students that in Spanish, each vowel in a dipthong is pronounced individually and that the *-yendo* ending helps avoid this mispronunciation.

55. 1. está durmiendo
2. está pidiendo
3. está oyendo
4. se están vistiendo / están vistiéndose

56. 1. haciendo   4. durmiendo
2. vistiendo   5. pidiendo
3. leyendo   6. escuchando

57. Answers will vary. Sample answers:
1. Patricia está leyendo un libro, bebiendo café y oyendo música.
2. Andy está vistiéndose y hablando por teléfono.
3. Mack y Tim están viendo la tele y bebiendo un jugo.

58. Answers will vary. Sample answers:
El Paso (passage), *San Francisco* (Saint Francis), *San Antonio* (Saint Anthony).

Additional Resources

Fans Online activities
Practice Workbook

HERITAGE LANGUAGE LEARNERS

• Have students think about a relative in their country of origin. Have them use the present progressive to talk about what that person is doing at this moment. Focus students' description on the differences and similarities between American and Hispanic daily routines.

MULTIPLE INTELLIGENCES:

Verbal-Linguistic Intelligence

• Have students write a children's poem using the present progressive. To force the rhyme, alternate verses should end in a verb conjugated in the present participle. You may ask them to ilustrate their poems. Compile their work in an anthology. For example:

Estoy en la escuela.
Estoy aprendiendo.
Me gusta aprender.
¿Estás escuchando?

Unit 6
DESAFÍO 3
Comunicación

Presentation

- In this section, students will practice:
  - Ways to express development of an action.
  - Vocabulary relating to technology and entertainment.
  - Words related to modes of communication.
  - Words related to artistic activities.
  - How to express a progressive action.
  - Irregular present participles.
  - The present progressive with object pronouns.

Activities	Standards	Resources
59.	1.2, 1.3	
60.	1.1, 1.2, 1.3	
61.	1.2, 1.3	Audio
62. Final del desafío	1.2, 1.3	

Teaching Suggestions

Warm-Up / Independent Starter

- Ask students to write a brief introduction to a suspense story using the present progressive. They should describe a suspenseful scene in 4–5 sentences. For example: *La mujer está caminando sola. Está llorando. Está lloviendo …*

Preparation

- Have students work in pairs to invite each other to different places, and then to refuse the invitation with an excuse written in the present progressive. For example:
  A. *¿Quieres ir a la tienda?*
  B. *No puedo. Estoy haciendo mi tarea.*

Activities

59. Ask students to write a brief e-mail to a friend in their class about what they are doing this year in school. For example: *Estoy estudiando español …* Then have students trade their e-mails with a partner.

61. Ask students to think of three things that each person is not doing in the picture.

62. Have students act out their versions of the final scene for the class.

118

DESAFÍO 3

Comunicación

59 Correos a casa

▶ **Lee y completa.** While traveling around the United States, Tess and Patricia send e-mails to their friends and family. Read the e-mail below and fill in how they are doing. Use the present progressive form.

Querido papá y hermanos:

¿Cómo estáis? Nosotras lo ___1___ muy bien en este Desafío y ___2___ mucho sobre la
   (pasar)   (aprender)
cultura hispana en los Estados Unidos. Yo ___3___ mucho en español y mamá ___4___
                                          (hablar)   (comer)
platos muy interesantes.

Todos los compañeros ___5___ muchas fotos. Tim y Andy también ___6___ videos.
                      (tomar)   (grabar)

Nos vemos pronto. Estas semanas nos ___7___ con más frecuencia. ¡Qué bien!
                                  (comunicarse)
Con mucho cariño,
Tess y mamá

60 Hablar de los otros

▶ **Escribe y habla.** Write sentences ordering the clues below. Then ask your partner what each person is doing.

Modelo		El señor Ramírez	escuchar

A. *¿Qué está haciendo el señor Ramírez?*
B. *El señor Ramírez está escuchando música.*

1. | Isabel | ver |
2. | Elisa | lavarse |
3. | usted | grabar |

4. | ellos | leer |
5. | tú | cepillarse |
6. | Teresa | preparar |

118 ciento dieciocho

Differentiated Instruction

DEVELOPING LEARNERS

- To practice vocabulary before doing the activities on this spread, have students create a picture dictionary for the following nouns: *foto, cámara, televisión, teatro, cine, película, radio, correo electrónico, teléfono.* If possible, encourage *students* to give examples of each of the different types of media. For example: *una película = Star Wars.*

EXPANDING LEARNERS

- Have students write an e-mail to a relative about what they are doing right now. Students should use the present progressive in their e-mails. After the e-mail is complete, have students highlight the tenses for clear recognition.

61 **Adivina qué**

▶ **Escucha e identifica.** Listen as the people give clues about what they are doing. According to the clues, guess what each person is doing.

Final del desafío

¡Aquí está mi cámara!

¡Tess, rápido, toma la foto!

Perdón, Juanes, ¿podemos sacarle una foto?

Están esperándome en el teatro. ¡Es muy tarde!

¡Por favor, por favor! Estamos participando en un desafío cultural...

62 **¿Qué pasa en la historia?**

▶ **Escribe y representa.** What happens in the last scene? Did Tess and Patricia get the last photo they needed? Write the dialogue and act out the final scene.

ciento diecinueve 119

AUDIO SCRIPT
See page 87L

Answer Key

59. 1. estamos pasando
2. estamos aprendiendo
3. estoy hablando
4. está comiendo
5. están tomando
6. están grabando
7. estamos comunicando

60. 1. A. ¿Qué está haciendo Isabel?
B. Está viendo una película.
2. A. ¿Qué está haciendo Elisa?
B. Está lavándose las manos.
3. A. ¿Qué está haciendo usted?
B. Estoy grabando una película.
4. A. ¿Qué están haciendo ellos?
B. Están leyendo un libro.
5. A. ¿Qué estás haciendo tú?
B. Estoy cepillándome el pelo.
6. A. ¿Qué está haciendo Teresa?
B. Está preparando sándwiches.

61. 1. Estás viendo una película.
2. Estás estudiando.
3. Estás comiendo.
4. Estás hablando por teléfono.
5. Estás tomando fotos.

62. Answers will vary.

Additional Resources

Fans Online activities
Practice Workbook

HERITAGE LANGUAGE LEARNERS

• Using the vocabulary from *Desafío 3*, have students do chain response drills to review the present progressive formation. For example: *escribir correos.*
¿Estás escribiendo correos ahora? → *Sí, estoy escribiendo correos a mis amigos.*
¿Está Sergio escribiendo correos ahora? → *No, está hablando con Jorge.*

SPECIAL-NEEDS LEARNERS

• Students with Attention Deficit Disorder (ADD) may benefit from TPR techniques for focusing their attention. Have students act out different action words from the new vocabulary. For example: *Está escuchando música.* Do this process as a class activity to reintegrate these students with the others.

Presentation

- In *Desafío 4*, Andy and Janet are in Dodger Stadium in Los Angeles, the home of the LA Dodgers. One participant will play with the team and try to hit a home run before time runs out.

- In this section, students will learn:
  - Sports vocabulary.
  - The verb *jugar*.

Activities	Standards	Resources
Fotonovela	1.2	Vis. Pres.
63.	1.2, 1.3	
64.	1.3	
65.	1.1, 1.2, 1.3	Audio
66. Cultura	1.1, 1.2, 2.1, 3.2	

Teaching Suggestions

Warm-Up / Independent Starter

- Ask students to list all the baseball terms they know. Have them write a brief definition for each.

Preparation

- Take a survey of the class to see how many like baseball. Students can rate how much they like the sport using the numbers 1–4 as below:
  - *Me gusta mucho.* (4)
  - *Me gusta.* (3)
  - *No me gusta.* (2)
  - *No me gusta nada.* (1)
- Create a pie chart with the information.

La fotonovela

Before Viewing

- Have a student read the introduction. Ask students to predict the answers to the questions: Who will play? Will that person hit the ball out of the park?

After Viewing

- Ask for volunteers to act out the scene for the class. They can also add a scene that would go before the *fotonovela* begins, and add an extra one at the end of the *fotonovela*.

¡Vamos a jugar!

Andy and Janet are in Dodger Stadium in Los Angeles, the home of the LA Dodgers. One of them will play with the team and try to hit a home run before time runs out. Who will play? Will he or she hit the ball out of the park?

¡Qué difícil, Andy! No juego bien al béisbol.

Vamos, Janet. Tú juegas mejor que yo.

¿Por qué no juegas tú? No tengo ganas de jugar.

Vale, Janet. ¡Yo juego!

¡Voy a jugar! Hay que hacer un jonrón.

¡Oh, no!

Continuará…

63   Detective de palabras

▶ **Completa.** The sentences below summarize the *fotonovela*. Complete each one with a word from the boxes.

1. Janet _____ al béisbol mejor que Andy.
2. Janet no tiene ganas de _____ .
3. Andy _____ primero.
4. Janet va a _____ para hacer un jonrón.

> jugar   jugar
>
> juega   juega

Differentiated Instruction

DEVELOPING LEARNERS

- Have students skim the text of the *fotonovela*. Ask them to stop each time they find one of the following words: *juego, juegas,* or *jugar*. Have them complete the following matching activity:

  1. … juego.   a. Me gusta
  2. … juegas.   b. Yo
  3. … jugar.   c. Tú

EXPANDING LEARNERS

- Use the phrases in activity 65 as a springboard to recycle the present progressive. Pair advanced students to interview each other about what they are doing this week. For example:

  A. *¿Estás haciendo ejercicio esta semana con tu hermana?*
  B. *No, estoy haciéndolo solo.*

  Require them to use direct object pronouns in their responses.

64 **¿De qué tiene ganas?**

▶ **Escribe.** What do the people below feel like doing? Write a sentence according to the pictures.

Modelo ¿Andy tiene ganas de comer empanada? 😠
→ *No, Andy no tiene ganas de comer empanada.*

😠 = no
😊 = sí

1. ¿El entrenador quiere perder tiempo? → 😠

2. ¿Tú y yo queremos jugar en el estadio? → 😊

3. ¿Andy y Tim quieren llevar sus guantes de béisbol? → 😊

4. ¿Los jugadores tienen ganas de ver la televisión? → 😠

5. ¿Tú quieres ver un partido de béisbol hoy? → 😊

6. ¿Ese fan del béisbol tiene ganas de jugar al fútbol? → 😠

 65 **Para estar en forma**

 ▶ **Escucha y escribe.** Listen to Janet's fitness plan and write down the advice she gives. You may find help in the box.

Modelo *Janet tiene que hacer ejercicio.*

dormir ocho horas	hacer ejercicio	comer bien
beber agua	tomar jugos de frutas	montar en bicicleta

 ▶ **Habla.** Now talk with a partner about the advice in the box. Which pieces of advice do you agree with? Which do you follow?

Modelo A. *¿Tú haces ejercicio?*
B. *Sí, hago ejercicio todos los días.*

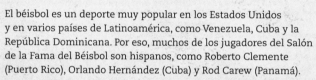 **CULTURA**

El béisbol

El béisbol es un deporte muy popular en los Estados Unidos y en varios países de Latinoamérica, como Venezuela, Cuba y la República Dominicana. Por eso, muchos de los jugadores del Salón de la Fama del Béisbol son hispanos, como Roberto Clemente (Puerto Rico), Orlando Hernández (Cuba) y Rod Carew (Panamá).

66 **Piensa.** What other Spanish-speaking sports figures do you know? What other sports do you enjoy watching?

ciento veintiuno 121

Activities

63. Ask students to write down the opposite of each sentence in this activity. For example: *Janet juega al béisbol mejor que Andy.* → *Janet no juega al béisbol mejor que Andy.*

 AUDIO SCRIPT
See page 87L

  CULTURA

El béisbol

Unlike most of the rest of Latin America, Venezuela's most popular sport is by far baseball, whereas in other Spanish-speaking countries soccer is king. There are currently eight professional teams in the national *Liga Venezolana de Béisbol Profesional*. The participants in this league also play against their Minor League counterparts every winter in the United States.

Answer Key

63. 1. juega   2. jugar   3. juega   4. jugar

64. 1. No, el entrenador no quiere perder tiempo.
2. Sí, tú y yo queremos jugar en el estadio.
3. Sí, Andy y Tim quieren llevar sus guantes de béisbol.
4. No, los jugadores no tienen ganas de ver la televisión.
5. Sí, yo quiero ver un partido de béisbol hoy.
6. No, ese fan del béisbol no tiene ganas de jugar al fútbol.

65. Janet tiene que hacer ejercicio.
Janet tiene que comer bien.
Janet tiene que beber agua.
Janet tiene que montar en bicicleta.
▶ Answers will vary.

66. Answers will vary.

HERITAGE LANGUAGE LEARNERS

• Have students think about a sport that is very popular in Latin America but is not as popular in the United States. Ask them to create a Venn diagram comparing and contrasting the two sports. For example, soccer and American football.

MULTIPLE INTELLIGENCES:
Musical Intelligence

• To raise interest in the topic, ask students if they have ever been to a soccer game. Discuss what types of sounds and music they heard while there. Bring in the lyrics to Ricky Martin's song "La copa de la vida" (the official song of the 1998 FIFA World Cup) and have students sing it together. Ask students to underline any of the vocabulary words that they see in the lyrics.

Additional Resources

Fans Online activities

Unit 6
DESAFÍO 4
Vocabulario – Los deportes

Presentation

- In this section, students will learn:
  - Words related to sports and game playing.
  - Words related to sports equipment.

Activities	Standards	Resources
Vocabulario	1.2	
67.	1.3	
68.	1.3	
69.	1.1, 1.2, 1.3	Audio
70. Cultura	1.1, 1.2, 3.2, 4.2	

Teaching Suggestions

Warm-Up / Independent Starter

- Have students sort the vocabulary words into columns according to categories. They can use a chart like the one below.

Deportes	Acciones	Equipo
el béisbol	ganar	el casco
la natación	perder	la raqueta

Preparation

- Have students make a separate list and divide sports in the United States by popularity: Most popular and Less popular. Then ask them to think about sports that are not popular in the United States, but that are popular in other countries. For example: rugby in Great Britain, or cricket in India.

- Have students choose one country and write five sentences comparing and contrasting the sports in that country with those in the United States.

Activities

67. To extend this activity, ask partners to act out a sport while the other partner states what sport he or she is playing using the present progressive. Then have them switch roles.

68. Have students create picture flashcards of the sports equipment and the sports with the pictures on the front and the words on the back. Then ask pairs to play matching games to match the equipment with the sport.

122

Vocabulario

Los deportes

Jugar al…

fútbol — el balón

fútbol americano — el casco

béisbol — el guante, el bate

baloncesto — el balón

tenis — la pelota, la raqueta

voleibol — la red

golf — la pelota

boliche — la bola

Practicar…

la natación

la piscina

La competición

el estadio

el jugador

ganar

el equipo

perder

el partido

67 **¿A qué están jugando?**

▶ **Escribe.** Andy and Janet play many sports. Write a sentence for each picture. Use the present progressive.

Modelo   *Andy y Janet están jugando al fútbol americano.*

① ② ③ ④

122 ciento veintidós

Differentiated Instruction

DEVELOPING LEARNERS

- Point out a few cognates in the new vocabulary, such as *béisbol, tenis, golf* and *voleibol.* Have the students name the English cognate. Ask them to create a picture dictionary of these cognates with the word and a picture to represent each sport. Next, have students scan the rest of the vocabulary for any additional Spanish to English connections.

EXPANDING LEARNERS

- Have students choose their favorite sport and write a script for a TV show that centers around that sport. They can take on the role of the host and even videotape their show to share with classmates. In their show, they should try to use as many of the vocabulary words as possible.

68 **¿Qué deporte?**

▶ **Escribe.** Andy and Janet are volunteering as P. E. teachers in a kindergarten class. Help them explain to the children which piece of equipment goes with each sport.

Modelo béisbol - bate → *Para jugar al béisbol necesitamos un bate.*

1. fútbol americano - casco
2. tenis - raqueta
3. voleibol - red
4. béisbol - guante
5. boliche - bola
6. baloncesto - balón

69 **¿Ver o jugar?**

 ▶ **Escucha y escribe.** Listen and fill in a chart like the one below with the sports the characters like to watch or play.

	①	②	③	④	⑤	⑥
ver						
jugar						

▶ **Escribe.** Now write sentences to tell which sports each participant likes to watch and which he or she likes to play.

Modelo *A Mack le gusta ver* **el baloncesto** *y le gusta jugar* **al fútbol**.

 ▶ **Habla.** Talk with a partner about the sports you like to watch and the ones you play. Share the information with your class.

 **CULTURA**

La popularidad de los deportes

El fútbol es el deporte más popular del mundo. Según las estadísticas, el fútbol tiene millones de fans en todo el mundo. En los Estados Unidos, el deporte más popular es el fútbol americano y el fútbol es el deporte número cuatro.

70 **Compara.** Why do you think soccer is so popular around the world? Why do you think soccer is not as popular in the United States as it is in the rest of the world?

ciento veintitrés 123

HERITAGE LANGUAGE LEARNERS

• Invite students to write a Wikipedia entry about the most popular sport in their country of origin. They should answer the following questions in their report:

1. *¿Cómo se llama el deporte?*
2. *¿Es un deporte para jugar en equipo? ¿Cuántos jugadores hay en un equipo?*
3. *¿Qué tipo de equipamiento necesita? (¿Una pelota, un guante, un bate...?)*
4. *¿Dónde se juega?*
5. *¿Cómo son los fans?*

SPECIAL-NEEDS LEARNERS

• Students with visual impairments may benefit from a touch and feel presentation of the vocabulary. Bring in objects that relate or represent the different vocabulary words. Pass the objects to the students and have them touch and explore them as you say the Spanish word that relates to each object. For example: use a pair of goggles or a swimming cap to represent *natación*. Make sure the students know the category of the new vocabulary before the actual touch and feel activity.

 AUDIO SCRIPT
See page 87L

 CULTURA

La popularidad de los deportes

The International Federation of Football Association (FIFA) is the principal body regulating soccer around the world. The FIFA has more countries affiliated with it than the United Nations. Its main tournament is the World Cup and takes place every four years.

Answer Key

67. 1. Andy y Janet están jugando al boliche.
2. Andy y Janet están jugando al béisbol.
3. Andy y Janet están jugando al baloncesto.
4. Andy y Janet están jugando al tenis.

68. Para jugar al...
1. fútbol americano necesitamos un casco.
2. tenis necesitamos una raqueta.
3. voleibol necesitamos una red.
4. béisbol necesitamos un guante.
5. boliche necesitamos una bola.
6. baloncesto necesitamos un balón.

69. 1. A Mack le gusta ver el baloncesto y le gusta jugar al fútbol.
2. A Andy le gusta ver el voleibol y le gusta jugar al tenis.
3. A Tess le gusta ver la natación en la tele y le gusta jugar al baloncesto.
4. A Janet le gusta ver los partidos de béisbol en el estadio y le gusta jugar al béisbol.
5. A Patricia le gusta ver el fútbol americano en la tele y le gusta jugar al golf.
6. A Tim le gusta ver el boliche en la televisión y le gusta jugar al béisbol.
▶ Answers will vary.

70. Answers will vary.

Additional Resources

Fans Online activities
Practice Workbook

123

Unit 6

DESAFÍO 4

Gramática – Verbos con raíz irregular (*u > ue*)

Presentation

- In this section, students will learn:
  - How to express habits.
  - How to express desires tied to sports.
  - How to conjugate and use the verb *jugar*.

Activities	Standards	Resources
Gramática	1.2, 3.1, 4.1	
71.	4.1	
72.	1.1, 1.3	
73.	1.2, 1.3	Audio
74.	1.1, 1.3, 5.1	
75. Cultura	1.2, 2.1, 3.1, 3.2	
Tu desafío	1.2, 3.2	

Teaching Suggestions

Warm-Up / Independent Starter

- Ask students to write a list of the sports they like to play using the stem *A mí me gusta jugar …*

Preparation

- Have students fill in a chart like the one below with the sports that their family members and friends like to play.

	Deporte
A mi hermano(a) le gusta jugar…	
A mi madre/padre le gusta jugar…	
A mis primos les gusta jugar…	
A mis abuelos les gusta jugar…	
A mis amigos les gusta jugar…	

- After learning about the verb *jugar*, students can write a sentence using the correct form of the verb, and the information from the chart and the Warm-Up / Independent Starter.

Activities

71. Ask students to write a sentence about the sports they play and the instruments they play. For example: *Yo juego al tenis y toco la guitarra.*

Gramática

Verbos con raíz irregular (*u > ue*)

- In the verb jugar *(to play)*, the u in the stem changes to ue in the present tense:

VERBO JUGAR (TO PLAY). PRESENTE

Singular		Plural	
yo	juego	nosotros nosotras	jugamos
tú	juegas	vosotros vosotras	jugáis
usted él ella	juega	ustedes ellos ellas	juegan

Note: As with other stem-changing verbs, all forms in the present tense are irregular except for nosotros, nosotras and vosotros, vosotras. This is another *boot* verb.

- The preposition a is used with jugar to talk about playing a sport or game.

  yo + jugar + a + el tenis $\rightarrow$ Yo juego al tenis.

  nosotros + jugar + a + el fútbol $\rightarrow$ Nosotros jugamos al fútbol.

- Jugar means "to play a sport or a game". It isn't used to refer to playing a musical instrument, as in English. Tocar *(to play)* is used for an instrument.

  Ellos **juegan** al tenis.   Yo **juego** al voleibol.

  Ellos **tocan** el piano.   Yo **toco** la guitarra.

71 **Piensa.** Why do you think that Spanish uses different verbs to refer to playing sports vs. playing a musical instrument?

72 **¿A qué juegas?**

▶ **Habla.** Andy plays tennis. With your partner, take turns asking and answering whether you play the following sports. If you don't play a sport, refer to someone you know that does.

Modelo A. *¿Juegas al baloncesto?*
B. *Sí, juego al baloncesto en la escuela.*
B. *No, no juego al baloncesto. Mi hermano juega al baloncesto.*

1. el tenis
2. el golf
3. el fútbol americano
4. el béisbol
5. el fútbol
6. el boliche

Differentiated Instruction

DEVELOPING LEARNERS

- Reinforce vocabulary and grammar acquisition by pointing out the relationship between *juego* (verb) and *juego* (noun). Highlight the differences using the words in different contexts. Have students use the verb and the noun in two different sentences of their own. Finally, ask students to create an illustration (or a visual representation using clip art) of one of the following sentences: *Juego a un juego. ¿Juegas a un juego? El chico juega a un juego. Jugamos a un juego. Ellos juegan a un juego.*

EXPANDING LEARNERS

- Have students play a game of association in small groups. One student calls out a sport or a musical instrument. The other students have to think fast to decide if they should use *jugar* or *tocar* in their sentence. For example:

  A. *la guitarra*
  B. *Toco la guitarra.*
  A. *el golf*
  B. *Juego al golf.*

73 Adivina…

▶ **Escucha y decide.** Listen and decide which sport the four pairs are going to play.

 Ⓐ
 Ⓑ
 Ⓒ
 Ⓓ

▶ **Escribe.** Now write a sentence to tell what sport each person plays, and where.

Modelo *Andy juega al béisbol en el parque.*

74 Deportes en familia

▶ **Escribe.** You and your family plan to play several sports over the next three days. Write what sports you will play, and when you will play them.

Modelo *Hoy mi familia juega al fútbol por la tarde.*
Mañana jugamos a…

▶ **Habla y presenta.** Now create a poster and present your schedule to the class.

CULTURA

El jai alai

El *jai alai* viene del País Vasco, del norte de España. Es conocido como «el deporte más rápido del mundo», por la velocidad *(speed)* de la pelota. Los jugadores juegan al *jai alai* con una pelota de cuero y una canasta *(basket)* atada *(tied)* al brazo. La cancha *(court)* de *jai alai* tiene tres paredes. En los Estados Unidos hay partidos de *jai alai* en el estado de Florida y en Connecticut.

75 **Investiga.** Go online and find out the rules of *jai alai*. When was it invented?

▶→ **TU DESAFÍO** Visit the website to learn more about *jai alai*.

74. After students present their posters, ask them to compare the information. Do their families play similar sports? What seems to be the most popular sport among them?

AUDIO SCRIPT
See page 87L

CULTURA

El *jai alai*

In the United States, *jai alai* is popular in Florida. The first fronton, or jai alai court, in the United States was built in Hialeah near Miami in 1924. Since then, this sport has expanded to other cities in the state. The organization World Jai Alai, which is based in Miami, has opened schools for amateur players in many places around the world.

Answer Key

71. Answers will vary.

72. Answers will vary.

73. Andy y Janet – C. Béisbol
Tim y Mack – D. Fútbol americano
Diana y Rita – A. Tenis
Tess y Patricia – B. Fútbol

▶ Andy / Janet juega al béisbol en el parque.
Tim / Mack juega al fútbol americano en el estadio.
Diana / Rita juega al tenis en el centro recreativo.
Tess / Patricia juega al fútbol en el parque.

74. Answers will vary.

▶ Answers will vary.

75. Answers will vary.

Additional Resources

Fans Online activities
Practice Workbook

HERITAGE LANGUAGE LEARNERS

• Have students think about some games that are popular in their home countries (if they are not sure, they can talk to a family member). Have students write a short report about the game by answering the following questions: ¿Cómo se llama el juego? ¿Quién juega a ese juego? ¿Dónde juega? ¿Cómo juega?

• Alternatively, have students give directions about how to play the game to the rest of the class.

MULTIPLE INTELLIGENCES:
Interpersonal Intelligence

• Have pairs of students take turns using the verb *jugar* to share opinions about famous sports figures. Remind students not to forget to use the preposition *a (a + el = al)* in their sentences. For example:

A. *Derek Jeter juega muy bien al béisbol.*
B. *No. Derek Jeter juega regular. Andy Pettitte juega muy bien al béisbol.*

125

Unit 6
DESAFÍO 4
Comunicación

Presentation

- In this section, students will practice:
  - Words related to sports and game playing.
  - Words related to sports equipment.
  - The verb *jugar*.

Activities	Standards	Resources
76.	1.2, 1.3	Audio
77.	1.1, 1.3, 5.1	
78.	1.1, 1.3	
79.	1.1, 1.3, 3.1, 5.2	
80. Final del desafío	1.2, 1.3, 3.1	
Tu desafío	1.2, 1.3	

Teaching Suggestions

Warm-Up / Independent Starter

- Have students find photos of famous people playing sports (they can use clip art or search online). Ask them to describe the sport the person is playing, what the person is wearing, etc. For example: *El hombre lleva un casco. Juega con un bate. Está jugando al béisbol.*

Preparation

- Tell students that they have been asked by the gym teacher to help organize the sports equipment in the gym. Have students put the equipment into the appropriate "bins" according to the label on each one. They can use a graphic organizer like the one below.

fútbol	baloncesto	béisbol	tenis

- Alternatively, students can cut photos out of the equipment (or use clip art or draw the objects) and glue them into the appropriate category boxes.

Activities

76. After completing the activity, have students work in pairs to create a dialogue between Andy and his sister Janet. Andy tries to convince his sister to let him play sports by giving an excuse for each task. Invite volunteers to role-play their dialogues in front of the class.

126

Comunicación

76 **Primero las tareas**

▶ **Escucha y relaciona.** Andy wants to play sports this weekend, but Janet reminds him of the household chores he has to do. Listen and match each sport with the chore that will replace it.

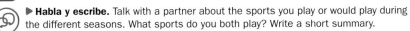

77 **Temporada de deportes**

▶ **Habla y escribe.** Talk with a partner about the sports you play or would play during the different seasons. What sports do you both play? Write a short summary.

Modelo A. ¿A qué juegas en invierno?
B. En invierno yo juego al baloncesto. ¿Y tú?
A. Yo practico la natación.

En invierno, yo practico la natación y Sonia juega al baloncesto.

78 **En la tienda de deportes**

▶ **Habla.** Andy and Janet go to the sporting goods store to buy some new equipment. With your partner, take turns pointing to the different equipment and saying what they will buy to play different sports.

Modelo Andy juega al béisbol. Va a comprar un bate nuevo.

Differentiated Instruction

DEVELOPING LEARNERS

- Go over vocabulary and grammar spreads before attempting the *Comunicación* activities. Call on volunteers to name a vocabulary category and three new words in it. Then have one student summarize the use of the verb *jugar*.

EXPANDING LEARNERS

- Have students pretend that they are sports commentators for the *Final del desafío* activity. As a fellow student presents pictures to the class, have the other students act as commentators. Before assigning this activity, discuss as a class which topics sports commentators talk about. For example, batting statistics, player histories or player positions.

79 Un día de deportes

▶ **Escribe.** Your school is planning an Olympic Day. Make a poster with the sports that you will play, the schedule of events, where each sport will take place, and the equipment needed.

 ▶ **Habla.** Present your poster to the class. Then talk with your classmates about what you will do at their events. Whose event sounds like the most fun?

Modelo *¡Bienvenidos a nuestro día de deportes! Hoy vamos a…*

Final del desafío

> Vamos, Janet, tú juegas bien al béisbol. ¡Tú puedes hacerlo!

> ¡Vamos, vamos, vamos! ¡Sal del campo!

> ¡Siiiiii! Voy a jugar al béisbol mañana también.

80 ¿Qué pasa en la historia?

▶ **Lee y dibuja.** Janet is up to bat. Using the speech bubbles, draw pictures to represent the end of the story. Then present your pictures to the class.

 → **TU DESAFÍO**   Earn points for your own challenge! Listen to the questions for your *Minientrevista Desafío 4* on the website and write your answers.

HERITAGE LANGUAGE LEARNERS

• Students should research and write a brief report about a famous athlete from their country of origin. Tell students to include the following: the athlete's name, sport, his team name, age, heritage, professional history, and greatest accomplishments. Encourage students to personalize the report by stating why they selected this particular sports figure.

MULTIPLE INTELLIGENCES:

Logical-Mathematical Intelligence

• Have students do Internet research to identify different measurements associated with sports. For example: a baseball field, a record, the length of an Olympic swimming pool, etc. Have them present their findings to the class.

Unit 6

DESAFÍO 4

Comunicación

78. Ask students to brainstorm a list of equipment that can be used for more than one sport. For example: *balón → baloncesto, voleibol, fútbol.*

79. Have students create a TV commercial / video advertisement for their Olympic Day. The students can work in groups and should be encouraged to use props and other means (posters that they make using pictures and sports vocabulary, fliers) to advertise their day to the audience. They should include information about what sports will be played and the equipment that participants should bring with them to the event. If possible, show the video projects to the rest of the class—and even other Spanish classes—and have the audience vote on the best commercial (funniest, most convincing, most entertaining, etc.).

 AUDIO SCRIPT
See page 87L

Answer Key

76. 1. C   2. A   3. B   4. D
77. Answers will vary. Sample answer:
    A. ¿A qué juegas en verano?
    B. En verano yo juego al béisbol. ¿Y tú?
    A. Yo juego al fútbol.
    En verano, yo juego al fútbol y mi compañero(a) juega al béisbol.
78. Answers will vary. Sample answer:
    Janet juega al tenis. Va a comprar una raqueta nueva.
79. Answers will vary.
    ▶ Answers will vary.
80. Answers will vary.

Additional Resources

Fans Online activities
Practice Workbook

127

Unit 6
Todo junto

Presentation

- This section combines all of the grammar, vocabulary, and communicative contexts from the entire unit and presents activities that involve students in integrated practice.

Activities	Standards	Resources
81.	1.1, 1.3	
82.	1.2, 1.3	
83.	1.1, 1.2, 1.3	Audio
84.	1.1, 1.2, 1.3, 3.1	

Teaching Suggestions

Warm-Up / Independent Starter

- Ask students to write questions for a fantasy interview with their favorite sports figure, movie star, singer, scientist, or other famous person.

Preparation

- Have students use their questions from the Warm-Up to interview a partner pretending to be that famous person. Monitor for use of Spanish in their conversations.

Activities

81. Have students create a video advertisement for their school's Olympic Week. They should work in small groups to write a script, and then they can act out their commercial and videotape it. Have students share their videos with the class. The class can even vote on their favorite ad (or the funniest, or the most convincing, etc.), favorite actress, favorite actor, best screenplay, etc.

82. Have pairs of students act out a dialogue between Mr. Goldberg and his scheduler. For example:
MR. GOLDBERG: ¿Qué voy a hacer hoy a las diez de la mañana?
SCHEDULER: Hoy a las diez va a hablar con el director.

84. Have small groups choose a painting they like from the slide show at http://www.joaquin-sorolla-y-bastida.org/slideshow.html. Invite volunteers to describe the painting to the class using the questions in this activity.

128

Todo junto

ESCRIBIR Y HABLAR

81 La semana de los deportes

▶ **Escribe.** Your school is celebrating an Olympic Week. Write a list of what the people are doing according to the picture.

Modelo *Orlando está jugando al fútbol. Kate está grabando el partido.*

 ▶ **Habla.** Now in a small group, take turns announcing the sports while your classmates say who is playing them.

Está jugando al fútbol.

¡Es Orlando!

ESCRIBIR

82 Una visita

 ▶ **Escribe.** It's Olympic Week, and Mr. Goldberg is visiting your school for two days. Write what you think he is going to do during his visit.

Modelo Hoy a las 10 a. m.
→ *Hoy a las diez de la mañana el señor Goldberg va a hablar con el director.*

1. Hoy a las 12 p. m.
2. Hoy a las 3 p. m.
3. Hoy a las 5 p. m.
4. Mañana a las 11 a. m.
5. Mañana a la 1 p. m.
6. Mañana a las 4 p. m.

128 ciento veintiocho

Differentiated Instruction

DEVELOPING LEARNERS

- Pair students up and have them list as much vocabulary, grammar and as many tasks from each *Desafío* as they can in a chart like the one below. They should use the book to help them to fill in each box.

	Desafío 1	Desafío 2	Desafío 3	Desafío 4
Vocabulario	el médico, la oficina			
Gramática	ten, haz, pon, ven			
Tema	el juego de dominó			

EXPANDING LEARNERS

- Have students write a skit between a professional and a client / customer / patient (for example: a doctor and a patient, a lawyer and a client, etc.). Encourage students to use as many commands and present progressive verbs in their skit as possible. For example:

DOCTOR: *Ven a mi consulta el mes próximo.*
PACIENTE: *Estoy estudiando. No puedo.*

ESCUCHAR, ESCRIBIR Y HABLAR

83 **¿Qué ves?**

 ▶ **Escucha y escribe.** Mack has taken some photos while in the United States. Listen and check whether Mack's descriptions match up with the photos. Write the differences.

Modelo 1. *Rita no está hablando por teléfono. Ella está leyendo un libro.*

 ▶ **Habla.** Compare what you have written with your partner's answers.

LEER, HABLAR Y ESCRIBIR

84 **Un cuadro de Sorolla**

Joaquín Sorolla es un famoso pintor español. Su pintura representa la luz y la vitalidad de su tierra, Valencia, junto al mar Mediterráneo. La Hispanic Society de Nueva York conserva muchas de sus obras.

▶ **Habla.** Talk about the painting with a partner. Answer the following questions:

1. ¿Dónde están las personas del cuadro?
2. ¿Qué están haciendo?
3. ¿Qué van a hacer después?

▶ **Escribe.** Write a conversation between the people in the painting.

Joaquín Sorolla. *Bajo el toldo, playa de Zarauz*, 1910.

 AUDIO SCRIPT
See page 87L

Answer Key

81. Orlando está jugando al fútbol.
Kate está grabando el partido.
Teo está jugando al béisbol.
Tom está corriendo.
Bill y Lola están viendo el partido.
Jesús está llamando a un amigo.
Karen y Susan están jugando al baloncesto.
Lisa está jugando al tenis.
Óliver está entrenando a un chico.
▶ Answers will vary.

82. Answers will vary. Sample answers:
1. Hoy a las doce del mediodía, el señor Goldberg va a comer con los directores.
2. Hoy a las tres de la tarde, el señor Goldberg va a ver los partidos de los estudiantes.

83. 1. Rita no está hablando por teléfono. Ella está leyendo un libro.
2. Andy no está escribiendo mensajes con el celular. Janet está escribiendo mensajes con el celular.
3. Tess no está hablando por teléfono. Ella está leyendo un libro.
▶ Answers will vary.

84. Answers will vary.
▶ Answers will vary.

Additional Resources

Fans Online activities
Practice Workbook

HERITAGE LANGUAGE LEARNERS

• Discuss professions with students. Ask them if their families have ever given them advice about which professions or jobs they should seek when they are older. Are certain jobs looked at as more important or worthwhile in their home cultures?

• Have them write a speech in the voice of a family member who has given them some job advice. Ask students to use *tú* commands in the speech. Have them share their speeches with the rest of the class.

MULTIPLE INTELLIGENCES:
Auditory Learners

• Have students write and record a radio advertisement for a game or sport. Encourage students to use vocabulary and grammar from this unit. If possible, the advertisement can include special sound effects. Play the ads to the class. For example: *¡Ven al partido de béisbol este sábado! Juegan los Diablos de San José contra los Ángeles de San Juan.*

129

Unit 6

El encuentro

Presentation

- In this section, students will use the communicative goals of the unit by writing an e-mail. They will
  - Speak about professions, use commands, and give advice.
  - Express intent.
  - Describe actions.
  - Talk about habits and sports.

Activities	Standards	Resources
Fotonovela	1.2	
85.	1.3	
86.	1.1	

Teaching Suggestions

Warm-Up / Independent Starter

- Have students answer these questions in writing.
  - *¿Cuál es la profesión de tu padre/madre? Descríbela.*
  - *¿Qué profesión quieres tener en el futuro?*
  - *¿Qué puedes hacer para lograr tus metas?*
  - *¿Cuáles son tus hábitos y deportes favoritos?*

Preparation

- Before teaching this spread, have students glance over the four *Desafíos* that make up this unit. Have students narrate what happened in each. They can also rank them from 1 to 4 using categories, such as most interesting, difficult, boring, etc. These rankings will help them justify their votes at the end of this spread.

La fotonovela

- Ask students to study the pictures, read them individually and then share their impressions with the class.
- Have students write the names of the different characters and how they feel or what they have achieved. Ask students to share their opinions about what the characters have achieved.
- Assign one of the four scenes to pairs of students to act out for the class. For each scene, have the partners divide the dialogue between both characters so that each student participates equally.

130

En Grant Park

The four pairs meet in Chicago after their individual tasks. Did all of them complete their tasks successfully? Who will win the challenge in the United States?

Este dominó es de Miami. ¡Ven a jugar con nosotros!

En el museo de la Sociedad Hispánica hay cuadros muy interesantes... ¡Voy a ir a clase de pintura!

Hum, la foto de Juanes no está muy clara... ¡Tess está cantando sus canciones todo el día!

Janet juega muy bien al béisbol. ¡Es una campeona!

130 ciento treinta

Differentiated Instruction

DEVELOPING LEARNERS

- Have students look at the four photos on page 130. Have them write one sentence for each photo that tells what the participants are doing using the following structure:

  Tim y Mack **están** *jugando* *al dominó.*
  (names of participants) (present participle) (extra information —optional)

EXPANDING LEARNERS

- Have students look at the four photos on page 130. Ask them to write commands for one of the participants (as if talking directly to him or her) related to what they are doing in each scene. For example: *Tim, pon el dominó en la mesa.*

¿Vamos al Festival de Música Latina? ¡Están tocando jazz latino!

85 **Al llegar**

▶ **Escribe.** Write an e-mail to your classmates summarizing each pair's performance. Be sure to include the following information:

- Where they go and the task they have to complete.

> Modelo Diana y Rita van a Nueva York. Tienen que pasar una noche en el museo de la Sociedad Hispánica de América.

- What they do to complete the task.

> Modelo Diana y Rita no pueden usar la computadora ni el teléfono en el museo. Durante la noche van a mirar los cuadros, van a leer libros y van a escuchar música.

- What each character is going to do in his or her leisure time while in the United States.

> Modelo Rita va a jugar al baloncesto con Andy y Tim.

86 **Las votaciones**

▶ **Decide.** Which pair has done the most multicultural challenge? Take a vote to decide!

Multicultural

ciento treinta y uno **131**

Unit 6

El encuentro

Activities

85. Before students complete this activity, review the *ir a* + infinitive structure to talk about future actions and plans. You may also want to go over some of the vocabulary used to talk about sports and free-time activities. Allow some time for students to write and revise their e-mails. Finally, have volunteer students read their e-mails to the class.

86. On the board, write the names of the members of each pair in the challenge and tally the results of the class vote for the winning pair. If time allows, let students present their findings to the class and explain briefly why they chose their winning team.

Answer Key

85. Answers will vary. Sample answer:

¡Hola! Os escribo porque quiero deciros qué Desafío me pareció el más multicultural. Para mí fue el primer Desafío. En este Desafío, Tim y Mack hablan con muchas personas interesantes en la Calle Ocho. Allí también juegan al dominó. En la foto están jugando con unos hombres muy graciosos. Creo que ellos van a ganar en los Estados Unidos.

86. Answers will vary.

HERITAGE LANGUAGE LEARNERS

- Students should research and write a brief report about a famous athlete or musician from their country of origin. Tell students to try to find information about the kind of advice this athlete/musician received throughout his or her career and/or the kind of advice he or she would give to aspiring athletes/musicians. Have students present the information and the advice to the class.

MULTIPLE INTELLIGENCES:

Logical-Mathematical Intelligence

- Have students play "Domino Math" in groups of 3–4 students. One student calls out a number in Spanish and the rest of the group has to find dominoes with that number of dots. For variation, students can call out commands like *Pon una ficha de dominó en la mesa que vale menos de/más de nueve.*

131

Unit 6
MAPA CULTURAL
Estados Unidos

Presentation

- This section presents the United States through snapshots of a variety of places around the country. We get a taste for different regions and cities of the United States (for example: San Antonio, Miami, Los Angeles, and New York) as well as a sense for the history of the country and its vibrant Latino heritage. The photos and graphic organizers serve to support the geographic, historical and demographic information for students.

Activities	Standards	Resources
Mapa cultural	1.2, 1.3, 2.2, 3.1, 3.2	Video
87.	1.3, 3.1	
88.	1.1, 1.3	

Teaching Suggestions

Warm-Up / Independent Starter

- Have students locate readings about one place they are particularly interested in. Ask them to fold their paper into three columns labeled: S (Sé) – Q (Quiero saber) – A (Aprendí). Before reading the section, ask students to write all the information they already know about that place in the S (Sé) column. Next have them write a list of questions they have about the place in the column marked Q (Quiero saber). Finally, ask students to read the section and then fill in the A (Aprendí) column with information they gleaned from the reading.

- You may want to pair the students who chose different places and have them exchange their papers.

Preparation

- Ask for volunteers to read each section of the Mapa cultural. Have students follow the map on the page or even the map in your classroom as they read this section.

- Ask students to read the two speech bubbles aloud. Have them mention as many United States cities that have Spanish names as they can in one minute. Write those names on the board. How many names did students mention?

Estados Unidos tiene una importante herencia hispana presente en la historia, en la arquitectura, en la gastronomía, en el arte y en los nombres de personas y lugares.

Según los datos de la Oficina del Censo para 2009, en los Estados Unidos hay 48 millones de personas de origen hispano. La presencia hispana es más importante en Florida, Texas, Nuevo México y California, y en las grandes ciudades como Nueva York o Chicago.

Algunos estados de la Unión tienen nombre español. Por ejemplo, Nevada, Florida y Colorado.

Y también muchos pueblos y ciudades.

87 **Los hispanos y los Estados Unidos**

▶ **Escribe.** Answer these questions.

- What contributions from Hispanics to the United States do you know?
- How many famous Hispanic people do you know? What are their professions?

132 ciento treinta y dos

Differentiated Instruction

DEVELOPING LEARNERS

- The United States is known as a "melting pot" of diversity. Discuss this term with students and brainstorm the various ethnicities that make up the United States. Help students identify the greatest areas of diversity by using a map. Have them use icons to represent each of the populations in the map.

EXPANDING LEARNERS

- Hispanic immigration to the United States has been a steady phenomenon since the country began. Have students research and discuss the social, economic and cultural effects of this phenomenon.

La presencia hispana en los Estados Unidos

1. Huellas hispanas en los Estados Unidos

Los nombres de algunos lugares, la arquitectura colonial, la gastronomía, ciertos movimientos culturales y los medios de comunicación en español son testimonios de la herencia hispana de los Estados Unidos.

2. Estados con historia hispana

Algunos territorios de los Estados Unidos tienen un pasado hispano. Florida y Texas fueron colonizados por españoles, y las regiones que ahora son California, Nevada, Arizona, Utah, Nuevo México y parte de Colorado fueron territorios de España y, más tarde, de México.

Misión de San José y San Miguel de Aguayo (San Antonio, Texas).

Espectadores en el Desfile del Día de Puerto Rico (Nueva York).

3. Concentración hispana en las ciudades

Los Ángeles, Nueva York, Miami y Chicago son ciudades con mucha población hispana. En estas ciudades y en todo el país se festeja, entre septiembre y octubre, el Mes de la Herencia Hispana, una celebración de las aportaciones de la comunidad hispana a los Estados Unidos.

88 ¿Es de origen hispano?

 ▶ **Completa.** Complete the chart with the information from the text.

 ▶ **Habla.** Should your state and/or your city be included in the chart? Why?

Presencia hispana en los Estados Unidos	
Estados de origen hispano	
Ciudades con mayor población hispana	
Huellas hispanas en los Estados Unidos	

HERITAGE LANGUAGE LEARNERS

• Encourage students to share what life is like for them and their families here in the United States. Ask if they identify with any of the communities showcased in the spread. Have them think about different reasons why it could be important or productive to associate in communities.

CRITICAL THINKING

• Have students think about how different the United States would be without its Hispanic populations. Think about what areas of life would be most affected. Would they personally experience these effects? How or why? Tell students to keep a record of their thoughts on this topic for a class discussion.

Activities

88. Have students work in small groups of 3–4 persons and assign a region, city or state to each group. Ask students to brainstorm all they know about their assigned region. Have each group report their information to the class and then make a group poster.

Answer Key

87. Answers will vary. Sample answers:
Some Hispanic contributions to the United States include:
– Jaime Escalante – education
– Placido Domingo – opera
– Chita Rivera – acting
– Lee Trevino – golf
– Franklin Chang-Rodriguez – NASA astronaut

88.

Presencia hispana en los Estados Unidos	
Estados de origen hispano	Florida, Texas, California, Nevada, Arizona, Utah, Nuevo México, Colorado.
Ciudades con mayor población hispana	Los Ángeles, Nueva York, Miami, Chicago.
Huellas hispanas en Estados Unidos	El Mes de la Herencia Hispana.

▶ Answers will vary.

133

MAPA CULTURAL

Estados Unidos

Presentation

- In this section, students will expand their knowledge and awareness of how Latino heritage has taken root in the United States, and the different ways in which this heritage continues to manifest and influence the rest of the country.
  - Students will learn about one of the United States' leading muralists, Judy Baca, creator of the *Great Wall of Los Angeles*.
  - Students will also read about the origin of Tex-Mex food.
  - In addition, students will explore Little Havana, the emblematic Hispanic neighborhood that is located in Miami.

Activities	Standards	Resources
Mapa Cultural	1.2, 1.3, 2.2, 3.1, 3.2	
89.	1.1, 1.2, 1.3, 3.1, 3.2	

Teaching Suggestions

Warm-Up / Independent Starter

- Have students complete the following sentences with information they know about the United States.
  - *La capital de los Estados Unidos es …*
  - *Los Estados Unidos tienen … estados.*
  - *Cuatro regiones con alta concentración hispana son …*
  - *Una ciudad estadounidense con un nombre en español es …*
  - *Una persona famosa de origen latino en este país es …*

Preparation

- Review this unit's cultural passages to make sure students are familiar with them. Explain that in this spread they will focus on other aspects that illustrate the Hispanic influence on this country. Talk about one of the features of this spread in detail and in a personalized way. For instance, you can mention that Tex-Mex food is your favorite, and you especially enjoy eating enchiladas. Motivate students to share and elaborate on their own experiences.

(1) La Gran Pared de Los Ángeles.

1. Judy Baca y el muralismo de Los Ángeles

En Los Ángeles, los chicanos pintan murales para expresar su identidad. El mural más importante es *La Gran Pared de Los Ángeles*, de la artista chicana Judy Baca. Este mural mide casi un kilómetro y representa la historia de California. Es un monumento a la armonía interracial.

2. La comida tex-mex

La expresión tex-mex originalmente procede de una compañía ferroviaria llamada *Texas-Mexican Railway*. Después se usó para describir un tipo de comida.

La comida tex-mex es una mezcla de las recetas de México y de Texas.

Los ingredientes básicos de esta cocina son la carne picada, la salsa de chile y el queso amarillo. Nachos, tacos crujientes, chili con carne y fajitas son algunas recetas tex-mex.

(2) Un restaurante de comida tex-mex.

The Hispanic World

Judy Baca y el muralismo de Los Ángeles

Judy Baca is a well-known Chicano artist from Los Angeles. Her most famous work is a large-scale mural called *The Great Wall of Los Angeles*. This mural consists of 41 segments where California's history is depicted from the perspective of groups, such as ethnic minorities, whose voices have been historically excluded. Judy Baca involves the community in the production of her murals as an example of an alternative to a society that focuses attention on individual success. Additional information can be found at: http://www.judybaca.com/now/index.php

La comida tex-mex

Tex-Mex cuisine in a full-fledged cuisine that stands on its own merits. It draws inspiration from Mexican dishes and Mesoamerican products, such as chili peppers, beans, tomatoes, avocadoes, and corn, but has been adapted by American cooks in Texas. Native-American, Mexican-Spanish, and local non-native populations have lived and traded along the southwestern border of the United States for hundreds of years, but Tex-Mex cuisine, as we know it today, is a 20th century phenomenon. Texas was the cradle of Tex-Mex food and it became mainstream American in the 1970s.

3. La Pequeña Habana

La Pequeña Habana es un área de Miami habitada principalmente por cubanos. En este barrio hay muchas actividades culturales: galerías de arte, teatros, espectáculos musicales y pasatiempos. En la Calle Ocho se celebra un famoso carnaval. Más de un millón de personas se reúnen para disfrutar de la música y el baile en la calle.

(3) Vista aérea del Festival de la Calle Ocho.

89 Nombres y nombres

▶ **Lee y clasifica.** Read the text and classify the names below by the graphic organizer provided.

> **Nombres de origen hispano**
>
> Muchos lugares de los Estados Unidos tienen un nombre de origen hispano. Algunos tienen nombres de santos, como San Diego; otros tienen nombres de ciudades españolas, como Toledo; hay nombres de animales o plantas de la zona, como Fresno, y otros describen el lugar que nombran, como Florida o Nevada.

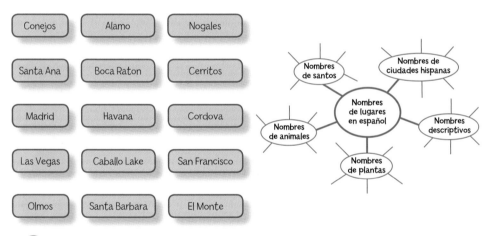

Conejos · Alamo · Nogales · Santa Ana · Boca Raton · Cerritos · Madrid · Havana · Cordova · Las Vegas · Caballo Lake · San Francisco · Olmos · Santa Barbara · El Monte

Nombres de lugares en español:
- Nombres de santos
- Nombres de ciudades hispanas
- Nombres de animales
- Nombres descriptivos
- Nombres de plantas

▶ **Habla.** Play a guessing game with your partner. Ask him or her where the places you added to your graphic organizer are and let him or her ask you back.

Activities

89. Elicit from students the definitions they already know for these Spanish place names. Encourage them to find these words and their definitions in a Spanish dictionary. Once students have located the words, inquire if the definition is meaningful and relevant to the place.

Answer Key

89.
- Nombres de santos: Santa Ana, Santa Barbara, San Francisco
- Nombres de ciudades hispanas: Madrid, Havana, Cordova
- Nombres de animales: Conejos, Boca Raton, Caballo Lake
- Nombres de plantas: Olmos, Alamo, Nogales
- Nombres descriptivos: Las Vegas, Cerritos, El Monte

Additional Resources

Fans Online activities
Practice Workbook

La Pequeña Habana

This Miami neighborhood has experienced many changes in its short history. During the 1930s, it had a thriving Jewish community. When Fidel Castro came to power in 1959, Cubans who opposed his regime began arriving in the United States. A large number of these exiles settled in this neighborhood, inspiring its current name of Little Havana. In the 1970s, they began moving to the suburbs. A second wave of immigrants from Cuba and Central America settled in Little Havana in the 1980s and 90s. Local neighbors, businesses, and government have worked together to preserved Little Havana's unique heritage.

Nombres de origen hispano en los Estados Unidos

The Spanish presence in the United States goes back to 1565 when the Spanish founded a permanent settlement in St. Augustine, Florida. In 1542, Juan Rodriguez Cabrillo—a Portuguese navigator working for the Spanish crown—led an expedition to explore what is now the coast of California. Until 1848, large sections of the southwestern United States were part of Mexico. It is not surprising to find an abundance of Spanish place names in the United States, with some as far north as Alaska where Madre de Dios Island is located.

135

LECTURA

Celebramos la Herencia Hispana

Presentation

- In this section, students will read about *Mes de la Herencia Hispana*, a month-long celebration of Hispanic heritage in the United States.

Activities	Standards	Resources
Lectura	1.2, 3.1, 3.2	
90.	1.3, 3.1	
91.	1.2, 1.3	
92.	1.3, 5.2	
Tu desafío	1.1, 1.3, 5.1	

Teaching Suggestions

Warm-Up / Independent Starter

- Have students look at the photos on the first page of the reading and see if they can identify each picture. They can fill in a question word chart like the one below with the information by answering questions such as:
  - *¿Qué?* (What is in the photo?)
  - *¿Quién?* (Who is in the photo?)
  - *¿Cuándo?* (When does the celebration take place?)
  - *¿Cómo?* (How are people celebrating?)
  - *¿Por qué?* (Why are people celebrating?)

¿Qué?	¿Quién?	¿Cuándo?

¿Cómo?	¿Por qué?

Preparation

- Have students predict which words and phrases they might need to use in Spanish to talk about the reading based on the photos. Ask them to see if they can find any of these new words and phrases in the text as they read.

Activities

90. Have students tell a friend about the connections they listed in this activity. Do they have any of the same connections? Which ones? Which connections are different?

LECTURA

Using prior knowledge

You use prior knowledge when you recall what you know about the topic, format, or language of the text, your personal experiences, and your knowledge of the world.

Before, during, and after reading, make connections to something you know. Bringing this prior knowledge to the text helps you understand it and learn new information.

---

1. Don't miss it!

136 ciento treinta y seis

Celebramos la Herencia Hispana

La cultura hispana está transformando los Estados Unidos. Su influencia está presente en la moda, en la comida, en la música, en el baile, en la forma de hablar de la gente y en el arte.

Del 15 de septiembre al 15 de octubre muchas ciudades celebran el Mes de la Herencia Hispana. En ese tiempo los Estados Unidos reconocen la contribución de la comunidad hispana al progreso de la nación.

Coloridos desfiles, música y danzas tradicionales, exposiciones, comida y mucha alegría muestran la riqueza y la diversidad de la cultura hispana. Es una fiesta para todos. ¡No te la pierdas![1]

Nuestra propuesta

En Chicago
DESFILE DEL DÍA DE INDEPENDENCIA DE MÉXICO
FECHA: 16 de septiembre
HORA: 7 p. m.
LUGAR: Chicago Cultural Center

En Los Ángeles
FESTIVAL DE CINE LATINO DE LOS ÁNGELES
FECHA: del 12 de septiembre al 19 de octubre
LUGAR: UCLA North Campus

En Nueva York
FIESTA DE LA JUVENTUD CARIBEÑA DE BROOKLYN
FECHA: 13 de septiembre
HORA: de 10 a. m. a 5 p. m.
LUGAR: 4th Street, Brooklyn

Differentiated Instruction

DEVELOPING LEARNERS

- Pair developing learners with more advanced students to promote peer support. Have them read *Celebramos la Herencia Hispana* to each other. As they read, encourage them to check their comprehension by asking each other *yes* and *no* questions.

EXPANDING LEARNERS

- Have students compare the Hispanic celebrations described in the reading with one from their family's cultural background. Draw a Venn diagram on the board and guide students in comparing and contrasting the celebrations.

ESTRATEGIA Utilizar el conocimiento previo

 Hacer conexiones

▶ **Escribe.** Write connections between topics, images, or details in the text and the things or experiences they remind you of.

En el texto...		Yo lo relaciono con...
Celebran el mes de la Herencia Hispana.	→	Tengo vecinos hispanos.
	→	
	→	
	→	

COMPRENSIÓN

 Los hispanos y los Estados Unidos

▶ **Corrige.** Correct the sentences so that they agree with the text.

1. El Mes de la Herencia Hispana es una celebración hispana en los Estados Unidos.
2. La influencia hispana en la vida de los Estados Unidos no es muy importante.
3. Los estadounidenses no hispanos no pueden participar en los festejos del Mes de la Herencia Hispana.
4. El Mes de la Herencia Hispana es una fiesta de la diversidad.

92 **Hispanos unidos**

▶ **Haz un cartel.**
In a small group, make an eye-catching poster about Hispanic Heritage.

 TU DESAFÍO Use the website to learn more about Hispanic Heritage.

ciento treinta y siete 137

Activities

92. Have students pretend that they are advertising executives. Have them verbally present their poster to the class, with the other students serving as the "clients." Encourage students to ask questions about the poster (for example, their choice of images, colors, fonts, and so on).

Answer Key

90. Answers will vary. Sample answer:
La influencia hispana está presente en la moda. → Me gusta la ropa de Carolina Herrera.

91. 1. Cierto. Desde 1988, los festejos en homenaje a la comunidad hispana duran un mes.
2. La influencia de la población hispana en la vida de Estados Unidos <u>es muy importante</u>.
3. <u>Todos los estadounidenses</u> pueden participar en los festejos del Mes de la Herencia Hispana.
4. Cierto. El Mes de la Herencia Hispana celebra la riqueza y la diversidad de la cultura hispana.

92. Answers will vary.

Additional Resources

Fans Online activities

HERITAGE LANGUAGE LEARNERS

• Ask if students know any other celebrations of Hispanic origin that take place in the United States (such as the Day of the Dead, *el Cinco de Mayo*, etc.). Have them compare these holidays to similar holidays in their countries of origin using a Venn diagram. Ask them to share their knowledge with the rest of the class.

MULTIPLE INTELLIGENCES:
Musical Intelligence

• Have students research two Christmas songs, one in Spanish and one in English (such as "Feliz Navidad" and "Have a Holly Jolly Christmas"). Have them compare and identify the genres and lyrics. Ask if any of the students play musical instruments, and if so, ask them to prepare an acoustic version of the song with two or three other students. Have them talk about the rhythm they chose for each song and why.

137

Unit 6

REPASO

Vocabulario

Presentation

- In this section, students will review all key vocabulary from the unit, organized by themes, to prepare for an assessment. Students will complete practice activities for each of the four *Desafíos*.

Activities	Standards	Resources
1.	1.2, 1.3	
2.	1.3	
3.	1.2, 1.3	
4.	1.2, 1.3	

Teaching Suggestions

Warm-Up / Independent Starter

- Students can review vocabulary by writing ten words that they remember from this unit. You may guide them by listing a few categories on the board.

Preparation

- Ask students to find photos or clip art of the free-time activities to use as flashcards. Have them practice the words by showing their photos and talking about their favorite ones with a partner. For example: *Me gusta escribir correos electrónicos porque es gratis.*

Activities

1. Have students pretend to be one of the professionals. Have them talk about what they do all day at their jobs until a classmate guesses their identity. For example: *Yo trabajo en el gimnasio. Trabajo con los deportistas…*

3. Have students work in small groups and brainstorm a problem they might have encountered at the Latin Grammy Awards if they had been assigned Tess and Patricia's task. Have students write the problem on a piece of paper and exchange it with another group. They should offer advice to solve each other's problems.

4. You may bring in a variety of sports equipment to the class. Have students categorize the equipment into the sports they represent.

138

El trabajo

Lugares de trabajo

la escuela	school
la fábrica	factory
el hospital	hospital
la obra	construction site
la oficina	office

Las profesiones

el/la abogado(a)	lawyer
el/la director(a)	director, principal
el/la entrenador(a)	coach
el/la ingeniero(a)	engineer
el/la maestro(a)	teacher
el/la médico(a)	doctor
el/la secretario(a)	secretary

Tiempo libre

escribir correos	to write e-mails
escuchar la radio	to listen to the radio
grabar	to tape, to record
ir al cine	to go to the movies
jugar a los videojuegos	to play video games
tomar/sacar fotos	to take pictures
ver películas	to see movies
la cámara de fotos	camera
la cámara de video	camcorder
la película	movie, film
el videojuego	video game

Los pasatiempos

actuar	to act
bailar	to dance
caminar	to walk
cantar	to sing
escribir mensajes	to send a text message
escuchar música	to listen to music
hacer deporte, practicar deportes	to play sports
leer un libro	to read a book
montar en bicicleta	to ride a bike
nadar	to swim
pintar	to paint
tocar el piano	to play the piano
viajar	to travel

Los deportes

Los deportes

el baloncesto	basketball
el béisbol	baseball
el boliche	bowling
el fútbol	soccer
el fútbol americano	football
el golf	golf
la natación	swimming
el tenis	tennis
el voleibol	volleyball
jugar (a), practicar	to play

El equipamiento

el balón	ball
el bate	bat
la bola	ball
el casco	helmet
el guante	glove
la pelota	ball
la raqueta	racket
la red	net

La competición deportiva

el partido	game
el estadio	stadium
el/la jugador(a)	player
el equipo	team
ganar	to win
perder	to lose

Differentiated Instruction

DEVELOPING LEARNERS

- Provide extra practice for developing learners by pairing them with advanced students to write a quiz like the one below. Or you may do this type of activity as an oral exercise, on a transparency, or on a handout.

Which one doesn't belong in this sequence? (For example: *la fábrica, la fotografía, la oficina.*)

1. *la ingeniera, el secretario, el teatro*
2. *caminar, escuchar música, nadar*
3. *pintar, el béisbol, el tenis*
4. *el guante, el cine, la pelota*
5. *la película, el teatro, la oficina*

EXPANDING LEARNERS

- Ask students about their favorite hobbies. Referring to the sports equipment and media vocabulary from the unit, have students brainstorm all the equipment or materials necessary to participate in their hobby. Have students share their information in small groups. For example: *Me gusta el tenis. Para jugar al tenis necesito una raqueta y una pelota, y tengo que ir a la cancha.*

DESAFÍO 1

1 **Profesiones.** Read the statements below and determine which person is talking from the people in the word bank.

> maestro   director   ingeniero   abogada   secretaria

1. Tengo que organizar el horario de la escuela y las reuniones con los padres.
2. Trabajo en una fábrica de coches. Hago muchos cálculos matemáticos y físicos.
3. Tengo muchas tareas en mi oficina: escribir cartas, hablar por teléfono…
4. Trabajo en una escuela. Tengo cinco clases cada día. Pongo notas.
5. Represento a mis clientes en asuntos legales.

DESAFÍO 2

2 **Preferencias.** Say what the first person likes to do and what the second person prefers.

Modelo   *A ellos les gusta bailar. Yo prefiero cantar.*

Ángel   yo

nosotros   ella

Rosa   usted

DESAFÍO 3

3 **Buenos consejos.** Solve the problems with the appropriate advice.

1. Quiero ver a Juanes en directo.
2. Tengo que tomar fotos.
3. No me gusta ver películas en la tele.
4. Tengo que contactar con mi maestro.
5. Esta noche no puedo ver la película.

a. Usa mi cámara.
b. Escríbele un correo electrónico.
c. Pues grábala.
d. Asiste a su concierto en el teatro.
e. Entonces ve al cine.

DESAFÍO 4

4 **Deportes.** Answer the following questions in complete sentences.

1. ¿Dónde juega al fútbol o al béisbol un equipo profesional?
2. ¿Qué necesitas para jugar al béisbol?
3. ¿Cuántos jugadores necesita un equipo de baloncesto?
4. ¿Dónde practicas la natación?
5. ¿Qué deporte practicas con una raqueta y una pelota?

ciento treinta y nueve 139

HERITAGE LANGUAGE LEARNERS

• In small groups, have students create a role-play situation centered around the vocabulary themes from Unit 6. For example, they can write a scene about sports, media, professions, etc. Instruct them to write a short script wherein they each play a part. Give students the opportunity to perform their plays for the group.

TOTAL PHYSICAL RESPONSE (TPR)

• Tell students that you are going to play a game. Break the class into small teams. Have the students assign a number to themselves. Have all Student 1s stand up from every group. Perform a gesture or an action (for example: pretend to swim) and watch as each student writes the word associated with that action on a mini/individual white board/chalkboard (or simply on a piece of paper). The first student to show the correct written answer wins a point for his or her team. The team with the most points wins.

Unit 6

REPASO

Gramática

Presentation

- Students will review the grammatical structures presented in the unit. The activities here provide systematic practice by *Desafío*.

Activities	Standards	Resources
5.	1.2, 1.3	
6.	1.2, 1.3	
7.	1.2, 1.3	
8.	1.3	
9. Cultura	1.3, 2.1, 2.2, 5.2	

Teaching Suggestions

Warm-Up / Independent Starter

- Have students use the following prompts to write five sentences:
  - *Mañana por la mañana…*
  - *Voy a…*
  - *Toma…*
  - *Estamos comiendo…*
  - *Juego…*

Preparation

- Ask students to review the irregular *tú* commands by playing a game of *Cambia la frase*. One student gives a command such as *Ve a la pizarra*. Another student changes the verb or the noun in the sentence, for example: *Ve a la tienda*. The next one says *Compra en la tienda*, and so on.

Activities

5. Have students come up with three commands an athlete would hear from his or her coach. For example: *Haz ejercicio*.

7. Ask students to look around the room and write two sentences, describing what their classmates are doing, using the present progressive.

8. Have students write a list of two sports they play and one sport they don't play. Then have them share their sports with a classmate (*Yo juego al béisbol y al fútbol americano. No juego al hockey*). Finally, ask students to report their partner's information to the class (for example: *Mi amigo Jaime juega al baloncesto y al fútbol. No juega al tenis*.)

140

REPASO **Gramática**

Imperativo afirmativo. Verbos irregulares (pág. 98)

Decir *(to say)*	di
Hacer *(to do)*	haz
Ir *(to go)*	ve
Poner *(to put)*	pon
Salir *(to leave)*	sal
Ser *(to be)*	sé
Tener *(to have)*	ten
Venir *(to come)*	ven

El presente continuo (pág. 114)

In Spanish the present progressive is formed as follows: *estar* + **gerundio**.

Estoy estudiando español.

El gerundio (pág. 116)

The present participle is formed this way:

▶ Add **-ando** to the stem of verbs ending in *-ar*.

▶ Add **-iendo** to the stem of verbs ending in *-er* and *-ir*.

VERBOS IRREGULARES EN GERUNDIO

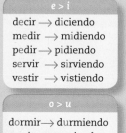

e > i

decir → diciendo
medir → midiendo
pedir → pidiendo
servir → sirviendo
vestir → vistiendo

o > u

dormir → durmiendo
morir → muriendo
poder → pudiendo

Ir a + infinitivo (pág. 106)

To express the intention to do something, use this structure: *ir a* + **infinitive**.

Vamos a viajar a Miami.

Expresiones temporales de futuro (pág. 106)

ahora	now
luego, después	later
hoy	today
esta mañana	this morning
esta tarde	this afternoon
esta noche	tonight
mañana	tomorrow
mañana por la mañana	tomorrow morning
mañana por la tarde	tomorrow afternoon/ evening
mañana por la noche	tomorrow night
la próxima semana, la semana que viene	next week
el próximo año, el año que viene	next year

Verbos con raíz irregular (u > ue) (pág. 124)

JUGAR

yo	juego	nosotros nosotras	jugamos
tú	juegas	vosotros vosotras	jugáis
usted él ella	juega	ustedes ellos ellas	juegan

140 ciento cuarenta

Differentiated Instruction

DEVELOPING LEARNERS

- Have students create picture flashcards for ten present progressive actions (five with regular present participles and five with irregular present participles). They should illustrate the actions using clip art, magazine cut-outs, or hand-drawn pictures. Have them quiz their classmates using their cards.

EXPANDING LEARNERS

- Have students play a game to pratice both the *tú* commands and the present progressive verbs in groups of threes. The first student gives a command to the second. The second student acts out the command. The third student reports what the second student is doing. For example:

A. *Ponte la tarea en la cabeza.*
B. (Puts his homework on top of his head)
C. *Está poniéndose la tarea en la cabeza.*

DESAFÍO 1

5 **Órdenes.** Change the following obligations into commands.

Modelo Tienes que salir de casa. → Sal de casa.

1. Tienes que poner la mesa.
2. Tienes que ser prudente.
3. Tienes que hacer la tarea.
4. Tienes que venir a la fiesta.
5. Tienes que ir a la oficina.
6. Tienes que decir la verdad.

 DESAFÍO 2

6 **Planes.** Ask and answer questions with a partner according to the model.

Modelo tú - esta tarde - jugar al fútbol → A. ¿Qué vas a hacer tú esta tarde?
B. Esta tarde voy a jugar al fútbol.

1. Rosa - esta noche - ver una película
2. ustedes - mañana - montar en bicicleta
3. María y Ana - el sábado - bailar
4. usted - ahora - tocar el piano

 DESAFÍO 3

7 **¿Qué están haciendo?** Rewrite the sentences changing the present tense into the present progressive and the direct object into a direct object pronoun.

Modelo Ella *escribe un mensaje.* → Ella *está escribiéndolo* o Ella *lo está escribiendo.*

1. Yo compro un casco.
2. Tú ordenas tu dormitorio.
3. Nosotros oímos las canciones.
4. Ella pide la carta.
5. Ellos graban una película.
6. Ustedes ven la televisión.

DESAFÍO 4

8 **¿Jugamos?** Say what sport the people play according the pictures. Use the verb *jugar*.

nosotros   yo   ellos   tú   Pilar

 **CULTURA**

9 **Estados Unidos hispano.** Answer the questions.

1. What is the Maximo Gomez Park in Miami better known as?
2. Which Hispanic artist has won the most Latin Grammy Awards?
3. Where does the Fiesta Noche del Río take place?
4. In what Hispanic countries is baseball the most popular?

ciento cuarenta y uno 141

HERITAGE LANGUAGE LEARNERS

- Have students record a conversation with a relative who speaks Spanish. Have them ask questions about what they are going to do in the future (*ir a* + infinitive). As they present their recordings to the class, have the other students raise their hands (or clap, or stomp their feet) whenever they hear the *ir a* + infinitive structure being used by the speaker.

SPECIAL-NEEDS LEARNERS

- For students with organizational or information processing difficulties, the amount of information presented on a review page may be overwhelming. Encourage these students to copy the information from each box onto its own page in their notebooks. Have them write a few original sentences using the grammar from each of the four boxes so that they can personalize and better internalize the information.

PROYECTO

Un hispano famoso

Presentation

- In this section, students will create a presentation to celebrate Hispanic heritage in the United States and to practice the vocabulary and grammar they have learned in Unit 6. The project offers an opportunity for students to demonstrate what they have learned. Students will follow step-by-step instructions.

Activities	Standards	Resources
Paso 1	1.2, 1.3, 3.1	
Paso 2	1.2, 1.3, 3.1	
Paso 3	1.3, 3.1, 5.2	
Paso 4	1.1, 1.3	

Teaching Suggestions

Warm-Up / Independent Starter

- Have students meet regularly in small groups to do peer reviews of their projects.

Preparation

- Ask students to brainstorm all the information they know about famous Hispanics in the United States. They should choose someone who they can look up to, or someone who inspires them on a personal level.

Step-by-Step Instructions

Paso 1

- Have students do an Internet search regarding famous Hispanics. Some excellent resources can be found at:
  - Hispanic Latino-Americans: http://www.personal.psu.edu/faculty/c/s/csr4/PSU3/Hispanic-Latino-Americans/Hispanic-Latino-Americans.html
  - Hispanic Americans @ InfoPlease: http://www.infoplease.com/spot/hhmbioaz.html

  They should answer the four questions using the information they find online or in library books.

Paso 2

- Encourage students to design a "story board" version of their poster before they begin as a way of designing the final product. They can use a piece of scratch paper and map out where each bit of text or imagery will appear on the final poster.

142

Un cartel sobre

un hispano famoso

In this project you will create a poster about a well-known person of Hispanic origin in the United States.

– First, you will research well-known native Spanish speakers.
– Secondly, in groups, decide on the person that interests you the most. Then prepare an illustrated poster to introduce the person selected.
– Thirdly, you will announce and then make your presentation to your classmates.

PASO 1 Investiga

- Find out about well-known people of Hispanic origin who are distinguished in fields such as medicine, sport, entertainment, and business. Look for information to answer these questions:
  – ¿De qué país es?   – ¿Qué profesión tiene?
  – ¿Dónde vive o trabaja ahora?   – ¿Por qué es famoso(a)?

Aquí tienes algunas ideas:

Pedro Duque, astronauta.   Sonia Sotomayor, jueza.   Gloria Estefan, cantante.   Carolina Herrera, diseñadora.   Isabel Allende, escritora.

PASO 2 Prepara tu cartel

- In a group, select the person that interests you the most.
- Write the answers to the questions in Step 1 in complete sentences and creatively copy them onto your poster.
- Find photos to illustrate the information.
- Write captions to describe what is happening in each photo.

El español Pau Gasol es un jugador de baloncesto muy conocido en los Estados Unidos.

Rubric for Evaluation

	Content	Organization	Presentation
1 point	Limited relevance. Information is incomplete or not based on research. Little Spanish is used.	Inefficient use of class time. Information is disorganized or unclear.	Communication is unclear. Many errors in vocabulary and grammar.
3 points	Basic information is correct. Relevant information but lacks significance. Spanish is used most of the time.	Class time is used well. Information and content are mostly organized but lack some clarity.	Good communication. Mostly correct vocabulary and grammar.

PASO 3 Anuncia tu presentación

• Prepare an advertisement for your presentation. Include the following information:
– The name of the person you are going to present.
– The time and place you will make your presentation.
– Whom your presentation will appeal to.

¡El baloncesto con un experto!

Fecha:
el 10 de octubre

Hora:
a las 3 de la tarde

Lugar:
en el gimnasio

Tema:
el jugador Pau Gasol

¿Te gusta el baloncesto?
¡Ven a mi presentación!

PASO 4 Presenta el cartel

• Present your poster to the class.
• Invite your classmates to ask you questions at the end.

¿Hay preguntas?
¿Quieren saber más?

Unidad 6

Autoevaluación

¿Qué has aprendido en esta unidad?

Use these questions to evaluate how well you have understood this unit's concepts.

Evaluate your skills. For each activity, say Very well, Well, or I need more practice.

a. Can you talk about professions?
▶ Talk to your partner about which profession you would prefer to have and why.

b. Can you tell someone what to do using verbs like *decir, salir, venir,* and *poner*?
▶ Write four *tú* commands using the verbs *decir, salir, venir,* and *poner*. Ask your partner to act them out.

c. Can you say what you are going to do in the future?
▶ Ask your partner what are his or her plans for next week.

d. Can you describe what someone is doing now?
▶ Say what three classmates are doing now.

e. Can you talk about sports?
▶ Ask two classmates what sports they like to watch or play.

	Content	Organization	Presentation
5 points	Relevant, interesting information. Many details and significance are highlighted. Spanish is used exclusively.	Class time is used wisely. Information and content are clearly organized visually and logically.	Clear communication. Correct and complete vocabulary and grammar.

PROYECTO

Un hispano famoso

Paso 3

▪ Students create advertisements related to their presentation. This is a way to encourage their classmates to come to their talks. Have students make the ads exciting and interesting by adding photos and important information about their presentations.

Paso 4

▪ Each student will give a presentation to the class. Have them remember to speak slowly and clearly, while also keeping a smile on their faces and making eye contact with the audience.

Evaluation

▪ Explain how the project will be evaluated by distributing copies of the rubric chart and discussing how it works.

▪ Encourage students to refer to the rubric as they prepare their projects. It may be helpful to correlate points with traditional grade scales and indicate how much the project counts toward the final grade.

Content

▪ Explain the importance of data collection (*Paso 1* and *Paso 2*). Students should select information that is interesting and relevant. To develop research skills, ask students to include their lists of sources, especially if they need to go back to them for more research.

Organization

▪ Let students decide which information to include, and then reflect on the length of their written script and the time needed to perform it. Decide whether you want to evaluate the project individually or by groups.

Presentation

▪ Students should use as much Spanish as possible. They should check grammar and vocabulary before completing the project.

▪ Rehearsals should enable them to present confidently and fluently, as well as guarantee a good grade. Encourage creativity and style to hold their classmates' attention.

143

Objectives

- To talk about past actions.
- To discuss the different modes of transportation.
- To use travel vocabulary.
- To express actions related to travel.
- To list travel necessities and accessories.
- To talk about destinations and accommodations.

- To express when actions happened in the past.
- To give negative commands.
- To tell locations and give directions.
- To explore cultural aspects of Argentina.

Contents

Vocabulary

- Modes of transportation.
- Public transportation facilities.
- Travel actions and information.
- Travel accessories.
- Destinations and accommodations.
- Places in a city.
- Directions.

Grammar

- Regular -ar verbs in the preterite tense.
- Regular -er and -ir verbs in the preterite tense.
- Adverbs that indicate time.
- Preterite tense of the verbs *ser* and *ir*.
- Negative *tú* commands.

Culture

- The geography and culture of Argentina.
- Buenos Aires.
- *El tren a las nubes.*
- Public transportation.
- La Pampa and gaucho tradition.
- The Marathon *A Pampa Traviesa.*
- Iguazu Falls.
- *La Plaza de Mayo.*
- *La Casa Rosada.*
- *La Pirámide de Mayo.*
- *El Teatro Colón.*
- The works of an Argentine author.

Evaluation Criteria

- Express actions in the past.
- Tell when the actions occurred.
- Show understanding of the use of *ser* and *ir* in the preterite.

- Organize travel plans and accommodations.
- Describe travel destinations.
- Talk about different forms of transportation for a trip and/or around a city.

- List items needed to prepare for a trip.
- Give and take driving and/or walking directions.
- Give and respond to negative commands.

Unit Plan

La llegada

Estimated time: 2 sessions.

Dialogue: *En Buenos Aires.*

Forms & functions:
- Travel necessities and accessories.
- Modes of transportation.
- Travel destinations and accommodations.
- Places in the city.
- Public transportation facilities.
- Expressing readiness.
- Expressing having something handy.

Culture:
- Buenos Aires.

DESAFÍO 1

Estimated time: 5 sessions.

Dialogue: *El tren a las nubes.*

Forms & functions:
- Modes of transportation and public transportation facilities.
- Expressing actions in the past: Regular -*ar* verbs in the preterite tense.

Culture:
- *El tren a las nubes.*
- *El transporte público: el metro.*

DESAFÍO 2

Estimated time: 5 sessions.

Dialogue: *Un gaucho de la Pampa.*

Forms & functions:
- Travel necessities and accessories.
- Expressing actions related to traveling: Regular -*er* and -*ir* verbs in the preterite tense.

Culture:
- *Los gauchos.*
- *La Pampa.*
- *A Pampa Traviesa.*

DESAFÍO 3

Estimated time: 6 sessions.

Dialogue: *Las cataratas del Iguazú.*

Forms & functions:
- Travel destinations and accommodations.
- Expressing when an action in the past took place: adverbs and expressions of time.
- Expressing actions in the past: Preterite tense of the verbs *ser* and *ir*.

Culture:
- *Las cataratas del Iguazú.*

DESAFÍO 4

Estimated time: 5 sessions.

Dialogue: *Sobres en la calle.*

Forms & functions:
- Places in the city and directions.
- To tell someone what not to do: Negative *tú* commands.

Culture:
- *La Plaza de Mayo.*
- *La Casa Rosada.*
- *La Pirámide de Mayo.*

Todo junto / El encuentro

Estimated time: 2 sessions.

Dialogue: *En el Teatro Colón.*

Forms & functions:
- Review of *Desafíos 1–4.*

Culture:
- *El Teatro Colón.*

MAPA CULTURAL / LECTURA

Estimated time: 2 sessions.

Mapa cultural: *Argentina.*

Reading: *La vuelta al mundo de Cinthia Scoch.*

REPASO

Estimated time: 2 sessions.

Vocabulary: *Repaso.*

Grammar: *Repaso.*

PROYECTO / EVALUACIÓN

Estimated time: 5 sessions.

Project: *Crónica de un viaje.*

Self-evaluation: *Autoevaluación.*

Standards for Learning Spanish

COMMUNICATION

1.1. Interpersonal mode
- Discuss and vote on the pairs' challenges.
- Talk to a partner about previous and/or future travel plans and preferences.
- Talk to a partner about travel preferences.
- Discuss purchases.
- Give a partner advice or directions using commands.
- Write a list, paragraph, or fill in a chart to summarize class findings.
- Listen to a conversation or a partner's questions and respond.
- Read a passage and discuss the critical thinking questions with a partner.
- Read a passage and compare items in the United States and in the Spanish-speaking world.

1.2. Interpretive mode
- Listen to an audio recording and take notes.
- Listen to a conversation and write sentences to summarize what was heard.
- Listen to a conversation and decide which character performed the action.
- Read a cultural passage and show comprehension by making comparisons with daily life.
- Read a passage and answer the questions based on personal experiences and/or preferences.

1.3. Presentational mode
- Act out a dialogue for the class.
- Write sentences or a story based on clues or questions.
- Use a picture story to answer comprehension questions.
- Take notes based on your or a partner's activities.

CULTURE

2.1. Practices and perspectives
- Understand the use and efficiency of public transportation.
- Understand the customs of an Argentinean gaucho.

2.2. Products and perspectives
- Relate pictures with cultural aspects of Argentina.
- Show comprehension of the history and culture of Argentina.
- Understand the reasoning for painting the *Casa Rosada* pink.

CONNECTIONS

3.1. Interdisciplinary connections
- Review the formation of the past tense in English.
- Create a short story based on clues provided.
- Compare geographical regions in the United States with Argentina's.
- Compare the locations of natural wonders in the United States with the rest of the Americas.
- Understand the history, nature, and purpose of a compass rose.
- Understand compound words in English and in Spanish.
- Convert kilometers to miles.

- Read and follow a map.
- Research the history and representations of statues in the United States.

3.2. Viewpoints through language/culture
- Discuss the advantages and disadvantages of public transportation in your town and in Spanish-speaking countries.
- Compare the lifestyles of Argentine gauchos and American cowboys.
- Compare the speed limits in Latin America with those in the United States.
- Decide what the color of the Presidential Palace in Argentina represents.

COMPARISONS

4.1. Compare languages
- Compare the formation of the past tense in English and Spanish.
- Understand compound words in English and Spanish.
- Compare the similarities and differences between negative commands in English and in Spanish.

4.2. Compare cultures
- Compare Argentine gauchos and American cowboys.
- Compare La Pampa with a region in the United States.
- Compare the Marathon *A Pampa Traviesa* with a race in your town.
- Name statues in the United States, like the *Pirámide de Mayo* in Argentina, that represent the liberation of a people.

COMMUNITIES

5.1. Spanish beyond the school setting
- Write a postcard to a friend to describe your travel experiences.
- View and describe your hometown.

5.2. Spanish for lifelong learning
- Research and present biographical information about a famous Argentine figure.
- Interview people and share information about previous and future travel plans.
- Convert the speed limits in Latin America from kilometers to miles.

Communicative Skills

Interpersonal Mode — Activities

Speaking	• Talk to a partner about travel plans and preferences. • Talk to a classmate about their activities in the past tense. • Give a partner advice or directions using commands. • Talk to a partner about means of transportation.	• 6, 12, 16, 53, *Proyecto* • 20, 28, 33, 48 • 68, 69, 71, 76 • 10
Writing	• Summarize class findings. • Write a passage to read aloud to a partner.	• 53, 57, 75 • 20, 28, 31, 33
Listening	• Understand questions and respond appropriately. • Obtain information from an oral exchange.	• 31 • 44, 53
Reading	• Read and understand a map.	• 71

Interpretive Mode — Activities

Listening	• Identify the main ideas of an oral text. • Evaluate or interpret oral information. • Demonstrate an understanding of an oral text.	• 3, 18, 24, 31, 55, 72, 75 • 8, 15, 44, 51 • 27, 49, 61, 63
Reading	• Relate the theme of a reading passage to your personal life or experiences. • Demonstrate an understanding of a reading passage. • Infer the meaning of a reading passage. • Identify the key concepts of a picture story.	• 13, 25, 29, 34, 42, 62, 70 • 11, 18, 35, 36, 40, 52, 56, 73, 77, 84 • 7, 23, 43, 59, 60 • 1, 2, 6, 22, R2, R3

Presentational Mode — Activities

Speaking	• Act out a dialogue for the class. • Conduct an interview in front of the class. • Present a cultural topic based on a poster.	• 17, 38, 68, 78 • 57, *Proyecto* • 36
Writing	• Write a story to present to the class. • Write a description.	• 17, 19, 26, 27, 32, 37, 41, 45, 49, 50, 51, 58, 63, 69, 72, 74, 76, 83 85, R4, R5, R6, R7, R8 • 61, 71, 73, 75, 78

Cross-Curricular Standards

Subject	Standard	Activities
Language Arts	• Identify and conjugate past tense of verbs. • Understand the difference between present- and past-tense verbs. • Implement reading strategies.	• 18, 35 • 14, 31, 39 • *Lectura*
Art	• Draw an original work of art.	• 85, *Proyecto*
Social Studies	• Explore geographical and political features of Argentina. • Draw and/or read a map or compass. • Become aware of public transportation's uses and efficiency.	• 29, 42, 62, 66, 70 • 46, 64, 65, 71, 80, *Proyecto* • 13
Math	• Convert kilometers to miles.	• 54

Lesson Plans (50-Minute Classes)

Day	Objectives	Sessions	Activities	Time	Standards	Resources/ Homework
1	To introduce Argentina	**Argentina** (145–146) • Warm-Up: Country orientation • Argentina • Images and functions		5 m. 15 m. 30 m.	1.2, 2.2, 4.1	Video Practice Workbook
2	To introduce Argentina and to discuss the pairs' challenges	**La llegada** (147–149) • Warm-Up: Independent Starter • Presentation: *En Buenos Aires* • *Expresiones útiles* and *¿Quién ganará?*	 1 2–5	5 m. 15 m. 30 m.	1.1, 1.2, 1.3, 4.1	Visual Presentation Audio Practice Workbook
3	To talk about modes of transportation and to talk about past actions	**Desafío 1 – El tren a las nubes** (150–151) • Warm-Up: Independent Starter • *Fotonovela: El tren a las nubes* • *Cultura: El tren a las nubes*	 6–8 9	5 m. 30 m. 15 m.	1.1, 1.2, 1.3, 3.1, 3.2, 4.2	Visual Presentation Audio Video
4	To learn modes of transportation and public transportation facilities	**Desafío 1 – Vocabulario** (152–153) • Warm-Up: Independent Starter • *Vocabulary: De viaje* • *Conexiones: El transporte público: el metro*	 10–12 13	5 m. 35 m. 10 m.	1.1, 1.2, 1.3, 3.1, 3.2	Practice Workbook
5	To conjugate regular *-ar* verbs in the preterite tense	**Desafío 1 – Gramática** (154–155) • Warm-Up: Independent Starter • *Grammar: Verbos regulares en -ar. Pretérito*	 14–17	5 m. 45 m.	1.1, 1.2, 1.3, 3.1, 4.1	Audio Practice Workbook
6	To integrate vocabulary and grammar	**Desafío 1 – Comunicación** (156–157) • Warm-Up: Independent Starter • *Comunicación*: Review main vocabulary and grammar	 18–20	5 m. 45 m.	1.1, 1.2, 1.3, 3.1	Audio Practice Workbook
7	To assess student proficiency	**Desafío 1 – Evaluación** (157) • Warm-Up: *Final del desafío* • Quiz on *Desafío 1*	 21	30 m. 20 m.	1.2, 1.3	*Tu desafío*
8	To talk about travel accessories and to talk about past actions	**Desafío 2 – Un gaucho de la Pampa** (158–159) • Warm-Up: Independent Starter • *Fotonovela: Un gaucho de la Pampa* • *Comparaciones: Los gauchos*	 22–24 25	5 m. 35 m. 10 m.	1.1, 1.2, 1.3, 2.1, 3.2, 4.2, 5.2	Visual Presentation Audio *Tu desafío*
9	To talk about objects and actions related to travel	**Desafío 2 – Vocabulario** (160–161) • Warm-Up: Independent Starter • *Vocabulary: Los viajes* • *Cultura: La Pampa*	 26–28 29	5 m. 35 m. 10 m.	1.1, 1.2, 1.3, 2.1, 3.1, 3.2, 4.2	Audio Practice Workbook
10	To conjugate regular *-er* and *-ir* verbs in the preterite tense	**Desafío 2 – Gramática** (162–163) • Warm-Up: Independent Starter • *Grammar: Verbos regulares en -er y en -ir. Pretérito* • *Cultura: A Pampa Traviesa*	 30–33 34	5 m. 35 m. 10 m.	1.1, 1.2, 1.3, 3.1, 3.2, 4.1, 4.2	Audio Practice Workbook

Day	Objectives	Sessions	Activities	Time	Standards	Resources/ Homework
11	To integrate vocabulary and grammar	**Desafío 2 – Comunicación** (164–165) • Warm-Up: Independent Starter • *Comunicación*: Review main vocabulary and grammar	35–37	5 m. 45 m.	1.2, 1.3, 3.1	Practice Workbook
12	To assess student proficiency	**Desafío 2 – Evaluación** (165) • Warm-Up: *Final del desafío* • Quiz on *Desafío 2*	38	30 m. 20 m.	1.2, 1.3, 3.1	
13	To learn travel destinations and accommodations, expressions of time, and past actions	**Desafío 3 – Las cataratas del Iguazú** (166–167) • Warm-Up: Independent Starter • *Fotonovela: Las cataratas del Iguazú* • *Cultura: Las cataratas del Iguazú*	39–41 42	5 m. 30 m. 15 m.	1.1, 1.2, 1.3, 3.1, 3.2, 4.2, 5.2	Visual Presentation Video *Tu desafío*
14	To learn travel destinations and accommodations	**Desafío 3 – Vocabulario** (168–169) • Warm-Up: Independent Starter • *Vocabulary: Destinos y alojamientos* • *Conexiones: La rosa de los vientos*	43–45 46	5 m. 35 m. 10 m.	1.1, 1.2, 1.3, 3.1, 3.2	Audio Practice Workbook
15	To learn adverbs and expressions of time	**Desafío 3 – Gramática** (170–171) • Warm-Up: Independent Starter • *Grammar: Marcadores temporales de pasado*	47–50	5 m. 45 m.	1.1, 1.2, 1.3, 3.1, 4.1	Audio Practice Workbook
16	To learn the preterite tense of the verbs *ir* and *ser*	**Desafío 3 – Gramática** (172–173) • Warm-Up: Independent Starter • *Grammar: Los verbos 'ser' e 'ir'. Pretérito* • *Conexiones: Las distancias: ¿millas o kilómetros?*	51–53 54	5 m. 35 m. 10 m.	1.1, 1.2, 1.3, 3.1, 3.2, 4.1	Audio Practice Workbook
17	To integrate vocabulary and grammar	**Desafío 3 – Comunicación** (174–175) • Warm-Up: Independent Starter • *Comunicación*: Review main vocabulary and grammar	55–57	5 m. 45 m.	1.1, 1.2, 1.3, 3.1, 5.1	Audio Practice Workbook
18	To assess student proficiency	**Desafío 3 – Evaluación** (175) • Warm-Up: *Final del desafío* • Quiz on *Desafío 3*	58	30 m. 20 m.	1.2, 1.3	*Tu desafío*
19	To learn the parts of the city, to give directions, and negative commands	**Desafío 4 – Sobres en la calle** (176–177) • Warm-Up: Independent Starter • *Fotonovela: Sobres en la calle* • *Cultura: La Plaza de Mayo*	59–61 62	5 m. 35 m. 10 m.	1.1, 1.2, 1.3, 3.1, 3.2	Visual Presentation Audio
20	To learn the parts of the city and to give directions	**Desafío 4 – Vocabulario** (178–179) • Warm-Up: Independent Starter • *Vocabulary: La ciudad* • *Cultura: La Casa Rosada*	63–65 66	5 m. 35 m. 10 m.	1.1, 1.2, 1.3, 3.1, 3.2	Audio Practice Workbook
21	To give negative *tú* commands	**Desafío 4 – Gramática** (180–181) • Warm-Up: Independent Starter • *Grammar: El imperativo negativo* • *Cultura: La Pirámide de Mayo*	67–69 70	5 m. 35 m. 10 m.	1.1, 1.2, 1.3, 3.1, 3.2, 4.1, 4.2	Practice Workbook

Day	Objectives	Sessions	Activities	Time	Standards	Resources/ Homework
22	To integrate vocabulary and grammar	**Desafío 4 – Comunicación** (182–183) • Warm-Up: Independent Starter • *Comunicación*: Review main vocabulary and grammar	71–73	5 m. 45 m.	1.1, 1.2, 1.3, 5.1	Audio Practice Workbook
23	To assess student proficiency	**Desafío 4 – Evaluación** (183) • Warm-Up: *Final del desafío* • Quiz on *Desafío 4*	74	30 m. 20 m.	1.2, 1.3	
24	To integrate language in context	**Todo junto** (184–185) • Warm-Up: Independent Starter • *Todo junto*	75–77	5 m. 45 m.	1.1, 1.2, 1.3, 5.1	Audio Practice Workbook
25	To integrate language in context	**El encuentro** (186–187) • Warm-Up: Independent Starter • *El encuentro: En el Teatro Colón*	78–79	5 m. 45 m.	1.1, 1.2, 1.3	
26	To learn about Argentine customs and traditions	**Mapa cultural – Argentina** (188–191) • Warm-Up: Independent Starter • *Mapa cultural: Argentina*	80–82	5 m. 45 m.	1.2, 1.3, 2.1, 2.2, 3.1, 3.2, 5.2	Video Practice Workbook
27	Read the works of an Argentine author	**Lectura – La vuelta al mundo de Cinthia Scoch** (192–193) • Warm-Up: Independent Starter • *Lectura: La vuelta al mundo de Cinthia Scoch*	83–85	5 m. 45 m.	1.2, 1.3, 3.1, 3.2	*Tu desafío*
28	To review vocabulary	**Repaso – Vocabulario** (194–195) • Warm-Up: Independent Starter • *Repaso: Vocabulario*	1–4	5 m. 45 m.	1.2, 1.3	Practice Workbook
29	To review grammar and culture	**Repaso – Gramática** (196–197) • Warm-Up: Independent Starter • *Repaso: Gramática*	5–9	5 m. 45 m.	1.3, 2.1, 2.2, 5.2	Practice Workbook
30	To prepare and illustrate a travelogue	**Proyecto – Un viaje** (198–199) • Warm-Up: Read the project outline • Work on project		5 m. 45 m.	1.1, 1.2, 1.3, 3.1, 5.2	
31	To prepare and illustrate a travelogue	**Proyecto – Un viaje** (198–199) • Warm-Up: Read the project outline • Work on project		5 m. 45 m.	1.1, 1.2, 1.3, 3.1, 5.2	
32	To present projects	**Proyecto – Un viaje** (198–199) • Warm-Up: Prepare presentations • Project presentations		5 m. 45 m.	1.1, 1.2, 1.3, 3.1, 5.2	
33	To present projects	**Proyecto – Un viaje** (198–199) • Warm-Up: Prepare presentations • Project presentations		5 m. 45 m.	1.1, 1.2, 1.3, 3.1, 5.2	
34	To assess student proficiency	**Assessment** • *Autoevaluación* (199) • Test on Unit 7		10 m. 40 m.	1.2, 1.3	

Lesson Plans (90-Minute Classes)

Day	Objectives	Sessions	Activities	Time	Standards	Resources/ Homework
1	To introduce Argentina and to discuss the pairs' challenges	**Estados Unidos / La llegada** (88–93) • Warm-Up: Country orientation • The United States • Images and functions • Presentation: *En Buenos Aires* • *Expresiones útiles* and *¿Quién ganará?*	 1 2–5	5 m. 10 m. 20 m. 20 m. 35 m.	1.1, 1.2, 1.3, 2.2, 4.1	Visual Presentation Video Audio Practice Workbook
2	To talk about modes of transportation and public transportation facilities and to talk about past actions	**Desafío 1 – El tren a las nubes / Vocabulario** (150–153) • Warm-Up: Independent Starter • *Fotonovela: El tren a las nubes* • *Cultura: El tren a las nubes* • Vocabulary: *De viaje* • *Conexiones: El transporte público: el metro*	 6–8 9 10–12 13	 5 m. 30 m. 15 m. 30 m. 10 m.	1.1, 1.2, 1.3, 2.1, 4.2, 5.1	Visual Presentation Audio Video Practice Workbook
3	To conjugate regular -ar verbs in the preterite tense and to integrate vocabulary and grammar	**Desafío 1 – Gramática / Comunicación** (154–157) • Warm-Up: Independent Starter • Grammar: *Verbos regulares en -ar. Pretérito* • *Comunicación*: Review main vocabulary and grammar	 14–17 18–20	 5 m. 40 m. 45 m.	1.1, 1.2, 1.3, 3.1, 4.1	Audio Practice Workbook
4	To assess student proficiency and to talk about objects and actions related to travel, and to talk about past actions	**Desafío 1 – Evaluación / Desafío 2 – Un gaucho de la Pampa** (157–159) • Warm-Up: *Final del desafío* • Quiz on *Desafío 1* • *Fotonovela: Un gaucho de la Pampa* • *Comparaciones: Los gauchos*	 21 22–24 25	 25 m. 20 m. 30 m. 15 m.	1.1, 1.2, 1.3, 2.1, 3.2, 4.2, 5.2	Visual Presentation Audio *Tu desafío*
5	To talk about travel accessories and information and to conjugate regular -er and -ir verbs in the preterite tense	**Desafío 2 – Vocabulario / Gramática** (160–163) • Warm-Up: Independent Starter • Vocabulary: *Los viajes* • *Cultura: La Pampa* • Grammar: *Verbos regulares en -er y en -ir. Pretérito* • *Cultura: A Pampa Traviesa*	 26–28 29 30–33 34	 5 m. 30 m. 10 m. 30 m. 15 m.	1.1, 1.2, 1.3, 2.1, 3.1, 3.2, 4.1, 4.2	Audio Practice Workbook
6	To integrate vocabulary and grammar and to assess student proficiency	**Desafío 2 – Comunicación / Evaluación** (164–165) • Warm-Up: Independent Starter • *Comunicación*: Review main vocabulary and grammar • *Final del desafío* • Quiz on *Desafío 2*	 35–37 38	 5 m. 45 m. 20 m. 20 m.	1.2, 1.3, 3.1	Audio Practice Workbook

Day	Objectives	Sessions	Activities	Time	Standards	Resources/Homework
7	To learn travel destinations and accommodations, adverbs and expressions of time, and to learn the preterite tense of the verbs *ir* and *ser*	**Desafío 3 – Las cataratas del Iguazú / Vocabulario** (166–169) • Warm-Up: Independent Starter • *Fotonovela: Las cataratas del Iguazú* • *Cultura: Las cataratas del Iguazú* • Vocabulary: *Destinos y alojamientos* • *Conexiones: La rosa de los vientos*	 39–41 42 43–45 46	 5 m. 30 m. 15 m. 30 m. 10 m.	1.1, 1.2, 1.3, 3.1, 3.2, 4.2, 5.2	Visual Presentation Audio Video Practice Workbook *Tu desafío*
8	To learn adverbs and expressions of time, and the preterite tense of the verbs *ir* and *ser*	**Desafío 3 – Gramática** (170–173) • Warm-Up: Independent Starter • Grammar: *Marcadores temporales de pasado* • Grammar: *Los verbos 'ser' e 'ir'. Pretérito* • *Conexiones: Las distancias: ¿millas o kilómetros?*	 47–50 51–53 54	 5 m. 40 m. 35 m. 10 m.	1.1, 1.2, 1.3, 3.1, 3.2, 4.1	Audio Practice Workbook
9	To integrate vocabulary and grammar and to assess student proficiency	**Desafío 3 – Comunicación / Evaluación** (174–175) • Warm-Up: Independent Starter • *Comunicación*: Review main vocabulary and grammar • *Final del desafío* • Quiz on *Desafío 3*	 55–57 58	 5 m. 45 m. 20 m. 20 m.	1.1, 1.2, 1.3, 3.1, 5.1	Audio Practice Workbook *Tu desafío*
10	To learn the parts of the city, to give directions, and to give negative *tú* commands	**Desafío 4 – Sobres en la calle / Vocabulario** (176–179) • Warm-Up: Independent Starter • *Fotonovela: Sobres en la calle* • *Cultura: La Plaza de Mayo* • Vocabulary: *La ciudad* • *Cultura: La Casa Rosada*	 59–61 62 63–65 66	 5 m. 30 m. 15 m. 30 m. 10 m.	1.1, 1.2, 1.3, 3.1, 3.2	Visual Presentation Audio Practice Workbook
11	To give negative *tú* commands and to integrate vocabulary and grammar	**Desafío 4 – Gramática / Comunicación** (180–183) • Warm-Up: Independent Starter • Grammar: *El imperativo negativo* • *Cultura: La Pirámide de Mayo* • *Comunicación*: Review main vocabulary and grammar	 67–69 70 71–73	 5 m. 30 m. 10 m. 45 m.	1.1, 1.2, 1.3, 3.1, 3.2, 4.1, 4.2, 5.1	Audio Practice Workbook
12	To assess student proficiency	**Desafío 4 – Evaluación** (183) • Warm-Up: *Final del desafío* • Last minute questions • Quiz on *Desafío 4*	 74	 40 m. 30 m. 20 m.	1.2, 1.3	
13	To integrate language in context	**Todo junto / El encuentro** (184–187) • Warm-Up: Independent Starter • *Todo junto* • *El encuentro: En el Teatro Colón*	 75–77 78–79	 5 m. 40 m. 45 m.	1.1, 1.2, 1.3, 5.1	Audio Practice Workbook

Day	Objectives	Sessions	Activities	Time	Standards	Resources/Homework
14	To learn about Argentine customs and traditions	***Mapa cultural / Lectura*** (188–193) • Warm-Up: Independent Starter • *Mapa cultural: Argentina* • *Lectura: La vuelta al mundo de Cinthia Scoch*	 87–89 90–92	 5 m. 45 m. 40 m.	1.2, 1.3, 2.1, 2.2, 3.1, 3.2, 5.2	Video Practice Workbook *Tu desafío*
15	To review vocabulary, grammar, and culture	***Repaso – Vocabulario / Gramática*** (194–197) • Warm-Up: Independent Starter • *Repaso: Vocabulario* • *Repaso: Gramática*	 1–4 5–9	 5 m. 40 m. 45 m.	1.2, 1.3, 2.1, 2.2, 5.2	Practice Workbook
16	To prepare and illustrate a travelogue	***Proyecto*** (198–199) • Warm-Up: Read the project outline • Work on project		 5 m. 85 m.	1.1, 1.2, 1.3, 3.1, 5.2	
17	To prepare and illustrate a travelogue	***Proyecto*** (198–199) • Warm-Up: Prepare presentations • Project presentations		 5 m. 85 m.	1.1, 1.2, 1.3, 3.1, 5.2	
18	To present projects and to assess student proficiency	***Proyecto / Assessment*** (198–199) • Warm-Up: Prepare presentations • Project presentations • *Autoevaluación* • Test on Unit 7		 5 m. 30 m. 10 m. 45 m.	1.1, 1.2, 1.3, 3.1, 5.2	

3 **Preguntas y respuestas**

1. Nos vamos. ¡Adiós!
2. ¿Están todos listos?
3. ¿Tienes el pasaporte?
4. ¿Compro yo los billetes?
5. El hotel está completo, no hay habitaciones libres.

8 **Preparativos para la excursión**

¡Hoy mi abuelo y yo vamos de paseo en el tren a las nubes! Ayer visitamos la agencia de viajes. También hablamos con mi abuela por teléfono. Luego compramos comida en el supermercado y preparamos unos sándwiches muy ricos. Después jugamos un partido de dominó en el parque y descansamos un poco. Y hoy estamos listos para comenzar el viaje. ¡Qué emocionante!

15 **¿Qué pasó?**

–Hola, Diana.

–Hola, Andy. ¿Qué tal el fin de semana?

–Muy bien. El sábado viajé a una isla en barco.

–¡Qué divertido! Yo llamé por teléfono a mi amiga Luisa. Ella vive cerca de aquí.

–Qué bien. ¿Y hablaste con Tess y con Tim?

–Sí. Ellos trabajaron mucho este fin de semana.

–¿Trabajaron?

–Sí. Tess compró un libro de Matemáticas porque tiene que estudiar para un examen. Y Tim limpió toda la casa.

–¡Qué tarea!

18 **¡Qué día!**

Hola, Tim. ¿Cómo estás? La semana pasada pasé mucho tiempo ocupada. El lunes tomé las fotos de la fiesta. Son muy bonitas. El martes visité la biblioteca para buscar unos libros sobre Argentina. El miércoles compré una computadora nueva, pero todavía no está conectada. El jueves preparé una comida para tus padres. El viernes hablé por teléfono con una amiga. El sábado visité el aeropuerto nuevo. ¡Es muy grande! Y el domingo descansé todo el día. Te llamo más tarde. Cuídate mucho.

24 **En el avión**

–Hola. Me llamo Diana.

–Hola, Diana. Yo soy Sabrina.

–Encantada, Sabrina. ¿Eres argentina?

–No, yo soy chilena. Mi esposo es argentino y vivimos en Buenos Aires.

–¿Es difícil ser asistente de vuelo?

–No. A mí me gusta viajar y trabajar en un avión es muy interesante.

–A mí también me gusta viajar.

–¿De dónde eres?

–Soy americana y voy con mi tía a Santa Rosa.

–¿Por qué van a Santa Rosa? ¿Van de vacaciones?

–¡Es una larga historia! Nosotras somos fans del español.

–Ah, qué interesante. Yo estudié inglés en Londres y viajé mucho por Europa. Diana, si van a estar en Santa Rosa mucho tiempo, pueden venir a visitarme. Tengo una casa allí.

–Gracias, Sabrina.

–De nada. Un placer conocerte, Diana. ¡Buen viaje!

27 **¿Estás lista para el viaje?**

Hola, Diana, habla mamá. Cuando viajas, todo tiene que estar en orden. Escucha.

Primero tienes que tener tu pasaporte listo. El pasaporte es necesario para entrar en otro país. Luego busca los billetes de avión. Puedes mirar ofertas en Internet. ¿Qué más? Ah, sí. Tienes que llevar una guía turística de Argentina para leer sobre los lugares interesantes del país. Otra cosa: prepara tu maleta dos o tres días antes. Ah, y lleva una chaqueta porque a veces hace frío en el avión.

Un beso, Diana. Te llamo más tarde. ¡Buen viaje!

31 **¿Presente o pasado?**

1. –¿Qué preparaste?
   –Seco de carne, un plato típico de Perú.
2. –Tengo un gato que se llama Berto.
   –Y yo tengo un perro que se llama Rambo. Paseo a mi perro todos los días.
3. –En el centro comercial compré una blusa bonita.
   –¡Yo también compré una blusa en el centro comercial!
4. –Para la cena cociné un pollo asado.
   –¡Qué rico! Mi mamá cocinó una sopa deliciosa.
5. –¿Qué haces?
   –Hablo con mi abuelo.

44 **¿Adónde vamos?**

1. Mack y Tim van al norte, a la montaña. Ellos prefieren ir en autobús. A Tim le gusta ir a la montaña.
2. Mi hermana Janet y yo vamos a la playa, al este, en coche. A nosotros nos gusta mucho el mar.
3. Diana y Rita van al sur, a la costa. Ellas tienen una reserva en un hotel grande. Diana y Rita viajan en avión.
4. Tess y Patricia prefieren ir al oeste. Van a la ciudad. Quieren visitar museos y lugares históricos. Ellas van en taxi.

49 **¿Qué hicieron?**

–Andy, vamos a recordar nuestras actividades en Argentina.

–De acuerdo.

–El mes pasado compramos una guía turística para conocer mejor el país. Y el martes pasado visitamos una playa muy bonita.

–Sí. Y el miércoles pasamos la noche en un cámping en la montaña.

–El jueves paseamos por la ciudad y visitamos museos y lugares muy interesantes.

–El sábado cenamos con Tim y Mack en un restaurante buenísimo.
Y ayer hablamos por teléfono con nuestros padres.

–Anoche yo usé la computadora hasta muy tarde. Les escribí correos
electrónicos a mis amigas.

–Y yo esta mañana me levanté temprano para montar en bicicleta con
Tim.

–¡Cuántas actividades!

51 Viajes por Argentina

1. Con Diana, mi sobrina, viajé en taxi hasta la costa este de Argentina.
¡Qué lindo lugar!
2. Tim y yo fuimos en tren a la montaña.
3. Andy y yo fuimos en autobús a un cámping.
4. Patricia y yo fuimos del campo a la ciudad en avión. A mi mamá y a mí
nos gustan las grandes ciudades como Buenos Aires.

55 Habla Andy

–Hola, Tess. Habla Andy. ¿Cómo estás?

–Hola, Andy. Estoy bien, gracias. ¿Y tú?

–Bien. Oye, Tess, ¿te gustó el hotel que reservé?

–Sí, me gustó mucho el hotel. La habitación es muy grande.

–¡Qué bien! ¿Y adónde fueron ayer?

–Yo me quedé en el hotel y escribí un correo a mi papá.

–¿Y tu mamá?

–Mi mamá salió de la habitación temprano para correr. ¿Y ustedes qué
hicieron?

–Yo pasé un rato en la playa. Y luego Janet y yo fuimos al oeste del
parque porque Janet miró mal el mapa.

–¿Miró mal el mapa? ¡Pobre Janet!

–Tess, te llamo después porque ahora vamos a comer.

–Está bien. Adiós, Andy.

–Adiós.

61 La ruta más corta

Comenzamos nuestro recorrido en la calle Balcarce. Vamos hacia el
norte por la calle Balcarce hasta la Avenida Hipólito Yrigoyen. Desde aquí
entramos en la famosa Plaza de Mayo. En el centro de la plaza podemos
ver la Pirámide de Mayo. Doblamos a la derecha y vamos a la Casa
Rosada, la sede presidencial de Argentina. Finalmente seguimos hacia el
este y terminamos nuestro paseo en el Parque Colón.

63 ¿Adónde fueron?

–Primero compré un boleto para ir al cine. Después devolví un libro en la
biblioteca. Por último, jugué al fútbol con Andy y Janet en el parque.

–Yo visité a un amigo en el hospital. Luego fui a esperar a mi amiga
Olivia al aeropuerto. Su avión llegó tarde.

72 Sugerencias

1. –Mamá, quiero estudiar en una escuela de baile este verano.
Me gusta mucho bailar.
–No, hija. No estudies en una escuela de baile. Estudia en una
escuela de música. Tocas muy bien el piano.
2. –¿Podemos pasar unas noches en un hotel este verano?
–Sí, yo también prefiero ir a un hotel.
3. –¿Vamos a ir mucho al teatro en Santa Rosa?
–Sí. Los teatros allí son impresionantes.
4. –Yo quiero viajar por todo el país en autobús.
–¡Ay no, Tess! Es mejor viajar en tren.
5. –¿Puedo visitar el parque?
–No, no visites el parque, está un poco lejos. Pero puedes visitar
la plaza, es muy bonita.
6. –Podemos pasear por el centro de la ciudad.
–Sí, de acuerdo.
7. –Mamá, quiero trabajar en el banco que está cerca de la plaza.
–Pero no tienes los estudios necesarios. Es mejor pensar en otro
trabajo.
8. –Quiero cenar todas las noches en el café de la calle Corrientes.
Me gusta mucho la comida argentina.
–No, Tess. No cenes hoy en el café, es muy caro. Hoy puedes cenar
en casa.

75 El viaje de tus sueños

Anunciamos nuestro gran concurso de verano. Entra y gana el viaje de
tus sueños. Solamente necesitas tu pasaporte y tu maleta. Tú decides
el lugar: la playa o la montaña. Puedes ir en tren o en avión. Y para
alojarte, puedes elegir un hotel o un cámping. En tu destino puedes
hacer excursiones y visitar museos e iglesias antiguas.

¿Adónde quieres ir? Graba un mensaje de voz con los detalles del viaje
de tus sueños. Incluye lo que vas a llevar, el medio de transporte, dónde
te vas a alojar y qué sitios quieres visitar. ¡Buena suerte!

Argentina

Argentina

En tierra de gauchos

The Unit

- The hemes for Unit 7 are means of transportation and travel.
- The participants meet in Buenos Aires, Argentina, with tango dancer Alina Aguilar, who will give them their individual tasks in each of the four cities that they will visit. The participants face the following challenges:
  - *Desafío* 1. Mack and Tim must travel on the Train to the Clouds and take a picture of each town they pass while the train is still moving.
  - *Desafío* 2. Diana and Rita are traveling to Santa Rosa, the capital of La Pampa. There they must find a man running a marathon in gaucho attire.
  - *Desafío* 3. Andy and Janet are taking a trip to Iguazu Falls where they must make a video guide of the Devil's Throat, a waterfall that lies between Argentina and Brazil.
  - *Desafío* 4. Tess and Patricia are in Buenos Aires. There they must collect four envelopes with the pieces of a puzzle in the *Plaza de Mayo*, the main square of the city.

Activities	Standards	Resources
Argentina	1.2, 2.2, 4.1	Video

Teaching Suggestions

Warm-Up / Independent Starter

- Ask students to answer the following personal questions:
  - Do you like to travel?
  - Do you prefer to travel by car or by train?
  - Where is your favorite place to travel?

Argentina

- Give students a map of Argentina with the following places labeled:
  - Salta
  - La Pampa
  - Iguazú
  - Buenos Aires

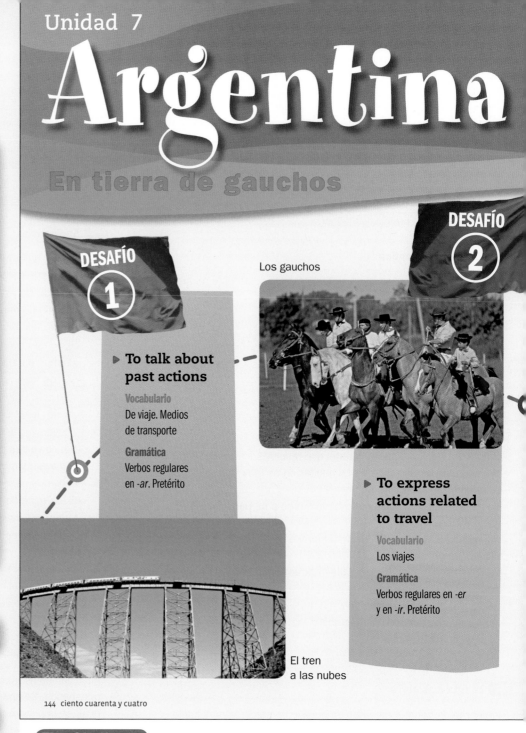

DESAFÍO 1

Los gauchos

DESAFÍO 2

▶ **To talk about past actions**

Vocabulario
De viaje. Medios de transporte

Gramática
Verbos regulares en -*ar*. Pretérito

▶ **To express actions related to travel**

Vocabulario
Los viajes

Gramática
Verbos regulares en -*er* y en -*ir*. Pretérito

El tren a las nubes

The Challenge

DESAFÍO 1

El tren a las nubes
The Train to the Clouds is the third highest railway in the world. It moves through 21 tunnels and over 29 bridges in its course from Salta to La Polvorilla. It owes its poetic name to the almost 14,000 foot climb.

DESAFÍO 2

Los gauchos
The gaucho, or Argentine cowboy, has a lifestyle of his own. For example, one of the most traditional drinks of the gaucho is *yerba mate*, an infusion made from an evergreen shrub that is native to the Argentine Pampas. Dry leaves are steeped in hot water, usually in a gourd made especially for drinking *mate*.

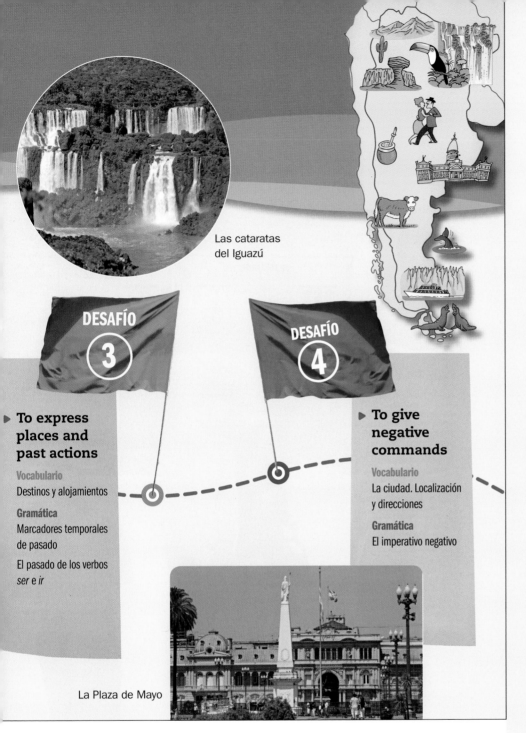

Argentina

Las cataratas del Iguazú

DESAFÍO 3

▶ **To express places and past actions**

Vocabulario
Destinos y alojamientos

Gramática
Marcadores temporales de pasado

El pasado de los verbos *ser* e *ir*

DESAFÍO 4

▶ **To give negative commands**

Vocabulario
La ciudad. Localización y direcciones

Gramática
El imperativo negativo

La Plaza de Mayo

■ Ask students to color code each place by team:
rojo – Tim *y* Mack   *amarillo* – Diana *y* Rita
azul – Tess *y* Patricia   *verde* – Andy *y* Janet.

Picture Discussion

El tren a las nubes

Ask students if they have ever experienced being up high—perhaps on a roller coaster, on a Ferris wheel, on a mountain, etc. Then ask them to fill in a senses chart like the one below with words that describe their memories.

ver	oír	oler	saborear	tocar

Los gauchos

The typical gaucho outfit has served as an inspiration for fashion designers. Have students look for photos of the pants that the gauchos of Argentina wear and the pants called *gaucho* on the Internet. How are they similar? How are they different? Ask students to think about any other articles of clothing that come from other countries or cultures.

Las cataratas del Iguazú

Iguazu Falls is even taller than Niagara Falls in New York state. Waterfalls are said to have mystical powers. Ask students if they have ever heard any folktales, myths or legends surrounding waterfalls. After sharing the Guarani legend of the Iguazu Falls with students (you can find it online), have them write their own creative folktale involving a waterfall.

La Plaza de Mayo

The *Plaza de Mayo* is in downtown Buenos Aires. This plaza has been the center of Argentine political life for many decades. It owes its name to the Independence Movement of May of 1810. Here the people of Buenos Aires gather to protest, celebrate, or people watch. Have students locate the *Plaza de Mayo* on a map of Buenos Aires and name the streets surrounding it. Have students think about why a place like this could become a political center.

Objectives

■ By the end of the unit, students will be able to use:
– The past tense of regular *-ar* verbs.
– The past tense of regular *-er* and *-ir* verbs.
– Markers of past tense, and the past tenses of *ser* and *ir*.
– Negative commands.

DESAFÍO 3

Las cataratas del Iguazú

The Iguazu Falls is one of the most popular tourist destinations in South America. Some of the largest falls in this system of waterfalls rise to close to 270 feet tall, though most are around 200 feet in height. This system of falls is arranged in a horseshoe shape along almost two miles of the Iguazu River. The Devil's Throat lies between Argentina and Brazil and is the largest fall in the Iguazu Falls system.

DESAFÍO 4

La Plaza de Mayo

The *Plaza de Mayo* is the main square in downtown Buenos Aires. On one side of the *Plaza de Mayo* is the Government House of Argentina, the *Casa Rosada*. The *Plaza de Mayo* is the political center of the city, and has been for much of Argentina's history. It is the site of a weekly protest march by the *Madres de la Plaza de Mayo*. These mothers began protesting the disappearance of their children during the Dirty War, the military dictatorship that took place in Argentina between 1976 and 1983.

La llegada

Presentation

- In this section, students will learn:
  - Travel and transportation vocabulary.
  - Past tense of regular *-ar* verbs.

Activities	Standards	Resources
Fotonovela	1.2	Vis. Pres.
1.	1.2, 1.3	

Teaching Suggestions

Warm-Up / Independent Starter

- Have students underline all the verbs in the following paragraph.

  Esta mañana, los estudiantes llegaron a la escuela a las ocho, entraron en sus salones de clase y estudiaron durante una hora. A las nueve, el inspector de la zona llegó y les entregó el examen. Ellos terminaron a las diez. ¡Qué mañana tan larga!

Presentation

- Have students list the infinitives of each of the verbs in the Independent Starter in the first column of a four-column chart. In the second column, have them write the conjugated form as it appears in the paragraph. In the third column, have them write the subject of the sentence and, in the fourth column, ask them to write the tense. Verify that students' charts look like the following chart. Invite volunteers to explain what is similar and different about the verbs in the second column.

llegar	llegaron	los estudiantes	pasado
entrar	entraron	los estudiantes	pasado
estudiar	estudiaron	los estudiantes	pasado
llegar	llegó	el inspector	pasado
entregar	entregó	el inspector	pasado
terminar	terminaron	los estudiantes	pasado

La fotonovela

Before Viewing

- Ask students to look at the photos. Have them try to predict each person's task.

After Viewing

- Have students summarize the dialogue in small groups. Each group can report their summary back to the class by re-enacting the *fotonovela*.

146

La llegada

En Buenos Aires

In Argentina, the four pairs gather in Buenos Aires, the capital. They come together at the *Plaza de Mayo*, in downtown Buenos Aires. There they meet Alina Aguilar, a tango dancer. She welcomes them and assigns each pair their task.

> Hola, soy Alina Aguilar. ¡Bienvenidos a Argentina, un país interesante y moderno!

> ¿Tienen sus pasaportes, sus maletas...? ¡Van a viajar mucho! En tren, en avión, en autobús...

> ¿Están listos? ¡Buen viaje a todos!

> ¡Qué bien!

146 ciento cuarenta y seis

Differentiated Instruction

DEVELOPING LEARNERS

- After students read the dialogue, have them write out the words that they recognize in their notebooks. Then have them classify them into two groups: "Recycled words" and "Cognates." Go through each phrase of the dialogue again and check for unknown words. Elicit possible meanings based on context.

EXPANDING LEARNERS

- Have students describe three things they do before going on a trip. Have students look at the pictures and use the new vocabulary in their descriptions.

Vamos a San Antonio de los Cobres en tren. Salimos de la estación de Salta.

¿Vamos a Salta en autobús? ¿Compramos billetes de ida y vuelta?

¡Tenemos que caminar mucho! Hay que encontrar un parque, una iglesia...

No olvides el plano, Tess.

Sí, y el pasaporte. Tenemos que enseñarlo en el aeropuerto.

¿Tienes a mano los billetes, tía?

Llamé al hotel. No hay habitaciones libres...

No importa. ¿Preguntaste en el cámping?

1 ¿Comprendes?

▶ **Une.** Match each question (column A) with the corresponding answer (column B).

Ⓐ

1. ¿Están preparados los personajes para el viaje?
2. ¿Viajan Tim y Mack en avión?
3. ¿Van Tess y Patricia en taxi a su destino?
4. ¿Reservó Andy una habitación en el hotel?
5. ¿Tienen Diana y Rita el pasaporte a mano?

Ⓑ

a. No, no hay habitaciones libres.
b. No, van caminando.
c. Sí, lo necesitan para viajar.
d. Sí, están listos.
e. No, viajan en tren.

ciento cuarenta y siete **147**

Activities

1. Have students write a list of all the documents that should be brought with you on a trip—some are mandatory, while others are optional. They can organize their words into two columns in a chart like the one below.

obligatorio	opcional
el pasaporte	la guía turística
los billetes	el plano

Answer Key

1. 1. d   2. e   3. b   4. a   5. c

Additional Resources

Fans Online activities
Practice Workbook

HERITAGE LANGUAGE LEARNERS

- Tell students to focus on the word *cámping* used in the dialogue. Inform them that this word is borrowed from English to Spanish. Ask them if this is the word used in their countries of origin to refer to the same activity. Students in Mexico, for example, may say they use *campamento* or *parque para acampar*. Have them think of other English words that they or their relatives used before coming to the United States.

SPECIAL-NEEDS LEARNERS

- Provide students with visual disabilities with the audio of the dialogue before class. During the presentation, make sure you provide verbal descriptions of the pictures as the rest of the students go through them.

147

Unit 7
La llegada

Presentation

- In this section, students will learn useful expressions to talk about travel.

Activities	Standards	Resources
Expresiones útiles	1.2, 4.1	
2.	1.2, 1.3	
3.	1.2, 1.3	Audio
4.	1.1, 1.2	
5.	1.1, 1.2, 1.3	

Teaching Suggestions

Warm-Up / Independent Starter

- Have students choose the best answers for the following questions:

  1. *¿Estás preparado para un examen hoy?*
     A. *Estoy listo.*
     B. *Tengo el examen a mano.*
  2. *¿Tienes un lápiz en tu mochila?*
     A. *No importa.*
     B. *Sí, lo tengo a mano.*
  3. *Voy a tomar el tren.*
     A. *¡Gracias!*
     B. *¡Buen viaje!*

Preparation

- Ask students to work in groups to practice creating sentences that use the *Expresiones útiles*. Have each group share their sentences with the class.

Activities

2. After students complete this activity, you may divide the class into four groups and ask them to act out each scenario. Invite volunteer groups to present their scenes to the class.
3. Before playing the audio, review the *Expresiones útiles*. Pronounce each expression and have students repeat them. Ask them to imagine different situations in which they would use these expressions. After students have completed the activity, have them improvise short conversations in pairs using the *Expresiones útiles*.

148

EXPRESIONES ÚTILES

Sí, tengo el pasaporte a mano.

To ask if someone is ready:
  Estar listo(a). / Estar preparado(a).

To express having something handy:
  Tener... a mano.

To talk about a round-trip ticket:
  Comprar un billete de ida y vuelta.

To say that something does not matter:
  No importa. / No pasa nada.

To wish someone a good trip:
  ¡Buen viaje!

2 Expresiones

▶ **Relaciona.** The expressions below don't correspond to the pictures under them. Match them appropriately.

a. ¿Tiene usted los documentos a mano? **b.** ¡Buen viaje, Carmen! **c.** Dos billetes de ida y vuelta, por favor. **d.** ¡Estamos listos!

3 Preguntas y respuestas

▶ **Escucha y relaciona.** Listen to the statements. Match each one with a logical response.

a. Sí, tranquilo. Lo tengo a mano.
b. Sí, estamos listos.
c. No pasa nada.
d. ¡Buen viaje!
e. Sí. Compra dos billetes de ida y vuelta.

148 ciento cuarenta y ocho

Differentiated Instruction

DEVELOPING LEARNERS

- Have students create a picture dictionary with the *Expresiones útiles*. They can illustrate each expression, use clip art, or cut images from a magazine to demonstrate that they understand each phrase.

EXPANDING LEARNERS

- In pairs, have students practice the expression *tener... a mano* with common classroom objects by playing a game in which one student calls out a question (for example: *¿Tienes el cuaderno a mano?*) and the partner is required to pick up the corresponding object and answer (for example: *Sí, tengo el cuaderno a mano*).

¿Quién ganará?

 4 **Los desafíos**

 ▶ **Habla.** What will be the challenge for each team? Think about this question and discuss it with your classmates.

**DESAFÍO ① **

Tim y Mack

El tren
a las nubes

**DESAFÍO ② **
Un gaucho
de la Pampa

Diana y Rita

**DESAFÍO ③ **
Las cataratas del Iguazú

Andy y Janet

**DESAFÍO ④ **
Sobres en la calle

Tess y Patricia

5 **Las votaciones**

▶ **Decide.** You decide. You will vote to choose the most amazing challenge. Who do you think will win?

Sorprendente

¿Quién ganará?

4. Have students look at the pictures and ask them if they can decide what the challenge will be for each pair. Elicit different answers.

Remind students of the different challenges:

1. Tim and Mack travel on the Train to the Clouds to take a picture of each town they pass.
2. Diana and Rita have to find a man running the Santa Rosa marathon in gaucho attire.
3. Andy and Janet must make a video guide of the Devil's Throat, a waterfall that is part of the Iguazu Falls.
4. Tess and Patricia have to collect four envelopes with the pieces of a puzzle in *Plaza de Mayo*, Buenos Aires.

5. Explain to students that at the end of this unit they will decide and vote on which challenge is the most amazing. Let the students discuss their different opinions and then help them to reach an agreement.

AUDIO SCRIPT
See page 143K

Answer Key

2. a. 4   b. 3   c. 2   d. 1
3. 1. d   2. b   3. a   4. e   5. c
4. Answers will vary.
5. Answers will vary.

Additional Resources

Fans Online activities
Practice Workbook

HERITAGE LANGUAGE LEARNERS

• Have students share other *Expresiones útiles* they may know that have related meanings. For example: *No te preocupes*, *Feliz viaje*, or *Comprar un boleto redondo*. Have them share these expressions with the class.

MULTIPLE INTELLIGENCES:
Verbal-Linguistic Intelligence

• Have students write a dialogue or skit using the expressions. This might be a scene from a *fotonovela* in which someone is going off on a trip or an advertisement for a travel service. Ask them to perform their dialogues for the class or record videos and share them. As classmates watch the skits or videos, have them raise their hands (or clap, etc.) each time they hear one of the *Expresiones útiles*.

DESAFÍO 1

Hablar de acciones pasadas

Presentation

- In *Desafío 1*, Tim and Mack are traveling on the Train to the Clouds, which is the third-highest railway in the world. Tim and Mack must take a picture of each town they pass while the train is still moving.

- In this section, students will learn:
  - Travel vocabulary.
  - Past tense of *-ar* verbs.

Activities	Standards	Resources
Fotonovela	1.2	Vis. Pres.
6.	1.1, 1.2, 1.3	
7.	1.2	
8.	1.2, 1.3	Audio
9. Cultura	1.1, 1.2, 3.1, 3.2, 4.2	Video

Teaching Suggestions

Warm-Up / Independent Starter

- To recycle the conjugation of *-ar* verbs in the present tense, have students conjugate the following verbs: *hablar, trabajar, bailar, cantar, pasear*.

Preparation

- Display a map of South America from a transparency or the Internet where students can see the location of Argentina. Explain that this sequence takes place in the northern part of Argentina, near the border with Chile and Bolivia. The Train to the Clouds connects Salta, in Argentina, to the border with Chile. Ask students to imagine riding on the train. What might they see from the windows of this high altitude train?

 ### La fotonovela

Before Viewing

- Ask a student volunteer to read the introduction to the task. Ask students to look at the pictures and tell what they find surprising or interesting. What problems do they think Tim might face when trying to take pictures with his camera?

150

El tren a las nubes

 Tim and Mack are traveling on the Train to the Clouds. This train is the third highest railway in the world. Tim and Mack must take a picture of each town they pass while the train is still moving.

> ¡Qué bien, abuelo, vamos de excursión en tren!

> Sí. El tren a las nubes pasa por el norte de Argentina. Vamos a ver paisajes fantásticos.

> ¿Te gusta viajar en tren, Tim? A mí me gusta mucho.

> Yo solo viajé en tren una vez y me gustó. Pero me gusta más viajar en avión.

> ¡Ay, abuelo, tomé una foto muy fea!

> Abuelo, ¿cuántas fotos tenemos que tomar?

> No sé... Necesitamos una foto de cada ciudad. ¡Y tenemos que tomar todas las fotos desde el tren!

> No importa, Tim. Toma otra foto, rápido. Estamos saliendo de esta ciudad...

Continuará...

6 **¿Comprendes?**

 ▶ **Completa.** Which verb or verb phrase from the dialogue matches these expressions?

I traveled	I liked it	I took a photo
1.	2.	3.

 ▶ **Habla.** Ask a partner about somewhere he or she has traveled.

Modelo A. *¿Viajaste a Miami?*
　　　　 B. *No, no viajé a Miami. Viajé a Orlando.*

Differentiated Instruction

DEVELOPING LEARNERS

- Ask students to work in pairs to act out phrases from the *fotonovela*. One student acts out the phrase / sentence, while the other guesses which one is being presented. Sample phrases to act out include: *Vamos de excursión en tren; Vamos a ver paisajes fantásticos; Toma otra foto, rápido.*

EXPANDING LEARNERS

- After completing the spread, have students answer the following questions in writing: *¿Alguna vez has viajado en tren? ¿Cuáles son las ventajas y desventajas de viajar en tren frente a otros medios de transporte?* Have them use as many of the new vocabulary words as possible. Students may jumpstart their writing with a compare and contrast table.

7 **¿Quién viajó?**

▶ **Decide.** Read these statements. Are they referring to Mack or to Tim?

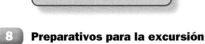

1. Él viajó en tren una vez.

2. A él le gustó viajar en tren.

3. Él tomó una foto muy fea.

8 **Preparativos para la excursión**

▶ **Escucha y decide.** Listen and decide which of these activities Tim and Mack did.

1. visitar la agencia de viajes
2. desayunar en un café
3. hablar por teléfono con la abuela
4. comprar comida en un supermercado
5. preparar unos sándwiches
6. tomar un taxi
7. jugar un partido de dominó
8. pasear por el parque
9. descansar

▶ **Escucha y escribe.** Listen again and write the verb forms that correspond to the infinitives you chose above.

Modelo 1. *visitamos*

CULTURA

El tren a las nubes

El tren a las nubes sale de la ciudad de Salta y va hasta el viaducto La Polvorilla. La excursión comienza a las 7 de la mañana y termina después de la medianoche. El tren pasa por veintinueve puentes *(bridges)*, veintiún túneles y dos zigzags. Se llama tren a las nubes porque sube a 4.200 metros sobre el nivel del mar.

9 **Piensa.** Have you ever taken a trip by train? What are the advantages and disadvantages of travelling by train versus other means of transportation?

ciento cincuenta y uno 151

After Viewing

▪ Ask students what problems Tim and Mack had on the train. Why? What might they do to make things run more smoothly?

Activities

6. To simplify this activity, have students write the questions and answers before they engage in a dialogue with their partner.

9. If students have never taken a train ride, ask them to describe a train ride they may have seen in a movie or even on a subway.

 AUDIO SCRIPT
See page 143K

CULTURA

El tren a las nubes

The *tren a las nubes* is a famous train in the northern part of Argentina. The province of Salta, where this train operates, is bordered by three countries: Chile, Bolivia, and Paraguay.

Answer Key

6. 1. viajé   2. me gustó   3. tomé
▶ Answers will vary.

7. Tim: 1, 2, 3

8. 1. visitar la agencia de viajes
3. hablar por teléfono con la abuela
4. comprar comida en un supermercado
5. preparar unos sándwiches
7. jugar un partido de dominó
9. descansar
▶ 1. visitamos   5. preparamos
3. hablamos   7. jugamos
4. compramos   9. descansamos

9. Answers will vary.

Additional Resources

Fans Online activities

151

HERITAGE LANGUAGE LEARNERS

• Have students talk about forms of transportation in other countries. Ask if one is more popular than the others. Have them describe places they have visited using such forms of transportation.

MULTIPLE INTELLIGENCES:

Interpersonal Intelligence

• Have students look at the pictures of Tim and Mack and focus on their body language. What do these pictures tell us about their relationship? Have students bring photos of a family vacation to class and share them. Have them talk about what these photos communicate.

DESAFÍO 1

Vocabulario – De viaje

Presentation

- In this section, students will learn:
  - Words related to travel.
  - Means of transportation.

Activities	Standards	Resources
Vocabulario	1.2	
10.	1.2, 1.3	
11.	1.2, 1.3	
12.	1.1, 1.3	
13. Conexiones	1.1, 1.2, 3.1, 3.2	

Teaching Suggestions

Warm-Up / Independent Starter

- Ask students to answer the following questions in complete sentences, according to their previous family vacations.
  1. ¿Viajaste en tus vacaciones?
  2. ¿Adónde viajaste?

Preparation

- Have students point to each image of the transportation vocabulary and repeat each word after you. Ask them to talk about traveling in the United States.

- Most major cities have some form of mass transit—either subways, trolley cars, or buses. An excellent way of introducing students to the subway or bus routes of a major city is by using a street map. Here's how to make one for your own classroom. Materials needed:
  - A shower curtain liner.
  - Permanent markers.
  - A projection of a subway map (for example: using an electronic whiteboard screen or an overhead screen with a projector).

  Hang the liner on the wall and project your map image onto it using an overhead projector or electronic whiteboard. Trace the streets, subway lines or landmarks that you want using permanent markers. When you are finished, use commands to have students move from one part of the city to another by using toy cars, buses, or trains to "travel around the city."

152

Vocabulario

De viaje

el avión

el barco

el tren

Me gusta ir a pie.

el metro

el autobús

el taxi

el coche

Nos vamos de vacaciones. ¡Nos gusta mucho viajar en avión!
el aeropuerto

Nos vamos de excursión. Vamos en tren.
la estación

10 El transporte ideal

▶ **Habla.** Mack and Tim are looking at the signs along the way. Read their notes and decide which would be the appropriate form(s) of transportation to take to each place.

Modelo   A. ¿Cómo pueden ir al Parque don Tomás?
B. Pueden ir a pie.

Distancias

Parque don Tomás	1 km
Buenos Aires	577 km
Las Mercedes	45 km
San Carlos	7 km
Córdoba	580 km

152   ciento cincuenta y dos

Differentiated Instruction

DEVELOPING LEARNERS

- Before the vocabulary presentation, developing learners may benefit from a review of the present tense conjugations of *ir*. Write the complete conjugation table on the board and leave it as a visual aid to help students respond to simple questions about the pictures. For example: *¿Quién va de viaje en esa foto?*

EXPANDING LEARNERS

- Challenge students to expand and elaborate on their answers to questions when appropriate. You may guide them with logical questions that stimulate a guided conversation, if necessary. For example: *¿Qué van a hacer Mack y Tim en el Parque don Tomás? → Mack y Tim van a practicar muchos deportes, como el fútbol y el tenis. Se van a divertir mucho.*

¡Cuántos viajeros!

▶ **Completa.** In the airport the four pairs heard many travelers talking around them. Complete their statements with a term from the boxes.

Modelo   Normalmente voy a la escuela en *autobús* .

| metro | coche | a pie | avión | barco |

1. ¡Mi _____ sale inmediatamente! ¿Dónde está la terminal internacional?
2. Voy al puerto de Miami. Voy a tomar un _____ para viajar por el Caribe.
3. Para moverme por Washington DC uso el _____. Es más rápido y barato que un taxi.
4. Tengo licencia para conducir. Podemos rentar un _____ para viajar por la región.
5. El hotel está muy cerca del centro de la ciudad. Podemos ir _____.

 ¿Qué haces durante las vacaciones?

 ▶ **Habla.** Talk with a classmate about the things you do during your summer break. Use the prompts below.

1. Me gusta ir de vacaciones a…
2. A mi familia y a mí nos gusta viajar a/por…
3. Vamos de excursión a/por…

CONEXIONES: CIENCIAS SOCIALES

El transporte público: el metro

Buenos Aires, igual que Nueva York, Madrid, la Ciudad de México y otras ciudades, tiene un servicio de transporte público muy popular: el metro o subte (de subterráneo). El metro argentino fue *(was)* el primero de Latinoamérica. Fue inaugurado en 1913.

13 **Piensa.** What are the public transportation services in your city or town? Are they efficient? What are the advantages of a public transportation system?

Activities

10. Remind students that the "km" at the end of measured distances means kilometers. You may connect this activity to math, asking them to convert the kilometers to miles.

12. Have students complete the sentences in their notebooks and rehearse their pronunciation before embarking on their conversations.

13. Ask students to find a map online, or bring one from home, that represents their public transportation system or one near their city. They can find public transportation maps on Google Maps, or on specific websites. For example, Los Angeles: http://www.metro.net.

CONEXIONES: CIENCIAS SOCIALES

El transporte público: el metro

The first metro in the world was the London Underground. This rapid transit system opened in 1863 and is still one of the busiest metro systems in the world. At present, more than 160 cities in Europe, Asia, and Latin America depend on metro systems.

Answer Key

10. Answers will vary. Sample answers:
   1. Pueden ir a Buenos Aires en avión.
   2. Pueden ir a Las Mercedes en coche.

11. 1. avión   4. coche
   2. barco   5. a pie
   3. metro

12. Answers will vary.

13. Answers will vary.

Additional Resources

Fans Online activities

HERITAGE LANGUAGE LEARNERS

• As you present the new vocabulary, ask heritage learners to use the words in complete sentences. You may write their sentences on the board and have the rest of the class read them aloud. Heritage speakers may then explain and elaborate on their sentences.

MULTIPLE INTELLIGENCES:

Visual Intelligence

• To assist students with auditory or listening disabilities, provide tactile representations of vocabulary whenever possible. For this set, you may bring toy models of trains, airplanes, and other forms of transportation. As you show students each object, go through a series of simple tasks that enable you to repeat the vocabulary word several times before having students repeat it. For example: *Toca el autobús* (walk over to one student and have that student touch the toy); *Pasa el autobús a Miguel* (have student pass the toy to another student).

153

DESAFÍO 1

Gramática – Verbos regulares en -*ar*. Pretérito

Presentation

- In this section, students will learn past tense forms of regular -*ar* verbs.

Activities	Standards	Resources
Gramática	1.2, 3.1, 4.1	
14.	3.1, 4.1	
15.	1.2, 1.3	Audio
16.	1.1	
17.	1.1, 1.3	

Teaching Suggestions

Warm-Up / Independent Starter

- Have students write five sentences based on this writing prompt:

  Me gusta viajar en … para ir a …
  (transportation) (travel destination)

Preparation

- Write the verbs *viajar, mirar*, and *caminar* on the board and ask for student volunteers to conjugate the verbs in the present tense. As you go through the grammar section, use the verbs on the board as a visual comparison between the present tense and the preterite tense.

Activities

14. Ask students to play a password game in groups. One student says a verb in the present tense and the partner must match that verb in the past tense. Students can start by using English verbs and then Spanish verbs. For example:

    1. A. sing   2. A. *canto*
       B. sang   B. *canté*

16. Using the questions from the activity, have students survey their classmates and create a class bar graph to indicate the most popular answers. Then ask students to write a short paragraph summarizing the results. For example: *Cinco estudiantes tomaron el metro, dos cenaron muy tarde. Sin embargo, nadie cantó en un karaoke.* Invite volunteers to read their paragraphs to the class.

Gramática

Verbos regulares en -*ar*. Pretérito

- To talk about completed actions in the past, we use the preterite tense.

PRESENTE	PRETÉRITO
Yo **compro** una blusa.	→ Yo **compré** una camisa.
Yo **viajo** en barco.	→ Yo **viajé** en metro.

- These are the preterite tense endings of -*ar* verbs.

VERBO COMPRAR (TO BUY). PRETÉRITO

Singular		Plural	
yo	**compré**	nosotros nosotras	**compramos**
tú	**compraste**	vosotros vosotras	**comprasteis**
usted él ella	**compró**	ustedes ellos ellas	**compraron**

Note: The nosotros form is the same in the preterite as in the present. Context will clarify the tense.

PRESENTE

Todos los días **viajamos** en tren.

PRETÉRITO

En marzo **viajamos** en autobús.

14 **Compara.** How do we form the past tense in English? Are there any cases where the present and past tenses of a verb look the same?

15 **¿Qué pasó?**

▶ **Escucha y escribe.** Andy and Diana are talking about what they and two other characters did over the weekend. Listen and write a sentence about what each person did. You may find clues in the pictures.

Modelo 1. *Andy viajó a una isla en barco.*

Differentiated Instruction

DEVELOPING LEARNERS

- After the grammar presentation, have students create three sets of index cards, each set of a different color. Have them use one set for personal pronouns, one for verb stems, and one for conjugation endings. Ask them to practice different combinations.

EXPANDING LEARNERS

- Have students talk about what they did yesterday. Challenge them to use as many verbs as possible. You may control the activity by eliciting examples from students and making sure they are using the correct forms. For example: *¿Qué preparaste ayer para la cena?* Possible answer: *Mi mamá y yo preparamos carne y arroz.*

16 **¿Compraste algo?**

▶ **Habla.** Find out what a classmate did on a recent vacation. Ask whether he or she did each of the following things.

Modelo viajar a Argentina ⟶ A. ¿Viajaste a Argentina?
                                              B. Sí, viajé a Argentina.

1. tomar el metro
2. hablar con la gente
3. escuchar música tradicional
4. bailar salsa
5. pintar un paisaje
6. cantar en un karaoke
7. cenar muy tarde
8. tomar platos típicos
9. comprar recuerdos

17 **Las compras**

▶ **Escribe.** The characters went shopping yesterday. Write what each person bought, according to the photos.

Modelo 1. Yo compré una bandera de Argentina.

① ② Mariano Mores ③ ④

yo   tú   Mack   nosotras

⑤   ⑥   ⑦

ustedes   Rita   Tim y Tess

▶ **Habla y presenta.** Imagine you bought one of the items above. Tell a partner which one you chose. Then, as a pair, report your purchases to the class.

Modelo

Yo compré una chaqueta de cuero. ¿Qué compraste tú?

Yo compré una bandera argentina.

Marta y yo compramos una chaqueta de cuero y una bandera de Argentina.

ciento cincuenta y cinco 155

17. Ask students to pretend that they bought each of the items in the photos. Have them set up a bartering system in which they trade objects with each other. They can use the following script as a guide for their interactions.

A. *Yo compré una bandera argentina, pero quiero una chaqueta de cuero.*

B. *Yo compré una chaqueta de cuero, pero quiero una bandera argentina. ¿Quieres cambiar?*

AUDIO SCRIPT
See page 143K

Answer Key

14. Answers will vary.

15. A. Tim limpió la casa.
    B. Andy viajó a una isla en barco.
    C. Diana llamó por teléfono a su amiga Luisa.
    D. Tess estudió para un examen.

16. Answers will vary. Sample answers:
    1. A. ¿Tomaste el metro?
       B. Sí, tomé el metro. / No, no tomé el metro.
    2. A. ¿Hablaste con la gente?
       B. Sí, hablé con la gente. / No, no hablé con la gente.

17. 1. Yo compré una bandera argentina.
    2. Tú compraste un CD de tangos.
    3. Mack compró una camiseta de fútbol.
    4. Nosotras compramos unos libros y unas películas.
    5. Ustedes compraron una chaqueta de cuero.
    6. Rita compró una bufanda.
    7. Tim y Tess compraron unas mochilas.
    ▶ Answers will vary.

HERITAGE LANGUAGE LEARNERS

• Ask heritage learners to describe a sequence of events in the past. They may talk about a trip or a vacation they took with their family. How did they prepare before the trip? What did they do the first day? Be sure students are only using the preterite tense.

MULTIPLE INTELLIGENCES:

Verbal-Linguistic Intelligence

• Select a random picture in the book and have students tell a story as if it happened yesterday. What are three things the characters did before the picture was taken? Encourage students to use their imaginations.

Additional Resources

Fans Online activities
Practice Workbook

155

DESAFÍO 1

Comunicación

Presentation

- In this section, students will practice:
  - Travel vocabulary.
  - Transportation words and phrases.
  - Past tense of regular *-ar* verbs.

Activities	Standards	Resources
18.	1.2, 1.3, 3.1	Audio
19.	1.2, 1.3, 3.1	
20.	1.1, 1.2, 1.3	
21. Final del desafío	1.3	
Tu desafío	1.2, 1.3	

Teaching Suggestions

Warm-Up / Independent Starter

- Have students think of three things that they did yesterday after school. Ask them to take a sheet of paper and hold it horizontally and then fold it into three columns. Have them draw the three activities (using stick figures or a quick sketch). Then ask them to write sentences describing each of the three activities on a separate sheet of paper. For example:

  Scene 1: *Hablé con la profesora.*
  Scene 2: *Estudié en la biblioteca.*
  Scene 3: *Visité a mi amiga Isabel.*

Preparation

- Ask students to exchange illustrations from the previous activity with a partner. Have the students write a sentence describing the activities on the backs of each of the scenes. For example:
  Scene 1: *Habló con la profesora.*
  Scene 2: *Estudió en la biblioteca.*
  Scene 3: *Visitó a su amiga Isabel.*

- Have students compare answers to see if they guessed correctly. Finally, ask students to write a short paragraph comparing what they did with what their partner did yesterday after school. For example: *Yo hablé con la profesora, pero Jennifer tocó el violín. Jennifer y yo estudiamos en la biblioteca.* Ask for volunteers to read their paragraphs to the class.

Comunicación

18 ¡Qué día!

▶ **Lee e identifica.** Tim wrote an e-mail about his trip on the Train to the Clouds. As you read it, identify the verbs in the past tense and create a list.

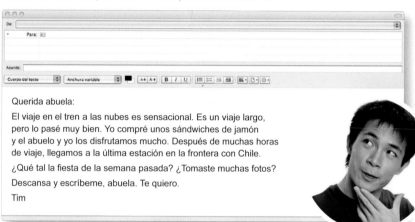

Querida abuela:

El viaje en el tren a las nubes es sensacional. Es un viaje largo, pero lo pasé muy bien. Yo compré unos sándwiches de jamón y el abuelo y yo los disfrutamos mucho. Después de muchas horas de viaje, llegamos a la última estación en la frontera con Chile.

¿Qué tal la fiesta de la semana pasada? ¿Tomaste muchas fotos?

Descansa y escríbeme, abuela. Te quiero.

Tim

 ▶ **Escucha y escribe.** Listen to the message Tim's grandmother left for him and take notes about what she did each day.

lunes	Ella tomó fotos.
martes	
miércoles	
...	

19 Una historia

▶ **Escribe.** Create a short story using the people and verb phrases below.

Modelo *Tomás y Carolina viajaron en tren...*

Tomás	hablar por teléfono tomar un refresco
Carolina	pasear grabar
Daniela	desayunar viajar
	cantar bailar

 ▶ **Lee y compara.** Now read your story to a classmate. Compare stories.

Differentiated Instruction

DEVELOPING LEARNERS

- Before starting with the *Comunicación* activities, have students organize what they learned in this *Desafío* in a two-column chart like the one below. Have them share their charts in pairs to add anything that they might have missed.

Vocabulario	Gramática
el aeropuerto el avión...	Compré, compraste, compró...

EXPANDING LEARNERS

- Have students look back through the previous units and talk about a *Desafío* they particularly liked. Then have them role-play the participants reminiscing about the experience. Encourage them to include information about where the *desafío* took place, what they saw, and what they did. For example:

  TIM: *Me gustó mucho el tren a las nubes. ¿Y a ti, abuelo?*

  MACK: *A mí también. Tomamos muchas fotos y yo compré algo bonito para tu abuela.*

20 **Tu semana**

▶ **Completa.** Fill in a chart like the one below using the preterite *yo* form of the verbs.

estudiar	comprar un regalo
escuchar música	ver la televisión
usar la computadora	llamar a un(a) amigo(a)

lunes	
martes	
miércoles	
...	

 ▶ **Habla.** Ask your partner what he or she did last week and take notes. Did you both do some of the same things?

Modelo A. ¿Estudiaste el domingo?
B. No. Estudié el sábado. ¿Compraste un regalo el lunes?
A. Sí.
B. ¡Yo también!

Final del desafío

① ② ③ ④

 21 **¿Qué pasa en la historia?**

▶ **Escribe.** Mack and Tim took the photos above during their trip. Write captions for each photo telling what they did. Use the verbs in the word bank.

hablar
comprar
viajar
mirar

→TU DESAFÍO Earn points for your own challenge! Listen to the questions for your *Minientrevista Desafío 1* on the website and write your answers.

ciento cincuenta y siete 157

HERITAGE LANGUAGE LEARNERS

- Ask students to pretend they took part in your school's student exchange program in Argentina last summer. Have them act out a phone conversation in which one person from the United States is talking on the phone to his or her "sister" or "brother" in Argentina. Have them reminisce about the events of last summer—what they did, ate, or saw; where they went; who they spent time with, etc. As they perform, you may write phrases or words that they use on the board that may be difficult for the rest of the class.

CRITICAL THINKING

- Break students into groups of four. Have each group brainstorm the advantages and disadvantages of each means of transportation that they have learned in this *Desafío*. Then ask students what the logical order for going to the following places would be: The Caribbean, Europe, Australia, Hawaii, Washington DC.

Activities

19. Have students create a picture book version of the story they wrote. They can design a paper version of the story with illustrations, a cover, and pages, or they can create a virtual picture book using PhotoStory or a free online program like Tikatok (http://www.tikatok.com/).

21. Ask students to read their captions to a partner and to help each other correct and improve their writing by using peer editing techniques.

AUDIO SCRIPT
See page 143K

Answer Key

18. pasé   llegamos
compré   tomaste
disfrutamos

▶ lunes: Ella tomó fotos.
martes: Visitó la biblioteca.
miércoles: Compró una computadora nueva.
jueves: Preparó una comida.
viernes: Habló con una amiga.
sábado: Visitó el aeropuerto nuevo.
domingo: Descansó todo el día.

19. Answers will vary. Sample answer:
Tómas desayunó temprano.
▶ Answers will vary.

20. Answers will vary. Sample answers:
lunes: Escuché música.
martes: Llamé a una amiga.
▶ Answers will vary.

21. 1. Tim compró una camiseta.
2. Tim y Mack viajaron en el tren a las nubes.
3. Tim y Mack miraron las fotos.
4. Mack habló con una mujer.

Additional Resources

Fans Online activities
Practice Workbook

DESAFÍO 2

Expresar acciones relacionadas con los viajes

Presentation

- In *Desafío 2*, Diana and Rita are in Santa Rosa, the capital of La Pampa, an Argentine province. They have been asked to make their way to the marathon and find a man running in gaucho attire who will give them proof of their completed task.

- In this section, students will learn:
  - Travel vocabulary.
  - Past tense of regular -er and -ir verbs.

Activities	Standards	Resources
Fotonovela	1.2, 2.1	Vis. Pres.
22.	1.2, 1.3	
23.	1.2, 1.3	
24.	1.2, 1.3	Audio
25. Comparaciones	1.1, 1.2, 3.2, 4.2	
Tu desafío	1.2, 5.2	

Teaching Suggestions

Warm-Up / Independent Starter

- Ask students to write what they will pack for each of the following travel destinations and temperatures: España (65°F), Argentina (45°F), Nicaragua (85°F).

Preparation

- Explain to students that the seasons in Argentina are the opposite of the seasons and weather in the United States. For example: when it is summer in New York, it is winter in Buenos Aires. Elicit from students that this is due to Argentina being in the Southern Hemisphere. Have them discuss and vote on which months would be the best ones to visit Argentina.

La fotonovela

Before Viewing

- Have students look at the photos. What do they think is happening? Do Diana and Rita look calm, or stressed out? Ask students to brainstorm reasons why travel might be stressful. What are some things that people can do to avoid stressful travel situations?

158

Un gaucho de la Pampa

Diana and Rita have to travel to Santa Rosa, the capital of La Pampa, an Argentine province. There they must make their way to the Marathon *A Pampa Traviesa*. They must find a man running in gaucho attire. He will give them proof of their completed task. Will they find him?

Diana, ¿vamos a Santa Rosa en avión o en coche?

Depende... ¿Tu licencia es válida en Argentina, tía?

Sí, pero ¿no prefieres viajar en avión?

Sí, prefiero ir en avión. ¿Compramos los billetes en la agencia de viajes?

¿Llevas a mano el pasaporte, Diana?

Sí, y llevo también la guía turística. Mira, habla del maratón...

Por favor, dos billetes de avión de Buenos Aires a Santa Rosa.

¿Ida y vuelta? ¿Clase turista? ¿Prefieren el vuelo por la mañana o por la tarde?

Continuará...

22 **Detective de palabras**

▶ **Relaciona.** What term from the dialogue corresponds to each image?

Differentiated Instruction

DEVELOPING LEARNERS

- Help students with reading comprehension by asking specific *yes* and *no* questions about the dialogue. For example: Does Diana prefer to travel by plane? Does Rita want to drive to Santa Rosa?

EXPANDING LEARNERS

- Have students act out the *fotonovela* without a script. In order to prepare, they can follow these steps:
  1. Have them read the *fotonovela* several times.
  2. Encourage students to read the *fotonovela* out loud, with different students reading the parts of Diana, Rita, and the travel agent.
  3. Ask students to write a list of the major actions / scenes.
  4. Finally, ask them to act out the scene without reading from a script or cue cards of any sort.

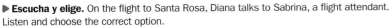

23 ¿Comprendes?

▶ **Decide.** Use the dialogue on page 158 to tell whether the statements below are true *(cierto)* or false *(falso)*. If they are false, revise them to express a true statement.

1. Diana y Rita van a Santa Rosa en autobús.
2. La licencia de conducir de Rita es válida en Argentina.
3. Van a comprar los billetes a la oficina de información y turismo.
4. Una agencia de viajes vende billetes de avión.
5. Rita y Diana pueden comprar billetes de ida y vuelta.

24 En el avión

▶ **Escucha y elige.** On the flight to Santa Rosa, Diana talks to Sabrina, a flight attendant. Listen and choose the correct option.

1. Sabrina es de _____
   a. Chile   b. Argentina   c. Perú

2. Su esposo es _____
   a. chileno   b. argentino   c. mexicano

3. Le gusta _____
   a. caminar   b. viajar   c. dormir

4. Ella viajó mucho por _____
   a. Australia   b. Asia   c. Europa

5. Ella tiene una casa en _____
   a. Santa Rosa   b. Buenos Aires   c. Santa Fe

COMPARACIONES

Los gauchos

Los gauchos son como los *cowboys* americanos. Viven en la Pampa argentina y en algunas regiones de Uruguay, Paraguay, Bolivia, Chile y Brasil. En Santa Rosa, la capital de la provincia de La Pampa, hay una Fiesta de la Tradición Gaucha durante el mes de noviembre.

25 **Piensa.** What do you think are some similarities between cowboys and gauchos?

→ TU DESAFÍO Visit the website to learn more about the Pampa and about the gaucho lifestyle.

After Viewing

▪ Ask students to talk about their favorite means of transportation when they travel. Take a class survey to find out how students prefer to travel. Then create a class pie chart with the information.

Activities

23. Ask students to write three more true/false sentences relating to the dialogue. Have them swap their sentences with a partner. Have students check their partner's answers. For example: *Diana prefiere viajar en coche.* (False)

AUDIO SCRIPT
See page 143K

COMPARACIONES

Los gauchos

The *Fiesta de la Tradición Gaucha* in Argentina has been celebrated uninterruptedly since 1939. The celebrations last many days and include bonfires to celebrate the cold nights of the Argentine Pampa, dancing at popular halls, parades, and large outdoor barbecues.

Answer Key

22. 1. pasaporte   2. billetes   3. guía turística

23. 1. Falso. Diana y Rita van en avión.
2. Cierto
3. Falso. Van a comprar los billetes en la agencia de viajes.
4. Cierto
5. Cierto

24. 1. a   2. b   3. b   4. c   5. a

25. Answers will vary.

Additional Resources

Fans Online activities

HERITAGE LANGUAGE LEARNERS

• Have students brainstorm a list of questions, other than the ones from the *fotonovela* that Rita and Diana may have for the travel agent. Have them write their questions and trade with another student to answer the questions.

MULTIPLE INTELLIGENCES:

Bodily-Kinesthetic Intelligence

• Have volunteers come up to the front of the class and perform the dialogues as you read them aloud. They must mimic the words in silence and act them out.

DESAFÍO 2

Vocabulario – Los viajes

Presentation

- In this section, students will learn words related to travel and tourism.

Activities	Standards	Resources
Vocabulario	1.2	
26.	1.2, 1.3	
27.	1.2, 1.3	Audio
28.	1.3	
29. Cultura	1.1, 1.2, 2.1, 3.1, 3.2, 4.2	

Teaching Suggestions

Warm-Up / Independent Starter

- Ask students to pretend they are Diana and Rita and that they traveled from Buenos Aires to La Pampa. Have them write a paragraph of at least four sentences telling how they got there, what they saw on their trip, what they bought along the way, and an interesting activity they did to pass the time. Remind students to use the preterite of the verbs.

Preparation

- Have students copy the vocabulary words into their notebook as you go over them. Once you have explained each item on the vocabulary list, have students close their books and make a list of as many of the words as they can remember. Then have them draw a corresponding picture next to each vocabulary word. They can either create a picture dictionary or a set of flashcards to help them learn the vocabulary from this *Desafío*.

Activities

26. After writing Rita's advice to Diana in full sentences, have students order the sentences based on when each activity happens during a typical trip. Alternatively, students can place the statements in order, according to how important they feel each suggestion is. For example:
    1. *Ve a la oficina de turismo.*
    2. *Mira la hora del vuelo.*
    3. *Llega al aeropuerto temprano.*

160

Vocabulario

Los viajes

el pasaporte   el billete   la maleta   la bolsa   la guía turística

la agencia de viajes   la oficina de turismo   el mostrador de información

facturar el equipaje   enseñar el pasaporte   comprar recuerdos

26 **Viajeros con experiencia**

▶ **Escribe.** Rita gave Diana a lot of travel advice, which Diana has written in her notebook. Use her notes to report what Rita told her to do.

Modelo   salir del metro con cuidado → *Sal del metro con cuidado.*

leer la guía turística	facturar pronto el equipaje
cerrar bien la maleta	ir a la oficina de turismo
mirar la hora del vuelo	visitar museos grandes y pequeños
llegar al aeropuerto temprano	comprar muchos recuerdos

160 ciento sesenta

Differentiated Instruction

DEVELOPING LEARNERS

- Have students personalize the vocabulary by creating their own picture dictionary. They may use index cards and cut outs from magazines. Have them play a memory game with a partner by mixing both sets of cards.

EXPANDING LEARNERS

- Ask students to write five things they like and five things they dislike about going on a trip. For example: *Me gusta comprar recuerdos para mis amigos or No me gusta ir a la oficina de turismo.* Have them work in pairs to talk about their lists. Then students should report on their partner's likes and dislikes.

27 ¿Estás lista para el viaje?

 ▶ **Escucha y ordena.** Listen to what Diana's mother says and decide in which order these items should be prepared for travel.

(A)   (B)   (C)   (D)   (E)

▶ **Escribe.** Write a note to yourself telling why you need to bring or buy each of the things shown above.

Modelo 1. *Tengo que llevar una chaqueta para no tener frío en el avión.*

> entrar en otro país
> no tener frío en el avión
> llevar toda la ropa
> tomar el avión
> saber más sobre Argentina

28 El itinerario del día

 ▶ **Escribe y habla.** You went on a fabulous vacation to Argentina! Write a list of the steps you took to prepare for the trip. Then tell your partner what you did before and during your vacation.

Modelo *Primero compré una guía turística…*

> **Mi viaje a Argentina**
> 1. Compré una guía turística.
> 2. …

 CULTURA

La Pampa

La Pampa es una provincia argentina importante por su agricultura y su industria. Está en el centro del país. A 30 kilómetros de Santa Rosa está la Reserva Natural Parque Luro. Allí puedes hacer cámping y practicar todo tipo de deportes.

29 **Compara.** Considering the presence of gauchos and the information above, what region of the U.S. would be most like La Pampa? Why? What differences might there be?

ciento sesenta y uno 161

27. Are there any suggestions missing from Diana's mother's list? Have students add three travel suggestions of their own to the list.

 AUDIO SCRIPT
See page 143K

CULTURA

La Pampa

Despite its large size (55,382 sq miles), La Pampa doesn't have a large population (less than 500,000). This is probably due to its geography. Most of the territory is used for agricultural purposes and lacks industry. The Pampa is the youngest of the Argentine provinces, becoming an official province in 1952. For a complete factual landscape of this Argentine region, visit the official site at www.lapampa.gov.ar.

Answer Key

26. Lee la guía turística.
Cierra bien la maleta.
Mira la hora del vuelo.
Llega al aeropuerto temprano.
Factura pronto el equipaje.
Ve a la oficina de turismo.
Visita museos grandes y pequeños.
Compra muchos recuerdos.

27. 1. C   2. D   3. E   4. B   5. A
▶ Answers will vary. Sample answer: Tengo que comprar una maleta para llevar toda la ropa.

28. Answers will vary.

29. Answers will vary.

Additional Resources

Fans Online activities
Practice Workbook

HERITAGE LANGUAGE LEARNERS

• Have students from different countries of origin share variations in the vocabulary of this *Desafío*. Students from Mexico, for example, may use *boleto* instead of *billete*. Students from Argentina may say *valija* instead of *maleta*.

CRITICAL THINKING

• Students may elaborate on the differences and similarities between American cowboys and Argentine gauchos. Have them create a two-column chart and work with a partner to complete it. Have students compare their work with other pairs in the class. Once they have created their lists of differences and similarities, ask them to think about possible reasons why these two groups might be similar and what might account for the differences. For example, they might be similar due to the types of jobs that they do, such as cattle herding and farm work.

Unit 7

DESAFÍO 2

Gramática – Verbos regulares en -*er* y en -*ir*. Pretérito

Presentation

- In this section, students will learn past tense forms of regular -*er* and -*ir* verbs.

Activities	Standards	Resources
Gramática	1.2, 3.1, 4.1	
30.	1.1, 4.1	
31.	1.1, 1.2, 1.3	Audio
32.	1.3	
33.	1.3	
34. Cultura	1.1, 1.2, 3.2, 4.2	

Teaching Suggestions

Warm-Up / Independent Starter

- Ask students to think about the best souvenir they ever bought during their travels. Have them write three sentences to describe their objects using the categories below:

¿Dónde compraste el recuerdo?	¿Cuánto costó el recuerdo?	¿Qué te gustó del recuerdo?
Lo compré en...		

Preparation

- Ask students to compare their answers to the previous activity. Create a class diagram with the information.

Activities

31. This activity can be extended using clips from Spanish TV channels or videos, poetry, or passages from written materials such as books or comics.

32. Ask students to choose a photo and write one thing that happened before the photo was taken, what was happening in the photo, and one thing that happened afterwards. For example, for photo 1:

– Antes: *La chica compró un billete para el vuelo.*

– Ahora: *La chica bebe agua.*

– Después: *La chica va a llegar a su destino.*

162

Gramática

Verbos regulares en -*er* y en -*ir*. Pretérito

- Regular -*er* and -*ir* verbs have the same endings in the preterite tense. Here is how they are conjugated:

VERBO COMER (TO EAT). PRETÉRITO

Singular		Plural	
yo	com**í**	nosotros nosotras	com**imos**
tú	com**iste**	vosotros vosotras	com**isteis**
usted él ella	com**ió**	ustedes ellos ellas	com**ieron**

VERBO ESCRIBIR (TO WRITE). PRETÉRITO

Singular		Plural	
yo	escrib**í**	nosotros nosotras	escrib**imos**
tú	escrib**iste**	vosotros vosotras	escrib**isteis**
usted él ella	escrib**ió**	ustedes ellos ellas	escrib**ieron**

Note: Just as with -*ar* verbs, the nosotros form of -*ir* verbs is the same in the preterite and the present tense. The context helps to determine the tense of the verb.

30 **Piensa.** What other clues would make you think that a sentence was in the past tense or the present tense?

31 **¿Presente o pasado?**

 ▶ **Escucha y decide.** Diana and Rita overheard conversations on the plane. Listen and decide whether the people are talking about something that happened in the past or something that normally happens.

A. Pasó en el pasado.   **B.** Normalmente pasa.

 ▶ **Escribe y habla.** Write three sentences using the preterite or present tense. Say them aloud to a partner. He or she will indicate whether you are talking about something that happened in the past or something that normally happens.

Modelo

Yo viajé a Argentina.   Pasó en el pasado.

162 ciento sesenta y dos

Differentiated Instruction

DEVELOPING LEARNERS

- For further practice with the past tense of regular -*er* and -*ir* verbs, make a list of ten verbs the students know well. Ask students to create conjugation tables on index cards for each one of the verbs. Remind students that some endings require accent marks.

EXPANDING LEARNERS

- Have students explain aloud what they did this morning before coming to class. Elicit at least five uses of the past tense from them. You may guide them by asking questions like *¿Te duchaste hoy o ayer por la noche? ¿Comiste manzanas esta mañana?*

32 **¿Qué hicieron?**

▶ **Escribe.** What did these people do before and during their flight? Write a sentence describing each action.

Modelo *El hombre prendió la luz.*

① la niña   ② la mujer   ③ los chicos   ④ Rita

33 **Hoy y antes**

▶ **Escribe y habla.** Write ten sentences to talk about the day's events. Write five sentences in the *nosotros* form of the present tense and five sentences in the *nosotros* form of the preterite. Share your sentences with a partner.

Modelo Presente ⟶ *Todos los días escribimos en la clase de Ciencias.*
Pretérito ⟶ *Esta mañana escribimos en la clase de Inglés.*

CULTURA

A Pampa Traviesa

A Pampa Traviesa es un maratón. Se celebra cada año en Santa Rosa, la capital de La Pampa. Los participantes corren veintiséis millas por la ciudad. No pueden correr más de mil personas.

Los atletas se reúnen delante del Edificio Mundial a las ocho de la mañana. Allí está la salida y también la llegada.

34 **Piensa.** What kind of training do you think it takes to run a marathon? What are the distances of the marathons and other races in your city or town?

Gramática – Verbos regulares en -*er* y en -*ir*. Pretérito

 AUDIO SCRIPT
See page 143K

CULTURA

A Pampa Traviesa

The main categories for participating in the *A Pampa Traviesa* marathon are: conventional, wheelchair, and visually impaired. The maximum number of participants is 1,000 athletes for two distances: 42 and 21 kilometers (approx. 26 and 13 miles each). The first-place prize for the winner of the race is 2,000 Argentine pesos (about US$525), but if the winner breaks the record he or she will get a bonus.

Answer Key

30. Past tense verbs + words like *ayer, anoche, la semana pasada, el año pasado*, etc.

31. 1. A 2. B 3. A 4. A 5. B
▶ Answers will vary. Sample answers:
A. Ayer comimos en un restaurante elegante.
B. Pasó en el pasado.

32. Answers will vary. Sample answers:
1. La niña bebió agua.
2. La mujer escribió un e-mail.
3. Los chicos subieron al avión.
4. Rita comió un sándwich.

33. Answers will vary. Sample answers:
Siempre estudiamos en la biblioteca.
Esta tarde estudiamos en casa.

34. Answers will vary.

Additional Resources

Fans Online activities
Practice Workbook

HERITAGE LANGUAGE LEARNERS

• Share the following quotes about travel with students. Have them choose one and write a response to the quote, telling whether they agree or disagree, and why.

"Se viaja no para buscar el destino sino para huir de donde se parte." (Miguel de Unamuno)

"Viajar es una buena forma de aprender y de superar miedos." (Luis Rojas Marcos)

"El que está acostumbrado a viajar, sabe que siempre es necesario partir algún día." (Paulo Coelho)

MULTIPLE INTELLIGENCES:

Intrapersonal Intelligence

• For further practice, have students write journal entries about how they feel when they travel. Encourage them to write about what they learn or ways in which they grow on a personal level when they are far away from their homes. Have students share portions of their journal entries with a partner.

163

DESAFÍO 2

Comunicación

Presentation

- In this section, students will learn:
  - Travel and tourism vocabulary.
  - Past tense forms of regular *-er* and *-ir* verbs.

Activities	Standards	Resources
35.	1.2, 1.3	
36.	1.2, 1.3, 3.1	
37.	1.3	
38. Final del desafío	1.2, 1.3, 3.1	

Teaching Suggestions

Warm-Up / Independent Starter

- Have students conjugate the following verbs and use them in sentences: *correr, salir, beber, abrir.*

Preparation

- Have students create signs that say *pasado* on one side and *presente* on the other (this can be created with a sheet of paper). Working in pairs, have students act out different verbs while flipping the signs to either the *pasado* or the *presente* sides. Their partners should guess the verb and say it in the proper tense (past or present). For example: (Sign is on the *pasado* side.)
  A. Acts out drinking a glass of water.
  B. Says: *Bebiste agua.*

Activities

35. Ask students to write an e-mail to a friend in another town, state, or country. Have them write a brief description of what they did on their last vacation using the preterite.

36. Have students create a skit to promote their trip to Argentina. Encourage students to record their skits to create videos. In the video they can show the poster they've created, act out some of the interesting facts from the memo, and add other details from this unit. They can even vote to determine which video is the class favorite!

37. Ask students to work with a partner to write about their trip. To extend this activity, have them write about things they both did and things only one of them did.

Comunicación

35 **Pasó en Argentina...**

▶ **Completa.** Diana's e-mail to her best friend is incomplete—some verbs are missing. Complete her message by filling in the blanks with the appropriate preterite forms.

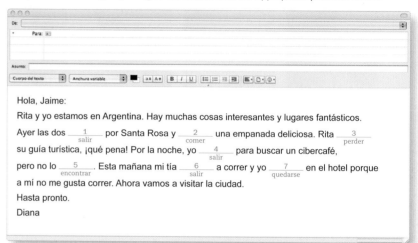

Hola, Jaime:

Rita y yo estamos en Argentina. Hay muchas cosas interesantes y lugares fantásticos.

Ayer las dos ___1___ (salir) por Santa Rosa y ___2___ (comer) una empanada deliciosa. Rita ___3___ (perder) su guía turística, ¡qué pena! Por la noche, yo ___4___ (salir) para buscar un cibercafé, pero no lo ___5___ (encontrar). Esta mañana mi tía ___6___ (salir) a correr y yo ___7___ (quedarse) en el hotel porque a mí no me gusta correr. Ahora vamos a visitar la ciudad.

Hasta pronto.

Diana

36 **Un viaje de estudios**

▶ **Lee y escribe.** Read the memo sent to parents about a student trip to Argentina and write two interesting facts about the excursion.

▶ **Crea un póster.** Now find pictures about Argentina in a magazine and create a poster to try to convince your classmates to go there this year.

Viaje de estudios a Argentina

Estimados padres y madres:

El verano pasado, la organización Gauchos Argentinos invitó a varias escuelas americanas a conocer Buenos Aires y otras ciudades de Argentina. Los estudiantes conocieron a muchas personas y aprendieron mucho sobre la vida de los gauchos.

El próximo verano nuestra escuela va a pasar dos semanas en Argentina con el mismo programa. Este viernes ustedes pueden asistir a una reunión informativa sobre el viaje. Todos son bienvenidos.

Atentamente,

El Departamento de Español

Differentiated Instruction

DEVELOPING LEARNERS

- Have pairs of students practice past tense conjugations by talking about different activities they did in the past. One student calls out an activity in the infinitive verb form and the partner says what he or she did for the activity. For example:
  A. *escribir*
  B. *Escribí mi tarea.*

EXPANDING LEARNERS

- Ask each of the students to explain orally what happened in this *Desafío.* Their summaries should be concise and include uses of the past tense.

37 ¡Tú también participas!

▶ **Escribe.** You and a friend went to Santa Rosa, like Diana and Rita.
Write about your trip using some the verbs below, in the preterite tense.

Modelo *En marzo viajamos a Santa Rosa. Comimos en todos los restaurantes famosos.*

comer	comprar	visitar
viajar	conocer	perder
correr	competir	ver

Final del desafío

Aquí hay mucha gente, tía. El gaucho ya ___1___ por aquí.

Sí, Diana, el gaucho ya ___2___ a la meta.

...uel hombre nos está ___3___. Es el gaucho, ...erdad?

¡Qué bien, tía! ¡El gaucho nos ___4___ su sombrero!

38 ¿Qué pasa en la historia?

▶ **Completa y representa.** Complete the dialogue with the correct forms of the verbs below.
Then, in a group, act out the ending of the *Desafío.*

| saludar | regalar | llegar | pasar |

---

38. To extend this activity, break the class into small groups and ask each group to come up with an additional line or two near the end of the dialogue. Invite groups to act out the dialogue for the class. You may want to have a vote on the most original dialogue.

Answer Key

35.
1. salimos
2. comimos
3. perdió
4. salí
5. encontré
6. salió
7. me quedé

36. Answers will vary. Sample answer:
Los estudiantes conocieron a muchas personas.
▶ Answers will vary.

37. Answers will vary. Sample answer:
Mi amigo visitó el museo nacional. Yo comí empanada argentina por primera vez.

38.
1. pasó
2. llegó
3. saludando
4. regaló

Additional Resources

Fans Online activities
Practice Workbook

HERITAGE LANGUAGE LEARNERS

• Instruct students to find information about an event in Argentina not mentioned in *Desafío 2.* Have them narrate the event as if they participated in it last year. Students may use images from the Internet to illustrate their presentations.

MULTIPLE INTELLIGENCES:

Naturalist Intelligence

• Have students use *Fans del español* or other Internet sites to learn about the Pampa. Students should create a brochure highlighting the region's flora and fauna. If resources allow it, print out their brochures and share them with the class. If not, students can work with transparency paper and all of their work can be shown to the class. Be sure students cite their Internet sources.

165

DESAFÍO 3

Expresar lugar y acciones pasadas

Presentation

- In *Desafío 3*, Andy and Janet are in Iguazu Falls. Their task is to make a video guide of the *Garganta del Diablo* (Devil's Throat), a waterfall located between Argentina and Brazil.

- In this section students will learn:
  - Destinations and travel accommodations.
  - Adverbs and time expressions.
  - The verbs *ir* and *ser* in the preterite tense.
  - Prepositions of place.

Activities	Standards	Resources
Fotonovela	1.2, 3.1	Vis. Pres.
39.	1.3	
40.	1.2, 1.3	
41.	1.2, 1.3	
42. Cultura	1.1, 1.2, 3.1, 3.2, 4.2	Video
Tu desafío	1.2, 5.2	

Teaching Suggestions

Warm-Up / Independent Starter

- Ask students to choose their favorite destination from the following list: the beach, the mountains, a large cosmopolitan city, a small town in the countryside.

Preparation

- Have students report their destinations to the class. Create a bar chart to show the students' choices. What is the most popular destination?

La fotonovela

Before Viewing

- Ask students to look at the photos in the *fotonovela* and try to suggest phrases they would expect to hear in the dialogues.

After Viewing

- Have students point to each photo and answer the questions in the chart below:

	¿Quién habla?	¿Qué dice?	¿Qué palabras nuevas hay?
1.	Janet	Sí, está aquí.	montaña, …

DESAFÍO 3 **Expresar lugar y acciones pasadas**

Las cataratas del Iguazú

Andy and Janet are taking a trip to Iguazu Falls, one of the most spectacular waterfalls in South America. Their task is to make a video guide of the *Garganta del Diablo* (Devil's Throat), a waterfall that lies between Argentina and Brazil.

No veo la Garganta del Diablo en el mapa. ¿Y tú?

¿Llamaste ayer al hotel para reservar una habitación?

No, finalmente reservé en el cámping.

Sí, está aquí, al sur de la montaña.

Perdimos la ruta... ¿Fuimos en la dirección correcta?

No sé... Ayer miré la ruta en Internet. La Garganta del Diablo está al norte...

¡Oh, no, Janet! ¡Miramos mal el mapa!

Continuará…

39 Detective de palabras

▶ **Completa.** Complete the sentences using the dialogue above.

1. _____ en el cámping.
2. _____ la ruta…
3. _____ en la dirección correcta?
4. _____ mal el mapa.

▶ **Piensa.** Are the verbs above in the present or in the past tense?

Differentiated Instruction

DEVELOPING LEARNERS

- Have students scan the *fotonovela* for cognates (for example: *mapa, hotel, reservar, cámping, ruta, correcta*). Have them list these words in their notebooks and find a clip art illustration to show the meaning of each word, then ask them to write a sentence to go along with each picture.

EXPANDING LEARNERS

- Ask students to rewrite the events and scenes in this *Desafío* in different genres. Possible genres include: adventure, horror, comedy, drama, documentary, infomercial, travelogue, or a reality show.

40 **¿Comprendes?**

▶ **Decide y escribe.** Decide whether these statements are true *(cierto)* or false *(falso)* and correct the false statements.

Modelo Janet reservó habitación en un hotel.
→ *Falso. Janet reservó habitación en un cámping.*

1. Andy y Janet perdieron la ruta.
2. Ayer Janet miró la ruta en una guía turística.
3. La Garganta del Diablo está al sur.
4. Andy y Janet miraron mal el mapa.

41 **Buscando la Garganta del Diablo**

▶ **Ordena.** Put these events in order according to the dialogue.

a. Andy buscó la Garganta del Diablo en el mapa.
b. Andy y Janet perdieron la ruta.
c. Andy y Janet se sentaron para pensar.
d. Janet encontró la Garganta del Diablo en el mapa.
e. Andy descubrió el error.
f. Andy y Janet caminaron mucho tiempo.
g. Andy miró bien el mapa.

▶ **Escribe.** Now write Andy and Janet's adventure in search of the Devil's Throat. Use the sentences you ordered and the following words to connect them.

| primero | después | luego | y | más tarde |

CULTURA

Las cataratas del Iguazú

Las cataratas *(waterfalls)* del río Iguazú son unas de las cataratas más impresionantes del mundo. Están entre Paraguay, Argentina y Brasil. En esa zona está el Parque Nacional Iguazú, formado por más de 275 cataratas.

42 **Piensa.** Have you ever seen a waterfall? Can you name some waterfalls in North America? Are they located in a national park like Iguazu Falls?

▶ TU DESAFÍO Visit the website to learn more about the *Parque Nacional Iguazú*.

Activities

39. Activate prior knowledge by asking students how they can tell if the verbs in the first column function for present or past tenses. Elicit from them that context helps to determine the correct tense.

CULTURA

Las cataratas del Iguazú

The Iguazu Falls are part of a river of the same name. This river and the Parana River make up the borders between Brazil, Argentina, and Paraguay. The Devil's Throat is at the center of the falls. The Tancredo Neves Bridge, also known as Fraternity Bridge, connects Argentina and Brazil over the Iguazu River.

Answer Key

39. 1. No, finalmente reservé
2. Perdimos
3. ¿Fuimos
4. Miramos
▶ 1. Past.
2. Past.
3. Past.
4. Both.

40. 1. Cierto
2. Falso. Miró la ruta en Internet.
3. Falso. La Garganta del Diablo está al norte.
4. Cierto

41. a, d, f, c, b, g, e.
▶ Answers will vary.

42. Answers will vary.

Additional Resources

Fans Online activities

HERITAGE LANGUAGE LEARNERS

• Heritage students can use compare and contrast charts to talk about a geographical feature in their country of origin and the Iguazu Falls. Have students prepare short presentations for the class. Encourage them to keep the language at the level of the rest of the class by using vocabulary and cognates that have been studied. Remind them to speak clearly and slowly.

CRITICAL THINKING

• Have students think about the name *Garganta del Diablo*. Ask them what type of place this might be and why people would give it such name. Allow students a few minutes to investigate and share information with their classmates. Then invite students to talk about whether they would visit a place with this or a similar name. Have them elaborate on their answers.

167

DESAFÍO 3

Vocabulario – Destinos y alojamientos

Presentation

- In this section, students will learn:
  - Words related to destinations.
  - Words related to travel accommodations.

Activities	Standards	Resources
Vocabulario	1.2	
43.	1.3	
44.	1.1, 1.2, 1.3	Audio
45.	1.2, 1.3	
46. Conexiones	1.1, 1.2, 3.1, 3.2	

Teaching Suggestions

Warm-Up / Independent Starter

- Write the cognates *montaña, costa, hotel, turismo,* and *cámping* on the board. Have students write an English definition for each.

Preparation

- Ask students to talk about some of their vacation destinations. Encourage them to describe where they went, where they stayed, who went with them, and how they got there.

Activities

43. To extend the activity and practice prior vocabulary and structures, have students create a list of the clothing that each contestant is wearing in each photo. Ask students to compare their list with that of a partner.

45. Ask students to create mini-posters to go along with their travel proposals. The posters should contain visuals that respond to all four questions. For example, if the answer to *¿Cómo van a viajar?* is *En tren*, students should include a visual of a train, using clip art, a photograph, or a drawing.

46. Work with the art teacher to have students create their own compass rose. Students should look at several highly decorative examples before creating their own designs. Some good examples can be found online.

168

Vocabulario

Destinos y alojamientos

el campo

la ciudad

Me gusta **hacer turismo** y conocer ciudades.

la playa

la montaña

¿Tienen una **habitación** para dos personas?

el hotel

el cámping

reservar habitación

43 **¿Adónde viajaron?**

▶ **Habla.** The characters visited different places during their vacations. According to what each one is wearing, where do you think they traveled?

Modelo

¿Adónde viajó Tim?

Tim viajó a la ciudad.

Differentiated Instruction

DEVELOPING LEARNERS

- Create simple flashcards to help support new vocabulary. Share images from magazines that represent the new vocabulary words. As you show students the images, ask them to call out the Spanish word for each one. Then write the words on the board and ask students to copy them into their notebooks.

EXPANDING LEARNERS

- Have students discuss their preferred forms of accommodation when traveling. Have them say why they like it and when was the last time that they stayed in such a place. Encourage them to include details and relevant information. For example: *Me gusta dormir en un hotel. Los hoteles son más cómodos que el cámping. No me gusta dormir en un cámping.*

44 **¿Adónde vamos?**

 ▶ **Escucha y escribe.** The characters are going to many places in Argentina. Listen to Andy coordinate their destinations and write a sentence to say where everyone goes, and how they will get there.

Modelo 1. *Mack y Tim van al norte, a la montaña, en autobús.*

 (A) (B)   (C) (D)

1. Mack y Tim	al norte	a la costa	en coche
2. Andy y Janet	al sur	a la montaña	en avión
3. Diana y Rita	al este	a la playa	en taxi
4. Tess y Patricia	al oeste	a la ciudad	en autobús

▶ **Habla.** Now tell a partner where and how the characters traveled.

Modelo A. *¿Adónde viajaron Mack y Tim?*
B. *Ellos viajaron al norte, a la montaña, en autobús.*

45 **Una propuesta de viaje**

▶ **Escribe.** Your family cannot decide where to go on vacation this year. Write a proposal that includes answers to the following questions.

1. ¿Adónde van a ir tu familia y tú?
2. ¿Qué van a hacer allí?
3. ¿Cómo van a viajar?
4. ¿Por qué quieres ir tú allí?

▶ **Lee.** In a small group, read your proposal. Then vote for the most convincing plan.

 CONEXIONES: GEOGRAFÍA

La rosa de los vientos

La rosa de los vientos representa los cuatro puntos cardinales (Norte, Sur, Este y Oeste). Puede mostrar también otras direcciones, como Noreste, Sureste, Noroeste y Suroeste. La rosa de los vientos se utiliza en muchos mapas.

46 **Piensa.** Why do you think that the compass rose is often highly decorative? If you were a mapmaker, what would your compass rose look like?

ciento sesenta y nueve 169

 AUDIO SCRIPT
See page 143K

 CONEXIONES: GEOGRAFÍA

La rosa de los vientos

The compass rose is called a "rose" because of the highly decorative and ornate images used to decorate early compasses. The first compass roses appeared on maps and charts in the 1300s. These early compasses had 32 points. There were eight major points: north, south, east, west, northeast, southeast, northwest, and southwest, which were then divided into four subpoints.

Answer Key

43. 1. A. ¿Adónde viajó Andy?
   B. Andy viajó a la playa.
2. A. ¿Adónde viajó Janet?
   B. Janet viajó a la costa.
3. A. ¿Adónde viajó Tess?
   B. Tess viajó a la montaña.

44. 1. Mack y Tim van al norte, a la montaña, en autobús.
2. Andy y Janet van al este, a la playa, en coche.
3. Diana y Rita van al sur, a la costa, en avión.
4. Tess y Patricia van al oeste, a la ciudad, en taxi.

45. Answers will vary. Sample answers:
1. Vamos a la playa de Cancún.
2. Allí vamos a nadar en el mar.
3. Vamos en avión.
4. Queremos ir a la playa porque es muy divertido.
▶ Answers will vary.

46. Answers will vary.

Additional Resources

Fans Online activities
Practice Workbook

 HERITAGE LANGUAGE LEARNERS

• Instruct students to research four locations in their country of origin, each representing a geographical point. Encourage them to find interesting information about each place, such as the climate, flora, and fauna. Have them present their findings in visual form, using a map. Alternatively, ask them to write a blog entry about the four places in the form of a travelogue.

MULTIPLE INTELLIGENCES:
Bodily-Kinesthetic Intelligence

• Play a game with students similar to "We're going on a bear hunt." The teacher models actions as sentences are called out and students repeat the actions and phrases immediately after the teacher.

	Says	Does
Teacher	*Vamos de viaje.*	Picks up a pretend suitcase and waves goodbye.
Students	*Vamos de viaje.*	Pick up pretend suitcases and wave goodbye.

Unit 7

DESAFÍO 3

Gramática – Marcadores temporales de pasado

Presentation

- In this section, students will learn adverbs and time expressions that refer to the past tense.

Activities	Standards	Resources
Gramática	1.2, 3.1, 4.1	
47.	1.1, 3.1, 4.1	
48.	1.1, 1.2, 1.3	
49.	1.2, 1.3	Audio
50.	1.2, 1.3	

Teaching Suggestions

Warm-Up / Independent Starter

- Have students write examples for each of the following words:

  la montaña → Mount St. Helens, Washington, U.S.
  la costa
  la playa
  el hotel

Preparation

- Bring objects to the class that are outdated; for example, a VCR, an old photo of yourself, or a page from an old calendar. Point to these objects as you introduce students to the adverbs they will soon learn. For example, as you point to the photo of your last birthday, say *el año pasado*, or as you point to the calendar page, say *el mes pasado*. Ask students to repeat each time expression after you model the pronunciation.

Activities

48. Ask students to create their own personalized timetable for the past week. Have them compare and contrast their table with that of a classmate. Did they do similar activities or not?

49. Have students use the activities under column B to write sentences about themselves. They should specify when they did the activities that apply to them. When they finish, have them organize their sentences chronologically.

170

DESAFÍO 3

Gramática

Marcadores temporales de pasado

- The adverbs *antes*, *ayer*, and *anoche* refer to the past tense:

antes · ahora · ayer anoche · hoy

Antes hablé con Juan. · Ayer cené en un restaurante.

- You can also use these expressions to refer to the past tense:

el año pasado · el mes pasado · la semana pasada

La semana pasada visité a mi abuela.

47 **Piensa.** The Spanish word *anteayer* is a compound word formed by two shorter words. What do you think it means? Is there an equivalent word in English?

48 **¿Cuándo pasó?**

▶ **Escribe.** Write sentences using this information.

Modelo 1. *Diana vio una película ayer.*

Actividades		
Quién	**Qué**	**Cuándo**
1. Diana	ver una película	ayer
2. Tim	hablar por teléfono	anoche
3. Janet	aprender una receta nueva	la semana pasada
4. Diana y Rita	comer en un restaurante	el mes pasado
5. Patricia y Tess	viajar en metro	el jueves pasado

 ▶ **Habla.** Now tell a partner when you last did these activities.

Modelo A. *¿Cuándo viste una película?*
B. *Vi una película la semana pasada.*

170 ciento setenta

Differentiated Instruction

DEVELOPING LEARNERS

- Have students create memory aids to remember the time expressions taught in this spread. Ask students if they know of any other words that might work in the same manner. You may give them examples like, *el lunes pasado,* or *la primavera pasada.* Elicit that the words *pasado* or *pasada* can modify any day of the week or season of the year.

EXPANDING LEARNERS

- Have students write down as many sentences as they can to describe what they did last year. Ask them to narrate the events chronologically and check for accuracy and use of the time expressions taught in this spread.

49 **¿Qué hicieron?**

 ▶ **Escucha y une.** Listen to Andy and Janet talk about what they did recently and match the elements in columns A and B.

Ⓐ

1. el mes pasado
2. el martes pasado
3. el miércoles
4. el jueves
5. el sábado
6. ayer
7. anoche
8. esta mañana

Ⓑ

a. visitar una playa
b. usar la computadora
c. cenar con Tim y Mack
d. comprar una guía turística
e. levantarse temprano
f. pasear y visitar museos
g. pasar la noche en un cámping
h. hablar con sus padres

▶ **Escribe.** Now write sentences about Andy and Janet's schedule.

Modelo 1. *El mes pasado compraron una guía turística.*

50 **Una agenda llena**

▶ **Escribe.** You are organizing your mom's birthday party. Write who did each thing and when they did it. (Note today's date on the agenda!)

Modelo *Esta mañana limpié mi habitación.*

JULIO
1 Lunes — *Organizar las invitaciones (los tíos).*
2 Martes
3 Miércoles — *Preparar la comida (papá y yo).*

JULIO
4 Jueves — *Escribir a los abuelos (Juliana).*
5 Viernes — *Por la mañana, comprar un regalo para mamá (yo). Por la tarde, llamar a la florería (Manuel).*
6 Sábado — *Limpiar mi habitación (yo).*
7 Domingo

ciento setenta y uno 171

 AUDIO SCRIPT
See page 143K

Answer Key

47. *Anteayer (antes + ayer)* literally means "before yesterday."

48. 1. Diana vio una película ayer.
2. Tim habló por teléfono anoche.
3. Janet aprendió una receta nueva la semana pasada.
4. Diana y Rita comieron en un restaurante el mes pasado.
5. Patricia y Tess viajaron en metro el jueves pasado.
▶ Answers will vary.

49. 1. d   5. c
2. a   6. h
3. g   7. b
4. f   8. e
▶ 1. El mes pasado compraron una guía turística.
2. El martes pasado visitaron una playa.
3. El miércoles pasaron la noche en un cámping.
4. El jueves pasearon y visitaron museos.
5. El sábado cenaron con Tim y Mack.
6. Ayer hablaron con sus padres.
7. Anoche Janet usó la computadora.
8. Esta mañana Andy se levantó temprano.

50. Ayer por la tarde Manuel llamó a la florería. Ayer por la mañana compré un regalo para mamá.
Anteayer Juliana escribió a los abuelos.
El miércoles pasado papá y yo preparamos la comida.
El lunes pasado los tíos organizaron las invitaciones.

Additional Resources

Fans Online activities
Practice Workbook

HERITAGE LANGUAGE LEARNERS

• Ask heritage learners to watch the news (*el noticiero*) in Spanish or on a Spanish-language TV station (or listen on the radio). Have them take notes on what happened yesterday, etc. (*ayer, anoche, la semana pasada*, etc.) based on what they saw / heard on the news. Have them report the information to the class.

MULTIPLE INTELLIGENCES:
Bodily-Kinesthetic Intelligence

• Have students play a game of charades with sentences in the past tense. They can use a large calendar page to indicate past times. For example, student mimes eating a hamburger and rubbing his or her stomach to illustrate the word *delicious*, then points to the previous day on the calendar. Classmates take turns guessing until they come to the correct sentence: *El lunes pasado comí una hamburguesa deliciosa.*

171

DESAFÍO 3

Gramática – Los verbos *ser* e *ir*. Pretérito

Presentation

- In this section, students will learn:
  - Irregular past tense of the verbs *ser* and *ir*.
  - Prepositions of place.

Activities	Standards	Resources
Gramática	1.2, 3.1, 4.1	
51.	1.2, 1.3	Audio
52.	1.2, 1.3	
53.	1.1, 1.3	
54. Conexiones	1.1, 1.2, 3.1, 3.2	

Teaching Suggestions

Warm-Up / Independent Starter

- Have students list five activities that they did in the past. Ask them to order the activities from earliest to latest (for example: *el año pasado → el mes pasado → la semana pasada → anteayer → ayer*) and then write a paragraph with the information.

Preparation

- Have students share their paragraphs with a partner. They must take notes on what they hear and report back to the class.
  El año pasado Marisa fue a Chicago.
  El mes pasado Marisa visitó Costa Rica.

Activities

52. Ask students to write a note to a friend about where they went today. Have students white out five words and give the note to their partner. Can their partner guess the missing words?

53. You may want to break students into small groups for this activity. Ask them to interview their classmates in the group and choose the travel experiences of one of them to act out. Have them write a short script summarizing this person's travel experiences and ask them to act it out for the class.

54. Have students research distances in South America in miles and kilometers on an online conversion site.

Gramática

Los verbos *ser* e *ir*. Pretérito

- The verbs *ser* and *ir* are irregular in the preterite and share the same forms.

VERBOS *SER* (TO BE) E *IR* (TO GO). PRETÉRITO

Singular		Plural	
yo	fui	nosotros nosotras	fuimos
tú	fuiste	vosotros vosotras	fuisteis
usted él ella	fue	ustedes ellos ellas	fueron

Prepositions of place

The verb *ir* can be used with prepositions to express various ideas.

- Remember, you can use *ir a* to say that you went to a certain place.

ir a + place

Fui a Buenos Aires en marzo.

- To express direction or destination, use these structures:

ir desde (from) + place + *hasta* (to) + place

Él fue **desde** México **hasta** Buenos Aires.

ir de (from) + place + *a* (to) + place

Yo fui **de** México **a** Buenos Aires.

51 **Viajes por Argentina**

 ▶ **Escucha y escribe.** The characters have traveled around Argentina. Listen and match each pair with their destination and transportation. Then write sentences.

Modelo 1. 2-C. *Diana y Rita fueron a la costa en taxi.*

Diana y Rita   Mack y Tim   Janet y Andy   Patricia y Tess

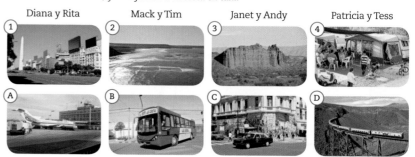

Differentiated Instruction

DEVELOPING LEARNERS

- Ask students to think about three places they and their family members visited last month. Have them use the past conjugations of *ir*, encouraging them to create one sentence using *yo*, one using *nosotros*, and one using *él/ella*, or *ellos/ellas*. For example: *Yo fui al centro comercial. Mi mamá y yo fuimos al cine. Mi papá fue al supermercado.*

EXPANDING LEARNERS

- Have students narrate the *Fans del español's* participants' journey up until now. List the events on the board as they mention them. Encourage them to embellish their narrations with interesting details about what happened in each location. For example: *Andy y Janet fueron a las cataratas del Iguazú. Fueron a la Garganta del Diablo.*

52 **Una nota incompleta**

▶ **Completa.** Andy left Janet a note about his activities. Fill in the missing parts using the words from the word bank.

(al) (fuimos) (a) (desde) (al) (fui) (al) (a)

¡Hola, Janet!

Hoy fui ___1___ supermercado para comprar fruta. Después,
___2___ ___3___ la calle Tres en autobús. Allí me encontré
con Carlos y ___4___ en metro ___5___ parque para jugar
al fútbol. ___6___ el parque fuimos en metro hasta una plaza
muy bonita para almorzar. Después del almuerzo regresé
___7___ hotel y ahora voy ___8___ la biblioteca. Nos vemos
pronto, hermana.

Andy

53 **Nuestros viajes**

 ▶ **Habla y escribe.** Where is the most interesting place you have gone? Interview your classmates to find out each person's answer. Then write a summary of everyone's travels.

Modelo Yo fui a Florida el año pasado. Catarina y Tommy fueron a Cancún.

 CONEXIONES: MATEMÁTICAS

Las distancias: ¿millas o kilómetros?

En los Estados Unidos y en Gran Bretaña utilizan las millas para medir las distancias. Pero en Latinoamérica y en muchos otros países usan el sistema métrico y los kilómetros.

Una milla equivale a 1,61 kilómetros. Un kilómetro es igual a 0,62 millas.

54 **Piensa.** Some standard speed limits in Argentina are 40 km/hr, 60 km/hr, 80 km/hr, and 120 km/hr. If you were in a car going these speeds, how fast would you be going in miles per hour?

ciento setenta y tres 173

 AUDIO SCRIPT
See page 143L

 CONEXIONES: MATEMÁTICAS

Las distancias: ¿millas o kilómetros?
The United States uses the official U.S. system of measurements. It is similar to British imperial units. On several occasions, the U.S. government has tried to come to a consensus about exclusively using the metric system in the United States, but we primarily continue to use the customary U.S. system today. If you look at any beverage container you will see the measurement in both units. This is to be able to trade and sell our goods to countries that only use the metric system.

Answer Key

51. 1. 2–C. Diana y Rita fueron a la costa en taxi.
2. 3–D. Mack y Tim fueron a la montaña en tren.
3. 4–B. Janet y Andy fueron a un cámping en autobús.
4. 1–A. Patricia y Tess fueron a la ciudad en avión.

52. 1. al   5. al
2. fui   6. Desde
3. a   7. al
4. fuimos   8. a

53. Answers will vary. Sample answers:
Yo fui a Cancún el verano pasado.
Mi maestra fue a Costa Rica.

54. 24.8 mph, 37.2 mph, 49.6 mph, and 74.4 mph.

Additional Resources

Fans Online activities
Practice Workbook

173

HERITAGE LANGUAGE LEARNERS

• Have students think about five heroes in the history of their family's country of origin. Have them use the verb *ser* to describe their professions. For example: *Simón Bolívar fue un héroe de la independencia.* Or *Benito Juárez fue el primer presidente indígena de México.*

MULTIPLE INTELLIGENCES:
Musical Intelligence

• Have students write a song using the past tense forms of *ser* and *ir*. You may allow them to work in groups and come up with a melody. They can use the template below to help write their song.

Song template	Example
Place you went	*Fui a Chile.*
When you went	*Fui a Chile en el mes de mayo.*
Place you went + how you went	*Fui a Chile en avión.*
Ay ay ay, la la la	*Ay ay ay, la la la*

Unit 7
DESAFÍO 3
Comunicación

Presentation

- In this section, students will practice:
  - Travel destinations and accommodations vocabulary.
  - Adverbs and time expressions.
  - The verbs *ir* and *ser* in the preterite.
  - Prepositions of place.

Activities	Standards	Resources
55.	1.2, 1.3	Audio
56.	1.2, 1.3, 3.1, 5.1	
57.	1.1, 1.2, 1.3	
58. Final del desafío	1.3	
Tu desafío	1.2, 1.3	

Teaching Suggestions

Warm-Up / Independent Starter

- Have students write a list of five places they visited in the past five years. Then ask them to list five places they hope to visit. They can fill in a chart like the one below with their information.

Fui a…	Quiero ir a…
Chicago	Costa Rica

Preparation

- Have students find three photos online of travel destinations and/or accommodations (alternatively, they can draw them or use clip art). Ask them to write captions for each one. Students must use vocabulary and grammar learned in this *Desafío*. Then ask students to read their captions to a partner who will try to guess which destination or accommodation is being described.

Activities

55. Have students describe their ideal hotel. They can work in pairs to brainstorm what the hotel would look like, where it would be located, what sports would be available, what amenities their rooms would have, etc. Then encourage them to create an advertisement for this "dream hotel" to share with the class.

174

Comunicación

55 **Habla Andy**

 ▶ **Escucha y decide.** Andy has called Tess to see how she and Patricia are doing. Listen to their conversation and decide whether the following statements are true *(cierto)* or false *(falso)*. Then correct the false statements.

1. Andy reservó un hotel perfecto.
2. Tess y Patricia viajaron ayer.
3. Tess escribió un correo a su papá.
4. Ayer Patricia salió temprano de la habitación para correr.
5. Andy pasó tiempo en la playa.
6. Andy y Janet fueron al sur del parque.

56 **Vacaciones increíbles**

▶ **Lee y escribe.** Have you ever had a bad travel experience? Read this postcard from Andy to his friend Manuel. Write three good things and three bad things that happened.

> *Querido Manuel:*
>
> *¿Qué tal estás? Yo estoy muy contento, lo estamos pasando muy bien.*
>
> *La semana pasada fuimos a conocer las cataratas del Iguazú. Estuvimos en un cámping en el Parque Nacional. Allí conocimos a unos italianos muy simpáticos.*
>
> *El lunes comimos unas frutas deliciosas. Por la noche llovió mucho y por eso descansamos mal.*
>
> *El martes me desperté temprano para tomar fotos, pero no encontré mi cámara. ¡Qué horror! Pero tomé unas fotos maravillosas con la cámara de Janet.*
>
> *¡Son unas vacaciones increíbles!*
>
> *Hasta pronto.*
>
> *Andy*

Manuel Ortiz
1234 5th Street
Santa Fe, NM 87507

▶ **Escribe.** Write a postcard to a friend about a particularly wonderful or horrible vacation experience. Don't forget to use the preterite tense!

174 ciento setenta y cuatro

Differentiated Instruction

DEVELOPING LEARNERS

- To practice the language in this section, have students write five questions for a partner using the grammar and vocabulary from this *Desafío*. Then have students switch papers and answer their partner's questions in writing. Encourage them to use the book and the glossary for reference if they forget any of the vocabulary or grammar.

EXPANDING LEARNERS

- Have students expand on Andy and Janet's adventure in the *Garganta del Diablo*. Encourage them to create a storyboard sequence titled *El día anterior*. They may use drawings or cut outs from magazines to illustrate what happened.

57 **Encuestas**

▶ **Habla y escribe.** What do you know about your classmates' activities? In a small group, conduct mini-interviews to find out who did the things below and when they did them. Then write a paragraph with your findings.

Modelo 1. A. *¿Cuándo viste una película en el cine?*
  B. *La semana pasada.*
  A. *Irene y John vieron una película en el cine la semana pasada.*

1. ¿Quién vio una película en el cine?
2. ¿Quién comió en un restaurante argentino?
3. ¿Quién compró algo en un centro comercial?
4. ¿Quién fue de vacaciones a otro país?
5. ¿Quién fue a un concierto?

Final del desafío

58 **¿Cuándo pasó?**

▶ **Ordena y escribe.** Put the scenes in the most logical order and write the script. What did Andy and Janet tell their friends after they got back to camp for the night?

▶ **TU DESAFÍO** Earn points for your own challenge! Listen to the questions for your *Minientrevista Desafío 3* on the website and write your answers.

ciento setenta y cinco **175**

56. Have students write the postcard as well as actually design and create one using an index card. The front should have a travel scene from their destination. The reverse side should include a stamp design that reflects the wonderful (or horrible) nature of their vacation experience, along with an imaginary address for their friend and their message.

🎧 **AUDIO SCRIPT**
See page 143L

Answer Key

55. 1. Cierto
2. Falso. Tess y Patricia no viajaron ayer.
3. Cierto
4. Cierto
5. Cierto
6. Falso. Andy y Janet fueron al oeste del parque.

56. Answers will vary. Sample answers:
Good things:
1. Fueron a un bonito cámping.
2. Conocieron a unos italianos simpáticos.
3. Comieron frutas deliciosas.
Bad things:
1. Llovió mucho.
2. Descansaron mal.
3. Andy no encontró su cámara.
▶ Answers will vary.

57. Answers will vary. Sample answers:
A. ¿Cuándo comiste en un restaurante argentino?
B. Anoche.
A. Alex comió en un restaurante argentino anoche.

58. 3, 1, 4, 2.
▶ Answers will vary.

Additional Resources

Fans Online activities
Practice Workbook

HERITAGE LANGUAGE LEARNERS

• Encourage heritage learners to imagine taking a trip to a Spanish-speaking country—or think about an actual trip that they may have already taken. Have them write down the name of the place, what they did there, and who was with them. Ask them to include as many details as possible. You may want them to share their writing with the rest of the class.

MULTIPLE INTELLIGENCES:
Visual-Spatial Intelligence

• Tell students to imagine they work as private detectives. One student pretends to be the client and shows the detective several pictures to serve as clues (the pictures should represent what a person did the previous week). Have the detective try to figure out a sequence of events for each day of the week based on the pictures. Students should take turns being the detective and the client.

Unit 7
DESAFÍO 4
Dar órdenes negativas

Presentation

- In *Desafío 4* Tess and Patricia are in Buenos Aires. Their task is to collect four envelopes with the pieces of a puzzle in the *Plaza de Mayo*, the main square in the city. Will they be able to find all the envelopes?

- In this section, students will learn:
  – Places in the city.
  – Directions.
  – Verbs of motion.
  – Negative commands.

Activities	Standards	Resources
Fotonovela	1.2	Vis. Pres.
59.	1.2, 1.3	
60.	1.2, 1.3	
61.	1.2, 1.3	Audio
62. Cultura	1.1, 1.2, 3.1, 3.2	

Teaching Suggestions

Warm-Up / Independent Starter

- Have students think about three landmarks in their town, city or state. Ask them to write the name of each place, where it is located, and to describe the landmark using descriptive words.

Preparation

- Ask students to share their lists of landmarks with the class by reading only the descriptions and locations. See if the rest of the class can guess which landmarks are being described.

La fotonovela

Before Viewing

- Have a volunteer read the introduction to the task. Ask students to brainstorm different types of puzzles with which they are familiar.

After Viewing

- Ask for volunteers to act out the scene for the class. They can also be encouraged to add a scene from before the *fotonovela* begins and to add one at the end of it. Have students "publish" their work on a bulletin board.

176

Sobres en la calle

Tess and Patricia are in Buenos Aires. Their task is to collect four envelopes with the pieces of a puzzle in the *Plaza de Mayo*, the main square in the city. Will they be able to find all the envelopes?

Continuará…

59 **Detective de palabras**

▶ **Completa.** Fill in the blanks to complete each negative statement.

1. No _____ por esa calle.
2. No lo _____ todavía.
3. No _____ tan rápido.
4. No _____ tan pesimista.

60 **¿Comprendes?**

▶ **Decide.** Decide if these statements about Tess and Patricia are true *(cierto)* or false *(falso)*. If they are false, correct them.

1. Comenzaron en la calle Rivadavia.
2. Encontraron cuatro sobres.
3. Cruzaron el parque.
4. No fueron a la calle Bolívar.
5. Tess caminó despacio.
6. No encontraron el tercer sobre.

Differentiated Instruction

DEVELOPING LEARNERS

- Write the verbs *caminar* and *celebrar* on the board. Ask students to skim the text in the *fotonovela* to find phrases that use those two verbs (for example: *No lo celebres todavía*, and *No camines tan rápido*). Next, have volunteers conjugate *caminar* and *celebrar* in the present tense and write their conjugations on the board. Ask students to point out if they notice anything different about the forms used in the dialogue (for example, the different endings of the command forms).

EXPANDING LEARNERS

- Have students pretend that they are reporters. Their task is to report what happened in the *fotonovela* in the past tense as if it were a TV news report. Have students record their reports on an MP3 or cassette recorder to use as a podcast, or on a digital video camera. Have students share their reports with the class.

61 **La ruta más corta**

 ▶ **Escucha e identifica.** Tess and Patricia are taking a tour of the *Plaza de Mayo* to help them find the envelopes with the clues. Listen to the tour guide and take notes.

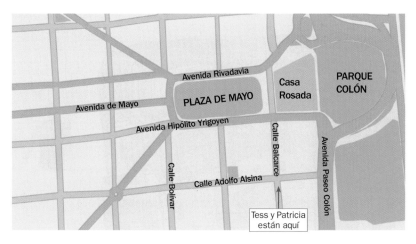

Avenida Rivadavia

Casa Rosada

PARQUE COLÓN

Avenida de Mayo

PLAZA DE MAYO

Avenida Hipólito Yrigoyen

Calle Balcarce

Calle Bolívar

Calle Adolfo Alsina

Avenida Paseo Colón

Tess y Patricia están aquí

 ▶ **Habla y escribe.** Now, with a partner, write a paragraph about the route they followed.

Modelo *Comenzaron aquí, en la calle Balcarce.*

 **CULTURA**

La Plaza de Mayo

La Plaza de Mayo es la plaza principal de Buenos Aires y está en el centro de la ciudad. Esta plaza es el lugar donde comenzó la revolución por la independencia de Argentina, en mayo del año 1810.

La Casa Rosada, sede *(seat)* de la presidencia del gobierno, está delante de la plaza. Por eso, la Plaza de Mayo se considera el centro de la vida política de Buenos Aires.

62 **Piensa.** Where is the center of political power in the United States? If you could create your own political party, what would it be called and where would it be located? Why?

ciento setenta y siete 177

HERITAGE LANGUAGE LEARNERS

• Discuss the *Plaza de Mayo*. Have students compare it with different plazas in other countries and in the United States. Prompt a discussion about the typical activities that go on in a town square / plaza, and their importance to the people of that particular place.

MULTIPLE INTELLIGENCES:

Bodily-Kinesthetic Intelligence

• Familiarize students with negative commands by playing a game of "Simon Says." Use negative commands of verbs they know and can easily recognize, such as *levantarse, sentarse, lavarse los dientes,* etc. As students play the game, exaggerate the vowel differences between the negative and affirmative commands.

Activities

59. Have students rewrite the sentences in the affirmative. For example:
No vayas por esa calle. → *Ve por esa calle.*

62. Ask students to look at a photo of the Casa Rosada. Ask them to describe what they see and to compare it with the U.S. Capitol in Washington DC.

 AUDIO SCRIPT
See page 143L

 CULTURA

La Plaza de Mayo

From its creation, the *Plaza de Mayo* has been the center of the political and social life in the city of Buenos Aires. This landmark has changed with the centuries. Each generation has beautified and added character to this plaza. For example, in 1811 an obelisk was built. In 1856, the obelisk was remodeled and topped with a figure representing Liberty. In 1977, the *Plaza de Mayo* became the center of protest for a group of mothers who wanted information about their children who were disappeared by the military dictatorship of that time.

Answer Key

59. 1. vayas   3. camines
       2. celebres   4. seas

60. 1. Falso. Comenzaron en la calle Balcarce.
       2. Falso. Encontraron tres sobres.
       3. Cierto
       4. Falso. Fueron a la calle Bolívar.
       5. Falso. Tess caminó muy rápido.
       6. Falso. Encontraron el tercer sobre.

61. Answers will vary.

62. Answers will vary.

Additional Resources

Fans Online activities

DESAFÍO 4

Vocabulario – La ciudad

Presentation

- In this section, students will learn:
  - Places in the city.
  - Directions.
  - Verbs of motion.

Activities	Standards	Resources
Vocabulario	1.2	
63.	1.2, 1.3	Audio
64.	1.2, 1.3, 3.1	
65.	1.3	
66. Cultura	1.1, 1.2, 3.1, 3.2	

Teaching Suggestions

Warm-Up / Independent Starter

- Have students write five yes/no questions about their city's landmarks. For example: a student from Los Angeles could write *¿Tenemos playas en Los Ángeles?*

Preparation

- As you go over the vocabulary for places in the city, have students "walk" from place to place with their forefingers and middle fingers over the map. When you get to the directions vocabulary have students move their heads in the direction you mention. For instance, when you say *doblar a la derecha,* students should turn their heads to the right.
- Have students create picture flashcards of all place words with the picture on the front and the word on the back.

Activities

63. Have students work in pairs to look at the photos and give a thumbs-up signal or thumbs-down signal, depending on each place. They should say sentences like *Me gusta el parque* or *No me gusta el hospital*.

64. Explain to students that Patricia will be waiting for Tess at the corner of calle del Pez and calle de América. Ask students to write their own instructions to Tess so that she can meet Patricia.

Vocabulario

La ciudad

el banco

la biblioteca

la calle

el hospital

la plaza

la iglesia

el café

Localización y direcciones

Por favor, ¿dónde está la catedral?

Tienes que seguir recto hasta la plaza y allí doblar a la derecha.

 seguir recto

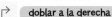 doblar a la derecha

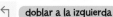 doblar a la izquierda

 cruzar

63 **¿Adónde fueron?**

▶ **Escucha y escribe.** On the phone, Tess and Patricia describe where they went yesterday. Write sentences about the places each one visited.

Modelo 1. *Tess fue al cine y…*

Differentiated Instruction

DEVELOPING LEARNERS

- Students may benefit from TPR clues to remember vocabulary. As you go through the list, repeat each word and make a gesture that relates to its meaning. For example, for *biblioteca* you may pretend you are opening a book. Have students say the word and repeat the physical response association.

EXPANDING LEARNERS

- Have students use the new vocabulary to describe their own city to a partner. Ask them to give as much relevant information as possible, such as their favorite places in the neighborhood (*el cine, la biblioteca*, etc.), the location of their homes in relation to different places and so on. Encourage them to work in pairs, drawing simple maps of the neighborhood based on these descriptions.

64 **Instrucciones para Tess**

▶ **Completa y adivina.** Tess is lost. Look at the map and complete the note Patricia left her.

Hola, Tess.

Para llegar al museo tienes que ___1___ recto por la calle Mayor. Luego tienes que ___2___ la plaza y caminar por la calle Larga. Después tienes que ___3___ a la izquierda y ___4___ por la avenida Principal hasta la plaza.

Yo te espero allí.

Patricia

65 **Direcciones**

▶ **Escribe.** Write simple instructions telling how to get from your Spanish classroom to the following places in your school.

- la cafetería
- la biblioteca
- el gimnasio
- el salón de computación
- la oficina de la enfermera
- la oficina principal

▶ **Dibuja.** Now, with a partner, try out your instructions. As he or she reads each one, draw a map to that place.

CULTURA

La Casa Rosada

La Casa Rosada es el palacio presidencial. Está en el centro de Buenos Aires. Es de color rosado desde el siglo XIX. Una teoría es que el presidente escogió este color, mezcla de los colores rojo y blanco, para representar la unión de dos partidos políticos en tensión.

66 **Piensa.** If you were the president of Argentina, what color would you choose for your house? What would that color represent?

ciento setenta y nueve 179

66. Ask students to draw an image of their "presidential home." Tell them that not only can they design their own homes as presidents of their country, but they can design their own neighborhoods to go around their homes! Have them label all the streets and landmarks that surround their "palace."

 AUDIO SCRIPT
See page 143L

CULTURA

La Casa Rosada

The official website of the Casa Rosada museum is located at http://www.museo.gov.ar. In this site, students can see 360° views of certain rooms and areas in the house, learn about its history, and see what buildings and landmarks are in the surrounding area. The site is organized to facilitate students' comprehension. The history link, for example, divides the Casa Rosada in four stages: the fort, the new *aduana*, the government house, and the museum.

Answer Key

63. 1. Tess fue al cine, a la biblioteca y al parque.
2. Patricia fue al hospital y al aeropuerto.

64. 1. seguir
2. cruzar
3. doblar
4. seguir

65. Answers will vary.
▶ Answers will vary.

66. Answers will vary.

Additional Resources

Fans Online activities
Practice Workbook

HERITAGE LANGUAGE LEARNERS

- Invite students to talk about the cities or towns from which their families came. Have them bring in maps of their hometowns and their current city to help make comparisons. Ask students if there are more differences than similarities between their cities of origin and where they live now. Encourage them to use vocabulary that the class will know, including recently learned vocabulary words, and to speak slowly so that other students can follow the conversation.

SPECIAL-NEEDS LEARNERS

- Students with visual impairments may benefit from a tactile presentation of the vocabulary. Bring in objects that can be used to create the model of a city. Ask students to design it according to their preferences. Guide them by asking them questions such as where would the plaza be?

DESAFÍO 4

Gramática – El imperativo negativo

Presentation

■ In this section, students will learn:
- Negative commands.
- Irregular negative commands of *ser* and *ir*.

Activities	Standards	Resources
Gramática	1.2, 3.1, 4.1	
67.	1.1, 3.1, 4.1	
68.	1.3	
69.	1.1, 1.3	
70. Cultura	1.1, 1.2, 3.1, 3.2, 4.2	

Teaching Suggestions

Warm-Up / Independent Starter

■ Ask students to draw a map of the area around their school, including several streets and landmarks. Have students label the map with the words *Mi escuela* and any other landmarks or buildings they know.

Preparation

■ Ask students to write a list of five things that they shouldn't do in the classroom or in school. Have them share their lists with a partner or the class to create a class list. For example:
- Don't talk when the teacher is talking.
- Don't eat in the classroom.
- Don't send text messages during class.

Activities

67. Using the list generated by the previous activity, have students create commands for a class poster. Ask students to illustrate the commands or find clip art to decorate the poster, and then hang it up in the classroom.
   - *¡No hables cuando habla la maestra!*
   - *¡No comas en el salón de clase!*
   - *¡No escribas mensajes electrónicos durante la clase!*

69. Have students create three more suggestions relating to their school. For example:
   Estudia por la mañana en la biblioteca.
   No estudies por la tarde en la cafetería.

180

Gramática

El imperativo negativo

- To tell someone what not to do or to prohibit something, Spanish uses the negative command form preceded by the word *no*.
   No viajes sin el pasaporte.
- To give someone a friendly command, use the negative *tú* commands:

VERBOS REGULARES. IMPERATIVO NEGATIVO

Comprar	Comer	Escribir
no compres	no comas	no escribas

- Negative commands do not generally include a subject pronoun.

Forming the negative commands

- The negative command forms are based on the *yo* form of the present tense, substituting the -o for these endings:
   - -es for -ar verbs
   - -as for -er and -ir verbs

Verbo	Presente	Imperativo negativo
comprar	yo compro	no compres
comer	yo como	no comas
escribir	yo escribo	no escribas

- The verbs *ser* and *ir* are an exception:

VERBOS SER E IR. IMPERATIVO NEGATIVO

Ser	Ir
no seas	no vayas

No seas pesimista.
No vayas a ese hotel.

67 **Piensa.** How do we form negative commands in English? How is this different from the negative commands in Spanish? How is this similar?

68 **¿Lo hago o no lo hago?**

 ▶ **Habla.** With a partner, take turns acting out different actions. Tell your friend not to do whatever he or she is doing.

Modelo *No abras el libro.*

180 ciento ochenta

Differentiated Instruction

DEVELOPING LEARNERS

- Play a game with students to practice the verbs. Seat students in rows and provide index cards to each student. Dictate a verb in its infinitive form. Students should write the negative informal command. Ask them to exchange their card with the classmate sitting directly behind them and check to see if the answer is correct. If the student closest to the front of the row is correct, nothing happens. If the student closest to the back of the row is correct, the two students switch seats. The students who make it to the front of their rows first win the game.

EXPANDING LEARNERS

- Negative informal commands are often used between parents and children (or teachers and students) and usually have to do with safety or behavior issues (for example: *¡No hagas eso! ¡No toques! ¡No corras!*). Have students write a list of situations in which these commands might be used, along with the negative commands themselves (for example: *Un estudiante corre en el pasillo. El profesor dice: ¡No corras!*). Ask students to act out several of the scenes for the class.

69 **Consejos para tu viaje**

▶ **Escribe.** Write sentences about what to do and what not to do according to the clues below. Use the *tú* commands.

Modelo 1. *No camines por el parque. Camina por la calle.*

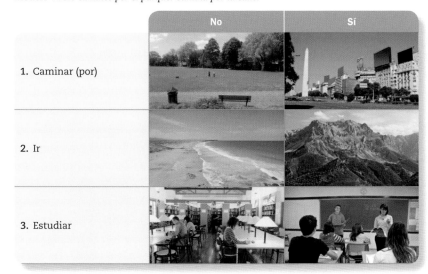

	No	Sí
1. Caminar (por)		
2. Ir		
3. Estudiar		

 ▶ **Habla.** Now offer your partner a suggestion about when not to do each thing.

Modelo 1. A. *Voy al parque.*
B. *No vayas al parque ahora. Hace mucho frío.*

 CULTURA

La Pirámide de Mayo

La Pirámide de Mayo es el monumento nacional más antiguo de Buenos Aires. Está situada en el centro de la Plaza de Mayo y fue construida en el año 1811 para celebrar el primer aniversario de la Revolución de Mayo. El 21 de mayo de 1942 la Pirámide de Mayo fue declarada monumento histórico.

70 **Piensa.** Can you think of any statues in the United States that represent a revolution or the liberation of people? Where are they located?

ciento ochenta y uno 181

HERITAGE LANGUAGE LEARNERS

• Have students write a list of the things their parents tell them not to do. If the entry is not written as an informal negative command, ask students to rewrite it. Have students share their lists with the rest of the class.

CRITICAL THINKING

• Draw students' attention to the city map in the book. Why do cities usually have a plaza in their center? Ask students to think of different reasons why cities are organized this way.

---

70. Ask students to research a famous statue from their town, city or state. Have them present a short report to the class, including a photo of the statue and an explanation regarding why they chose it. Ask them to address these questions: *¿Cómo se llama la estatua? ¿Dónde está? ¿Qué representa?*

 CULTURA

La Pirámide de Mayo

On the top of this obelisk sits a statue that represents Liberty. There are four other figures placed at the four corners of the obelisk that represent Industry, Commerce, Science and the Arts. On December 8, 2005, the ashes of the founder of the Mothers of the *Plaza de Mayo* were buried at the base of this obelisk.

Answer Key

67. Answers will vary. Sample answer:
In English, we form negative commands by simply adding the word *no* to an affirmative command. In Spanish, the conjugation of the verb changes along with the addition of the word *no*.

68. Answers will vary. Sample answer:
Your partner starts to sing. → You say: *No cantes.*

69. Answers will vary. Sample answers:
1. No camines por el parque. Camina por la calle.
2. No vayas a la playa. Ve a la montaña.
3. No estudies en la biblioteca. Estudia en la clase.
▶ Answers will vary.

70. Answers will vary.

Additional Resources

Fans Online activities
Practice Workbook

DESAFÍO 4

Comunicación

Presentation

- In this section, students will practice:
  - Places in the city and directions.
  - Verbs of motion.
  - Negative commands.

Activities	Standards	Resources
71.	1.1, 1.3	
72.	1.2, 1.3	Audio
73.	1.2, 1.3, 5.1	
74. Final del desafío	1.2, 1.3	

Teaching Suggestions

Warm-Up / Independent Starter

- Have students match the following sentences:

1. Yo como muchos dulces.
2. Mis amigas gastan demasiado dinero.
3. Juan Carlos grita en la biblioteca.
4. Ellas escriben mensajes en clase.
5. Tú bebes muchos refrescos.

A. Yo digo: "¡No bebas tantos refrescos!".
B. La bibliotecaria dice: "¡No grites!".
C. La maestra dice: "¡No escriban mensajes en clase!".
D. Yo les digo: "¡No gasten tanto dinero!".
E. Mi mamá me dice: "¡No comas tantos dulces!".

Preparation

- Now have students use the vocabulary words to create five more situations for which they would need a command. Then they will exchange their papers with a partner. For example:
  A. Mi hermano está cantando en la biblioteca.
  B. No cantes en la biblioteca.

Activities

71. Have students work in pairs to mark three more locations on their maps. They should give each other directions about how to get there.

72. Ask students to write a list of three things that they would like to do this summer. Have them read their lists to each other and make recommendations about the activities using affirmative and negative commands.

Comunicación

71 **¿Dónde está el hospital?**

▶ **Escribe.** Look at the map and write how to get to the places below. Use the *tú* commands.

Modelo el cine
→ Para ir al cine, sigue recto, cruza la plaza y dobla a la derecha en la calle Libreros.

1. la plaza   2. el hospital   3. la biblioteca   4. el Banco Central

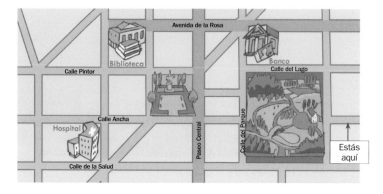

 ▶ **Habla.** Using the map, ask your partner how to get to other places in the city. Take turns.

Modelo A. Por favor, ¿cómo puedo ir al teatro?
B. Para ir al teatro, sigue recto...

72 **Sugerencias**

 ▶ **Escucha y decide.** Tess wants to do many things this summer. Listen and decide whether Patricia agrees with Tess about each item on her list.

1. estudiar en una escuela de baile
2. pasar unas noches en un hotel
3. ir mucho al teatro
4. viajar por todo el país en autobús
5. visitar el parque
6. pasear por el centro de la ciudad
7. trabajar en el banco
8. cenar todas las noches en el café

▶ **Escribe.** For each activity that Patricia disapproves of, write her negative command and give a possible alternative.

Modelo No estudies en una escuela de baile. Estudia en una escuela de música.

182 ciento ochenta y dos

Differentiated Instruction

DEVELOPING LEARNERS

- Before attempting the communication activities, review the directional vocabulary by asking students to navigate with their fingers on a map of your town or city. Tell students where to start on the map. Then give simple directions such as *Dobla a la derecha*, or *Cruza la calle*. After a few directions, check if students arrived at the correct place on the map.

EXPANDING LEARNERS

- Have students think about mistakes they have made, and what advice they might give to someone else based on those mistakes. Ask them to write a list of five things that they do, but would tell someone else not to do. Ask students to share their advice with the class. For example:

  Yo compro ropa cara. No compres ropa cara.
  Yo como mucha comida rápida. No comas comida rápida.

73 **Mi ciudad**

▶ **Lee y contesta.** Read this description of Patricia's hometown and answer the questions.

Mi ciudad

Mi ciudad es grande y bonita.
Me gustan mucho las calles
anchas con árboles y flores.
En el centro, los edificios son
muy altos y elegantes.
Las calles están llenas de
cafés. Mi cine favorito está
en el centro, cerca del teatro.
¡Es divertido salir por la noche
en mi ciudad!

1. ¿Qué piensa Patricia de su ciudad?
2. ¿Cómo son los edificios del centro?
3. ¿Qué hay en las calles del centro?
4. ¿Dónde está el cine?

▶ **Escribe.** Now write a description of your city or town. Include landmarks and direction words.

Final del desafío

…há, estoy cansada.
…inamos todo el día
…cando los sobres.
…demos sentarnos?

Sí. Mira, allí hay un café. Pero no comas todavía y comemos juntas después, ¿quieres?

No bebas tan rápido. Tenemos tiempo. La plaza está allí.

¡Es cierto! ¿Ves la biblioteca?

74 **¿Qué pasó en la historia?**

▶ **Escribe.** Look at the scenes above. Decide what happens in the next scene and write a summary of what happened in this *Desafío*.

Modelo *Tess y Patricia caminaron todo el día buscando los sobres…*

ciento ochenta y tres 183

HERITAGE LANGUAGE LEARNERS

• If there are students in your class from an Argentine background or who know Argentina, ask them to talk about the country and give advice to potential visitors. Encourage them to use positive and negative commands such as: *Toma muchas fotos. No gastes mucho dinero en ropa de cuero.* Have the rest of the students collaborate on writing one list of questions that they may still have after reading the information about Argentina in the chapter.

MULTIPLE INTELLIGENCES:

Naturalist Intelligence

• Have students research environmental issues in Argentina and create posters aimed at educating the public about those problems. A good site for beginning research is the World Wildlife Fund's website.

---

73. Students can turn their descriptions into a guessing game. Assign values according to difficulty and organize the descriptions into clearly marked categories on the board. Divide the class into teams and have them take turns selecting and answering questions.

 AUDIO SCRIPT
See page 143L

Answer Key

71. Answers will vary. Sample answer:
   1. Para ir a la plaza, cruza el parque y sigue recto por la calle Ancha.
   ▶ Answers will vary.

72. 1. No está de acuerdo.
   2. Sí está de acuerdo.
   3. Sí está de acuerdo.
   4. No está de acuerdo.
   5. No está de acuerdo.
   6. Sí está de acuerdo.
   7. No está de acuerdo.
   8. No está de acuerdo.
   ▶ 1. No estudies en una escuela de baile. Estudia en una escuela de música.
   4. No viajes en autobús. Viaja en tren.
   5. No visites el parque. Visita la plaza.
   7. No trabajes en el banco. Piensa en otro trabajo.
   8. No cenes en el café. Cena en casa.

73. 1. Su ciudad es grande y bonita.
   2. Los edificios son muy altos y elegantes.
   3. Hay muchos cafés.
   4. Está en el centro, cerca del teatro.
   ▶ Answers will vary.

74. Answers will vary.

Additional Resources

Fans Online activities
Practice Workbook

Unit 7

Todo junto

Presentation

- In this section, students will review how to
  - Talk about past actions.
  - Express actions related to travel.
  - Express places and directions.
  - Give negative commands.

Activities	Standards	Resources
75.	1.2, 1.3, 5.1	Audio
76.	1.1, 1.2, 1.3	
77.	1.2, 1.3	

Teaching Suggestions

Warm-Up / Independent Starter

- Have students list three things that they would take with them to the following destinations: *las montañas, la playa, la ciudad.* Ask students to share their lists with the class. Is there something that most students take with them on their trip?

Preparation

- Ask students to share their answers for the previous activity with the class. Poll the class, item by item, to determine the most popular class answers. Write the results from most popular to least popular.

Activities

75. Have students create their own passports for their dream trip.

76. For additional practice of the past tense, have students do a skit of a parent or teacher talking to a child / student. One gives commands while the other responds. For example:
MOTHER: *Estudia para el examen.*
SON: *Ya estudié.*

77. Ask students to think of a place they visited on a trip. Have them jot down in their notebooks what they remember about the trip (for example: means of transport, how long it took, things they saw and did, etc.). Then ask students to use their notes to write their own diary entries. Invite volunteers to share their entries with the class.

Todo junto

ESCUCHAR, ESCRIBIR Y HABLAR

 75 **El viaje de tus sueños**

 ▶ **Escucha y elige.** Your local radio station is sponsoring a contest to win a fantasy trip. First listen to the advertisement that explains the rules of the contest. Then choose the answer that was NOT mentioned in the advertisement.

1. Necesitas...   a. el pasaporte   b. la maleta   c. el billete de ida y vuelta
2. Tú escoges ir a...   a. la montaña   b. la ciudad   c. la playa
3. Puedes ir en...   a. tren   b. taxi   c. avión
4. Te quedas en un...   a. hotel   b. hostal   c. cámping
5. Visitas...   a. museos   b. teatros   c. iglesias

▶ **Escribe.** Write the script for your contest entry, describing the "trip of your dreams." Be sure to include answers to the following questions:

1. ¿Adónde quieres ir?
2. ¿Qué vas a llevar?
3. ¿Cómo vas a viajar?
4. ¿Dónde te vas a quedar?
5. ¿Qué piensas visitar?

 ▶ **Presenta.** When you have written your script, record it on an MP3 player or onto a CD. Then play your contest entry for the class. As you listen to your classmates, fill in a chart like the one below to keep track of the most popular places.

¿Adónde quieres ir?

a la montaña	a la playa	a la ciudad
Karen y Bill		

Differentiated Instruction

DEVELOPING LEARNERS

- Have students make personal connections to some of the places in the city vocabulary by connecting a proper name from their town or city with each word. For example:
la calle = Elm Place
el café = Starbucks
el hospital = Good Samaritan

EXPANDING LEARNERS

- Have students find an authentic street map on the Internet. Some possible cities might include Madrid, Buenos Aires, or Mexico City. Ask them to break into pairs and find some important city sites on the map. Then one partner should give verbal directions for getting from one place to another. The other partner should trace the directions with his or her finger on the map until reaching the correct destination. They can even narrate where they are going in the first person. Then they can switch roles and repeat the exercise.

HABLAR

76 ¡Ya viajé a la costa!

 ▶ **Habla.** With a partner, take turns telling each other what not to do and what you already did and when. Follow the model.

No viajes a la costa.

¡Viajé a la costa la semana pasada!

1. ir a la ciudad en tren
2. comer en ese restaurante
3. pasear de noche por ese parque
4. viajar a la playa

5. comprar recuerdos en la terminal
6. comprar un billete de ida y vuelta
7. beber agua del río
8. escribir en el libro

LEER

77 ¡Tocamos las nubes!

 ▶ **Lee y contesta.** Read the following extract from Tim's diary about their trip on the Train to the Clouds, and answer the questions.

Lunes, 3 de marzo

¡Tocamos las nubes!

Primero mi abuelo y yo viajamos en autobús desde Buenos Aires hasta Salta. En Salta tomamos el tren a las nubes. El viaje duró casi doce horas.

Cuando el tren alcanza los 3.000 metros (9,000 feet) casi no se puede respirar.

San Antonio de los Cobres fue nuestra última estación. Está situada a 4.000 metros de altura (12,000 feet). ¡Allí puedes tocar las nubes!

1. ¿Cómo viajaron Tim y Mack desde Buenos Aires hasta Salta?
2. ¿Desde dónde sale el tren a las nubes?
3. ¿Cuánto tiempo duró el viaje en el tren a las nubes?
4. ¿Qué pasa cuando el tren alcanza los 3.000 metros?
5. ¿Por qué llaman a este tren el tren a las nubes?

ciento ochenta y cinco 185

 AUDIO SCRIPT
See page 143L

Answer Key

75. 1. c   2. b   3. b   4. b   5. b

▶ Answers will vary. Sample answers:
1. Quiero ir a la playa de Cancún.
2. Voy a llevar un traje de baño y unas gafas de sol.
3. Voy a viajar en avión.
4. Me voy a quedar en un hotel de lujo.
5. Pienso visitar las pirámides de Chichén Itzá.

▶ Answers will vary.

76. Answers will vary. Sample answers:
1. A. No vayas a la ciudad en tren.
   B. Fui a la ciudad en tren ayer.
2. A. No comas en ese restaurante.
   B. Comí en ese restaurante el mes pasado.
3. A. No pasees de noche por ese parque.
   B. Paseé de noche por ese parque anteayer.
4. A. No viajes a la playa.
   B. Viajé a la playa el año pasado.
5. A. No compres recuerdos en la terminal.
   B. Compré recuerdos en la terminal el martes pasado.
6. A. No compres un billete de ida y vuelta.
   B. Compré un billete de ida y vuelta la semana pasada.
7. A. No bebas agua del río.
   B. Bebí agua del río ayer.
8. A. No escribas en el libro.
   B. Escribí en el libro el lunes pasado.

77. 1. Viajaron en autobús.
2. Sale desde Salta.
3. Duró casi doce horas.
4. Casi no se puede respirar.
5. Porque puedes tocar las nubes.

Additional Resources

Fans Online activities
Practice Workbook

HERITAGE LANGUAGE LEARNERS

• Have students interview members of the Spanish-speaking community who work at different places in the city (*el banco, el hospital, la iglesia*, etc.). Ask them to share information about where they work, what types of jobs they do, and what they like most about their work / job. Encourage students to ask them for advice (using affirmative and negative commands) as though the students were prospective employees at their places of business.

MULTIPLE INTELLIGENCES:

Spatial Intelligence

• Have students find three authentic subway or bus maps on the Internet. Ask them to make a list of the colors used in the maps for different train lines and to think about why these kinds of colors are used in transportation maps. Now have them imagine that they are going to hire a designer to create a mass transit map for an imaginary city. Have them create a list of affirmative and negative commands for the designer, giving directions about the colors and numbers they want to be used for their maps and why.

185

Unit 7

El encuentro

Presentation

▪ This section combines all of the grammar, vocabulary, and communicative contexts from the entire unit and presents activities to involve students in integrated practice.

Activities	Standards	Resources
Fotonovela	1.2	
78.	1.1, 1.3	
79.	1.1	

Teaching Suggestions

Warm-Up / Independent Starter

▪ Have students silently read the speech bubbles for each photo and write their opinions of each team's completion of the task.

Preparation

▪ Break students into groups of four. Be sure to place students with different skill levels together. Before doing the activities ask students to choose the following roles: Team Leader, Reader, Writer, and Presenter. The team leader will make sure the group stays on task, the reader will read the *fotonovela* and the prompts for the activity, the writer will write the team's responses, and the presenter will present the final work to the class. All group members will contribute to the activity and be equally responsible for the final product.

La fotonovela

▪ Ask students to study the pictures. Let them read the dialogues individually and then share their impressions with the class.

▪ Have students write the names of the different characters and what they have achieved. Ask students to share their opinions about what the characters have achieved.

▪ Have students point to the characters and imagine aloud how they feel. Then ask pairs of students to read the dialogue aloud, and include the characters' projected feelings in their reading. Alternatively, students can act out the dialogues.

En el Teatro Colón

The four pairs meet in Buenos Aires after attempting to complete their individual tasks. Did all the pairs successfully carry out their assignments?

Mira, tomamos muchas fotos. ¡Viajamos por todas estas ciudades en un solo día!

¡Encontramos al gaucho! ¡Él corrió rápido, pero nosotras corrimos más rápido que él!

Ayer fuimos a Iguazú. ¡Qué impresionante! Nos perdimos, pero grabamos un video.

Encontramos todos los sobres en la ciudad. ¡Cuidado, Tess, no los pierdas!

186 ciento ochenta y seis

Differentiated Instruction

DEVELOPING LEARNERS

• Divide the students into groups of four. Ask one student in the group to read a line from one of the speech bubbles out loud. The other three students have to listen and point to the corresponding picture as fast as they can identify it. The first person to point to the right scene goes next. Continue the game until all lines are read. The person with the most correct answers will assign a person from the group to read all the speech bubbles.

EXPANDING LEARNERS

• Have students practice the verbs *ser* and *ir* in the preterite by writing a description in the past tense similar to those posted on social networks. Ask them to pick a famous person and describe him or her as if they were writing that persons's profile page. For example: *Eva Perón – Fui la esposa del presidente de Argentina.*

186

¡Qué lástima! Nuestros amigos no probaron nuestro postre más tradicional: el dulce de leche.

78 Al llegar

▶ **Habla.** In a small group, play charades by choosing one scene and acting it out for the rest of your classmates. See if they can guess which scene is being portrayed.

▶ **Escribe.** After reviewing the scenes and the task that each pair faced, choose a winning team and try to convince the other students why they deserve to win. Write a description answering the following questions:

- ¿De dónde salieron?
- ¿Adónde fueron?
- ¿Cómo llegaron?
- ¿Qué encontraron?
- ¿Qué lugares visitaron?

Modelo

> Andy y Janet fueron desde Buenos Aires hasta Iguazú en avión. Visitaron las cataratas del Iguazú, pero...

79 Las votaciones

▶ **Decide.** Which pair has done the most amazing challenge in Argentina? Take a vote to decide!

Sorprendente

Activities

78. Have students present arguments in support of their favorite pair to win this challenge. After all students have presented their arguments, take a final vote.

79. On the board, write the names of the participants in the challenge and tally the results of the class vote for the most amazing challenge. If time allows, let each of the students briefly explain why they chose their winning team.

Answer Key

78. Answers will vary.

79. Answers will vary.

HERITAGE LANGUAGE LEARNERS

- Have students think about a traditional dessert from a country with which they are familiar. Ask them to find a recipe for the dessert and rewrite it using simple affirmative and negative commands. Collect student recipes and "publish" a recipe book for the class to take home.

MULTIPLE INTELLIGENCES:
Bodily-Kinesthetic Intelligence

- Ask students to try to learn the tango by researching the dance online. Then ask them to teach the dance steps to the rest of the class by using affirmative and negative commands.

187

Unit 7
MAPA CULTURAL
Argentina

Presentation

- This section presents Argentina by using scenes from different regions and important sites throughout the country. The map of the country serves as a reference point for additional cultural readings and activities.

Activities	Standards	Resources
Mapa cultural	1.2, 3.1, 3.2, 5.2	Video
80.	1.3	
81.	1.3	

Teaching Suggestions

Warm-Up / Independent Starter

- Have students pick a person, place, or thing in the *Mapa cultural* that they would like to learn more about. Ask them to do some research online about their choices. Then they should write five important facts that they learned.

Preparation

- Have students make a short verbal presentation of their five facts from the previous activity. Students can improvise visual aids and may use key cards as they speak.

- Invite students to summarize some of the things they have learned about Argentina in this unit, including facts they gathered from their classmates' presentations. Then share the following information with them if it has not yet been mentioned.

- Argentina is a federal republic divided into 23 provinces. The capital of Argentina is the autonomous city of Buenos Aires. The name Argentina comes from the Latin word *argentum*, which means "silver." The currency is the Argentine peso. Argentina is rich in natural resources and has well-developed agricultural and industrial sectors. It was one of the world's wealthiest countries a century ago. However, a series of economic crises during the 20th and 21st centuries have undermined the country's economic strength.

- Ask for volunteers to read each section of the *Mapa cultural*. Have students follow the map on the page or even the map in your classroom as they read this section.

188

MAPA CULTURAL

Argentina es una república situada en el sur de América. La capital de la nación es Buenos Aires.

Argentina es el país hispanohablante más grande del mundo, aunque no es el más poblado: tiene aproximadamente 40 millones de habitantes. El 86 % de la población desciende de europeos, especialmente de españoles e italianos.

¿Sabes que la montaña más alta de América está en Argentina?

¡Claro! Se llama Aconcagua y mide 6.959 metros.

80 **¿Exactamente dónde?**

▶ **Elige.** Look at the map and choose the appropriate ending for each sentence.

1. Argentina está…
   - a. al sur de Paraguay
   - b. al norte de Paraguay
2. Buenos Aires está…
   - a. en el centro del país
   - b. en el este del país
3. Las cataratas del Iguazú están cerca de…
   - a. Chile
   - b. Paraguay
4. El glaciar Perito Moreno está lejos de…
   - a. Chile
   - b. Brasil

188 ciento ochenta y ocho

Differenciated Instruction

DEVELOPING LEARNERS

- To ensure comprehension, have students work together and analyze the information presented on this page. Ask them to find specific things on the map or in the resources they have available. Have students use a two-column chart to compare the information presented here about Argentina with corresponding information about the United States. Give them support when needed.

EXPANDING LEARNERS

- Ask students to relate what they have learned about Argentina so far with what they know about the United States. You may want to use the following prompts:
  - Where are the two countries located?
  - How big are they, comparatively?
  - What kinds of climate and topography do they each have?
  - What are some of the similarities and differences between their capital cities, forms of government, demographics, etc.?

Los paisajes de Argentina

Argentina está atravesada de norte a sur por la cordillera de los Andes. Tiene tres regiones muy diferentes: el Chaco, la Pampa y la Patagonia.

1. El Chaco

El Chaco es una región cálida de bosques y selvas en el norte de Argentina. Es una de las zonas menos pobladas.

En el noroeste, en la frontera con Brasil, están las **cataratas del Iguazú**.

(1) Cataratas del Iguazú.

(2) Avenida 9 de Julio (Buenos Aires).

2. La Pampa y Buenos Aires

En el centro de Argentina está **la Pampa**. Es una llanura muy extensa cubierta de hierba. En el este de esta región está **Buenos Aires**, la capital.

(3) Glaciar Perito Moreno.

3. La Patagonia

La Patagonia ocupa el sur de Argentina. Es una región árida de glaciares. El glaciar más espectacular es el **Perito Moreno**, en la frontera con Chile.

81 **Así es Argentina**

▶ **Escribe.** What are the three regions like? Put the adjectives in the corresponding boxes.

¿Cómo es cada región?	
El Chaco	
La Pampa	
La Patagonia	

cálida   fría

extensa   llana

Activities

80. Before doing this activity, have students use the expressions of place (*al sur, al norte, en el centro, en el este, cerca de,* and *lejos de*) to describe landmarks in their city. Ask for volunteers to play a guessing game by describing the location of different landmarks in their city and having the rest of the class guess which landmarks are being described.

81. You may allow students to expand on the information about these places by summarizing what they have learned throughout the unit.

Answer Key

80. 1. a   3. b
        2. b   4. b

81. El Chaco – cálida
        La Pampa – extensa, llana
        La Patagonia – fría

HERITAGE LANGUAGE LEARNERS

• Encourage heritage students to describe one of the regions or landscapes of their own country of origin. Have them share geographical and historical information about the region. Encourage them to compare and contrast that region with a similar area in the United States.

CRITICAL THINKING

• Buenos Aires is often called the Paris of South America. Ask students what they think this means. Engage them in a discussion about the characteristics that could apply to both cities.

189

MAPA CULTURAL

Argentina

Presentation

- In this section, students will continue to learn about Argentina by exploring cultural icons.

Activities	Standards	Resources
Mapa cultural	1.2, 2.1, 2.2, 3.1, 3.2, 5.2	
82.	1.3, 3.1, 5.2	

Teaching Suggestions

Warm-Up / Independent Starter

- Have students view the photos from this spread and select the most attractive one. Ask them to explain their choices. What makes this photo interesting?

Preparation

- In this section, students learn about the tango, Mafalda, Buenos Aires, and the *ñoquis del 29* tradition.

- Review the photos with the class. Focus students' attention on the image of the couple dancing the tango and ask them if they have ever seen or heard the tango. Invite volunteers to share what they know about the tango. You may bring a recording to class and allow students to listen to it. Ask students if they are familiar with the idiomatic expression "It takes two to tango." What might this expression mean? Why do they think the tango is used as a metaphor in this expression?

- Point out that Mafalda is a well-known comic strip in the Spanish-speaking world. You may want to bring one of the Mafalda comics to class and explain this character's kind of sense of humor. Have students talk about the similarities and differences in the way cultures express humor. Did they find Mafalda funny? Witty? Have them explain their reasoning.

- Tell students about the Argentine tradition of eating *ñoquis* on the 29th of every month. It is believed that leaving a peso under a plate of this pasta brings good luck. Ask students to brainstorm other traditions or beliefs from their own cultures. What is believed to bring good uck in their cultures? Ask for volunteers to share their traditions with the class.

190

---

1. El tango

El **tango** es un tipo de música y de baile conocido en todo el mundo. Su origen es en los barrios populares de Buenos Aires y de otras ciudades de Argentina y de Uruguay.

Los tangos hablan del amor, del paso del tiempo, del barrio, etc.

El instrumento básico de los tangos es el bandoneon.

(1) Una orquesta tocando tangos.

Una pareja bailando un tango.

2. Mafalda

Mafalda es el personaje principal de la historieta gráfica más famosa de Argentina. El autor de esas historietas es Quino (Joaquín Salvador Lavado).

Durante años, las historietas de Mafalda sirvieron para denunciar con humor los problemas de los argentinos.

Quino, el creador de Mafalda.

(2) Un dibujo de Mafalda.

190 ciento noventa

The Hispanic World

El tango

The tango originated in the 19th century in the *Río de la Plata* area of Buenos Aires, Argentina and Montevideo, Uruguay. In the beginning it was associated with the working class and shunned by high society. Eventually, the tango became fashionable and today it is enjoyed throughout the world. There have been several prominent tango singers, but none as famous as Carlos Gardel. He helped popularize the tango in Europe and the United States through his recordings and films.

Mafalda

The comic strip Mafalda ran for only ten years in various newspapers in Argentina, but it soon became very popular throughout the Spanish-speaking world, Europe, and Asia. It has been translated into more than 30 languages. The main character, Mafalda, is a bright young girl who does not shy away from sharing her opinions on family life, school, friendship, and even world events.

3. Buenos Aires

Buenos Aires, la capital de Argentina, es una gran ciudad. Sus habitantes dicen que tienen la avenida más ancha del mundo (la avenida **9 de Julio**) y la más larga (la avenida **Rivadavia**).

Entre los barrios de Buenos Aires está el famoso barrio obrero de **La Boca**. En su calle Caminito, el pintor **Benito Quinquela** organizó un museo al aire libre.

(3) La Plaza de Mayo, en el centro de Buenos Aires.

(4) Una familia comiendo ñoquis.

4. Los ñoquis del 29 del mes

Tradicionalmente, los argentinos comen **ñoquis** el día **29** de cada mes. Ese día colocan dinero debajo del plato de ñoquis; los argentinos creen que así atraen a la suerte. Esta costumbre se llama «ñoquis del 29».

82 **Mitos argentinos**

▶ **Investiga y escribe.**
Search for information about one of these people and write a brief summary of his or her life.

Include photos and biographical information such as main achievements and music, literature, or movie tributes.

Jorge Luis Borges.

Eva Perón (Evita).

Activities

82. Have students take on the role of either Jorge Luis Borges or Eva Perón and present an "autobiography" to the rest of the class in the first person singular. They must include information from their reports.

Answer Key

82. Answers will vary.

Additional Resources

Fans Online activities
Practice Workbook

Buenos Aires

Buenos Aires, like many other metropolitan areas worldwide, has several picturesque neighborhoods. La Boca is perhaps the best known of these *barrios*. It was settled by European immigrants who arrived in Argentina during the 19th century looking for a better future. La Boca is home to tango performers, artists, and the Boca Juniors, a world-famous soccer team.

Los ñoquis del 29 del mes

The word *ñoqui* comes from the Italian word *gnocchi*, a traditional Italian pasta. Argentina received a large influx of Italian immigrants during the 19th and 20th centuries whose cuisine impressed the Argentines. One legend about this tradition of eating *ñoquis* says that by the 29th of each month, the day before payday, working-class families were broke, but with some flour and potatoes, both cheap, they could enjoy *ñoquis*. These days, restaurants are full on the 29th of every month, and patrons leave a peso under their dishes to attract prosperity.

LECTURA

La vuelta al mundo de Cinthia Scoch

Presentation

- In this section, students will read a children's fantasy story in which a young girl takes a trip around the world in search of the corner grocery store.

Activities	Standards	Resources
Lectura	1.2, 3.1, 3.2	
83.	1.3	
84.	1.2, 1.3	
85.	1.3	
Tu desafío	1.3, 3.1	

Teaching Suggestions

Warm-Up / Independent Starter

- Have students look at a globe. Ask them to imagine that their teacher asked them to go to the library to study for an upcoming test, but instead of going to the right, they went to the left and had to circumnavigate the globe to arrive at the library. What countries would they cross en route to reach their hometown library?

Preparation

- Before reading the story, point to the Reading Strategy text and read it aloud to the class. Review what the story elements are, and write the Spanish terms on the board: *marco, personajes, argumento.* Tell the class that after reading, they will complete a story map detailing the different elements of Cinthia Scoch's story.

- Tell students that this is a fantasy story. Invite them to share what they know about this literary genre. If necessary, explain that a fantasy is a type of fiction that contains elements that could not exist in real life. Examples might include talking animals, time travel, supernatural powers, magical settings, etc.

- Have students think about a story they read recently or that they loved as a child. Ask them to list the elements (setting, characters, and plot) for that story.

La vuelta al mundo
de Cinthia Scoch

READING STRATEGY
Story elements

Narrative texts have three common components:

- Setting—the time and place in which the events of the story occur (when and where).
- Characters—the people or sometimes the animals in the story (who).
- Plot—the sequence of events (what).

Cinthia Scoch es una chica muy obediente. Un día, su madre la mandó a comprar un kilo de azúcar.

–Anda al almacén[1] de la derecha –le indicó la señora Scoch.

Cinthia pensó: «En realidad, el almacén está a la izquierda», pero, para no contradecir a su madre, caminó hacia la derecha.

Oliendo el lindo aroma de los tilos[2] de su barrio, caminó una, dos, tres cuadras[3], pero no encontró el almacén.

A las tres horas llegó al puerto de Buenos Aires. Allí tomó un barco con ruta de navegación hacia la derecha.

El barco navegó días y días y al fin llegó a un puerto de Australia. Cinthia Scoch bajó a tierra. Continuó hacia la derecha. Cruzó toda Australia. En la ciudad de Sidney no encontró ningún almacén, así que tomó otro barco, también hacia la derecha.

Llegó al puerto de Valparaíso, en Chile. Continuó hacia la derecha. Cruzó los Andes. Llegó a Mendoza y cruzó las provincias de San Luis y Santa Fe.

Llegó a Buenos Aires, y siempre caminando hacia la derecha, finalmente se encontró[4] en su barrio. Así completó la vuelta al mundo y de nuevo olió el lindo aroma de los tilos de su barrio. Una cuadra antes de su casa, encontró el almacén. Es decir, a la izquierda de su casa. «Mamá está equivocada[5]», pensó.

Differentiated Instruction

DEVELOPING LEARNERS

- Developing learners may benefit from a guided reading of the story. Ask volunteers to read it sentence by sentence. After each pause, you may turn the sentence into a yes / no question and check for comprehension.

EXPANDING LEARNERS

- Have students talk about the events in the story. Ask if they think this story could have been real. Which elements of the story are reasonable? What elements of the plot seem hard to believe? Encourage students to use as much of the target language as they can in their discussion.

Compró un kilo de azúcar.

Entró en casa y le entregó⁶ el paquete a la señora Scoch.

La madre de Cinthia guardó el azúcar en un tarro⁷.

–Hija –le dijo a Cinthia–, ¡cuánto tardaste⁸!

RICARDO MARIÑO, *Botella al mar* (texto adaptado).

1. grocer's shop	2. lime trees	3. blocks	4. was
5. wrong	6. gave	7. jar	8. it took you so long!

ESTRATEGIA Elementos de la narración

 Una historia con muchos elementos

▶ **Escribe.** Complete the story map with the different elements of Cinthia Scoch's story.

Título y autor:

Marco (setting)	Tiempo (when):
	Lugar (where):
Personajes (characters)	
Argumento (plot)	

COMPRENSIÓN

 ¿Está claro?

▶ **Completa.** Complete these sentences.

a. Cinthia salió a la calle para…
b. Cinthia caminó hacia la derecha para…
c. Cinthia caminó por su barrio, pero…
d. En el puerto de Buenos Aires…

e. Cinthia cruzó…
f. Cinthia encontró el almacén…
g. En el almacén…
h. En su casa…

85 **Un resumen**

▶ **Escribe.** Write a summary of Cinthia's travels. Include the main elements of the story. If you wish, illustrate the story with a drawing.

 TU DESAFÍO Earn points for your own challenge! Visit the website to take a virtual tour around Argentina and describe your trip in a letter to a friend.

HERITAGE LANGUAGE LEARNERS

• Have students write a similar story using themselves as the main characters. Encourage them to employ exaggeration and fantasy to achieve a similar tone. You may use the story map in the book to facilitate the organization of the writing task.

CRITICAL THINKING

• Even though the main character knew that her mother was wrong, she decided to follow her order to go to the right—thus causing her to travel around the world. Ask students to think about why Cinthia chose to do that. Do they think that they would have done the same? Why or why not? What might be the moral to this story?

Activities

83. Have students share the information from their story maps with the class.

84. Using a globe, have students trace the trip that Cinthia Scoch took in the story. Use your fingers to represent the trip on the globe, or on a separate map as students answer the questions aloud.

Answer Key

83. Answers will vary. Sample answer:
Título y autor: "La vuelta al mundo de Cinthia Scoch", Ricardo Mariño.
Marco: un pueblo o un barrio argentino.
Personajes: Una niña llamada Cinthia Scoch y su madre.
Argumento: La madre de Cinthia la manda a comprar un kilo de azúcar en el almacén cerca de su casa. Buscando el almacén, da la vuelta al mundo. Cuando regresa, encuentra el almacén y compra el azúcar para su madre.

84. a. … comprar un kilo de azúcar.
b. … no contradecir a su madre.
c. … no encontró el almacén.
d. … tomó un barco.
e. … toda Australia.
f. … una cuadra antes de su casa.
g. … compró el kilo de azúcar.
h. … le entregó el paquete a su madre.

85. Answers will vary.

Additional Resources

Fans Online activities

193

Unit 7

REPASO

Vocabulario

Presentation

- In this section, students will review all key vocabulary from the unit organized by themes, to prepare for an assessment. Students will complete practice activities for each of the four *Desafíos*.

Activities	Standards	Resources
1.	1.3	
2.	1.2, 1.3	
3.	1.2, 1.3	
4.	1.2, 1.3	

Teaching Suggestions

Warm-Up / Independent Starter

- Ask students to imagine that they have taken a fantasy trip to any place in the world. Then have them answer the following questions:
  - ¿Adónde fuiste?
  - ¿Cómo fuiste?
  - ¿Cuándo fuiste?
  - ¿Qué llevaste contigo?

Preparation

- Have students review the vocabulary of the unit by creating flashcards with cut outs from magazines. One student should show a card to his or her partner and the other should try to associate it with a vocabulary word.

Activities

1. Ask students to work in pairs to complete this activity. Have them write a list of *destinos* (*la costa, la montaña*, etc.) for their partner. Then ask their partner to fill in the *medios de transporte* that they would need to take in order to get to each place.

2. To extend this activity, add the following two places and ask students what actions they would perform in these places: *aeropuerto, estación*.

3. Have students work in small groups. Ask them to choose one of the four places and pretend they visited this place on their last vacation. Have them come up with four statements to say what they did during their vacation there.

194

De viaje

Medios de transporte
(ir) a pie	on foot, walking
el autobús	bus
el avión	plane
el barco	boat
el coche	car
el metro	subway
el taxi	taxi
el tren	train

Acciones
ir de vacaciones	to go on vacation
ir de excursión	to go on an excursion
viajar	to travel

Lugares
el aeropuerto	airport
la estación	station

Los viajes

Objetos
el billete	ticket
la bolsa	bag
la guía turística	travel guide, guidebook
la maleta	suitcase
el pasaporte	passport

Acciones
comprar recuerdos	to buy souvenirs
enseñar el pasaporte	to show your passport
facturar el equipaje	to check the baggage

Lugares
la agencia de viajes	travel agency
la oficina de turismo	tourist office
el mostrador de información	information desk

Destinos y alojamientos

el campo	countryside
la ciudad	city, town
la costa	coast
la montaña	mountain
la playa	beach
el cámping	campsite
el hotel	hotel
reservar habitación	to reserve a room
hacer turismo	to be a tourist

La ciudad

Lugares
el banco	bank
la biblioteca	library
el café	café
la calle	street
el hospital	hospital
la iglesia	church
la plaza	square, plaza

Localización y direcciones
cruzar la calle	to cross the street
doblar a la derecha	to turn right
doblar a la izquierda	to turn left
seguir recto	to go/walk straight ahead

194 ciento noventa y cuatro

Differentiated Instruction

DEVELOPING LEARNERS

- Play a game of "Slap" with the students. Flash an index card with the image of a vocabulary word and ask the students to slap their desks if they know the word. Assign points to each student who gets the correct answer.

EXPANDING LEARNERS

- Ask students to write a composition using all of the vocabulary taught in this unit. Students may select any genre for their composition (a travelogue, a diary entry, an adventure story, a love story, etc.). Encourage them to be creative and to use peer support as they write. When the compositions are done, have students exchange and review each other's work and offer commentary on it.

DESAFÍO 1

1 **Respuestas lógicas.** Complete each sentence with the most logical answer.

1. En Buenos Aires yo viajo casi siempre…
   a. en tren   b. en avión   c. en metro
2. Yo vivo lejos y casi nunca voy a la escuela…
   a. a pie   b. en tren   c. en avión
3. Para viajar desde Buenos Aires hasta Nueva York tengo que ir…
   a. en autobús   b. en metro   c. en avión
4. Cuando voy de excursión con mi clase, normalmente vamos…
   a. a pie   b. en autobús   c. en barco

 ## DESAFÍO 2

2 **De viaje.** Match each place with the corresponding actions.

1. En una tienda

2. En una agencia de viajes

3. En una oficina de turismo

a. compras los billetes de avión.
b. pides un plano de la ciudad.
c. compras recuerdos.
d. pagas el viaje.
e. pides información de la ciudad.
f. compras una maleta.

DESAFÍO 3

3 **Las vacaciones.** Match each statement with the corresponding picture.

1. El año pasado nos alojamos en un cámping.
2. Este verano pasamos las vacaciones en la playa.
3. En Navidad fuimos a esquiar a la montaña.
4. La semana pasada reservamos habitación en un hotel.

 ## DESAFÍO 4

4 **¿Adónde vas?** Answer the questions in complete sentences. Use the word bank.

1. ¿Adónde vas si necesitas dinero?
2. ¿Adónde vas si estás muy enfermo?
3. ¿Adónde vas si tienes mucha hambre?
4. ¿Adónde vas si quieres leer un libro?

 restaurante   banco

hospital   biblioteca

ciento noventa y cinco   195

Unit 7
REPASO
Vocabulario

4. Ask students to draw a map of their town, labeling all the places (for example: *el banco, la biblioteca,* etc.). Break them into pairs and place a "toy person" (they can use a coin or any other small object to represent the person) somewhere on their maps. Their partners must give them directions to a different place on the map while they follow these directions and move the "toy person" accordingly. For example:

A. *Sigue recto por la calle Rosa. Cruza el parque. Dobla a la derecha en la calle Verde. ¿Dónde estás?*
B. *En la biblioteca.*
A. *¡Sí!*

Answer Key

1. 1. c   2. a   3. c   4. b
2. 1. c, f
   2. a, d
   3. b, e
3. 1. D   2. C   3. A   4. B
4. 1. Voy al banco.
   2. Voy al hospital.
   3. Voy al restaurante.
   4. Voy a la biblioteca.

Additional Resources

Fans Online activities
Practice Workbook

HERITAGE LANGUAGE LEARNERS

• Have heritage learners create a travel show about Argentina. Have them research cultural topics not covered in this unit, such as food. They should write a script and record their program or perform it for the class.

COOPERATIVE LEARNING

• Place developing learners in mixed-level groups with expanding learners to play a game of "Connect Four." The advanced learners in the group will create a quiz consisting of 20 multiple choice questions based on the vocabulary from the unit. Each of the slower-paced learners will draw a 9 x 9 grid on poster board using a particular color. The advanced students will take turns reading the quiz questions aloud to two slower-paced learners in the group. For every correct answer they may place a piece on the grid. The first one to connect four pieces wins.

195

REPASO

Gramática

Presentation

- Students will review the grammatical structures presented in the unit. The activities here provide systematic practice by *Desafío*.

Activities	Standards	Resources
5.	1.3	
6.	1.2, 1.3	
7.	1.2, 1.3	
8.	1.2, 1.3	
9. Cultura	1.3, 2.1, 2.2, 5.2	

Teaching Suggestions

Warm-Up / Independent Starter

- Have students practice the preterite of the verb *ir*. Ask them to write a list of who went to each of the following places: *tienda, restaurante, café, banco, cine*. For example: *Yo fui a la tienda. Mi amigo fue al restaurante.*

Preparation

- Have students illustrate one of the sentences from the Warm-Up. Using the picture, have students play a guessing game. One student tells the other what they bought there (using *comprar* in the preterite tense), and the other guesses where her partner went (using *ir* in the preterite tense). For example:
  A. *Compré una chaqueta para mi viaje en ese lugar.*
  B. *Fuiste a la tienda.*

Activities

5. Before completing this activity, have students write a list of everything they did over the past year using time expressions in the past such as *ayer, anoche, antes, la semana pasada*, etc.

7. Have students rank their activities from the most interesting to the least interesting. Focus on one of the time expressions (for example: *anoche*), and ask students to share their answers with the class. What activity did the students do most?

8. Students can add three more recommendations based on the structures of the ones provided.

196

Verbos regulares. Pretérito (págs. 154, 162)

	COMPRAR	COMER	ESCRIBIR
yo	compré	comí	escribí
tú	compraste	comiste	escribiste
usted él ella	compró	comió	escribió
nosotros nosotras	compramos	comimos	escribimos
vosotros vosotras	comprasteis	comisteis	escribisteis
ustedes ellos ellas	compraron	comieron	escribieron

Marcadores temporales de pasado (pág. 170)

anteayer	the day before yesterday
antes	before
ayer	yesterday
anoche	last night
la semana pasada	last week
el mes pasado	last month
el año pasado	last year

Los verbos *ser* e *ir*. Pretérito (pág. 172)

singular		plural	
yo	fui	nosotros nosotras	fuimos
tú	fuiste	vosotros vosotras	fuisteis
usted él ella	fue	ustedes ellos ellas	fueron

Preposiciones de lugar (pág. 172)

a	to
de... a...	from ... to ...
desde... hasta...	from ... to/until ...

El imperativo negativo (pág. 180)

Verbos regulares

Comprar	Comer	Escribir
no compres	no comas	no escribas

Verbos *ser* e *ir*

Ser	Ir
no seas	no vayas

Differentiated Instruction

DEVELOPING LEARNERS

- Have students create a matching card game like "Concentration" for some of the past tense verbs discussed in the unit. One card should show the grammar information (for example: *tú/comprar*) and a matching card should be made with the conjugated verb (for example: *compraste*). Have students spread the cards face down on their desks. Each student turns over one card and then tries to match it. When they find a match, they get to keep those cards. The student with the most matches at the end of the game wins.

EXPANDING LEARNERS

- Invite students to demonstrate the use of the grammar topics in their original contexts. They can use the past tense, for example, to talk about what they did last year. In order to use the negative informal commands they have learned they can mention the rules they have to observe at home.

DESAFÍO 1

5 **Nuestro fin de semana.** Write sentences about what everyone did last weekend.

Modelo 1. *Yo viajé en avión.*

   yo   ellas   nosotros   usted   tú

DESAFÍO 2

6 **Experiencias.** Answer the questions in complete sentences.

Modelo ¿Escribiste el correo electrónico a tus abuelos?
    → *Sí, escribí el correo electrónico a mis abuelos.*

1. ¿Comiste en un restaurante argentino?   3. ¿Fuiste a otro país?
2. ¿Leíste el último libro de Harry Potter?   4. ¿Participaste en un maratón?

DESAFÍO 3

7 **Recuerda.** Write what you did at the times indicated below.

1. antes   3. ayer   5. el lunes pasado   7. el mes pasado
2. anoche   4. anteayer   6. la semana pasada   8. el año pasado

DESAFÍO 4

8 **Órdenes.** Write negative commands based on the information provided.

Modelo Si abres **la puerta**, hace frío. (abrir) → *No abras la puerta.*

1. **Esa carne** está mala. (comer)   3. Tus amigos no van **al cine** esta noche. (ir)
2. **Ese libro** es muy aburrido. (leer)   4. **Esa mochila** es muy cara. (comprar)

CULTURA

9 **¡Descubre Argentina!** Answer the questions.

1. Why is *tren a las nubes* well named?
2. What do you know about the Pampa region?
3. Where is Iguazu Falls located?
4. What color is the Presidential Palace in Buenos Aires?
5. Describe the different geographical regions in Argentina.

Answer Key

5.
1. Yo viajé en avión.
2. Ellas escucharon música.
3. Nosotros preparamos un sándwich.
4. Usted cortó el césped.
5. Tú paseaste al perro.

6. Answers will vary. Sample answers:
1. Sí, comí en un restaurante argentino.
2. Sí, leí el último libro de Harry Potter.
3. Sí, fui a otro país.
4. No, no participé en un maratón.

7. Answers will vary. Sample answers:
1. Antes hablé con mi amiga.
2. Anoche comí una empanada deliciosa.

8.
1. No comas esa carne.
2. No leas ese libro.
3. No vayas al cine esta noche.
4. No compres esa mochila.

9. Answers will vary. Sample answers:
1. Because this train reaches such a high altitude that it seems to travel through the clouds.
2. The Pampa is a rich farmland region located in central Argentina.
3. Iguazu Falls is located in the northeastern part of the country.
4. The Presidential Palace in Buenos Aires is pink.
5. Argentina has three distinct regions: the Chaco, the Pampas, and Patagonia. The Chaco is a warm region of forests and jungles located in northern Argentina. The Pampas, located in central Argentina, are vast grass plains where cattle are raised. Patagonia is a dry, cold region located in southern Argentina. Some spectacular glaciers are located in this region.

Additional Resources

Fans Online activities
Practice Workbook

HERITAGE LANGUAGE LEARNERS

- Have students try to guess the answer to this riddle or *adivinanza*: *Fui y no soy, no soy y fui; mañana seré y hablarán de mí.* (*El día de ayer*).

- Have students try to create their own *adivinanzas* using the verbs *ser* or *ir* in the preterite.

SPECIAL-NEEDS LEARNERS

- Students diagnosed with Asperger's Syndrome may benefit from an environment free of sound stressors. For a student with AS, it is very important to present material to them in a clear manner and to give them time to absorb what is said. To expect an AS student to listen, take notes, and read the blackboard all at the same time is often too much. Present them with notes prior to the class so they can truly listen and learn.

PROYECTO

Un viaje

Presentation

- In this section, students will create an illustrated travelogue to practice the vocabulary and grammar they learned in Unit 7. The project offers an opportunity for students to demonstrate what they have learned. Students will follow step-by-step instructions.

Activities	Standards	Resources
Paso 1	1.2, 3.1	
Paso 2	1.1, 1.2, 5.2	
Paso 3	1.3	
Paso 4	1.3	
Paso 5	1.3, 5.2	

Teaching Suggestions

Warm-Up / Independent Starter

- Have students read over the project outline to themselves.

Preparation

- Ask students to brainstorm all the information they know about the different regions / areas of Argentina. They should think about the regions that the participants visited and the regions that most interest or intrigue them.

Step-by-Step Instructions

Paso 1

- Have students do an Internet search for different travelogues. Some excellent resources can be found at:
  – Argentina, Yours Truly
  – Journey to the End of the World
  – Travelogue Buenos Aires

Paso 2

- Ask students to view video travelogues and try to answer the questions in the box. A sample video travelogue can be found online at: http://www.vimeo.com/channels/argentina.

Paso 3

- Have students use an online timeline maker to help with this step. You can find templates and generators by searching online.

PROYECTO

Crónica de

un viaje

In this project you will prepare an illustrated travelogue. The traveler can be someone in your family, a person in your community, or a famous person. You will present your travelogue to your classmates, who will vote for the best trip in each of these categories: most interesting, most fun, and most dangerous.

PASO 1 Decide qué viaje vas a describir

- Decide what trip you are going to describe. For example:
  – El viaje de una persona de tu familia.
  – El viaje de una persona de tu comunidad.
  – Un viaje histórico.

> **Viaje a la Patagonia**
>
> En 1978 una expedición viajó a la Patagonia, en Argentina, para recordar los viajes de Francisco P. Moreno, cien años antes.

PASO 2 Busca información sobre el viaje

- Interview people or do research on the Internet to find information.

> El viaje de...
>
> ¿Adónde viajó?
> ¿Cuándo viajó?
> ¿Cómo viajó? En tren, en avión, en coche…
> ¿Qué objetos llevó? Pasaporte, cámara…
> ¿Qué ocurrió en el viaje?
> ¿Qué vio?

- Gather documents to illustrate the trip:
  – Fotos de los viajeros.
  – Un mapa o un plano para dibujar el itinerario.
  – Postales, billetes, recuerdos…

Rubric for Evaluation

	Content	Organization	Presentation
1 point	Limited relevance. Information is incomplete or not based on research. Little Spanish is used.	Inefficient use of class time. Information is disorganized or unclear.	Communication is unclear. Many errors in vocabulary and grammar.
3 points	Basic information is correct. Relevant information but lacks significance. Spanish is used most of the time.	Class time is used well. Information and content are mostly organized but lack some clarity.	Good communication. Mostly correct vocabulary and grammar.

PASO 3 Escribe la crónica

- Organize all your information in chronological order and write one or two sentences to describe the information.

En noviembre de 1979, la expedición visitó el glaciar Perito Moreno. El glaciar se llama así en honor al perito Francisco P. Moreno.

PASO 4 Presenta la crónica

- Present your report and answer your classmates' questions.

¿Qué ropa llevan?

Llevan chaquetas, gorros, guantes y botas.

PASO 5 Vota la mejor crónica

- Take a vote to decide which travelogue is the best in each category: *más interesante, más divertido, más peligroso*. Give reasons for your vote.

El viaje de la expedición al glaciar Perito Moreno es el más interesante: viajaron en coche y en barco a este glaciar del sur de Argentina.

Unidad 7

Autoevaluación

¿Qué has aprendido en esta unidad?

Do the following activities to evaluate how well you get along in Spanish.

Evaluate your skills. For each item, say Very well, Well, or I need more practice.

a. Can you talk about what you did yesterday?
- ▶ Tell your partner what you did before and after breakfast yesterday.

b. Can you talk about where you live?
- ▶ Ask your partner to name three important places where you live.
- ▶ Tell your partner the location of the same three places.

c. Can you say how people travel in your region?
- ▶ Ask your partner how his or her family goes shopping.
- ▶ Say how you get to school.

Paso 4
- Each student will give a presentation to the class. Have them remember to speak slowly and clearly, while also interacting with the audience.

Paso 5
- Allow students to explain why they voted in the way they did.

Evaluation
- Explain how the project will be evaluated by distributing copies of the rubric chart and discussing it.
- Encourage students to refer to the rubric as they prepare their projects. It may be helpful to correlate points with traditional grade scales and indicate how much the project counts toward the final grade.

Content
- Students should select information that is interesting and relevant. To develop research skills, ask students to prepare a list of sources, including Internet sites. If students quote a person they have interviewed, ask them to follow the correct format when writing the quote.

Organization
- Every part of the outline in the instructions should be included in the presentation.

Presentation
- Students should use as much Spanish as possible. They should check grammar and vocabulary. Encourage creativity and a presentation style that will hold their classmates' attention.

	Content	Organization	Presentation
5 points	Relevant, interesting information. Many details and significance are highlighted. Spanish is used exclusively.	Class time is used wisely. Information and content are clearly organized visually and logically.	Clear communication. Correct and complete vocabulary and grammar.

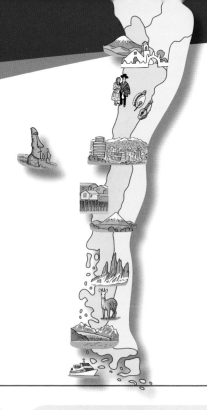

Objectives

- To wish someone good luck, to express admiration, and to state quantity.
- To learn about the universe through the text.
- To express cause.
- To describe the geographical and political divisions of a country.

- To quantify in uncertain terms.
- To describe nature and the environment.
- To reflect on past actions.
- To express permission and prohibition.
- To explore the cultural aspects of Chile.

Contents

Vocabulary

- Useful expressions to wish someone good luck, to express admiration, and to state quantity.
- The universe.
- Geographical terms.
- Political divisions.
- Numbers 101–1,000.
- Nature.
- The environment.
- Recycling and recyclables.

Grammar

- Expressing cause using the conjunction *porque* and the preposition *por*.
- Expressing quantity: Indefinite words.
- Irregular verbs *decir* and *hacer* in the past tense.
- Irregular verbs *estar* and *tener* in the past tense.
- Expressing permission and prohibition.

Culture

- The geography and culture of Chile.
- *La Chascona.*
- Atacama Desert and the *Valle de la Luna.*
- *La Isla de Pascua* and the moai.
- Valparaiso and *El Maratón de las Escaleras.*
- Currency in Chile.
- Economic and symbolic value of lapis lazuli.
- Viña del Mar and *El Festival Internacional de la Canción de Viña del Mar.*
- Torres del Paine National Park.
- A Chilean poet: Pablo Neruda.

Evaluation Criteria

- Express luck, admiration, and quantity.
- Describe the elements of the universe.
- Ask for a reason using *por qué.*
- Express cause or reason using the conjunction *porque* followed by a sentence.
- Express cause or reason using the preposition *por.*

- Describe the geography of a place and its political divisions.
- Express quantity using indefinite adjectives.
- Express past actions using irregular verbs *decir*, *hacer*, *estar* and *tener.*
- Describe items in nature and the environment.

- Asking for permission, giving permission, and denying permission using *poder.*
- Describe Chile's customs, geographical aspects, and historical facts.

Unit Plan

La llegada

Estimated time: 2 sessions.

Dialogue: *En Santiago de Chile.*

Forms & functions:
- To wish someone good luck.
- To show admiration.
- To stress quantity.
- Irregular verbs in the preterite.
- Recycling.

Culture:
- Santiago, Chile.
- *La Chascona.*

DESAFÍO 1

Estimated time: 5 sessions.

Dialogue: *Las estrellas de Atacama.*

Forms & functions:
- The universe.
- Expressing cause: The conjunction *porque* and the preposition *por.*

Culture:
- *El Valle de la Luna.*
- *San Pedro de Atacama.*

DESAFÍO 2

Estimated time: 5 sessions.

Dialogue: *Una estatua falsa.*

Forms & functions:
- Geographical terms.
- To express quantity: Indefinite adjectives.

Culture:
- *La Isla de Pascua.*
- *Un balneario en Chile.*

DESAFÍO 3

Estimated time: 6 sessions.

Dialogue: *El Maratón de las Escaleras.*

Forms & functions:
- Political divisions.
- Numbers from 101 to 1,000.
- Expressing actions in the past: Irregular verbs in the preterite *decir, estar, hacer,* and *tener.*

Culture:
- *El Maratón de las Escaleras de Valparaíso.*
- *El dinero chileno.*
- *El lapislázuli.*
- *El Festival Internacional de la Canción de Viña del Mar.*

DESAFÍO 4

Estimated time: 5 sessions.

Dialogue: *La famosa Ruta W.*

Forms & functions:
- Nature and the environment.
- Expressing permission and prohibition using *poder.*

Culture:
- *Parque Nacional Torres del Paine.*

Todo junto / El encuentro

Estimated time: 2 sessions.

Dialogue: *En la Plaza de Armas.*

Forms & functions:
- Review of *Desafíos 1–4.*

Culture:
- *La Plaza de Armas*, Santiago.

MAPA CULTURAL / LECTURA

Estimated time: 2 sessions.

Mapa cultural: *Chile.*

Reading: *Oda a la manzana.*

REPASO

Estimated time: 2 sessions.

Vocabulary: *Repaso.*

Grammar: *Repaso.*

PROYECTO / EVALUACIÓN

Estimated time: 5 sessions.

Project: *Un póster sobre animales en peligro.*

Self-evaluation: *Autoevaluación.*

Standards for Learning Spanish

 COMMUNICATION

1.1. Interpersonal mode
- Summarize classmates' answers.
- Share personal views with classmates.
- Interview classmates.
- Write diary entry or personal reflection.
- Write questions to ask a partner.
- Write about yourself or your opinions.
- Read a blog.
- Read someone's notes.

1.2. Interpretive mode
- Read a blog on a visit to a Chilean desert.
- Determine if statements are true / false based on descriptions.
- Listen and answer questions.
- Listen and report findings.
- Listen and interpret.
- Read a cultural text.
- Answer reading comprehension questions.
- Read and extract main ideas.

1.3. Presentational mode
- Summarize cultural information in a text.
- Write a list of facts for inclusion in a promotional poster about Chile.
- Share a list of personal information with classmates.
- Present the results of research.
- Write a summary or paragraph.
- Relay information based on pictures.

 CULTURE

2.1. Practices and perspectives
- Explore reasons for the deforestation of Easter Island.
- Analyze the reasons for the existence of the Stairs Marathon.
- Analyze the benefits of singing competitions around the Spanish-speaking world.

2.2. Products and perspectives
- Discover the meaning of the moai for the Rapanui people.
- Understand the use and production of *lapislázuli* in Chile.
- Understand the role of a significant Chilean artist and his work.
- Use a popular Mexican game show as inspiration to create a survey.

CONNECTIONS

3.1. Interdisciplinary connections
- Convert Chilean currency to dollars.
- Research the best months to vacation in Chile.
- Explore the possibility of life on other planets.
- Understand how geographical positions influence one's view of the night sky.
- Explain the survival tactics of plants and animals according to their environments.
- Discuss the causes and effects of deforestation.

3.2. Viewpoints through language / culture
- Analyze Chileans' views on nature based on their national parks.
- Discover Chilean geography.
- Understand the significance of statues made by Pre-Columbian peoples.
- Explain the reasons why animals are on the endangered species list in Chile.

COMPARISONS

4.1. Compare languages
- Compare reasons for spelling changes in Spanish verbs with English verbs.
- Compare indefinite adjectives in English with those in Spanish.
- Describe the similarities and differences in the way cause is expressed in English and in Spanish.
- Explain how to determine the meaning of a Spanish verb that has two different definitions in English.

4.2. Compare cultures
- Compare music competitions in Chile with those in the United States.
- Compare views on animals in danger of extinction in Chile and in the United States.

 COMMUNITIES

5.1. Spanish beyond the school setting
- Write a paragraph about the conservation of natural resources.
- Convert the price of a school lunch in your school into Chilean pesos.
- Compare the places in your community that make handmade jewelry with the lapis lazuli workshops in Chile.

5.2. Spanish for lifelong learning
- Write a blog entry speculating about the end of a story.
- Design a promotional poster advertising a television program.

Communicative Skills

Interpersonal Mode | Activities

Speaking	• Engage in basic conversations with a partner.	• 19, 20, 25, 36, 38, 47, 51, 61, 69, 78, 84
	• Share personal views with classmates.	• 11, 21, 32, 37, 45
	• Interview students to gather information.	• 38, 43, 62
Writing	• Write a blog entry.	• 21
	• Write questions to ask a partner.	• 9, 51, 84
	• Compare answers with a partner.	• 92
Listening	• Understand a classmate's answers.	• 20, 51
	• Interpret a classmate's oral display.	• 38, 62, 84, *Proyecto*
Reading	• Determine the meaning of else's notes.	• 36, 73

Interpretive Mode | Activities

Listening	• Identify key concepts of a listening passage.	• 10, 18, 29, 42
	• Demonstrate an understanding of an audio recording.	• 24, 34
	• Summarize an oral text.	• 37, 47, 50, 69, 79
	• Interpret the meaning of a passage.	• 52, 66, 74, 83
Reading	• Determine the overall meaning of a reading passage.	• 8, 12, 17, 26, 30, 35, 36, 44, 48, 54, 59, 67, 71, 76
	• Obtain literal information from a narrative.	• 1, 6, 23, 41
	• Use the context in order to complete a text.	• 9, 40, 53, 65, 68, 77, 82, R1
	• Infer the meaning of a text.	• 7, 64, 81, 91, R5
	• Extract the main ideas from a passage.	• 21, 36, 84, 91

Presentational Mode | Activities

Speaking	• Share information with classmates.	• 45, 75
	• Present the results of research.	• 38, *Proyecto*
Writing	• Write a summary or paragraph.	• 73, 79, 80, 81, 91, 93, R8
	• Write descriptions or narratives based on pictures.	• 14, 39, 56, 60, 63, 70, R2
	• Respond to oral comprehension questions in writing.	• 1, 6, 23, 41
	• Present information in a table, graph or chart.	• 27, 38, 46, 62, 75, 92, R4
	• Write sentences based on clues.	• 11, 22, R3, R7

Cross-Curricular Standards

Subject	Standard	Activities
Social Studies	• Discuss production and distribution of arts and crafts.	• 54
	• Research about Chilean cultural topics.	• 89, 90, 92
Fine Arts	• Discuss musical venues and their functions.	• 59
Math	• Convert currencies and distances.	• 48, 61
Science	• Discuss reasons for deforestation.	• 35

Lesson Plans (50-Minute Classes)

Day	Objectives	Sessions	Activities	Time	Standards	Resources/ Homework
1	To introduce Chile	**Chile** (200–201) • Warm-Up: Country orientation • Chile • Images and functions		5 m. 15 m. 30 m.	1.2, 2.2, 4.1	Video Practice Workbook
2	To introduce Chile and to discuss the pairs' challenges	**La llegada** (202–205) • Warm-Up: Independent Starter • Presentation: *En Santiago de Chile* • *Expresiones útiles* and *¿Quién ganará?*	1 2–4	5 m. 15 m. 30 m.	1.1, 1.2, 1.3, 3.1	Visual Presentation Audio Practice Workbook
3	To talk about the universe and to express cause	**Desafío 1 – Las estrellas de Atacama** (206–207) • Warm-Up: Independent Starter • *Fotonovela: Las estrellas de Atacama* • *Cultura: El Valle de la Luna*	5–7 8	5 m. 35 m. 10 m.	1.1, 1.2, 1.3, 3.1, 3.2	Visual Presentation
4	To talk about the universe	**Desafío 1 – Vocabulario** (208–209) • Warm-Up: Independent Starter • Vocabulary: *El universo* • *Cultura: San Pedro de Atacama*	9–11 12	5 m. 35 m. 10 m.	1.1, 1.2, 1.3, 3.1, 3.2	Audio Practice Workbook
5	To express cause using *porque* and *por*	**Desafío 1 – Gramática** (210–211) • Warm-Up: Independent Starter • Grammar: *Expresar causa* • *Conexiones: El salar de Atacama*	13–16 17	5 m. 35 m. 10 m.	1.1, 1.2, 1.3, 3.1, 3.2, 4.1, 5.1	Practice Workbook
6	To integrate vocabulary and grammar	**Desafío 1 – Comunicación** (212–213) • Warm-Up: Independent Starter • *Comunicación*: Review main vocabulary and grammar	18–20	5 m. 45 m.	1.1, 1.2, 1.3, 3.1, 5.1	Audio Practice Workbook
7	To assess student proficiency	**Desafío 1 – Evaluación** (213) • Warm-Up: *Final del desafío* • Quiz on *Desafío 1*	21	30 m. 20 m.		
8	To talk about geography and to express quantity	**Desafío 2 – Una estatua falsa** (214–215) • Warm-Up: Independent Starter • *Fotonovela: Una estatua falsa* • *Cultura: La Isla de Pascua*	22–25 26	5 m. 30 m. 15 m.	1.1, 1.2, 1.3, 2.2, 3.1, 3.2	Visual Presentation Audio Video
9	To speak about geography	**Desafío 2 – Vocabulario** (216–217) • Warm-Up: Independent Starter • Vocabulary: *Geografía* • *Conexiones: Un balneario en Chile*	27–29 30	5 m. 35 m. 10 m.	1.1, 1.2, 1.3, 3.1, 3.2	Audio Practice Workbook
10	To learn and use indefinite adjectives to express quantity	**Desafío 2 – Gramática** (218–219) • Warm-Up: Independent Starter • Grammar: *Expresar cantidad. Los indefinidos* • *Conexiones: La deforestación*	31–34 35	5 m. 35 m. 10 m.	1.1, 1.2, 1.3, 3.1, 3.2, 4.1	Audio Practice Workbook

Day	Objectives	Sessions	Activities	Time	Standards	Resources/ Homework
11	To integrate vocabulary and grammar	**Desafío 2 – Comunicación** (220–221) • Warm-Up: Independent Starter • *Comunicación*: Review main vocabulary and grammar	36–38	5 m. 45 m.	1.1, 1.2, 1.3, 3.1, 5.1	Audio Practice Workbook
12	To assess student proficiency	**Desafío 2 – Evaluación** (221) • Warm-Up: *Final del desafío* • Quiz on *Desafío 2*	39	30 m. 20 m.	1.3, 3.1	*Tu desafío*
13	To describe the political divisions of land and to use irregular verbs in the past tense	**Desafío 3 – El Maratón de las Escaleras** (222–223) • Warm-Up: Independent Starter • *Fotonovela: El Maratón de las Escaleras* • *Cultura: El Maratón de las Escaleras de Valparaíso*	40–43 44	5 m. 30 m. 15 m.	1.1, 1.2, 1.3, 2.1	Visual Presentation Audio Video *Tu desafío*
14	To describe the political divisions of land and to use numbers from 101–1,000	**Desafío 3 – Vocabulario** (224–225) • Warm-Up: Independent Starter • Vocabulary: *Divisiones políticas. Números del 101 al 1.000* • *Conexiones: El dinero chileno*	45–47 48	5 m. 35 m. 10 m.	1.1, 1.2, 1.3, 3.1, 3.2, 5.1	Audio Practice Workbook
15	To use irregular verbs in the past tense	**Desafío 3 – Gramática** (226–227) • Warm-Up: Independent Starter • Grammar: *Verbos irregulares en el pasado. 'Decir' y 'hacer'* • *Comunidades: El lapislázuli*	49–53 54	5 m. 35 m. 10 m.	1.1, 1.2, 1.3, 2.2, 3.1, 3.2, 4.1, 5.1	Audio Practice Workbook
16	To use irregular verbs in the past tense	**Desafío 3 – Gramática** (228–229) • Warm-Up: Independent Starter • Grammar: *Verbos irregulares en el pasado. 'Estar' y 'tener'* • *Conexiones: El Festival Internacional de la Canción de Viña del Mar*	55–58 59	5 m. 35 m. 10 m.	1.1, 1.2, 1.3, 2.1, 3.1, 3.2, 4.1, 4.2	Practice Workbook
17	To integrate vocabulary and grammar	**Desafío 3 – Comunicación** (230–231) • Warm-Up: Independent Starter • *Comunicación*: Review main vocabulary and grammar	60–62	5 m. 45 m.	1.2, 1.3, 3.1	Audio Practice Workbook
18	To assess student proficiency	**Desafío 3 – Evaluación** (231) • Warm-Up: *Final del desafío* • Quiz on *Desafío 3*	63	30 m. 20 m.	1.3	
19	To talk about nature and the environment, and to express permission and prohibition	**Desafío 4 – La famosa Ruta W** (232–233) • Warm-Up: Independent Starter • *Fotonovela: La famosa Ruta W* • *Cultura: Parque Nacional Torres del Paine*	64–66 67	5 m. 35 m. 10 m.	1.1, 1.2, 1.3, 3.1, 3.2, 5.1	Visual Presentation Audio
20	To talk about nature and the environment	**Desafío 4 – Vocabulario** (234–235) • Warm-Up: Independent Starter • Vocabulary: *La naturaleza y el medio ambiente* • *Conexiones: ¡A reciclar!*	68–70 71	5 m. 35 m. 10 m.	1.1, 1.2, 1.3, 3.1, 3.2, 5.1	Audio Practice Workbook

Unit 8 Chile

Day	Objectives	Sessions	Activities	Time	Standards	Resources/Homework
21	To express permission and prohibition	**Desafío 4 – Gramática** (236–237) • Warm-Up: Independent Starter • Grammar: *Expresar permiso y prohibición* • *Conexiones: Animales en peligro de extinción*	72–75 76	5 m. 35 m. 10 m.	1.1, 1.2, 1.3, 3.1, 3.2, 4.1	Audio Practice Workbook
22	To integrate vocabulary and grammar	**Desafío 4 – Comunicación** (238–239) • Warm-Up: Independent Starter • *Comunicación*: Review main vocabulary and grammar	77–80	5 m. 45 m.	1.1, 1.2, 1.3, 3.1, 5.1	Audio Practice Workbook
23	To assess student proficiency	**Desafío 4 – Evaluación** (239) • Warm-Up: *Final del desafío* • Quiz on *Desafío 4*	81	30 m. 20 m.	1.1, 1.2, 1.3	*Tu desafío*
24	To integrate language in context	**Todo junto** (240–241) • Warm-Up: Independent Starter • *Todo junto*	82–84	5 m. 45 m.	1.1, 1.2, 1.3, 5.2	Audio Practice Workbook
25	To integrate language in context	**El encuentro** (242–243) • Warm-Up: Independent Starter • *El encuentro: En la Plaza de Armas*	85–86	5 m. 45 m.	1.1, 1.3, 3.1	
26	To learn about Argentine customs and traditions	**Mapa cultural – Chile** (244–247) • Warm-Up: Independent Starter • *Mapa cultural: Chile*	87–90	5 m. 45 m.	1.1, 1.2, 1.3, 2.2, 3.1, 3.2	Video Practice Workbook
27	To read the works of a Chilean poet	**Lectura – Oda a la manzana** (248–249) • Warm-Up: Independent Starter • *Lectura: Oda a la manzana*	91–94	5 m. 45 m.	1.2, 1.3, 3.1, 3.2	*Tu desafío*
28	To review vocabulary	**Repaso – Vocabulario** (250–251) • Warm-Up: Independent Starter • *Repaso: Vocabulario*	1–4	5 m. 45 m.	1.2, 1.3	Practice Workbook
29	To review grammar and culture	**Repaso – Gramática** (252–253) • Warm-Up: Independent Starter • *Repaso: Gramática*	5–9	5 m. 45 m.	1.2, 1.3, 2.1, 2.2, 3.1, 5.2	Practice Workbook
30	To conduct research and present findings on a poster	**Proyecto – Animales en peligro** (254–255) • Warm-Up: Read project outline • Work on project		5 m. 45 m.	1.1, 1.2, 1.3, 3.1, 5.1, 5.2	
31	To conduct research and present findings on a poster	**Proyecto – Animales en peligro** (254–255) • Warm-Up: Review project outline • Work on project		5 m. 45 m.	1.1, 1.2, 1.3, 3.1, 5.1, 5.2	
32	To present projects	**Proyecto – Animales en peligro** (254–255) • Warm-Up: Prepare presentations • Project presentations		5 m. 45 m.	1.1, 1.2, 1.3, 3.1, 5.1, 5.2	
33	To present projects	**Proyecto – Animales en peligro** (254–255) • Warm-Up: Prepare presentations • Project presentations		5 m. 45 m.	1.1, 1.2, 1.3, 3.1, 5.1, 5.2	
34	To assess student proficiency	**Assessment** • *Autoevaluación* (255) • Test on Unit 8		5 m. 45 m.	1.2, 1.3	

Lesson Plans (90-Minute Classes)

Day	Objectives	Sessions	Activities	Time	Standards	Resources/ Homework
1	To introduce Chile and to discuss the pairs' challenges	**Chile / La llegada** (200–205) • Warm-Up: Country orientation • Chile • Images and functions • Presentation: *En Santiago de Chile* • *Expresiones útiles* and *¿Quién ganará?*	 1 2–4	 5 m. 10 m. 20 m. 20 m. 35 m.	1.1, 1.2, 1.3, 2.2, 3.1, 4.1	Visual Presentation Video Audio Practice Workbook
2	To talk about the universe and to express cause	**Desafío 1 – Las estrellas de Atacama / Vocabulario** (206–209) • Warm-Up: Independent Starter • *Fotonovela: Las estrellas de Atacama* • *Cultura: El Valle de la Luna* • Vocabulary: *El universo* • *Cultura: San Pedro de Atacama*	 5–7 8 9–11 12	 5 m. 30 m. 10 m. 35 m. 10 m.	1.1, 1.2, 1.3, 3.1, 3.2	Visual Presentation Audio Practice Workbook
3	To express cause using *porque* and *por,* and to integrate vocabulary and grammar	**Desafío 1 – Gramática / Comunicación** (210–213) • Warm-Up: Independent Starter • Grammar: *Expresar causa* • *Conexiones: El salar de Atacama* • *Comunicación*: Review main vocabulary and grammar	 13–16 17 18–20	 5 m. 40 m. 10 m 35 m.	1.1, 1.2, 1.3, 3.1, 4.1, 5.1	Audio Practice Workbook
4	To assess student proficiency, to talk about geography, and to express quantity	**Desafío 1 – Evaluación / Desafío 2 – Una estatua falsa** (213–215) • Warm-Up: *Final del desafío* • Quiz on *Desafío 1* • *Fotonovela: Una estatua falsa* • *Cultura: La Isla de Pascua*	 21 22–25 26	 25 m. 20 m. 30 m. 15 m.	1.1, 1.2, 1.3, 2.2, 3.1, 3.2	Visual Presentation Audio Video
5	To speak about geography, and to learn and use indefinite adjectives to express quantity	**Desafío 2 – Vocabulario / Gramática** (216–219) • Warm-Up: Independent Starter • Vocabulary: *Geografía* • *Conexiones: Un balneario en Chile* • Grammar: *Expresar cantidad. Los indefinidos* • *Conexiones: La deforestación*	 27–29 30 31–34 35	 5 m. 30 m. 10 m. 30 m. 15 m.	1.1, 1.2, 1.3, 3.1, 3.2, 4.1	Audio Practice Workbook
6	To integrate vocabulary and grammar, and to assess student proficiency	**Desafío 2 – Comunicación / Evaluación** (220–221) • Warm-Up: Independent Starter • *Comunicación*: Review main vocabulary and grammar • *Final del desafío* • Quiz on *Desafío 2*	 36–38 39	 5 m. 45 m. 20 m. 20 m.	1.1, 1.2, 1.3, 3.1, 5.1	Audio Practice Workbook *Tu desafío*

Day	Objectives	Sessions	Activities	Time	Standards	Resources/ Homework
7	To describe the political divisions of land, to use numbers 101–1,000, and to express irregular verbs in the past tense	**Desafío 3 – El Maratón de las Escaleras / Vocabulario** (222–225) • Warm-Up: Independent Starter • Fotonovela: El Maratón de las Escaleras • Cultura: El Maratón de las Escaleras de Valparaíso • Vocabulary: Divisiones políticas. Números del 101 al 1.000 • Conexiones: El dinero chileno	 40–43 44 45–47 48	 5 m. 30 m. 15 m. 30 m. 10 m.	1.1, 1.2, 1.3, 2.1, 3.1, 3.2, 5.1	Visual Presentation Audio Video Practice Workbook *Tu desafío*
8	To use irregular verbs in the past tense	**Desafío 3 – Gramática** (226–229) • Warm-Up: Independent Starter • Grammar: Verbos irregulares en el pasado. 'Decir' y 'hacer' • Comunidades: El lapislázuli • Grammar: Verbos irregulares en el pasado. 'Estar' y 'tener' • Conexiones: El Festival Internacional de la Canción de Viña del Mar	 49–53 54 55–58 59	 5 m. 30 m. 15 m. 30 m. 10 m.	1.1, 1.2, 1.3, 2.1, 2.2, 3.1, 3.2, 4.1, 4.2, 5.1	Audio Practice Workbook
9	To integrate vocabulary and grammar and to assess student proficiency	**Desafío 3 – Comunicación / Evaluación** (230–231) • Warm-Up: Independent Starter • Comunicación: Review main vocabulary and grammar • Final del desafío • Quiz on Desafío 3	 60–62 63	 5 m. 45 m. 20 m. 20 m.	1.1, 1.2, 1.3, 2.1, 3.1, 3.2, 4.1, 4.2	Audio Practice Workbook
10	To talk about nature and the environment and to express permission and prohibition	**Desafío 4 – La famosa Ruta W / Vocabulario** (232–235) • Warm-Up: Independent Starter • Fotonovela: La famosa Ruta W • Cultura: Parque Nacional Torres del Paine • Vocabulary: La naturaleza y el medio ambiente • Conexiones: ¡A reciclar!	 64–66 67 68–70 71	 5 m. 30 m. 15 m. 30 m. 10 m.	1.1, 1.2, 1.3, 3.1, 3.2, 5.1	Visual Presentation Audio Practice Workbook
11	To express permission and prohibition and to integrate vocabulary and grammar	**Desafío 4 – Gramática / Comunicación** (236–239) • Warm-Up: Independent Starter • Grammar: Expresar permiso y prohibición • Conexiones: Animales en peligro de extinción • Comunicación: Review main vocabulary and grammar	 72–75 76 77–80	 5 m. 30 m. 10 m. 45 m.	1.1, 1.2, 1.3, 3.1, 3.2, 4.1, 5.1	Audio Practice Workbook
12	To assess student proficiency	**Desafío 4 – Evaluación** (239) • Warm-Up: Final del desafío • Last minute questions • Quiz on Desafío 4	 81	 40 m. 30 m. 20 m.	1.1, 1.2, 1.3	*Tu desafío*

Day	Objectives	Sessions	Activities	Time	Standards	Resources/ Homework
13	To integrate language in context	**Todo junto / El encuentro** (240–243) • Warm-Up: Independent Starter • *Todo junto* • *El encuentro: En la Plaza de Armas*	 82–84 85–86	 5 m. 40 m. 45 m.	1.1, 1.2, 1.3, 3.1, 5.2	Audio Practice Workbook
14	To learn about Chilean customs and traditions, and to read the works of a Chilean poet	**Mapa cultural / Lectura** (244–249) • Warm-Up: Independent Starter • *Mapa cultural: Chile* • *Lectura: Oda a la manzana*	 87–90 91–94	 5 m. 45 m. 40 m.	1.1, 1.2, 1.3, 2.2, 3.1, 3.2	Video Practice Workbook *Tu desafío*
15	To review vocabulary, grammar, and culture	**Repaso – Vocabulario / Gramática** (250–253) • Warm-Up: Independent Starter • *Repaso: Vocabulario* • *Repaso: Gramática*	 1–4 5–9	 5 m. 40 m. 45 m.	1.2, 1.3, 2.1, 2.2, 3.1, 5.2	Practice Workbook
16	To conduct research and present findings on a poster	**Proyecto** (254–255) • Warm-Up: Review project outline • Work on project		 5 m. 85 m.	1.1, 1.2, 1.3, 3.1, 5.1, 5.2	
17	To present projects	**Proyecto** (254–255) • Warm-Up: Prepare presentations • Project presentations		 5 m. 85 m.	1.1, 1.2, 1.3, 3.1, 5.1, 5.2	
18	To present projects and to assess student proficiency	**Proyecto / Assessment** (254–255) • Warm-Up: Prepare presentations • Project presentations • *Autoevaluación* • Test on Unit 8		 5 m. 30 m. 10 m. 45 m.	1.1, 1.2, 1.3, 3.1, 5.1, 5.2	

10 Errores

1. La Tierra es el planeta donde vivimos.
2. El Sol se mueve alrededor de la Tierra.
3. Los eclipses ocurren todos los días.
4. El Sol es muy importante para los animales y las plantas.
5. El trabajo de un astronauta es explorar el espacio.
6. El planeta Marte es el más grande del sistema solar.

18 Nuestro universo

¡Bienvenidos a nuestra exposición de Astronomía!

Hoy vamos a observar el espacio. Aquí está el Sol. El Sol es la estrella más cercana al planeta Tierra. Nuestro planeta forma parte del sistema solar. Desde la Tierra se pueden ver otros planetas, como Venus, Marte y Saturno. Saturno es un planeta con anillos. Y Júpiter es el planeta más grande del sistema solar. Los cometas también forman parte de nuestro sistema solar. Están formados por hielo y otras sustancias. Este es Neil Armstrong. Él fue el primer hombre que caminó por la Luna.

24 Una isla espectacular

–¡Vamos a visitar la Isla de Pascua! Tengo muchas ganas de ver los moáis, las famosas esculturas de esa isla. También quiero practicar un poco de rapanui.

–¿Rapanui?

–Sí, rapanui. En la Isla de Pascua hablan dos lenguas: el español y el rapanui.

–Ah, qué interesante. Creo que es un lugar con una geografía espectacular. La isla principal está formada por tres volcanes.

–¡Tres volcanes! ¿Y todos están activos?

–No, Tess, no hay ningún volcán activo en la isla.

–La isla principal tiene forma de triángulo y está rodeada de pequeñas islas.

–Sí, se llaman islotes.

–En la Isla de Pascua hay pocos árboles porque no llueve con frecuencia. La isla está casi deforestada.

–¡Qué triste!

29 Una guía para turistas

–Tess, en los Estados Unidos hay playas muy bonitas, ¿verdad?

–Sí, Claudia, en los Estados Unidos tenemos mar al este y al oeste. Mis playas favoritas están en la costa oeste, en el estado de California.

–¿Y conoces Nueva York?

–Sí, fuimos allí el verano pasado. Manhattan me encantó. ¿Sabes que Manhattan es una isla?

–¿Una isla? ¡Qué interesante! Tengo muchas ganas de visitar el norte del continente americano: Canadá, los Estados Unidos y México.

–Los tres países son muy bonitos. Hay paisajes preciosos y muy variados.

–Oye, Tess, ¿hay algún bosque tropical en los Estados Unidos?

–No, no hay ninguno. Hay otro tipo de bosques, pero no hay ningún bosque tropical. Solo hay bosques tropicales en Puerto Rico.

–¿Y desiertos? ¿Hay desiertos en los Estados Unidos?

–Sí, tenemos desiertos. En el oeste de los Estados Unidos hay un gran desierto: el desierto de Arizona.

–Tengo muchas ganas de conocer tu país.

34 Impresiones y experiencias

–¿A ustedes les gusta caminar por las montañas? A mí me encanta.

–Sí, Tess, a mí también me gusta.

–¿Y a ti, Andy?

–No, a mí no me gusta caminar por las montañas.

–Tenemos que ir a la ciudad. Quiero comprar muchos recuerdos de nuestro viaje, pero en especial quiero un moái. ¿Alguien sabe dónde puedo comprar una miniatura?

–Sí, claro. En todas las tiendas de turistas hay moáis en miniatura. Son típicos. Uf, ya estoy un poco cansado de viajar. ¿Ustedes no?

–Sí. A Tess y a mí nos gusta mucho viajar, pero también estamos un poco cansadas y extrañamos a nuestra familia.

–Claro. A mí también me gusta mucho viajar, pero tengo ganas de volver a casa.

37 Similitudes y diferencias

La situación ecológica de la Isla de Pascua es muy triste. La isla está casi deforestada. Hay muy pocos árboles. Llueve muy poco y la falta de agua afecta a las plantas y a los animales. Además, por su situación geográfica, hay pocas especies animales.

42 ¿Qué viste?

–¡Hola, Daniel! ¿Cómo estás?

–Hola, Julia. Estoy bien, gracias.

–¿Te gusta el Maratón de las Escaleras?

–Sí. Me parece muy interesante.

–¡Ya vienen los participantes! Hay un hombre muy alto. ¿Lo ves?

–Sí. ¡Mira, y hay un hombre vestido de gaucho!

–Ah, sí. ¡Y también hay un niño corriendo! Mira, ahora están pasando cerca de la zapatería.

–No veo nada…

–Es que hay mucha gente.

–¡El próximo año yo también voy a participar en el Maratón de las Escaleras!

47 A sumar y restar

–¿Qué vas a comprar en el supermercado, Tess?

–Necesito un sobre para escribir una carta. Vale 200 pesos, pero solo tengo 175 pesos. Mamá, ¿tú qué vas a comprar?

–Estoy pensando… Tengo 980 pesos y me gusta mucho ese chocolate. Cuesta 795 pesos. Sí, lo voy a comprar.

–Yo tengo 460 pesos y quiero comprar una bolsa de papas fritas. Pero las papas cuestan 900 pesos… Y tú, Rita, ¿qué quieres comprar?

–Yo quiero comprar una botella de agua. Tengo 715 pesos y el agua
cuesta 354 pesos.

–Yo quiero un jugo, igual que mi nieto Tim. Tengo 625 pesos y el jugo
cuesta 600 pesos. ¿Y tú, Diana?

–Yo tengo 860 pesos y quiero comprar unas manzanas.

–¿Cuánto cuestan?

–499 pesos.

50 Tim dijo que...

–Valparaíso es una ciudad muy bonita, ¿no?

–¿Qué dijiste, abuelo? No te escuché.

–Dije que esta ciudad es muy bonita.

–Sí, a mí me gusta mucho Valparaíso. Es una ciudad fascinante.

–Hoy hay mucha gente. ¿Es por el maratón?

–Sí. En el anuncio dijeron que hay más de mil personas aquí.

–Este maratón es muy emocionante.

–¿Cómo se les ocurrió la idea de correr por las escaleras, abuelo?
Son muy altas.

–Un participante me dijo que es un buen ejercicio.

52 ¿Qué hicieron?

–Tim, Mack, ¿qué hicieron este fin de semana?

–Mi abuelo y yo fuimos a un taller de artesanía. Hicimos unas figuras
de cerámica muy bonitas para mi abuela. ¿Y tú, Diana?

–Yo conocí a una chica muy simpática. Ahora tengo una nueva amiga.

–¡Qué bueno! ¿Y tú, Rita, qué hiciste?

–Yo hice un viaje a la costa. ¡Y me gustó mucho!

–Andy, Janet, ¿qué hicieron ustedes?

–Hicimos una cena deliciosa. Andy hizo una ensalada y yo hice pasta
con vegetales.

–¡Qué rico! ¿Y ustedes qué hicieron, Tess?

–Mi mamá y yo hicimos planes para el verano porque mi familia viaja
con frecuencia.

66 Fotos del parque

¡Hola, mamá! ¿Cómo estás? ¿Recibiste mis fotos? ¡El parque Torres
del Paine es precioso! Al llegar, hicimos muchas fotos de animales.
Luego caminamos por la famosa Ruta W y llegamos a un lago muy
grande. Es un lago muy bonito, pero no recuerdo el nombre. Después
de pasear por el lago vimos a unos chicos dejando basura en el parque.
No se puede botar la basura en el parque, porque es muy malo para
las plantas y para los animales. La tía Rita y yo la vamos a recoger.
Creo que mis fotos te van a gustar mucho. ¡Nos vemos pronto!

69 ¿Oíste algo?

–Tengo miedo, tía.

–No tengas miedo, Diana. Estamos en un parque muy seguro.

–¿Oíste eso?

–Sí, lo oí. No te preocupes, solo fue el aire.

–¡Qué susto!

–Escucha... ¿Qué animal es ese?

–¿Qué animal, tía? ¿Es peligroso?

–No, es un pájaro muy bonito. Tranquila, Diana. [pausa]

–Mira esta hoja, es muy suave. Tócala.

–Sí, es muy suave.

–¡Ay! ¡Algo me está tocando!

–Solo es un insecto, tía. El insecto te tocó.

–¡Qué susto!

74 Empacando para el viaje

–Tía, quiero llevar mi radio al parque para escuchar música.

–No se puede escuchar la radio en el parque, Diana.

–Entonces voy a llevar un libro. ¿Se puede leer en el parque?

–Sí, claro.

–También quiero llevar mi balón para jugar al fútbol.

–No se puede jugar con un balón en el parque, es peligroso.

–¿Y puedo llevar un videojuego?

–Sí. Pero ¿piensas jugar con el videojuego en el parque?

–No lo sé todavía, pero quiero saber si se puede o no se puede.
¿Y puedo llevar unas botellas de refrescos?

–Sí, pero tienes que reciclar las botellas. No se puede dejar basura
en el parque.

–Está bien. ¡Ah! No puedo olvidar mi cámara. Yo sé que allí se pueden
tomar fotos.

79 ¿Qué puede hacer ella?

Hoy me siento inspirada. Quiero hacer más cosas para cuidar el medio
ambiente.

Primero voy a plantar un árbol. Y pienso proteger a todos los insectos.
Ahora sé que los insectos y los animales son muy importantes para
el medio ambiente. Además, voy a botar siempre la basura en el lugar
correcto. Y voy a reciclar el metal, el vidrio, el plástico y el papel. Reciclar
es muy importante. Y también puedo colaborar con las organizaciones
que ayudan a proteger la naturaleza.

83 Un programa especial

Esta noche en «Descubre el espacio» vamos a conocer el espacio
y nuestro sistema solar. Muchas personas creen que hay vida en otros
planetas. ¡Vamos a explorar esta posibilidad! ¿Hay plantas o animales
en Venus, Marte o Júpiter? ¿Hay océanos, lagos y continentes en otros
planetas? ¿Creen que hay vida en planetas de otros sistemas solares?
¿Pueden imaginar países y ciudades en otros lugares del espacio? Esta
noche en «Descubre el espacio». En el canal 300, a las nueve de la noche.

Chile

The Unit

- The theme of this unit is the physical world in the context of different regions of Chile. The participants will perform a variety of tasks relating to nature, geography, and other aspects of ecological interest as they visit different parts of Chile.

- The pairs will perform different tasks given to them by Héctor Basualdo, their Chilean host.

  – *Desafío 1.* Andy and Janet are in the *Valle de la Luna* in the Atacama Desert. Their task is to spend the night looking for a rock formation in the shape of a howling dog.

  – *Desafío 2.* Tess and Patricia are on Easter Island. They have to find and topple a fake moai.

  – *Desafío 3.* Tim and Mack are at the *Maratón de las Escaleras* in Valparaiso. They have to run this challenging race.

  – *Desafío 4.* Diana and Rita are visiting the Torres del Paine National Park. They have to hike the W route and collect five pounds of trash as they do it.

Activities	Standards	Resources
Chile	1.2, 2.2, 4.1	Video

Teaching Suggestions

Warm-Up / Independent Starter

- Have students divide a piece of paper into four sections. Students will use the *Vocabulario* for each *Desafío* as a heading for each section. For example, the first section will be labeled *Desafío 1: El universo.* They should write five things they would like to learn under each category.

Chile

- Chile is located in South America. It is the longest, north to south, country in the world. Because of its elongated shape, its geography and climate are varied. Chile is a representative democracy and is one of the most prosperous countries in South America.

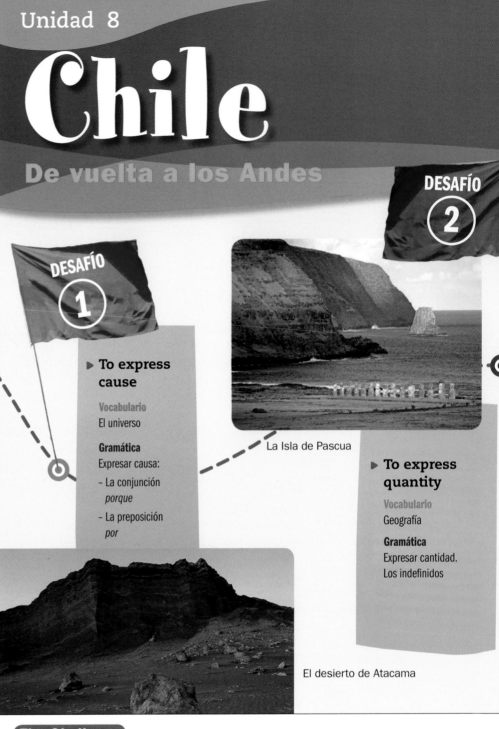

Unidad 8

Chile

De vuelta a los Andes

DESAFÍO 1

▶ **To express cause**

Vocabulario
El universo

Gramática
Expresar causa:
- La conjunción *porque*
- La preposición *por*

El desierto de Atacama

DESAFÍO 2

La Isla de Pascua

▶ **To express quantity**

Vocabulario
Geografía

Gramática
Expresar cantidad.
Los indefinidos

The Challenge

DESAFÍO 1

El desierto de Atacama

The Atacama Desert is one of the driest places in the world. It is 50 times drier than Death Valley in California. Research suggests that some places in the Atacama Desert have not had rainfall for over 400 years. Although this desert occupies 40,600 square miles, it is not an empty territory. In fact, it is estimated that more than a million people live in the different towns, villages, and cities dotting this desert. San Pedro de Atacama—an old village oasis with a population of approximately 2,000 permanent residents—is one of those towns.

DESAFÍO 2

La Isla de Pascua

This Polynesian island is a territory of Chile, annexed in 1888. It is world famous for its moai statues, the legacy of the Rapanui native people. While the first Europeans to arrive on Eastern Island in 1722 were amazed by the moai statues, not much was known about the Rapanui people. Large numbers of islanders were taken by Peruvian slave ships in the 1800s. This slave trade as well as diseases brought to the island by successive migrations of people from other places killed off most of the population. Today the Rapanui population is around 1,500 people.

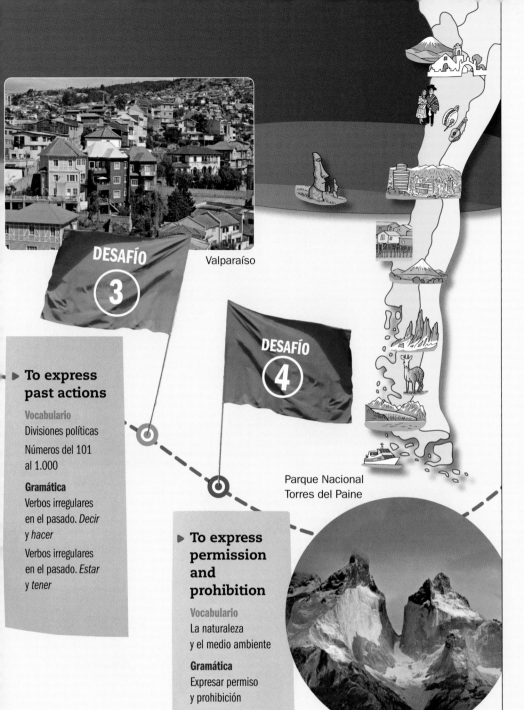

Valparaíso

DESAFÍO 3

▶ **To express past actions**

Vocabulario
Divisiones políticas

Números del 101 al 1.000

Gramática
Verbos irregulares en el pasado. *Decir* y *hacer*

Verbos irregulares en el pasado. *Estar* y *tener*

DESAFÍO 4

Parque Nacional Torres del Paine

▶ **To express permission and prohibition**

Vocabulario
La naturaleza y el medio ambiente

Gramática
Expresar permiso y prohibición

⚑ **DESAFÍO 3**

Valparaíso

The *Maratón de las Escaleras* in Valparaiso was started in 2008. It is called "the Stairs Marathon" because the course includes stairs in an urban setting. Despite its name, the race is 5 km (3 miles) and it includes 526 steps in three stairways. The race was not run in 2009, however, there are plans being made to make this an annual event.

⚑ **DESAFÍO 4**

Parque Nacional Torres del Paine

This park in southern Chile has many geographic features of great scientific interest, including mountains, lakes, rivers, and glaciers. The mountain range *Cuernos del Paine* is one of its most representative landmarks. Also included in the park are campsites, dormitory-style lodgings, and world-class hotels so that tourists can choose their own comfort level while still enjoying the park.

- Have students look at a map of Chile. Ask them to locate each of the four places to which the participants will travel. According to what they know about geography and the illustrations on the map, have students describe how they think these places look.

Picture Discussion

- Have students look at the photos on pages 200–201. Ask them to work in pairs to describe what they see in the pictures. Then have them predict what this unit will be about. They should try to answer questions such as: What do they think will be asked of the participants? How long will each task take? Which tasks would they like to take part in?

El desierto de Atacama

- Working in pairs, have students discuss what they know about deserts. They can write their information on a three-column chart with the headings "I know for a fact," "I am almost sure," and "I am not that sure." As they present their information to the class, you can clarify and check for accuracy.

La Isla de Pascua

- Have students think about why people create sculptures or art in general. Have them summarize their conclusions in a bulleted paragraph. Ask them if any of their answers could apply to the building of moai on Easter Island.

Valparaíso

- Based on the picture, discuss the reason for the existence of a "Stairs Marathon" in Valparaiso. Ask them to vote for the best answer and the most imaginative one.

Parque Nacional Torres del Paine

- Ask students to pretend that they are park rangers. Ask them to list the vocabulary they would need to know for explaining the features of this park to visitors.

Objectives

- In this unit students will learn about nature and geography. By the end of the unit students will be able to
  - Express cause.
  - Use the conjunction *porque* and the preposition *por*.
  - Express quantity.
  - Use the past tense forms of irregular verbs.
  - Express that something can be done or not.

La llegada

Presentation

- This section presents the main themes for the unit. The participants meet in Santiago de Chile with Héctor Basualdo, their Chilean host, who will share their individual tasks with them in each of the four places that they will visit.

- The dialogue previews:
  - Geographical features vocabulary.
  - Nature and ecology vocabulary.
  - Use of the past tense forms.
  - Asking if something can be done.

Activities	Standards	Resources
Fotonovela	1.2	Vis. Pres.
1.	1.2, 1.3	

Teaching Suggestions

Warm-Up / Independent Starter

- Have students write a sentence with each of the following cognates: *montaña, universo, océano, desierto,* and *maratón.* Have students with expanding abilities write a story to read to the class.

 La fotonovela

Before Viewing

- Ask students to look at the photos on page 202. Have them scan the text for words they know or they can identify, such as *casa, museo, poeta,* and *artista.* Have students explain how these words help them understand the meaning of the dialogue.

While Viewing

- As students watch and listen to the dialogue, ask them to focus on complete (contextual) meaning rather than on individual words. Have them write down clues that may help them retell what happened in the dialogue.

After Viewing

- In small groups, have students retell the dialogue as a story. They should write at least five lines in the preterite tense. Then each group can report their story back to the class by re-enacting the *fotonovela.* Compare the different "versions" of the story.

202

En Santiago de Chile

 In this unit the four pairs are in Santiago, the capital of Chile. Héctor Basualdo, their Chilean host, welcomes them at *La Chascona.* This house was once owned by Pablo Neruda, a Nobel Prize-winning poet.

202 doscientos dos

Differentiated Instruction

DEVELOPING LEARNERS

- After reading the *fotonovela*, check for comprehension by asking students to match the following key words to each of the pairs' tasks: *desierto* (Andy y Janet), *estatuas* (Tess y Patricia), *maratón* (Tim y Mack), and *reciclar* (Diana y Rita).

EXPANDING LEARNERS

- In small groups, have students choose a speech bubble from the *fotonovela* to recite. Group members should first guess who made the statement and then tell what they looked like or what they were holding in the *fotonovela.* For example:
  - A. *"No sé. ¡Todos parecen iguales!".*
  - B. *Lo dice Patricia. Está mirando un póster de la Isla de Pascua.*

La llegada

¡Tenemos que pasar una noche en el desierto!

¡Qué impresionante!

¡Cuántas estatuas! ¡Son enormes! ¿Cómo vamos a encontrar el moái falso?

No sé. ¡Todos parecen iguales!

¿Puedo botar una botella de plástico en este contenedor?

Este maratón va por las calles de la ciudad...

Sí, es un circuito de cinco kilómetros. Lo vi por televisión.

¡No, hay que reciclarla!

1 **¿Comprendes?**

▶ **Responde.** Answer the questions according to what you read.

1. ¿Qué es La Chascona? ¿Por qué es famosa?
2. ¿Quién es Matilde?
3. ¿Cómo son las estatuas?
4. ¿Qué quiere botar Diana en el contenedor de basura?

Activities

1. Have students use the dialogue to create two more questions. Ask for volunteers to read their new questions aloud, and select those that promote critical thinking to discuss as a class. For example: *¿Por qué es la casa de Pablo Neruda un museo?*

Answer Key

1. 1. Es la casa del poeta chileno Pablo Neruda. Ahora es un museo.
2. La esposa de Pablo Neruda.
3. Los moáis son enormes.
4. Diana quiere botar una botella de plástico.

Additional Resources

Fans Online activities
Practice Workbook

HERITAGE LANGUAGE LEARNERS

• Have students look at the portrait Diego Rivera made of Pablo Neruda's wife, Matilde, at http://redescolar.ilce.edu.mx/redescolar/biblioteca/literatura/trabajosydias/neruda/retrato.htm. Ask them to write a short poem based on the painting. Have them share their poems with the class.

CRITICAL THINKING

• Ask students to think about the following essential question: Why might someone have a painting of another person made? Have students look at a variety of commissioned paintings on the Internet. Do these paintings have anything in common? If you knew Diego Rivera or another famous painter, who would you ask to make a painting for you? Why?

203

Unit 8
La llegada

Presentation

■ In this section, students will use expressions to
  – Wish someone good luck.
  – Show admiration.
  – Stress quantity.

Activities	Standards	Resources
Expresiones útiles	1.2, 1.3, 4.1	
2.	1.3	
3.	1.1, 1.2	
4.	1.1, 1.2, 1.3	

Teaching Suggestions

Warm-Up / Independent Starter

■ Have students pair the following sentences with an expression they already know. They may use their books to scan previous units.
  1. *La maestra de Ciencias está enferma.*
  2. *No tengo dinero en la cartera.*
  3. *¡Esta barra de chocolate cuesta diez dólares!*
  4. *Señora vendedora, me gusta esta falda.*
  5. *Tengo una A en mi clase de Español.*

Preparation

■ Review the *Expresiones útiles* by using them in personalized contexts. You can write the following paragraph on the board:
Voy a correr en un maratón. Mi madre tiene setenta años y va a correr también. El maratón tiene 26 millas. Van a participar 10,000 personas. Have students plug in the *Expresiones útiles* in the paragraph that would apply in each situation.

Activities

2. Expand this activity by having students create original contexts for the four expressions. Ask them to illustrate the context and exchange their drawings with a partner to resolve the activity. In pairs, ask students to act out the original contexts they have created. Have the rest of the class say what would be the appropriate expression for each context. Invite students who guessed correctly to write the expressions on the board. Make sure they include the inverted exclamation point at the beginning of each expression.

204

EXPRESIONES ÚTILES

¡Cuántas estatuas!

To wish someone good luck:
  ¡Suerte!

To show admiration:
  ¡Qué impresionante!

To stress quantity:
  ¡Cuánto dinero!
  ¡Cuánta gente!
  ¡Cuántos moáis!
  ¡Cuántas estatuas!

2 Expresiones

▶ **Escribe.** Match each expression with the corresponding picture.

a. ¡Suerte!	b. ¡Qué impresionante!	c. ¡Cuánta gente!	d. ¡Qué grande!

204 doscientos cuatro

Differentiated Instruction

DEVELOPING LEARNERS

• To practice adjective-noun agreement, have students practice the *¡Cuántas estatuas!* expression using different nouns in place of *estatuas*. Have them use a chart like the one below for organization.

Cuánta	comida
Cuántas	…
Cuánto	…
Cuántos	…

EXPANDING LEARNERS

• Have students think of situations in which the *Expresiones útiles* would be used in their own lives. Have them choose one expression and act out a short dialogue in which the expression can serve as the last line. For example:
  A. *Tengo que ir a la clase de Ciencias.*
  B. *¿Tienes mucho que estudiar para esa clase?*
  A. *Sí. Tengo que escribir tres trabajos sobre los experimentos de la semana pasada.*
  B. *¡Cuánta tarea!*

¿Quién ganará?

3 Los desafíos

 ▶ **Habla.** What will be the challenge for each pair? Think about this question and discuss it with your classmates.

DESAFÍO ①

Las estrellas de Atacama

Andy y Janet

DESAFÍO ②

Una estatua falsa

Tess y Patricia

DESAFÍO ③

El Maratón de las Escaleras

163   164

Tim y Mack

DESAFÍO ④

Diana y Rita

La famosa Ruta W

4 Las votaciones

 ▶ **Decide.** Who will win this unit's challenge? Vote to choose the most enriching task.

Enriquecedor

HERITAGE LANGUAGE LEARNERS

- There are many ways of expressing admiration or positive feelings in Spanish that start with the interjection ¡Qué …! Have heritage students create a list of these different expressions. Ask them to combine all their expressions into one big class list and post it in the classroom. Students can also label each expression with its country or countries of use. For example:
  - ¡Qué chulo! (Mexico)
  - ¡Qué guay! (Spain)
  - ¡Qué chévere! (Colombia, Venezuela)

COOPERATIVE LEARNERS

- Have expanding learners work with developing learners to practice situations in which the expressions might be used. Expanding students should think of a sentence that would prompt one of the expressions and the partner should then use it in his or her response. For example:
  - A. Tengo que hacer un examen hoy.
  - B. ¡Suerte!

¿Quién ganará?

3. Encourage students to share their ideas and elicit answers if they are unsure about the different desafíos.

Remind them that:
1. Andy and Janet have to spend the night in the Atacama Desert looking for a rock formation in the shape of a howling dog.
2. Tess and Patricia have to find a fake moai on Easter Island and topple it.
3. Tim and Mack have to run the Stairs Marathon in Valparaiso.
4. Diana and Rita have to collect five pounds of trash as they hike the W route in the Torres del Paine National Park.

4. Ask students to think about the word *enriching*. As a class, discuss what this word means to students and the criteria they use to judge how enriching something is. Based on the pictures on the page, the responses on the board, and your class discussion about this word, have students vote for the team they believe will perform the most enriching challenge.

Answer Key

2. a. 4   b. 3   c. 2   d. 1
3. Answers will vary.
4. Answers will vary.

Additional Resources

Fans Online activities
Practice Workbook

DESAFÍO 1

Expresar causa

Presentation

■ In *Desafío 1*, Andy and Janet are in the *Valle de la Luna* in the Atacama Desert. Their task is to spend the night there looking for a rock formation in the shape of a howling dog. Students will learn:
  – Universe and space vocabulary.
  – The preposition *por* and sentences with *porque*.

Activities	Standards	Resources
Fotonovela	1.2, 3.1	Vis. Pres.
5.	1.2	
6.	1.2, 1.3	
7.	1.2, 1.3	
8. Cultura	1.1, 1.2, 3.1, 3.2	

Teaching Suggestions

Warm-Up / Independent Starter

■ To recycle informal commands, have students rewrite the following dialogue.
  —... *(mirar) las rocas, Janet. ¡Tengo frío!*
  —... *(sacar) el suéter de la mochila y ... (beber) chocolate caliente.*
  —... *(cuidar) la cámara un momento.*

Preparation

■ Display a map of Chile from a transparency or the Internet where students can see the location of the Atacama Desert. Explain that this desert is considered the driest place on Earth. Have students use what they know about deserts to extrapolate on how the surroundings affect Andy and Janet. Will this be a difficult task?

La fotonovela

Before Viewing

■ Ask a volunteer to read the introduction to the task. Have students look at the pictures and tell what they find surprising or interesting. Then ask them to point to words they recognize in the dialogue and share their meanings with the class.

After Viewing

■ Ask students if they think Andy and Janet will complete the task. Have them explain their reasons.

Las estrellas de Atacama

Andy and Janet are in the *Valle de la Luna*, a moon-like landscape in the Atacama Desert. They will spend the night there searching for a rock formation in the shape of a howling dog.

Estamos en el Valle de la Luna, Janet. ¡Vamos a explorarlo!

¡Allí hay gente... pero no se mueve!

No se mueven porque no son personas, Janet. Son rocas.

Estas rocas son interesantes...

¡Cuántas estrellas! El cielo está muy limpio.

¡Mira, aquello es el planeta Marte!

Vamos, Janet, tenemos que buscar las rocas para resolver la prueba.

Tengo la cámara lista para tomar fotos...

Continuará...

5 **Detective de palabras**

▶ **Relaciona.** What word from the dialogue relates to each of these images?

 ①  ②  ③

Differentiated Instruction

DEVELOPING LEARNERS

• Have students create a timeline with the main action from the *fotonovela*. For example:

| Janet ve gente. | Andy dice que no son personas. | Exploran las rocas. | Andy mira el cielo ... |

EXPANDING LEARNERS

• Have expanding students write an alternative *fotonovela* in the style of a science fiction movie or TV show. They might make the rock formations come to life, have Andy ride in a spaceship to the stars, or have a UFO land in the desert. Ask students to act out their science fiction story or videotape it to share with the class.

6 ¿Comprendes?

▶ **Escribe.** Use the dialogue in the *fotonovela* to answer these questions.

1. ¿Dónde están Andy y Janet?
2. ¿Qué van a hacer Andy y Janet?
3. ¿Qué ve Janet?
4. ¿Cómo está el cielo de Atacama?
5. ¿Qué tienen que hacer Andy y Janet?

7 Cada oveja con su pareja

▶ **Une.** Match each sentence in column A with the corresponding ending in column B according to the *fotonovela*.

Ⓐ

1. Este lugar se llama Valle de la Luna
2. Las figuras no se mueven
3. Andy y Janet ven muchas estrellas
4. Janet va a tomar fotos
5. Andy y Janet tienen que buscar unas rocas

Ⓑ

a. porque la cámara está lista.
b. porque quieren resolver la prueba.
c. porque su paisaje es similar al de la Luna.
d. porque no son personas. ¡Son rocas!
e. porque el cielo está muy limpio.

CULTURA

El Valle de la Luna

El Valle de la Luna está cerca de San Pedro de Atacama. El valle tiene ese nombre porque su aspecto es muy similar al paisaje de la Luna. Este valle es considerado uno de los lugares más secos de la Tierra. ¡En algunas áreas no llueve nunca!

8 Piensa. Do you think there is life on the Moon or on other planets? If so, what kind of life forms would live there?

HERITAGE LANGUAGE LEARNERS

• Latin American folklore abounds with tales that describe the origins of some feature of the natural world (e.g., why the ocean is blue or why the sun shines during the day and the moon at night?). Have students find one of these "why stories" from their own cultures that describes the origin of some natural feature from their countries of origin. Have them share their stories with the class.

MULTIPLE INTELLIGENCES:

Naturalistic Intelligence

There is archaeological evidence that humans have lived in the Atacama Desert since pre-Columbian times. Tulor Village (*Aldea de Tulor*), located in the municipality of San Pedro de Atacama, is a good example of this. Have students research this archaeological site and ask them to create a report for the class. They may present their findings in a slideshow or on a poster.

Activities

5. You may use the answers to this activity to review previous grammar topics, such as masculine nouns that end in *-a* (*el planeta*), or the gender and number of nouns (*las rocas*).

6. Ask students to answer the questions in writing before attempting a discussion.

8. Have students share their theories on extraterrestrials with the class. Do they know about and/or believe in Area 51 or UFOs?

CULTURA

El Valle de la Luna

The *Valle de la Luna* is a fascinating feature of the Atacama Desert. It is located 12 km from San Pedro de Atacama. This valley owes its name to its amazing similarities to a moon landscape. The most impressive hours to visit are at sunrise and sunset, when the salts of its dry lakes reflect the sunlight in different tones and colors. These salts formed interesting protuberances, giving the valley the appearance of a garden of sculptures.

Answer Key

5. 1. estrellas, cielo
   2. planeta
   3. rocas

6. Answers will vary. Sample answers:
   1. En el Valle de la Luna, en el desierto de Atacama.
   2. Van a explorarlo.
   3. Janet ve gente, pero no es gente, son rocas.
   4. El cielo de Atacama está muy limpio.
   5. Tienen que buscar las rocas para resolver la prueba.

7. 1. c   2. d   3. e   4. a   5. b

8. Answers will vary.

Additional Resources

Fans Online activities

207

Unit 8

DESAFÍO 1

Vocabulario – El universo

Presentation

- In this section, students will learn:
  - Words related to the universe and space.
  - Verbs associated with scientific research.

Activities	Standards	Resources
Vocabulario	1.2, 3.1	
9.	1.2, 1.3	
10.	1.2, 1.3	Audio
11.	1.2, 1.3	
12. Conexiones	1.1, 1.2, 3.1, 3.2	

Teaching Suggestions

Warm-Up / Independent Starter

- Have students use *Me gusta* and *No me gusta* to express their opinions about the following subjects in complete sentences:
  1. *Observar el mundo natural.*
  2. *Estudiar Ciencias Sociales.*
  3. *Discutir con mis amigos.*
  4. *Leer libros sobre el universo.*
  5. *Tomar fotos de paisajes naturales.*

Preparation

- Ask students to look at the new vocabulary. Have them organize it alphabetically.
- Ask students simple questions using the most obvious cognates. For example: *¿Quieres ser astronauta?* or *¿Te gusta explorar las montañas?*

Activities

9. Have students work in small groups to come up with additional sentences to describe the rest of the words in this vocabulary list (e.g., *cometa, Tierra, sistema solar,* and *astronauta*). Invite groups to read their sentences to the class and have the class complete the sentences with the missing vocabulary words.

10. After students have finished with the second part of this activity, have them read their "clues" to a partner as a guessing game. For example:
    A. *Es azul. Los pájaros y los aviones vuelan por él.*
    B. *Es el cielo.*

Vocabulario

El universo

9 Tus conocimientos

▶ **Completa.** Complete the sentences with the vocabulary above.

1. _____ es una estrella.
2. _____ brillan en el cielo por la noche.
3. _____ giran alrededor del Sol.
4. _____ es el satélite de la Tierra.
5. _____ pueden ser de sol o de luna.

Differentiated Instruction

DEVELOPING LEARNERS

- Have students classify the vocabulary words into three columns: person, place, and thing. They can use a chart like the one below.

Persona	Lugar	Objeto
el astronauta	el planeta Marte	el cometa

EXPANDING LEARNERS

- Have students write the names of the planets in English and in order from closest to the sun to farthest from the sun. Then tell them the planets in Spanish and see if they can match them to their English equivalents. Finally, ask them to invent a sentence in Spanish like the ones used to remember the order of the planets in English (e.g., "My Very Educated Mother Just Served Us Noodles").

Planets	Sentence	Planetas	Frase
Mercury	My	Mercurio	Mi
Venus	Very	Venus	Valiente
Earth	Educated	Tierra	Tía

10 Errores

 ▶ **Escucha y decide.** Janet has learned about space, but she seems to have confused some facts. Listen and decide whether her statements are true *(cierto)* or false *(falso)*.

▶ **Escribe.** Write facts that you know about each of the following topics.

Modelo el cielo ⟶ *El cielo es azul.*

1. la Tierra   2. las estrellas   3. la Luna   4. el Sol

11 Las actividades típicas

▶ **Escribe.** Use the prompts below to write four sentences about the things you like to do during the seasons of the year.

1. En primavera me gusta…
2. Me gusta el verano porque puedo…
3. El otoño es especial para…
4. Durante el invierno puedo…

 ▶ **Habla.** Compare your answers with a partner's. What activities do you have in common?

Modelo   A. *A mí me gusta el invierno porque puedo esquiar. ¿Y a ti?*
       B. *A mí también.*

 CONEXIONES: CIENCIAS

San Pedro de Atacama

San Pedro de Atacama es un pueblo del norte de Chile famoso por su situación geográfica. Está a casi 8.000 pies sobre el nivel del mar (más alto que muchas montañas). El pueblo también es famoso por su cielo nocturno: ¡en el cielo de San Pedro de Atacama se pueden ver millones de estrellas!

12 **Piensa.** How do you think San Pedro's geographic situation influences its view of the night sky? How does the geographic situation in your city or town influence your view of the night sky?

doscientos nueve   209

11. Turn this activity into a class poll to decide which activities are the most popular each season.

 AUDIO SCRIPT
See page 199K

 CONEXIONES: CIENCIAS

San Pedro de Atacama

San Pedro de Atacama is a small desert town that has been inhabited since pre-Columbian times. Many consider it to be the archeological capital of Chile. Its geography is world famous as a small oasis in the Atacama Desert. The two industries that sustain the local economy are tourism and agriculture.

Answer Key

9. 1. El Sol
   2. Las estrellas
   3. Los planetas
   4. La Luna
   5. Los eclipses

10. 1. Cierto   4. Cierto
   2. Falso   5. Cierto
   3. Falso   6. Falso
   ▶ Answers will vary.

11. Answers will vary. Sample answers:
   1. En primavera me gusta salir al campo.
   2. Me gusta el verano porque puedo ir a la playa.
   3. El otoño es especial para pasear por el parque.
   4. Durante el invierno puedo llevar abrigos y suéteres.
   ▶ Answers will vary.

12. Answers will vary.

Additional Resources

Fans Online activities
Practice Workbook

HERITAGE LANGUAGE LEARNERS

• There have been many Latino astronauts throughout the history of space exploration: Joseph M. Acabá (Puerto Rico), Fernando Caldeiro (Argentina), Franklin Chang-Díaz (Costa Rica), Sidney M. Gutierrez (Mexico), Carlos I. Noriega (Peru), Ellen Ochoa (Mexico), and George D. Zamka (Colombia). Have students choose one of these astronauts (or another of their choosing) and write a short biography in the first person (as if the student were the astronaut). Ask them to perform a monologue in which they share their "autobiography" with the class.

TOTAL PHYSICAL RESPONSE (TPR)

• Play the song "La Luna" by Belinda Carlisle. Ask students to count aloud the number of times she says *la luna* in her song (15). Then have students work together to translate one verse of the song. You can assign verses or allow students to choose their own.

Unit 8
DESAFÍO 1

Gramática – Expresar causa

Presentation

- In this section, students will learn:
  - The conjunction *porque*.
  - The preposition *por*.

Activities	Standards	Resources
Gramática	1.2, 3.1, 4.1	
13.	1.3, 4.1	
14.	1.2, 1.3	
15.	1.2, 1.3	
16.	1.3, 5.1	
17. Conexiones	1.1, 1.2, 3.1, 3.2	

Teaching Suggestions

Warm-Up / Independent Starter

- Have students match each question with its appropriate answer.
  1. *¿Cómo se llama nuestro planeta?*
  2. *¿Cuándo se produce un eclipse?*
  3. *¿Quién explora el cielo?*
  4. *¿Cuál es la estrella más grande?*

  a. *El Sol.*
  b. *El/La astronauta.*
  c. *La Tierra.*
  d. *Si la Luna pasa frente al Sol.*

Preparation

- Recycle the interrogative *¿Por qué?* with familiar questions, such as *¿Por qué estudias español?*, or *¿Por qué llevas pantalones cortos en verano?* Have students ask you questions following this pattern. Answer them using *porque*, and stress the difference in intonation and spelling.

- The preposition *por* may be a little harder to explain. Let students know that *por* is associated with the words "for" (positive) and "because of" (negative). For example:
  A. *¿Por qué vas a la fiesta?* (Why are you going to the party?)
  B. *Voy a la fiesta <u>por</u> la música.* (I'm going to the party <u>for</u> the music.)
  A. *¿Por qué no fuiste a la fiesta?* (Why didn't you go to the party?)
  B. *No fui <u>por</u> el mal tiempo.* (I didn't go <u>because of</u> the bad weather.)

210

DESAFÍO 1

Gramática

Expresar causa

La conjunción *porque*

- To express cause, use the conjunction *porque* followed by a sentence with a conjugated verb.

  Lily sabe muchas cosas **porque** lee mucho.

- To ask for a reason, use the question *¿Por qué...?* To respond, use the word *porque*.

  –**¿Por qué** no puedes ir a la fiesta?
  –**Porque** estoy enfermo.

La preposición *por*

- The preposition *por* sometimes expresses cause or reason.

  No fuimos a la playa **por** el viento.

- The preposition *por* is usually followed by a noun.

  Le compré un regalo **por su cumpleaños**.

13 **Compara.** How do we state cause in English? Describe similarities and differences in the way we express this concept in English and in Spanish.

14 **Razones para todo**

▶ **Relaciona y escribe.** Match the actions below with the corresponding picture. Write sentences using *por*.

Modelo 1. → B. *Janet fue a ese café por los helados.*

1. Janet fue a ese café...
2. Janet bebió mucha agua...
3. Janet visitó Chile...
4. Janet vio las rocas de noche...
5. Janet compró unas gafas...

la luna llena

los helados

una oferta especial

el calor

sus paisajes

Differentiated Instruction

DEVELOPING LEARNERS

- Have students look at the interrogative *¿por qué?* and the conjunction *porque*. Ask them to list three differences that they see between the two terms (i.e., the question marks, two words versus one word, the accent on the letter e). To practice the two terms, ask them to write two sentences, one using the question word and one using an appropriate response. For example: *¿Por qué no te gusta el invierno? Porque hace mucho frío.*

EXPANDING LEARNERS

- Ask students to play a game of "What's My Line?" using the preposition *por* and the conjunction *porque*. Sitting in a small group, the first student begins with a sentence starter like *No voy a la playa hoy* ... The next student continues the sentence by adding a cause or reason like *porque no tengo mi traje de baño*. Then the next student repeats the last part as the beginning of a new sentence: *No tengo mi traje de baño* ..., and the next student finishes it by adding, for example, *por olvidarlo*. The game continues until someone can't continue the sentence.

15 **Los motivos de Andy y Janet**

▶ **Completa.** Complete the sentences with *por* or *porque*.

1. Andy y Janet fueron al desierto _____ el desafío.

2. Janet tiene miedo _____ es de noche.

3. Andy lleva su cámara _____ le gusta tomar fotos.

4. El cielo está bonito _____ hay muchas estrellas.

5. Andy y Janet pasan mala noche _____ el frío del desierto.

16 **¡A conocernos!**

▶ **Escribe.** Read the following topics and choose five. Then write a sentence about yourself in relation to each topic.

Modelo 1. la familia → *Nunca estoy solo(a) porque mi familia es muy grande.*

1. la familia
2. los deportes
3. las películas
4. la escuela
5. el arte
6. el trabajo
7. los amigos
8. la música
9. la comunicación
10. las fiestas
11. las compras
12. la casa

CONEXIONES: CIENCIAS

El salar de Atacama

El salar de Atacama es el depósito de sal más grande de Chile. Está situado al sur de San Pedro de Atacama. Casi todo el depósito está permanentemente seco, pero hay lagunas. Gracias a ellas muchas aves y otros animales viven allí.

17 **Piensa.** Plant and animal life has adapted to live in this area, which, in some places, has never had rainfall recorded. What kinds of plants and animals would be able to survive? What adaptations would they have to make?

HERITAGE LANGUAGE LEARNERS

• Have heritage students research environmental problems in their countries of origin. They should start with the question *¿Por qué…?* (e.g., *¿Por qué está en peligro de extinción el jaguar?*) and research the causes of the problem (e.g., *Porque hay deforestación de su hábitat.*). Ask all students to share their findings with the class. Create a class poster with the issues and their causes.

CRITICAL THINKING

• Often times, problems have more than one direct cause or reason. Have students think of a world problem (e.g., *el hambre, la polución, la guerra*) and then write a list of several different reasons for these problems. Ask students to stage a debate about one problem, with some taking one side of the debate (the *pro* side) and others taking the other side (the *contra* side). Ask them to consider this question: Is it ever possible for both the *pro* and the *contra* sides to be right?

Activities

14. Have students turn their answers into direct speech. For example: *Janet, te duele el estómago porque comiste mucho helado.*

15. To make sure students understand the differences between *porque* and *por*, have them write an example of each in their notebooks.

16. Tell students that they may use *porque* to express their opinions about the topics they have selected. For example: *El arte es importante porque comunica los sentimientos de un artista.*

CONEXIONES: CIENCIAS

El salar de Atacama

The Atacama Salt Flat is one of the largest salt deposits in the world. Its brines are rich in lithium, a metallic element that is essential to the manufacture of rechargeable batteries. A lake lies below the jagged crust of bizarrely twisted and curved salt formations. There are, however, numerous openings, or lagoons, in this thick salt crust. Wildlife is abundant in these lagoons. *Laguna de Chaxa*, for example, is home to three of the five known species of flamingos.

Answer Key

13. Answers will vary. (Students should be able to identify the uses of *why, because,* and *for* in English with its Spanish equivalents.)

14. 1. B → … por los helados.
2. D → … por el calor.
3. E → … por sus paisajes.
4. A → … por la luna llena.
5. C → … por una oferta especial.

15. 1. por   3. porque   5. por
2. porque   4. porque

16. Answers will vary. Sample answer:
Me gusta mucho ir al cine porque me gustan las películas de terror.

17. Answers will vary.

Additional Resources

Fans Online activities
Practice Workbook

Unit 8

DESAFÍO 1

Comunicación

Presentation

- In this section, students will practice:
  - Vocabulary about the universe and space.
  - The preposition *por* and the conjunction *porque*.

Activities	Standards	Resources
18.	1.2, 3.1	Audio
19	1.1, 1.3, 5.1	
20.	1.1, 1.2, 1.3	
21. Final del desafío	1.2, 1.3, 3.1, 5.1	

Teaching Suggestions

Warm-Up / Independent Starter

- Have students answer the following questions in a paragraph of three to four sentences:
  ¿Van a completar su desafío Janet y Andy?
  ¿Por qué?

Preparation

- Before attempting the *Comunicación* activities, make sure students have mastered the communicative goals of this unit. To do this, have students prepare flashcards for vocabulary and grammar and walk around the classroom quizzing each other. Follow this activity with a summary of the grammar and vocabulary from this unit.

Activities

18. Ask students to read the sentences before listening to the passage, as they may know some of the answers before listening.

19. Before beginning this activity, have students read their questions to each other. Each pair will choose the best five questions for their interview.

20. Extend this activity by having volunteers read their essays aloud to the class. Focus on pronunciation and intonation. After a few volunteers read, have a question and answer time for students to discuss the essays.

21. Have students give at least three reasons why things happened the way they did in their blogs.

Comunicación

18 **Nuestro universo**

 ▶ **Escucha y decide.** Listen to a scientist talk about space. Then decide whether the statements below are true *(cierto)* or false *(falso)*.

> **Prueba tus conocimientos sobre el espacio**
> 1. El Sol es una estrella.
> 2. El planeta Tierra no está en el sistema solar.
> 3. Desde la Tierra no pueden verse otros planetas.
> 4. Saturno es un planeta con anillos.
> 5. Júpiter es el planeta más grande de nuestro sistema solar.
> 6. No hay cometas en nuestro sistema solar.
> 7. Los cometas están formados por hielo y otras sustancias.
> 8. Neil Armstrong fue el primer hombre en caminar por la Luna.

19 **Una entrevista de radio**

▶ **Escribe.** You are interviewing a space scientist for the school's Internet Radiocast. Write five questions you would like to ask about his or her work.

Modelo
> **1.** ¿Por qué estudias el universo?

 ▶ **Habla.** With your partner, role-play the interview. You ask the questions and he or she answers. Then switch roles.

> ¿Por qué estudias el universo?

> Porque en el universo hay muchas cosas interesantes.

Differentiated Instruction

DEVELOPING LEARNERS

- Before starting with the *Comunicación* activities, have students create a picture dictionary of the vocabulary words from this *Desafío*.

EXPANDING LEARNERS

- Ask students to create a comic strip using the theme of *El universo* and *El sistema solar* that deals with a particular issue of cause and effect. For example, a sad comic where an astronaut causes a Martian to get lost or a comic where a cloud causes the sun to sneeze. Students can illustrate their own comic strips or use an online comic generator.

20 **¿Razones o excusas?**

▶ **Habla.** What excuses do your classmates have for not doing the chores below? Ask five friends.

poner la mesa   barrer el suelo   ordenar el garaje   cocinar   limpiar el baño

Modelo A. ¿Qué excusa tienes para no limpiar tu dormitorio?
B. Yo no limpio mi dormitorio porque estoy cansado.

▶ **Escribe.** Using your classmates' answers, write a short essay of five sentences about their excuses.

Modelo Jim no limpia su dormitorio porque está cansado...

Final del desafío

El blog de Andy

3 de marzo. San Pedro de Atacama

Observar el cielo de Atacama fue fantástico. El cielo allí es muy claro y puedes ver muchas estrellas. También puedes ver Marte y otros planetas.

En Chile estamos en verano, pero las noches son frías. Anoche fue difícil dormir en la tienda de campaña por el frío.

Janet y yo hablamos mucho de la Luna, de los eclipses y de los cometas, y por la noche soñé con ser astronauta. Quiero descubrir y explorar nuevos mundos.

¡Ah! Janet tomó la foto de las rocas en forma de perro porque queremos ganar el desafío.

21 ¿Qué pasa en la historia?

▶ **Escribe.** Andy and Janet spent the night in the Atacama Desert. Read Andy's blog and see if they accomplished their task. Then write your own blog entry describing what you think happened to Andy and Janet the following day when they woke up. Share your blog with the class.

doscientos trece 213

AUDIO SCRIPT
See page 199K

Answer Key

18. 1. Cierto   5. Cierto
2. Falso   6. Falso
3. Falso   7. Cierto
4. Cierto   8. Cierto

19. Answers will vary.
▶ Answers will vary.

20. Answers will vary.
▶ Answers will vary.

21. Answers will vary.

Additional Resources

Fans Online activities
Practice Workbook

HERITAGE LANGUAGE LEARNERS

- Have students take on the role of one of the eight planets and write a statement starting with the words: *Yo soy el planeta... Estoy... Soy...* Ask students to create a video with all eight planets represented. Upload the video to the school or department webpage to share with other classes and / or parents.

MULTIPLE INTELLIGENCES:
Musical Intelligence

- Many songs have been written about outer space and space travel. In English, there are popular songs like "Space Odyssey" by David Bowie and "Man on the Moon" by R.E.M. Have students listen to the song "Espacio Sideral" by Jesse y Joy. Then ask them to write their own songs about space travel. Have students share their songs—and even sing them, if they can—with the class. The class can vote on their favorite song.

213

Unit 8
DESAFÍO 2
Expresar cantidad

Presentation

- In *Desafío 2*, Tess and Patricia are on Easter Island. They have to find and topple a fake moai.
- In this section, students will learn:
  – Words for geographical features.
  – Indefinite articles and adjectives.

Activities	Standards	Resources
Fotonovela	1.2, 2.2	Vis. Pres.
22.	1.2, 1.3	
23.	1.2, 1.3	
24.	1.2, 1.3	Audio
25.	1.1, 1.2, 1.3	
26. Cultura	1.1, 1.2, 2.2, 3.1, 3.2	Video

Teaching Suggestions

Warm-Up / Independent Starter

- Have students write a short paragraph of three to four sentences about Easter Island and the Rapanui people.

Preparation

- Choose one of the topics from the Independent Starter and call on students to read their paragraphs. Have the class vote for the most informative paragraph.

La fotonovela

Before Viewing

- Ask partners to take turns reading the speech bubbles aloud. Circulate throughout the room to help with proper intonation and pronunciation.

After Viewing

- Ask students to talk about which difficulties Tess and Patricia might have completing their challenge. How does their challenge compare with Andy and Janet's challenge?

Activities

24. Before listening to the audio, have students write the complete sentences surrounding the responses. For example:
  1. *Tess tiene ganas de ver …*

214

Una estatua falsa

Tess and Patricia are on Easter Island, Chile. There they have to find and topple a fake moai. The native Rapanui people believed that the moai offered them protection.

La Isla de Pascua tiene unos paisajes extraordinarios.

Sabemos muy poco sobre la cultura rapanui...

¡Sí! Tiene volcanes, pero no están activos.

Mira, ahí hay algunos moáis. Todos parecen auténticos, ¿verdad?

Camina con cuidado, la costa es rocosa.

Ahí no está el moái falso. Tenemos que buscar un lago...

Continuará…

22 Detective de palabras

▶ **Identifica.** What nouns from the dialogue relate to these images?

①    ②    ③    ④

▶ **Escribe.** Write one sentence for each noun.

Differentiated Instruction

DEVELOPING LEARNERS

- Have students work in pairs to read the speech bubbles from the *fotonovela* aloud. Encourage them to use gestures, facial expressions and vocal intonation in accordance with the meaning of the words they are speaking. After each statement, ask the students to talk about what each scene means.

EXPANDING LEARNERS

- Ask students to imagine that they are going to take a trip to Easter Island. Have them write a list of the things they would pack for this trip and the questions they might ask the tour guide as they view the ancient moai.

23 ¿Comprendes?

▶ **Escribe.** Answer the questions in complete sentences.

1. ¿Cómo son los paisajes de la Isla de Pascua según Patricia?
2. ¿Cómo es la costa de la isla?
3. ¿De qué cultura son los moáis?
4. ¿Qué pista tienen Tess y Patricia para encontrar el moái falso?

En la isla no llueve con frecuencia.

24 Una isla espectacular

▶ **Escucha y contesta.** Before their trip, Tess and Patricia talked about Easter Island. Listen to the conversation and answer the questions.

1. ¿Qué tiene ganas de ver Tess?
2. ¿Cuántas lenguas hablan en la Isla de Pascua?
3. ¿Cuántos volcanes no activos hay en la isla?
4. ¿Cómo se llaman las islas que rodean a la isla principal?
5. ¿Por qué hay pocos árboles en la Isla de Pascua?

25 Algunas cosas

▶ **Habla.** Do you know the names of any of the following? Make a list, then ask a partner if he or she knows of any.

Modelo   A. ¿Conoces algún lago?
         B. Sí, conozco el lago Ontario.

1. ¿Conoces alguna isla?
2. ¿Conoces alguna estatua?
3. ¿Conoces algún volcán?
4. ¿Conoces algún bosque tropical?

 CULTURA

La Isla de Pascua

La Isla de Pascua está en el océano Pacífico, en la Polinesia. Esta isla forma parte de Chile. Allí viven los descendientes de la civilización rapanui. Sabemos poco sobre esta antigua cultura. En 1877 quedaron en la isla poco más de cien personas. Hoy la población es de cuatro mil habitantes aproximadamente. Las imágenes de los moáis de la isla son famosas en todo el mundo.

26 Piensa. What would you like to find out about the Rapanui? Why?

doscientos quince **215**

HERITAGE LANGUAGE LEARNERS

• Ask heritage students to research the Rapanui culture and moai online, and have them write a short report in Spanish. They may use the questions the expanding learners created to help them write their reports. Have them share their findings with the class.

MULTIPLE INTELLIGENCES:

Visual-Spatial / Linguistic Intelligence

• Have students look at cartoons featuring the moai from Easter Island. Ask them to choose one and write an appropriate caption for it in Spanish. Encourage them to try to make their captions humorous.

---

25. You can turn this activity into a competition. Divide students into groups of two or three. Once all the groups are set you will say *Go* for all the groups to begin. The first group to come up with all four correct answers wins.

 AUDIO SCRIPT
See page 199K

CULTURA

La Isla de Pascua

Trees are scarce on Easter Island, but the islanders were greeted with a lush paradise when they first discovered it. Trees were cut for agriculture, houses, fires, and the devices used to move and erect the moai. This caused the soil to erode and the clans turned on one another fighting for scarce resources.

Answer Key

22. 1. (el/un) lago   3. (el/un) moái
       2. (el/un) volcán   4. (la/una) isla
       ▶ Answers will vary.

23. 1. Los paisajes son extraordinarios.
       2. La costa de la isla es rocosa.
       3. Los moáis son de la cultura rapanui.
       4. Para encontrar el moái falso Tess y Patricia tienen que buscar un lago.

24. 1. Tess tiene ganas de ver los moáis.
       2. En la Isla de Pascua hablan dos lenguas: el español y el rapanui.
       3. Hay tres volcanes no activos en la isla.
       4. Las islas pequeñas que rodean a la isla principal se llaman islotes.
       5. Porque no llueve con frecuencia y la isla está casi deforestada.

25. Answers will vary.

26. Answers will vary.

Additional Resources

Fans Online activities

DESAFÍO 2

Vocabulario – Geografía

Presentation

■ In this section, students will learn:
  – Geographical features.
  – Words to describe geographical features.

Activities	Standards	Resources
Vocabulario	1.2, 1.3	
27.	1.2, 3.1	
28.	1.3	
29.	1.2, 1.3	Audio
30. Conexiones	1.1, 1.2, 3.1, 3.2	

Teaching Suggestions

Warm-Up / Independent Starter

■ Ask students to classify the vocabulary with a Venn diagram by "Cognates" (left), "Not cognates" (right), and "I don't know" (common).

Preparation

■ Write the vocabulary words *el continente, la montaña, el desierto,* and *el bosque* on the board. Have volunteers write the names of all the geographical locations until you have listed three under each category. Proceed to introduce the vocabulary.

Activities

27. To extend this activity, ask students to research the most interesting places for each category in the table. They may use the Internet or their science books to make a list of three interesting and exotic places for each category. When students have finished, ask for volunteers to share their lists with the rest of the class.

28. Ask students to create a dialogue between Tess and Patricia in which they talk about visiting these places. Call on volunteers to perform their dialogues in front of the class.

29. Have students create an informative report on one geographical feature from their birth cities or states. Have students find images that represent their geographical features and ask them to paste them onto a large class map.

Vocabulario

Geografía

¿Viajamos por tierra o por mar?

el continente

la isla

el océano

la montaña

el valle

el lago

el río

El desierto es seco.

El bosque es tropical.

27 **¿Dónde vivimos?**

▶ **Clasifica.** Classify the places by the geographic feature(s) that each represents. Then add one more place that you know to each column.

el Sahara   el Mississippi   el Amazonas   Hawái   Asia

el Mediterráneo   Yellowstone   el Atlántico   Bermudas   África

océanos	continentes	islas	ríos	desiertos	mares	bosques

Differentiated Instruction

DEVELOPING LEARNERS

• Have students practice the vocabulary by playing "Password" in pairs. One student gives their partner clues for guessing which word is being described. For example, if the word is *(el) océano*, clues would be *Pacífico, Atlántico,* etc. Take turns until all the words are practiced.

EXPANDING LEARNERS

• Have students create a travel brochure for a region of the world that they have visited or would like to visit one day. Ask them to use as many of the *Vocabulario* words as possible. Tell students that they should use the words in complete sentences. Encourage them to illustrate their brochures with drawings or photos. The brochures can be used as reference material in class, or can be displayed in the room.

28 La geografía chilena

▶ **Escribe.** These are the places Tess and Patricia would like to visit in Chile. What kind of geographic features are they?

Modelo los Andes → *Los Andes son montañas.*

1. Atacama
2. Loa
3. Viña del Mar
4. Rupanco
5. El Pacífico

29 Una guía para turistas

▶ **Escucha y decide.** Tess is describing geographic features of the United States to a friend in Chile. Listen and tell if the statements below are true *(cierto)* or false *(falso)*. If they are false, correct them.

1. Hay mar al este y al oeste.
2. California es un estado de la costa este.
3. Manhattan es una isla.
4. Los Estados Unidos forman parte del continente americano.
5. En los Estados Unidos no hay bosques tropicales.
6. En el este de los Estados Unidos hay un gran desierto.

CONEXIONES: GEOGRAFÍA

Un balneario en Chile

Viña del Mar es una ciudad balneario *(beach resort)* famosa en todo el mundo. Tiene un clima mediterráneo similar al de California: las estaciones lluviosas son el otoño y el invierno. Pero, recuerda, Chile está en el hemisferio sur de nuestro planeta. Por eso sus estaciones son opuestas a las nuestras.

30 **Piensa.** During which months would it be safe to visit Viña del Mar if you want to minimize your chances of rain?

doscientos diecisiete **217**

HERITAGE LANGUAGE LEARNERS

• Have heritage students write a list of places in their country of origin that match the vocabulary words. For example, a student from Colombia might talk about *el río Amazonas* or *la Isla de San Andrés*. Then ask them to choose one place and present a weather report for that region of the world. For example: *Hoy la temperatura es de 85 grados en la Isla de San Andrés, con mucho sol y humedad alta…*

SPECIAL-NEEDS LEARNERS

• Create a series of flashcards for each of the vocabulary words to show to students with language processing disabilities. The card should be large (at least 8.5" × 11") and have just the image. On index cards, write or type the accompanying words for each image. Ask students to match the word cards with the picture cards to practice the vocabulary.

🎧 **AUDIO SCRIPT**
See page 199K

CONEXIONES: GEOGRAFÍA

Un balneario en Chile

Viña del Mar is a popular tourist destination in Chile. It is also known as *Ciudad Jardín* (Garden City). Founded in 1878, Viña del Mar was once a vineyard, but it has grown into a modern city with a subway that connects it to neighboring Valparaiso. There are ten beaches, the most popular of which is Reñaca. Viña del Mar and Sausalito, in California, are sister cities.

Answer Key

27. océanos: el Atlántico
continentes: África, Asia
islas: Hawái, Bermudas
ríos: el Mississippi, el Amazonas
desiertos: el Sahara
mares: el Mediterráneo
bosques: Yellowstone, el Amazonas

28. 1. Atacama es un desierto.
2. Loa es un río.
3. Viña del Mar es una ciudad.
4. Rupanco es un lago.
5. El Pacífico es un océano.

29. 1. Cierto
2. Falso. California está en la costa oeste.
3. Cierto
4. Cierto
5. Cierto
6. Falso. En el oeste de los Estados Unidos hay un gran desierto: el desierto de Arizona.

30. Durante los meses de primavera y verano.

Additional Resources

Fans Online activities
Practice Workbook

DESAFÍO 2

Gramática – Expresar cantidad. Los indefinidos

Presentation

- In this section, students will learn:
  - How to express quantity.
  - Indefinite adjectives.
  - Indefinite pronouns.

Activities	Standards	Resources
Gramática	1.2, 3.1, 4.1	
31.	1.1, 3.1, 4.1	
32.	1.3	
33.	1.2, 1.3	
34.	1.2, 1.3	Audio
35. Conexiones	1.1, 1.2, 3.1, 3.2	

Teaching Suggestions

Warm-Up / Independent Starter

- Have students unscramble the lines of words to form logical sentences.
  1. cinco / comprar / a / voy / de / azúcar / kilogramos
  2. dos / necesito / lápices / para / examen / el
  3. estudiantes / los / mochila / una / tienen / todos

Preparation

- Have volunteers read their sentences aloud. Ask them to identify how many of each item there are. Let them know that the number is definite. Today they will learn to talk about the same items in indefinite terms.
- Go over the grammar presentation with students. Then ask students to rewrite the sentences from the Independent Starter with indefinite adjectives.

Activities

31. Students can demonstrate this comparison with the use of a three-column table similar to the following:

Indefinidos – español / inglés	Similitudes	Diferencias
ningún, ninguno, ninguna / not, (not) any		

Gramática

Expresar cantidad. Los indefinidos

- In many cases, nouns can be counted using specific numbers.

  Tengo **tres** libros de español.   Hay **veinte** estudiantes en la clase.

  It is possible, however, to refer to nouns using nonspecific terms of number. These terms are called *indefinites*.

  Hay **algunos** libros de español allí.   **Muchas** personas visitaron el museo ayer.

- These are the most common indefinites:

  PRINCIPALES INDEFINIDOS

| ningún ninguno(a) | algún alguno(a) algunos(as) | poco(a) pocos(as) | mucho(a) muchos(as) | todo(a) todos(as) |

  ¿Hay **algún** estudiante en la escuela?   En el desierto hay **poca** agua.
  No veo **ningún** lago en la isla.   Hay **muchas** estatuas en la Isla de Pascua.
  Tengo **algunos** libros sobre Chile.   **Todas** las parejas viajaron a Chile.

Uso de los indefinidos

- Before a masculine singular noun, use *algún* or *ningún* instead of *alguno* or *ninguno*.
  –¿Tienes **algún** amigo chileno?
  –Sí, tengo **alguno**.

- *Ningún, ninguno,* and *ninguna* are used only in negative sentences.
  Hoy **no** hay **ninguna** estrella en el cielo.

- *Todo, toda, todos,* and *todas* are used as follows:

  | todo + artículo + nombre | Hay estatuas en **toda** la isla.

31 **Compara.** Think about the concept of indefinites in English. Describe similarities and differences between the forms in Spanish and English. Give examples.

32 **Tus compañeros**

 ▶ **Habla.** Talk with a partner about your classmates' characteristics.

1. Todos los compañeros…
2. Algunos compañeros…
3. Muchos compañeros…
4. Ningún compañero…

Differentiated Instruction

DEVELOPING LEARNERS

- Have students illustrate each of the indefinite adjectives as a means of visualizing and personalizing these different terms for expressing quantity. For example:
  – ninguna comida
  – muchos dulces
  – algunas nubes

EXPANDING LEARNERS

- Have students practice the indefinite adjectives with classroom objects. Have them go on a scavenger hunt to find the following items and then count them: *estudiantes, libros, cuadernos, lápices, profesores, sillas, mesas, pizarras, mochilas.* After they gather the information, ask them to write a sentence about each item. For example: *Hay muchos estudiantes. Hay pocas pizarras.*

33 **Durante el viaje a Chile**

▶ **Completa.** Complete the statements with the appropriate word.

Modelo *No hay ninguna estación de trenes en la isla.*

 muchos   ningún   ninguno   todos   poca   algún

1. No tengo _____ libro sobre Chile.
2. _____ los chilenos están orgullosos de su país.
3. En Chile descubrimos _____ lugares maravillosos.
4. ¿Ves _____ lago? En el centro de la isla no hay _____.
5. Hay _____ información sobre la cultura rapanui.

34 **Impresiones y experiencias**

 ▶ **Escucha y contesta.** Listen to the characters talk about their experience in Chile and answer the following questions in complete sentences.

1. ¿A algún personaje le gusta caminar por las montañas?
2. ¿Hay moáis en alguna tienda turística?
3. ¿Algún personaje está cansado de viajar?
4. ¿Alguno tiene muchas ganas de ver a su familia?
5. ¿A alguno le gusta viajar?

 CONEXIONES: CIENCIAS

La deforestación

La deforestación de la Isla de Pascua es un fenómeno estudiado por los científicos. Algunos fósiles indican que existieron bosques tropicales en esta isla. Hoy no hay bosques. Llueve poco en la isla y esto contribuye a la deforestación.

35 **Piensa.** What other reasons can account for the disappearance of the rainforest on Easter Island, and in other parts of the world?

doscientos diecinueve 219

HERITAGE LANGUAGE LEARNERS

• Have heritage students compare the geographic features of a state or province from their country of origin to the geographic features of the state in the United States where they live now using a Venn diagram and the *indefinidos*. For example: *En el estado de mis padres en México hay algunos bosques tropicales. En mi estado de los Estados Unidos no tenemos ninguno.* Have students compare their information with that of their classmates in groups of three or four.

MULTIPLE INTELLIGENCES:

Interpersonal Intelligence

• Ask students to interview each other about their music collections using the following sentence starters:
A. *¿Tienes algún disco de...?*
B. *Sí, tengo algunos discos de.../No, no tengo ningún disco de...*
A. *¿Tienes alguna canción de... ?*
B. *Sí, tengo alguna canción de.../No, no tengo ninguna canción de...*

Gramática – Expresar cantidad. Los indefinidos

34. To personalize this activiy, have students elaborate on each response with their own opinions. Take this oportunity to recycle *porque* and *por* from the previous *Desafío*.

🎧 **AUDIO SCRIPT**
See page 199K

 CONEXIONES: CIENCIAS

La deforestación

Deforestation is a worldwide problem. Human use of timber has contributed to the economy of many countries through the centuries, but many of these natural resources are non-renewable. Organizations focused on the protection of the environment estimate that in the last two centuries, humans have killed half of the forests on our planet.

Answer Key

31. Answers will vary. Sample answer: English indefinites don't have gender or number.

32. Answers will vary. Sample answer:
1. Todos los compañeros son estudiosos.

33. 1. ningún   3. muchos   5. poca
2. Todos   4. algún; ninguno

34. 1. Sí, a Tess y a Janet les gusta caminar por las montañas.
2. Sí, hay moáis en miniatura en todas las tiendas turísticas.
3. Sí, Andy está cansado de viajar.
4. Patricia, Tess y Janet tienen ganas de ver a su familia.
5. A Tess, a Patricia y a Janet les gusta viajar.

35. Answers will vary.

Additional Resources

Fans Online activities
Practice Workbook

DESAFÍO 2

Comunicación

Presentation

- In this section, students will practice:
  - Words for geographical features.
  - Indefinite adjectives and pronouns.

Activities	Standards	Resources
36.	1.1, 1.2, 1.3, 5.1	
37.	1.1, 1.2, 1.3, 3.1	Audio
38.	1.3, 3.1	
39. Final del desafío	1.2, 1.3	
Tu desafío	1.1, 1.2, 1.3, 5.1	

Teaching Suggestions

Warm-Up / Independent Starter

- Have students complete the following sentences using the indefinites below.

  muchas   algún   toda   ninguna   pocos

  1. ... día voy a visitar Chile.
  2. La Isla de Pascua tiene ... árboles.
  3. ... la geografía chilena es sensacional.
  4. Tess y Diana hicieron ... amigas en Chile.
  5. Por las nubes, hoy no hay ... estrella en el cielo.

Preparation

- After students have completed their Independent Starter, have them write a short report on Easter Island. Have them compare any aspect discussed in this *Desafío* to their life in the United States and share their ideas with the class.

Activities

36. Divide the class into groups of three students. Each student in the group should research one fact for a group poster. Have them compile their facts and present the poster to the class.

37. Turn the *Habla* section of this activity into a class discussion about deforestation and the environment. Provoke critical thinking by asking what reasons people have for not believing that the planet is facing any ecological catastrophes. Ask students for *pro* and *contra* points of view.

Comunicación

36 **Un boletín escolar**

 ▶ **Lee y escribe.** Read Tess's notes and write a list of the three facts that would be most interesting in a promotional poster for Chile.

 ▶ **Habla.** With a partner, ask thought-provoking questions about each fact to guide your research.

Modelo Los Andes son unas montañas altas.
A. ¿Qué actividades puedes hacer en las montañas?
B. En las montañas puedes caminar y ver animales.

▶ **Crea un póster.** Create a poster with the facts you chose and some images and other information about Chile.

Chile, simplemente espectacular

- Chile tiene 2.700 millas de costa.
- El desierto de Atacama es uno de los desiertos más secos del mundo.
- Los Andes son unas montañas altas.
- Viña del Mar es una ciudad balneario con playas sensacionales. Tiene un festival de música muy famoso.
- Los moáis están en la Isla de Pascua.
- Chile tiene al oeste el océano Pacífico.
- Tiene ríos para practicar deportes acuáticos.

37 **Similitudes y diferencias**

 ▶ **Escucha y escribe.** Listen as Tess describes the major ecological problems on Easter Island. Write down the problems she discusses.

- La isla está casi deforestada.

▶ **Habla.** With a partner, compare the environmental problems of Easter Island with those of the United States. What are some possible solutions?

Differentiated Instruction

DEVELOPING LEARNERS

- Using coins (candies, beans, or small pebbles are acceptable as well), have students demonstrate the meanings of several different indefinite adjectives to each other. For example, one student places 20 coins on the table; the partner says *muchas monedas*. Students should practice until all the indefinite adjectives have been represented.

EXPANDING LEARNERS

- Have students play a guessing game to practice the indefinites and the new vocabulary. One student describes a geographical region (e.g., *el desierto*) by making statements like *Hay mucho sol, hay poca agua, tiene pocas plantas*. The student who guesses what region they are talking about first is the next to describe a different geographical area.

38 **Encuesta general**

 ▶ **Habla.** You want to find out your classmates' travel history. Ask each student if he or she has gone to the places below.

Modelo *¿Fuiste a algún río?*

1. una isla
2. un bosque
3. una montaña
4. un desierto
5. un mar
6. otro continente

 ▶ **Presenta.** Create a chart like this one to display your classmates' answers.

	una isla	un bosque	una montaña	...
todos	✔			
algunos		✔		
ninguno			✔	

Final del desafío

El diario de Tess

39 **¿Qué pasa en la historia?**

▶ **Escribe.** Tess forgot to write in her diary last night. Look at the images and write a short description of what happened.

▶ **TU DESAFÍO** | Earn points for your own challenge! Listen to the questions for your *Minientrevista Desafío 2* on the website and write your answers.

doscientos veintiuno 221

38. You can finish this activity by asking students if they have traveled outside of the United States. Then ask who has traveled to two countries. Three? Four? The student who has been to the most countries can tell the class about his or her experiences using as much of the new vocabulary as he or she can.

🎧 **AUDIO SCRIPT**
See page 199K

Answer Key

36. Answers will vary.
▶ Answers will vary.
▶ Answers will vary.

37. • La isla está casi deforestada.
• Hay muy pocos árboles.
• Llueve muy poco.
• La falta de agua afecta a las plantas y a los animales.
• Por su situación geográfica, hay pocas especies animales.
▶ Answers will vary.

38. Answers will vary.
▶ Answers will vary.

39. Answers will vary.

Additional Resources

Fans Online activities
Practice Workbook

HERITAGE LANGUAGE LEARNERS

• Have heritage students think about the animals that live in different geographical regions of their countries of origin. Then ask them to write sentences describing the quantities of each animal in those places. For example: *En el río Amazonas hay muchos peces, pero hay pocos delfines rosados. Los delfines rosados están en peligro de extinción.*

COOPERATIVE LEARNING

• Ask students to work together to practice the indefinite adjectives by interviewing each other about their classes in school. Have students swap schedules and create five sentences about each other's school day, asking if each sentence is correct or not. For example:
A. *Tú tienes muchas clases de Ciencias, ¿verdad?*
B. *Sí. Y tú tienes algunas clases de Arte, ¿no?*
A. *Sí, me gusta el arte.*

221

Unit 8
DESAFÍO 3
Expresar acciones pasadas

Presentation

- In *Desafío 3*, Tim and Mack are in Valparaiso. Their task is to participate in the Stairs Marathon.
- In this section students will learn:
  - Irregular past tense forms of *decir, hacer, estar,* and *tener*.
  - Political divisions.
  - Numbers from 101 to 1,000.

Activities	Standards	Resources
Fotonovela	1.1, 1.2, 2.1	Vis. Pres.
40.	1.2, 1.3	
41.	1.2, 1.3	
42.	1.2	Audio
43.	1.1	
44. Cultura	1.1, 1.2	Video
Tu desafío	1.2, 5.2	

Teaching Suggestions

Warm-Up / Independent Starter

- Have students complete the following sentences using the correct preterite conjugation of the verbs in parentheses.
  1. *Ayer mi abuelo y yo ... (correr) dos kilómetros.*
  2. *Tim y Mack ... (desayunar) en el hotel.*
  3. *El abuelo ... (probar) una comida chilena deliciosa.*
  4. *Pablo Neruda ... (vivir) en la Chascona.*

Preparation

- Have students name some marathons or other races in your town or state. Are there any stairs involved? Ask students to research the most unique marathons around the world to compare to the *Maratón de las Escaleras*.

La fotonovela

Before Viewing

- Ask a volunteer to read the introduction to the task. Have students look at the pictures and say what they find suprising or interesting. Have them scan the title and the speech bubbles for cognates and known words. Ask them to read the dialogue silently and note the words they don't understand.

222

El Maratón de las Escaleras

 Tim and Mack are in Valparaiso, Chile, to participate in the *Maratón de las Escaleras* (the Stairs Marathon). Their task is to run this challenging race!

Tim, este maratón es muy difícil. ¿Viste las escaleras?

Héctor Basualdo dijo que Valparaíso es la capital de esta provincia y una de las ciudades más importantes del país.

Sí, abuelo, las vi. Hay escaleras porque la ciudad de Valparaíso está en la montaña.

Abuelo, ¿dónde estuviste?

Bueno, abuelo, ¿cómo vamos a correr el maratón?... ¿Abuelo?

Vamos, abuelo. Tenemos que continuar.

Estoy cansado.

Estuve con una señora. ¡Me dijo que hay más de quinientos escalones!

Continuará...

---

40 Detective de palabras

▶ **Completa.** Fill in each blank with the appropriate word, according to the dialogue above.

La ciudad de Valparaíso

1. La _____ de Valparaíso está en la montaña.
2. Valparaíso es la _____ de esta _____.
3. Es una de las ciudades más importantes del _____.

Differentiated Instruction

DEVELOPING LEARNERS

- Have students look at the photos in the *fotonovela*. Ask them to describe what they see in each scene with simple vocabulary using a chart like the one below.

Personas	Lugares	Objetos
Tim	montañas	camiseta
Mack	la ciudad	tenis

EXPANDING LEARNERS

- Ask students to imagine that they are newspaper reporters who have been asked to cover the marathon. Have students conduct "interviews" between a runner and a newspaper reporter, asking ten questions about the athlete's training and the race.

Expresar acciones pasadas

41 ¿Comprendiste?

▶ **Contesta.** Answer the questions in complete sentences.

1. ¿Dónde están Tim y Mack?
2. ¿Dónde está Valparaíso?
3. ¿Qué tienen que hacer allí?
4. ¿Por qué es difícil su tarea?
5. ¿Cuántos escalones hay?
6. ¿Por qué está cansado Mack?

42 ¿Qué viste?

▶ **Escucha y escribe.** Two spectators are commenting on the marathon. Listen and write whether or not they saw the following people and things.

1. un hombre muy alto
2. un gaucho
3. un niño corriendo
4. la Luna
5. una papelería
6. una montaña
7. una entrenadora de fútbol

43 ¿Dónde estuviste?

▶ **Habla.** Find out where five classmates were on a significant date in the past year.

Modelo A. ¿Dónde estuviste el 1 de enero?
B. Estuve en Nueva York, en Times Square.

CULTURA

El Maratón de las Escaleras de Valparaíso

El Maratón de las Escaleras es un evento especial. Tiene lugar en Valparaíso, una ciudad en la costa de Chile. En el maratón, la gente corre por la ciudad. Los corredores suben y bajan más de quinientos escalones. Hay muchas personas y la carrera se divide en varios grupos por el peligro de accidentes. Las camisetas tienen códigos para identificar a cada corredor.

44 **Piensa.** Have you ever run a race? Why or why not?

→ TU DESAFÍO Use the website to learn more about the *Maratón de las Escaleras*.

HERITAGE LANGUAGE LEARNERS

- There are many special sporting events in different countries around the world. Ask heritage students to investigate a sporting event of interest from their country of origin or from another Spanish-speaking country. Ask them to write a blog entry about this special event.

TOTAL PHYSICAL RESPONSE (TPR)

- Do some TPR Storytelling with the class. Tell students the following story and include all the gestures / movements with each sentence. Then read the story again and have students join in.

Tim y Mack se pusieron los zapatos. (Bend over and tie shoes.)

Mack fue a hablar con una señora. (Make the "blah blah" sign with your hand.)

Tim le preguntó a su abuelo: "¿Dónde estuviste?". (Shrug shoulders and raise hands as if to say "what happened?".)

Tim y Mack subieron las escaleras. (Climb up stairs in place.)

After Viewing

- Check for global comprehension. Verify that students have gathered meaning despite not understanding some words. Have them write four-sentence paragraphs that summarize the *fotonovela*.

Activities

40. Have students create a mini dictionary for all the words in this dialogue. They should include at least three examples of usage for each entry.

41. Have students use their questions and answers to prepare for an oral interview. Ask volunteers to perform the activity in front of the class as if they were on a talkshow. Challenge them to make their presentations without their notebooks.

44. Students may present their responses aided by a graphic organizer. Suggest a two-column chart using the headings *porque* and *porque no*.

AUDIO SCRIPT
See page 199K

Answer Key

40. 1. ciudad   2. capital; provincia   3. país

41. 1. Tim y Mack están en Valparaíso, Chile.
2. Valparaíso está en la montaña.
3. Tienen que participar en el Maratón de las Escaleras.
4. Porque hay que subir escaleras.
5. Hay más de quinientos escalones.
6. Porque corrió mucho.

42. 1. Sí   3. Sí   5. No   7. No
2. Sí   4. No   6. No

43. Answers will vary.

44. Answers will vary.

Additional Resources

Fans Online activities

DESAFÍO 3

Vocabulario – Divisiones políticas

Presentation

- In this section, students will learn:
  - Political divisions (cities, states, regions, etc.).
  - Numbers from 101 to 1,000.

Activities	Standards	Resources
Vocabulario	1.2, 1.3, 3.1	
45.	1.3	
46.	1.3	
47.	1.1, 1.2, 1.3	Audio
48. Conexiones	1.1, 1.2, 1.3, 3.1, 3.2, 5.1	

Teaching Suggestions

Warm-Up / Independent Starter

- Ask students to write the following quantities in words to review numbers from 1 to 100.
  - 28 niños
  - 1 maestra
  - 50 dólares
  - 30 mascotas
  - 81 carros
  - 17 años
  - 45 refrescos
  - 34 manos
  - 12 huevos

Preparation

- Have students look at a map of the United States. Ask them to describe places as you point to them. For example, if you point to Washington DC, students should say: *Washington DC es la capital de los Estados Unidos.* Repeat this until you have used all the new vocabulary.

- After students have said the vocabulary in Spanish, go back to the map and talk about distances between cities. Allow students to guess how many miles there are between two points and write the number out on the board.

Activities

45. After students have finished this activity, have them write an e-mail to a friend in Chile describing their birthplace.

46. Use the categories from this activity to hold a "Geography Bee." Prompt each student with a category from the activity. If the student cannot name a place that hasn't been mentioned yet, he or she should sit down. The last student standing wins.

Vocabulario

Divisiones políticas

Números del 101 al 1.000

101 ciento uno	200 doscientos	500 quinientos	800 ochocientos
110 ciento diez	300 trescientos	600 seiscientos	900 novecientos
132 ciento treinta y dos	400 cuatrocientos	700 setecientos	1.000 mil

45 **Yo soy de...**

▶ **Piensa y escribe.** What are the geographic divisions where you were born? Write this information in your notebook.

Mi país: _____   Mi estado: _____

La capital de mi país: _____   Mi ciudad o pueblo: _____

 ▶ **Presenta.** Now share this information with the class. Does everyone have the same information?

224 doscientos veinticuatro

Differentiated Instruction

DEVELOPING LEARNERS

- Ask students to give examples from their town or city for each of the vocabulary words. For instance, *el país: los Estados Unidos; el estado: Kentucky*, and so on. Have students share their information with the class and create a class list of examples for each word.

EXPANDING LEARNERS

- Have students practice the numbers and the political divisions by playing a map game. Using a map of Chile (or South America) and a small toy car, ask them to give commands to each other regarding places and distances to travel. For example: *Comenzando en Santiago, viaja cien millas al sur. ¿Qué pueblo es?* The classmate should "travel" with the toy car on the map to find out what town is 100 miles south of Santiago. (*San Fernando*)

46 **Lluvia de ideas**

▶ **Escribe.** Can you give examples of each part of our world? Take two minutes and write as many examples of each term as you can brainstorm.

país	capital	ciudad	pueblo
Chile Los Estados Unidos			

montaña	océano	isla	río
	Atlántico		

47 **A sumar y restar**

▶ **Escucha y escribe.** Listen to the characters and write the things they want to buy in the supermarket, and how much they cost.

Modelo   Tim - 540 pesos
→ *Quiere comprar un jugo en el supermercado. El jugo cuesta 600 pesos.*

1. Tess - 175 pesos
2. Patricia - 980 pesos
3. Andy - 460 pesos
4. Rita - 715 pesos
5. Mack - 625 pesos
6. Diana - 860 pesos

▶ **Habla.** Now look at the amount of pesos each person brought and talk with a partner about whether that person can purchase the items he or she wants, and why or why not.

Modelo   A. *¿Tim puede comprar el jugo?*
B. *No, porque solo tiene quinientos cuarenta pesos.*

CONEXIONES: MATEMÁTICAS

El dinero chileno

La moneda de Chile es el peso. Hay monedas de 10, 50 y 100 pesos. Los billetes son de 500, 1.000, 5.000 y 10.000 pesos. Un dólar americano tiene un valor aproximado de 500 pesos chilenos.

48 **Piensa.** Do the math to convert your school's lunch menu prices into Chilean pesos. Can you find a pattern in order to estimate the conversion without using a calculator?

HERITAGE LANGUAGE LEARNERS

• Have heritage students ask family and community members if they have any examples of currency from their countries of origin. Encourage them to bring some coins or bills to school and share information about its value in American dollars using the number words. They can also describe who or what is represented on the bills and / or coins.

MULTIPLE INTELLIGENCES:

Logical-Mathematical Intelligence

• Test students' knowledge of numbers 101–1,000 by playing a game of "Around the World." Use a set of cards with mathematical equations. The cards may have addition, subtraction, or multiplication equations. Two students will compete at a time. The first person to solve the problem will continue. The person who does not guess correctly must sit down. The first student to get back to their original seat or go "around the world," wins.

AUDIO SCRIPT
See page 199K

Answer Key

45. Answers will vary.
▶ Answers will vary.

46. Answers will vary.

47. 1. Quiere comprar un sobre. El sobre cuesta 200 pesos.
2. Quiere comprar chocolate. El chocolate cuesta 795 pesos.
3. Quiere comprar una bolsa de papas fritas. Las papas cuestan 900 pesos.
4. Quiere comprar una botella de agua. El agua cuesta 354 pesos.
5. Quiere un jugo. El jugo cuesta 600 pesos.
6. Quiere comprar unas manzanas. Las manzanas cuestan 499 pesos.

▶ 1. A. ¿Tess puede comprar el sobre?
B. No, porque solo tiene ciento setenta y cinco pesos.
2. A. ¿Patricia puede comprar el chocolate?
B. Sí, porque tiene novecientos ochenta pesos.
3. A. ¿Andy puede comprar las papas?
B. No, porque solo tiene cuatrocientos sesenta pesos.
4. A. ¿Rita puede comprar el agua?
B. Sí, porque tiene setecientos quince pesos.
5. A. ¿Mack puede comprar el jugo?
B. Sí, porque tiene seiscientos veinticinco pesos.
6. A. ¿Diana puede comprar las manzanas?
B. Sí, porque tiene ochocientos sesenta pesos.

48. Answers will vary.

Additional Resources

Fans Online activities
Practice Workbook

DESAFÍO 3

Gramática – Verbos irregulares en el pasado. *Decir* y *hacer*

Presentation

■ In this section, students will learn:
   – Irregular past tense forms of *decir* and *hacer*.

Activities	Standards	Resources
Gramática	1.2, 3.1, 4.1	
49.	1.1, 1.2, 4.1	
50.	1.2, 1.3	Audio
51.	1.1, 1.3, 2.2	
52.	1.2, 1.3	Audio
53.	1.2, 1.3	
54. Comunidades	1.1, 1.2, 2.2, 3.1, 3.2, 5.1	

Teaching Suggestions

Warm-Up / Independent Starter

■ Have students write the opposite idea of each sentence using the following words: *algunos, ninguna, pocos, nunca.*
   1. *Patricia escribió muchos correos electrónicos.*
   2. *Andy se levanta temprano todos los días.*
   3. *Algunas personas compraron ropa cara.*
   4. *Ningún participante subió las escaleras.*

Preparation

■ Review the formation of the regular past tense forms by going around the classroom and asking a few students *¿Qué desayunaste hoy?* Then have pairs of students do the same thing with each other.

■ Write the complete conjugations of the verbs used as examples on the board and discuss how some verbs don't follow these patterns.

Activities

51. Use the polls created in this activity to play a game of *"Los estudiantes de la clase dijeron."* Follow the format of *Family Feud.*

53. Have students play "Telephone" by sitting in a circle and whispering the message in another student's ears. The student who receives the message should write it down. Once students have written their messages let them share them with the class. Are they the same?

Gramática

Verbos irregulares en el pasado. *Decir* y *hacer*

● The verbs decir *(to say)* y hacer *(to do, to make)* are irregular in the preterite. Here are their conjugations:

VERBO DECIR (TO SAY). PRETÉRITO

Singular		Plural	
yo	dije	nosotros nosotras	dijimos
tú	dijiste	vosotros vosotras	dijisteis
usted él ella	dijo	ustedes ellos ellas	dijeron

VERBO HACER (TO DO, TO MAKE). PRETÉRITO

Singular		Plural	
yo	hice	nosotros nosotras	hicimos
tú	hiciste	vosotros vosotras	hicisteis
usted él ella	hizo	ustedes ellos ellas	hicieron

Héctor **dijo** que Valparaíso es la capital.　　Ayer **hice** una comida chilena.

49 **Piensa.** Why does the *c* change to a *z* in the form hizo? How would that form be pronounced if it kept the letter *c*?

50 **Tim dijo que…**

 ▶ **Escucha y escribe.** Tim and Mack are talking at a water stand. Listen and note who makes each statement. Then write a sentence about each.

Modelo　Valparaíso es muy grande.
　　　　→ *Tim y Mack dijeron que Valparaíso es muy grande.*

   1. La ciudad es muy bonita.
   2. Le gusta mucho Valparaíso.
   3. Hay mucha gente.
   4. El maratón es emocionante.
   5. Las escaleras son altas.

51 **Cinco estudiantes dijeron**

 ▶ **Habla y escribe.** The game show *Cien mexicanos dijeron* has asked you to poll your class for their next show. Create three questions to ask your classmates, then compile their answers in writing.

Modelo　A. *¿Cuál es tu bebida favorita?*
　　　　B. *Mi bebida favorita es el jugo de naranja.*
　　　　A. *Dos estudiantes dijeron que el jugo de naranja es su bebida favorita.*

Differentiated Instruction

DEVELOPING LEARNERS

• Have students play a game like "Telephone." The first student in a row whispers a word or phrase from the vocabulary to the second student in that same row. The second student then whispers the word/phrase and adds another word to the third student who adds another word and so on. When the word/phrase reaches the last student in the row, that student reports the entire sequence aloud by saying: *"Dijiste… (word/phrase)."* Was the message passed correctly? Can the students trace the phrase and added words back (by saying *"Dijiste…"*)? Repeat the activity with another word/phrase.

EXPANDING LEARNERS

• Ask students to read a comic strip in Spanish. Then ask them to describe what happened in the comic strip to a partner. Ask them to use preterite forms of *hacer* and *decir* in their descriptions. See if their partners can draw the comic strip based on the spoken description.

52 ¿Qué hicieron?

 ▶ **Escucha y une.** Listen to the characters talk about what they did last weekend. Match the participants with their activities.

Ⓐ
1. Tim y Mack
2. Diana
3. Rita
4. Andy y Janet
5. Tess y Patricia

Ⓑ
a. una cena deliciosa
b. una nueva amiga
c. unas figuras de cerámica
d. un viaje a la costa
e. planes para el verano

▶ **Escribe.** Now write a complete sentence telling what the character(s) did.

Modelo *Tim y Mack hicieron…*

53 Mensaje perdido

▶ **Escribe.** Mack took a phone message from Martin, Tim's friend from home. Read the note and fill in the missing forms of the verbs *ver* and *decir*.

> ¡Hola, Tim! Soy Mack.
>
> Tu amigo Martín llamó desde San Francisco. Él ___1___ (decir) que anoche te ___2___ (ver) en las noticias. ¡Qué emoción! Yo le ___3___ (decir) que tu mamá me llamó ayer para decirme lo mismo. Martín ___4___ (decir) que ustedes ___5___ (hacer) planes para el verano. ¿ ___6___ (hacer, tú) todas tus tareas? Nos vemos luego.

 COMUNIDADES

EL LAPISLÁZULI

El lapislázuli es una piedra (*stone*) semipreciosa usada en trabajos de artesanía y en joyas (*jewelry*). Su color azul simboliza la pureza, la salud, la suerte y la nobleza. La producción de lapislázuli es muy importante en Chile.

54 **Relaciona.** Is there a place in your city or town where people make jewelry by hand? If there is, where is this jewelry sold?

doscientos veintisiete **227**

Unit 8

DESAFÍO 3

Gramática – Verbos irregulares en el pasado. *Decir* y *hacer*

 AUDIO SCRIPT
See page 199L

 COMUNIDADES

El lapislázuli

Chile is an important source of lapis lazuli coming from the Andes Mountains. Chilean artisans make jewelry with this semiprecious stone. The quality depends on the purity of the blue color. It became the national stone of Chile on 1984.

Answer Key

49. Because the letter *c* in front of *o* sounds like a *k*.

50. 1. Mack dijo que la ciudad es muy bonita.
2. Tim dijo que le gusta mucho Valparaíso.
3. Mack dijo que hay mucha gente.
4. Mack dijo que el maratón es emocionante.
5. Tim dijo que las escaleras son altas.

51. Answers will vary.

52. 1. c   2. b   3. d   4. a   5. e
▶ 1. Tim y Mack hicieron unas figuras de cerámica.
2. Diana hizo una nueva amiga.
3. Rita hizo un viaje a la costa.
4. Andy y Janet hicieron una cena deliciosa.
5. Tess y Patricia hicieron planes para el verano.

53. 1. dijo   3. dije   5. hicieron
2. vio   4. dijo   6. hiciste

54. Answers will vary.

Additional Resources

Fans Online activities
Practice Workbook

227

DESAFÍO 3

Gramática – Verbos irregulares en el pasado. *Estar* y *tener*

Presentation

- In this section, students will learn:
  - Irregular past tense forms of *estar* and *tener*.

Activities	Standards	Resources
Gramática	1.2, 3.1, 4.1	
55.	1.1, 4.1	
56.	1.3	
57.	1.2, 1.3	
58.	1.2, 1.3	
59. Conexiones	1.1, 1.2, 2.1, 3.1, 3.2, 4.2	

Teaching Suggestions

Warm-Up / Independent Starter

- Have students write five sentences using the verb *hacer* and the prompts below.
  1. *El año pasado…*
  2. *Ayer…*
  3. *Esta mañana…*
  4. *Anoche…*
  5. *La semana pasada…*

Preparation

- Review the present tense conjugations of the verbs *estar* and *tener*. Elicit examples of usage from students. Then write the preterite tense conjugations of the same verbs. This will help students make the transition to the past tense. Invite volunteers to come up with examples of usage of *estar* and *tener* in the past tense.

Activities

55. You may help students visualize these differences by circling or underlining the endings you want to be contrasted.

57. Ask students to write three additional sentences in which they use *estar* and *tener* to describe a trip they took.

58. Have students use the activity as a jumpstart to write a paragraph for a personal composition. Encourage them to use transition words to avoid a list of disconnected sentences.

Gramática

Verbos irregulares en el pasado. *Estar* y *tener*

- Two more commonly used irregular verbs in the preterite tense are estar *(to be)* and tener *(to have)*. Here are their conjugations:

VERBO ESTAR (TO BE). PRETÉRITO

Singular		Plural	
yo	estuve	nosotros nosotras	estuvimos
tú	estuviste	vosotros vosotras	estuvisteis
usted él ella	estuvo	ustedes ellos ellas	estuvieron

VERBO TENER (TO HAVE). PRETÉRITO

Singular		Plural	
yo	tuve	nosotros nosotras	tuvimos
tú	tuviste	vosotros vosotras	tuvisteis
usted él ella	tuvo	ustedes ellos ellas	tuvieron

Estuvimos en la costa con nuestros amigos.

Andy y Janet **tuvieron** un resfriado en Chile.

55 **Piensa.** What differences do you notice between the endings of the regular preterite verbs and the endings of these irregular preterite verbs?

56 **¡Inclúyame!**

▶ **Escribe.** Your teacher has asked your class to digitally paste yourselves into pictures with the characters in Chile. Using the pictures below, describe where each person was.

Modelo 1. *Mi amigo Pepe estuvo con Tess en la playa.*

① Pepe  ② Julia y yo  ③ yo  ④ ellos

228 doscientos veintiocho

Differentiated Instruction

DEVELOPING LEARNERS

- Have students choose a verb (*estar* or *tener*) and create a verb conjugation chart for each of the six subjects, including a sentence for each. They can use a chart like the one below.

Yo estuve en la costa.	*Nosotros estuvimos* en el río.
Tú estuviste en la playa.	*Vosotros estuvisteis* en la capital.
Ella estuvo en la ciudad.	*Ellos estuvieron* en las montañas.

EXPANDING LEARNERS

- Ask students to write an e-mail to a friend to describe a special trip they took in the past. They should include the places where they were (*estuve en…*) and what they had to do (*tuve que…*). Students may invent an answer if they have not been on a recent trip. Ask students to share their e-mail messages with a partner.

57 **¿Qué tuviste?**

▶ **Une y escribe.** Match the columns and write sentences with the preterite of the verb *tener*.

(A)	(B)
1. Liliana	a. ganas de viajar a Chile.
2. Mi papá y yo	b. un buen viaje.
3. Tú	c. dos perros y un pájaro.
4. Mi mamá	d. hambre esta mañana.
5. Mis hermanos	e. una amiga chilena en la escuela.
6. Yo	f. sed después de hacer deporte.

Modelo 1. *Liliana tuvo un buen viaje.*

58 **Viajes**

▶ **Escribe.** Write where the people below were, or what they had, using the appropriate forms of *estar* or *tener*.

Modelo *Juan estuvo en la capital.*

1. Mi abuela _____ en una playa muy bonita.
2. Nosotros _____ en las montañas.
3. Tú _____ una fiesta fantástica en el hotel.
4. Yo _____ en otro país.
5. Ellas _____ buen tiempo durante el viaje.
6. Carlos y Marta _____ en una isla tropical.
7. Mi familia y yo _____ algún problema en el viaje.

CONEXIONES: MÚSICA

El Festival Internacional de la Canción de Viña del Mar

El Festival Internacional de la Canción de Viña del Mar se celebra anualmente desde 1959. Incluye conciertos y un concurso de música popular y folclórica. Este festival es muy importante y en él participan artistas de todo el mundo. Los jueces del concurso son cantantes y músicos famosos.

59 **Piensa.** Can you think of any music competitions in the United States or around the world? How do they help aspiring artists?

HERITAGE LANGUAGE LEARNERS

• Have heritage students write a short biography about a family or community member and his or her experiences immigrating to the United States. Have students include information about where the person came from, what struggles he or she had in coming to the United States (if any), and why that person decided to leave his or her country of origin to come to the United States.

SPECIAL-NEEDS LEARNERS

• For students who are visually challenged, ask classmates to create a large print version of the conjugation grids from the two grammar presentations on poster board. Make sure that all of the text is written in large letters.

DESAFÍO 3

Gramática – Verbos irregulares en el pasado. *Estar* y *tener*

CONEXIONES: MÚSICA

El Festival Internacional de la Canción de Viña del Mar

One of the peculiarities of the Viña del Mar Music Festival is its audience. Viña's audience is loud and rambunctious, and it does not shy away from expressing its approval or disapproval freely. In fact, many recognized artists have been booed off the stage. The importance that both artists and media attach to Viña's audience is perhaps best exemplified by the fact that it has been given a name: *El Monstruo* (The Monster).

Answer Key

55. Elicit from students that these verbs do not follow the patterns already learned. They use some of the *-er* and *-ir* endings.

56. 1. Mi amigo Pepe estuvo con Tess en la playa.
2. Julia y yo estuvimos con Andy en el bosque.
3. Yo estuve con Mack en la ciudad.
4. Ellos estuvieron con Diana en la montaña.

57. Answers will vary. Sample answers:
2. Mi papá y yo tuvimos hambre esta mañana.
3. Tú tuviste dos perros y un pájaro.
4. Mi mamá tuvo una amiga chilena en la escuela.
5. Mis hermanos tuvieron sed después de hacer deporte.
6. Yo tuve ganas de viajar a Chile.

58. 1. estuvo   5. tuvieron
2. estuvimos   6. estuvieron
3. tuviste   7. tuvimos
4. estuve

59. Answers will vary.

Additional Resources

Fans Online activities
Practice Workbook

229

Unit 8
DESAFÍO 3
Comunicación

Presentation

- In this section, students will practice:
  - Irregular past tense forms of *decir, hacer, estar,* and *tener.*
  - Political divisions.
  - Numbers from 101 to 1,000.

Activities	Standards	Resources
60.	1.3	
61.	1.2, 1.3	
62.	1.2, 1.3, 3.1	
63. Final del desafío	1.3	

Teaching Suggestions

Warm-Up / Independent Starter

- Have students rewrite the following sequence of events in their logical order.
  1. *Mañana voy a llevar tenis.*
  2. *Mamá me dijo: "Son las diez de la mañana".*
  3. *Hice pocas cosas por la mañana.*
  4. *Ayer me levanté tarde.*

Preparation

- Ask students to write the preterite tense conjugation of the verbs *estar, decir, hacer,* and *tener* on a sheet of paper. They may not use their books or their notes. After five minutes have students trade papers with a partner and correct each other's work. After two minutes have students trade with another partner and correct each other's work. Finally, pass the papers back to their original owners. Write the verb conjugations on the board. Did students get them correct the first time? Did they finally end up with the correct answers if not? Discuss the results as a class.

Activities

60. Ask students to use their sentences, and other necessary phrases, to write a coherent paragraph about Mark's day. Invite volunteers to read their paragraphs aloud.

61. Ask students to research distances between their home cities and five state capitals in the United States. Have them report their findings to the class.

230

Comunicación

60 **¿Qué hizo Mark ayer?**

▶ **Escribe.** Write about Mark's day according to the pictures and the clues below.

Modelo 1. *Ayer hizo sol.*

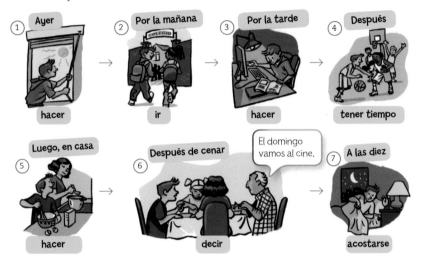

61 **¿Qué distancia hay?**

 ▶ **Lee y habla.** With a partner, take turns asking and answering questions about the distance between these cities in Chile.

Modelo A. *¿Qué distancia hay de Iquique a Arica?*
B. *Hay trescientos dos kilómetros.*

Ciudades	Distancias
Santiago de Chile - Valparaíso	120 km
Chillán - Temuco	270 km
Iquique - Arica	302 km
Chillán - Santiago de Chile	407 km
Villarica - Castro	527 km
Calama - Arica	600 km
Viña del Mar - Temuco	796 km
Santiago de Chile - Valdivia	841 km

▶ **Piensa y escribe.** A kilometer is roughly 0.6 miles (*millas*). Convert the distances above into miles.

Modelo 1. *De Santiago de Chile a Valparaíso = 120 km*
→ 120 × 0.6 = 72
→ *De Santiago a Valparaíso hay setenta y dos millas.*

230 doscientos treinta

Differentiated Instruction

DEVELOPING LEARNERS

- Have students review the numbers by counting by 100s in pairs. For example:
  A. *cien*
  B. *doscientos*
  A. *trescientos…*

EXPANDING LEARNERS

- Ask students to design a travel itinerary through Chile that includes one city, one border, one town, and one region. Ask them to create a travel brochure using the itinerary, including the distances between each of the four places.

62 Tú, el detective

▶ **Habla.** Imagine you are a detective in charge of solving a mystery. Interview five witnesses about where they were, what they did there, and what they saw.

Modelo A. *¿Dónde estuviste el martes?*
B. *Estuve en el parque.*
A. *¿Qué hiciste allí?*
B. *Hice mi tarea y hablé con Manuel.*
A. *¿Qué viste?*
B. *Vi a mucha gente corriendo.*

▶ **Escribe.** Now fill in a detective notebook with a chart of information like the one below.

Nombre(s)	¿Dónde estuvo / estuvieron?	¿Qué hizo / hicieron?	¿Qué vio / vieron?
Paola	Estuvo en el parque.	Hizo su tarea. Habló con Manuel.	Vio a mucha gente corriendo.

Final del desafío

63 ¿Dónde estuvieron?

▶ **Escribe.** Describe what is happening in each scene. Write about where the characters were, what they did, what they saw, and what they said.

doscientos treinta y uno 231

Answer Key

60. Answers will vary. Sample answers:
2. Mark fue a la escuela por la mañana.
3. Por la tarde, Mark hizo la tarea.
4. Después tuvo tiempo para jugar un partido de baloncesto.
5. Luego, en casa, Mark hizo la cena con su madre.
6. Después de cenar, su padre dijo: "El domingo vamos al cine".
7. Mark se acostó a las diez.

61. 1. A. ¿Qué distancia hay de Santiago de Chile a Valparaíso?
B. Hay ciento veinte kilómetros.
2. A. ¿Qué distancia hay de Chillán a Temuco?
B. Hay doscientos setenta kilómetros.
4. A. ¿Qué distancia hay de Chillán a Santiago de Chile?
B. Hay cuatrocientos siete kilómetros.
5. A. ¿Qué distancia hay de Villarica a Castro?
B. Hay quinientos veintisiete kilómetros.
6. A. ¿Qué distancia hay de Calama a Arica?
B. Hay seiscientos kilómetros.
7. A. ¿Qué distancia hay de Viña del Mar a Temuco?
B. Hay setecientos noventa y seis kilómetros.
8. A. ¿Qué distancia hay de Santiago de Chile a Valdivia?
B. Hay ochocientos cuarenta y un kilómetros.

▶ 2. Ciento sesenta y dos millas.
3. Ciento ochenta y una millas.
4. Doscientas cuarenta y cuatro millas.
5. Trescientas dieciséis millas.
6. Trescientas sesenta millas.
7. Cuatrocientas setenta y siete millas.
8. Quinientas cuatro millas.

62. Answers will vary.
▶ Answers will vary.

63. Answers will vary.

Additional Resources

Fans Online activities
Practice Workbook

HERITAGE LANGUAGE LEARNERS

• Ask heritage students to write a creative short story about a travel experience. The story can center around a funny or silly incident on a trip or be an adventure story, and should use the preterite forms of *estar*, *tener*, *decir*, and *hacer* wherever possible. Encourage students to illustrate their stories and then read them to a classmate.

MULTIPLE INTELLIGENCES:
Intrapersonal Intelligence

• Have students write a Facebook wall post or a Twitter "tweet" in which they comment on an opportunity that they once had, but that they missed. For example: *Tuve la oportunidad de ir a Hawái con mis padres, pero me quedé en casa para pasar las vacaciones con mis amigos.* Ask students to share their posts with the class.

231

Unit 8
DESAFÍO 4
Expresar permiso y prohibición

Presentation

- In *Desafío 4*, Diana and Rita are visiting the Torres del Paine National Park in Patagonia. Their task is to collect five pounds of litter from the W trail.

- In this section, students will learn:
  - Nature and environmental vocabulary.
  - Words related to recycling.
  - The use of the verb *poder* to ask for and give permission or express prohibition.

Activities	Standards	Resources
Fotonovela	1.2	Vis. Pres.
64.	1.2	
65.	1.2	
66.	1.2, 1.3	Audio
67. Cultura	1.1, 1.2, 3.1, 3.2, 5.1	

Teaching Suggestions

Warm-Up / Independent Starter

- Have students read and rewrite the speech bubbles in the *fotonovela* in scrambled order in their notebooks.

Preparation

- Once students have finished with the Independent Starter, have them close their books and work with a partner to put the speech bubbles back into a logical order. Students' repeated reading of the dialogue will aid in comprehension.

 La fotonovela

Before Viewing

- Have a student read the introduction to the task. Ask students if they have visited a National Park and what their impression is when they see litter. Have students talk about the effects of human indifference on the environment.

After Viewing

- Ask students to say what they think happened before the scene begins and after the scene ends. Students will draw and caption a scene before the *fotonovela* begins, and add one at the end of it.

232

La famosa Ruta W

 Diana and Rita are visiting the Torres del Paine National Park in Patagonia, Chile. They are going to hike the W Route, the most popular route in the park. They must collect five pounds of litter from the trail … and hike back with it!

> El guía dijo que tenemos que tomar la Ruta W.

> ¿Por qué se llama así?

> Hola, chicas. Aquí tienen sus bolsas para la basura.

> Porque tiene forma de W.

> Hay flores y pájaros muy bonitos. ¿Podemos tomar fotos de los animales y las plantas durante la ruta?

> Mira, tía, esos chicos están dejando mucha basura.

> Sí, pero no podemos tocarlos.

> ¡Oigan, se puede comer en el parque, pero no se puede dejar la basura!

Continuará…

64 Detective de palabras

▶ **Relaciona.** Using the dialogue, match the images below with words from the box.

flor
planta
pájaro
basura

① ② ③ ④

Differentiated Instruction

DEVELOPING LEARNERS

- Have students work in groups of three (one student for Rita, one for Diana, one for the park ranger) to act out the *fotonovela* by reading the speech bubbles aloud to each other. Encourage students to use appropriate inflections and gestures as they read.

EXPANDING LEARNERS

- Have students work in groups of three and use the categories *flor*, *planta*, *pájaro*, and *basura* to write the names of all the flowers, plants, birds, and types of trash / recyclables they know in Spanish. If they cannot think of any, have students research the categories on the Internet.

65 ¿Comprendes?

▶ **Elige.** Decide which things can and cannot be done while walking along the W Route. Choose the correct option to complete each sentence.

1. En la ruta _____ tomar fotos de los animales.
   se pueden/no se pueden

2. En la ruta _____ tocar a los animales.
   se puede/no se puede

3. _____ comer en el parque.
   Se puede/No se puede

4. _____ dejar la basura en el parque.
   Se puede/No se puede

66 Fotos del parque

 ▶ **Escucha y ordena.** Diana sent some picture messages to her mom. Listen to the voice mail she left and put the photos in the order you hear about them.

 C

A

B

CULTURA

Parque Nacional Torres del Paine

El Parque Nacional Torres del Paine está en la cordillera del Paine, en la Patagonia chilena. El pico (peak) más alto, Cerro Paine Grande, mide casi 3.000 metros de altura. Hay tres picos famosos, llamados las Torres del Paine. El parque tiene una gran variedad de paisajes: montañas, valles, ríos, lagos y glaciares. La flora y la fauna del parque son muy ricas.

67 Piensa. Have you ever hiked up a tall mountain? If so, how did it feel? If not, would you like to one day?

HERITAGE LANGUAGE LEARNERS

- In many parts of the Spanish-speaking world, recycling takes on different meanings. In the United States, we collect our recyclables and put them in special bins to be hauled off to special treatment and sorting facilities. In much of Latin America, things like cardboard, paper, aluminum and glass are collected and sorted by people suffering economic hardships and then sold to businesses that do the recycling. Ask students to talk about how materials are recycled in their countries of origin and to share this information with the class.

CRITICAL THINKING

- Ask students to consider why it is important to recycle. Have them create a flow chart showing what would happen if we all continued to consume without recycling.

Unit 8
DESAFÍO 4

Expresar permiso y prohibición

Activities

64. You can modify this activity by having students write original sentences. Take the opportunity to review subject-verb agreement.

67. Have students use *porque* and *por* to explain their reasons. Before doing the activity you may write these words on the board and have students spend a few minutes reviewing how to use them.

 AUDIO SCRIPT
See page 199L

CULTURA

Parque Nacional Torres del Paine

The official site of the Torres del Paine National Park recommends wearing proper clothing when visiting. Strong winds, rain, and snow are very common in the area. The weather in Patagonia can be quite extreme, with temperatures ranging from highs in the mid-sixties in springtime to lows below freezing during the fall and winter. There are roads and trails, and a park ranger station where visitors can gather maps and information.

Answer Key

64. 1. planta
2. flor
3. basura
4. pájaro

65. 1. se pueden
2. no se puede
3. Se puede
4. No se puede

66. 1. B 2. C 3. A

67. Answers will vary.

Additional Resources

Fans Online activities

233

DESAFÍO 4

Vocabulario – La naturaleza y el medio ambiente

Presentation

- In this section, students will learn:
  - Nature and environmental vocabulary.
  - Words related to recycling.

Activities	Standards	Resources
Vocabulario	1.2, 1.3, 3.1	
68.	1.2	
69.	1.2, 1.3	Audio
70.	1.3, 3.1	
71. Conexiones	1.1, 1.2, 3.1, 3.2, 5.1	

Teaching Suggestions

Warm-Up / Independent Starter

- Have students create illustrated flashcards for five terms in the new vocabulary. On the backs of the cards, students should write the vocabulary words and one sentence using each of them.

Preparation

- Introduce the new words with the flashcards from the Independent Starter modeling their pronunciation. You may have students act out the terms with gestures. *El pájaro*, for example, could be represented by a student flapping his or her arms as if they were wings. This can be a fun way to introduce vocabulary, as some of the terms may trigger students' creativity.

Activities

68. Before proceeding with the activity, have students point out which terms are cognates. Have them name the English word and identify the similarities and differences between the terms.

69. Have students help you review the endings for the past tense before completing the activity. Then give students a conjugation chart with the verbs *oír* and *sentir*.

70. Have students add five things they could put in each category. Working with a partner, students should tell why each item belongs in its particular category.

Vocabulario

La naturaleza y el medio ambiente

¡Me gustan mucho las plantas y los animales!

El reciclaje

Hay que reciclar para cuidar el medio ambiente.

68 **Flora y fauna**

▶ **Completa.** Complete the sentences with the correct option.

1. ¡Qué bien huelen estas _____!   a. animales   b. flores
2. Ese río tiene el _____ muy limpia.   a. agua   b. aire
3. Muchos _____ viven en los árboles.   a. peces   b. pájaros
4. Los mosquitos son un tipo de _____.   a. insectos   b. peces
5. Ese contenedor es para reciclar el _____.   a. medio ambiente   b. vidrio

Differentiated Instruction

DEVELOPING LEARNERS

- Developing learners often learn better with visual cues. Have students create a picture dictionary using the words from the new vocabulary and images from clip art, magazines, or hand-drawn illustrations. Collate the images and create a class picture dictionary.

EXPANDING LEARNERS

- Have students use the new vocabulary to talk about their favorite places in nature with a classmate. As they describe this favorite place, their partner should try to guess which place is being described. For example:
  A. *Tiene muchos peces.*
  B. *¿Es la costa?*
  A. *No. Tiene muchos árboles.*
  B. *¿Es el bosque?*

69 **¿Oíste algo?**

 ▶ **Escucha y dibuja.** Diana and Rita could not see well in the forest. Copy the chart below and fill it in with drawings of what they heard and felt.

Modelo

Sentido		
Elemento del bosque		

 ▶ **Habla.** Now tell a partner what Diana and Rita experienced.

Modelo A. *¿Qué oyó Diana?*
B. *Diana oyó el sonido del aire.*

70 **¿Botar o reciclar?**

▶ **Escribe.** Decide whether these materials are recyclable or not and write complete sentences.

Modelo *Las botellas de vidrio son para reciclar.*

① ② ③ ④

para reciclar   para botar a la basura

 CONEXIONES: ECOLOGÍA

¡A reciclar!

Para salvar nuestro planeta, es muy importante reducir la cantidad de basura y reciclar. En nuestras casas podemos reciclar el plástico, el metal, el vidrio y el papel. Si reciclamos estos materiales, podemos ayudar a conservar nuestros recursos naturales.

71 **Compara.** What items do you recycle in your home? Do you help separate your trash at home? What other ways can you think of to keep trash from ending up in our landfills?

HERITAGE LANGUAGE LEARNERS

• Ask heritage students to write a poem in which they describe the natural landscapes in your state. They should include vocabulary words from the book as well as other words and phrases. They may use their dictionaries to look up and use new vocabulary that they don't know. Encourage students to recite their poems to the class, or to share them in writing.

MULTIPLE INTELLIGENCES:

Visual-Spatial Intelligence

• Ask students to write a list of items that they can recycle in your town. Then using the list, ask them to create a recycling poster labeling the images of the items with the expression *Se puede reciclar…* Hang the posters around the school.

Vocabulario – La naturaleza y el medio ambiente

 AUDIO SCRIPT
See page 199L

CONEXIONES: ECOLOGÍA

¡A reciclar!

The most important environmental group in the United States is the U.S. Environmental Protection Agency (EPA). The EPA handles programs and hosts frequent competitions to raise awareness of how human consumption affects the environment. Visit the official EPA website to find resources and information regarding recycling, including information on a program for young citizens called "Planet Protectors."

Answer Key

68. 1. b   2. a   3. b   4. a   5. b
69. Answers will vary.
▶ A. ¿Qué oyó Diana?
B. Diana oyó el sonido del aire.
A. ¿Qué oyó Rita?
B. Rita oyó el sonido de un pájaro muy bonito.
A. ¿Qué tocó Diana?
B. Diana tocó una hoja muy suave.
A. ¿Qué tocó a Rita?
B. ¡La tocó un insecto!
70. 1. Las botellas de plástico son para reciclar.
2. La piel de la fruta es para botar a la basura.
3. Las latas son para reciclar.
4. El papel es para reciclar.
71. Answers will vary.

Additional Resources

Fans Online activities
Practice Workbook

DESAFÍO 4

Gramática – Expresar permiso y prohibición

Presentation

- In this section, students will learn the use of the verb *poder* to ask for and give permission or express prohibition.

Activities	Standards	Resources
Gramática	1.2, 3.1, 4.1	
72.	1.1, 4.1	
73.	1.2, 1.3	
74.	1.2, 1.3	Audio
75.	1.2, 1.3, 3.1	
76. Conexiones	1.1, 1.2, 3.1, 3.2	

Teaching Suggestions

Warm-Up / Independent Starter

- Have students complete the following sentences with the correct forms of the verb *poder* in the present tense.
  1. *Yo … caminar diez kilómetros sin cansarme.*
  2. *Nosotros … ayudar con la basura.*
  3. *Ellos no … completar el desafío.*
  4. *Señor, ¿… enseñarme el mapa?*

Preparation

- Preview the structure *se puede* + infinitive with signs from the real world. You may draw them on the board. At this point, students see the sign as they repeat your interpretation of it. Use phrases like *Se puede nadar, Se puede pasear con perros, No se puede entrar,* etc.

- Have students develop three rules for a classroom poster. Elicit the sentence *No se puede hablar inglés en clase.*

Activities

74. Students may add three more items according to what they know about visiting this type of park. Ask them *¿Qué más se puede llevar?*

75. Use the activity to provoke a class discussion. Ask students what would happen if there were no rules in a national park. Have them decide if it would be ever appropriate to break a rule there. When would that be?

236

DESAFÍO 4

Gramática

Expresar permiso y prohibición

Expresar permiso

- Use the verb *poder* to ask for and to give permission.
  - –¿**Puedo** salir este fin de semana?
  - –Sí, **puedes** salir después de hacer tus tareas.

- When you want to express permission in general terms, use these formulas:

se puede + infinitivo *(with singular object)*	**Se puede** dar comida a los peces.
se puede(n) + infinitivo *(with plural object)*	**¿Se puede(n)** tomar fotos en el museo?

- The verb *poder* means *can* or *to be able to*.
  - **Puedes** reciclar el plástico aquí.   **Podemos** hacer la excursión en bicicleta.

Expresar prohibición

- The negative form of *poder* can be used to deny permission or express prohibition.
  - **No puedes** usar la computadora aquí.   **No puedes** volver tarde a casa.

- When you want to express prohibition in general terms, use these formulas:

no se puede + infinitivo	No se puede botar basura en el suelo.
no se puede(n) + infinitivo	No se puede(n) botar las botellas de vidrio a la basura.

72 **Piensa.** *Poder* is also the Spanish word for *power*. How are the two definitions —*to be able to* and *power*— related?

73 **Reglas para la casa**

▶ **Escribe.** The notes below were brainstormed during a family meeting prior to drawing up some house rules. Write the rules of what is allowed or prohibited.

Modelo *No se puede correr por la casa.*

Se puede
Se pueden
No se puede
No se pueden

😠 bailar encima de las mesas
🙂 comer pizza una vez a la semana
😠 escuchar música hasta muy tarde
😠 ver películas violentas
🙂 ver la televisión los fines de semana
🙂 jugar después de hacer las tareas
😠 leer el correo de otros
🙂 estudiar en el jardín

236 doscientos treinta y seis

Differentiated Instruction

DEVELOPING LEARNERS

- Have students write a list of ten things that they can or cannot do at home using the word *poder*. For example: *Se puede hablar por teléfono. No se puede usar la computadora.*

EXPANDING LEARNERS

- Ask students to write a list of ten things that they can or cannot do in their school or their class using the phrases *Se puede* and *No se puede*. For example: *En la clase de español, se puede hablar español. No se puede hablar inglés.*

74 Empacando para el viaje

 ▶ **Escucha y decide.** Diana wants to know what items she can bring with her to Torres del Paine National Park. Listen to her conversation with Rita and decide if these things are allowed or not allowed in the park.

① ② ③
④ ⑤ ⑥

▶ **Escribe.** Write sentences to tell if each of the items above is permitted or not.

75 ¿Lo hago o no lo hago?

▶ **Escribe.** Using a chart like the one below, list five things that you are allowed to do and five things that you are not allowed to do in a national park.

En el parque se puede…	En el parque no se puede…
leer un libro	jugar al hockey

▶ **Habla.** Now tell a partner the park rules that you came up with.

Modelo   *En el parque se puede leer un libro, pero no se puede jugar al hockey.*

CONEXIONES: CIENCIAS

Animales en peligro de extinción

Muchos animales están en peligro de extinción por factores como el desarrollo humano y la contaminación. En Chile están en peligro aves como el pájaro carpintero y el ñandú; mamíferos, como la vicuña y la chinchilla cordillera; y mamíferos marinos, como algunas ballenas y delfines.

76 **Piensa y busca.** What other reasons might account for these animals' status on the endangered-species list? Find out what animals are in danger where you live.

doscientos treinta y siete **237**

Gramática – Expresar permiso y prohibición

AUDIO SCRIPT
See page 199L

CONEXIONES: CIENCIAS

Animales en peligro de extinción

There are more than forty endangered species in Chile. Most of these species live in the Valdivian Coastal Range, a region of Chile where scientists believe some animal species took refuge during the last Ice Age. As a result, the Valdivian Coastal Range still harbors Chile's highest concentrations of species found nowhere else on Earth.

Answer Key

72. Answers will vary. Elicit from students that to have *power* means *to be able to* do things.

73. Se puede…
  – comer pizza una vez a la semana.
  – ver la televisión los fines de semana.
  – jugar después de hacer las tareas.
  – estudiar en el jardín.
  No se puede…
  – bailar encima de las mesas.
  – escuchar música hasta muy tarde.
  – leer el correo de otros.
  No se puede(n) ver películas violentas.

74. Se puede: 2, 4, 5, 6.
  No se puede: 1, 3.
  ▶ 1. No se puede escuchar la radio.
   2. Se puede leer un libro.
   3. No se puede jugar con el balón.
   4. Se puede jugar con un videojuego.
   5. Se puede(n) llevar botellas de refresco, pero hay que reciclar las botellas.
   6. Se puede llevar la cámara porque se pueden tomar fotos en el parque.

75. Answers will vary.
  ▶ Answer will vary.

76. Answers will vary.

Additional Resources

Fans Online activities
Practice Workbook

DESAFÍO 4

Comunicación

Presentation

- In this section, students will practice:
  - Nature and environmental vocabulary.
  - Words related to recycling.
  - The use of the verb *poder* to ask for and give permission or express prohibition.

Activities	Standards	Resources
77.	1.2	
78.	1.1	
79.	1.2, 1.3, 3.1	Audio
80.	1.3, 3.1, 5.1	
81. Final del desafío	1.1, 1.2, 1.3	
Tu desafío	1.2, 1.3	

Teaching Suggestions

Warm-Up / Independent Starter

- Have students write paragraphs of four to five sentences about what they can and cannot do in the library.

Preparation

- Have students read their paragraphs from the Independent Starter in small groups. Once they have finished reading, students should stay in their groups to do the *Comunicación* activities. You may want to turn it into a competition. At the end of the class, the group with the most correct answers wins.

Activities

77. Have students extend each sentence in writing by using *por* and *porque* to explain the reasons behind each correct answer. For example:
1. *Es importante reciclar las latas de metal porque es bueno para el planeta.*
2. *Hay que plantar más árboles por el bien del medio ambiente.*

79. Have students turn their reflections into a podcast for a recycling program. The students can work in groups and should be encouraged to use sound effects.

Comunicación

77 ¿Qué podemos hacer?

▶ **Elige.** There are many ways we can help save our environment. Choose the correct word to complete each sentence.

1. Es importante reciclar las latas de _____   a. papel   b. metal
2. Hay que plantar más _____   a. animales   b. árboles
3. Debemos escribir en los dos lados de una hoja de _____   a. planta   b. papel
4. Hay que mantener limpio el aire para proteger a los _____   a. pájaros   b. peces
5. Siempre hay que apagar la luz para no gastar _____   a. metal   b. electricidad

78 ¿Se puede reciclar?

▶ **Habla.** Look at the items below. Talk with your partner about what they are made of and ask if they can be recycled or not.

Modelo   A. ¿De qué es esta botella?   A. ¿Se puede reciclar?
          B. Es de plástico.   B. Sí, se puede.

①    ②    ③    ④    ⑤

79 ¿Qué puede hacer ella?

▶ **Escucha y dibuja.** Diana was inspired by the Torres del Paine National Park. Listen to her plans and draw pictures of four things she will do to help the environment.

▶ **Escribe.** Now reflect on Diana's plans and write what you too can do at home.

Modelo

En casa yo puedo reciclar el papel.
También puedo plantar un árbol.

Differentiated Instruction

DEVELOPING LEARNERS

- To practice the vocabulary words, have students go on a scavenger hunt around the classroom to identify things that represent as many of the vocabulary words as possible. For example, students can point to the garbage can (*basura*), the window (*vidrio*), a notebook (*papel*), and a tree through the window (*árbol*). To turn this into a competition, see which team of students can identify the most items.

EXPANDING LEARNERS

- Ask each student to write a contract regarding all the things that he or she can do to save the environment. The contract should include five items (e.g., *Puedo reciclar plástico. Puedo ahorrar energía*). Have students share their contracts with the rest of the class. Compile the statements to create a class contract, and then ask the students to sign it and hang it in the classroom.

80 **¿Qué puedo hacer yo?**

▶ **Escribe.** Everyone can do something to help conserve our natural resources. Write a short statement about what you can do to help.

Todos podemos conservar los recursos naturales del mundo. Por ejemplo, se puede(n)...
Pero no se puede(n)...
Por eso, yo puedo...

Final del desafío

①

②

③

a. Sí, tía. Tenemos que reciclarlas.

b. Vamos, Diana. Ya tenemos nuestras cinco libras de basura. Si caminamos más rápido, podemos llegar a tiempo.

c. ¡Qué horror! ¡Mira cuántas latas y cuántas botellas de plástico! No podemos dejarlas aquí.

81 **¿Qué pasó?**

▶ **Habla y escribe.** Look at the scenes above and decide which caption corresponds to each. Do you think Diana and Rita made it to the park entrance to turn in their five pounds of trash? Write a final caption to tell what you think happened.

🚩→ **TU DESAFÍO** Earn points for your own challenge! Listen to the questions for your *Minientrevista Desafío 4* on the website and write your answers.

HERITAGE LANGUAGE LEARNERS

• Have students write a newspaper article or editorial about items made from recycled materials. They might include answers to questions like the following: Which materials are most frequently recycled? What items are most often made from recycled materials? Is it important to buy items that are made from recycled materials? Why or why not? They can also research this theme on the Internet, where they may find some surprising items made from recycled materials. Ask them to share these with the class.

MULTIPLE INTELLIGENCES:
Bodily-Kinesthetic Intelligence

• Have students play a game of "Mother May I?" in groups of four. One student plays *la madre* while the other three line up a few feet away. The "mother" gives various commands using *puedes* and the classmates follow the commands asking for permission. The student that reaches the mother first, wins. If they move without asking, they lose a turn. For example:

MADRE: *Tomás, puedes reciclar las botellas.*
TOMÁS: *Madre, ¿puedo reciclar las botellas?*
MADRE: *Tomás, sí puedes.* (Tomás then takes a step forward.)

---

80. You may divide the class into small groups and assign a different natural resource to each group (e.g., tropical forests, the ocean, oil, etc.). Have each group write a short statement saying what they can do to conserve their assigned natural resource. When they finish, invite groups to share their statements with the class.

🎧 **AUDIO SCRIPT**
See page 199L

Answer Key

77. 1. b 2. b 3. b 4. a 5. b

78. 2. A. ¿De qué es esta botella?
B. La botella es de vidrio.
A. ¿Se puede reciclar?
B. Sí, se puede.

3. A. ¿De qué son estas revistas?
B. Las revistas son de papel.
A. ¿Se pueden reciclar?
B. Sí, se pueden.

4. A. ¿De qué es esta lata?
B. Esta lata es de metal.
A. ¿Se puede reciclar?
B. Sí, se puede.

5. A. ¿De qué es este suéter?
B. Este suéter es de lana.
A. ¿Se puede reciclar?
B. Sí, se puede.

79. Answers will vary.
▶ Answers will vary.

80. Answers will vary.

81. 1. c 2. a 3. b
▶ Answers will vary.

Additional Resources

Fans Online activities
Practice Workbook

Todo junto

Presentation

- In this section, students will review:
  - Vocabulary for the universe and space, geographic features, political divisions, nature, the environment, and recycling.
  - Sentences with *por* and *porque*.
  - Irregular past tense of *decir, hacer, estar,* and *tener*.
  - Numbers from 101 to 1,000.
  - The use of the verb *poder*.

Activities	Standards	Resources
82.	1.2, 1.3	
83.	1.2, 1.3, 5.2	Audio
84.	1.1, 1.2, 1.3	

Teaching Suggestions

Warm-Up / Independent Starter

- Students should review the unit's grammar and vocabulary before getting started. Tell students they are taking an interplanetary journey. Have them describe in writing five things that they see on their adventure.

Preparation

- Have volunteers read their descriptions aloud to a partner. Allow the class to select the five best descriptions. Students can use these to create a more elaborate class story or a class comic book.
- Review the main vocabulary and grammar for the entire unit before beginning the activities in this section. Take five minutes per topic to review and answer any questions students may have.

Activities

82. Complete this activity as a class. Have two volunteers read the conversation aloud and pause when they get to a blank. The rest of the class will call out the correct answer. Readers should not continue reading until they get the correct answer.

84. For listening practice, have students close their books and read the textbook entry to them. Students should take notes as you read. Verify comprehension with questions about the main idea and the supporting details. For example: *¿Cuál es la idea principal del texto?*

240

LEER Y ESCRIBIR

82 Las aventuras de Bill y de Ted

▶ **Lee y elige.** Bill and Ted are on separate cross-country trips. Read their conversation and fill in the blanks, choosing the correct option for each.

> BILL: Yo ayer _____1_____ en Chicago, en el estado de Illinois.
> estuvieron / estuve
>
> TED: ¿Sí? Yo fui al sur del país. _____2_____ tiempo de ver ciudades y zonas naturales
> Tuvo / Tuve
> muy interesantes.
>
> BILL: ¡Qué bien! ¿ _____3_____ calor?
> Hicieron / Hizo
>
> TED: No, pero mi papá me _____4_____ que en el sur normalmente hace mucho calor.
> dijo / dije
> ¡Casi parece un bosque tropical!
>
> BILL: Estoy muy cansado porque _____5_____ cuatrocientas millas ayer.
> viajó / viajé
>
> TED: ¡Cuatrocientas millas! ¿Y adónde _____6_____ antes de ir a Chicago?
> viajamos / viajaste
>
> BILL: Viajé por tres estados. La semana pasada _____7_____ algunos parques nacionales.
> visitasteis / visité
>
> TED: ¿Sabes si _____8_____ entrar en los parques nacionales por la noche?
> se puede / se pueden
> Quiero ver las estrellas desde Yellowstone.

▶ **Escribe.** How does the conversation between Bill and Ted continue? Write it.

ESCUCHAR Y ESCRIBIR

83 Un programa especial

▶ **Escucha y escribe.** There is a special show on television tonight about life on other planets. Listen to the preview and take notes.

▶ **Diseña un cartel.** Design the promotional poster that will be used for advertising. Include images, words, phrases, and sentences to show the program's content.

¿HAY VIDA EN OTROS PLANETAS?

Hoy a las 9:00 p. m., programa especial

240 doscientos cuarenta

Differentiated Instruction

DEVELOPING LEARNERS

- Have students fill in a *cuento loco,* like the one below, with preterite tense forms of the verbs in parentheses. Have them write some more sentences to finish the story.
  El año pasado, mi familia y yo … (pasar) las vacaciones en un lugar muy bonito. Nosotros … (tener) muy buen tiempo e … (hacer) muchas cosas divertidas …

EXPANDING LEARNERS

- Ask students to imagine that they are students in a school that does not have a recycling program. Have them write a letter to the principal of the school in which they outline the reasons for recycling and inform him or her of the items that students could recycle. Have students share their letters with the class. (If your school doesn't have a recycling program, encourage students to give their letters to the principal.)

LEER, ESCRIBIR Y HABLAR

84 **Un libro de texto chileno**

▶ **Lee e identifica.** Tim borrowed a social studies textbook from a friend in Chile. Read the pages and identify the most important facts and issues about Chile.

Los paisajes de Chile

Chile es un país con diferentes paisajes: costas, montañas, desiertos, valles y volcanes.

La capital de Chile es Santiago de Chile, que fue fundada por los españoles en el año 1541.

Santiago de Chile

La ciudad de Santiago de Chile tiene problemas de contaminación del aire, especialmente en invierno (junio, julio y agosto). También hay contaminación del agua a causa de la industria y la agricultura. Es muy importante reciclar para ayudar a limpiar el aire y el agua.

▶ **Escribe.** Write a five-question quiz to give a partner. You should test whether your partner learned the key information from the textbook pages.

Modelo

¿Por qué hay contaminación del agua en Santiago de Chile?

 ▶ **Habla.** Ask a partner your quiz questions. He or she should point out where the answers can be found on the textbook pages.

doscientos cuarenta y uno 241

> **AUDIO SCRIPT**
> See page 199L

Answer Key

82 1. estuve   5. viajé
2. Tuve   6. viajaste
3. Hizo   7. visité
4. dijo   8. se puede
▶ Answers will vary.

83. Answers will vary.
▶ Answers will vary.

84. Answers will vary. Sample answers:
– Chile tiene costas, valles, montañas, desiertos y volcanes.
– La capital de Chile es Santiago de Chile.
– Santiago de Chile tiene problemas de contaminación del aire y del agua.
▶ Answers will vary.
▶ Answers will vary.

Additional Resources

Fans Online activities
Practice Workbook

HERITAGE LANGUAGE LEARNERS

• Have students think of other words that describe nature and natural landscapes (e.g., *la quebrada, el cerro*, etc.). Ask them to create flashcards with images and share these new words with the class.

MULTIPLE INTELLIGENCES:

Naturalistic Intelligence

• Ask students to investigate what happens when certain kinds of garbage reach natural areas on our planet. For example, when six-pack plastic rings reach the ocean, dolphins and small whales can get their beaks caught in the rings and can suffocate and die. Ask students to create a poster that is aimed at educating the general public about a safety or environmental hazard involving garbage. Display the posters around the school.

241

Unit 8
El encuentro

Presentation

■ The four pairs meet in the *Plaza de Armas* in Santiago de Chile to show the results of their individual challenges. Students will vote for the team who completed the most enriching challenge. In this section students will use their communicative goals to write a story.

Activities	Standards	Resources
Fotonovela	1.2	
85.	1.3, 3.1	
86.	1.1, 1.3	

Teaching Suggestions

Warm-Up / Independent Starter

■ Have students answer the following questions using complete sentences.

1. ¿Cuántos planetas hay en nuestro sistema solar?
2. ¿Cómo se dice river, lake y mountain en español?
3. ¿Cuál es la capital de tu estado? ¿A cuántas millas está de tu ciudad?
4. ¿Por qué hay que proteger el medio ambiente?
5. ¿Cómo se puede ayudar al medio ambiente?

Preparation

■ Before teaching this spread, have students glance over the four *Desafíos* that make up this unit. Have students narrate what happened in each one. They should say what each pair did, said, what they had to do, and where they were.

La fotonovela

■ Ask students to study the pictures. Let them read the dialogues individually and then share their impressions with the class.

■ Have students write the names of the different characters and what they achieved. Ask students to share their opinion about what the characters have achieved.

■ Have students point to the characters and say how they might feel. Then ask pairs of students to read the dialogues aloud and include the characters' projected feelings into their reading.

242

En la Plaza de Armas

The four pairs meet in Santiago de Chile after completing their individual tasks. Did they all carry out their challenges successfully?

¡Fue fantástico observar el cielo en el desierto!

¡Y encontramos las rocas en forma de perro!

Corrimos como unos campeones, ¿verdad?

¡Sí, hicimos el circuito completo y llegamos a la meta!

Caminamos por toda la isla hasta llegar a un lago. ¡Allí encontramos el moái falso!

¡Sí, cuánta basur para reciclar!

Después de caminar mucho llenamos las bolsas de basura.

242 doscientos cuarenta y dos

Differentiated Instruction

DEVELOPING LEARNERS

• Have students look at the photos and write three words to describe each one. Then one student can read a description and see if the other students can guess which image is being described. Encourage students to use words from this unit's vocabulary.

EXPANDING LEARNERS

• Ask students to write a summary of each pair's task in this unit, using the preterite tense. For example: *En el desierto, Andy y Janet miraron las estrellas. Pasaron mala noche por el frío.*

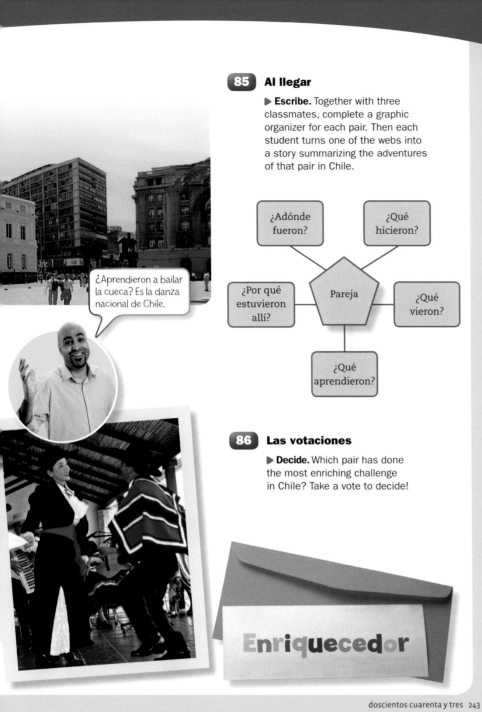

85 Al llegar

▶ **Escribe.** Together with three classmates, complete a graphic organizer for each pair. Then each student turns one of the webs into a story summarizing the adventures of that pair in Chile.

¿Aprendieron a bailar la cueca? Es la danza nacional de Chile.

¿Adónde fueron?

¿Qué hicieron?

¿Por qué estuvieron allí?

Pareja

¿Qué vieron?

¿Qué aprendieron?

86 Las votaciones

▶ **Decide.** Which pair has done the most enriching challenge in Chile? Take a vote to decide!

Enriquecedor

Activities

85. Have students complete the graphic organizer by themselves first to ensure that they all understand the themes of this unit. Then break students into groups. Make sure to mix students with different skill levels to ensure that everyone who needs help has someone in the group to assist them.

86. Before they vote, ask students for their personal definitions of *enriquecedor*. Write their answers on the board and have them vote for the best responses as a class. This way all students will be using the same criteria for the class vote about which team completed the most enriching task.

Answer Key

85. Answers will vary.

86. Answers will vary.

HERITAGE LANGUAGE LEARNERS

• Have students think about or research traditional dances from their countries of origin. Ask students to describe one of these dances to their classmates. Alternatively, encourage students to demonstrate a few steps from this traditional dance.

MULTIPLE INTELLIGENCES:
Musical Intelligence

• Have students write song lyrics using the word *enriquecedor* for their inspiration. The song might include a list of things that are enriching (e.g., "My Favorite Things" from *The Sound of Music*). Encourage students to add a melody to their lyrics. For example:

"Las cosas enriquecedoras de la vida"
Es enriquecedora la playa cuando hace sol.
El bosque, con sus árboles, es enriquecedor.

243

Unit 8

MAPA CULTURAL

Chile

Presentation

■ This section presents Chile through snapshots of a variety of places around the country. We get a taste of different regions and cities, as well as a sense of the history of the country. The photos and map support the geographic, historical, and demographic information for students.

Activities	Standards	Resources
Mapa cultural	1.2, 1.3, 2.2, 3.1, 3.2	Video
87.	1.2	
88.	1.1, 1.3, 3.1	

Teaching Suggestions

Warm-Up / Independent Starter

■ Have students look at the map of Chile. Ask them which of the five cities mentioned they would like to visit in Chile and why.

Preparation

■ Allow students to talk about the places they selected in the Independent Starter. As a class, talk about which places received the most interest and why.

■ Ask students to create a chart with two columns. The first column is for things they already know about Chile and the second column is for the things they have just learned about Chile. Have students fill in the first column before you read through the *Mapa cultural* and fill in the second column after.

■ Write the following on the board. How does Chile compare to your state?
  – Country: Chile
  – Capital: Santiago
  – Official Language: Spanish
  – Government: Representative democracy
  – Area: 291,930 square miles
  – Population: 16,602,000 (2009 est.)
  – Currency: Chilean peso
  – Highest Point: Mount Ojos del Salado 22,614 ft.
  – Length from north to south: approx. 2,700

Chile es una república situada en el suroeste de América del Sur. Su capital es Santiago de Chile.

Chile se extiende a lo largo de la costa del océano Pacífico. Es un país muy estrecho y muy largo, y está atravesado por dos cordilleras: los Andes y la cordillera de la Costa. También forman parte de Chile algunos archipiélagos y la Isla de Pascua *(Easter Island)*, situada en la Polinesia.

Chile tiene casi 17 millones de habitantes. El 90% vive en las ciudades.

¡Chile es un país muuuuy largo!

Sí, tiene más de 4.300 kilómetros de norte a sur. Es el país más largo del mundo.

87 ¿Cuál es la ruta?

▶ **Decide.** Look at the map and decide if the statements are true *(cierto)* or false *(falso)*.

1. Para ir de Atacama a la Patagonia chilena tengo que pasar por Valparaíso.
2. Para ir desde Santiago de Chile hasta la Isla de Pascua debo cruzar el océano Atlántico.
3. Para ir de Valparaíso a Punta Arenas hay que cruzar el desierto.
4. Para conocer el norte de Chile, puedo pasar por el desierto de Atacama.

244 doscientos cuarenta y cuatro

Differentiated Instruction

DEVELOPING LEARNERS

• Have students look at a map of Chile online. Ask them to point to five different political divisions (e.g., *el país, la región, la provincia, la ciudad, el pueblo, la capital*), other than the ones mentioned in the book.

EXPANDING LEARNERS

• Have students look at the map and the photos of Chile. Have them pretend to be an alien who just landed in Chile. Using vocabulary from the chapter and the preterite tense, ask students to write a short report home to their alien leader about where they were, what the people said, what they did, and what they had.

Los paisajes de Chile

De norte a sur, Chile tiene tres regiones muy distintas: el árido norte, el fértil Valle Central y el sur.

1. El árido norte

En el norte de Chile está el **desierto de Atacama**, el lugar del mundo donde menos llueve.

(1) El desierto de Atacama.

(2) Santiago de Chile.

2. El fértil Valle Central y Santiago de Chile

El centro es la zona más activa del país. Allí están las ciudades más importantes: **Valparaíso**, **Viña del Mar** y **Santiago de Chile**.

Santiago de Chile, la capital, está en un valle entre los Andes y la cordillera de la Costa.

(3) Lago Rupanco y volcán Osorno.

3. El sur

El sur de Chile se divide en dos zonas: la **Araucanía**, llena de volcanes, lagos y bosques, y la **Patagonia**, un laberinto de canales, montañas, islas y glaciares.

88 Con lupa

▶ **Completa.** Fill in the chart according to the text.

 ▶ **Habla.** Are there any regions in Chile that are similar to regions in other Spanish-speaking countries? Think of Argentina and Mexico and discuss similarities with a partner.

| bosques | glaciares | desierto |
| ciudades | lagos | |

El norte	El centro	El sur

Activities

87. Have students use the map to write three more possible routes between different places in Chile.

88. Assign a region, city, or province to volunteer readers. Then ask students to mention additional information they recall about each topic. Students are not allowed to look back through the unit.

Answer Key

87. 1. Cierto
2. Falso
3. Falso
4. Cierto

88. El norte – desierto.
El centro – ciudades.
El sur – bosques, lagos, glaciares.
▶ Answers will vary.

HERITAGE LANGUAGE LEARNERS

• Ask students to draw a map of their countries of origin with several important sites drawn in (e.g., the capital, places of interest, different towns and provinces, etc.). Have the students share their maps with a classmate.

CRITICAL THINKING

• Have students read this quote about travel by Albert Camus: "Travel, which is like a greater and graver science, brings us back to ourselves." Ask students what this quote means. Then ask them why they think people travel. Have students brainstorm a list of reasons—and compile their answers on the board.

MAPA CULTURAL

Chile

Presentation

- In this section, students will explore Easter Island and learn about the giant statues built by the Rapanui on the island. Students will also learn about Pablo Neruda, a world-famous Chilean poet. Then, students will explore the city of Viña del Mar, best known for its music festival.

Activities	Standards	Resources
Mapa cultural	1.2, 1.3, 2.2, 3.1, 3.2	
89.	1.3, 3.1	
90.	1.3, 3.1	

Teaching Suggestions

Warm-Up / Independent Starter

- List the three main topics of this spread on the board. Have students write five questions or five facts they know about each of them.
  1. *La Isla de Pascua*
  2. *Pablo Neruda*
  3. *El Festival Internacional de la Canción de Viña del Mar*

Preparation

- Use the Independent Starter as a springboard to the spread. Have students add this information to their information charts. Remember that the first column is for information they already know and the second column is for things they have learned.

Activities

89. Encourage students to provide accurate and interesting information. They may want to use the Internet as a source beyond their textbook. Tell students that a great place to look is the country's official website.

90. Allow students to share their ads or posters with the class. Have them select one song they like and create a video for it. Remind them that the Internet has many sites where they can find the lyrics to most songs. Also let them know that they should not illegally download songs for this assignment.

246

MAPA CULTURAL **Chile**

1. La Isla de Pascua

La **Isla de Pascua** es la isla más grande de Chile. Está en la Polinesia, en el océano Pacífico.

En la Isla de Pascua hay unas estatuas gigantescas de piedra llamadas **moáis**. Los moáis fueron construidos por los primeros pobladores de la Isla de Pascua.

(1) *Playa de Anakena (Isla de Pascua).*

(2) *Casa de Pablo Neruda en Valparaíso.*

2. Pablo Neruda

Pablo Neruda (1904–1973) es el poeta más conocido de Chile. A los veinte años publicó su obra *Veinte poemas de amor y una canción desesperada.* Ganó el **Premio Nobel de Literatura** en 1971.

Pablo Neruda.

The Hispanic World

La Isla de Pascua

Easter Island is famous for its monumental statues, or moai. These statues are found all over the island, but it is not clear how they were moved. Some scholars believe the statues were placed on wooden sledges and moved along using log rollers. But a Rapanui legend claims that the moai just walked from the quarry to their current locations. It is difficult to know the exact number of moai because many are still buried beneath the soil, but the estimates vary from 800 to 1,000. The moai vary in size from 6 feet to over 30 feet.

Pablo Neruda

Pablo Neruda's real name was Neftalí Ricardo Reyes Basoalto (1904-1973). It is believed that the poet changed his name to hide his poetry writing from his father, who did not approve of his son not having a "real job." Neruda was not always a well-liked person. In 1943 he was elected to the Senate and joined the Communist Party until the government outlawed communism in 1948. He had to flee the country for his life through the mountains. This, however, did not stop him from becoming one of the best and most well-known poets of all time.

(3) Escenario del Festival de Viña del Mar.

(3) Viña del Mar.

3. El Festival Internacional de la Canción de Viña del Mar

Viña del Mar es una localidad costera muy turística situada en el centro de Chile. Desde 1959, allí se celebra anualmente el *Festival Internacional de la Canción de Viña del Mar*, el evento musical más importante de Hispanoamérica. Los países compiten en dos categorías: música popular y música folclórica.

89 **Los moáis de la Isla de Pascua**

▶ **Investiga y explica.** Search for information and explain the following:

1. Who built the moai? Why?
2. How did they build them?
3. Why have the moai intrigued scientists?

90 **Un concierto de música chilena**

▶ **Investiga y escribe.** Search for information about Chilean music and make an advertisement. You may follow these steps:

1. Search for information about Chilean music and about current Chilean bands.
2. Write down the genre and the groups you like.
3. Organize the information in a poster or ad. Include images and other elements to promote the concert.
4. As a class, organize a Chilean music festival featuring each concert.

doscientos cuarenta y siete **247**

Answer Key

89. Answers will vary. Sample answers:

1. The moai were built by the Rapanui, Easter Island's earliest inhabitants. It is probable that these huge statues were built in honor of Polynesian gods or to immortalize individuals from the island's history.
2. The moai statues were sculpted from volcanic rock (rock formed by the solidification of molten lava). This stone was readily available, easy to sculpt, and durable enough to withstand time and the elements.
3. These statues have intrigued scientists because no one knows for certain how the giant statues were moved miles away from where they were created. One theory is that the moai were built by extraterrestrial beings.

90. Answers will vary.

Additional Resources

Fans Online Activities
Practice Workbook

Viña del Mar

Viña del Mar, also known as *Ciudad Jardín*, is located in the Valparaiso Province. It is a coastal city and a popular tourist vacation spot. The beaches are pristine and world-renowned. Viña del Mar is a modern city that boasts numerous shopping malls, well-known restaurants, various parks, and a modern amphitheater where the annual Viña del Mar International Song Festival is held.

El Festival Internacional de la Canción de Viña del Mar

This five-night festival takes place every year in February. It has come a long way from its humble beginnings in 1959, when it started as a collaboration among local musicians who played outdoors while the audience sat on the ground. Today the show attracts artists from many different countries and is held at the Quinta Vergara, one of Viña's oldest estates that is now a cultural center and a museum. This festival has been celebrated uninterruptedly for more than 50 years, but the last day of the 2010 festival was canceled due to a large earthquake that devastated some areas of Chile.

LECTURA

Oda a la manzana

Presentation

■ In this section students will read "Oda a la manzana," an ode by celebrated Chilean poet, Pablo Neruda.

Activities	Standards	Resources
Lectura	1.2, 3.1, 3.2	
91.	1.3	
92.	1.3, 3.1	
93.	1.3	
94.	1.3	
Tu desafío	1.3	

Teaching Suggestions

Warm-Up / Independent Starter

■ Have students scan Pablo Neruda's "Oda a la manzana" for the ten longest words. They should list them in their notebooks from longest to shortest and put a check mark by each word they know.

Preparation

■ Have students explain how they know the words they checked for their Independent Starter. Ask them to share their words with a partner. Do they have the same words?

■ Before reading the story, point to the Reading Strategy text and read it aloud to the class. Ask what the reading strategies were in the past units (asking questions, using prior knowledge, determining the story elements). Ask students to explain how these strategies help them understand their reading.

■ Explain that an ode is a celebratory poem that addresses a particular person or thing and is usually written for a solemn occasion. The ode form belongs to the long and varied tradition of lyric poetry. It originated in Ancient Greece and it used to be accompanied by music and dance. Examples in English include "Ode on a Grecian Urn" by John Keats and "Ode, Intimations of Immortality" by William Wordsworth. Discuss with students why Pablo Neruda would write an ode to an apple.

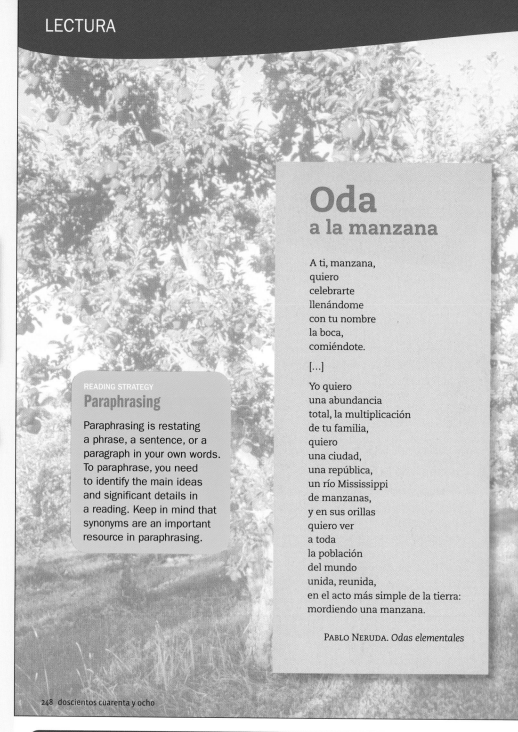

READING STRATEGY
Paraphrasing

Paraphrasing is restating a phrase, a sentence, or a paragraph in your own words. To paraphrase, you need to identify the main ideas and significant details in a reading. Keep in mind that synonyms are an important resource in paraphrasing.

Oda
a la manzana

A ti, manzana,
quiero
celebrarte
llenándome
con tu nombre
la boca,
comiéndote.

[...]

Yo quiero
una abundancia
total, la multiplicación
de tu familia,
quiero
una ciudad,
una república,
un río Mississippi
de manzanas,
y en sus orillas
quiero ver
a toda
la población
del mundo
unida, reunida,
en el acto más simple de la tierra:
mordiendo una manzana.

PABLO NERUDA. *Odas elementales*

Differentiated Instruction

DEVELOPING LEARNERS

• Have students break the poem into smaller parts. Ask students to stop at different points to comment about their understanding of the poem. Continue reviewing students' understanding. This would be a good time to talk a little about poetic devices such as metaphors and similes. Make it brief.

EXPANDING LEARNERS

• Ask students to write their own odes to a fruit they love or to another "simple thing" using what they know about the style. Encourage them to recite (or read) their poem aloud to a classmate or to the entire class. Alternatively, students can record themselves performing their poems and create a group podcast.

LECTURA

Oda a la manzana

ESTRATEGIA Parafrasear

91 **Con mis palabras**

▶ **Escribe.** State the meaning of the poem *Oda a la manzana* using your own words. You may write more than one sentence.

92 **Tu investigación**

▶ **Escribe.** Find information about Pablo Neruda and fill in a chart like the one below.

> Nombre: Pablo Neruda
> Fecha y lugar de nacimiento:
> Algunos datos de su biografía:
>
> Algunos títulos de sus obras:

COMPRENSIÓN

93 **La manzana y la vida**

▶ **Relaciona y escribe.** Relate each picture to a main idea expressed in the poem. Then put them in order and write a sentence summarizing each idea.

(1)

(2)

94 **El mensaje del poema**

▶ **Escribe.** Write another title for the poem. Then compare it with your partner's.

 TU DESAFÍO Earn points for your own challenge! Visit the website to learn more about Pablo Neruda.

doscientos cuarenta y nueve 249

HERITAGE LANGUAGE LEARNERS

• Ask students to share a poem in Spanish from a poet they enjoy, or an appropriate Neruda poem. Why did they choose this poem / poet? Have them read the poem for the class.

COOPERATIVE LEARNING

• Have students help each other to interpret different parts of the poem. Pair students with different skill levels. On the board, compile all the different ways students interpreted and / or understood the same phrase / stanza. Have students vote on the interpretation that they think best represents this phrase / stanza.

Activities

91. You may want students to use a Spanish Thesaurus or a *Diccionario de sinónimos* to complete this activity.

92. Let students know that Pablo Neruda changed his name from Neftalí Ricardo Reyes Basoalto. Encourage students to look him up by his given name and see if the information differs from what they find by using his elected name.

94. After students are done writing their titles, have them list three reasons for their choices. When students have finished, they may compare their work with a partner's. If time allows, have students share their titles and reasons with the class while you create a class list of new titles.

Answer Key

91. Answers will vary.

92. Answers will vary. Sample answers:
- Neftalí Ricardo Reyes Basoalto or Pablo Neruda.
- 12 de julio de 1904. Parral, Chile.
- Vivió en Chile y en muchos otros países porque fue diplomático. Ganó el Premio Nobel de Literatura en 1971. Murió en Santiago de Chile el 23 de septiembre de 1973.
- *Veinte poemas de amor y una canción desesperada, Odas elementales, Los versos del capitán, Confieso que he vivido.*

93. Answers will vary.

94. Answers will vary.

Additional Resources

Fans Online Activities

REPASO

Vocabulario

Presentation

- In this section, students will review all key vocabulary from the unit to prepare for an assessment. Students will complete practice activities for each of the four *Desafíos*.

Activities	Standards	Resources
1.	1.2, 1.3	
2.	1.2, 1.3	
3.	1.2, 1.3	
4.	1.2, 1.3	

Teaching Suggestions

Warm-Up / Independent Starter

- Students can create a vocabulary booklet to practice the four categories learned in this unit. Each page of the booklet should be dedicated to a category or subcategory. You may want to provide students with construction paper to make their booklets more durable. They may also illustrate their booklets.

Preparation

- Ask students to play vocabulary games such as "Memory" or "Hangman" with the vocabulary of the unit. You may turn this into a class activity by asking volunteers to compete against each other on the board. To raise the level of difficulty in "Hangman," you may use simple sentences that use two or three of the vocabulary words in context. For example: *El desierto es un lugar seco con pocos animales.*

Activities

1. Have students write similar clues for the rest of the vocabulary in this category. Have them work in pairs and compete against each other to try to guess the words.

2. You may bring more pictures to display on the board and have students write additional descriptions. Have volunteers read their descriptions aloud and ask the class to identify the picture being described. Once you have verified its accuracy, have that student dictate his or her description to the class.

250

El universo

el universo	universe
el sistema solar	solar system
el cielo	sky
el cometa	comet
el eclipse	eclipse
la estrella	star
el planeta	planet
el Sol	Sun
la Luna	Moon
la Tierra	Earth
el/la astronauta	astronaut
descubrir	to discover
explorar	to explore

Geografía

Geografía	Geography
el bosque	forest
el continente	continent
el desierto	desert
la isla	island
el lago	lake
el mar	sea
la montaña	mountain
el océano	ocean
el río	river
la roca	rock
la tierra	land
el valle	valley
seco	dry
tropical	tropical

Divisiones políticas

la capital	capital
la ciudad	city
la frontera	border
el país	country
la provincia	province
el pueblo	town
la región	region

Los números

cien	one hundred
doscientos	two hundred
trescientos	three hundred
cuatrocientos	four hundred
quinientos	five hundred
seiscientos	six hundred
setecientos	seven hundred
ochocientos	eight hundred
novecientos	nine hundred
mil	one thousand

La naturaleza y el medio ambiente

la naturaleza	nature
el medio ambiente	environment
el agua	water
el aire	air
el animal	animal
el insecto	insect
el pájaro	bird
el pez	fish
el árbol	tree
la flor	flower
la hoja	leaf
la planta	plant

El reciclaje

el reciclaje	recycling
la basura	trash
el contenedor	container
la electricidad	electricity
el metal	metal
el papel	paper
el plástico	plastic
el vidrio	glass
botar	to throw away
reciclar	to recycle

Differentiated Instruction

DEVELOPING LEARNERS

- Have students choose ten vocabulary words and write an original sentence for each one. They must use at least two words from each section. Ask students to share their work with a classmate and proofread each other's work.

EXPANDING LEARNERS

- Have students write a story using ten vocabulary words from the *Repaso* section. Ask students to read their stories aloud to the class. Each time students hear one of the vocabulary words, they should clap (or stomp their feet, for example).

DESAFÍO 1

1 **El sistema solar.** Use the clues to identify each part of the solar system.

1. El _____ es la persona que explora y observa el universo.
2. Hay ocho _____ y uno de ellos se llama Júpiter.
3. En una noche clara se pueden ver las _____
4. Si la Luna pasa frente al _____ se produce un eclipse.
5. La _____ es el nombre de nuestro planeta.

DESAFÍO 2

2 **Paisajes.** Which geographic features do the photos represent? Identify the features by writing a sentence and a short description of each.

Modelo 1. *Es un bosque tropical. En él hay árboles y animales.*

DESAFÍO 3

3 **Distancias.** Write the distance from Washington DC to the following places in the U.S.

Modelo el condado de Fairfax (16 millas)
→ *El condado de Fairfax está a dieciséis millas de Washington.*

1. la capital de Pennsylvania (123 millas)
2. la ciudad de Chicago (699 millas)
3. la frontera con Canadá (560 millas)
4. la ciudad de Nueva York (204 millas)
5. el país de Canadá (624 millas)
6. el pueblo de Ashland, KY (428 millas)

DESAFÍO 4

4 **Ecología.** Classify these items according to whether they are natural or unnatural in a park.

una botella de plástico	un río
un árbol	un insecto
una lata de metal	un pájaro
una flor	una botella de vidrio
una hoja	una planta

☺	☹
un pez	basura

HERITAGE LANGUAGE LEARNERS

• Ask students to review the vocabulary list and try to think of synonyms for at least ten of the words. For example: *el animal = la bestia; la ciudad = la metrópolis*, and so on. Have them create posters with their synonyms to hang around the classroom.

MULTIPLE INTELLIGENCES:
Verbal-Linguistic Intelligence

• Play a game of charades with the class using the vocabulary from this unit. Choose a student volunteer to act out one of the vocabulary words with gestures and mime. The student who guesses the word correctly is the next student to act out a word. Play the game until most of the words have been acted out.

---

3. Have students convert their answers to kilometers by multiplying the miles value by 1.61. This will provide extra practice with numbers.

4. Ask students to elaborate on why they classified each item as they did.

Answer Key

1. 1. astronauta
2. planetas
3. estrellas
4. Sol
5. Tierra

2. Answers will vary. Sample answers:
1. Es un bosque tropical. En él hay árboles y animales
2. Es un río. El río es largo. En el río nadan los peces.
3. Es una isla. La isla está rodeada de mar por todas partes. Chile tiene una isla con paisajes extraordinarios: la Isla de Pascua.
4. Es un lago. Los lagos pueden ser enormes, como el Lago Ontario.

3. 1. La capital de Pennsylvania está a ciento veintitrés millas de Washington.
2. La ciudad de Chicago está a seiscientas noventa y nueve millas de Washington.
3. La frontera con Canadá está a quinientas sesenta millas de Washington.
4. La ciudad de Nueva York está a doscientas cuatro millas de Washington.
5. El país de Canadá está a seiscientas veinticuatro millas de Washington.
6. El pueblo de Ashland, KY está a cuatrocientas veintiocho millas de Washington.

4. Natural: un árbol, una flor, una hoja, un río, un insecto, un pájaro, una planta.
No natural: una botella de plástico, una lata de metal, una botella de vidrio.

Additional Resources

Fans Online activities
Practice Workbook

251

REPASO

Gramática

Presentation

- Students will review the grammatical structures presented in the unit. The activities here provide systematic practice by *Desafío*.

Activities	Standards	Resources
5.	1.2, 1.3	
6.	1.2	
7.	1.2, 1.3	
8.	1.3, 3.1, 5.2	
9. Cultura	1.3, 2.1, 2.2, 5.2	

Teaching Suggestions

Warm-Up / Independent Starter

- Have students use the following prompts to write five sentences.
  1. *No puedo comer pescado porque…*
  2. *Mamá me dijo…*
  3. *Algunas personas no…*
  4. *Yo tuve que conducir quinientas…*
  5. *En el parque se puede…*

Preparation

- On the board, write the sentence *Hoy se pueden llevar sandalias porque hace calor.* Have students tell you which two grammar points seen in this unit can be reviewed with this sentence. When the students come up with the answer, have them write three more sentences that combine two or more grammar points.

Activities

5. Have students share their excuses with a classmate. Use peer correction as grammar point reinforcement.

7. Have students re-create the sentences to say what they did on each day. They must write in complete sentences and use the preterite tense.

8. You may want to have students research Yellowstone's rules before attempting the activity.

9. Ask students to complete this activity without referring back to their textbooks. Who can answer the most questions correctly without looking?

REPASO Gramática

Expresar causa (pág. 210)

- Conjunción porque + oración con verbo conjugado

  ¿Por qué no puedes ir?

  No puedo ir porque estoy enferma.

- Conjunción por + sustantivo

  No fuimos por el mal tiempo.

Expresar cantidad. Los indefinidos (pág. 218)

ningún, ninguno(a)	*no, (not) any*
algún, alguno(a), algunos(as)	*one, some, any, a few*
poco(a), pocos(as)	*some, few*
mucho(a), muchos(as)	*many, a lot of*
todo(a), todos(as)	*all, every, throughout*

Verbos irregulares en el pasado (págs. 226, 228)

DECIR

yo	dije	nosotros / nosotras	dijimos
tú	dijiste	vosotros / vosotras	dijisteis
usted él ella	dijo	ustedes ellos ellas	dijeron

HACER

yo	hice	nosotros / nosotras	hicimos
tú	hiciste	vosotros / vosotras	hicisteis
usted él ella	hizo	ustedes ellos ellas	hicieron

ESTAR

yo	estuve	nosotros / nosotras	estuvimos
tú	estuviste	vosotros / vosotras	estuvisteis
usted él ella	estuvo	ustedes ellos ellas	estuvieron

TENER

yo	tuve	nosotros / nosotras	tuvimos
tú	tuviste	vosotros / vosotras	tuvisteis
usted él ella	tuvo	ustedes ellos ellas	tuvieron

Expresar permiso y prohibición (pág. 236)

Expresar permiso

se puede + infinitivo — Se puede dar comida a los animales.

se puede(n) + infinitivo — Se puede(n) tomar fotos en el museo.

Expresar prohibición

no se puede + infinitivo — No se puede botar la basura en el suelo.

no se puede(n) + infinitivo — No se puede(n) botar las botellas de vidrio a la basura.

Differentiated Instruction

DEVELOPING LEARNERS

- Have students practice the irregular preterite verbs by using words and gestures. One student gestures the subject pronoun (e.g., points at oneself for *yo*, points to the partner for *tú*, and so on). Then the student says a verb in the infinitive form (e.g., *tener*) and the partner must conjugate the verb correctly and say it aloud with the subject pronoun (e.g., *yo tuve*).

EXPANDING LEARNERS

- Have students practice indefinite adjectives and nouns by writing their daily routines. For example:
  - *No voy al gimnasio ningún día.*
  - *Algunas tardes estudio en la biblioteca.*
  - *Todos los fines de semana veo una película.*

DESAFÍO 1

5 **Causas.** Match the columns and write five sentences. Use *por* or *porque*.

Modelo *No quiero ir a la fiesta porque tengo que estudiar.*

1. ir a la fiesta
2. hacer ejercicio
3. leer
4. comer
5. salir a pasear

a. estar cansado
b. el dolor de estómago
c. tener que estudiar
d. la lluvia
e. doler la cabeza

DESAFÍO 2

6 **¿Qué comemos?** Choose the words that logically complete the dialogue.

> CARMEN: ¡Mira cuánta comida! Hay (pocos / muchos) tipos de carnes, verduras y postres.
>
> SARAH: Sí. Y (poco / algún) postre tiene chocolate blanco, mi favorito.
>
> CARMEN: No me gusta el chocolate blanco. ¿Hay (alguno / ninguno) sin chocolate?
>
> SARAH: ¡Claro que sí! Creo que hay (ninguno / algunos) con fruta.
>
> CARMEN: ¡Perfecto! (Muchos / Todos) los postres con fruta me gustan mucho.

DESAFÍO 3

7 **¿Qué hicieron?** Create sentences about what each person did and when.

Modelo Miguel - estar - ciudad - sábado $\rightarrow$ *El sábado Miguel estuvo en la ciudad.*

1. Yo - hacer la tarea - biblioteca - miércoles
2. Nosotros - tener que hacer - examen - lunes
3. Vosotros - estar - centro de la ciudad - sábado
4. Ella - decir la verdad - escuela - viernes

DESAFÍO 4

8 **Reglas.** Write a memorandum about what is allowed and what is not allowed in your rental cabin in Yellowstone National Park.

Modelo *En mi cabaña se puede cocinar, pero no se puede hacer fuego...*

CULTURA

9 **Está en Chile.** Answer the questions.

1. What is the land of the *Valle de la Luna* compared to? Why?
2. Who constructed the moai on Easter Island?
3. Compare the Torres del Paine National Park with a national park in the United States.
4. Who was Pablo Neruda? Why is he significant?

doscientos cincuenta y tres 253

Answer Key

5. Answers will vary. Sample answers:
   1. No quiero ir a la fiesta porque tengo que estudiar.
   2. No quiero hacer ejercicio porque estoy cansado.
   3. No quiero leer porque me duele la cabeza.
   4. No quiero comer por el dolor de estómago.
   5. No quiero salir a pasear por la lluvia.

6. 1. muchos
   2. algún
   3. alguno
   4. algunos
   5. Todos

7. 1. El miércoles yo hice la tarea en la biblioteca.
   2. El lunes nosotros tuvimos que hacer un examen.
   3. El sábado vosotros estuvisteis en el centro de la ciudad.
   4. El viernes ella dijo la verdad en la escuela.

8. Answers will vary.

9. Answers will vary. Sample answers:
   1. The *Valle de la Luna* is compared to the moon because it is extremely dry.
   2. The native Rapanui people.
   3. The Torres del Paine National Park can be compared to Yellowstone National Park. They are both open to the public, they both have waterfalls, and they both have several species of plants and animals living within the confines of the park.
   4. Pablo Neruda was a famous Chilean writer. He was significant because he was one of the most influential writers of the 20th century and he won the Nobel Prize for Literature in 1971.

Additional Resources

Fans Online activities
Practice Workbook

HERITAGE LANGUAGE LEARNERS

• Have students find a poem in Spanish that uses the preterite tense (have them print it out and underline all the examples of the preterite tense). Encourage them to share the poem with the class.

SPECIAL-NEEDS LEARNERS

• For a student with Asperger's syndrome, it is very important to present material in a clear manner and to give them time to absorb what is said. To expect an AS student to listen, take notes, and read the blackboard all at the same time is often too much. Present them with notes prior to the class so that they can truly listen to the instructor and learn.

PROYECTO

Animales en peligro

Presentation

- In this section, students will create a poster about endangered animal species to practice the vocabulary and grammar presented in this unit. Students will follow step-by-step instructions.

Activities	Standards	Resources
Paso 1	1.3, 3.1	
Paso 2	1.3, 3.1, 5.2	
Paso 3	1.2, 1.3, 5.1	
Paso 4	1.1, 5.2	

Teaching Suggestions

Warm-Up / Independent Starter

- Have students read the introduction to the project and all the tasks involved, then begin brainstorming about which endangered animal they would like to cover in this project.

Preparation

- Have students list five resources they could use to research the topic. After each, have them write a brief explanation detailing why they think this is a good resource. (Wikipedia is *not* a reliable source.)
- Ask students to brainstorm all the information they know about endangered animals. This activity can be done independently or as a class.

Step-by-Step Instructions

Paso 1

- Have students do an Internet search regarding endangered animal species. You may narrow their search by suggesting a specific region for each student. Encourage students to find animals they have never heard of. These are some good information sources: http://www.nature.org/wherewework/southamerica/chile/work/art5116.html and http://www.worldwildlife.org/what/wherewework/southernchile/species.html.

Paso 2

- Encourage students to work out the information on scrap paper first. Then encourage them to print a practice map and picture, so they can freely arrange the elements before pasting them on poster board.

Un póster sobre

animales en peligro

There are endangered animals throughout the world. In Chile alone, there are more than forty endangered species.

In this project you are going to do research on an endangered animal. Your research involves learning about the animal and its habitat, discovering why it is endangered, and indicating what people can do to protect it. Your final goal is to display all your work on a poster.

Nutria de río.

PASO 1 Investiga sobre los animales en peligro de extinción en Chile y selecciona un animal

- Research the endangered mammals, fish, and birds in Chile.
- Choose one animal to research. These criteria may help you decide:
  - you like its appearance;
  - it is also an endangered animal where you live;
  - it lives in extreme climatic conditions: desert, mountain, tiny island.
- Select several photos and find out the animal's name in Spanish.

Vicuña.

PASO 2 Busca información para una ficha y un mapa

- Organize your information on a file card, and make a map to show the animal's habitat.

Albatros ojeroso.

Nombre	Ballena azul
Descripción física Color Peso Tamaño	Negro, azul 181.500 kg (400,000 lb.) 24–27 m (80–100')
Población	3.000–5.000
Hábitat	Océano Pacífico
Alimentación	Pequeños crustáceos, krill
Dato curioso	Come 3.600 kg (8,000 lb.) de krill al día. Es más grande que 25 elefantes.

Rubric for Evaluation

	Content	Organization	Presentation
1 point	Limited relevance. Information is incomplete or not based on research. Little Spanish is used.	Inefficient use of class time. Information is disorganized or unclear.	Communication is unclear. Many errors in vocabulary and grammar.
3 points	Basic information is correct. Relevant information but lacks significance. Spanish is used most of the time.	Class time is used well. Information and content are mostly organized but lack some clarity.	Good communication. Mostly correct vocabulary and grammar.

PASO 3 Explica por qué ese animal está en peligro y prepara sugerencias para protegerlo

- Why is the animal endangered? Summarize two or three of the most important causes. Some of the most common causes are:

  – Los cambios en el hábitat. Por ejemplo, la temperatura.
  – La intervención de los seres humanos. Por ejemplo, la contaminación o la caza *(hunting)*.
  – Causas naturales. Por ejemplo, las enfermedades.

  > – *Cazaron muchas ballenas por su carne.*
  > – *Ahora hay menos krill porque la temperatura del agua está cambiando.*

- Suggest some ways to protect this endangered animal. For example:

  – Prohibir la caza de ballenas.
  – Controlar los cambios del clima.

PASO 4 Organiza toda la información en tu póster y preséntala a la clase

- Arrange all your information in a logical way on your poster.

- Practice presenting your information aloud. Then present it to your classmates. Answer their questions.

¿A las ballenas azules les gusta el agua fría?

Sí. Prefieren el agua fría.

Unidad 8

Autoevaluación

¿Qué has aprendido en esta unidad?

Do the following activities to evaluate how well you can manage in Spanish.

Evaluate your skills. For each item, say Very well, Well, or I need more practice.

a. Can you talk about the seasons and the solar system?
  ▶ Draw three items in space and ask your partner to identify them.
  ▶ Say what season your birthday falls in.

b. Can you express cause or reason?
  ▶ Write three reasons to visit Chile. Use *por* or *porque*.

c. Can you describe the geography of Chile?
  ▶ Describe land and water features. Use words like *alguno*, *todo*, *mucho*, and *poco*.

d. Can you talk about where you live?
  ▶ Choose three cities in your country and guess how far they are from you.

e. Can you narrate past events?
  ▶ Ask your partner what living things he or she saw yesterday.

f. Can you explain how to protect the environment?
  ▶ Tell three things that are allowed or prohibited with regard to the environment.

	Content	Organization	Presentation
5 points	Relevant, interesting information. Many details and significance are highlighted. Spanish is used exclusively.	Class time is used wisely. Information and content are clearly organized visually and logically.	Clear communication. Correct and complete vocabulary and grammar.

PROYECTO

Animales en peligro

Paso 3

- Let students know that the most important thing when summarizing is to identify the main idea. Supporting details must reinforce the main ideas, so they must choose the most relevant ones.

Paso 4

- Each student will give a presentation to the class. Have them remember to speak slowly and clearly, while also keeping smiles on their faces and making eye contact with the audience.

Evaluation

- Distribute copies of the rubric to students. Discuss the evaluation criteria and explain how this project will be graded. Encourage students to refer to the rubric as they prepare their projects. It may be helpful to correlate the points with the traditional grade scale and indicate how much each project counts towards the final grade.

Content

- Make sure students have chosen an animal that is in fact on the endangered species list. Have them check the date of their source before choosing it. These lists are updated frequently, and thankfully some animals are removed each year.

- Explain the importance of good data collection. Students should collect information that is interesting and relevant.

- To develop research skills, ask students to provide quotes in the correct format and include a list of sources, especially if they need to go back to them for more research.

Organization

- Students should make sure that all questions (*Paso 1*), geographical information (*Paso 2*), reasons and suggestions for the endangered animal (*Paso 3*), and presentational information (*Paso 4*) are addressed completely before presenting the project.

Presentation

- Students should use as much Spanish as possible. They should check grammar and vocabulary before completing the project.

- Rehearsals should enable them to present confidently and fluently, as well as guarantee a good grade. Encourage creativity and a style that holds their classmates' attention.

TAREA FINAL

- As a final task, students may complete the following culminating activities. These activities are fun way for students to review the countries visited during the two courses, stay up to date with the characters and their challenges, and put their cultural and linguistic knowledge to the test.

- The teacher can copy these activities to complete in class or to assign as homework. Each activity was designed with the flexibility to be completed individually, in pairs, or in small groups.

¿Eres un verdadero fan del español?

1 El mundo en español

▶ **Colorea.** What countries have Tim and Mack, Andy and Janet, Tess and Patricia, and Diana and Rita gone to? Color them in the map provided.

▶ **Escribe.** Write which country you like the most and why.

_____

_____

_____

_____

_____

Amigos en español

▶ **Completa.** In small groups, complete the table with facts from each country the four pairs visited. The first person to complete the table wins.

País	Ciudad	Tradición	Monumento	Personaje

▶ **Relaciona y escribe.** ¿With what country do you associate the following pictures? Write the name of the country in the space provided.

1

_____

2

_____

3

_____

4

_____

TAREA FINAL

3 **Amigos en español**

▶ **Escribe.** Describe your favorite pair and why you like them.

_____

_____

_____

_____

_____

_____

▶ **Escribe.** Write an e-mail to your favorite participant. Be sure to introduce yourself, tell him or her about your favorite challenge, and describe your experience as a _fan del español_.

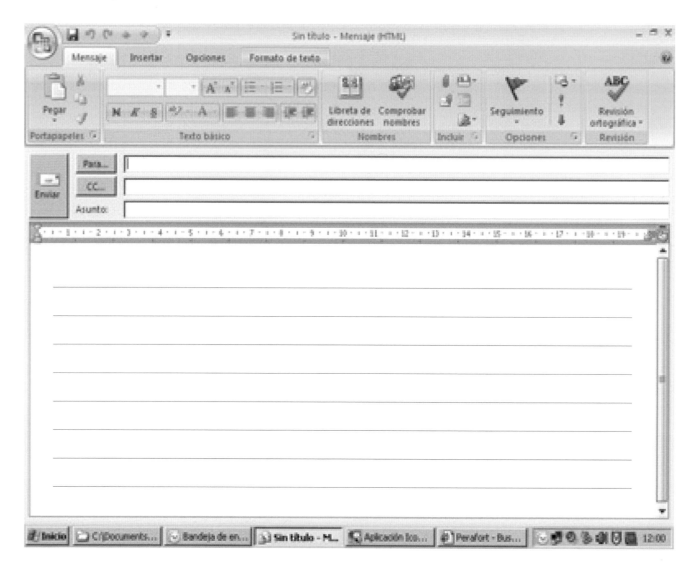

4 **Desafíos en español**

▶ **Escribe y habla.** Describe the challenge you found most interesting. Write your reasoning and share it with a partner.

_____

_____

_____

_____

_____

_____

▶ **Escribe.** Invent a new challenge for your favorite team by completing the form below.

País: _____

Ciudad: _____

Descripción de la prueba: _____

_____

_____

Foto o dibujo:

TAREA FINAL

5 **Presente y futuro en español**

▶ **Responde.** Answer each question in complete sentences.

1. What do you like most about studying Spanish?

_____

_____

_____

2. What is the hardest part about learning Spanish?

_____

_____

3. Now are you a true *fan del español*? Why?

_____

_____

4. Do you want to continue studying Spanish?

_____

_____

5. Which Spanish-speaking countries would you like to visit with your friends? Why?

_____

_____

_____

6 ¿Qué sabes hacer en español?

▶ **Responde.** Answer each question in complete sentences.

1. ¿Qué dices para presentarte? ¿Y para presentar a tu compañero(a)?

2. ¿Qué dices para preguntar el precio de una camisa?

3. ¿Qué dices para pedir un plato en un restaurante?

4. ¿Qué dices en la consulta del médico?

5. ¿Qué dices para comprar un billete de tren?

6. ¿Qué dices para hablar de tus planes para las vacaciones?

¿Cómo es tu nivel de español?

☐ Muy bueno   ☐ Bueno   ☐ Aceptable   ☐ Necesito mejorar

RESUMEN DE GRAMÁTICA

Nouns and articles

Gender of nouns

In Spanish all nouns are **masculine** or **feminine**. Most nouns that end in -o are masculine, and most nouns that end in -a are feminine. Nouns that end in -e or in a consonant can be either masculine or feminine.

Nouns that refer to people have a masculine and a feminine form. The feminine is usually formed by changing the -o of the masculine form to an -a, or by adding an -a.

Masculine form	Feminine form	Examples
Ends in -o.	Changes -o to -a.	el niño → la niña
Ends in a consonant.	Adds -a.	el profesor → la profesora

Plural of nouns

Nouns can be **singular** (one person or thing) or **plural** (more than one person or thing). To form the plural, add -s to the singular form if the noun ends in a vowel. If it ends in a consonant, add -es.

Singular form	Plural form	Examples
Ends in a vowel.	Adds -s.	el edificio → los edificios
Ends in a consonant.	Adds -es.	el ascensor → los ascensores

Articles

Definite articles refer to a specific noun. In English the definite article has only one form: the. In Spanish there are four forms: el, la, los, and las.

Indefinite articles refer to a nonspecific noun. In Spanish, the indefinite article has four forms: un, una (a or an) and unos, unas (some or a few).

DEFINITE ARTICLES

	Masculine	Feminine
Singular	el	la
Plural	los	las

INDEFINITE ARTICLES

	Masculine	Feminine
Singular	un	una
Plural	unos	unas

Contractions

The combination of the prepositions a and de with the definite article el results in a contraction.

a + el → al	de + el → del

Adjectives

Agreement with nouns

Adjectives describe nouns. Spanish adjectives can be masculine or feminine, singular or plural. They must agree with the noun both in gender and in number.

GENDER

Masculine form	Feminine form	Examples
Ends in -o.	Changes -o to -a.	niño simpático → niña simpática
Ends in -e or in a consonant.	Does not change.	niño inteligente → niña inteligente

NUMBER

Singular form	Plural form	Examples
Ends in a vowel.	Adds -s.	amigo simpático → amigos simpáticos
Ends in a consonant.	Adds -es.	amigo joven → amigos jóvenes

Demonstrative adjectives

Demonstrative adjectives indicate where something or someone is located in relation to the person speaking.

Distance from speaker	Singular		Plural	
	Masculine	Feminine	Masculine	Feminine
Near	este	esta	estos	estas
At a distance	ese	esa	esos	esas
Far away	aquel	aquella	aquellos	aquellas

Possessive adjectives

Possessive adjectives express ownership. They agree with the noun they accompany. They agree with the thing (or person) possessed, not with the owner.

mi mis	my	nuestro, nuestra nuestros, nuestras	our
tu tus	your (informal)	vuestro, vuestra vuestros, vuestras	your (informal)
su sus	his, her, your	su sus	their, your

Indefinite adjectives

Indefinite adjectives express number of nouns in nonspecific terms.

ningún, ninguno(a)	no, (not) any
algún, alguno(a), algunos(as)	one, some, any, a few
poco(a), pocos(as)	some, few
mucho(a), muchos(as)	many, a lot of
todo(a), todos(as)	all, every, throughout

Comparatives

Comparisons of inequality and equality

To express a difference regarding one characteristic, use más... que (more ... than) or menos... que (less ... than). To express equality, use tan... como (as ... as).

más + adjetivo + que
menos + adjetivo + que
tan + adjetivo + como

Comparative adjectives

Mejor and peor are used just like the English words *better* and *worse* to indicate a comparative degree.

bueno	→	mejor, mejores	malo	→	peor, peores
good		*better*	*bad*		*worse*

Pronouns

Subject pronouns

Subject pronouns identify the person who is performing an action.

Singular		Plural	
yo	I	nosotros nosotras	we
tú	you (informal)	vosotros vosotras	you (informal)
usted él ella	you (formal) he she	ustedes ellos ellas	you they they

Direct object pronouns

To avoid repeating words that have already been mentioned, you can replace the direct object with a pronoun.

Singular		Plural	
Masculine	**Feminine**	**Masculine**	**Feminine**
lo — him, it	la — her, it	los — them	las — them

Indirect object pronouns

To avoid repeating words that have already been mentioned, you can replace the indirect object with a pronoun.

Indirect object pronouns are the same as those used with the verb gustar.

Singular		Plural	
me	to me	nos	to us
te	to you (informal)	os	to you (informal)
le	to him, to her, to you (formal)	les	to them, to you

Adverbs and prepositions

Adverbs of frequency

These adverbs and adverbial phrases express how often something is done:

nunca	*never*	muchas veces	*usually, normally*
casi nunca	*almost never*	casi siempre	*many times, often*
rara vez	*seldom, rarely*	siempre	*always*
a veces	*sometimes*	todos los días	*every day*

Adverbs of quantity

These adverbs express a quantity:

nada	poco	bastante	mucho
not at all	*little, not much*	*quite, enough*	*a lot, much*

Adverbs and phrases of location

aquí	*here*	encima de	*on, on top of*
ahí	*there*	debajo de	*under*
allí	*over there*	delante de	*in front of*
al lado de	*next to*	detrás de	*behind*
a la derecha de	*to the right of*	cerca de	*near, close to*
a la izquierda de	*to the left of*	lejos de	*far from*

Adverbs and phrases about the future

When you express intention or future plans you can use these adverbs or expressions:

		mañana	*tomorrow*
ahora	*now*	mañana por la mañana	*tomorrow morning*
luego, después	*later*	mañana por la tarde	*tomorrow afternoon / evening*
		mañana por la noche	*tomorrow night*
hoy	*today*	la próxima semana, la semana que viene	*next week*
esta mañana	*this morning*		
esta tarde	*this afternoon*	el próximo año, el año que viene	*next year*
esta noche	*tonight*		

Adverbs and phrases about the past

These adverbs and time expressions refer to the past tense:

antes	*before*	la semana pasada	*last week*
anoche	*last night*	el mes pasado	*last month*
ayer	*yesterday*	el año pasado	*last year*
anteayer	*the day before yesterday*		

Prepositions of place

en	*at, in, on, inside* (to express location)
a	*to* (after the verb *ir* indicating destination) *(not translated in English before direct and indirect objects)*
de	*from* (to express origin)
desde... hasta de... a	*from … to* (to express direction or destination)

Conjunctions

Sentences with *si*

In order to express what you do if something happens, use this formula:

Si + condition...

The conjunction *porque*

To express cause, use the conjunction porque or the preposition por:

porque + sentence

por + noun

Interrogatives

Interrogative words

Interrogatives are question words.

¿Qué?	¿Quién?	¿Cómo?	¿Cuándo?	¿Dónde?	¿Cuánto(a)? ¿Cuántos(as)?	¿Por qué?
What?	*Who?*	*How?* *What?*	*When?*	*Where?*	*How much?* *How many?*	*Why?*

Verbs: present tense

Regular verbs: *lavar, prender, abrir*

Lavar *(to wash)*			
Singular		**Plural**	
yo	**lav**o	nosotros nosotras	**lav**amos
tú	**lav**as	vosotros vosotras	**lav**áis
usted él ella	**lav**a	ustedes ellos ellas	**lav**an

Prender *(to switch on)*			
Singular		**Plural**	
yo	**prend**o	nosotros nosotras	**prend**emos
tú	**prend**es	vosotros vosotras	**prend**éis
usted él ella	**prend**e	ustedes ellos ellas	**prend**en

Abrir *(to open)*			
Singular		**Plural**	
yo	**abr**o	nosotros nosotras	**abr**imos
tú	**abr**es	vosotros vosotras	**abr**ís
usted él ella	**abr**e	ustedes ellos ellas	**abr**en

Irregular verbs: *ser, estar, tener, ir*

Ser *(to be)*			
Singular		**Plural**	
yo	soy	nosotros nosotras	somos
tú	eres	vosotros vosotras	sois
usted él ella	es	ustedes ellos ellas	son

Estar *(to be)*			
Singular		**Plural**	
yo	estoy	nosotros nosotras	estamos
tú	estás	vosotros vosotras	estáis
usted él ella	está	ustedes ellos ellas	están

Tener (to have)

Singular		Plural	
yo	tengo	nosotros nosotras	tenemos
tú	tienes	vosotros vosotras	tenéis
usted él ella	tiene	ustedes ellos ellas	tienen

Ir (to go)

Singular		Plural	
yo	voy	nosotros nosotras	vamos
tú	vas	vosotros vosotras	vais
usted él ella	va	ustedes ellos ellas	van

Ir a + infinitive

To express the intention to do something, use this structure:

ir a + infinitive

The verb *gustar*

The verb *doler*

Gustar (to like)

	Singular	Plural
(A mí)	me **gust**a	me **gust**an
(A ti)	te **gust**a	te **gust**an
(A usted) (A él) (A ella)	le **gust**a	le **gust**an
(A nosotros) (A nosotras)	nos **gust**a	nos **gust**an
(A vosotros) (A vosotras)	os **gust**a	os **gust**an
(A ustedes) (A ellos) (A ellas)	les **gust**a	les **gust**an

Doler (to hurt, to ache)

	Singular	Plural
(A mí)	me **duele**	me **duelen**
(A ti)	te **duele**	te **duelen**
(A usted) (A él) (A ella)	le **duele**	le **duelen**
(A nosotros) (A nosotras)	nos **duele**	nos **duelen**
(A vosotros) (A vosotras)	os **duele**	os **duelen**
(A ustedes) (A ellos) (A ellas)	les **duele**	les **duelen**

Stem-changing verbs

Cerrar (e > ie) (to close)		
Singular	**Plural**	
yo **cierro**	nosotros nosotras	**cerramos**
tú **cierras**	vosotros vosotras	**cerráis**
usted él ella **cierra**	ustedes ellos ellas	**cierran**

Poder (o > ue) (to be able to)		
Singular	**Plural**	
yo **puedo**	nosotros nosotras	**podemos**
tú **puedes**	vosotros vosotras	**podéis**
usted él ella **puede**	ustedes ellos ellas	**pueden**

Pedir (e > i) (to ask)		
Singular	**Plural**	
yo **pido**	nosotros nosotras	**pedimos**
tú **pides**	vosotros vosotras	**pedís**
usted él ella **pide**	ustedes ellos ellas	**piden**

Jugar (u > ue) (to play)		
Singular	**Plural**	
yo **juego**	nosotros nosotras	**jugamos**
tú **juegas**	vosotros vosotras	**jugáis**
usted él ella **juega**	ustedes ellos ellas	**juegan**

The verb *sentirse*

Sentirse (to feel)		
Singular	**Plural**	
yo **me siento**	nosotros nosotras	**nos sentimos**
tú **te sientes**	vosotros vosotras	**os sentís**
usted él ella **se siente**	ustedes ellos ellas	**se sienten**

Verbs with irregular yo forms

Hacer (to do, to make)

Singular		Plural	
yo	hago	nosotros nosotras	hacemos
tú	haces	vosotros vosotras	hacéis
usted él ella	hace	ustedes ellos ellas	hacen

Poner (to put)

Singular		Plural	
yo	pongo	nosotros nosotras	ponemos
tú	pones	vosotros vosotras	ponéis
usted él ella	pone	ustedes ellos ellas	ponen

Traer (to bring)

Singular		Plural	
yo	traigo	nosotros nosotras	traemos
tú	traes	vosotros vosotras	traéis
usted él ella	trae	ustedes ellos ellas	traen

Salir (to leave)

Singular		Plural	
yo	salgo	nosotros nosotras	salimos
tú	sales	vosotros vosotras	salís
usted él ella	sale	ustedes ellos ellas	salen

Irregular verbs: *ver, oír, oler,* and *decir*

Ver (to see)

Singular		Plural	
yo	veo	nosotros nosotras	vemos
tú	ves	vosotros vosotras	veis
usted él ella	ve	ustedes ellos ellas	ven

Oír (to hear)

Singular		Plural	
yo	oigo	nosotros nosotras	oímos
tú	oyes	vosotros vosotras	oís
usted él ella	oye	ustedes ellos ellas	oyen

Oler *(to smell)*

	Singular		Plural
yo	huelo	nosotros nosotras	olemos
tú	hueles	vosotros vosotras	oléis
usted él ella	huele	ustedes ellos ellas	huelen

Decir *(to say)*

	Singular		Plural
yo	digo	nosotros nosotras	decimos
tú	dices	vosotros vosotras	decís
usted él ella	dice	ustedes ellos ellas	dicen

Reflexive verbs

Lavarse *(to wash oneself)*

	Singular		Plural
yo	me **lav**o	nosotros nosotras	nos **lav**amos
tú	te **lav**as	vosotros vosotras	os **lav**áis
usted él ella	se **lav**a	ustedes ellos ellas	se **lav**an

Other reflexive verbs are:

acostarse (ue) *(to go to bed)* → yo me acuesto

despertarse (ie) *(to wake up)* → yo me despierto

dormirse (ue) *(to fall asleep)* → yo me duermo

levantarse *(to get up)* → yo me levanto

Expressions of obligation

hay que + infinitive	tener que + infinitive
a general obligation; rules or norms	*a personal obligation*

Expressions of permission and prohibition

Expressing permission:	**Expressing prohibition:**
se puede + infinitive (with singular object) se puede(n) + infinitive (with plural object)	no se puede + infinitive no se puede(n) + infinitive

Verbs: the present participle

Regular present participle forms

The *gerundio* (present participle) is formed by adding the following endings to the verb stem:

-ando	for -*ar* verbs	escuchar	→	escuchando
-iendo	for -*er*, -*ir* verbs	hacer escribir	→ →	haciendo escribiendo

Irregular present participle forms

e > ie				*o > u*		
decir → diciendo	servir → sirviendo			dormir → durmiendo		
medir → midiendo	vestir → vistiendo			morir → muriendo		
pedir → pidiendo				poder → pudiendo		

When the stem of an -*er* or -*ir* verb ends in a vowel (*leer*, *creer*, *oír*), the ending -*iendo* becomes -*yendo*.

leer → leyendo	creer → creyendo	oír → oyendo

Verbs: the present progressive

The present progressive is formed with *estar* + *gerundio* (present participle):

Trabajar *(to work)*			
Singular		**Plural**	
yo	estoy trabajando	nosotros nosotras	estamos trabajando
tú	estás trabajando	vosotros vosotras	estáis trabajando
usted él ella	está trabajando	ustedes ellos ellas	están trabajando

Verbs: commands

Affirmative *tú* commands

REGULAR VERBS

Caminar *(to walk)*	Comer *(to eat)*	Escribir *(to write)*
camina	come	escribe

IRREGULAR VERBS

Tener *(to have)*	Hacer *(to do)*	Poner *(to put)*	Venir *(to come)*	Salir *(to leave)*	Ser *(to be)*	Decir *(to say)*	Ir *(to go)*
ten	haz	pon	ven	sal	sé	di	ve

Negative *tú* commands

REGULAR VERBS

Comprar *(to buy)*	Comer *(to eat)*	Escribir *(to write)*
no compres	no comas	no escribas

IRREGULAR VERBS *SER* AND *IR*

Ser *(to be)*	Ir *(to go)*
no seas	no vayas

Verbs: the preterite tense

Regular verbs (*-ar, -er, -ir*)

	Comprar *(to buy)*	Comer *(to eat)*	Escribir *(to write)*
yo	compré	comí	escribí
tú	compraste	comiste	escribiste
usted él ella	compró	comió	escribió
nosotros nosotras	compramos	comimos	escribimos
vosotros vosotras	comprasteis	comisteis	escribisteis
ustedes ellos ellas	compraron	comieron	escribieron

Irregular verbs

Ser (to be) e ir (to go)

Singular		Plural	
yo	fui	nosotros nosotras	fuimos
tú	fuiste	vosotros vosotras	fuisteis
usted él ella	fue	ustedes ellos ellas	fueron

Decir (to say)

Singular		Plural	
yo	dije	nosotros nosotras	dijimos
tú	dijiste	vosotros vosotras	dijisteis
usted él ella	dijo	ustedes ellos ellas	dijeron

Hacer (to do, to make)

Singular		Plural	
yo	hice	nosotros nosotras	hicimos
tú	hiciste	vosotros vosotras	hicisteis
usted él ella	hizo	ustedes ellos ellas	hicieron

Estar (to be)

Singular		Plural	
yo	estuve	nosotros nosotras	estuvimos
tú	estuviste	vosotros vosotras	estuvisteis
usted él ella	estuvo	ustedes ellos ellas	estuvieron

Tener (to have)

Singular		Plural	
yo	tuve	nosotros nosotras	tuvimos
tú	tuviste	vosotros vosotras	tuvisteis
usted él ella	tuvo	ustedes ellos ellas	tuvieron

GLOSARIO ESPAÑOL-INGLÉS

A

a *to* 16
a causa de *because of* 241
a diario *daily* 73
A la(s)… *At … (time)* 22
a la derecha de *to the right of* 16
a la izquierda de *to the left of* 16
a la vez *at the same time* 117
a lo largo de *along* 113
¿A qué hora abre…? *What time does … open?* 22
¿A qué hora cierra…? *What time does … close?* 22
¿A qué te dedicas? *What do you do for living?* 92
a veces *sometimes* 18
abajo *down* 80
abierto(a) *open* 22
el/la **abogado(a)** *lawyer* 96
abrir *to open* 18
la **abuela** *grandmother* 2
el **abuelo** *grandfather* 2
los **abuelos** *grandparents, grandfathers* 2
la **abundancia** *abundance* 77
aburrido(a) *boring* 69
el **accidente** *accident* 38
la **acción** *action* 12
el **aceite** *oil* 67
el **acento** *accent* 99
el **acordeón** *accordion* 115
acostarse (o > ue) *to go to bed* 50
la **actividad** *activity* 14
las **actividades de ocio** *leisure activities* 14
activo(a) *active* 214
el **acto** *act* 248
el **actor** *actor* 113
actuar *to act* 104
acuático(a) *aquatic* 109
además *what's more* 43
la **adivinanza** *riddle* 45
adivinar *to guess* 119
el **adjetivo** *adjective* 6
los **adjetivos posesivos** *possessive adjectives* 8
la **adolescencia** *adolescence* 51
¿Adónde? *Where to?* 43
los **adverbios de cantidad** *adverbs of quantity* 26
los **adverbios de frecuencia** *adverbs of frequency* 18
los **adverbios de lugar** *adverbs of location* 16

el **aeropuerto** *airport* 152
afeitarse *to shave* 48
afirmativo(a) *affirmative* 68
la **agencia de viajes** *travel agency* 160
la **agenda** *agenda* 97
agosto *August* 241
la **agricultura** *agriculture* 161
agrio(a) *sour* 24
el **agua** *water* 24
las **aguas termales** *hot springs* 52
ahí *there* 16
ahora *now* 17
el **aire** *air* 234
al *to the* 16
al aire libre *outdoors, in the open air* 191
al fin *finally* 192
al lado de *next to* 16
al llegar *upon arriving* 75
el **albatros** *albatross* 254
alcanzar *to reach* 185
la **alegría** *joy* 136
algo *something* 54
el **algodón** *cotton* 23
algún, alguno(a)(os)(as) *a few, any, one, some* 218
la **alimentación** *feeding* 254
los **alimentos** *food* 61
allí *there (far)* 16
el **almacén** *grocery store* 192
almorzar (o > ue) *to have lunch* 69
el **almuerzo** *lunch* 108
el **alojamiento** *accomodations* 168
alojarse *to stay* 195
alrededor de *around* 208
alto(a) *tall* 4 *loud* 43
la **altura** *height* 185
amargo(a) *bitter* 24
amarillo(a) *yellow* 22
americano(a) *American* 159
el/la **amigo(a)** *friend* 2
los **amigos** *friends (males, males and females)* 8
el **amor** *love* 35
anaranjado(a) *orange* 22
ancho(a) *wide* 183
andar *to go, to walk* 192
el **anillo** *ring* 212
el **animal** *animal* 234
el **aniversario** *anniversary* 181
anoche *last night* 170
anteayer *the day before yesterday* 170
antes (de) *before* 48

antiguo(a) *old* 37
anualmente *annually* 229
el **anuncio** *ad* 73
el **año** *year* 8
apagar *to turn off* 43
el **apellido** *last name* 85
la **aportación** *contribution* 133
aprender *to learn* 44
aprovechar *to take advantage* 100
aproximadamente *approximately* 188
aproximado(a) *rough* 225
aquel, aquella *that (far away)* 30
aquello *that (neutral)* 206
aquí *here* 16
árabe *Arab* 47
el **árbol** *tree* 234
el **archipiélago** *archipelago* 76
el **área** *area* 135
argentino(a) *Argentinian* 153
el **argumento** *plot* 193
árido(a) *arid, dry* 189
el **arma** *weapon* 242
el **armario** *closet* 12
la **armonía** *harmony* 134
el **aroma** *scent* 192
la **arquitectura** *architecture* 65
el **arroz** *rice* 24
el **arte** *art* 103
la **artesanía** *handicraft* 227
el **artículo** *article* 10
el/la **artista** *artist* 103
artístico(a) *artistic* 43
el **ascensor** *elevator* 12
así que *so that* 192
asistir *to attend* 100
el/la **astronauta** *astronaut* 208
el **asunto** *matter* 139
atado(a) *tied* 125
Atentamente. *Sincerely yours,* 52
atlántico(a) *Atlantic* 76
el/la **atleta** *athlete* 97
atlético(a) *athletic* 4
atraer *to attract* 191
atravesado(a) *crossed* 189
atrevido(a) *daring* 4
aunque *although* 188
los **auriculares** *headphones* 96
auténtico(a) *authentic* 214
el **autobús** *bus* 152
la **autoevaluación** *self-evaluation* 87

el/la **autor(a)** *author* 190

el **autorretrato** *self-portrait* 41

el **ave** *bird* 211

la **avenida** *avenue* 79

la **aventura** *adventure* 78

el **avión** *plane* 152

¡Ay! *Ouch!* 58

ayer *yesterday* 170

ayudar *to help* 51

el **azúcar** *sugar* 24

azul *blue* 22

el **azulejo** *tile* 37

B

bailar *to dance* 104

el **baile** *dance* 114

bajar *to get off* 192 *to go down* 223

bajo(a) *short* 4

la **ballena** *whale* 237

el **balneario** *beach resort* 217

el **balón** *ball* 122

el **baloncesto** *basketball* 122

la **banana** *banana* 27

el **banco** *bank* 178

la **banda** *band* 115

la **bandera** *flag* 155

el **bandoneón** *Argentinian large accordion* 190

bañar *to bathe* 77

bañarse *to take a bath* 48

la **bañera** *bathtub* 12

el **baño** *bathroom* 12

barato(a) *cheap* 153

el **barco** *ship* 152

barrer *to sweep* 14

el **barrio** *neighborhood* 95

básico(a) *basic* 66

bastante *quite, enough* 26

la **basura** *garbage* 14

el **bate** *bat* 122

beber *to drink* 25

la **bebida** *drink* 24

el **béisbol** *baseball* 122

la **belleza** *beauty* 69

bello(a) *beautiful* 79

el **beso** *kiss* 17

la **biblioteca** *library* 178

bien *well* 2 *properly* 160 *correctly* 167

Bienvenido(a). *Welcome.* 57

bilingüe *bilingual* 97

el **billete** *ticket* 160 *bill* 225

blanco(a) *white* 22

la **blusa** *blouse* 22

la **boca** *mouth* 40

la **bola** *ball* 122

el **boletín** *bulletin* 220

el **boleto** *ticket* 108

el **boliche** *bowling* 122

el **bolígrafo** *ballpoint* 17

la **bolsa** *bag* 160

bonito(a) *pretty* 11

el **bosque** *forest* 216

botar *to throw away* 234

la **botella** *bottle* 24

el **brazo** *arm* 40

brillar *to shine* 208

la **broma** *joke* 46

la **brutalidad** *brutality* 80

buen, bueno(a) *good* 10

¡Buen fin de semana! *Have a nice weekend!* 19

¡Buen viaje! *Have a good trip!* 148

Bueno, … *Well …* 17

buscar *to find, to look for* 13

C

el **caballo** *horse* 80

la **cabaña** *cabin* 253

la **cabeza** *head* 40

cada *each* 14

el **café** *coffee* 25 *cafe* 178

la **cafetería** *cafeteria* 100

los **calcetines** *socks* 22

el **cálculo** *calculation* 139

el **calendario** *calendar* 106

cálido(a) *warm* 189

caliente *hot* 24

la **calle** *street* 178

la **cama** *bed* 12

la **cámara de fotos** *camera* 112

la **cámara de video** *camcorder* 112

cambiar *to change* 49

el **cambio** *change* 51

caminar *to walk* 66

el **camino** *way* 55

la **camisa** *shirt* 22

la **camiseta** *T-shirt* 22

el/la **campeón(a)** *champion* 130

el **cámping** *campsite* 168

el **campo** *countryside* 39 *field* 127

el **canal** *canal* 245

la **canasta** *basket* 125

la **cancha** *court (sports)* 125

la **canción** *song* 113

cansado(a) *tired* 4

el/la **cantante** *singer* 111

cantar *to sing* 104

la **cantidad** *quantity* 218

la **capital** *capital city* 224

la **cara** *face* 40

la **característica** *feature* 4

característico(a) *characteristic, typical* 78

caribeño(a) *Caribbean* 136

el **cariño** *love* 118

el **carnaval** *carnival* 135

la **carne** *meat* 24

la **carrera** *race* 39

la **carta** *menu* 24

el **cartel** *poster* 137

la **casa** *house* 12

el **casco** *helmet* 122

casi *almost* 134

casi nunca *almost never* 18

casi siempre *most of the time* 18

el **castillo** *castle* 77

las **cataratas** *waterfalls* 145

la **catedral** *cathedral* 57

la **categoría** *category* 247

católico(a) *Catholic* 33

la **causa** *cause* 210

la **caza** *hunting* 255

cazar *to hunt* 255

la **celebración** *celebration* 133

celebrar *to celebrate* 9

cenar *to have dinner* 31

central *central* 182

el **centro** *downtown* 21 *middle, center* 76

el **centro comercial** *shopping center, mall* 99

cepillarse *to brush (one's hair, teeth)* 48

el **cepillo** *hairbrush* 48

el **cepillo de dientes** *toothbrush* 48

la **cerámica** *ceramics, pottery* 227

cerca de *close to* 16

los **cereales** *cereals* 67

cerrado(a) *closed* 22

cerrar (e > ie) *to close* 20

el **césped** *lawn* 14

el **champú** *shampoo* 48

la **chaqueta** *jacket* 22

la **chica** *girl* 2

el/la **chicano(a)** *Chicano* 134

el **chico** *boy* 2

los **chicos** *boys, boys and girls* 116

el **chile** *chili* 134

chileno(a) *Chilean* 159

la **chinchilla** *chinchilla* 237

el **chocolate** *chocolate* 25

el **cibercafé** *cybercafe* 164

ciclista *cycling* 32

el/la **ciclista** *cyclist* 39

el **cielo** *sky* 208

la(s) **ciencia(s)** *science* 61

el/la **científico(a)** *scientist* 219

cierto(a) *true* 5 *certain* 133

el **cine** *movie theater* 112 *cinematography* 114

el **circuito** *track* 203

la **ciudad** *city* 168

civil *civil* 80

la **civilización** *civilization* 215

Claro. *Of course.* 64

claro *clearly* 99

claro(a) *clear* 130

la **clase** *classroom* 17 *class* 21

la **clase turista** *coach class* 158

la **clave** *key* 99

el/la **cliente(a)** *customer* 25 *client* 97

el **clima** *climate* 77

el **coche** *car* 152

la **cocina** *kitchen* 12 *cuisine* 134

cocinar *to cook* 213

el **código** *code* 223

la **colección** *collection* 103

colocar *to place* 191

colombiano(a) *Colombian* 69

colonizar *to colonize* 133

el **color** *color* 22

colorido(a) *colorful* 136

el/la **comentarista** *announcer* 38

comenzar (e > ie) *to begin* 151

comer *to eat* 51 *to have lunch* 73

comer bien *to eat well* 66

el **cometa** *comet* 208

la **comida** *meal* 24 *food* 31

como *like* 9

¿Cómo? *How?* 25

¿Cómo es? *What does he/she/it look like? (physical characteristics); What is he/she/it like? (personality traits)* 4

¿Cómo está/estás? *How are you?* 2

¿Cómo te llamas? *What's your name?* 2

¿Cómo te sientes? *How are you feeling?* 36

la **cómoda** *dresser* 12

cómodo(a) *comfortable* 50

el/la **compañero(a)** *classmate* 18

la **compañía** *company* 10

la **comparación** *comparison* 26

la **competición** *competition* 39

la **competición deportiva** *sport competition* 138

competir (e > i) *to compete* 20

completar *to complete* 2

comprar *to buy* 17

las **compras** *shopping* 155

comprender *to understand* 35

la **comprensión** *comprehension* 81

la **computadora** *computer* 8

la **comunicación** *communication* 44

la **comunidad** *community* 97

con *with* 5

la **concentración** *concentration* 133

el **concierto** *concert* 107

el **concurso** *contest* 229

el **condado** *county* 251

conducir *to drive* 153

la **conexión** *connection* 51

confesar (e > ie) *to confess* 44

la **conjunción** *conjunction* 210

conmigo *with me* 117

conocer *to be acquainted, to know* 30

el **conocimiento** *knowledge* 137

el/la **consejero(a)** *advisor* 101

el **consejo** *advice* 64

conservar *to preserve* 117

considerar *to consider* 177

la **construcción** *building* 79 *construction* 97

construir *to build* 181

la **consulta** *doctor's office* 61

contactar *to contact* 139

la **contaminación** *pollution* 237

contar (o > ue) *to count* 20

el **contenedor** *container* 234

contento(a) *happy* 4

el **continente** *continent* 216

continuar *to continue* 192

contradecir *to contradict* 192

la **contribución** *contribution* 136

contribuir *to contribute* 219

controlar *to control* 255

conversar *to talk, to chat* 95

convertir (e > ie) *to convert* 77

el **corazón** *heart* 99

la **cordillera** *mountain chain* 189

el **coro** *choir* 65

correcto(a) *correct* 166

el/la **corredor(a)** *runner* 223

el **correo electrónico** *e-mail* 85

correr *to run* 66

cortar *to cut* 14

corto(a) *short* 41

la **cosa** *thing* 10

la **costa** *coast, shore* 168

costar (o > ue) *to cost* 20

costero(a) *coastal* 247

la **costumbre** *custom* 73

crear *to create* 45

creer *to believe* 110

la **crema de afeitar** *shaving cream* 48

el/la **cristiano(a)** *Christian* 57

la **crónica** *chronicle* 198

crujiente *crunchy* 134

el **crustáceo** *crustacean* 254

cruzar *to cross* 178

el **cuaderno** *notebook* 17

la **cuadra** *block* 192

el **cuadro** *painting* 40

cuando *when* 5

¿Cuándo? *When?* 81

¡Cuánto(a)(os)(as)…! *How much/many …!* 204

¿Cuánto cuesta? *How much is it?* 23

¿Cuántos(as)? *How many?* 17

el **cuarto** *room* 44

cubano(a) *Cuban* 95

cubierto(a) *covered* 189

el **cubismo** *cubism* 43

cubista *cubist* 43

la **cuchara** *spoon* 24

el **cuchillo** *knife* 24

la **cueca** *Chilean national dance* 243

el **cuello** *neck* 40

el **cuero** *leather* 125

el **cuerpo** *body* 40

el **cuidado** *care* 160

¡Cuidado! *Watch out!* 38

cuidar *to take care of* 14

cuidarse *to take care of oneself* 66

la **cultura** *culture* 39

cultural *cultural* 76

el **cumpleaños** *birthday* 9

la **cuna** *birthplace* 78

curar *to cure* 97

la **curiosidad** *curiosity* 108

curioso(a) *curious* 254

D

la **danza** *dance* 136

dar *to give* 64

el **dato** *piece of information* 132

de *of* 3 *than* 47 *from* 172

de ida y vuelta *round trip* 148

de nuevo *again* 192

de viaje *on a trip* 152

debajo de *under* 16

deber *must* 238

débil *weak* 54

decidir *to decide* 25

decir *to say, to tell* 42

declarar *to declare* 181

decorar *to decorate* 47

dedicarse a *to do for a living* 92

el **dedo** *finger, toe* 40

defender (e > ie) *to defend* 97

la **deforestación** *deforestation* 219

dejar *to leave (smething)* 232

del *of the* 5

delante de *in front of* 16

el **delfín** *dolphin* 237

delgado(a) *thin* 4

delicioso(a) *delicious* 164

los/las **demás** *rest* 61

los **demostrativos** *demonstratives* 30

dentro *inside* 64

denunciar *to denounce* 190

el **departamento** *department* 164

el **deporte** *sport* 122

el **depósito** *deposit* 211

el **desafío** *challenge* 32

el **desarrollo** *development* 110

desayunar *to have breakfast* 69

el **desayuno** *breakfast* 28

descansar *to rest* 50

el **descanso** *rest* 47

descender (e > ie) *to descend* 188

el/la **descendiente** *descendant* 215

describir *to describe* 2

descriptivo(a) *descriptive* 135

descubrir *to discover* 208

desde *from* 43 *since* 57

desesperado(a) *desperate* 80

el **desfile** *parade* 133

el **desierto** *desert* 216

el **desodorante** *deodorant* 48

despacio *slowly* 176

despertarse (e > ie) *to wake up* 50

después *later on* 53

después de *after* 69

el **destino** *destination* 168

destruir *to destroy* 80

el/la **detective** *detective* 38

detrás de *behind* 16

el **día** *day* 43

el **diablo** *devil* 166

el **diario** *diary* 221

diario(a) *daily* 53

el **dibujo** *drawing* 190

el **diente** *tooth* 40

la **dieta** *diet* 51

la **diferencia** *difference* 220

diferente *different* 49

difícil *difficult* 41

el **dinero** *money* 191

la **dirección** *direction* 166

el/la **director(a)** *director* 96 *principal* 128

dirigir *to direct, to run* 97

el **disco** *disc* 117

diseñar *to design* 67

el **diseño** *design* 47

disfrutar *to enjoy* 76

la **distancia** *distance* 152

distinto(a) *different* 26

la **diversidad** *diversity* 136

divertido(a) *fun* 9

divertirse (e > ie) *to enjoy oneself* 113

dividir *to divide* 223

la **división** *division* 224

doblar a la derecha/izquierda *to turn to the right/left* 178

el/la **doctor(a)** *doctor* 34

el **documental** *documentary* 85

el **documento** *document* 148

el **dólar** *dollar* 23

doler (o > ue) *to hurt* 58

el **dolor** *ache, pain* 56

el **domingo** *Sunday* 157

el **dominó** *dominoes* 88

don *Mr.* 5

¿Dónde? *Where?* 12

dormir (o > ue) *to sleep* 61

dormirse (o > ue) *to fall asleep* 50

el **dormitorio** *bedroom* 12

la **ducha** *shower* 12

ducharse *to take a shower* 48

dulce *sweet* 24

el **dulce de leche** *milk caramel typical of Argentina and other countries in the Rio de la Plata region* 187

durante *for* 39 *during* 49

durar *to last* 185

E

el **eclipse** *eclipse* 208

la **ecología** *ecology* 251

el **edificio** *building* 12

el **ejemplo** *example* 97

él *he* 6

el, la *the* 10

el año pasado *last year* 170

el año que viene *next year* 106

el mes pasado *last month* 170

la **electricidad** *electricity* 238

eléctrico(a) *electric* 115

el **elefante** *elephant* 254

elegante *elegant* 183

el **elemento** *element* 193

ella *she* 6

ellas *they (feminine)* 6

ellos *they (males, males and females)* 6

emocionado(a) *excited* 4

emocionante *exciting* 37

empacar *to pack* 237

la **empanada** *pie* 111

empezar (e > ie) *to begin, to start* 20

el/la **empleado(a)** *employee* 96

el/la **empresario(a)** *businessman, businesswoman* 95

en *in* 16

en brazos *in one's arms* 80

en cambio *instead* 105

en directo *live* 139

en el centro de *in the middle of* 161

en general *in general* 73

en realidad *actually* 192

Encantado(a). *Nice to meet you.* 2

encima de *on, on top of* 16

encontrar (o > ue) *to find* 46

encontrarse (o > ue) *to feel* 60

encontrarse (o > ue) con *to run into, to meet with* 173

el **encuentro** *meeting, encounter* 74

la **encuesta** *survey* 43

la **energía** *energy* 61

enero *January* 223

la **enfermedad** *illness* 56

el/la **enfermero(a)** *nurse* 56

enfermo(a) *sick* 4

el/la **enfermo(a)** *patient* 56

enloquecido(a) *mad* 80

enojado(a) *angry* 4

enorme *huge* 203

enriquecedor(a) *enlightening* 205

la **ensalada** *salad* 27

enseñar *to teach* 97

enseñar el pasaporte *to show one's passport* 160

entender (e > ie) *to understand* 20

entonces *then* 25

entrar *to enter* 31

entre *between* 73 *among* 103

entregar *to give* 193

el/la **entrenador(a)** *coach* 96

entretener *to entertain* 34

la **entrevista** *interview* 212

la **época** *age* 46

equilibrado(a) *well-balanced* 51

el **equipaje** *baggage* 160

el **equipamiento** *equipment* 138

el **equipo** *team* 122

equivaler *to be equivalent* 173

equivocado(a) *wrong* 192

el **error** *mistake* 167

la **escalera** *stairs* 12

el **escalón** *step* 222

el **escenario** *scenario* 78

escoger *to choose* 35

escolar *school* 220

escribir *to write* 3

escribir correos *to write e-mails* 112

escribir mensajes *to write instant messages* 104

escuchar *to listen* 3

el **escudo** *shield* 37

la **escuela** *school* 96

ese, esa *that (nearby)* 30

esos(as) *those (nearby)* 30

el **espacio** *space* 212

la **espada** *sword* 80

la **espalda** *back* 56

el **español** *Spanish (language)* 6

español(a) *Spanish* 73

el/la **español(a)** *Spaniard* 43

especial *special* 25

especialmente *specially* 79

la **especialidad** *specialty* 25

espectacular *spectacular* 189

el **espectáculo** *show* 43

el/la **espectador(a)** *spectator* 133

la **esperanza** *hope* 80

esperar *to wait for* 35

espontáneo(a) *spontaneous* 4

la **esposa** *wife* 202

el **esposo** *husband* 159

el **esquema** *diagram* 67

esquiar *to ski* 195

esta mañana *this morning* 106

esta noche *tonight, this evening* 106

esta tarde *this afternoon/ evening* 106

la **estación** *station* 152 *season* 217

el **estadio** *stadium, arena* 122

las **estadísticas** *statistics* 123

el **estado** *condition* 54 *state* 76

los **Estados Unidos** *United States* 9

el/la **estadounidense** *American (noun)* 137

la **estantería** *bookcase* 12

estar *to be* 6

estar en forma *to be in shape* 66

estar listo(a) *to be ready* 148

estar preparado(a) *to be ready* 148

la **estatua** *statue* 103

este, esta *this* 30

el **este** *east* 169

Este(a) es... *This is ...* 2

el **estilo** *style* 43

Estimado(a)... *Dear...* 49

esto *this (neutral)* 77

el **estómago** *stomach* 56

Estoy enfermo(a). *I am sick.* 36

la **estrategia** *strategy* 81

la **estrella** *star* 208

el/la **estudiante** *student* 2

los **estudiantes** *students (males, males and females)* 97

el **estudio** *study* 164

estudioso(a) *studious* 4

la **estufa** *stove* 12

la **etapa** *stage* 38

el/la **europeo(a)** *European* 188

el **evento** *event* 46

evitar *to avoid* 61

exactamente *exactly* 188

el **examen** *test* 5

la **excursión** *excursion, field trip* 48

la **excusa** *excuse* 69

la **existencia** *existence* 16

existir *to exist* 219

el **éxito** *success* 99

la **expedición** *expedition* 198

la **experiencia** *experience* 160

experto(a) *expert* 94

explorar *to explore* 208

la **exposición** *exhibition* 108

expresar *to express* 8

la **expresión** *expression* 16

extenderse (e > ie) *to spread out* 78

extenso(a) *vast* 77

la **extinción** *extinction* 237

extraordinario(a) *extraordinary* 108

F

la **fábrica** *factory* 96

la **fachada** *front, facade* 59

facturar el equipaje *to check the luggage* 160

las **fajitas** *fajitas* 134

la **falda** *skirt* 22

fallado(a) *failed* 53

falso(a) *false* 25

la **familia** *family* 2

familiar *family* 9

famoso(a) *famous* 31

el/la **famoso(a)** *celebrity* 93

el/la **fan** *fan* 44

fantástico(a) *fantastic* 117

la **farmacia** *pharmacy, drugstore* 56

la **fauna** *fauna* 233

favorito(a) *favorite* 105

la **fecha** *date* 136

femenino(a) *feminine* 10

el **fenómeno** *phenomenon* 219

feo(a) *ugly* 5

ferroviario(a) *railway* 134

festejar *to celebrate* 133

el **festejo** *festivity* 137

el **festival** *festival* 131

la **ficha** *domino* 101 *file card* 254

la **fiebre** *fever* 56

la **fiesta** *party* 9

la **figura** *figure* 207

fijarse *to notice* 43

el **fin de semana** *weekend* 15

el **final** *end* 45

finalmente *finally* 166

físico(a) *physical* 4

el **flamenco** *flamenco* 43

la **flor** *flower* 234

la **flora** *flora* 233

la **florería** *flower shop* 171

folclórico(a) *folk* 229

la **forma** *way* 61

formado(a) por *formed by* 167

formar parte de *to be part of* 215

el **fósil** *fossil* 219

la **foto** *photo, picture* 11

la **fotografía** *photo, picture* 43
photography 92

el/la **fotógrafo(a)** *photographer* 91

la **fotonovela** *photonovel* 38

el **francés** *French (language)* 92

la **frecuencia** *frequency* 18

frente a *in front of* 251

frío(a) *cold* 24

la **frontera** *border* 224

la **fruta** *fruit* 24

el **fuego** *fire* 80

fuerte *strong* 38

funcionar *to function, to work* 15

fundado(a) *founded* 103

el **fútbol** *soccer* 122

el **fútbol americano** *football* 122

el **futuro** *future* 106

las **gafas** *glasses* 210

la **gala** *gala* 111

la **galería** *gallery* 95

ganar *to win* 37

el **garaje** *garage* 12

la **garganta** *throat* 56

gastar *to waste* 238

la **gastronomía** *gastronomy* 132

el **gato** *cat* 8

el **gaucho** *gaucho* 144

el **gel** *gel* 48

general *general* 221

la **gente** *people* 17

la **geografía** *geography* 216

geográfico(a) *geographical* 209

geométrico(a) *geometric* 47

el **germen** *germ* 61

el **gerundio** *present participle* 116

gigantesco(a) *gigantic* 246

el **gimnasio** *gym* 67

girar *to turn* 208

el **glaciar** *glacier* 188

el **gobierno** *government* 67

el **golf** *golf* 122

el **golpe** *knock* 38

gordo(a) *fat* 4

el **gorro** *cap* 22

grabar *to tape, to record* 112

gracias *thank you* 3

gracias a *thanks to* 99

gracioso(a) *funny* 4

el **grado** *degree* 26

la **graduación** *graduation* 113

la **gramática** *grammar* 6

gran, grande *big* 13   *great* 77

Gran Bretaña *Great Britain* 173

gratis *free (of charge)* 47

la **gripe** *flu* 61

el **grupo** *group* 86

el **guante** *glove* 122

guapo *handsome* 5

guardar *to put … away* 193

la **guerra** *war* 80

el/la **guía** *guide* 108

la **guía turística** *tourist guide* 160

la **guitarra** *guitar* 42

gustar *to like* 26

los **gustos** *likes* 22

haber *auxiliary verb* 16

la **habitación** *room* 47

habitado(a) *inhabited* 135

el/la **habitante** *inhabitant* 188

el **hábitat** *habitat* 254

el **hábito** *habit* 51

habitual *habitual* 12

hablar *to talk* 3

hablar por teléfono *to talk on the phone* 14

Hace frío. *It's cold.* 197

Hace sol. *It's sunny.* 5

hacer *to do, to make* 30

hacer deporte *to play sports* 66

hacer ejercicio *to exercise* 66

hacer turismo *to travel around* 168

hacia *towards* 78

la **hamburguesa** *burger* 98

hasta *up to* 151   *to* 172   *until* 236

Hasta pronto. *See you soon.* 9

hay *there is, there are* 16

hay que… *one has to …* 28

el **helado** *ice cream* 24

el **hemisferio** *hemisphere* 217

la **herencia** *heritage* 79

la **hermana** *sister* 2

el **hermano** *brother* 2

los **hermanos** *brothers, siblings* 2

el **héroe** *hero* 100

hidratante *moisturizing* 50

el **hielo** *ice* 212

la **hierba** *grass* 189

la **higiene** *hygiene* 48

la **hija** *daughter* 2

el **hijo** *son* 2

los **hijos** *son and daughter, sons* 2

hispánico(a) *Hispanic* 88

hispano(a) *Hispanic* 95

hispanohablante *Spanish speaker* 188

la **Historia** *history (subject)* 101

la **historia** *story* 45

histórico(a) *historical* 181

la **historieta gráfica** *comic strip* 190

el **hockey** *hockey* 237

la **hoja** *leaf* 234

Hola. *Hello.* 2

el **hombre** *man* 2

honesto(a) *honest* 99

el **honor** *honor* 199

la **hora** *hour* 65

el **horario** *schedule* 23

el **horror** *horror* 80

el **hospital** *hospital* 56

el **hostal** *guest house* 33

el **hotel** *hotel* 168

hoy *today* 106

la **huella** *influence* 133

el **huevo** *egg* 24

humano(a) *human* 69

el **humor** *humor* 190

la **idea** *idea* 49

ideal *ideal* 109

la **identidad** *identity* 134

identificar *to identify* 2

la **iglesia** *church* 178

igual *same* 69   *equal* 173

igual que *similar to* 153

la **imagen** *image* 215

el **imperativo** *imperative (tense), command (tense)* 68

importante *important* 39

la **impresión** *impression* 219

impresionante *impressive* 167

inaugurar *to inaugurate* 153

incluir *to include* 228

increíble *incredible* 110

los **indefinidos** *indefinites* 218

la **independencia** *independence* 136

indicar *to indicate* 192

indígena *indigenous* 31

la **industria** *industry* 161

la **influencia** *influence* 79

la **información** *information* 94

mal *badly* 36 *wrongly* 166

la **maleta** *suitcase* 160

mal, malo(a) *bad* 43

la **mamá** *mom, mommy* 21

el **mamífero** *mammal* 237

mandar *to order* 192

la **mano** *hand* 40

el **mantel** *tablecloth* 24

mantener *to keep* 51

el **manuscrito** *manuscript* 103

la **manzana** *apple* 71

mañana *tomorrow* 9

la **mañana** *morning* 23

mañana por la mañana *tomorrow morning* 106

mañana por la noche *tomorrow night* 106

mañana por la tarde *tomorrow afternoon/evening* 106

el **mapa** *map* 76

maquillarse *to make (oneself) up* 48

el/la **mar** *sea* 216

el **maracuyá** *passion fruit* 50

el **maratón** *marathon* 158

maravilloso(a) *marvelous* 174

el **marco** *setting* 193

marinero(a) *sailor* 77

marino(a) *marine* 237

Marte *Mars* 208

el **martes** *Tuesday* 53

marzo *March* 154

más *more* 15

el/la **más** *most* 41

más de *more than* 47

más... que *more ... than* 26

más tarde *later on* 133

la **mascota** *pet* 14

masculino(a) *masculine* 10

las **Matemáticas** *math* 5

matemático(a) *mathematical* 139

el **material** *material* 235

mayo *May* 95

mayor *old* 4

el/la **mayor** *biggest* 76 *adult* 107

me *(to) me* 28 *myself* 50

Me duele/duelen... *I have a ... ache* 56

Me llamo... *My name is ...* 2

Me siento bien. *I feel fine.* 36

Me siento mal. *I don't feel well.* 36

la **medianoche** *midnight* 151

el **medicamento** *medication, medicine* 66

la **Medicina** *medicine (science)* 57

el/la **médico(a)** *doctor* 56

el **medio** *middle* 80

el **medio ambiente** *environment* 234

el **mediodía** *noon* 73

los **medios de comunicación** *mass media* 133

los **medios de transporte** *means of transport* 194

medir (e > i) *to measure* 20

mediterráneo(a) *Mediterranean* 79

mejor *better* 69

el/la **mejor** *best* 9

menos *less* 27

menos... que *less ... than* 26

el **mensaje** *message* 227

el **mensaje electrónico** *text message* 44

la **menta** *mint* 49

mental *mental* 51

el **merengue** *merengue* 108

el **mes** *month* 133

la **mesa** *table* 12

el/la **mesero(a)** *server, waiter/ waitress* 24

la **meseta** *plateau* 77

la **mesita de noche** *night stand* 12

la **meta** *finish lane* 165

el **metal** *metal* 234

el **metro** *meter* 151 *subway* 152

la **mezcla** *mixture* 134

la **mezquita** *mosque* 79

mi, mis *my* 8

el **microondas** *microwave* 12

el **miércoles** *Wednesday* 156

miles *thousands* 57

la **milla** *mile* 163

el **millón** *million* 123

el **mineral** *mineral* 50

el **minuto** *minute* 35

mirar *to look at* 38

mismo(a) *same* 164

el **mito** *myth* 191

el **moái** *monolithic human figures carved from rock on the Polynesian island of Easter Island, Chile* 203

la **mochila** *backpack* 46

la **moda** *fashion* 136

modernista *modernist* 79

moderno(a) *modern* 78

el **molino de viento** *windmill* 78

la **monarquía** *monarchy* 76

el **monasterio** *monastery* 33

la **moneda** *currency* 225

el **monje** *monk* 65

el **monstruo** *monster* 45

la **montaña** *mountain* 168

montar en bicicleta *to ride a bike* 104

el **monumento** *monument* 134

morado(a) *purple* 22

morder (o > ue) *to bite* 248

moreno(a) *brunet(te)* 4

morir (o > ue) *to die* 116

el **mostrador de información** *information desk* 160

mostrar (o > ue) *to show* 136

el **motivo** *motive* 211

mover (o > ue) *to move* 108

el **movimiento** *movement* 16

muchas veces *usually, normally, many times* 18

mucho *a lot, much* 26

mucho(a)(os)(as) *many, a lot of* 218

Mucho gusto. *It's a pleasure.* 2

los **muebles** *furniture* 14

las **muelas** *teeth (molars)* 54

la **muerte** *death* 80

el/la **muerto(a)** *dead* 80

la **mujer** *woman* 2

la **multiplicación** *multiplication* 248

el **mundo** *world* 57

el **mural** *mural* 134

el **muralismo** *muralism* 134

el **museo** *museum* 21

la **música** *music* 14

musical *musical* 111

el/la **músico(a)** *musician* 111

muy *very* 9

¡Muy bien! *Very well!* 92

nacer *to be born* 78

los **nachos** *nachos* 134

el **nacimiento** *birth* 249

la **nación** *nation* 136

nacional *national* 167

nada *nothing* 26

nadar *to swim* 104

la **naranja** *orange* 24

la **nariz** *nose* 40

la **narración** *narration* 193

la **natación** *swimming* 122

natural *natural* 41

la **naturaleza** *nature* 234

navegar   to sail 192

la **navegación**   navigation 192

necesario(a)   necessary 97

necesitar   to need 15

negativo(a)   negative 176

el **negocio**   business 95

negro(a)   black 22

neoyorquino(a)   New Yorker 108

nervioso(a)   nervous 15

nevar (e > ie)   to snow 5

ni   nor 43

los **nietos**   grandchildren, grandsons 2

ningún, ninguno(a)   no, (not) any 218

la **niña**   girl 2

el **niño**   boy 2

los **niños**   boys, boys and girls 10

el **nivel**   level 151

No importa.   It does not matter. 148

No pasa nada.   It does not matter. 148

la **nobleza**   nobility 227

la **noche**   night 23

nocturno(a)   night, nocturnal 209

nombrar   to name 135

el **nombre**   noun 10   name 30

el **noreste**   northeast 169

normalmente   usually, normally 19

el **noroeste**   northwest 55

el **norte**   north 41

nos   (to) us 28   ourselves 50

nosotros(as)   we 6

la **nota**   grade 139   note 173

la **noticia**   news 113

la **novela**   novel 78

la **novia**   girlfriend 2

noviembre   November 159

el **novio**   boyfriend 2

la **nube**   cloud 144

nuestro(a)   our 8

nuevo(a)   new 17

el **número**   number 123

nunca   never 18

la **nutria**   otter 254

la **nutrición**   nutrition 67

el **ñandú**   rhea 237

los **ñoquis**   Argentinian pasta similar to gnocchi 191

el **oasis**   oasis 107

obediente   obedient 192

el **objeto**   object 43

las **obligaciones**   duties 49

la **obra**   construction site 96

la **obra de arte**   work of art 102

obrero(a)   working-class 191

observar   to observe 213

el **océano**   ocean 216

octubre   October 133

ocurrir   to happen 198

el **oeste**   west 169

la **oferta**   offer 210

la **oficina**   office 96

la **oficina de turismo**   tourist office 160

la **Oficina del Censo**   Census Bureau 132

ofrecer   to offer 107

los **oídos**   ears 56

oír   to hear 40

el **ojo**   eye 40

oler   to smell 40

olvidar   to forget 147

la **oportunidad**   opportunity 100

opuesto(a)   opposite 217

la **oración**   sentence 84

la **orden**   order 64

ordenar   to tidy 15

las **orejas**   ears 40

la **organización**   organization 103

organizado(a)   organized 52

organizar   to organize 97

orgulloso(a)   proud 219

el **origen**   origin 95

original   original 69

originalmente   originally 55

la **orilla**   bank (river) 248

la **orquesta**   orchestra 190

os   (to) you (informal, plural) 28   yourselves (informal) 50

el **otoño**   fall 111

otro(a)   other 32

la **oveja**   sheep 207

la **paciencia**   patience 98

el/la **paciente**   patient 34

el **padre**   father 2

los **padres**   parents 2

la **paella**   traditional rice dish from Spain 25

pagar   to pay 195

la **página**   web site 67

el **país**   country 224

el **paisaje**   landscape 77

el **pájaro**   bird 234

el **pájaro carpintero**   woodpecker 237

la **palabra**   word 38

el **palacio**   palace 47

los **pantalones**   pants 22

los **pantalones cortos**   shorts 22

el **papá**   dad 30

la **papa**   potato 24

el **papel**   paper 234

la **papelería**   stationery store 223

el **paquete**   package 193

para   for 15   to 25   in order to 25

el **parador**   state-run hotel 55

parafrasear   to paraphrase 249

parecer   to seem 69   to look like 203

la **pared**   wall 54

la **pareja**   pair 35   couple 190   partner 207

parlamentario(a)   parliamentary 76

el **parque**   park 35

la **parte**   part 40

el/la **participante**   participant 43

participar   to participate 39

la **partida**   match, game 93

el **partido**   match, game 122

el **partido político**   political party 179

el **pasado**   past 133

pasado(a)   past 170

el **pasaporte**   passport 160

pasar   to pass 41   to happen 45   to spend (time) 107

pasar la aspiradora   to vacuum 14

pasarlo bien   to have a good time 118

el **pasatiempo**   pastime, hobby 104

pasear   to stroll 14

el **paseo**   avenue 77   walk, stroll 113

el **paso**   step 86   passage 190

la **pasta de dientes**   toothpaste 48

pedir (e > i)   to ask for 20

peinarse   to comb (one's hair) 48

el **peine**   comb 48

la **película**   movie 112

el **peligro**   danger 223

el **punto cardinal** *cardinal point* 169
la **pureza** *purity* 227

¿Qué? *What?* 5
¡Qué bien! *Great!* 118
¡Qué día! *What a day!* 156
¡Qué dolor! *How painful!* 38
¡Qué emoción! *How exciting!* 227
¡Qué horror! *How awful!* 174
¡Qué impresionante! *How impressive!* 204
¡Qué lástima! *What a pity!* 187
¡Qué pena! *What a shame!* 164
¡Qué suerte! *How lucky!* 113
¿Qué tal? *How are you doing?* 3
Que te mejores. *Get well.* 36
¿Qué te pasa? *What's wrong?* 36
quedar *to fit* 39
quedarse *to stay* 164
querer (e > ie) *to want* 20 *to love* 156
Querido(a)... *Dear...* 101
el **queso** *cheese* 5
¿Quién? *Who?* 3
la **quinceañera** *fifteen year old girl's party* 9

R

la **radio** *radio* 112
la **raíz** *stem* 20
rapanui *native Polynesian inhabitants of Easter Island* 214
rápido *quickly* 64
rápido(a) *quick* 125
la **raqueta** *racket* 122
rara vez *rarely* 18
raro(a) *rare* 103
el **rasgo** *feature* 4
la **razón** *reason* 210
real *royal* 47
la **receta** *recipe* 15
el **reciclaje** *recycling* 234
reciclar *to recycle* 234
recomendar (e > ie) *to recommend* 67
reconocer *to recognize* 136
recordar (o > ue) *to remember* 20
recorrer *to cover* 57
el **recuerdo** *souvenir* 155
el **recurso** *resource* 235
la **red** *net* 122

reducir *to reduce* 235
el **refresco** *refreshment, soda* 24
el **refrigerador** *refrigerator* 12
regalar *to give a present* 165
el **regalo** *gift* 22
la **región** *region* 77
regresar *to come back* 173
regular *regular* 18
regularmente *regularly* 65
relajarse *to relax* 47
el **remedio** *remedy* 66
rentar *to rent* 153
el **repaso** *review* 82
repetir (e > i) *to repeat* 20
representar *to perform* 25 *to represent* 43
la **república** *republic* 188
la **reserva** *reserve* 161
reservar habitación *to reserve a room* 168
el **resfriado** *cold* 56
resolver (o > ue) *to solve* 206
respirar *to breathe* 185
responder *to reply* 49
responsable *responsible* 98
la **respuesta** *answer* 148
restar *to subtract* 225
el **restaurante** *restaurant* 25
el **retrato** *portrait* 43
la **reunión** *meeting* 139
reunirse *to meet, to gather* 95
la **revista** *magazine* 14
la **revolución** *revolution* 177
el **rey** *king* 33
rico(a) *rich* 233
el **río** *river* 216
la **riqueza** *richness* 136
el **ritmo** *rhythm* 108
la **roca** *rock* 206
rocoso(a) *rocky* 214
rodear *to surround* 215
rojo(a) *red* 22
romano(a) *Roman* 47
la **ropa** *clothing* 22
la **rosa de los vientos** *compass rose* 169
rosado(a) *pink* 22
rubio(a) *blond(e)* 4
la **ruta** *route* 166
la **rutina** *routine* 48

el **sábado** *Saturday* 141
los **sábados** *on Saturdays* 19

saber *to know how* 30
el **sabor** *flavor* 24
saborear *to taste* 40
sacar *to take out* 14
sacudir *to dust* 14
la **sal** *salt* 24
la **sala** *living room* 12 *lounge* 47
salado(a) *salty* 24
el **salar** *salt flat* 211
la **salida** *start* 163
salir *to leave* 30
el **salón** *living room* 202
el **Salón de la Fama** *Hall of Fame* 121
la **salsa** *salsa (dance)* 108 *sauce* 134
la **salud** *health* 57
saludable *healthy* 61
saludar *to greet* 165
salvar *to save* 235
el **sándwich** *sandwich* 26
sano(a) *healthy* 26
el/la **santo(a)** *saint* 135
el **satélite** *satellite* 208
se *himself, herself, itself, yourselves, themselves* 50
se puede/pueden *it is allowed* 236
seco(a) *dry* 216
el/la **secretario(a)** *secretary* 96
Secundaria *secondary (high school)* 94
la **sede** *seat, venue* 177
seguir (e > i) recto *to keep (walking/driving) straight* 178
según *according to* 67
el/la **segundo(a)** *second* 176
la **selva** *jungle* 189
la **semana** *week* 39
semiprecioso(a) *semi-precious* 227
sensacional *sensational* 156
sentarse (e > ie) *to sit* 31
los **sentidos** *senses* 38
sentirse (e > ie) *to feel* 60
el **señor** *Sir* 25
la **señora** *Madam* 31
septiembre *September* 44
ser *to be* 6
ser de *to be from* 99
serio(a) *serious* 4
la **servilleta** *napkin* 24
servir (e > i) *to serve* 116
si *if* 60
sí *yes* 13

tu, tus   your (informal) 8
el   túnel   tunnel 151
el   turismo   tourism 77
el/la   turista   tourist 55
turístico(a)   touristic 53

último(a)   last 117
un, una   a, an 10
Un momento.   Just a moment. 31
unido(a)   united 137
el   universo   universe 208
unos, unas   some 10
usar   to use 19
usted   you (singular, formal) 6
ustedes   you (plural) 6
útil   useful 36
utilizar   to utilize 137

las   vacaciones   holidays, vacations 109
Vale.   All right. 120
válido(a)   valid 158
el   valle   valley 206
el   valor   value 225
variado(a)   varied 77
la   variedad   variety 233
el   vaso   glass 24
el/la   vecino(a)   neighbor 137

la   velocidad   speed 125
vender   to sell 159
venir   to come 17
la   ventana   window 28
ver   to watch 14   to see 40
ver películas   to see movies 112
el   verano   summer 103
el   verbo   verb 6
la   verdad   truth 98
¿Verdad?   Right? 64
verde   green 22
las   verduras   vegetables 24
el   vestido   dress 22
vestir (e > i)   to dress 20
vestirse (e > i)   to get dressed 48
la   vez   time 85
el   viaducto   viaduct 151
viajar   to travel 104
el   viaje   trip 147
el/la   viajero(a)   traveler 153
la   vicuña   vicuna 237
la   vida   life 65
el   video   video 113
el   videojuego   videogame 112
el   vidrio   glass 234
el   viento   wind 210
el   viernes   Friday 164
el   viñedo   vineyard 77
violento(a)   violent 236
la   visita   visit 55
el/la   visitante   visitor 73
visitar   to visit 21
la   vitalidad   vitality 129

la   vitamina   vitamin 69
vivir   to live 61
el   vocabulario   vocabulary 2
volar (o > ue)   to fly 20
el   volcán   volcano 214
el   voleibol   volleyball 122
volver (o > ue)   to return 20
vosotros(as)   you (plural, informal) 6
la   votación   voting 37
el   vuelo   flight 158
la   vuelta al mundo   around the world 192
la   vuelta ciclista   cycling race 32
vuestro(a)   your (plural, informal) 8

y   and 2
ya   already 165
yo   I 2
Yo soy...   I am … 2

la   zapatería   shoe store 22
los   zapatos   shoes 22
el   zigzag   zigzag 151
la   zona   area, region 41   zone 47

Los números

uno	1	trece	13	veinticinco	25	cien	100
dos	2	catorce	14	veintiséis	26	ciento uno	101
tres	3	quince	15	veintisiete	27	ciento diez	110
cuatro	4	dieciséis	16	veintiocho	28	doscientos	200
cinco	5	diecisiete	17	veintinueve	29	trescientos	300
seis	6	dieciocho	18	treinta	30	cuatrocientos	400
siete	7	diecinueve	19	cuarenta	40	quinientos	500
ocho	8	veinte	20	cincuenta	50	seiscientos	600
nueve	9	veintiuno	21	sesenta	60	setecientos	700
diez	10	veintidós	22	setenta	70	ochocientos	800
once	11	veintitrés	23	ochenta	80	novecientos	900
doce	12	veinticuatro	24	noventa	90	mil	1000

Órdenes para hacer las actividades

Adivina	Guess	Escucha	Listen
Analiza	Analyze	Explica	Explain
Anuncia	Announce	Habla	Speak
Busca	Look for	Haz	Do
Clasifica	Classify	Identifica	Identify
Compara	Compare	Investiga	Research
Completa	Complete. Fill in the blank	Lee	Read
Conecta	Connect	Ordena	Put in order
Contesta	Answer	Organiza	Organize
Corrige	Correct	Piensa	Think
Crea	Create	Prepara	Prepare
Decide	Decide	Presenta	Present
Define	Define	Relaciona	Relate. Connect. Match.
Dibuja	Draw	Representa	Act out
Diseña	Design	Responde	Respond
Elige	Choose	Selecciona	Select
Escoge	Choose	Une	Match
Escribe	Write		

GLOSARIO INGLÉS-ESPAÑOL

comparison   la comparación 26
compass rose   la rosa de los vientos 169
to **compete**   competir (e > i) 20
competition   la competición 39
to **complete**   completar 2
comprehension   la comprensión 81
computer   la computadora 8
concentration   la concentración 133
concert   el concierto 107
condition   el estado 54
to **confess**   confesar (e > ie) 44
conjunction   la conjunción 210
connection   la relación 40 la conexión 51
to **consider**   considerar 177
construction   la construcción 97
construction site   la obra 96
to **contact**   contactar 139
to **contain**   llevar 25
container   el contenedor 234
contest   el concurso 229
continent   el continente 216
to **continue**   continuar 192
to **contradict**   contradecir 192
to **contribute**   contribuir 219
contribution   la contribución 136
to **control**   controlar 255
to **convert**   convertir (e > ie) 77
to **cook**   cocinar 213
corn   el maíz 24
correct   correcto(a) 166
correctly   bien 167
to **cost**   costar (o > ue) 20
cotton   el algodón 23
cough   la tos 56
to **count**   contar (o > ue) 20
country   el país 224
countryside   el campo 39
couple   la pareja 190
course (meal)   el plato 25
court (sports)   la cancha 125
cousin   el/la primo(a) 2
to **cover (distance)**   recorrer 57
covered   cubierto(a) 189
to **create**   crear 45
credit card   la tarjeta de crédito 29
to **cross**   cruzar 178
crossed   atravesado(a) 189
crunchy   crujiente 134
crustacean   el crustáceo 254
to **cry**   llorar 80
Cuban   cubano(a) 95
cubism   el cubismo 43
cubist   cubista 43
cuisine   la cocina 134

cultural   cultural 76
culture   la cultura 39
cup   la taza 24
to **cure**   curar 97
curiosity   la curiosidad 108
curious   curioso(a) 254
currency   la moneda 225
custom   la costumbre 73
customer   el/la cliente(a) 25
to **cut**   cortar 14
cybercafe   el cibercafé 164
cycling   ciclista 32
cycling race   la vuelta ciclista 32
cyclist   el/la ciclista 39

dad   el papá 30
daily   diario(a) 53   a diario 73
dance   el baile 114   la danza 136
to **dance**   bailar 104
danger   el peligro 223
daring   atrevido(a) 4
date   la fecha 136
daughter   la hija 2
day   el día 43
dead   el/la muerto(a) 80
Dear ...   Estimado(a)... 49 Querido(a)... 101
death   la muerte 80
to **decide**   decidir 25
to **declare**   declarar 181
to **decorate**   decorar 47
to **defend**   defender (e > ie) 97
deforestation   la deforestación 219
degree   el grado 26
delicious   delicioso(a) 164
demonstratives   los demostrativos 30
to **denounce**   denunciar 190
deodorant   el desodorante 48
department   el departamento 164
deposit   el depósito 211
to **descend**   descender (e > ie) 188
descendant   el/la descendiente 215
to **describe**   describir 2
descriptive   descriptivo(a) 135
desert   el desierto 216
design   el diseño 47
to **design**   diseñar 67
desperate   desesperado(a) 80
dessert   el postre 24
destination   el destino 168
to **destroy**   destruir 80

detective   el/la detective 38
development   el desarrollo 110
devil   el diablo 166
diagram   el esquema 67
diary   el diario 221
to **die**   morir (o > ue) 116
diet   la dieta 51
difference   la diferencia 220
different   distinto(a) 26 diferente 49
difficult   difícil 41
to **direct**   dirigir 97
direct object pronouns   los pronombres de objeto directo 28
direction   la dirección 166
directions   las instrucciones 179
director   el/la director(a) 96
dirty   sucio(a) 85
disc   el disco 141
to **discover**   descubrir 208
dish   el plato 24
dishwasher   el lavaplatos 12
distance   la distancia 152
diversity   la diversidad 136
to **divide**   dividir 223
division   la división 224
to **do**   hacer 30
to **do for a living**   dedicarse a 92
to **do well in school**   ir bien 101
doctor   el/la doctor(a) 34 el/la médico(a) 56
doctor's office   la consulta 61
document   el documento 148
documentary   el documental 85
dog   el perro 14
dollar   el dólar 23
dolphin   el delfín 237
domino   la ficha 101
dominoes   el dominó 88
Don't worry.   Tranquilo(a). 148
door   la puerta 12
down   abajo 80
downtown   el centro 21
drawing   el dibujo 190
dream   el sueño 184
to **dream**   soñar (o > ue) 213
dress   el vestido 22
dresser   la cómoda 12
drink   la bebida 24
to **drink**   beber 25 tomar 121
to **drive**   conducir 153
drugstore   la farmacia 56
dry   árido(a) 189   seco 216
during   durante 49
to **dust**   sacudir 14
duties   las obligaciones 49

E

early   temprano 51
ears   las orejas 40   los oídos 56
Earth   la Tierra 208
to eat   tomar 25   comer 51
to eat well   comer bien 66
eclipse   el eclipse 208
ecology   la ecología 251
egg   el huevo 24
electric   eléctrico(a) 115
electricity   la electricidad 238
elegant   elegante 183
element   el elemento 193
elemental   elemental 248
elephant   el elefante 254
elevator   el ascensor 12
e-mail   el correo electrónico 85
employee   el/la empleado(a) 96
encounter   el encuentro 74
end   el final 45
to end   terminar 151
energy   la energía 61
engineer   el/la ingeniero(a) 96
English (language)   el inglés 92
to enjoy   disfrutar 76
to enjoy oneself   divertirse (e > ie) 113
enlightening   enriquecedor(a) 205
enough   bastante 26
to enter   entrar 31
to entertain   entretener 34
envelope   el sobre 149
environment   el medio ambiente 234
equal   igual 173
European   el/la europeo(a) 188
evening   la tarde 23
event   el evento 46
every   todo(a) 218
everything   todo 210
exactly   exactamente 188
example   el ejemplo 97
to exchange   intercambiar 105
excited   emocionado(a) 4
excursion   la excursión 48
excuse   la excusa 69
Excuse me.   Perdón. 35
to exercise   hacer ejercicio 66
exhibition   la exposición 108
to exist   existir 219
existence   la existencia 16
expedition   la expedición 198
experience   la experiencia 160
expert   el/la experto(a) 94
   el/la perito(a) 199
to explore   explorar 208
to express   expresar 8
expression   la expresión 16
extinction   la extinción 237
extraordinary   extraordinario(a) 108
eye   el ojo 40

F

facade   la fachada 59
face   la cara 40
factory   la fábrica 96
failed   fallado(a) 53
fajitas   las fajitas 134
fall (season)   el otoño 111
to fall asleep   dormirse (o > ue) 50
false   falso(a) 25
family   la familia 2
famous   famoso(a) 31
fan   el/la fan 44
fantastic   fantástico(a) 117
far away   lejos 64
far from   lejos de 16
fashion   la moda 136
fat   gordo(a) 4
father   el padre 2
fauna   la fauna 233
favorite   favorito(a) 105
feature   la característica, el rasgo 4
feeding   la alimentación 254
to feel   encontrarse (o > ue) 60
   sentirse (e > ie) 60
to feel like ...   tener ganas de... 14
feminine   femenino(a) 10
festival   el festival 131
festivity   el festejo 137
fever   la fiebre 56
few   poco(a)(os)(as) 218
field   el campo 127
field trip   la excursión 48
figure   la figura 207
file card   la ficha 254
to fill   llenar 248
finally   finalmente 166   al fin 192
to find   buscar 13   encontrar (o > ue) 46
finger   el dedo 40
to finish   terminar 71
finish line   la llegada 163 la meta 165
fire   el fuego 80
first   primer, primero(a) 30
first floor   el primer piso 12
first of all   primero 15

fish   el pescado 24
fish (alive)   el pez 234
fishing   la pesca 77
to fit   quedar 39
flag   la bandera 155
flavor   el sabor 24
flight   el vuelo 158
floor   el suelo 14
flora   la flora 233
flower   la flor 234
flower shop   la florería 171
flu   la gripe 61
to fly   volar (o > ue) 20
folk   folclórico(a) 229
food   la comida 31
foot (body)   el pie 40
foot (measurement)   el pie 209
football   el fútbol americano 122
footprint   la huella 133
for   para 15   durante 39   por 44
for example   por ejemplo 17
forest   el bosque 216
to forget   olvidar 147
to forgive   perdonar 74
fork   el tenedor 24
formed by   formado(a) por 167
fossil   el fósil 219
founded   fundado(a) 103
free   libre 147
free (of charge)   gratis 47
French   el francés 92
frequency   la frecuencia 18
Friday   el viernes 164
friend   el/la amigo(a) 2
friendly   simpático(a) 4
from   desde 43   de 172
front   la fachada 59
fruit   la fruta 24
full   lleno(a) 61
fun   divertido(a) 9
to function   funcionar 15
funny   gracioso(a) 4
furniture   los muebles 14
future   el futuro 106

G

gala   la gala 111
gallery   la galería 95
game   la partida 93   el juego 101   el partido 122
garage   el garaje 12
garbage   la basura 14
garden   el jardín 47
gastronomy   la gastronomía 132
to gather   reunirse 95

gaucho *el gaucho* 144
gel *el gel* 48
general *general* 221
geographical *geográfico(a)* 209
geography *la geografía* 216
geometric *geométrico(a)* 47
germ *el germen* 61
to **get dressed** *vestirse (e > i)* 48
to **get off** *bajar* 192
to **get up** *levantarse* 48
Get well. *Que te mejores.* 36
gift *el regalo* 22
gigantic *gigantesco(a)* 246
girl *la chica, la niña* 2
girlfriend *la novia* 2
to **give** *dar* 64 *entregar* 193
glacier *el glaciar* 188
glass *el vaso* 24 *el vidrio* 234
glasses *las gafas* 210
glove *el guante* 122
to **go** *ir* 16 *andar* 192
to **go by …** *ir en…* 152
to **go down** *bajar* 223
to **go on an excursion** *ir de excursión* 152
to **go on foot** *ir a pie* 152
to **go on vacation** *ir de vacaciones* 152
to **go shopping** *ir de compras* 22
to **go to …** *ir a…* 106
to **go to bed** *acostarse (o > ue)* 50
to **go to the movies** *ir al cine* 112
to **go up** *subir* 223
golf *el golf* 122
good *buen, bueno(a)* 10
Good luck! *¡Buena suerte!* 204
government *el gobierno* 67
grade *la nota* 139
to **grade** *poner notas* 139
graduation *la graduación* 113
grammar *la gramática* 6
grandchildren *los nietos y las nietas* 2
grandfather *el abuelo* 2
grandmother *la abuela* 2
grandparents *los abuelos* 2
grandsons *los nietos* 2
grass *la hierba* 189
great *gran, grande* 77
Great! *¡Qué bien!* 118
Great Britain *Gran Bretaña* 173
green *verde* 22
to **greet** *saludar* 165
grocery store *el almacén* 192
group *el grupo* 86
to **guess** *adivinar* 119
guest *el/la invitado(a)* 9

guest house *el hostal* 33
guide *el/la guía* 108
guitar *la guitarra* 42
gym *el gimnasio* 67

habit *el hábito* 51
habitat *el hábitat* 254
habitual *habitual* 12
hair *el pelo* 40
hairbrush *el cepillo* 48
ham *el jamón* 5
hand *la mano* 40
handicraft *la artesanía* 227
handsome *guapo* 5
to **happen** *pasar* 45 *ocurrir* 198
happy *contento(a)* 4
harmony *la armonía* 134
harbor *el puerto* 77
hat *el sombrero* 165
to **have** *tener* 8
to **have a good time** *pasarlo bien* 118
Have a good trip! *¡Buen viaje!* 148
Have a nice weekend! *¡Buen fin de semana!* 19
to **have breakfast** *desayunar* 69
to **have dinner** *cenar* 31
to **have handy** *tener a mano* 148
to **have lunch** *almorzar (o > ue)* 69 *comer* 73
to **have to …** *tener… que* 8
he *él* 6
head *la cabeza* 40
headphones *los auriculares* 96
health *la salud* 57
healthy *sano(a)* 26 *saludable* 61
to **hear** *oír* 40
heart *el corazón* 99
height *la altura* 185
Hello. *Hola.* 2
helmet *el casco* 122
to **help** *ayudar* 51
hemisphere *el hemisferio* 217
her *la* 28 *su* 8
(to) her *le* 26
here *aquí* 16
heritage *la herencia* 79
hero *el héroe* 100
herself *se* 50
him *lo* 28
(to) him *le* 26
himself *se* 50
his *su* 8

Hispanic *hispánico* 88 *hispano(a)* 95
historic *histórico(a)* 181
history *la Historia* 101
hygiene *la higiene* 48
hobby *el pasatiempo* 104
hockey *el hockey* 237
holidays *las vacaciones* 109
home run *el jonrón* 120
homeland *la tierra* 129
homework *la tarea* 99
honest *honesto(a)* 99
honor *el honor* 199
hope *la esperanza* 80
horror *el horror* 80 *el terror* 112
horse *el caballo* 80
hospital *el hospital* 56
hot *caliente* 24
hot (spicy) *picante* 24
hot springs *las aguas termales* 52
hotel *el hotel* 168
hour *la hora* 65
house *la casa* 12
housework *las tareas domésticas* 14
How? *¿Cómo?* 25
How are you? *¿Cómo está/ estás?* 2
How are you doing? *¿Qué tal?* 3
How are you feeling? *¿Cómo te sientes?* 36
How awful! *¡Qué horror!* 174
How big! *¡Qué grande!* 204
How exciting! *¡Qué emocionante!* 227
How impressive! *¡Qué impresionante!* 204
How lucky! *¡Qué suerte!* 113
How many …? *¿Cuántos(as)…?* 17
How much/many …! *¡Cuánto(a)(os)(as)!* 204
How much is it? *¿Cuánto cuesta?* 23
How painful! *¡Qué dolor!* 38
huge *enorme* 203
human *humano(a)* 69
humor *el humor* 190
to **hunt** *cazar* 255
hunting *la caza* 255
to **hurt** *doler (o > ue)* 58
husband *el esposo* 159

I *yo* 2
I am … *Yo soy…* 2

I am sick. *Estoy enfermo(a).* 36
I am sorry. *Lo siento.* 35
I don't feel well. *Me siento mal.* 36
I feel fine. *Me siento bien.* 56
I have a … ache. *Me duele/ duelen…* 56
ice *el hielo* 212
ice cream *el helado* 24
idea *la idea* 49
ideal *ideal* 109
to **identify** *identificar* 134
identity *la identidad* 134
if *si* 60
illness *la enfermedad* 56
image *la imagen* 215
imperative (tense) *el imperativo* 68
important *importante* 39
impression *la impresión* 219
impressive *impresionante* 167
in *en* 16
in a healthy way *saludablemente* 61
in front of *delante de* 16 *frente a* 251
in general *en general* 73
in one's arms *en brazos* 80
in order to *para* 25
in the middle of *en el centro de* 161
in the open air *al aire libre* 191
to **inaugurate** *inaugurar* 153
to **include** *incluir* 228
incredible *increíble* 110
indefinites *los indefinidos* 218
independence *la independencia* 136
to **indicate** *indicar* 192
indigenous *indígena* 31
indirect object pronouns *los pronombres de objeto indirecto* 28
industry *la industria* 161
influence *la influencia* 79
information *la información* 94
information desk *el mostrador de información* 160
informative *informativo(a)* 164
ingredient *el ingrediente* 134
inhabited *habitado(a)* 135
inhabitant *el/la habitante* 188
insect *el insecto* 234
inside *dentro* 64
instead *en cambio* 105
instrument *el instrumento* 115
intelligent *inteligente* 4

intense *intenso(a)* 78
intention *la intención* 102
interior *el interior* 77
interesting *interesante* 65
international *internacional* 39
interracial *interracial* 134
intervention *la intervención* 255
interview *la entrevista* 212
introduction *la presentación* 2
intruder *el/la intruso(a)* 13
invitation *la invitación* 171
to **invite** *invitar* 9
irregular *irregular* 20
irritated *irritado(a)* 43
island *la isla* 216
it *lo, la* 28
It doesn't matter. *No importa, No pasa nada.* 148
it is allowed *se puede/pueden* 236
Italian *el/la italiano(a)* 174
itinerary *el itinerario* 161
It's a pleasure. *Mucho gusto.* 2
It's cold. *Hace frío.* 197
It's sunny. *Hace sol.* 5
itself *se* 50

jacket *la chaqueta* 22
January *enero* 223
jar *el tarro* 193
jersey *el jersey* 39
jewel *la joya* 227
job *el trabajo* 97
joke *la broma* 46
journalist *el/la periodista* 99
joy *la alegría* 136
judge *el/la juez(a)* 99
juice *el jugo* 24
July *julio* 189
June *junio* 241
jungle *la selva* 189
Just a moment. *Un momento.* 31

to **keep** *mantener* 51
to **keep driving/walking straight** *seguir (e > i) recto* 178
key *la clave* 99
kilogram *el kilo* 192
kilometer *el kilómetro* 134
king *el rey* 33
kiss *el beso* 17
kitchen *la cocina* 12

knife *el cuchillo* 24
knock *el golpe* 38
to **know** *conocer* 30
to **know how** *saber* 30
knowledge *el conocimiento* 137

L

lagoon *la laguna* 211
lake *el lago* 216
land *la tierra* 216
landscape *el paisaje* 77
language *la lengua* 78
last *último(a)* 117
to **last** *durar* 185
last month *el mes pasado* 170
last name *el apellido* 85
last night *anoche* 170
last week *la semana pasada* 170
last year *el año pasado* 170
late *tarde* 50
later *luego* 106
later on *después* 53 *más tarde* 133
Latin American *latinoamericano(a)* 108
Latino *latino(a)* 89
lawn *el césped* 14
lawyer *el/la abogado(a)* 96
to **lead** *llevar* 57
leader *el/la líder* 38
leaf *la hoja* 234
to **learn** *aprender* 44
leather *el cuero* 125
to **leave** *salir* 30
leg *la pierna* 40
legal *legal* 139
legumes *las legumbres* 67
leisure activities *las actividades de ocio* 14
leisure time *el tiempo libre* 112
lemon *el limón* 27
less *menos* 27
less … than *menos… que* 26
lesson *la clase* 94
Let me introduce … to you. *Te presento a…* 2
level *el nivel* 151
liberty *la libertad* 103
library *la biblioteca* 178
license *la licencia* 153
life *la vida* 65
light *la luz* 129
like *como* 9
to **like** *gustar* 26
likes *los gustos* 22

next   el/la próximo(a) 106
next to   al lado de 16
  junto a 129
next week   la próxima semana,
  la semana que viene 106
next year   el próximo año, el año
  que viene 106
Nice to meet you.   Encantado(a).
  2
niece   la sobrina 11
night   la noche 23
  nocturno(a) 209
night stand   la mesita de noche 12
no   ningún, ninguno(a) 218
nobility   la nobleza 227
nocturnal   nocturno(a) 209
noon   el mediodía 73
nor   ni 43
normally   normalmente 19
  muchas veces 18
north   el norte 41
northeast   el noreste 169
northwest   el noroeste 55
nose   la nariz 40
not any   ningún, ninguno(a) 218
not much   poco 26
note   la nota 173
notebook   el cuaderno 17
nothing   nada 26
to **notice**   fijarse 43
noun   el nombre 10
novel   la novela 78
November   noviembre 159
now   ahora 17
number   el número 123
nurse   el/la enfermero(a) 56
nutrition   la nutrición 67

oasis   el oasis 107
obediente   obediente 192
object   el objeto 43
to **observe**   observar 213
occupation   la profesión 96
ocean   el océano 216
October   octubre 133
ode   la oda 248
of   de 3
Of course.   Claro. 64
of the   del 5
offer   la oferta 210
to **offer**   ofrecer 107
office   la oficina 96
oil   el aceite 67
old   mayor 4   antiguo(a) 37

on   encima de 16   sobre 80
on a trip   de viaje 152
on top of   encima de 16
one has to ...   hay que... 28
only   solo 54
open   abierto(a) 22
to **open**   abrir 18
opportunity   la oportunidad 100
opposite   opuesto(a) 217
orange   anaranjado(a) 22   la
  naranja 24
orchestra   la orquesta 190
order   la orden 64
to **order**   mandar 192
organization   la organización 103
to **organize**   organizar 97
organized   organizado(a) 52
origin   el origen 95
original   original 69
originally   originalmente 55
other   otro(a) 32
Ouch!   ¡Ay! 58
our   nuestro(a) 8
ourselves   nos 50
outdoors   al aire libre 191
ownership   la posesión 8

P

to **pack**   empacar 237
package   el paquete 193
pain   el dolor 56
painter   el/la pintor(a) 43
painting   el cuadro 40
  la pintura 69
pair   la pareja 35
palace   el palacio 47
pants   los pantalones 22
paper   el papel 234
parade   el desfile 133
to **paraphrase**   parafrasear 249
parents   los padres 2
park   el parque 35
parliamentary   parlamentario(a) 76
part   la parte 40
participant   el/la participante 43
to **participate**   participar 39
partner   la pareja 207
party   la fiesta 9
to **pass**   pasar 41
passage   el paso 190
passion fruit   el maracuyá 50
passport   el pasaporte 160
past   el pasado 133   pasado(a)
  170
pastime   el pasatiempo 104

patience   la paciencia 98
patient   el/la paciente 34
  el/la enfermo(a) 56
to **pay**   pagar 195
peak   el pico 233
people   la gente 17
pepper   la pimienta 24
Perfect!   ¡Perfecto! 92
to **perform**   representar 25
perfume   el perfume 40
period   el período 51
permanently   permanentemente
  211
permission   el permiso 236
person   la persona 2
personal   personal 46
personality   la personalidad 4
to **personalize**   personalizar 44
perspective   la perspectiva 43
pessimistic   pesimista 176
pet   la mascota 14
pharmacy   la farmacia 56
phenomenon   el fenómeno 219
to **phone**   llamar 147
photo   la foto 11   la fotografía 43
photographer   el/la fotógrafo(a) 91
photography   la fotografía 92
photonovel   la fotonovela 38
physical   físico(a) 4
piano   el piano 104
picture   la foto 11   la fotografía
  43
pie   la empanada 111
piece of information   el dato 132
pilgrim   el/la peregrino(a) 55
pink   rosado(a) 22
pizza   la pizza 5
place   el sitio 14   el lugar 16
to **place**   colocar 191
plain   la llanura 189
plan   el plan 53
plane   el avión 152
plastic   el plástico 234
plateau   la meseta 77
to **play games**   jugar (u > ue) 122
to **play sports**   practicar deportes 104
  jugar (u > ue) a/al 122
to **play videogames**   jugar (u > ue)
  a los videojuegos 112
player   el/la jugador(a) 122
plaza   la plaza 178
please   por favor 25
plot   el argumento 193
plural   el plural 6
poem   el poema 246
policeman   el policía 97
policewoman   la policía 97

political político(a) 177
political party el partido político 179
pollution la contaminación 237
popular popular 73
popularity la popularidad 123
populated poblado(a) 188
population la población 133
port el puerto 79
portrait el retrato 43
possession la posesión 8
possessive adjectives los adjetivos posesivos 8
poster el póster 86   el cartel 137
potato la papa 24
pottery la cerámica 227
pound la libra 239
to **prefer** preferir (e > ie) 20
preference la preferencia 22
preparations los preparativos 151
to **prepare** preparar 28
presence la presencia 132
present presente 132
present participle el gerundio 116
present progressive el presente continuo 114
present tense el presente 6
presentation la presentación 143
to **preserve** conservar 117
president el presidente 179
presidential presidencial 179
prestigious prestigioso(a) 111
preterite tense el pretérito 154
pretty bonito(a) 11
previous previo(a) 137
principal el/la director(a) 128
prize el premio 246
problem el problema 38
product el producto 47
production la producción 227
profession la profesión 96
professional profesional 91
progress el progreso 136
prohibition la prohibición 236
project el proyecto 86
to **promote** promover (o >ue) 103
properly bien 160
proposal la propuesta 136
to **protect** proteger 238
province la provincia 159
prudent prudente 141
public público(a) 153
to **publish** publicar 246
purity la pureza 227
purple morado(a) 22
to **put** poner 30
to **put … away** guardar 193

to **put on a good face** poner buena cara 94
pyramid la pirámide 67

quantity la cantidad 218
question la pregunta 21
quick rápido(a) 125
quickly rápido 64
quite bastante 26

race la carrera 39
racket (sports) la raqueta 122
radio la radio 112
railway ferroviario(a) 134
rain la lluvia 225
to **rain** llover (o > ue) 174
rainy lluvioso(a) 217
rare raro(a) 103
rarely rara vez 18
to **reach** alcanzar 185
to **read** leer 14
reading la lectura 80
ready listo(a) 206
reason la razón 210
recipe la receta 15
to **recognize** reconocer 136
to **recommend** recomendar (e > ie) 67
to **record** grabar 112
to **recycle** reciclar 234
recycling el reciclaje 234
red rojo(a) 22
to **reduce** reducir 235
refreshment el refresco 24
refrigerator el refrigerador 12
region la zona 41   la región 77
regular regular 18
regularly regularmente 65
to **relax** relajarse 47
relevant relevante 149
remedy el remedio 66
to **remember** recordar (o > ue) 20
to **rent** rentar 153
to **repeat** repetir (e > i) 20
to **reply** responder 49
to **represent** representar 43
republic la república 188
research la investigación 79
reserve la reserva 161
to **reserve a room** reservar habitación 168

resource el recurso 235
responsible responsable 98
rest el descanso 47   los/las demás 61
to **rest** descansar 50
restaurant el restaurante 25
to **return** volver (o > ue) 20
review el repaso 82
revolution la revolución 177
rhythm el ritmo 108
rice el arroz 24
rich rico(a) 233
richness la riqueza 136
riddle la adivinanza 45
to **ride a bike** montar en bicicleta 104
Right? ¿Verdad? 64
ring el anillo 212
river el río 216
rock la roca 206
rocky rocoso(a) 214
Roman romano(a) 47
room el cuarto 44   la habitación 47
rough aproximado(a) 225
round trip de ida y vuelta 148
route la ruta 166
routine la rutina 48
royal real 47
rule la regla 236
to **run** correr 66   dirigir 97
to **run into** encontrarse (o > ue) con 173

sad triste 4
to **sail** navegar 192
sailor marinero(a) 77
saint el/la santo(a) 135
salad la ensalada 27
salsa (dance) la salsa 108
salt la sal 24
salt flat el salar 211
salty salado(a) 24
same igual 69   mismo(a) 164
sandwich el sándwich 26
satellite el satélite 208
Saturday el sábado 141
sauce la salsa 134
to **say** decir 42
scenario el escenario 78
scent el aroma 192
schedule el horario 23
school la escuela 96   escolar 220
science las ciencias 61   la ciencia 67
scientist el/la científico(a) 219

sea   el/la mar 216

season   la temporada 126
   la estación 217

seat (government)   la sede 177

second   el/la segundo(a) 176

secondary (school)   Secundaria 94

secretary   el/la secretario(a) 96

to see   ver 40

to see movies   ver películas 112

See you soon.   Hasta pronto. 9

to seem   parecer 69

self-evaluation   la autoevaluación 87

self-portrait   el autorretrato 41

to sell   vender 159

sensational   sensacional 156

senses   los sentidos 38

sentence   la oración 84

September   septiembre 44

serious   serio(a) 4

to serve   servir (e > i) 116

server   el/la mesero(a) 24

to set the table   poner la mesa 29

setting   el marco 193

settler   el/la poblador(a) 246

shampoo   el champú 48

to shave   afeitarse 48

shaving cream   la crema de afeitar 48

she   ella 6

sheep   la oveja 207

shield   el escudo 37

to shine   brillar 208

ship   el barco 152

shirt   la camisa 22

shoe store   la zapatería 22

shoes   los zapatos 22

shopping   las compras 155

shopping center   el centro comercial 99

shore   la costa 168

short   bajo(a) 4   corto(a) 41

shorts   los pantalones cortos 22

show   el espectáculo 43
   el programa 43

to show   mostrar (o > ue) 136

to show one's passport   enseñar el pasaporte 160

shower   la ducha 12

shy   tímido(a) 4

siblings   los hermanos 2

sick   enfermo(a) 4

side   el lado 32

similar   similar 46

similar to   igual que 153

similarity   la similitud 220

simple   simple 248

since   desde 57

Sincerely yours.   Atentamente. 52

to sing   cantar 104

singer   el/la cantante 111

singular   el singular 6

sink   el lavabo 12

Sir   el señor 25

sister   la hermana 2

to sit   sentarse (e > ie) 31

size   el tamaño 254

to ski   esquiar 195

skirt   la falda 22

sky   el cielo 208

to sleep   dormir (o > ue) 61

slowly   despacio 176

small   pequeño(a) 41

to smell   oler 40

smile   la sonrisa 91

sneakers   los tenis 22

to snow   nevar (e > ie) 5

so   tan 176

so that   así que 192

soap   el jabón 48

soccer   el fútbol 122

social   social 46

society   la sociedad 88

socks   los calcetines 22

soda   el refresco 24

sofa   el sofá 12

Solar System   el sistema solar 208

to solve   resolver (o > ue) 206

some   unos, unas 10   algún, alguno(a)(os)(as) 218
   poco(a)(os)(as) 218

something   algo 54

sometimes   a veces 18

son   el hijo 2

son and daughter   los hijos 2

song   la canción 113

soon   pronto 50

soup   la sopa 24

sour   agrio(a) 24

south   el sur 47

southeast   el sureste 169

southwest   el suroeste 169

souvenir   el recuerdo 155

space   el espacio 212

Spaniard   el/la español(a) 43

Spanish (language)   el español 3

Spanish   español(a) 73

Spanish speaker   hispanohablante 188

special   especial 25

specially   especialmente 79

specialty   la especialidad 59

spectacular   espectacular 189

spectator   el/la espectador(a) 133

speed   la velocidad 125

to spend (time)   pasar 107

spontaneous   espontáneo(a) 4

spoon   la cuchara 24

sport   el deporte 122

sport competition   la competición deportiva 138

to spread out   extenderse (e > ie) 78

spring   la primavera 209

square   la plaza 178

stadium   el estadio 122

stage   la etapa 38

stairs   las escaleras 12

star   la estrella 208

start (race)   la salida 163

to start   empezar (e > ie) 20

state   el estado 76

state-run hotel   el parador 55

station   la estación 152

stationery store   la papelería 223

statistics   las estadísticas 123

statue   la estatua 103

to stay   quedarse 164   alojarse 195

to stay in shape   estar en forma 66

stem   la raíz 20

step   el paso 86   el escalón 222

stomach   el estómago 56

stone   la piedra 227

store   la tienda 22

story   la historia 45

stove   la estufa 12

strategy   la estrategia 81

street   la calle 178

stroll   el paseo 113

to stroll   pasear 14

strong   fuerte 38

student   el/la estudiante 2

studious   estudioso(a) 4

study   el estudio 164

style   el estilo 43

substance   la sustancia 212

to subtract   restar 225

subway   el metro 152

success   el éxito 99

sugar   el azúcar 24

suggestion   la sugerencia 72

suitcase   la maleta 160

summer   el verano 103

Sun   el Sol 208

Sunday   el domingo 157

supermarket   el supermercado 24

to surprise   sorprender 73

to surround   rodear 215

survey   la encuesta 43

sweater   el suéter 28

to sweep   barrer 14

sweet   dulce 24

to **swim**   nadar 104
swimming   la natación 122
swimming pool   la piscina 122
sword   la espada 80
symbol   el símbolo 80
symbolism   el simbolismo 80
symptom   el síntoma 56

table   la mesa 12
tablecloth   el mantel 24
tacos   los tacos 134
to **take a bath**   bañarse 48
to **take a means of transport**   tomar 151
to **take a shower**   ducharse 48
to **take advantage**   aprovechar 100
to **take care of**   cuidar 14
to **take care of oneself**   cuidarse 66
to **take medicines**   tomar medicamentos 66
to **take out**   sacar 14
to **take pictures**   tomar fotos 112
to **take place**   tener lugar 223
to **take time**   tardar 193
to **talk**   hablar 3   conversar 95
to **talk on the phone**   hablar por teléfono 14
tall   alto(a) 4
to **tape**   grabar 112
task   la tarea 97
to **taste**   saborear 40
taxi   el taxi 152
tea   el té 71
to **teach**   enseñar 97
teacher   el/la profesor(a) 2   el/la maestro(a) 96
team   el equipo 122
teeth (molars)   las muelas 58
telephone   el teléfono 14
television   el televisor 12   la televisión 14
to **tell**   decir 42
temperature   la temperatura 5
temple   el templo 79
temporal   temporal 106
tennis   el tenis 122
tension   la tensión 179
tent   la tienda de campaña 213
terminal   la terminal 153
territory   el territorio 76
test   el examen 5   la prueba 53
testimony   el testimonio 133
Texan   tejano(a) 115

text message   el mensaje electrónico 44
textbook   el libro de texto 241
than   de 47
thank you   gracias 3
thanks to   gracias a 99
that   ese, esa 30
that (far)   aquel, aquella 30
that (far, neutral)   aquello 206
the   el, la, los, las 10
the day before yesterday   anteayer 170
theater   el teatro 21
their   su 8
them   los, las 28
(to) them   les 28
theme   el tema 143
themselves   se 50
then   entonces 25
there   ahí 16
there (far)   allí 16
there is/are   hay 16
they   ellas, ellos 6
thin   delgado(a) 4
thing   la cosa 10
to **think**   pensar (e > ie) 20   parecer 69
third   el tercer, el/la tercero(a) 176
this   este, esta 30
this (neutral)   esto 77
this afternoon   esta tarde 106
this evening   esta tarde, esta noche 106
this morning   esta mañana 106
those (nearby)   esos(as) 30
thousands   miles 57
throat   la garganta 56
to **throw away**   botar 234
Thursday   el jueves 170
ticket   el boleto 108   el billete 160
to **tidy**   ordenar 15
tied   atado(a) 125
tile   el azulejo 37
time   el tiempo 46   la vez 85
timid   tímido(a) 4
tin   la lata 238
tired   cansado(a) 4
title   el título 249
to   a 16   para 25   hasta 172
to the   al 16
to the left of   a la izquierda de 16
to the right of   a la derecha de 16
today   hoy 106
toe   el dedo 40
together   junto 72

tomorrow   mañana 9
tomorrow afternoon/evening   mañana por la tarde 106
tomorrow morning   mañana por la mañana 106
tomorrow night   mañana por la noche 106
tonight   esta noche 106
tooth   el diente 40   la muela 54
toothbrush   el cepillo de dientes 48
toothpaste   la pasta de dientes 48
total   total 248
to **touch**   tocar 40
tourism   el turismo 77
tourist   el/la turista 55
tourist guide   la guía turística 160
tourist office   la oficina de turismo 160
touristic   turístico(a) 53
tournament   el torneo 108
towards   hacia 78
towel   la toalla 48
town   el pueblo 224   la localidad 247
track   el circuito 213
tradition   la tradición 9
train   el tren 152
to **transform**   transformar 136
transformation   la transformación 71
transportation   el transporte 152
travel agency   la agencia de viajes 160
to **travel around**   hacer turismo 168
traveler   el/la viajero(a) 153
tree   el árbol 234
trip   el viaje 147
tropical   tropical 216
true   cierto(a) 5
truth   la verdad 98
to **try**   probar (o > ue) 187
T-shirt   la camiseta 22
Tuesday   el martes 53
to **turn**   girar 208
to **turn off**   apagar 43
to **turn on**   prender 18
to **turn to the right/left**   doblar a la derecha/izquierda 178
TV   la tele 139
type   el tipo 67
typical   típico(a) 43   característico(a) 78

ugly   feo(a) 5
uncle   el tío 2

under *debajo de* 16

to **understand** *entender (e > ie)* 20 *comprender* 35

united *unido(a)* 137

United States *los Estados Unidos* 9

universe *el universo* 208

until *hasta* 236

up to *hasta* 151

upon arriving *al llegar* 75

(to) us *nos* 28

to **use** *usar* 19

useful *útil* 36

usually *normalmente* 19 *muchas veces* 18

to **utilize** *utilizar* 137

vacations *las vacaciones* 109

to **vacuum** *pasar la aspiradora* 14

valid *válido(a)* 158

valley *el valle* 206

value *el valor* 225

varied *variado(a)* 77

variety *la variedad* 233

vast *extenso(a)* 77

vegetables *las verduras* 24

venue *la sede* 177

verb *el verbo* 6

very *muy* 9

Very well! *¡Muy bien!* 92

viaduct *el viaducto* 151

video *el video* 113

videogame *el videojuego* 112

vineyard *el viñedo* 77

violent *violento(a)* 236

visit *la visita* 55

to **visit** *visitar* 21

visitor *el/la visitante* 73

vitality *la vitalidad* 129

vitamin *la vitamina* 69

vocabulary *el vocabulario* 2

volcano *el volcán* 214

volleyball *el voleibol* 122

voting *la votación* 37

to **wait for** *esperar* 35

waiter/waitress *el/la mesero(a)* 24

to **wake up** *despertarse (e > ie)* 50

to **walk** *pasear* 14 *caminar* 66 *andar* 192

wall *la pared* 54

to **want** *querer (e > ie)* 20

war *la guerra* 80

warm *cálido(a)* 189

to **wash** *lavar* 18

to **wash oneself** *lavarse* 50

to **waste** *gastar* 238

to **watch** *ver* 14

Watch out! *¡Cuidado!* 38

water *el agua* 24

waterfalls *las cataratas* 145

way *el camino* 55 *la forma* 61

we *nosotros(as)* 6

weak *débil* 54

weapon *el arma* 242

to **wear** *llevar* 23

Wednesday *el miércoles* 156

week *la semana* 39

weekend *el fin de semana* 15

weight *el peso* 254

Welcome. *Bienvenido(a).* 57

well *bien* 2

Well ... *Bueno...* 17

well-balanced *equilibrado(a)* 51

west *el oeste* 169

whale *la ballena* 237

What? *¿Qué?* 5

What a day! *¡Qué día!* 156

What a lot of money! *¡Cuánto dinero!* 204

What a lot of people! *¡Cuánta gente!* 204

What a pity! *¡Qué lástima!* 187

What a shame! *¡Qué pena!* 164

What do you do for living? *¿A qué te dedicas?* 92

What does he/she/it look like? *¿Cómo es?* 4

What is he/she/it like? *¿Cómo es?* 4

What time does ... close? *¿A qué hora cierra...?* 22

What time does ... open? *¿A qué hora abre...?* 22

what's more *además* 43

What's your name? *¿Cómo te llamas?* 2

What's wrong? *¿Qué te pasa?* 36

when *cuando* 5

When? *¿Cuándo?* 81

Where? *¿Dónde?* 12

Where to? *¿Adónde?* 43

white *blanco(a)* 22

Who? *¿Quién?* 3

Why? *¿Por qué?* 210

wide *ancho(a)* 183

wife *la esposa* 202

to **win** *ganar* 37

wind *el viento* 210

windmill *el molino de viento* 78

window *la ventana* 28

winter *el invierno* 126

with *con* 5

with me *conmigo* 117

without *sin* 115

woman *la mujer* 2

woodpecker *el pájaro carpintero* 237

word *la palabra* 38

work *el trabajo* 96

to **work** *funcionar* 15 *trabajar* 114

work of art *la obra de arte* 102

worker *el/la trabajador(a)* 100

working-class *obrero(a)* 191

world *el mundo* 57

to **worry** *preocuparse* 54

to **write** *escribir* 3

to **write e-mails** *escribir correos* 112

to **write instant messages** *escribir mensajes* 104

wrong *equivocado(a)* 192

wrongly *mal* 166

yard *el jardín* 12

year *el año* 8

yellow *amarillo(a)* 22

yes *sí* 13

yesterday *ayer* 170

yet *todavía* 176

you *tú (informal) usted (formal) vosotros(as) (informal, plural) ustedes (plural)* 6

(to) you *te* 28 *le (formal)* 28 *les* 28 *os (informal, plural)* 28

young *joven* 4

young man *el joven* 94

young woman *la joven* 94

your *su (formal, singular) sus (plural) tu (informal, singular) tus (plural) vuestro(a) (informal, plural)* 8

yourself *te* 50

yourselves *os (informal)* 50 *se* 50

youth *la juventud* 136

zigzag *el zigzag* 151

zone *la zona* 47

ÍNDICE GRAMATICAL

CRÉDITOS FOTOGRÁFICOS (TEACHER'S EDITION)

Cubierta I. Preysler/Atrezzo: Helen Chelton; Alfio Garozzo, Robert Harding/Michael Busselle/CuboImages/CORDON PRESS; Pat Canova, Luis Castañeda/A. G. E. FOTOSTOCK; **Contracubierta** Vincent Villafañe/EFE; J. Lucas; Guy Christian, Robert Harding/Marco Simoni/CuboImages/ CORDON PRESS; **T1** I. Preysler/Atrezzo: Helen Chelton; **T4** I. Preysler/Atrezzo: Helen Chelton; Jordi Camí/A. G. E. FOTOSTOCK; **T5** ISTOCKPHOTO; Miguel Rajmil/EFE; F. Ontañón; **T6** Javier Larrea/A. G. E. FOTOSTOCK; **T7** I. Preysler/Atrezzo: Helen Chelton; Javier Larrea/ A. G. E. FOTOSTOCK; **T11** I. Preysler/Atrezzo: Helen Chelton; **T16** I. Preysler/Atrezzo: Helen Chelton; **T18** Amos Morgan/A. G. E. FOTOSTOCK; **T21** Panoramic Images/GETTY IMAGES SALES SPAIN; **255B** José Fuste Raga/A. G. E. FOTOSTOCK; C. Díez Polanco; J. Crespo; J. Lucas; **255E** ISTOCKPHOTO; **255F** HIGHRES PRESS STOCK; AbleStock.com/HIGHRES PRESS STOCK; ARCHIVO SANTILLANA.

CRÉDITOS FOTOGRÁFICOS (STUDENT BOOK)

Cubierta: Preysler/Atrezzo: Helen Chelton; Alfio Garozzo, Robert Harding/Michael Busselle/CuboImages/CORDON PRESS; Pat Canova, Luis Castañeda/A. G. E. FOTOSTOCK; **Contracubierta:** Vincent Villafañe/EFE; J. Lucas; Guy Christian, Robert Harding/Marco Simoni/CuboImages/ CORDON PRESS: **I** Preysler/Atrezzo: Helen Chelton; **IV** Preysler/Atrezzo: Helen Chelton; ISTOCKPHOTO; S. Jiménez; **V** Preysler/Atrezzo: Helen Chelton; Gavin Hellier/Getty Images Sales Spain; F. Morera; **VI** ISTOCKPHOTO; Miguel Ángel Muñoz/A. G. E. FOTOSTOCK; **VII** ISTOCKPHOTO; **X** O. Torres; **XI** J. Lucas; GARCÍA PELAYO/Juancho; F. Ontañón; Horizon, Laurent Guerinaud, Kord.com/A. G. E. FOTOSTOCK; SEIS x SEIS; Preysler/Atrezzo: Helen Chelton; O. Torres; **XII** Hayden Roger Celestin/EPA/EFE; **XIII** Horizon, Laurent Guerinaud, Kord.com/A. G. E. FOTOSTOCK; SEIS x SEIS; Philippe Renault/CORDON PRESS; Preysler/Atrezzo: Helen Chelton; Hayden Roger Celestin/EPA; Patrick Frilet/SIPA-PRESS/EFE; **XIV** Mary Kate Denny/Getty Images Sales Spain; **XV** Horizon, Laurent Guerinaud, Johnny Stockshooter, Kord.com/A. G. E. FOTOSTOCK; SEIS x SEIS; Preysler/Atrezzo: Helen Chelton; J. Lucas; Edgar Dominguez/EFE; J. Ramallo; **XVI** Tips/Luis Castaneda, John Warburton-Lee/ FOTONONSTOP; **XVII** Tips/Luis Castaneda, Walter Bibikow/FOTONONSTOP; Horizon, Laurent Guerinaud, Kord.com/A. G. E. FOTOSTOCK; SEIS x SEIS; Patricio Cabezas Vieyra; Preysler/Atrezzo: Helen Chelton; **000** Preysler/Atrezzo: Helen Chelton; **002** AbleStock.com/HighRes Press Stock, COVER; J. Jaime; Prats i Camps; **003** Andersen Ross/A. G. E. FOTOSTOCK, J. Jaime; **004** AbleStock.com/HighRes Press Stock; A. Toril; ISTOCKPHOTO; J. Jaime; J. M.ª Escudero; STOCKBYTE/SERIDEC PHOTOIMAGENES CD; **005** AbleStock.com/HighRes Press Stock; Prats i Camps; **007** AbleStock.com/HighRes Press Stock; Glowimages/Getty Images Sales Spain; Image Source Limited/SERIDEC PHOTOIMAGENES CD; AbleStock/Jupiterimages; ISTOCKPHOTO; Prats i Camps; Preysler/Atrezzo: Helen Chelton; S. Enríquez; S. Padura; **008** ISTOCKPHOTO; **009** ISTOCKPHOTO; **011** AbleStock.com/HighRes Press Stock; A. G. E. FOTOSTOCK; COMSTOCK; Photos.com Plus/Getty Images Sales Spain; **012** Prats i Camps; Preysler/Atrezzo: Helen Chelton; **013** AbleStock.com/HighRes Press Stock; ISTOCKPHOTO; Prats i Camps; **014** AbleStock.com/ HighRes Press Stock; Ryan McVay/Getty Images Sales Spain; COMSTOCK; ISTOCKPHOTO; J. M.ª Escudero; PHOTOALTO/SERIDEC PHOTOIMAGENES CD; Prats i Camps; Preysler/Atrezzo: Helen Chelton; S. Enríquez; **015** F. Orte; ISTOCKPHOTO; J. Jaime; S. Enríquez; **017** J. Jaime; Prats i Camps; **018** J. M.ª Escudero; **019** Preysler/Atrezzo: Helen Chelton; **021** ISTOCKPHOTO; J. Jaime; Preysler/Atrezzo: Helen Chelton; **022** KAIBIDE DE CARLOS FOTÓGRAFOS; A. Toril; COMSTOCK; FOTONONSTOP; ISTOCKPHOTO; J. Jaime; MATTON-BILD; Prats i Camps; Preysler/Atrezzo: Helen Chelton; **023** ISTOCKPHOTO; Preysler/Atrezzo: Helen Chelton; **024** GARCÍA-PELAYO/Juancho; Christian Schwier, David Innes, Dirk Pieters/A. G. E. FOTOSTOCK; A. Toril; C. Díez Polanco; C. Roca; HighRes Press Stock; ISTOCKPHOTO; J. Jaime; J. Lucas; MATTON-BILD; Preysler/Atrezzo: Helen Chelton; S. Enríquez; **025** AbleStock.com/HighRes Press Stock; Preysler/Atrezzo: Helen Chelton; J. Jaime; MATTON-BILD; PHOTODISC, STOCKBYTE/SERIDEC PHOTOIMAGENES CD; S. Enríquez/Cafetería Alverán, Boadilla del Monte; **027** MATTON-BILD; Dirk Pieters, K. Arras/A. G. E. FOTOSTOCK; COMSTOCK; HighRes Press Stock; J. Jaime; Preysler/Atrezzo: Helen Chelton; **028** COMSTOCK; ISTOCKPHOTO; MATTON-BILD; Preysler/Atrezzo: Helen Chelton; **029** AbleStock.com/HighRes Press Stock; ISTOCKPHOTO; J. Jaime; SERIDEC PHOTOIMAGENES CD; **030** Prats i Camps; **032** Manuel Bruque/EFE; J. Lucas; **033** R. Matina/A. G. E. FOTOSTOCK; S. Padura; **034** GARCÍA-PELAYO/Juancho; Prats i Camps; **035** ISTOCKPHOTO; Preysler/Atrezzo: Helen Chelton; S. Enríquez; **036** AbleStock.com/HighRes Press Stock; Moodboard/CORBIS/CORDON PRESS; ISTOCKPHOTO; Preysler/Atrezzo: Helen Chelton; **037** EFE; ISTOCKPHOTO; Preysler/Atrezzo: Helen Chelton; S. Padura; T. Arias; **038** Imago sportfotodienst/Sirotti, REUTERS/Víctor Fraile/CORDON PRESS; Preysler/Atrezzo: Helen Chelton; **039** Hugo Philpott/EPA/EFE; Sirotti/Imago/CORDON PRESS; A. G. E. FOTOSTOCK; T. Albir/EFE; David Taylor/AGENCE D.P.P.I./FERY-PRESS; JOHN FOXX IMAGES/SERIDEC PHOTOIMAGENES CD; **040** AbleStock.com/HighRes Press Stock; Heather Weston, Robert Harding World Imagery/ Sergio Pitamitz, Tetra Images, Image Source/David Ryle, www.sylent-press.de/CORBIS/CORDON PRESS; PHOTOALTO/SERIDEC PHOTOIMAGENES CD; ISTOCKPHOTO; M.ª A. Ferrándiz; S. Enríquez; **041** Tim De Waele/CORBIS/CORDON PRESS; Preysler/Atrezzo: Helen Chelton; **043** Patrick Morin/SIPA-PRESS/SIPA ICONO/EFE; Preysler/Atrezzo: Helen Chelton; **045** Prats i Camps; Preysler/Atrezzo: Helen Chelton; **046** Adam Woolfitt/A. G. E. FOTOSTOCK, Preysler/Atrezzo: Helen Chelton; **047** ISTOCKPHOTO; Melba Agency; Prats i Camps; **048** ISTOCKPHOTO; J. Jaime; PHOTOALTO/SERIDEC PHOTOIMAGENES CD; Prats i Camps; **049** ISTOCKPHOTO; **050** A. Prieto/Agencia Estudio San Simón; **051** STOCKPHOTO; Preysler/Atrezzo: Helen Chelton; **052** J. Lucas; Prats i Camps; **053** C. Pérez; J. Jaime; P. Esgueva; Preysler/Atrezzo: Helen Chelton; **054** A. Toimil; Preysler/Atrezzo: Helen Chelton; **055** Nik Wheeler/CORBIS/CORDON PRESS; Ken Cavanagh/A. G. E. FOTOSTOCK; C. Pérez; ISTOCKPHOTO; PHOTODISC/SERIDEC PHOTOIMAGENES CD; **056** Cham/SIPA-PRESS/EFE; Pixtal, ARCO/Rudolf/A. G. E. FOTOSTOCK; Blend Images/J. L. Pelaez, Inc./CORBIS/CORDON PRESS; ISTOCKPHOTO; J. Jaime; KAIBIDE DE CARLOS FOTÓGRAFOS; Prats i Camps; S. Enríquez; **057** J. Jaime; **058** Preysler/Atrezzo: Helen Chelton; **059** A. Toimil; ISTOCKPHOTO; **060** Roberto Schmidt/AFP/Getty Images Sales Spain; Pixtal/A. G. E. FOTOSTOCK; ISTOCKPHOTO; **061** S. Enríquez; **062** SERIDEC PHOTOIMAGENES CD; **063** A. Toimil; Preysler/Atrezzo: Helen Chelton; T. Arias; **064** Preysler/Atrezzo: Helen Chelton; S. Padura; **065** AbleStock.com/HighRes Press Stock; José Ramón San Sebastián/ EFE; Preysler/Atrezzo: Helen Chelton; SERIDEC PHOTOIMAGENES CD; **066** Jupiterimages/Getty Images Sales Spain; Pixtal/A. G. E. FOTOSTOCK; ISTOCKPHOTO; J. Escandell.com; S. Enríquez; SERIDEC PHOTOIMAGENES CD; **067** My Pyramid.gov/United Status Department of Agriculture (USD A)AbleStock.com/HighRes Press Stock; **068** AbleStock.com/HighRes Press Stock; C. Pérez; ISTOCKPHOTO; MATTON-BILD; **069** akg-images/ALBUM; J. Martin/MUSEUM ICONOGRAFÍA; **070** AbleStock.com/HighRes Press Stock; Kate Kunz/CORBIS/CORDON PRESS; A. G. E. FOTOSTOCK; ISTOCKPHOTO; P. Esgueva; Preysler/Atrezzo: Helen Chelton; SERIDEC PHOTOIMAGENES CD; **071** Prats i Camps; Preysler/Atrezzo: Helen Chelton; S. Padura; SERIDEC PHOTOIMAGENES CD; **072** Prats i Camps; S. Enríquez; **073** COMSTOCK; D. López; ISTOCKPHOTO; Prats i Camps; Preysler/Atrezzo: Helen Chelton; **074** Panoramic Images/Getty Images Sales Spain; A. Toimil; F. Ontañón; Preysler/Atrezzo: Helen Chelton; **075** F. Ontañón; Preysler/Atrezzo: Helen Chelton; **076** ISTOCKPHOTO; **077** Javier Larrea/A. G. E. FOTOSTOCK; J. C. Muñoz; J. Navarro; **078** J. L. G. Grande; O. Torres; S. Enríquez; **079** GARCÍA-PELAYO/Juancho; S. Vannini/SYGMA/CONTIFOTO; O. Boé; **080** ORONOZ/ MUSEO NACIONAL CENTRO DE ARTE REINA SOFÍA; Dalmas/SIPA-PRESS/EFE; **081** ORONOZ/MUSEO NACIONAL CENTRO DE ARTE REINA SOFÍA; **083** ISTOCKPHOTO; Preysler/Atrezzo: Helen Chelton; **085** J. Martin/MUSEUM ICONOGRAFÍA; Preysler/Atrezzo: Helen Chelton; **086** Prats i Camps; **087** MATTON-BILD; **088** Alamy Images/ACI AGENCIA DE FOTOGRAFÍA; J. M.ª Escudero; **089** Joseph Sohm/Corbis/Visions of America/CORDON PRESS; **090** ISTOCKPHOTO; S. Enríquez; **091** ISTOCKPHOTO; Preysler/Atrezzo: Helen Chelton; SEIS x SEIS; **092** Preysler/Atrezzo: Helen Chelton; S. Enríquez; **093** ISTOCKPHOTO; AbleStock.com/HighRes Press Stock; Tophan/CORDON PRESS; ISTOCKPHOTO; Preysler/Atrezzo: Helen Chelton; **094** Dennis MacDonald/A. G. E. FOTOSTOCK; J. Jaime; Preysler/Atrezzo: Helen Chelton; SEIS x SEIS; **095** Prats i Camps; SEIS x SEIS; **096** AbleStock.com/HighRes Press Stock; A. G. E. FOTOSTOCK; COVER; ISTOCKPHOTO; J. Jaime; MARGEN FOTOGRAFÍA; S. Enríquez; SERIDEC PHOTOIMAGENES CD; STOCK PHOTOS; **097** Preysler/Atrezzo: Helen Chelton; S. Enríquez; SERIDEC PHOTOIMAGENES CD; **098** COMSTOCK; ISTOCKPHOTO; SERIDEC PHOTOIMAGENES CD; STOCK PHOTOS; **099** Wirelmage/Dave Rossman/Getty Images Sales Spain; FOTONONSTOP; Preysler/Atrezzo: Helen Chelton; **100** J. Jaime; MATTON-BILD; S. Enríquez; **101** Preysler/Atrezzo: Helen Chelton; **102** Preysler/ Atrezzo: Helen Chelton; Miguel Rajmil/EFE; Topham/CORDON PRESS; **103** DigitalVision/SERIDEC PHOTOIMAGENES CD; T. Abad/A. G. E. FOTOSTOCK; **104** AbleStock.com/HighRes Press Stock; Luis Castilla/EFE; ISTOCKPHOTO; J. Jaime; PHOTODIS/SERIDEC PHOTOIMAGENES CD; Prats i Camps; **105** C. Díez Polanco; HighRes Press Stock; M. Barcenilla; **107** AbleStock.com/HighRes Press Stock; J. Jaime; M. Barcenilla; MATTON-BILD; Preysler/Atrezzo: Helen Chelton; S. Enríquez; **108** S. Enríquez; **109** Miguel Rajmil/EFE; ISTOCKPHOTO; Preysler/Atrezzo: Helen Chelton;

World Language Program AP* Themes

AP THEMES ADDRESSED - LEVELS 1-4						
	Personal & Public Identities	Families & Communities	Beauty & Aesthetics	Contemporary Life	Science and Technology	Global Challenges
LEVEL 1						
Unit 1	*	*		*		
Unit 2		*	*	*		
Unit 3			*	*		
Unit 4				*	*	
Unit 5				*	*	
Unit 6				*	*	
Unit 7				*	*	
Unit 8					*	*
LEVEL 2						
Unit 1	*	*		*		
Unit 2		*	*	*	*	
Unit 3			*	*		
Unit 4				*	*	
Unit 5				*	*	
Unit 6				*	*	*
Unit 7				*	*	
Unit 8					*	*
LEVEL 3						
Unit 1	*	*		*		
Unit 2				*		
Unit 3		*	*	*		
Unit 4				*	*	
Unit 5				*	*	
Unit 6				*	*	
Unit 7					*	*
Unit 8	*			*		*
LEVEL 4						
Unit 1	*	*		*		
Unit 2		*		*	*	
Unit 3				*		*
Unit 4				*	*	
Unit 5	*			*		*
Unit 6			*			

*AP is a registered trademark of the College Board, which was not involved in the production of, and does not endorse, this product.

SANTILLANA USA
Language Education Experts
www.santillanausa.com 2023 NW 84th Avenue, Doral, FL 33122
Phone 1-800-245-8584 - Fax 1-888-248-9518 I customerservice@santillanausa.com
978-1-63113-249-0